Erin Doherty

ADOLESCENT LITERACY RESEARCH AND PRACTICE

SOLVING PROBLEMS IN THE TEACHING OF LITERACY

Cathy Collins Block, *Series Editor*

Recent Volumes

ADOLESCENT LITERACY RESEARCH AND PRACTICE

Edited by
Tamara L. Jetton
Janice A. Dole

THE GUILFORD PRESS
New York   London

© 2004 The Guilford Press
A Division of Guilford Publications, Inc.
72 Spring Street, New York, NY 10012
www.guilford.com

Printed in the United States of America

This book is printed on acid-free paper.

Last digit is print number: 9   8   7   6   5   4   3

Library of Congress Cataloging-in-Publication Data available from the Publisher.
ISBN 1-59385-021-2 (paper)
ISBN 1-59385-022-0 (cloth)

About the Editors

Tamara L. Jetton, PhD, teaches in the Secondary Program at James Madison University and has previously held positions at the University of Utah and Texas A&M University. Her research interests include understanding how adolescents learn with text in content-area domains and the strategies that teachers use to help students learn with text. Dr. Jetton has published in several journals, including *Reading Research Quarterly, Journal of Educational Psychology, Review of Educational Research, Educational Psychology,* and *Educational Psychology Review,* and in such edited volumes as the *Handbook of Reading Research* and the *Handbook of Discourse Processes.* She serves as a member of the Reading Committee for the National Assessment for Educational Progress.

Janice A. Dole, PhD, teaches in the Department of Teaching and Learning at the University of Utah and has held positions at the Center for the Study of Reading at the University of Illinois at Urbana–Champaign, Michigan State University, and the University of Denver. Her research interests include school reform in reading, professional development, and comprehension instruction. Dr. Dole has published widely in research and educational journals and has worked on educational reform in Estonia and Lithuania. She served for the past 10 years as a member of the reading development panel for the National Assessment for Educational Progress and was also a panel member of the recent RAND Reading Study Group. Recently, Dr. Dole has been involved in Utah's Reading Excellence Act, first as codirector and then in a technical assistance capacity. She is currently coevaluator for Utah's Reading First project.

Contributors

Peter Afflerbach, PhD, Department of Curriculum and Instruction, University of Maryland, College Park, Maryland

Patricia A. Alexander, PhD, Department of Human Development, University of Maryland, College Park, Maryland

Donna E. Alvermann, PhD, Department of Reading Education, University of Georgia, Athens, Georgia

Thomas W. Bean, PhD, Department of Curriculum and Instruction, University of Nevada, Las Vegas, Nevada

Alicia D. Beth, MA, Department of Educational Psychology, University of Texas, Austin, Texas

Mary E. Curtis, PhD, Center for Special Education, Lesley University, Cambridge, Massachusetts

Janice A. Dole, PhD, Department of Teaching and Learning, University of Utah, Salt Lake City, Utah

Georgia Earnest García, PhD, Department of Curriculum and Instruction, University of Illinois, Urbana–Champaign, Illinois

Michael F. Graves, PhD, Department of Curriculum and Instruction, University of Minnesota, Minneapolis, Minnesota

Heriberto Godina, PhD, Division of Curriculum and Instruction, University of Iowa, Iowa City, Iowa

Helen J. Harper, PhD, Faculty of Education, University of Western Ontario, London, Ontario

Kathleen Hinchman, PhD, Reading and Language Arts Center, School of Education, Syracuse University, Syracuse, New York

Tamara L. Jetton, PhD, Secondary Program, College of Education, James Madison University, Harrisonburg, Virginia

Michael L. Kamil, PhD, Psychological Studies in Education, School of Education, Stanford University, Stanford, California

Helen S. Kim, PhD, Psychological Studies in Education, School of Education, Stanford University, Stanford, California

Janette K. Klingner, PhD, School of Education, University of Colorado, Boulder, Colorado

Elizabeth Birr Moje, PhD, School of Education, University of Michigan, Ann Arbor, Michigan

Jeffery D. Nokes, MEd, Department of Teaching and Learning, University of Utah, Salt Lake City, Utah

P. David Pearson, PhD, Graduate School of Education, University of California, Berkeley, California

Michael Pressley, PhD, Department of Teacher Education, Michigan State University, East Lansing, Michigan

JoyLynn Hailey Reed, PhD, Office of Graduate Studies, University of Texas at Dallas, Richardson, Texas

Leslie S. Rush, PhD, Department of Secondary Education, University of Wyoming, Laramie, Wyoming

Diane Lemonnier Schallert, PhD, Department of Educational Psychology, University of Texas, Austin, Texas

Cynthia Shanahan, EdD, College of Education, University of Illinois at Chicago, Chicago, Illinois

Timothy Shanahan, PhD, College of Education, University of Illinois at Chicago, Chicago, Illinois

Wayne H. Slater, PhD, Department of Curriculum and Instruction, University of Maryland, College Park, Maryland

Steven A. Stahl, PhD, Department of Curriculum and Instruction, University of Illinois, Urbana–Champaign, Illinois

Emily Anderson Swan, PhD, Department of Teaching and Learning, University of Utah, Salt Lake City, Utah

Carol Ann Tomlinson, EdD, Leadership, Foundations and Policy Studies, University of Virginia, Charlottesville, Virginia

Terry Underwood, PhD, Department of Teacher Education, California State University, Sacramento, California

Sharon Vaughn, PhD, College of Education, University of Texas, Austin, Texas

Althea L. Woodruff, PhD, Department of Educational Psychology, University of Texas, Austin, Texas

Contents

Part III. **Critical Issues in Adolescent Literacy**

Part IV. **Reflections on Theory and Current Practice**

Introduction

TAMARA L. JETTON
JANICE A. DOLE

Jan and I came to this experience of editing a book on adolescent literacy from quite different perspectives. I was a middle and high school teacher for 10 years prior to becoming a reading professor at a university. My experiences as a teacher of adolescents have continued to influence the ways in which I research literacy practices in the schools. Jan, in contrast, had focused much of her research in the area of K–3 literacy reform, particularly with her work pertaining to the Reading Excellence Act and Reading First. However, through her graduate course work and subsequent work with preservice and inservice teachers of adolescent literacy, Jan has realized the need for more research that examines adolescent literacy. It is through our past experiences as educators and researchers that we have come together to edit this book. As we examine our past experiences that led to our desire to edit this book, we also flesh out some of the central issues that educators face as they continue to strive for excellence in literacy education for adolescents.

TAMARA'S EXPERIENCES

My experiences in middle and secondary education began with my employment as a secondary English teacher at the now defunct Spring

1

Branch High School in Houston, Texas. Poorly trained to help adolescents with the difficulties they encountered reading the required texts in the curriculum, I felt extremely ineffective as a teacher. All I knew how to do was give students the book and create questions for them to answer. I was left with many of my own questions about how to increase student learning in my classroom. How could I motivate these students to read when they struggled with these difficult texts? What kinds of activities would increase their understanding of the stories and novels? How could I teach the literary elements when students had difficulty gleaning even the literal understanding of the stories?

I began to think back on my own journey through middle and high school. Did I receive any instruction that enabled me to read the assigned texts? I know that my teachers expected me to summarize, answer questions, and discuss the stories that we read, but I do not remember any instruction in *how* to summarize, effectively answer text questions, and talk about the main themes and character motivations in the story. As Durkin (1978–1979) found years ago, teachers assessed students' abilities to use effective comprehension strategies such as summarization and questioning, but they rarely taught the students how to perform these strategies effectively with text.

I consider myself fortunate that in spite of the lack of instruction for gleaning meaning from text, I was able to read well enough to get by with the tasks and assignments of middle and high school and the university. Yet, not until I was a graduate student, acquiring my M.A. in English, did I begin to use the strategies available to me for understanding these complex narratives. My professors trained me to think for myself and critically analyze the texts that I read.

When I look back on the transformation in my reading skills that ultimately enabled me to further my education, I realize how much time I lost in middle and high school. What kind of a reader would I have become if I had possessed the repertoire of reading strategies that I finally acquired at the age of 23 in graduate school? In my experiences as a reading professor who teaches reading to preservice and inservice teachers, I get this same question every semester from at least one of my students. Why were we not taught these reading strategies when we needed them in middle and high school?

Although there are many answers to this question, one answer is to go back and take a look at my own training as a secondary preservice teacher at a university. I did not even have to take a reading class to graduate with a secondary education degree. At that time, Texas, where I received my initial teaching license, did not even require that I possess course work in reading in order to teach English in the middle or high school. Ironically, as a person who received my degree from a university in Illinois, I only had to take two additional courses to earn my teaching certificate in Texas— Texas history and government. Thus, although the state wanted to make sure that I knew the great history of Texas and its political process, it placed no value on my ability to help students read for meaning.

How much has changed since my initial experiences as a secondary teacher? In my subsequent experiences as an instructor at three universities, I still believe that most secondary preservice teachers receive very little training that will enable them to help adolescents learn the requisite literacy skills needed in the middle and high schools. Because the emphasis is on acquiring the content necessary to teach subject areas such as history, math, and science, the major concentration of courses that preservice teachers take is in their own content areas. At some universities, secondary students receive as little as a 1-hour course focused on literacy whereas at other universities, they received a 3-hour course in literacy. Currently at James Madison University, we are attempting to rectify this lack of training by providing preservice middle and secondary teachers with the reading training they will need to enhance the literacy skills of adolescents. Secondary teachers of all content areas are required to take 6 hours of reading course work and attend practica that enable them to practice literacy strategies in middle and high school classrooms.

Like myself, many teachers who entered the school system with little training have expectations of students as readers that are not supported by the reality of middle and secondary classrooms. For example, I just assumed, as did other teachers with whom I worked, that students would be able to read their content-area texts independently. Thus, when we assigned the texts to be read at home, we were surprised that many students would not complete the homework assignment. I, in my ignorance, assumed they were unmotivated and just did not care. For many adolescents, this is far from the case. Many of them cannot read their history and science texts without some help. Furthermore, teachers often lack the knowledge of effective instruction that they can employ to increase student success with these complex content-area texts.

Teacher training is certainly not the only solution to eliminating the literacy difficulties that adolescents confront when they try to learn in their content-area classrooms. Another problem is the increasing difficulty with the texts. As adolescents progress through the middle and secondary grades, the texts become increasingly difficult. The technical jargon that science students need to know to understand their biology texts is overwhelming. During my dissertation, I worked with six biology teachers who were using a biology textbook that contained technical vocabulary and complex sentence structure. When I examined the readability of this text, I found that it was beyond the highest level of the readability graph—the 17th-grade level (Fry, 1989). Faced with such obstacles, these knowledgeable biology teachers created their own texts that students could read.

With texts becoming increasingly difficult as adolescents move from middle to high school and on to college, it is not prudent to think that all students can be reading proficiently by grade 3, as some politicians would have the general public believe. Students need to be taught effective reading strategies explicitly throughout their educational career, including college. My graduate students still encounter very difficult text, particularly when they must learn to read the statistical methods and procedures in scientific studies. I continue to facilitate the use of effective reading strategies for helping them understand these texts.

Another factor related to the increasing difficulty that middle and high school students face with texts is the growing amount of information in the world, and the numerous and diverse ways in which we read this information in the 21st century; that is, students increasingly gain information by logging onto the Internet and searching topics on the World Wide Web. Students find it difficult to navigate through the complexity of the information on the Internet (Alexander & Jetton, 2003). Furthermore, students need to be able to judge the credibility of the sources of information that they acquire on the Net (Brem, Russell, & Weems, 2001). In Chapter 16, this volume, Kim and Kamil point to the literacy issues pertaining to literacy and technology.

An additional problem faced by many secondary teachers related to literacy is the diversity of literacy skills that adolescents possess in middle and secondary classrooms. As Stanovich (1986) showed in his study of the "Matthew effect," when students do not acquire the requisite literacy skills in elementary school, the gap between these students and the students who have acquired such skills gets bigger and bigger as they progress through school. Students who lack these requisite literacy competencies oftentimes do not gain as much knowledge in the various content areas, because they have difficulty acquiring the knowledge through reading. Thus, middle and secondary teachers face classrooms of adolescents with very diverse literacy skills.

Although most teachers are aware of these diverse literacy skills, many of them have no idea just how diverse adolescents' skills really are, because there are no assessments in place to determine such literacy skills. At my university, the preservice teachers who take my literacy course are placed in a practicum that occurs in one of three different schools—two high schools and a middle school. One of the high schools in rural Virginia conducts no reading assessments to determine the reading and writing strengths and needs of their students. As a result, many students are misplaced into remedial classes, because the school personnel identify them as having low motivation and/or behavioral problems. Because the teachers do not know the grade level at which these students are reading, they treat all students the same. All students receive intensive instruction in phonics skills. When my preservice teachers administered informal reading inventories to these students, they found that many of them possessed adequate phonics skills but had difficulty with reading comprehension. Thus, the preservice teachers found a mismatch between the students' literacy needs and the kind of instruction occurring in the classroom. Tomlinson asserts in Chapter 11, this volume, that students require differentiated instruction to meet these diverse needs.

At the other high school at which my preservice teachers attend a practicum, several assessments are administered to ensure that students are matched appropriately to the kind of instruction they need. However, the assessments have revealed that these secondary teachers face daunting challenges given that two thirds of their population of 1,250 students read at the first- through fifth-grade levels. Many of these students have very different needs than those students who struggle with text at the eighth-grade reading level. Once again, with the scant reading training that they receive, secondary teachers feel ill-prepared to deal with these challenges. Many of these students face language difficulties because English is not their native language. As Garcia and Godina (Chapter 14, this volume) and Klingner and Vaughn (Chapter 9, this volume) point out, teachers must be aware of the challenges that these students face, and the methods by which they can learn effectively in content-area classrooms.

JAN'S EXPERIENCES

My first experiences with adolescent literacy began with my work with migrant middle school students in Colorado. At the time, I was a doctoral student at the University of Colorado. I spoke some Spanish, and another doctoral student and I were assigned to a special education middle school classroom to work with a master teacher, Ms. Emerson.

Many migrant students were placed, often inappropriately, in Ms. Emerson's special education classroom because of their second-language status. To be sure, some students were bilingual and also had learning disabilities. But many more were just bright, capable Hispanic students who happened to speak English as a second language. Some of the students learned to read Spanish in Mexico before coming to the United States, then learned to read English when they came here. Others never learned to read Spanish but were taught to read Spanish and English in U.S. bilingual programs that were popular at that time. Still others learned to read only English. Regardless of when and where they learned English, what was common to all these migrant students was their struggle in reading English, and in their academic learning in junior high school.

Teaching these students was a moving reminder of the power of instruction. Over time, we watched them blossom as they learned English words and idioms, and as they learned how to read. Powerful intervention methods worked with these students, and they worked well. Gains were made; students progressed. They learned that they *could* learn. Ms. Emerson, my colleague, and I made a difference in that classroom of migrant children. We did so because we used powerful intervention methods that have stood the test of time.

I also remember with great affection the many secondary reading and content teachers with whom I have worked over the years. I marvel at the wisdom and knowledge of so many of these teachers, and their continuing desire to seek better instruction for their students. I have had so many middle and secondary teachers ask me for more research, more articles, more journals—for anything and everything they could get their hands on to learn more about how to help their students. These teachers' dedication has renewed my own dedication to them and to adolescents as well.

Finally, I recognize that middle and secondary teachers have a right to the same quality and quantity of research knowledge as do K–3 primary teachers. Yet, unfortunately, we cannot provide the same level of research in terms of quality or quantity as we can for primary-grade teachers. This has become more of a problem over the last 5 or 6 years, as books such as the National Research Council's *Preventing Reading Difficulties in Young Children* (Snow, Burns, & Griffin, 1998) have become more popular and have made their way into the public domain, and as federal programs such as the Reading Excellence Act and *Reading First* have provided millions of dollars to primary grade schools and children. I have no answers for my many colleagues who ask me, "What about my students, my middle and secondary school students who can't read their biology texts and can't read their U.S. history texts or can't read even at a third grade level? What are we supposed to do with them? Where is help for us?" There should be an answer for these teachers too, but there is not.

As of 2003, there is not a body of research to tell us appropriate interventions that will help struggling middle and secondary school readers who can barely read. As of 2003, we still do not have a body of research to provide us with appropriate interventions to help high school readers who can read fluently but remain 3 or 4 years below grade level in reading.

Although the research and the knowledge base may be many years away, we know enough to do better many things that we currently do in middle and secondary classrooms. If you are unconvinced of this, read Larry Cuban's (1993), *How Teachers Taught*, in which he argues that, with very few exceptions, secondary schools and classrooms are virtually unchanged from what existed 100 years ago. Certainly, we know more than teachers did 100 years ago. Certainly, members of the education field know more than they did 100 years ago. Yet what we know is not being implemented in middle and secondary classrooms.

PURPOSES FOR CONSTRUCTING THIS EDITED BOOK

Although Jan and I paint a rather bleak picture of research on adolescent literacy, we are encouraged by the attention that adolescent literacy is receiving. The International Reading Association Committee on Adolescent Literacy (1999) has highlighted the importance of examining adolescent literacy. In this statement, the association recommends that adolescent learners do the following:

- Read a wide variety of literature that appeals to their interests.
- Receive modeling and explicit instruction from expert teachers for the skills and motivation to read complex materials.
- Work with teachers who understand the complex nature of individual adolescent readers.
- Participate in assessments that determine their strengths and needs.
- Work with a reading specialist, if they have difficulty learning how to read.
- Receive support from their home, community, and the nation.

Some recent publications have also highlighted the importance of examining adolescent literacy. For example, in *Reconceptualizing the Literacies in Adolescents' Lives*, Alvermann, Hinchman, Moore, Phelps, and Waff (1998) and her colleagues invite educators of adolescents to consider a broader view of adolescent literacies that encompasses gender, race, ethnicity, and social class. More recently, Alvermann (2002) highlighted several critical issues pertaining to adolescent literacy instruction. In her article, she has argued for instruction that takes into account students' self-efficacy and engagement with an array of texts in many different settings.

The U.S. Department of Education and the National Institute of Child Health and Human Development (NICHD) has committed the next several years to research and development of projects and programs designed to understand the development of adolescent readers, and to implement and evaluate instruction and intervention programs to improve the reading and writing abilities of adolescent readers and writers. This group is devoting a massive amount of time and money, with a commitment to providing secondary teachers with the same kind of knowledge and research base as that provided for primary grade teachers. In particular, Peggy McCardle at the NICHD is committed to assist researchers in beginning to answer the kinds of questions that will help middle and secondary teachers down the road to understand the nature of language development and second-language acquisition in reading and writing, as well as literacy for adolescents in academic settings.

Despite recent publications, and public and professional attention, the area of adolescent literacy deserves much more attention. One reason is the lack of professional publications that attempt to examine several issues pertaining to adolescent literacy. Three years ago, I was asked to help one of the local school districts consider important issues in adolescent literacy, so that it could make careful and critical decisions about its upcoming text adoption. One request was that I list some professional publications that summarize many of these critical issues. Other than the traditional content-area textbooks and the work of Alvermann and her colleagues (1998), I could not cite a plethora of books that synthesize some of the critical issues in adolescent literacy. I finally had to compile a list of articles that focus on specific aspects of adolescent literacy.

The idea for this book evolved from this experience. I wanted educators to have an additional source pertaining to adolescent literacy that included many of the critically important issues in this area. Although this particular edited volume is certainly not complete in its examination of adolescent literacy, Jan and I strove to include chapters within the book that reflect critical themes that have emerged in the area of adolescent literacy. We wanted to compile from the best researchers in the field a summary and synthesis of adolescent literacy research and practice. This compilation of research and practice focuses on four key issues:

1. What do we reliably know about adolescent readers and writers?
2. How do we know this?
3. What do we know about literacy instruction for adolescents?
4. What do we still need to know?

The first issue, then, was to compile, summarize, and synthesize the research on various aspects of reading and writing that are critical to the needs of adolescents. Second was the issue of documenting clearly how we know what we know. The third issue was to focus on best practices for enhancing adolescent literacy based on the research we have. The last issue was to delineate clearly future questions that need to be addressed and answered in order to improve the reading and writing performance of adolescent learners.

ORGANIZATION OF THE BOOK

We have organized this book into four parts. In Part I, we have gathered together several chapters around the general academic organization of middle and secondary schools—content-area instruction. In an overview, Jetton and Alexander (Chapter 1) relate content area learning to domains of knowledge and discuss the important of content knowledge of subject areas, as well as knowledge of how to teach the subject areas. In Chapter 2, Slater discusses the traditional curriculum of the English teacher and calls for a radical change from English teaching as discussions of literary texts to English teaching as critical thinking, reading, and writing. This theme is further advanced by Shanahan (Chapter 3), who wants us to reconsider the teaching of writing as a learning process in addition to a thinking process. Through writing, argues Shanahan, students process content more deeply and gain a better understanding of what they learn. Two chapters on teaching science and social studies follow. In Chapter 4 on science, Shanahan shows readers how recent research suggests a new way of thinking about teaching students to think and work like scientists. In Chapter 5 on social studies, Stahl and Shanahan show readers how to teach students to think like historians.

In Part II of our book, we turn from the general academic organization of middle and secondary school to those students about whom many of us care deeply, but who receive far too little of our time and attention—*adolescents who struggle with literacy.* Curtis (Chapter 6) discusses current research and practice on adolescents who struggle with word identification—no small group of middle and high school students. Then, Underwood and Pearson (Chapter 7) identify four different levels of intervention for assisting readers in comprehension and describe several successful projects at these different levels. Nokes and Dole (Chapter 8) discuss the research on explicit strategy instruction and its positive effects on reading comprehension for adolescent readers. Klingner and Vaughn (Chapter 9) describe research and practical ideas for struggling second-language readers, a group of readers becoming more prominent in our schools today. Then, Alvermann and Rush (Chapter 10) identify and critique several commercially available programs for struggling middle and secondary school students. Finally, Tomlinson (Chapter 11) evaluates and critiques the research on differentiating instruction to meet the needs of all learners, especially those who need special attention.

In Part III, we have gathered together chapters on a number of related issues, practices, and programs relevant to adolescents and their literacy needs. Reed, Schallert, Beth, and Woodruff (Chapter 12) discuss the critically important issue of motivation—the first issue secondary teachers ask about when we talk to them about adolescent learning. Swan (Chapter 13) then makes the Reed et al. discussion come to life by describing high school classrooms that have implemented research-based best practices in the form of concept-oriented reading instruction (CORI). In Chapter 14, García and Godina include, but move beyond, motivation to describe the special needs of English-language learners (ELLs). Then, Moje and Hinchman (Chapter 15) describe culturally sensitive pedagogy for all adolescents—an idea that suits not only ELLs, but also all learners. Kim and Kamil discuss the new media and technology in which adolescents are immersed and about which we have a lot to learn in terms of how and what adolescents learn. Afflerbach (Chapter 17) discusses assessment of reading—another critical issue for teachers. Finally, Bean and Harper (Chapter 18) present an alternative, new view of teacher education that may change our current outmoded and largely ineffective model of teacher preparation.

Finally, in Part IV, we have asked two senior researchers to reflect on adolescent literacy from the perspective of the whole picture of K–12. In the penultimate chapter, Pressley (Chapter 19) reflects on years of visiting both elementary and secondary classrooms with a K–12 perspective and lens. Last, Graves (Chapter 20) discusses theories that have made a difference but could have made more of a difference. Perhaps they will yet.

REFERENCES

Alexander, P. A. & Jetton, T. L. (2003). Learning from traditional and alternative texts: New conceptualizations for the information age. In A. C. Graesser, M. A. Gernsbacher & S. R. Goldman (Eds.), *Handbook of discourse processes* (pp. 199–241). Mahwah, NJ: Erlbaum.

Alvermann, D. E. (2002). Effective literacy instruction for adolescents. *Journal of Literacy Research, 34,* 189–208.

Alvermann, D. E., Hinchman, K. A., Moore, D. W., Phelps, S. F., & Waff, D. R. (Eds.) (1998). *Reconceptualizing the literacies in adolescents' lives.* Mahwah, NJ: Erlbaum.

Brem, S. K., Russell, J., & Weems, L. (2001). Science on the web: Student evaluations of scientific arguments. *Discourse Processes, 32,* 191–213.

Cuban, L. (1993). *How teachers taught: Constancy and change in American classrooms 1890–1990* (2nd ed.). New York: Teachers College Press.

Durkin, D. (1978–1979). What classroom observations reveal about reading comprehension instruction. *Reading Research Quarterly, 14,* 481–533.

Fry, E. (1989). Reading formulas—maligned but valid. *Journal of Reading, 32,* 292–297.

International Reading Association. (1999). *Summary of adolescent literacy, a position statement for the Commission on Adolescent Literacy of the International Reading Association.* Retrieved from *http://www.reading.org/positions/adol_lit.html*

Snow, C. E., Burns, M. S., & Griffin, P. (Eds.). (1998). *Preventing reading difficulties in young children.* Washington, DC: National Academy Press.

Stanovich, K. (1986). Matthew effects in reading: Some consequences of individual differences in the acquisition of literacy. *Reading Research Quarterly, 21,* 360–407.

PART I

Teaching Content Domains through Literacy

1

Domains, Teaching, and Literacy

TAMARA L. JETTON
PATRICIA A. ALEXANDER

Those concerned with adolescent literacy inevitably find themselves immersed in the topic of reading in subjects such as history, mathematics, or science. These subject areas contain specialized knowledge that is organized in a specific way. For example, in biology, students read about classifications of organisms into what is known in this content area as phyla. In American history, students read about how particular bills and acts affected the lives of people during a historical time period. Because each subject area has specific knowledge organized in a unique way, we often refer to these subject areas as subject-matter domains.

Educators are concerned with the difficulty that students face as they try to read textual materials in these subject-matter domains. The reasons for this concern are understandable. As students progress through school, they are required to learn from printed materials that are often increasingly complex, less personally relevant, and conceptually dense. Paradoxically, just as the linguistic demands of text-based learning are expanding, academic supports for students in the forms of explicit reading instruction are diminishing (Alexander & Jetton, 2000).

Caught within this paradoxical situation are the students who must rely on their abilities to understand, interpret, and use demanding subject-matter texts if they are to grow and develop academically. In order to guide adolescent readers in their text-based learning, educators must recognize the influences that domains exert on learning and teaching. They need to realize that the very forms of texts that students read, along with their central purposes, differ across domains.

Teachers face another paradox as they design and implement practice within a subject-matter domain. Teachers may use linguistically demanding texts to facilitate learning, but they may lack the depth of knowledge required to bring the text content to life for their students. Furthermore, they may not know how to design sound teaching practices that not only enable students to utilize strategies for learning with text but also engage students in the process of the learning the content (Wade & Moje, 2000); that is, it takes the careful orchestration of content and pedagogical knowledge for teachers to engage adolescents successfully in the process of text-based learning (Jetton & Alexander, 1997).

If teachers are to aid students in their learning, they must appreciate the complex relations between domains and texts that are at the heart of text-based learning. To serve that end, we explore four central questions:

- What are domains?
- Why do domains matter?
- What do we know about reading in academic domains?
- What do we know about the role of the teacher in domain learning?

WHAT ARE DOMAINS?

The term *domain* has many meanings. In the educational literature, domains represent specialized fields of study as varied as dance and physics (Alexander, 1997). Those concerned with adolescent literacy are most interested in academic domains such as history, literature, reading, science, and mathematics, which are centerpieces of the educational experiences. In educational practice, domains are represented by courses or academic majors. It is within these academic domains that students regularly confront the demands of learning from texts meant to convey the specialized knowledge, processes, and vocabulary deemed as essential understandings by experts and society (VanSledright, 2002).

All academic domains involve a specialized body of knowledge most often acquired through formal education or training (Alexander, 1998). That knowledge is organized around core concepts or principles that distinguish one domain from another (Matthews, 1994; Stahl, Hynd, Glynn, & Carr, 1996; West & Pines, 1985). For example, the study of human biology is frequently organized around systems (e.g., circulatory or digestive) and subsystems (e.g., organs, tissues, or cells), whereas history is structured around specific time periods or geographic areas (e.g., early American history or ancient European civilizations). Those core concepts and principles are often determined by acknowledged experts and subsequently authorized or sanctioned through sociocultural practice (Phillips, 1987, 1995). Educational standards established for many academic domains are part of this authorization process (e.g., National Academy of Science, 1995; National Council of Teachers of Mathematics, 2000).

Domains also have their own lexicons or vocabulary that students must negotiate if they are to perform competently (Lampert & Blunk, 1998). Within the domain of history, for instance, words such as *acts, bills,* and *enactments* carry a meaning that might not be obvious or significant to those outside the domain. Similarly, terms such as *base ten, regrouping,* and *patterning* communicate to persons in the domain of mathematics. Students who do not become fluent in the "language" of academic domains are unlikely to achieve competence (Alexander & Jetton, 2003).

Modes of inscription central to domains are part of students' domain fluency. *Mode of inscription* refers to the way concepts and processes associated with an academic domain are represented in symbolic form (Goldin, 1992; Kulikowich, O'Connell, Rezendes, & Archambault, 2000). The primary mode of inscription for many domains, such as language arts and history, is linguistic, or the language of words, phrases, and sentences. For other domains, such as science and mathematics, that inscription is more often numeric or graphic in form (Alexander & Kulikowich, 1994). Those who read mathematics must understand numbers and equations. Even for those domains in which key concepts and processes are typically codified in numeric or graphic form, language remains important in their instruction (Alexander & Kulikowich, 1991). This is one reason that reading is regarded as a threshold domain. Competence in the domain of reading is required for learning in other domains to some degree given that so much domain knowledge is preserved and communicated via written or oral language (Alexander, 2003).

Just as domains are distinguished by their modes of inscription and lexicons, they are recognized by the tasks or problems at the core of schooling. Precisely because these tasks and problems are so common to student learning, they have been described as *schooled* (Stewart, 1987). For example, in the domain of English or language arts, a schooled task in which students often engage is to analyze the character of a story. In mathematics, students solve typical numeric problems involving rate, time, and distance. Some of the consistency in domain tasks comes about as a result of the national, state, and local standards and curricula that shape the educational experience. Although these typical school tasks change across grade levels and over time, they inevitably bestow a character on student learning (Alexander, 1998).

One feature of typical domain problems is their structuredness, which has to do with whether a problem is presumed to have an agreed-upon solution or not. Structuredness also pertains to how one arrives at the solution (Frederiksen, 1984). Well-structured problems, common in mathematics and science education, typically have one or limited "right" answers, arrived at by the application of specific algorithms or formulae. For domains such as language arts and history, however, tasks are more ill-structured or ill-defined (Alexander, 1998). In language arts, an ill-structured problem might be to write about how Stephen Crane uses imagery in his story to convey the reality of a Civil War battle. In addressing this problem, students arrive at different solutions, because they can select from a variety of images in the story to complete the task. The structuredness of domain problems is important, because it influences how and for what purpose students engage in reading. In science, for example, students might read to locate data, or confirm or disconfirm hypotheses, whereas in mathematics, texts may serve to explain numeric or graphic data, or pose problems for practice (Kulikowich et al., 2000). Within history classes, texts are essential for understanding varied perspectives on historical events that exist and establishing plausible interpretations based on available evidence. Those texts may be written by participants or eyewitnesses (primary source), or they can be interpretations or summaries of events (secondary source).

Finally, all academic domains arose from the human need to survive and thrive in the world (Durant, 1954). For example, the domain of history grew out of society's need to document its customs and traditions for posterity and to frame particular events in a certain perspective. What we now call *science* began as an effort to discern the patterns in nature upon which survival hinged, such as planting cycles and movements of the tides. Similarly, ancient societies' desire to count, weigh, and measure commodities with some consistency is the root of modern mathematics. Sadly, because domains are often treated as abstracted, disembodied bodies of knowledge, much of their practical value has been lost in modern-day instruction.

WHY DO DOMAINS MATTER?

With all the demands on teachers today to deal with both external mandates and internal needs of their students, why saddle them with yet another set of expectations regarding academic domains? In response to this legitimate concern, we discuss several reasons why knowledge of domains matters. Specifically, we consider the assessment and organizational power of domains and the synergy that exists between learning to read and reading to learn.

There is some debate in the literature as to whether domains are natural configurations of knowledge and skills that result from man's interaction with nature or are purely human contrivances (Alexander, 1998). Although the debate about whether domains are rooted in nature or are sociocultural creations is intriguing, it does not alter their power within schools and society at large. Academic domains are the arenas in which educational experiences play out and the platform for determining student achievement. Within postindustrial societies, students' educational abilities are judged by their demonstrated knowledge and skills (e.g., National Assessment of Educational Progress, 2002; National Reading Panel, 2000). Students who cannot deal with the print demands inherent in domain-specific learning will undoubtedly struggle educationally.

Academic domains are also powerful means of organizing vast bodies of related knowledge and experience. It is almost impossible to conceive of teaching or learning in today's information age without some means of organizing the universe of information that exists (Alexander, Murphy, & Woods, 1996). Domains are meaningful systems of information organizing, especially when their practical roots and value are kept in the forefront. Domains underpin much of our sociocultural identities and help shape the world in which we live. Therefore, domains are valuable sociocultural tools that enable students to navigate the academic world (VanSledright, 2002).

It has long been the practice to separate the domain of reading into two distinct stages: learning to read and reading to learn (Alexander & Jetton, 2000; Chall, 1995). However, such a dichotomy does not represent the reality of reading development (Alexander, 2002). In actuality, the processes of learning to read (e.g., breaking the code and discovering the meaningfulness of oral and written language) and reading to learn (e.g., using reading abilities to seek knowledge) are inextricably tied together. Specifically, as students begin to unravel the mysteries of language, they are simultaneously building their knowledge base. Similarly, as students pursue knowledge in reading or other academic domains, they are building a deeper and richer understanding of language (Alexander, 2002).

This reciprocity between learning to read and reading to learn has serious ramifications for literacy policy and practice. For one thing, their coupling fights the public misperception that individuals are "complete" as readers once they have acquired basic phonological skills in elementary school. For another, it argues against the isolation that often exists between those who teach reading and those who teach subject-matter content.

Many of the chapters in this volume attest to the continuing and nonproductive divorce between the very parties who should be partners in fostering students' academic development.

WHAT DO WE KNOW ABOUT READING IN DOMAINS?

Armed with an understanding of the nature and value of domains, we now turn to the question of what it means to engage in competent reading in academic fields. Our response to this question draws on the extant literature in text-based learning (e.g., Kamil, Mosenthal, Pearson, & Barr, 2000), as well as the research on developing expertise in academic domains (e.g., Chi, Glaser, & Farr, 1988). Both of these sources show that knowledge, strategies, and motivations are central to a student's ability to handle the demands of domain-specific reading. We first examine each of these dimensions separately, then consider how they interface and play out differently as individuals become more competent in a subject-area domain.

Knowledge

Students must possess two bodies of knowledge to deal well with domain-specific texts: linguistic knowledge and subject-matter knowledge. Linguistic knowledge encompasses all knowledge and skills required in the processing and use of written language. That universe of knowledge includes such basics as phonological ability, the ability to decode words by using letters and their corresponding sounds and vocabulary knowledge in understanding the conceptual meaning of words. (Adams, 1991; Stanovich, 1986). Linguistic knowledge also concerns an understanding of language conventions such as satire, text structures, and genres or text types (Britton, 1981; Goldman & Rakestraw, 2000; Jetton, Rupley, & Willson, 1995). Whereas basics such as decoding proficiency and a rich vocabulary allow students to process texts fluently and rather effortlessly, knowledge of text conventions, structures, and genres permit readers to recognize paragraph structures (e.g., descriptive or cause–effect; Armbruster, 1984) or claim–warrant–evidence patterns (Chambliss, 1995) typical of subject-matter texts.

Subject-matter knowledge, which is a special form of prior knowledge, also plays a significant part in students' domain reading (Alexander, Jetton, & Kulikowich, 1995). Two forms of subject-matter knowledge, in particular, influence students' text-based learning, and domain and topic knowledge. Domain knowledge represents the breadth of knowledge in a given field of study, such as history or biology (e.g., Alexander, 1997; Stahl et al., 1996), whereas topic knowledge describes the readers' background knowledge relative to the subject of a particular selection of text and to concepts included in that text (Alexander, Schallert, & Hare, 1991).

Let us say that Maribella, a seventh grader, is reading a chapter in her science textbook about amphibians. Her ease of processing and comprehension of that chapter depends on her knowledge of science, her knowledge of amphibians, and the specific concepts mentioned in that chapter. Teachers may occasionally encounter students who have a reasonably strong base of both domain and topic knowledge. However, given the stress on new versus familiar content in curricula, teachers are more likely to have students with either limited or variable subject-matter knowledge. By *variable*, we mean that some students may have a good base of domain knowledge but know little about the specific topic, or have relatively strong topic knowledge but lack a breadth of knowledge.

Strategies

Maribella must also possess cognitive and metacognitive or self-regulatory strategies as she learns with text in a subject-matter domain. She needs to employ cognitive strategies such as predicting, questioning, and summarizing to gain a deeper understanding of the content (Pressley, Goodchild, Fleet, Zajchowski, & Evans, 1989). She also needs to use metacognitive or self-regulatory processes (e.g., self-testing or self-evaluation; Winne, 1995; Zimmerman, 1995) to determine how well she is learning. There are two ways to categorize the strategies that students use during the processing of domain-specific texts. One categorization has to do with the generalizability or mobility of strategies, whereas the other is based on the degree of thinking or text manipulation involved.

General and Domain-Specific Strategies

Most of the strategies studied within the text-processing literature fit the category of *general* strategies. They are called general because they can be broadly applied to a range of tasks in many domains (Alexander & Judy, 1988; Garner, 1987). Predicting, summarizing, and self-questioning are examples of these general strategies. Whether students are reading a history text or math books, their learning benefits from predicting what is to come, summarizing what was read, and questioning their understanding.

By comparison, certain processing strategies are quite specific to the domain and its typical tasks or problems (Pressley et al., 1989). Although these domain-specific strategies are powerful learning tools in that context, they do not "travel" well to other domains or tasks. Every domain comes with its own set of these domain-specific strategies. As Maribella enters her seventh-grade language arts class, she must employ domain-specific strategies for reading stories. For example, she needs to understand how the bird's death in "The Scarlet Ibis" is used by the author to foreshadow the death of one of the main characters (Hurst, 2000). Analyzing the text for the use of foreshadowing is not a strategy that Maribella can transfer to her mathematics class.

Surface-Level and Deep-Processing Strategies

General strategies involved in text-based learning can be further categorized into surface-level and deep-processing strategies (Alexander, Sperl, Buehl, Fives, & Chiu, 2002; Murphy & Alexander, 2002; VanSledright & Alexander, 2002). Surface-level strategies are those that readers use to access and literally comprehend the written text. For example, as Maribella reads in her science class, she might reread sections of the text, omit unfamiliar words, or alter her rate of reading to understand the basic meaning of the science chapter. Deep-processing strategies, by comparison, are those that involve personalizing or transforming the texts being read. Questioning the author, sourcing, representing the text in another way, and intertextual comparisons are among those strategies that allow readers to get deeper into the message. Thus, as Maribella reads her science text to gain a deeper meaning, she draws a graphic depiction of the information in the text and relates the information she is reading to information that she has read in other science texts.

Motivation

Most educators would readily agree that text-based learning is a demanding cognitive process. But competence in domain-specific reading is also a motivational–affective enterprise. Educators may realize that motivation is a potent factor in students' domain learning but narrowly conceptualize motivation in terms of students' attentiveness, or their excitement or engagement in the lesson at hand (e.g., Oldfather & Wigfield, 1996). Thus, the teacher's role is to excite or promote students' interest and involvement (Mitchell, 1997). Situational interest or this kind of immediate and temporal excitement is certainly one aspect of motivation, but it is by no means the only or the most important motivational concern (Alexander & Jetton, 2000). Other key motivational constructs that are influential include students' personal interest in the domain or topic (Hidi, 1990) and their goals for learning (Ames, 1992; Dweck & Leggett, 1988).

Interest: Situational and Individual

Often, when educators define *interest*, they are talking about students' positive responses to specific persons, objects, or activities (e.g., "I am interested in the writings of J. R. R. Tolkien"), although interest can encompass negative reactions (e.g., a morbid fascination) as well (Schiefele, 1991). The relation between interest and text-based learning has been well documented in the literature (Dewey 1913; Renninger, Hidi, & Krapp, 1992). For example, we know that readers pay particular attention to segments of the text they find interesting (Reynolds, 1992; Reynolds & Shirey, 1988; Shirey, 1992). We also know that students' involvement in reading and their level of engagement are related to achievement (Almasi, McKeown, & Beck, 1996; Guthrie et al., 1996; Reed & Schallert, 1993; Reed, Schallert, & Goetz, 1993).

It is helpful to think in terms of two forms of interest that have different purposes and effects on domain learning: situational and individual interest. As we mentioned, situational interest has more to do with the feelings or reactions triggered by environmental conditions, such as when Maribella becomes intrigued by the hands-on activity that precedes the science lesson on circuits and electricity (Alexander, 1997; Hidi & Anderson, 1992). Because situational interest can succeed in getting learners' attention and exciting them, it can be a positive force in students' text-based learning. Indeed, no student deals well with learning environments that are bland and unstimulating (Mitchell, 1997). However, situational interest can have instructional side effects, such as when students spend valuable instructional time being excited and enthused about tangential information, or when teachers fail to build on students' initial interest to promote understanding of lesson content (Jetton & Alexander, 1997; Schellings & van Hout-Wolters, 1995).

In contrast to the fleeting nature of situational interest, individual interest is enduring and comes from students' personal and long-term investment in a domain, topic, or activity (Jetton & Alexander, 2001). The hobbies or careers people pursue are indicative of their individual interests (Alexander, 1997). Furthermore, these deep-seated interests have been strongly linked to students' domain knowledge, strategic processing, self-concepts, and personal goals (Alexander et al., 1995; Meece & Holt, 1993; Murphy & Alexander, 2002; Pintrich, 1994). Thus, the teacher concerned with students' text-based learning not only sparks their interest and arouses their curiosity but also makes the lesson personally relevant by connecting to the interests and concerns students bring into the classroom.

Goals and Goal Orientations

We know that students engage in text processing for many reasons (Schunk, 1991; Wigfield & Eccles, 1992). For example, our case student, Maribella, wants to learn all she can about the subject matter or master whatever academic challenges are put before her (Murphy & Alexander, 2002). Motivation researchers would describe students like Maribella as learning- or mastery-oriented in terms of their achievement goals (Nicholls, 1984, 1989).

Maribella's classmate, Alicia, wants to perform well in the classroom, but her motivations have more to do with her desire to look good to others or to compete well against her peers (Dweck & Leggett, 1988). We would classify students like Alicia as having a performance approach in their goal orientations (Meece & Holt, 1993). Alicia's friend, Mark, is similarly concerned about his performance rather than learning, but his incentive has more to do with not looking bad or not disappointing others. Because of the more negative tone of their goals, students like Mark would be described as performance avoidant (Pintrich, 2000). Finally, there are those for whom learning and performance matter little. Rather, for such students, the overall goal is to do as little as required within the learning environment. Such students are aptly described as work avoidant (Meece, Blumenfeld, & Hoyle, 1988).

It may not be surprising to learn that students' goal orientations are linked to their school achievement (Pintrich & Schunk, 2001). Students like Maribella and Alicia, who manifest learning/mastery or performance approach goals, achieve better in school than do students, like Mark, who are either performance or work avoidant. Of course, not all student goals are directly related to their learning or achievement. For example, some goals are more about students' friendships or relationships with teachers and classmates (Wentzel, 1991, 1993). Even though these social goals are not directly about learning, they still influence student achievement, such as when students work for a good grade to please their teachers or family, or act up in classes to impress their peers.

Knowledge, Strategies, and Motivation: Putting It Together

It is not simply the case that knowledge, strategies, and motivations independently influence students' text-based learning in academic domains (Alexander, 2003). These three components are intricately related. Moreover, the nature of their relationship changes as students become increasingly more competent in a given domain (Alexander, in press). For example, knowledge and strategies are linked in several ways. First, when students have limited knowledge in a domain, they understandably encounter more comprehension problems when processing domain-specific texts. This means that these students will need to use strategies frequently during processing, and will likely rely heavily on surface-level strategies to gain understanding. Reciprocally, students who have a better developed repertoire of general strategies are better able to use those strategies to build their knowledge base in a new or unfamiliar domain of study than are less strategically equipped students.

Of course, motivation comes into play in this knowledge–strategy relationship. Students who have an interest in the domain or topic may be more willing to exert the effort required to read strategically than students who are neither situationally or individually interested. Similarly, students who have learning or performance approach goals may be more strategically engaged in text-based learning than students who have performance avoidant or work avoidant goals.

Knowledge and interest have been linked in the research literature in other ways as well. For example, students with more subject-matter knowledge consistently display higher interest in the specific topic or domain (Alexander, 2002). In addition, as students become more competent in a domain, this bond between knowledge and individual interest becomes stronger as the need to be situationally interested lessens. When they achieve domain competence, students not only have the facility to explore a domain in greater depth but they also are likely have the desire to do so, which makes for an ideal learning situation (Alexander, 1997).

WHAT DO WE KNOW ABOUT THE ROLE OF THE TEACHER IN DOMAIN LEARNING?

Those who study teacher education within academic domains assert that teachers must possess at least two forms of knowledge, content and pedagogical knowledge, in order to engage students successfully in domain learning (Shulman, 1986). First, teachers must possess a depth of subject-matter knowledge in order to know the principles of the domain, the syntax used by writers and speakers of the domain, and how the target domain relates to other domains. Shulman and Quinlan (1996) refer to this as *content knowledge*. This thorough knowledge of the domain is essential when teachers face teaching a topic about which they know little.

Second, teachers must be able to communicate that knowledge in a way that adolescents find understandable and memorable. Teachers must be able to take a text considered inconsiderate, because it lacks a cohesive structure, and communicate the information in an alternative way to facilitate learning. Teachers must also be able to use forms of representation such as analogies, examples, demonstrations, and discussions that best represent the subject matter of the domain. This kind of knowledge has often been called pedagogical *knowledge* (Shulman, 1986). In this section, we explore the interplay of content and pedagogical knowledge as teachers engage in the process of teaching within a domain.

Content Knowledge

In order for teachers to apprentice adolescents successfully into the culturally accepted principles of a domain, they must first understand the principles of that domain worthy of knowing, and how those principles are organized within the domain. For example, according to the National Council of Teachers of Mathematics (NCTM; 2000) standards for high school mathematics, students must understand the connections among algebra, geometry, statistics, probability, and discrete mathematics. They need to comprehend the fundamental mathematical concepts of function and relation, invariance, and transformation, and they need to become competent in visualizing, describing, and analyzing situations in mathematical terms. Teachers must possess a depth of knowledge about those concepts to determine ways to represent the content to their students. Similarly, high school English/language arts teachers must be familiar with a wide range of print materials from many time periods and written in many diverse genres, such as poetry, drama, short story, and novels. They must also possess a knowledge of the strategies to comprehend, interpret, evaluate, and appreciate these print materials (National Council of Teachers of English, 1996).

Teachers must understand the particular syntax and semantics of writing and speaking within the domain (Lemke, 1990). As Lemke points out, the language of science entails particular rhetorical structures that include passive voice and particular figures of speech. The domain of science also has its own special text forms that include experimental reports and laboratory notes. In contrast, the text of history can be quite different. When they use history texts in the classroom, teachers must understand the rhetorical structures and devices of both primary and secondary sources. In analyzing the primary sources, teachers must know how the sociocultural events of the era influenced the rhetorical devices used during that time period. For example, to read the Declaration of Independence, one would need to know not only the views of the Americans and the English during that time but also understand the particular rhetorical devices Jefferson used to construct this document. Only by understanding the ways in which language is presented and organized can one devise the particular patterns of meaning within the domains of mathematics, science, literature, and history.

Teachers must also understand how the principles of their own domains relate to the principles of other domains. The chemistry teacher must possess not only a thorough knowledge of scientific equations but he or she must also know the mathematical calculations to use in order to balance an equation. Assume, for example, that a chemist is examining the reaction between sulfuric acid (H_2SO_4) and sodium hydroxide (NaOH) to form sodium sulfate (Na_2SO_4) and water. This reaction could be written as $NaOH + H_2SO_4 - H_2O + Na_2SO_4$, but it would not be a balanced equation, and a chemist can only make calculations if an equation is balanced. It takes some mathematical knowledge of equations to understand how one could balance the equation by placing a 2 in front of the NaOH to form the balanced equation $2NaOH_{(aq)} + H_2SO_4 - 2H_2O_{(l)} + Na_2SO_{4(aq)}$. Thus, the teacher must bring together his or her knowledge of the domains of both science and mathematics to solve problems necessary in chemistry (Center for Science, Mathematics, and Engineering Education, 1995).

English teachers must also understand how history and literature come together in such novels as *A Tale of Two Cities,* in which Dickens depicts the plight of both the English and French during the French Revolution. Many of the key historical personages of that time are depicted in that book, among them some of the French leaders, as well as the reasons for unrest among the populace during that era, and the methods of execution.

In some of our research, we have observed the ramifications on student learning when teachers lacked sufficient content knowledge to facilitate domain learning with adolescents (Jetton & Alexander, 1997). In one study, we examined the discussions and assessments of three physical science teachers as they taught information from an article about Stephen Hawking and his explorations in astrophysics. One of the teachers, Ms. King, claimed to possess very little knowledge of the topic. During her discussion of the black holes in the article, Ms. King was unable to answer several questions posed, and she offered several misconceptions about the topic. When asked by a student where black holes go if you cannot see them, she responded, "I frankly don't know, and I don't know if that's what Mr. Hawking is looking for" (Jetton & Alexander, 1997, p. 301). The students in Ms. King's classroom left with a distorted notion of what was important in this particular topic of astrophysics and a body of knowledge that included inaccuracies and misconceptions.

Another physical science teacher in our study, Ms. Meyer, also reported that she had very little subject-matter knowledge of the topic. Because of her limited domain knowledge, she relied heavily on the textbook as the repository for information, and she elaborated very little on the context. Thus, the students in her class came away with limited under-standing of Stephen Hawking and his theories. It is the subject–matter knowledge that forms the basis on which teachers employ the second form of knowledge, pedagogical knowledge; that is, teachers must use their understanding of the content to design effective pedagogy that engages adolescents in the domain. Thus, content and pedagogical knowledge need to work in tandem for students to receive optimal instruction for learning.

Teachers must come to understand that the content of the domain can be changed either by the sociocultural norms that society sets or by new content that adds to the field. History, for example, changes over time as society interprets historical events. For example, one would just have to look back at a history text written right after the Bay of Pigs incident and at a history book of today that details the same event. In science, we are constantly gathering new information that adds to our knowledge of the field and changes the theories that we once held as truth.

Teachers must also realize that with the advent of the Information Age, the content of a domain is increasing rapidly. Experts in the domain would be hard-pressed to keep up with the amount of information circu-lating throughout the world in traditional print and hypertext alone. It is for these two reasons—the dynamic nature of domains and the wealth of information that has exploded within each domain—that teachers must devote themselves to lifelong learning. They must be willing to access con-tent knowledge as often as possible. Acquiring the knowledge of the domain is crucial if teachers are to keep abreast of important contributions that arise in a field of study.

How can teachers acquire the knowledge to remain experts in the domain? One way is to join organizations for the particular domains, such as the NCTM or the National Council of Teachers of English. Organiza-tions such as these provide literature in the forms journals, pamphlet, and newspapers that inform their readership of the current knowledge within the field. Another important source for information within a domain is the Internet, but teachers need to know how to be critical consumers of the information on the World Wide Web (Brem, Russell, & Weems, 2001).

Pedagogical Knowledge

Simply defined, *pedagogy* means "the art or science of teaching" (Agnes, 2003, p. 475). Pedagogical knowledge refers to the knowledge that teachers possess for teaching (Shulman, 1986; Shulman & Quinlan, 1996). Teachers must know not only the content but also how to represent and formulate the subject matter so that it understandable to others. Representations and transformations can take on multiple forms that include lectures, analogies, illustrations, discussions, explanations, and demonstrations. Pedagogical knowledge also means understanding what makes a specific topic within a domain easy or difficult and what kinds of preconceptions and misconceptions students have of the content. Furthermore, teachers must know strategies for facilitating the learning of easy and difficult concepts, and for overcoming students' initial conceptions or misconceptions.

Teaching Approaches

One aspect of pedagogical knowledge that is important to consider for adolescent learning is the type of approach the teacher takes in facilitating subject-matter learning. As Alvermann (2002) and others have noted, a teacher-centered approach is the most widespread model is middle and high schools. The teacher-centered approach to transforming domain knowledge into pedagogy involves the teacher conveying "authorized or official" knowledge to the students (Wade & Moje, 2000, p. 611). This approach has also been labeled the *transmission approach* to learning (Wade & Moje, 2000). Teachers control the content in order to achieve specific learning objectives. The classroom interaction usually involves the teacher calling on students to respond in one-word answers to a set of predetermined questions designed by the teacher (Cazden, 1986; Dillon, 1981; Lemke, 1990). The text is viewed as a repository of official information that students must memorize (Alvermann, 2002).

The alternative approach is the *transactional* or *participatory approach* to subject-matter learning (Alvermann, 2002; Wade & Moje, 2000). Through this approach, teachers facilitate domain learning by providing opportunities for adolescents to engage in classroom structures that promote peer interaction and increase the likelihood that students will begin to construct the knowledge for themselves. When teachers employ this approach, they provide students with a variety of texts, including linear or traditional texts, nonlinear or hypertexts, and the texts of peer-led discussions to explore the content of a particular domain. By exploring a wide range of texts, students are able to search for important information within the domain, in order to construct a mental model of the concepts (Stahl et al., 1995). In using the participatory approach, teachers also ask students to construct their knowledge of the subject matter by writing in a variety of forms that include both their own sociocultural experiences and more sanctioned texts of the classroom (Wade & Moje, 2000).

Although these approaches might appear to be dichotomous choices that teachers make, that is, with teachers determining whether the content should be transmitted *or* facilitated, we believe there are inherent dangers in privileging one or the other approach as the sole pedagogy of the classroom. Rather, we believe that both approaches can be effectively implemented in the classroom environment. For example, if a teacher needs to provide a brief, direct explanation of a certain procedure or theory, the transmission approach might be best. On the contrary, when teachers want to engage students in problem solving, the transactional approach achieves more interactive reasoning among participants and might be the best approach for that situation.

It is clear in the research of adolescent classrooms, particularly in high schools, that the sole use of the transmission approach occurs too frequently (Alvermann, O'Brien, & Dillon, 1990; Cazden, 2001; Jetton, 1994). Those teachers who choose transmission as the sole approach risk seriously disengaging adolescents from the content. In our study of the high school physical science teachers, we found one teacher who had an in-depth understanding of the content. She was very enthusiastic about the content and provided numerous elaborations of the important scientific principles within the article on Stephen Hawking and his astrophysical studies. However, she did most of the talking during the entire lesson (Jetton & Alexander, 1997). The students' passive participation left us wondering whether these adolescents would be able to know the important information in any depth and apply or synthesize this knowledge to other situations, because they were given no chance to participate in the subject-matter learning.

We also believe that a classroom in which the participatory approach is the sole pedagogy could potentially be just as detrimental to student learning. Sometimes students need the teacher, as a more knowledgeable other, to provide a minilecture on a particular principle within the domain (Vygotsky, 1934/1986). In our observations of classroom discussions, we found that when students within a peer-led discussion reached an impasse in their knowledge, the discussion became unproductive and frustrating to them. The teacher would then ask students to pause their discussions, and she would provide a short lecture about the content (Alexander & Jetton, 2003; Jetton, 1994). In this way, she could elaborate on an important concept that would make it easier for the students to go back to their peer-led discussions and construct knowledge in a more participatory way. Other researchers have also noted that the transmission and participatory approaches are not necessarily oppositional in the classroom (Moore, 1996). We go a step further by saying that in our research of domain learning in science classrooms, both approaches are necessary, justified, and complementary according to the goals set by the teachers and students for learning (Jetton & Alexander, 1997).

Engagement

Whether the teacher uses a transmission or participatory approach to teach the content of a domain, we know from research that teachers must practice pedagogy that engages adolescents in domain learning (Guthrie,

McGough, Bennett, & Rice, 1996). A teacher must implement practices that facilitate adolescents' acquisition of new knowledge, motivate them to learn the content of the domain, teach them how to employ a variety of strategies to comprehend the principles of that domain, and allow them to learn through social interaction (Guthrie et al., 1996; Guthrie & Wigfield, 1999). As teachers implement practice within the domain, they motivate students by communicating clear learning goals, promoting understanding, and valuing the content over performance outcomes (Ames, 1992; Dweck & Leggett, 1988); that is, learning the content of a domain is more important than receiving a good grade or having correct answers. Effective domain teachers also engage students by including a wide range of texts in the classroom, so that students can find texts of particular interest to them (Guthrie et al., 1996). Many high school English teachers read a variety of narrative texts, without taking into account that some of the students would benefit from reading nonfiction materials.

Furthermore, teachers must value and teach general and domain-specific strategies for learning the content. For example, the history teacher must teach students the domain-specific strategies that historians employ to construct a mental model of the domain (Stahl et al., 1996). Processes such as evaluating historical documents, and integrating information from such documents, are key strategies in thinking like historians. Teachers can facilitate instruction of these strategies in an environment of collaboration, in which students have ample opportunities to talk to one another and their teacher about the content and their own mental processes.

Teachers use instructional strategies such as semantic maps or KWL (Know–Want to know–Learned) charts to model how to learn content and use general and domain-specific strategies within a domain (Ogle, 1986). The benefit of these instructional strategies is that they are designed to increase content knowledge in a domain and at the same time model for students how to strategically process the information. For example, a science teacher might engage students in a KWL chart about the central nervous system. As she introduces the "K," she asks students to brainstorm all of the information they already know about this topic. As students generate information from their prior knowledge, they are conveying content information to the chart and activating their prior knowledge, a critical literacy strategy. Similarly, as the teacher asks students to tell her what they want to know about the central nervous system, under the "W," students are thinking about the knowledge of the content that they do not possess. Finally, as students write what they learned about the topic from the text, under the "L," they are noting important content information to remember as they are determining importance, another critical reading strategy. Thus, the benefit of these instructional strategies is that they increase content knowledge at the same time that students are learning how to think strategically.

The use of instructional strategies in domain learning must be conscious and reflective. Teachers can become routinized in one or two particular instructional strategies, much to the detriment of student learning (Jetton, 1994). In one study conducted with six biology teachers, Jetton found that these teachers used a concept map almost every day for 12 weeks (Jetton & Alexander, 1997). These concept maps had become such a part of the classroom routine that the teachers had stopped using them in a strategic way to facilitate learning of particular concepts. When pedagogical practices become routinized rather than reflective, teachers may forget the theoretical reasons they are using a specific instructional strategy. Teachers should have a theoretical and practical purpose behind the use of these instructional strategies; that is, they should know that when they use particular instructional strategies, such as the KWL or brainstorming, they are modeling for students how strategic readers activate prior knowledge before they start reading. Likewise, when teachers implement an instructional strategy such as Reciprocal Teaching, they should know that this strategy facilitates practice of four powerful strategies: determining importance through summarizing, clarifying ideas, asking questions, and predicting future information (Palinscar & Brown, 1984). Instructional strategies can become very effective ways to model how students learn the content as long as teachers know what the strategies teach, how the strategies might be used in particular situations in the classroom, and when they would be most advantageous to employ.

Pedagogical knowledge also entails decisions about how much content needs to be taught and how best to teach it (Shulman, 1986). In the current atmosphere of statewide testing, teachers can get caught up in teaching less and less about more and more topics. Durkin (1978–1979) referred to this practice as "mentioning" rather than teaching. Such teaching increases the likelihood that students achieve only a superficial understanding of the domain. DiSessa (1988) advocates teaching more about less. Teachers and students work together to select content and particular strategies carefully and to explore these in greater depth. The idea is that students who participate in this kind of instruction will develop an understanding of the principled roots of the domain.

CONCLUDING THOUGHTS ABOUT THE FUTURE OF DOMAIN LEARNING AND TEACHING

Learning within a domain can be a fruitful and rewarding experience for adolescents who are adding to their content base, developing an interest in the subject matter, and employing strategic behavior. Likewise, educators who devote their professional lives to facilitating subject-matter learning for adolescents take pleasure in this lofty goal. During the past three decades, we have learned a great deal about how adolescents learn within a domain. However, we know little about the development of domain learning as individuals progress from a state of acclimation or naivete to a more competent state. Future research needs to focus on the developmental nature of learning within particular domains. For example, we need to conduct longitudinal studies of individuals as they progress through a domain from acclimation to competence to expertise. Through these studies, we can begin to examine the individual and contextual factors that contribute to an individual's movement from one phase of domain learning to another. Certainly, one of the factors that influences how individuals move through these phases is literacy. We need to understand better the complex interplay of knowledge, interest, and strategic processing as readers engage in text at each of the phases of learning.

We also need to understand how teachers can facilitate domain learning through literacy instruction. For example, we know that despite decades of research on strategies that enhance text-based learning, few teachers facilitate the use of comprehension strategies with their students in their classrooms (Dole, 2000; Pressley, 2002). We need to examine why teachers of adolescents are not utilizing text-based strategies to help their students learn the content from subject-matter texts. We can surmise that a host of reasons will emerge from this study, including lack of exposure to these strategies, or teachers' reluctance to use the strategies because they are obsessed with covering the content.

Another crucial issue that remains unanswered is how teachers can most effectively employ these literacy strategies in their content-area classrooms. How much and what kind of content should be read? With the trend of instruction focused on hands-on activities that engage learners, we need to examine how texts can be an effective part of a variety of instructional activities intended to enhance domain learning. How explicit or implicit do teachers need to be in teaching text-based strategies to their students? Very little research exists that examines how teachers employ literacy strategies in middle and high school classrooms to increase student learning. Thus, we know little about what that instruction looks like.

As state and national testing become even more prominent in the next few years, issues related to domain learning in science, mathematics, history, and English will become even more central and crucial to the lives of students and their teachers. Furthermore, adolescents will be required to read increasingly more difficult textual materials, and teachers will need to find ways to support these students as they confront these daunting challenges.

REFERENCES

Adams, M. J. (1991). *Beginning to read.* Cambridge, MA: MIT Press.

Agnes, M. (Ed.). (2003). *Webster's new world dictionary.* New York: Pocket Books.

Alexander, P. A. (2003). The development of expertise: The journey from acclimation to proficiency. *Educational Researcher, 32,* 10–14.

Alexander, P. A. (2002, January). *The struggling adolescent reader: A new perspective on an enduring problem.* Keynote address presented at the Adolescent Literacy Workshop sponsored by the National Institute of Child Health and Human Development, Washington, DC.

Alexander, P. A. (1998). The nature of disciplinary and domain learning: The knowledge, interest, and strategic dimensions of learning from subject-matter text. In C. Hynd (Ed.), *Learning from text across conceptual domains* (pp. 263–287). Mahwah, NJ: Erlbaum.

Alexander, P. A. (1997). Stages and phases of domain learning: The dynamics of subject-matter knowledge, strategy knowledge, and motivation. In C. E. Weinstein & B. L. McCombs (Eds.), *Strategic learning: Skill, will, and self-regulation* (Vol. 10, pp. 213–250). Mahwah, NJ: Erlbaum.

Alexander, P. A., & Jetton, T. L. (2000). Learning from text: A multidimensional and developmental perspective. In M. L. Kamil, P. B. Mosenthal, P. D. Pearson, & R. Barr (Eds.), *Handbook of reading research* (Vol. 3, pp. 285–310). Mahwah, NJ: Erlbaum.

Alexander, P. A., & Jetton, T. L. (2003). Learning from traditional and alternative texts: New conceptualizations for the information age. In A. C. Graesser, M. A. Gernsbacher, & S. R. Goldman (Eds.), *Handbook of discourse processes* (pp. 199–241). Mahwah, NJ: Erlbaum.

Alexander, P. A., Jetton, T. L., & Kulikowich, J. M. (1995). Interrelationship of knowledge, interest, and recall: Assessing a model of domain learning. *Journal of Educational Psychology, 87,* 559–575.

Alexander, P. A., & Judy, J. E. (1988). The interaction of domain-specific and strategic knowledge in academic performance. *Review of Educational Research, 58,* 375–404.

Alexander, P. A., & Kulikowich, J. M. (1991). Domain knowledge and analogic reasoning ability as predictors of expository text comprehension. *Journal of Reading Behavior, 23,* 165–190.

Alexander, P. A., & Kulikowich, J. M. (1994). Learning from physics text: A synthesis of recent research. *Journal of Research in Science Teaching, 31,* 895–911.

Alexander, P. A., Murphy, P. K., & Woods, B. S. (1996). Of squalls and fathoms: Navigating the seas of educational innovation. *Educational Researcher, 25*(3), 31–36, 39.

Alexander, P. A., Schallert, D. L., & Hare, V. C. (1991). Coming to terms: How researchers in learning and literacy talk about knowledge. *Review of Educational Research, 61,* 315–343.

Alexander, P. A., Sperl, C. T., Buehl, M. M., Fives, H., & Chiu, S. (2002, June). *Modeling domain learning: Profiles from the field of special education.* Manuscript submitted for publication.

Almasi, J. F., McKeown, M. G., & Beck, I. L. (1996). The nature of engaged reading in classroom discussions of literature. *Journal of Literacy Research, 28,* 107–146.

Alvermann, D. E. (2002). Effective literacy instruction for adolescents. *Journal of Literacy Research, 34,* 189–208.

Alvermann, D. E., O'Brien, D. G., & Dillon, D. R. (1990). What teachers do when they say they're having discussions of content area reading assignments: A qualitative analysis. *Reading Research Quarterly, 25,* 297–322.

Ames, C. (1992). Classrooms: Goals, structures, and student motivation. *Journal of Educational Psychology, 84,* 261–271

Armbruster, B. B. (1984). The problem of "inconsiderate texts." In G. G. Duffy, L. R. Roehler, & J. Mason (Eds.), *Theoretical issues in reading comprehension* (pp. 202–217). New York: Longman.

Brem, S. K., Russell, J., & Weems, L. (2001). Science on the web: Student evaluations of scientific arguments. *Discourse Processes, 32,* 191–213.

Britton, B. K. (1981, April). *Use of cognitive capacity in reading.* Paper presented at the annual meeting of the American Educational Research Association, Los Angeles, CA.

Cazden, C. B. (2001). *Classroom discourse: The language of teaching and learning.* Portsmouth, NH: Heinemann.

Center for Science, Mathematics, and Engineering Education. (1995). *National science education standards.* Washington, DC: National Academy Press.

Chall, J. S. (1995). *The stages of reading development* (2nd ed.). New York: Wadsworth.

Chambliss, M. (1995). Text cues and strategies successful readers use to construct the gist of lengthy written arguments. *Reading Researcher Quarterly, 30,* 778–807.

Chi, M. T. H., Glaser, R., & Farr, M. J. (Eds.). (1988). *The nature of expertise.* Hillsdale, NJ: Erlbaum.

Dewey, J. (1913). *Interest and effort in education.* Boston: Riverside.

Dillon, J. T. (1981). Duration of response to teacher questions and statements. *Contemporary Educational Psychology, 6,* 1–11.

diSessa, A. A. (1988). What will it mean to be "educated" in 2020? In R. S. Nickerson & P. P. Zodhiates (Eds.), *Technology in education: Looking toward 2020* (pp. 43"66). Hinsdale, NJ: Erlbaum.

Dole, J. A. (2000). Explicit and implicit instruction in comprehension. In B. M. Taylor, M. F. Graves, & P. van den Broek (Eds.), *Reading for meaning: Fostering comprehension in the middle grades* (pp. 52–69). New York: Teachers College Press.

Durant, W. (1954). *Story of civilization: Part I. Our Oriental heritage.* New York: Simon & Schuster.

Durkin, D. (1978–1979). What classroom observations reveal about reading comprehension instruction. *Reading Research Quarterly, 14,* 481–533.

Dweck, C. S., & Leggett, E. L. (1988). A social-cognitive approach to motivation and personality. *Psychological Review, 95,* 256–273.

Frederiksen, N. (1984). Implications of cognitive theory for instruction in problem solving. *Review of Educational Research, 54,* 363–407.

Garner, R. (1987). *Metacognition and reading comprehension.* Norwood, NJ: Ablex.

Goldin, G. A. (1992). Toward an assessment framework for school mathematics. In R. Lesh & S. J. Lamon (Eds.), *Assessments of authentic performance in elementary mathematics* (pp. 63–88). Washington, DC: American Association for the Advancement of Science.

Goldman, S. R., & Rakestraw, J. A., Jr. (2000). Structural aspects of constructing meaning from text. In M. L. Kamil, P. B. Mosenthal, P. D. Pearson, & R. Barr (Eds.), *Handbook of reading research* (Vol. 3, pp. 311–335). Mahwah, NJ: Erlbaum.

Guthrie, J. T., McGough, K., Bennett, L., & Rice, M. E. (1996). Concept-oriented reading instruction: An integrated curriculum to develop motivations and strategies for reading. In L. Baker, P. Afflerbach, & D. Reinking (Eds.), *Developing engaged readers in school and home communities* (pp. 165–190). Mahwah, NJ: Erlbaum.

Guthrie, J. T., Van Meter, P., McCann, A. D., Wigfield, A., Bennett, L., Poundstone, C. C., et al. (1996). Growth of literacy engagement: Changes in motivations and strategies during concept-oriented reading instruction. *Reading Research Quarterly, 31,* 306–332.

Guthrie, J. T., & Wigfield, A. (1999). How motivation fits into a science of reading. *Scientific Studies of Reading, 3,* 199–205.

Hidi, S. (1990). Interest and its contribution as a mental resource for learning. *Review of Educational Research, 60,* 549–571.

Hidi, S., & Anderson, V. (1992). Situational interest and its impact on reading and expository writing. In K. A. Renninger, S. Hidi, & A. Krapp (Eds.), *The role of interest in learning and development* (pp. 215–238). Hillsdale, NJ: Erlbaum.

Hurst, J. (2000). The scarlet ibis. In *Elements of literature: Third course* (pp. 315–323). Austin, TX: Holt, Rinehart & Winston.

Jetton, T. L. (1994). *Teachers' and students' understanding of scientific exposition: How importance and interest influence what is accessed and what is discussed.* Unpublished doctoral dissertation, Texas A&M University, College Station.

Jetton, T. L., & Alexander, P. A. (1997). Instructional importance: What teachers value and what students learn. *Reading Research Quarterly, 32,* 290–308.

Jetton, T. L., & Alexander, P. A. (2001). Interest assessment and the content area literacy environment: Challenges for research and practice. *Educational Psychology Review, 13,* 303–318.

Jetton, T. L., Rupley, W. H., & Willson, V. L. (1995). Comprehension of narrative and expository texts: The role of content, topic, discourse, and strategy knowledge. In K. A. Hinchman, D. H. Leu, & C. K. Kinzer (Eds.), *Perspectives on literacy research and practice* (pp. 197–204). Chicago: National Reading Conference.

Kamil, M. L., Mosenthal, P. B., Pearson, P. D., & Barr, R. (Eds.). (2000). *Handbook of reading research* (Vol. 3). Mahwah, NJ: Erlbaum.

Kulikowich, J. M., O'Connell, A. A., Rezendes, G., & Archambault, F. X. (2000, April). Many theories, many methodologies: Blending quantitative and qualitative procedures in the study of classroom dynamics involving technology. In K. Squire (Chair), *The merits of multiple theories of learning in the study of technology use in classroom settings.* Symposium presented at the annual meeting of the American Educational Research Association, New Orleans, LA.

Lampert, M., & Blunk, M. L. (1998). *Talking mathematics in schools.* Cambridge, UK: Cambridge University Press.

Lemke, J. L. (1990). *Talking science: Language, learning, and values.* Norwood, NJ: Ablex.~

Matthews, M. R. (1994). *Science teaching: The role of history and philosophy of science.* New York: Routledge.

Meece, J. L., Blumenfeld, P. C., & Hoyle, R. H. (1988). Students' goal orientations and cognitive engagement in classroom activities. *Journal of Educational Psychology, 80,* 514–523.

Meece, J. L., & Holt, K. (1993). A pattern analysis of students' achievement goals. *Journal of Educational Psychology, 85,* 582–590.

Mitchell, M. (1997, April). *Interest and anxiety in mathematics.* Paper presented at the annual meeting of the American Educational Research Association, Chicago. Dordrecht, the Netherlands: Kluwer Academic.

Moore, D. W. (1996). Contexts for literacy in secondary schools. In D. J. Leu, C. K. Kinzer, & K. A. Hinchman (Eds.), *Literacies for the 21st century: Research and practice: Forty-fifth yearbook of the National Reading Conference* (pp. 15–46). Chicago: National Reading Conference.

Murphy, P. K., & Alexander, P. A. (2002). What counts?: The predictive power of subject-matter knowledge, strategic processing, and interest in domain-specific performance. *Journal of Experimental Education, 70,* 197–214.

National Academy of Science. (1995). *National Science Education Standards.* Available online at *http://www.nap.edu/readingroom/books/nseslhtml/*

National Assessment of Educational Progress. (2002). *The nation's report card: Reading 2002.* Washington, DC: National Center for Education Statistics. Available online at *http://nces.ed.gov/pubsearch/pubsinfo.asp?pubid=2003521.*

National Council of Teachers of English. (1996). *Standards for the English language arts.* Urbana, IL: Author.

National Council of Teachers of Mathematics. (2000). *Principles and standards for school mathematics.* Retrieved January 3, 2004 from *http://standards.nctm.org/document/index.htm*

National Reading Panel. (2000). *Report of the National Reading Panel.* Washington, DC: National Institute of Child Health and Human Development. Available online at *http://www.nichd.nih.gov/publications/pubskey.cfm?from=nrp*

Nicholls, J. G. (1984). Achievement motivation: Conceptions of ability, subjective experience, task choice, and performance. *Psychological Review, 91,* 328–346.

Nicholls, J. G. (1989). *The competitive ethos and democratic education.* Cambridge, MA: Harvard University Press.

Ogle, D. M. (1986). K-W-L: A teaching model that develops active reading of expository text. *Reading Teacher. 39,* 564–570.

Oldfather, P., & Wigfield, A. (1996). Children's motivations to read. In L. Baker, P. Afflerbach, & D. Reinking (Eds.), *Developing engaged readers in school and home communities* (pp. 89–113). Mahwah, NJ: Erlbaum.

Palincsar, A. S., & Brown, L. (1984). Reciprocal teaching of comprehension fostering and comprehension-monitoring activities. *Cognition and Instruction, 1,* 117–175.

Phillips, D. C. (1987). *Philosophy, science, and social inquiry.* Oxford, UK: Pergamon.

Phillips, D. C. (1995). The good, the bad, and the ugly: The many faces of constructivism. *Educational Researcher, 24*(7), 5–12.

Pintrich, P. R. (1994). Continuities and discontinuities: Future directions for research in educational psychology. *Educational Psychologist, 29,* 137–148.

Pintrich, P. R. (2000). An achievement goal theory perspective on issues in motivation terminology, theory, and research. *Contemporary Educational Psychology, 25,* 92–104.

Pintrich, P. R., & Schunk, D. H. (2001). *Motivation in education: Theory, research, and applications* (2nd ed.). Englewood Cliffs, NJ: Prentice-Hall.

Pressley, M. (2002). Comprehension strategies instruction: A turn-of-the-century report. In C. C. Block & M. Pressley (Eds.), *Comprehension instruction: Research-based best practices* (pp. 11–27). New York: Guilford Press.

Pressley, M., Goodchild, F., Fleet, J., Zajchowski, R., & Evans, E. D. (1989). The challenges of classroom strategy instruction. *Elementary School Journal, 89,* 301–342.

Reed, J. H., & Schallert, D. L. (1993). The nature of involvement in academic discourse. *Journal of Educational Psychology, 85,* 253–266.

Reed, J. H., Schallert, D. L., & Goetz, E. T. (1993, April). *Interest happens but involvement takes effort: Distinguishing between two constructs in academic discourse tasks.* Paper presented at the annual meeting of the American Educational Research Association, Atlanta, GA.

Renninger, K. A., Hidi, S., & Krapp, A. (1992). *The role of interest in learning and development.* Hillsdale, NJ: Erlbaum.

Reynolds, R. E. (1992). Learning important information from text: The role of selective attention. *Review of Educational Psychology, 4,* 345–391.

Reynolds, R. E., & Shirey, L. L. (1988). The role of attention in studying and learning. In C. E. Weinstein, E. T. Goetz, & P. A. Alexander (Eds.), *Learning and study strategies: Issues in assessment, instruction, and evaluation* (pp. 77–100). San Diego: Academic Press.

Schellings, G. L. M., & van Hout-Wolters, B. H. A. M. (1995). Main points in an instructional text, as identified by students and their teachers. *Reading Research Quarterly, 30,* 742–756.

Schiefele, U. (1991). Interest, learning, and motivation. *Educational Psychologist, 26,* 299–323.

Shulman, L. S. (1986). Those who understand: Knowledge growth in teaching. *Educational Researcher, 24,* 9–17.

Shulman, L. S., & Quinlan, K. M. (1996). The comparative psychology of school subjects. In D. C. Berliner & R. C. Calfee (Eds.), *Handbook of educational psychology* (pp. 399–422). New York: Simon & Schuster/Macmillan.

Schunk, D. (1991). Self-efficacy and academic motivation. *Educational Psychologist, 26,* 207–231.

Shirey, L. L. (1992). Importance, interest, and selective attention. In K. A. Renninger, S. Hidi, & A. Krapp (Eds.), *The role of interest in learning and development* (pp. 281–296). Hillsdale, NJ: Erlbaum.

Stahl, S. A., Hynd, C. R., Glynn, S. M., & Carr, M. (1996). Beyond reading to learn: Developing content and disciplinary knowledge through texts. In L. Baker, P. Afflerbach, & D. Reinking (Eds.), *Developing engaged readers in school and home community* (pp. 139–163). Mahwah, NJ: Erlbaum.

Stanovich, K. E. (1986). Matthew effects in reading: Some consequences of individual differences in the acquisition of literacy. *Reading Research Quarterly, 21,* 360–406.

Stewart, I. (1987). *The problem of mathematics.* New York: Oxford University Press.

VanSledright, B., & Alexander, P. A. (2002). *Historical knowledge, thinking, and beliefs:*

Evaluation component of the Corps of Historical Discovery Project (No. S215X010242). Washington, DC: U.S. Department of Education.

VanSledright, B. A. (2002). *In search of America's past: Learning to read history in elementary school*. New York: Teachers College Press.

Vygotsky, L. (1986). *Thought and language* (A. Kozulin, Trans.). Cambridge, MA: MIT Press. (Original work published 1934)

Wade, S. E., & Moje, E. B. (2000). The role of text in classroom learning. In M. L. Kamil, P. B. Mosenthal, P. D. Pearson, & R. Barr (Eds.), *Handbook of reading research* (Vol. 3, pp. 609–627). Mahwah, NJ: Erlbaum.

Wentzel, K. R. (1991). Relations between social competence and academic achievement in early adolescence. *Child Development, 62,* 1066–1078.

Wentzel, K. R. (1993). Social and academic goals at school: Motivation and achievement in early adolescence. *Journal of Early Adolescence, 13,* 4–20.

West, L. H. T., & Pines, A. L. (1985). *Cognitive structures and conceptual change*. New York: Academic Press.

Wigfield, A., & Eccles, J. (1992). The development of achievement task values: A theoretical analysis. *Developmental Review, 12,* 265–310.

Winne, P. H. (1995). Inherent details in self-regulated learning. *Educational Psychologist, 30,* 173–187.

Zimmerman, B. J. (1995). Self-regulation involves more than metacognition: A social cognitive perspective. *Educational Psychologist, 30,* 217–221.

Teaching English from a Literacy Perspective
The Goal of High Literacy for All Students

WAYNE H. SLATER

The teaching of English in U.S. secondary schools has focused extensively on the study of U.S., British, and world literature, with a greater emphasis recently on literature by women and minorities. In addition, English teachers pay some attention to written and oral communication, English usage and style (edited American English), generic reading comprehension strategies, and listening (Applebee, 1974; Squire, 2003). Clearly, the predominant focus in English classrooms is the study of literature, which, of course, reflects the emphasis of most English teacher preparation programs (Applebee, 1993; Squire, 2003; Squire & Applebee, 1968). The study of literature permeates the English classroom to such an extent that one begins to believe that the purpose and function of English instruction in America is to train the next generation of literary scholars rather than to provide an increasingly diverse student population with a knowledge base and strategies necessary to help all students achieve the compelling goal of high literacy. For the purpose of this chapter, *high literacy* is defined as the educational goal of teaching all students to think, read, and write critically.

In this chapter, I examine current research findings on reading and writing, published by the National Assessment of Educational Progress

(NAEP), that strongly suggest that English instruction in America is failing to address all students' high literacy needs in both reading and writing. I then describe a classroom study that suggests what successful English classrooms that achieve high literacy look like. I then make the case for cognitive strategy instruction in English classrooms, with an emphasis on reciprocal teaching. Next, I briefly describe the Maryland English teacher preparation program designed to focus on language and cognitive strategy instruction. Finally, I focus on research that needs to be done on effective literacy instruction, cognitive strategy instruction, and English teacher preparation to help us achieve the goal of high literacy for all students.

THE NATIONAL ASSESSMENT OF EDUCATIONAL PROGRESS FINDINGS IN READING

The current NAEP reading assessment was initiated in 1992, and the recent 2002 NAEP reading results are not encouraging (Grigg, Daane, Jin, & Campbell, 2003). For my purposes, examining changes in scores for students at higher, middle, and lower performance levels provides a more comprehensive view of student progress. An examination of scores at different percentiles on the 0–500 reading scale at each grade level indicates whether or not the changes seen in the national average score results are found in the performance of lower, middle, and higher performing students. The percentile indicates the percentage of students whose scores fell below a particular score. At grade 4, scores at the 10th, 25th, and 50th percentiles were higher in 2002 than in 1998 and 2000 but were not significantly different from 1992. The score at the 75th percentile was higher than that in 1992. At grade 8, scores were higher in 2002 than in 1992 at all but the 90th percentile. However, only scores for lower performing students at the 10th and 25th percentiles were higher in 2002 than in 1998. At grade 12, the decline in performance since 1992 was evident across most of the score distribution (at the 10th, 25th, 50th, and 75th percentiles). Performance at the 90th percentile declined between 1998 and 2002.

The average reading scores for male and female fourth graders were higher in 2002 than in 1998, but were not found to be significantly different from the 1992 scores. The average reading scores of both male and female eighth graders were higher in 2002 than in 1992 and 1994. Although the reading score for eighth-grade males increased between 1998 and 2002, the average score for females in 2002 was not found to be significantly different from that in 1998. The average reading scores for both male and female 12th graders decreased between 1998 and 2002, resulting in average scores that were lower than those in 1992 for both groups.

Finally, the average reading scores were reported by race/ethnicity. At grade 4, both white students and black students had higher average reading scores in 2002 than in any of the previous assessment years. The average score for Hispanic students in 2002 was higher than in 1994, 1998, and 2000, but was not found to differ significantly from the 1992 score. The average score in 2002 was higher than that in 1992 for Asian/Pacific Islander students. At grade 8, average reading scores in 2002 were higher than those in 1992 and 1994 for white, black, and Hispanic students. At grade 12, the average scores for white and black students in 2002 were lower than those in 1992. In 2002, white students and Asian/Pacific Islander students had higher average scores than black and Hispanic students, and white students outperformed Asian/Pacific Islander students at all three grade levels. In addition, white and Asian/Pacific Islander students scored higher on average than native American/Alaska Native students at grades 4 and 8.

THE NATIONAL ASSESSMENT OF EDUCATIONAL PROGRESS FINDINGS IN WRITING

The current NAEP writing assessment was initiated in 1998, and, similar to the reading results, the 2002 NAEP writing results are not impressive (Persky, Daane, & Jin, 2003). Again, examining changes in scores for students at upper and lower performance levels provides a more comprehensive understanding of student progress. An examination of scores at different percentiles on the 0–300 writing scale at each grade level indicates whether the changes seen in the national average score results are reflected in the performance of lower, middle, and higher performing students. Increases in fourth-grade writing scores were observed for lower, middle, and higher performing students. Gains were found among the middle and higher performing eighth graders at the 50th, 75th, and 90th percentiles. At grade 12, only scores at the 90th percentile increased since 1998, whereas scores of the lower performing students in the 10th and 25th percentiles were lower in 2002.

At grades 4 and 8, the average writing scores of both male and female students were higher in 2002 than in 1998. However, at grade 12, the average scores for male students declined since 1998, whereas the apparent increase in the average scores for female students during the same period was not found to be statistically significant. Female students outperformed male students at all three grade levels.

Finally, at grades 4 and 8, white, black, and Hispanic students had higher average writing scores in 2002 than in 1998. Increases for fourth-

and eighth-grade Asian/Pacific Islander students were not found to be statistically significant. At grade 12, no significant changes were detected for any of the racial/ethnic groups from 1998 to 2002. In 2002, Asian/Pacific Islander students outperformed all other groups at grade 4, and both Asian/Pacific Islander and white students outperformed black and Hispanic students at grades 4 and 8. At grade 12, white and Asian/Pacific Islander students scored higher on average than black and Hispanic students, and Hispanic students had higher scores than black students.

WHAT DO THE NAEP 2002
READING AND WRITING FINDINGS SUGGEST?

Although it is not the purpose here to interpret the NAEP findings in depth, I think I can safely say that the 2002 results in both reading and writing have important implications for establishing a literacy perspective for English instruction. First, we are making some progress in certain areas in both reading and writing, but that progress is not sufficiently robust and universal to meet the high literacy needs of all students. Second, many more students who are currently scoring at *Basic* (this level denotes partial mastery of prerequisite knowledge and skills that are fundamental for proficient work at each grade) and *Proficient* (this level represents solid academic performance for each grade assessed; students reaching this level have demonstrated competence in challenging subject matter, including subject-matter knowledge, application of such knowledge to real-world situations, and analytical skills appropriate to the subject matter levels) should be scoring at the *Advanced* level (which signifies superior performance); that is, if we expect all students to attain high literacy, so that they can flourish in higher education, the competitive world of work, and our free society, many more need to be achieving at the *Advanced* level (College Entrance Examination Board, 2003; National Reading Panel, 2000). In the next section, I discuss a classroom study that suggests what successful English classrooms in which students achieve high literacy look like.

WHAT RESEARCH TELLS US ABOUT MIDDLE SCHOOL
AND HIGH SCHOOL ENGLISH CLASSES
THAT ACHIEVE HIGH LITERACY FOR ALL STUDENTS

In a seminal, 5-year study focused on middle school and high school English classes that achieve high literacy for all students, Langer (2001) examined English language arts programs in schools that have been trying to increase student performance in reading, writing, and English, comparing those schools whose students perform higher than demographically comparable schools with schools whose scores are more typical. For historically important studies in this same line of inquiry, refer to Squire and Applebee's (1968) examination of 158 programs in the 1960s, Hillocks (1986) research on writing instruction, and Applebee's (1993) research on literature instruction.

For her theoretical framework, Langer (2001) warranted her socio-cognitive perspective with the thinking of Bakhtin (1981) and Vygotsky (1987). From this perspective, student learning is hypothesized to be influenced by the values, experiences, and actions that manifest themselves within the larger environment. Students' and teachers' experiences and voices make a contribution to what is learned and how it is learned. In his theoretical perspectives on dialogical thinking and the multivocal nature of language, Bakhtin (1981) provides researchers and practitioners with a way to think about high literacy and its development. Instead of viewing high literacy as comprising independent skills or proficiencies that students muster when needed, he articulates a position in which the educated person has access to a multilayered history of experiences with language and content across many contexts. Multiple and competing voices and interpretations add depth to emerging thinking and ideas. He argues that the discourse of any nation includes an awareness of the rhetoric and experiences of many subgroups; that is, if we are to achieve high literacy for all students, these students must recognize and respond differently, he says, to the prose characteristics of teachers, lawyers, doctors, or clergy. These ways of communicating and interpreting must achieve a dialogue with one another rather than being reduced to a single, unified discourse. Such diverse voices also occur both within and across classrooms and subject areas (Applebee, 1996). Students use the voices of their out-of-school experiences, as well as conversations within their particular courses, to parse the topic being discussed in class. It is in the classroom that students are enculturated to use different voices and perspectives, and they become more proficient through interactions in intellectually challenging classroom environments. From interactions in these diverse contexts, students learn what counts as appropriate knowledge and effective communication. They develop the ability to comprehend multiple sources, understand an author's purpose, and generate warranted propositions and arguments that allow them to develop even further intellectually.

Vygotsky's (1987) sociocultural framework provides a means to conceptualize learning that occurs in a context in which both student and teacher can participate together in thoughtful discourse about language and content, because it is an inherent part of the social dynamic of any educational setting and the manner in which work is completed. These notions relate to the ideal that the way in which people learn content and strategies is dependent on the environment in which the learning takes place. This linguistically rich, interactive learning environment is fundamental in mediating what is learned, how it is used, and how it is interpreted. It is from the Bakhtin (1981) and Vygotsky (1987) perspectives that Langer (2001) examined teaching and learning in more and less successful middle and high school English classrooms.

The Langer (2001) study took place over a 5-year period. For the study, 25 schools, 44 teachers, and 88 classes were selected to participate, with a focus on one class for each of the teachers in each of 2 consecutive years. Recommendations were solicited from university and school communities in four states: Florida, New York, California, and Texas. These states were selected because they included diversity in student populations, educational problems, and approaches to improvement. Fourteen of the 25 participating schools were places where students were beating the odds, performing better on state-administered, high-stakes reading and writing tests than schools rated as demographically comparable by statewide data. The other 11 schools were also places that came highly recommended, with administrators and teachers who were trying hard to improve student performance, but the school literacy scores were more typical of other schools with similar demographics. This study used a nested, multicase design, with each English program comprising a case and the class including the teachers and student informants as cases within each case. None of the schools studied were dysfunctional, and none of the teachers were considered to be other than good. Data were analyzed by a system of constant comparison, in which patterns were identified and tested both within and across cases.

The results supported the theoretical warrants of the study and identified the following distinguishing features of instruction in the higher performing schools: (1) Strategies, skills, and knowledge are taught in multiple types of lessons; (2) tests are deconstructed to inform curriculum and instruction; (3) within curriculum and instruction, connections are made across content and structure to ensure coherence; (4) strategies for thinking and performing are emphasized; (5) generative learning is encouraged; and (6) classrooms are organized to foster collaboration and shared cognition (Langer, 2001). These features dominated the higher achieving English and language arts programs. In contrast, some aspects of these features were present in some of the more typical schools part of the time and other features, none of the time. According to Langer, "It is the 'whole cloth' environment, the multi-layered contribution of the full set of these features to the teaching and learning interactions, that distinguishes the higher achieving programs from the others" (p. 876). At the higher achieving schools, teachers always believed in students' abilities to be able and enthusiastic learners. These teachers believed that all students could learn and that they, as teachers, could make a difference. They created substantial and challenging instructional settings in which intellectually rich discussions about English language, literature, and writing could take place. Constructing a web of integrated and interconnected learning experiences, teachers used direct instruction, direct explanation, and contextualized learning experiences for their students' knowledge, strategy, and skills development. Finally, these teachers cultivated student independence in the acquisition of knowledge; that is, they relentlessly focused their efforts on scaffolding student learning in such a way that students would internalize the learning of knowledge, strategies, and skills to use on their own as mature, highly literate individuals at school, as well as at home and in their future academic and work experiences. These findings cut across high-poverty areas in inner cities as well as middle-class suburban communities. At the same time, it is important to note that because this was a qualitative study, the findings cannot be warranted by causal links. However, it does add to our knowledge of the differences between schools and classrooms whose students are attaining higher levels of literacy achievement and those whose students are not.

THE NEED FOR COGNITIVE STRATEGY INSTRUCTION IN ENGLISH CLASSROOMS: RECIPROCAL TEACHING

In rehearsing the need for cognitive strategy instruction in English classrooms, more specifically, reciprocal teaching, it is important to remember four key findings from Langer's (2001) research with schools achieving high literacy across a range of socioeconomic contexts: (1) Strategies, skills, and knowledge are taught in multiple types of lessons; (2) strategies for thinking and performing are emphasized; (3) generative learning is encouraged; and (4) classrooms are organized to foster collaboration and shared cognition.

Research tells us that students in English classes at the middle school and high school level face important changes and new responsibilities in their secondary school settings (Bruer, 1993; McGilly, 1996; Wiske, 1998). Unlike elementary school students who usually have one teacher who provides instruction in all subjects for one group of students, middle and high school students may encounter a variety of traditional and/or block schedules. Despite differences in scheduling formats, most middle and high school students are usually taught by a different teacher in each subject area. Such a change in the way instruction is delivered creates new learning responsibilities for students (Wood, Woloshyn, & Willoughby, 1995). Because one teacher is no longer solely responsible for student learning, all students must become more aware, strategically monitor their progress in learning, and assume greater responsibility for their learning. These new responsibilities for learners are even more formidable for those attending schools in urban and rural settings.

Because all learners in middle school and high school need to be effective and self-directed students, in order to acquire a wide range of learning strategies and achieve high literacy, they need to know when and how to use these strategies in specific learning contexts. Current research in cognitive psychology is focusing on how to help students become more aware, involved, and responsible for their learning in school (Bransford, Brown, & Cocking, 2000; Pressley & McCormick, 1995; Resnick, 1987). This cognitive strategy perspective focuses on making learners aware of their relevant background knowledge, enhancing their ability to monitor their learning as they complete instructional tasks and solve problems, and acquiring a repertoire of cognitive strategies which they can apply appropriately to learning tasks (Pinker, 1994; Pressley, 1998; Slater & Horstman, 2002).

Cognitive strategies are designed to help all students actively organize the information they are required to learn and to achieve high literacy. Research based, empirically validated cognitive strategies are grounded in information-processing models of learning (Bransford et al., 2000; Rosenshine & Meister, 1994; Wiske, 1998). These models specify that learners manipulate information as it passes through a series of learning operations. The level of processing, or manipulation of information, ranges from the simple processing of surface-level information to the deeper, critical, conceptual processing of higher level information (Wood et al., 1995). The type of cognitive strategy the student uses can facilitate this level of processing. Research tells us that the more complex the strategy, the deeper the processing the learner achieves with its use (Bransford et al., 2000).

Teaching a variety of cognitive strategies is important to ensure that learners use the most strategic intervention possible to address the specific demands of a particular learning task. All students need to learn and master a range of strategies, so that they will be able to select from an extensive repertoire that addresses their particular learning needs and abilities (Meichenbaum, 1977; Pressley, 1998; Pressley & McCormick, 1995; Pressley, Harris, & Marks, 1992). At the same time, it is important to remember that not all strategies can be used effectively by all students. If, after receiving careful instruction with numerous examples and modeling, students find a strategy difficult or impossible to use, the strategy may involve a level of complexity and demands that are too difficult for the students. Sometimes teachers can resolve these difficulties by providing more instruction and examples. If additional instruction does not prove beneficial, students can then be introduced to a simplified version of the strategy, or to other strategies that are not as cognitively complex and demanding (Pressley & McCormick, 1995).

Reciprocal Teaching

Given the range of cognitive strategies available, research tells us that reciprocal teaching is the one best suited to assist all students in becoming better, more strategic learners in their quest for high literacy. The four supporting strategies rehearsed within reciprocal teaching—questioning, clarifying issues, summarizing, and predicting—provide important scaffolding for learners in their engagement with course content.

As initially conceptualized, reciprocal teaching (Palincsar & Brown, 1984) is a cooperative–learning cognitive strategy in which students and a teacher work together to improve students' understanding of texts. At the same time, the goal is to improve students' general ability to monitor their comprehension and to learn from texts. This extensively researched strategy has produced positive results with first graders (Palincsar & David, 1991), sixth and seventh graders (Palincsar & Brown, 1984), and college students (Fillenworth, 1995). Studies show that students who work with reciprocal teaching increase their group participation and use of the strategies taught, learn from the passages studied, and increase their learning when reading independently. The studies also demonstrate that the strategy could be used in various settings and that students maintain the gains they achieve (Rosenshine & Meister, 1994).

The strategy uses four carefully selected supporting strategies: generating questions, clarifying issues, summarizing, and making predictions. Each of these strategies serves one or more definite purposes. Questioning focuses students' attention on main ideas and provides a check on their current understanding of what they are reading. Clarifying requires students to be actively engaged as they are reading and helps them to unpack ambiguous, confusing sections of text. Summarizing requires students to focus on the major content of the selection and determine what is important and what is not. Predicting requires students to rehearse what they have learned thus far in their reading and begin the next section of the text with some expectations of what is to come (Graves & Graves, 2003; Slater & Horstman, 2002).

When first implemented in a class, reciprocal teaching is teacher-directed. At first, the teacher or some other experienced reader, such as a classroom aide or trained tutor, serves as the leader of the group, taking the central role in explaining the strategies and modeling them for others in the group. The leader's task includes modeling the strategies students are expected to learn, monitoring students' learning and understanding, scaffolding their efforts, providing students with feedback, and tailoring the session to students' existing level of competence.

It is important to note that one primary purpose of reciprocal teaching is to convince all students to become actively involved in using the strategies themselves (Pressley et al., 1992; Rosenshine & Meister, 1994; Rosenshine, Meister, & Chapman, 1996). The goal is to have students eventually do the questioning, clarifying, summarizing, and predicting themselves. To accomplish this goal, the teacher, from the beginning, increasingly hands over responsibility to the students in the group. As soon as possible, the teacher steps out of the leadership role, and each student in the group takes his or her turn as group leader. Research findings tell us that when students assume the leadership role, they do some of their best learning. The teacher, however, continues to monitor the group as much as possible and intervenes when necessary to keep students on track and to facilitate the discussion (Pressley & McCormick, 1995; Wood et al., 1995).

The Four Supporting Strategies Included in Reciprocal Teaching

The instructional session begins with the leader reading aloud a short segment of text, typically a paragraph or two. Then, the leader follows these four steps in the following specific order:

1. *Questioning.* Once the text segment has been read, the leader or other group members generate several questions prompted by the passage just read, and members of the group answer the questions.
2. *Clarifying issues.* If the passage or questions produce any problems or misunderstandings, the leader and other group members clarify matters.
3. *Summarizing.* After all the questions have been answered and any misunderstandings have been clarified, the leader or other group members summarize the text segment.
4. *Predicting.* Based on the segment just read, segments that have preceded it, and the discussion thus far, the leader or other group members make predictions about the contents of the upcoming section of text.

The sequence of reading, questioning, clarifying, summarizing, and predicting is then repeated with subsequent sections of text. Research tells us that with extensive practice on a daily basis, students will master the four supporting strategies included in reciprocal teaching, and more importantly, will use them independently for all of their classroom assignments (Palincsar, 1986; Palincsar & Brown, 1984; Rosenshine & Meister, 1994).

In a recent research study, Slater (2003) examined the effects of reciprocal teaching through scaffolded reading experiences on high school English-language learners' comprehension of expository text (August & Hakuta, 1998; Schleppegrell & Colombi, 2002). Forty-one participants in two intact English Bridge classes in a suburban Maryland high school read two expository passages, one in the treatment condition and the other in a comparison condition. Treatment order was counterbalanced. In the treatment condition, participants engaged in reciprocal teaching in which questioning, clarifying, summarizing, predicting, and writing about the text were emphasized. Using a gradual release of responsibility model of instruction (Pearson & Gallagher, 1983), the teacher modeled reciprocal teaching and each of the four strategies, worked jointly with students on the strategies, then turned the locus of control over to students to work independently. The teacher–student, student–student interactions were characterized as dialogical, focused, and problem-solving in nature (Bakhtin, 1981; Moll, 1990; Pressley et al., 1992; Vygotsky, 1987). In the comparison group, participants were asked to start reading the text in class; the teacher asked them relevant comprehension questions, then unpacked the meanings of difficult words. Participants were also told to highlight important ideas in their texts. At the conclusion of the reading, participants in both conditions were asked to complete a posttest focused on their understanding of the reading.

As can be seen in Table 2.1, results indicated that participants in the treatment condition comprehended the texts better than did those in the comparison group condition ($p = .000$). In addition, participants in the treatment condition outperformed those in the comparison group condition on the higher level cognitive task items on the posttests ($p = .000$) (Anderson & Krathwohl, 2001). These results with English-language learn-

TABLE 2.1. English-Language Learners' Posttest Comprehension Scores

	Reciprocal teaching mean (SD)	Comparison group mean (SD)	Test statistics	
			t test	p
Violence in the media	67.65 (14.56)	50.95 (11.56)	−4.075	.000*
Death penalty	71.00 (10.54)	54.85 (11.78)	4.629	.000*

* statistical significance

ers lend support to previous research findings on the efficacy of cognitive strategy instruction through reciprocal teaching for improving students' learning and higher level comprehension of text.

Given Langer's (2001) findings in highly effective English classrooms and the goal of high literacy for all students, five powerful instructional concepts are inherent in reciprocal teaching: (1) The instructional focus on helping students acquire comprehension-enhancing strategies rather than simply asking them comprehension questions; (2) the concentration of instructional time on four research-validated, robust, comprehension-enhancing cognitive strategies rather than on dozens of strategies, many of which lack research support; (3) the requirement for practicing the strategies while reading authentic texts; (4) the increasing use of procedures for scaffolding or supporting students as they develop their strategy use; and (5) the increasing implementation of the constructivist notion of students providing support for each other in reading and other learning experiences. While many of these ideas are not new, the reciprocal teaching approach packages and presents them in a coherent manner for both students and teachers (Slater & Horstman, 2002).

To sum up, cognitive strategy instruction in general and reciprocal teaching in particular offer English teachers powerful, research-based strategies and approaches for helping all students to achieve high literacy in their classrooms. To be sure, a criticism of cognitive strategy instruction is that it is reductionist, forcing students to replicate the processing of others rather than to construct their own approaches to important cognitive tasks, such as reading and writing. To refute this criticism, research tells us that cognitive strategy instruction conducted effectively is student-sensitive, motivating students to experiment with strategies and to construct their own personalized versions of efficient information processing. Adaptation of strategies occurs continually as strategies are used flexibly in coordination with diverse knowledge to accomplish diverse goals in diverse situations (Elbers, 1991; Iran-Nejad, 1990; Pressley et al., 1992; Wittrock, 1992).

If the teacher explanations of cognitive strategies do not make explicit the personalized nature of strategy use, then reteaching and additional explanations warranted by student difficulties in strategy use should do so. Additional explanations and modeling require the teacher to model adapting the strategies to different situations (Meichenbaum, 1977; Pressley & McCormick, 1995; Pressley et al., 1992; Rosenshine & Meister, 1994). These additional explanations are dialogical, with the student and teacher working together to determine how to apply strategies to a situation that poses difficulty for the student. The teacher is not satisfied until the student understands what he or she is doing; that is, the additional explanations are focused on helping students understand the situation rather than simply showing them how to make correct responses. Finally, cognitive strategies are not forced on students. Instead, students are taught procedures that permit them greater success with less effort. Students come to value the strategies, because they recognize that strategies are intellectually powerful. Good strategy instruction delivers the message that students can control how they do academically, with much gained by creatively applying the cognitive strategies taught to them. Good strategy instruction encourages student reflection (Pressley et al., 1992). This type of instruction provides students with tools that permit reflective comprehension of texts, creation of reflective stances through writing, and reflective decision making about whether and how to use cognitive strategies they know in tackling new situations. These are the types of intellectual experiences, models, and tools that all students need to achieve high literacy.

COGNITIVE STRATEGY INSTRUCTION AND
ENGLISH TEACHER PREPARATION: THE MARYLAND PROGRAM

As I mentioned earlier, the goal of English instruction in America's schools should be high literacy for all students. Again, *high literacy* is defined for the purpose of this chapter as the goal of teaching all students to think, read, and write critically. Central to achieving this goal is preparing the type of English teacher who can deliver and design appropriate instruction needed by students to achieve this goal. Given the focus here on English literacy instruction, the Maryland Program is designed to revise the classic English major, with its focus on literature, literary history, and literary criticism (Squire, 2003). This traditional model has created a formidable disconnect between the academic and professional preparation of English teachers and the compelling literacy needs of students in America's classrooms.

Based on theory, research, and best practice, the Maryland Program, an undergraduate double-major in English and English Education, has reconfigured the English major for teaching in a manner that emphasizes English language and linguistics, reading, and oral and written communication (Bransford et al., 2000; Bruer, 1993; Cooper & Odell, 1999; Flood, Lapp, Squire, & Jensen, 2003; Pinker, 1994; Shavelson & Towne, 2002; Stanovich & Stanovich, 2003; Wigfield & Eccles, 2002; Wiske, 1998). Language study is central in the Maryland Program, because it serves as the mediator for all learning and instruction (Bransford et al., 1999; Hale & Keyser, 2002; Perelman & Olbrechts-Tyteca, 1958/1969; Pinker, 1989, 1994). Cognitive strategy instruction is emphasized in the professional education sequence in the program, because it is warranted by theory and research.

In the Maryland Program's language strand, students are required to complete an intermediate mastery of a modern or classical language, an introductory course in linguistics, and an advanced course in language and linguistics. In addition, they take a professional education course on bases for English-language instruction that includes theory, knowledge, best practice, and cognitive strategy instruction appropriate for English-language instruction.

In the reading strand of the program, students are required to complete a configuration of World, British, and American literature courses; a course in critical methods in the study of literature; a course in the major works of Shakespeare; courses in minority literature and literature by women; and a senior seminar. In addition, in their professional education sequence, students take one course in literature for adolescents and two courses that emphasize cognitive bases for instruction in reading: cognition and motivation in reading, and reading in the secondary school.

Then, in the program's oral and written communication sequence, students are required to take two courses in speech communication, with an emphasis on discussion and argumentation, and one course in foundations of rhetoric. In their professional education sequence, students take a course in teaching writing that emphasizes cognitive and rhetorical bases for writing instruction (Bereiter & Scardamalia, 1987; College Entrance Examination Board, 2003; Enos & Miller, 2003; Hillocks, 1986; Kellogg, 1994; Murphy, 2001; National Commission on Writing in America's Schools and Colleges, 2003; Ravitch, 2003; Warnick, 2002) and a general English methods course that integrates theory, research, and best practice for teaching literacy using cognitive strategy instruction for language, reading, writing, speaking, and listening instruction.

Finally, in the yearlong internship, students in this double-major apply their knowledge of language-focused subject-matter content and professional education courses, with their emphasis on cognitive strategy instruction, in their field placements and full-time internship (student teaching) at both the middle school and high school level.

To be sure, the Maryland Program for English teacher preparation, with its emphasis on language, reading, oral and written communication, and cognitive strategy instruction in the professional education sequence is a beginning in addressing the disconnect in English teacher preparation in the past with the high literacy needs of students in classrooms today. Much research is needed to validate the efficacy of the Maryland Program and to modify it in ways that better prepare teachers to design and construct the instruction necessary for all students, so that they can achieve high literacy.

NEEDED RESEARCH TO MOVE US FORWARD

To be sure, much systematic, well-funded research needs to examine the components of effective, challenging English instruction; effective, cognitive-based instruction; and relevant, literacy-focused English teacher preparation. Of course, the number of potential confounding variables in this needed research will be formidable.

To be specific, in the case of the Langer (2001) research on effective English classrooms that beat the odds, we need to remember that this was a qualitative, observational study that cannot establish causality.

• We need follow-up research that investigates micro-level issues on both teacher and class differences. These studies would help us better understand what differences in teachers and instruction can be allowed before achievement is diminished.

• We need well-designed and -documented instructional interventions that attempt to implement Langer's findings in her odds-beating schools in lower performing school settings that do not manifest this type of high literacy instruction. Of course, the central question will be does this instruction in lower performing schools affect student achievement.

• We need to focus on the kinds of theory-based, research-driven professional and instructional development that is needed to implement best practice in lower performing schools (Langer, 2001; Richardson, 2001). In the case of cognitive strategy research, most researchers would contend that much remains to be done (Berliner & Calfee, 1996; Bransford et al., 2000; Kamil, 2000; Kellogg, 1994; Pressley, 1998; Rosenshine & Meister, 1994; Snow, 2001).

• We need to learn more about the changes in internal cognitive processes that result from cognitive strategy instruction.

• We need to know more about the critical instructional factors for teaching cognitive strategies; that is, what specific instructional factors in various approaches to cognitive strategy instruction are the most effective, and what accounts for their effectiveness? In addition, which instructional procedures are most effective for teaching cognitive strategies? Finally, which and how many cognitive strategies are most productive for student learning?

• We need to focus in our research initiatives on the effects of teaching individual strategies and groups of strategies.

Finally, in the case of teacher preparation in general, and English teacher preparation more specifically, we need to face the daunting challenge of systematic study (Flood et al., 2003; Lincoln & Denzin, 2000; Meltzoff, 1997; Richardson, 2001; Shavelson & Towne, 2002). The research issues are formidable, and the theoretical and research base is fairly thin. We need to focus on the appropriate configuration of courses in the subject-matter major that address not only the liberal arts goals of a university education but also the literacy subject-matter preparation needed for preservice teachers who will be teaching diverse students in public school settings. We also need to focus on the appropriate configuration of courses and field experiences in professional education for all preservice teachers, but, in this instance, especially preservice English teachers. These courses and field experiences should provide preservice teachers with the grounding and relevant experiences needed to ensure that they have the instructional expertise to achieve the goal of high literacy for all students in our nation's classrooms.

- For English majors who wish to teach, what is the appropriate configuration of courses in the subject matter-major (e.g., language and linguistics, literature, literary criticism, rhetoric, written communication, and speech communication)?
- What is the appropriate configuration of courses and field experiences for preservice teachers in professional education (e.g., English methods, reading, writing, bases for language instruction, cognitive bases for instruction, assessment, philosophy, sociology, etc.)?
- What is the impact of a particular focus in an academic major and professional education on a teacher's ability to plan effective instruction for all students in a range of public school settings?

To conclude, and as I have said repeatedly in this chapter, much research remains to be done to achieve our goal of high literacy for all students: the goal of teaching all students to think, read, and write critically (National Research Council, 1999).

REFERENCES

Anderson, L. W., & Krathwohl, D. R. (Eds.). (2001). *A taxonomy for learning, teaching, and assessing: A revision of Bloom's taxonomy of educational objectives.* Boston: Allyn & Bacon.

Applebee, A. N. (1974). *Tradition and reform in the teaching of English: A history.* Urbana, IL: National Council of Teachers of English.

Applebee, A. N. (1993). *Literature in the secondary school.* Urbana, IL: National Council of Teachers of English.

Applebee, A. N. (1996). *Curriculum as conversation: Transforming traditions of teaching and learning.* Chicago: University of Chicago Press.

August, D., & Hakuta, K. (Eds.). (1998). *Educating language-minority children.* Washington, DC: National Academy Press.

Bakhtin, M. M. (1981). *The dialogic imagination.* Austin: University of Texas Press.

Bereiter, C., & Scardamalia, M. (1987). *The psychology of written composition.* Hillsdale, NJ: Erlbaum.

Berliner, D. C., & Calfee, R. C. (Eds.). (1996). *Handbook of educational psychology.* New York: Macmillan.

Bransford, J. D., Brown, A. L., & Cocking, R. R. (Eds). (2000). *How people learn: Brain, mind, experience, and school: Extended edition.* Washington, DC: National Academy Press.

Bruer, J. T. (1993). *Schools for thought: A science of learning in the classroom.* Cambridge, MA: MIT Press.

College Entrance Examination Board. (2003, April). *Report of the National Commission on Writing in America's schools and colleges: The neglected "R": The need for a writing revolution.* New York: Author.

Cooper, C. R., & Odell, L. (Eds.). (1999). *Evaluating writing: The role of teachers' knowledge about text, learning, and culture.* Urbana, IL: National Council of Teachers of English.

Elbers, E. (1991). The development of competence and its social context. *Educational Psychology Review, 3,* 73–94.

Enos, T., & Miller, K. D. (Eds.). (2003). *Beyond postprocess and postmodernism: Essays on the spaciousness of rhetoric.* Mahwah, NJ: Erlbaum.

Fillenworth, L. I. (1995). *Using reciprocal teaching to help at-risk college freshmen study reading.* Unpublished doctoral dissertation, University of Minnesota, Minneapolis.

Flood, J., Lapp, D., Squire, J. R., & Jensen, J. M. (Eds.). (2003). *Handbook of research on teaching the English language arts* (2nd ed.). Mahwah, NJ: Erlbaum.

Graves, M., & Graves, B. (2003). *Scaffolding reading experiences: Designs for student success* (2nd ed.). Norwood, MA: Christopher-Gordon.

Grigg, W., Daane, M. C., Jin, Y., & Campbell, J. R. (2003, June). *The nation's report card: Reading 2002.* Washington, DC: U.S. Department of Education, Institute of Education Sciences.

Hale, K., & Keyser, S. J. (2002). *Prolegomenon to a theory of argument structure.* Cambridge, MA: MIT Press.

Hillocks, G. W., Jr. (1986). *Research on written composition.* Urbana, IL: National Council of Teachers of English.

Iran-Nejad, A. (1990). Active and dynamic self-regulation of learning processes. *Review of Educational Research, 60,* 573–602.

Kamil, M. L. (Ed.). (2000). *Handbook of reading research* (Vol. 3). Mahwah, NJ: Erlbaum.

Kellogg, R. T. (1994). *The psychology of writing.* New York: Oxford University Press.

Langer, J. A. (2001). Beating the odds: Teaching middle and high school students to read and write well. *American Educational Research Journal, 38*(4), 837–880.

Lincoln, Y. S., & Denzin, N. K. (Eds.). (2000). *Handbook of qualitative research* (2nd ed.). Thousand Oaks, CA: Sage.

McGilly, K. (Ed.). (1996). *Classroom lessons: Integrating cognitive theory and classroom practice.* Cambridge, MA: MIT Press.

Meichenbaum, D. (1977). *Cognitive behavior modification: An integrative approach.* New York: Plenum Press.

Meltzoff, J. (1997). *Critical thinking about research: Psychology and related fields.* Washington, DC: American Psychological Association.

Moll, L. C. (Ed.). (1990). *Vygotsky and education: Instructional implications and applications of sociohistorical psychology.* Cambridge, UK: Cambridge University Press.

Murphy, J. J. (Ed.). (2001). *A short history of writing instruction: From ancient Greece to modern America* (2nd ed.). Mahwah, NJ: Hermagoras Press.

National Commission on Writing in America's Schools and Colleges. (2003, April). *The neglected "R": The need for a writing revolution.* New York: College Entrance Examination Board.

National Reading Panel. (2000). *Report of the National Reading Panel: Teaching children to read: An evidence-based assessment of the scientific research literature on reading and its implications for reading instruction: Reports of the subgroups.* Washington, DC: National Institute of Child Health and Human Development.

National Research Council. (1999). *Improving student learning: A strategic plan for education research and its utilization.* Washington, DC: National Academy Press.

Palincsar, A. S. (1986). The role of dialogue in providing scaffolded instruction instruction. *Educational Psychologist, 21,* 73–98.

Palincsar, A. S., & Brown, A. L. (1984). Reciprocal teaching of comprehension and monitoring activities. *Cognition and Instruction, 1*(2), 117–175.

Palincsar, A. S., & David, Y. M. (1991). Promoting literacy through classroom dialogue. In E. Hiebert (Ed.), *Literacy for a diverse society: Perspectives, programs, and policies.* New York: Teachers College Press.

Pearson, P. D., & Gallagher, M. C. (1983). The instruction of reading comprehension. *Contemporary Educational Psychology, 8,* 317–344.

Perelman, C., & Olbrechts-Tyteca, L. (1969). *The new rhetoric: A treatise on argumentation* (J. Wilkinson & P. Weaver, Trans.). Notre Dame, IN: University of Notre Dame Press. (Original work published in 1958 as *La Nouvelle Rhétorique: Traité de l'Argumentation*)

Persky, H. R., Daane, M. C., & Jin, Y. (2003, July). *The nation's report card: Writing 2002.* Washington, DC: U. S. Department of Education, Institute of Education Sciences.

Pinker, S. (1989). *Learnability and cognition: The acquisition of argument structure.* Cambridge, MA: MIT Press.

Pinker, S. (1994). *The language instinct: How the mind creates language.* New York: HarperCollins.

Pressley, M. (1998). *Reading instruction that works: The case for balanced teaching.* New York: Guilford Press.

Pressley, M., Harris, K. R., & Marks, M. B. (1992). But good strategy instructors are constructivists! *Educational Psychology Review, 4,* 3–31.

Pressley, M., & McCormick, C. B. (1995). *Advanced educational psychology: For educators, researchers, and policymakers.* New York: HarperCollins.

Ravitch, D. (2003). *The language police: How pressure groups restrict what students learn.* New York: Knopf.

Resnick, L. B. (1987). *Education and learning to think.* Washington, DC: National Academy Press.

Richardson, V. (Ed.). (2001). *Handbook of research on teaching* (4th ed.). Washington, DC: American Educational Research Association.

Rosenshine, B., & Meister, C. (1994). Reciprocal teaching: A review of the research. *Review of Educational Research, 64*(4), 479–530.

Rosenshine, B., Meister, C., & Chapman, S. (1996). Teaching students to generate questions: A review of intervention studies. *Review of Educational Research, 66,* 181–221.

Schleppegrell, M. J., & Colombi, M. C. (Eds.). (2002). *Developing advanced literacy in first and second languages: Meaning with power.* Mahwah, NJ: Erlbaum.

Shavelson, R. J., & Towne, L. (Eds.). (2002). *Scientific research in education.* Washington, DC: National Academy Press.

Slater, W. H. (2003). *The effects of reciprocal teaching on high school English language learners' comprehension of persuasive text.* Manuscript in preparation. College Park: University of Maryland.

Slater, W. H., & Horstman, F. R. (2002, Summer). Teaching reading and writing to struggling middle school and high school students: The case for reciprocal teaching. *Preventing School Failure, 46*(4), 163–166.

Snow, C. E. (2001). *Reading for understanding: Toward an R&D program in reading comprehension.* Santa Monica, CA: RAND Education.

Squire, J. R. (2003). The history of the profession. In. J. Flood, D. Lapp, J. R. Squire, & J. M. Jensen (Eds.), *Handbook of research on teaching the English language arts* (2nd ed., pp. 3–14). Mahwah, NJ: Erlbaum.

Squire, J. R., & Applebee, R. K. (1968). *High school English instruction today.* New York: Appleton–Century–Crofts.

Stanovich, P. J., & Stanovich, K. E. (2003, May). *Using research and reason in education: How teachers can use scientifically based research to make curricular and instructional decisions.* Portsmouth, NH: RMC Research Corporation, National Institute for Literacy, National Institute of Child Health and Human Development, U. S. Department of Education, U. S. Department of Health and Human Services.

Vygotsky, L. S. (1987). Thinking and speech. In R. Rieber & A. Carton (Eds.), *The collected works of L. Vygotsky.* New York: Plenum Press.

Warnick, B. (2002). *Critical literacy in a digital era: Technology, rhetoric, and the public interest.* Mahwah, NJ: Erlbaum.

Wigfield, A., & Eccles, J. S. (Eds.). (2002). *Development of achievement motivation.* San Diego: Academic Press.

Wiske, M. S. (Ed.). (1998). *Teaching for understanding: Linking research with practice.* San Francisco: Jossey-Bass.

Wittrock, M. C. (1992). Generative learning processes of the brain. *Educational Psychologist, 27,* 531–542.

Wood, E., Woloshyn, V. E., & Willoughby, T. (Eds.). (1995). *Cognitive strategy instruction: For middle and high schools.* Cambridge, MA: Brookline.

3

Overcoming the Dominance of Communication
Writing to Think and to Learn

TIMOTHY SHANAHAN

I have a hunch. If you were to ask a bunch of teens (and their teachers) why they need to know how to read, most would tell you something about using reading to learn or to find things out. The value of reading, when you are trying to learn history or science or literature, seems pretty obvious. Okay, now stay with me. Let's ask these same students and teachers about the value of writing. My guess on this one is that a very different answer emerges. These replies will have more to do with communication than with thinking or learning. Again, the answer probably seems self-evident: We write so that we can tell stuff to other people. But this self-evident position would be wrong!

Most teens are surprised to find out that writing is more than a social performance. It is more than just getting the words in the right order in sentences, or putting the punctuation in the right places so others can make sense of what we have to say. These are good things to be able to do, but they are somewhat (more on this later) outside the realm of this chapter. So let's start from a premise that will be alien to most teens—and possibly to their teachers as well: We write for the same reasons that we read. A student is asked to read a history chapter about the early days of the American Civil War. The teacher hopes that this reading will lead to a greater understanding of what caused the war and how the earlier events precipitated the later ones. Fair enough. But let's imagine a class where the students are writing essays on the early days of the American Civil War. No, not writing to divulge whether the students read the chapter or paid attention to the classroom lecture, but writing intended to lead to greater understanding of what caused the war and how the earlier events led to the later ones. In other words, we are talking about a writing assignment with learning, rather than communication, as the major point.

The confusion—among teachers, students, and parents—over the role of writing in the middle and secondary school curriculum is part of a larger argument that has raged for nearly 50 years among scholars in linguistics, psychology, and the cognitive sciences. The larger argument, instigated by the work of Noam Chomsky (1957), is not about reading and writing, but about the purpose of language. Historically, most scholars accepted the notion that language developed in humans because of our needs to communicate and that to understand language would require a careful analysis of the communicative functions of language. Chomsky challenged this idea, arguing that language developed for thinking, and that the communicative uses of language were tertiary at best. For Chomsky, the trick was to strip language of its social dimensions so that we could understand the more central role that language plays in cognition.

Those arguments about the role of language in cognition continue to reverberate in many fields of study, but even without a final resolution, they have revealed the major role language can play within thinking. The practical ramification of this somewhat abstract argument cuts to the heart of the secondary school literacy curriculum. If language is primarily for the purposes of communication, then certainly we should devote lots of instructional resources (usually within the English class) to making certain that our students can communicate effectively. Given this social aim, we might expect a writing-for-communication curriculum to focus heavily on how students write, how they learn to handle conventional aspects of the writing system, and so on. We probably would not see much writing demand on students until they had developed adequate basic writing skills. In other words, the science teacher wouldn't want students to write labs *until* the English teachers had sufficiently worked their magic on the students to ensure that they could handle the grammar, punctuation, spelling, and other conventional—social-communicative—aspects of writing.

But what if my premise that writing is primarily about thinking and learning is correct? That notion leads to some very different conclusions about how and where writing would fit into the curriculum. For example, if the purpose were more cognitive than communicative, one would expect to see writing instruction and activity taking place in all of the disciplines. Of course, there would still be a place for writing within the English class, but it is hard to imagine anyone willing to segregate science or history or mathematics from thinking and, therefore, from writing! Much of the instructional work on writing would not deal with how to write for others (though that would still have a place), but it would focus to a much greater extent on how students could learn most effectively through writing. Study skills courses have long been *au courant* in high school, and these typically teach students how to read and study in certain ways. Writing would move to center stage in such courses, because teachers and parents would want students to know how to learn most effectively, and writing would clearly have a role to play in that regard.

CRITICAL RESEARCH ON WRITING TO LEARN

We can imagine anything we want, of course, but the ultimate question is whether any convincing empirical evidence shows that writing leads to greater learning—especially in the disciplines. In fact, there is quite a bit of this kind of evidence (McGee & Richgels, 1990; Tierney & Shanahan, 1991). For instance, various studies have shown that the writing of summaries or précis lead to better recall and understanding of content information (Bean & Steenwyck, 1984; Taylor & Beach, 1984), and writing can take a central role in various study procedures that have been found to be effective (Martin, Konopak, & Martin, 1986). Several studies have suggested that writing does more than just improve recall of the factual information in the text, and that it actually increases the quality of student understanding (Copeland, 1987; Hayes, 1987). These positive outcomes have been evident in various subject matters including those least obviously connected to literacy: mathematics (Buerger, 1997) and science (Mason, 2001; Monopli, 2002).

   In fact, there have been so many studies showing that writing improves learning that it appears to be a closed question, not generating much recent research attention. Although the potency of writing for improving learning is apparently no longer in doubt, how writing generates this positive impact is very much an issue. Two fundamentally different theories have emerged for how writing affects learning, and although they overlap in important regards, each suggests differences in how writing might best be treated in content-area classrooms. However, either of them could turn out to be more correct in the end, and both appear to be worthwhile in helping to establish either a school writing program or a future research agenda.

The first theory—the one that has generated more empirical investigation—is derived from the work of Judith Langer and Arthur Applebee, and their students and colleagues (Langer & Applebee, 1987). Their position, to put it succinctly, is that writing activities engage or involve *specific* thinking skills or abilities. A good analogy for this theory would be the relationship that weight lifting has to muscle building. Particular physical exercises bring different sets of muscles into play and, thus, develop different strengths: Bench pressing builds the pectorals, curls strengthen triceps, and so on. Langer and Applebee hypothesized that particular kinds of writing activities will stimulate particular cognitive activity, and that just as weight lifting increases muscle mass, writing builds thinking.

In a multi-year investigation, Langer and Applebee (1987) themselves showed that excellent secondary teachers across the disciplines present their students with a wide array of writing assignments. These teachers, however, tended to assign writing that required more short-term rehearsal of information than deeper analysis of it. Writing generally was found to lead to more subject-matter learning in these classrooms than did reading or studying alone, but, importantly, different kinds of writing led students to focus on different kinds of information, to think about it in different ways, and to learn different information. For example, writing answers to short-answer study questions led students to focus on the kind of specific, declarative information that could be used to answer *wh-* questions, and this improved student recall of such information for the short term. Analytical writing, that is, writing that required students to analyze topics into their parts or to compare and contrast alternatives, led to a more thoughtful focus on information in more complex ways. This kind of writing failed to provide an immediate boost to short-term recall but led to longer lasting recall of more complex information.

Various scholars have replicated this basic finding again and again—and with various types of text, especially literary text. Marshall (1987), for example, looked at the effects of extended writing (essays) versus restricted writing (short answers to questions) in 11th grade. Students read short stories, then, without classroom discussion or teacher presentation, engaged in either restricted or extended writing. He found that on tests given on the third day of working with the story and on end-of-unit tests, the students learned more from the extended writing. In a couple of similar studies (Newell & Winograd, 1989, 1995) focusing on history texts and other expository materials, the superiority of extended writing as a way to learn from text was obvious as well. Writing short answers to study questions, reviewing the text information, or engaging in note taking alone did not lead to as much learning or to learning that lasted as long as what resulted from the extended essay writing. Extended writing had a powerful and consistent impact on students' abilities to apply concepts from the original texts.

If this *specific cognitive outcomes theory* is correct—that particular types of writing require students to activate different types and amounts of cognition (Langer & Applebee, 1987) and that these activations emphasize some aspects of the curriculum while de-emphasizing others (Newell, 1986)—then it becomes possible for teachers to prescribe writing assignments that encourage students to think in productive and effective ways, and to avoid writing that fails to do so. This holds the possibility that teachers in the various disciplines might stress different kinds of writing that better fit the cognitive goals of their discipline.

But that writing can guide students to thinking in particular ways does not guarantee particular learning outcomes (Penrose, 1992). This study revealed that even sound writing assignments sometimes led to less appropriate cognitive processing and less learning for the students than traditional reading-oriented study procedures. The reason for the failure was shown to be due to students' interpretation—or misinterpretation—of the writing tasks and the audience demands for the writing. This means that it is not enough to craft a writing task that will lead to particular cognitive experiences, but it is critical that such tasks be discussed with students ahead of time to ensure that they engage in the intended mental activities rather than in some alternative ones. Students, who think the purpose is to communicate effectively in terms of the conventions of text, will plan differently, engage the content more shallowly, and the purpose of the writing will be subverted, no matter what the teacher or curriculum designer intended.

In fact, there have been some inconsistent findings for the various writing prescriptions for use in literature classes. Marshall (1987), for example, found that two forms of extended writing, personal (interpreting a text in terms of one's own personal experiences and background) and formal (analyzing a text using formal categories of analysis such as comparison–contrast), both led to superior performance. However, Newell has consistently found personal writing superior to formal writing. For example, in one study (Newell, Suszynski, & Weingart, 1989), personal writing led to qualitatively more effective responses than did formal writing. The personal responses were more fluent and were constructed with a wider range of responses, but the formal essays led to a more consistent review of the text elements. Unfortunately, this study provided no additional measure of student learning than what was evident in the writing itself. In a more recent study, Newell (1996) had high school students read a story, participate in a discussion, and write an essay. One group was involved in a teacher-led discussion that focused on formal analysis, and the writing assignment was an extended form of this analysis. The second group was involved in similar activities, but instead of being taught a specific analytical approach by the teacher, the students were left to their own devices in setting up their analysis for making sense of the story in the discussion and writing. The personal writing in this case had the better outcomes, though this might have been due in part to the differences in the discussion groups as much as the writing, because students could respond to and challenge each others' interpretations in both venues.

From this brief review, it should be clear that writing can be prescribed to some extent, and particular kinds of writing experiences may lead to particular types of learning outcomes. However, it should also be evident that this is a complex issue that still needs to be sorted out in much greater detail with regard to many factors, including the specific impacts of public/formal versus personal/informal writing, the effects of writing audiences on the outcomes, the influence that writing revision might have, as well as how assignments can best encourage analytical or critical responses.

A very different approach to the role of writing in learning has been taken by Robert Tierney and his colleagues (e.g., McGinley & Tierney, 1989). They have been critical of the idea that writing (or reading, for that matter) can be properly engaged in with a predetermined set of learning goals, and argue for the use of a more complex, and less prescribed, student-centered writing. In other words, instead of seeing the variant outcomes earlier described by Penrose (1992) or Newell (1996) as limitations of the specific outcomes theory, Tierney and his colleagues argue that these are just examples of the different ways that readers might choose to use writing; consequently Tierney has explored the idea of *self-directed* uses of writing for learning—rather than teacher-given assignments.

McGinley and Tierney (1989) posited that "when students are involved in directing their own reading and writing activities . . . in pursuit of some other learning, they are able to avail themselves of the different perspectives and ways of thinking that more elaborate combinations of each of these activities will permit" (p. 245). Thus, it might be possible to prescribe writing assignments to students that would lead to particular engagement, but it would be even more valuable to allow students to assemble a complex repertoire of combined reading and writing activities that would better support individual learning.

If the specific outcomes theory can be compared to weight lifting, then the self-directed approach is well described as crossing a landscape (Tierney, Soter, O'Flahavan, & McGinley, 1989). In this analogy drawn from the philosopher Wittgenstein (1953), the landscape is tantamount to a domain of knowledge that can be traversed in many ways:

By criss-crossing the complex topical landscapes, the twin goals of highlighting multifacetedness and establishing multiple connections are attained. Also, awareness of variability and irregularity is heightened, alternative routes of traversal of the topic's complexity are illustrated, multiple routes for later information retrieval are established, and the general skill of working around that particular landscape is developed. . . . It builds flexible knowledge. (p. 8)

In other words, the more often you cross a landscape, and the more different ways you cross it, the better will be your understanding of that landscape. By using multiple ways of examining a problem or issue and combining these different examinations into varied and complex combinations, the learner has the opportunity to traverse the landscape of a knowledge domain. In this theory, the important idea is not that writing has particular specific outcomes, but that repeated readings and writings on a topic provide multiple opportunities to cross the learning landscape, and that each crossing, if it is done in a qualitatively different way, will provide a different perspective for learning.

A couple of examples of self-directed writing and its outcomes should suffice. In one study (Tierney et al., 1989), for example, college students were given a text to learn but were allowed to combine reading and writing in a variety of ways. On various passes, the reading and writing experiences gave students the opportunity to generate or access information; to alter opinions; to clarify, refine, or confirm; to evaluate ideas and arguments; to structure information for further learning; to react; and to make connections. Unfortunately, the learning in this study was only measured through the writing itself, but writing emerged as a tool through which students seemed to allow their own "ideas to come to fruition and [to] resolve disputes" (p. 166). Because the researchers were interested in a more student-centered approach to learning, they interviewed students after the study and were told things like: "Writing made me choose an opinion on the issue and bring up all the facts and opinions" or writing "polarized my opinion more than it had been originally" (p. 166).

In another study, McGinley (1989) tracked how college students combined reading and writing into a source of learning. He found that students used writing to create a kind of social community around course content that allowed them to exchange information and views. This suggests an interesting role for writing that is central to both learning and the development of thought, while still being highly communicative. The difference between this kind of writing and the communicative focus evident in Penrose's earlier discussed study (1992) has to do with who is the audience. When students share their writing with teachers, or with other adults more advanced than they may be in mechanics, usage, grammar, and spelling, they emphasize the form or surface of the writing and fail to engage the deep structure. However, when they are in control of the situation and are sharing with an audience better matched in skills and authority, as McGinley's students were, they seem to share the information with much less distraction over communicative details (it is also possible that these issues were just less of a problem generally for the college students versus the high school ones, so the skills demands did not distract in the one case but did in the other).

Whether it turns out that we, as a field, come to a highly specific understanding of how particular writing assignments shapes thinking, and subsequently, learning, or whether we develop an understanding of the choices that students make and how the various combinations of reading and writing activities enrich student understanding, is not yet known. However, one thing should be absolutely clear from this brief discussion: Writing leads to learning, and how it does this is both specific and complex. Given these findings, how can we best encourage writing to learn in the classroom?

APPLYING WHAT WE KNOW ABOUT LEARNING FROM WRITING

Middle school and secondary school teachers cannot yet rely on the "learning from writing" research to provide a detailed specification of a curriculum or even of a single well-validated teaching routine. However, this literature is full of clues as to what good instruction would look like, and it is from this literature that I suggest the following eight guidelines for using writing well to stimulate student learning. Because the theoretical disagreements noted earlier have not been resolved, and each approach has successfully led to student learning, I have drawn these guidelines from both of the programs of research I have described.

Students Need Frequent Opportunities to Engage in Writing

The case for the value of writing in learning has been made, but nothing has been said about how much writing. According to the National Assessment of Educational Progress (Greenwald, Persky, Campbell, & Mazzeo, 1999), 97% of elementary school students indicate that they spend 3 hours a week or less on writing assignments of all types, which is 15% less time than they spend watching television. The situation in high school is not much better. Half of 12th-graders say that they are assigned a paper of three or more pages once or twice per month, and about 40% of seniors say they never, or hardly ever, have such assignments (National Commission on

Writing, 2003). Writing to learn is a skill, and like any skill, it is best developed through practice. Writing should be a regular part of the activities in all content-area classes, so that students' experience with writing is sufficient to allow them to understand how to use writing effectively to accomplish learning.

Students Need Opportunities to Engage in *Extended* Writing

Opportunities to engage in critical writing are essential to stimulate learning. It is not that there is no benefit to writing summaries, notes, or paragraph-long answers to specific questions, because learning accrues from these as well. However, in every study that has compared extended essay writing—of many different types—with briefer forms of writing, extended writing won out (Marshall, 1987; Newell, 1989; Newell & Winograd, 1989). Extended writing creates the ground for extended learning. Such writing allows for a wider choice of approaches (personal, analytical, critical), and it requires a more thorough coordination of information from the source text, presentation, or discussion.

Think of it this way: If you assigned some reading to students about a topic such as stem cell research and asked them to take a position, they are unlikely to do much more than state an ill-formed position in a short paragraph. But in a more extensive essay, the student is forced to do more than take a position. He or she will need to contrast that position with other possible positions, marshal an evidentiary case, and entertain the use of hedges or cautions to temper a position, and so on. In other words, extended writing demands both a depth of thought and a more thorough consideration and coordination of information.

Students Should Take a Perspective When They Write

Writing-to-learn assignments should require a point or perspective. Students should take a position. It is this writing that is most likely to lead students to deeper conceptual understanding—beyond just pouring in new facts (Hynd, McWhorter, Phares, & Suttles, 1994). Too often, teachers craft writing assignments strictly to determine whether the student "knows" the information. So the student who can successfully summarize the facts from a science chapter is purported to be the one who has exhibited solid science knowledge. Unfortunately, students can do such writing without actually having such knowledge—mindlessly culling information from a text or lecture. The issue ultimately isn't whether the student can successfully spit such stuff out (and then promptly forget it), but whether the student knows the information well enough to use it, or translate it into a usable form. When writing requires students to take a position, they are forced to do more than summarize the facts, but they have to control these facts in a flexible way that allows them to support and defend a position (McGinley, 1989; Tierney et al., 1989). Students obviously can argue over whether a character from a short story is sympathetic or below contempt, can champion or demonize a historical figure, or can take a position in a scientific controversy or current events debate. But they also can argue for why multiplication is a better procedure than repeated addition, or can provide an argument for a particular solution for a simultaneous equation.

According to the student-centered approach described earlier, writing is a way of traversing a landscape. By crossing a domain of knowledge from the perspective accorded by writing, it becomes possible to connect ideas to personal experience, to evaluate, critique, and criticize, and to compare positions. Writing assignments should encourage students to engage in such activities, particularly with a critical sense of evaluating information and making sense of its value and meaning.

Revision Is Central to Using Writing to Extend Learning

Often, writing revision is an activity that is relegated to the English class—even in schools where a great deal of writing is evident in the other content areas. This is a problem, because revision affords an important opportunity for making sense of the information that is under study. Revision is not primarily about correcting mechanics, usage, grammar, and spelling, but is more about revisiting, re-visioning, and rethinking the original composition. According to a study conducted by the National Assessment, students at grades 8 and 12 who were always asked to write more than one draft of a paper had higher average scale scores in writing than did their peers who were never asked to do this, or who were only sometimes asked to do it (Greenwald et al., 1999). This speaks to the value of revision for improving writing skills, but what about content learning? In a review of research on learning from writing, it was concluded that approaches requiring some kind of revision were more effective than approaches that did not (McGee & Richgels, 1990). Because revision is about refining one's thinking, it has a role to play in any disciplinary learning. Here, revision may include both highly formal and elaborate approaches to making changes in a manuscript, or it can involve much less formal discussions of the ideas that were included in the students' papers without actual rewriting.

The point here is to have students thinking and rethinking the content information. To do this, feedback is important, as are chances to integrate new information into the picture. The idea of revision that I'm proposing won't necessarily lead to the development of a polished final draft, though there can be some value to that. Instead, the goal is to use writing as a way of ending up with a more refined and polished understanding. It is the mind that is being composed here, not a paper or project.

Writing Should Encourage Personalization

Research has indicated that it is important for students to write in a manner that personalizes a subject (McGee & Richgels, 1990; Newell & Winograd, 1995). The point of this approach is not to make it easy or even to motivate active participation, though it certainly may do both. The real reason for encouraging personalized responses is that they require students to link the information in the course with what they already know, to examine it through the lens of past knowledge and experience. The use of prior knowledge forces a student to confront misconceptions, to reformulate current understandings, and to incorporate new information. Assignments that require students to confront potential confusion (What is the difference between an inference and an observation?), to compare new information to previously learned information (Explain the difference between theorem x—an already studied theorem—and theorem y—a newly introduced one), or to apply the information to some new circumstance (How would Reconstruction have been different if Lincoln had lived?) is the ticket for getting students to personalize in appropriate ways.

Writing Should Be One of Many Ways of Thinking about a Subject

Writing certainly provides students with an excellent opportunity for thinking more deeply about a subject. However, it is not the only way that information can be analyzed (in fact, that is why it is often left out). The point of this chapter is not to argue that writing should become the only or even the primary locus of learning. The point is that writing is a particularly valuable way of encouraging deep thinking, but it is likely to be even better when used in combination with other ways of thinking (including reading, speaking, listening, viewing). The earlier presented metaphor of traversing a landscape is a useful way to think about learning. Learning occurs best from criss-crossing a landscape several times and from several different perspectives (Tierney et al., 1989). Having students write and rewrite about some aspect of a concept is valuable. Having them do this in the context of reading, interacting with peers, hearing presentations, trying to apply the information in a lab, viewing a videotape, comparing two articles, and so on, is much more powerful.

Writing—like speaking—is a way of externalizing one's ideas. It can be easier for some students to do this when the social partners are more obvious. (Writing can seem awfully lonely and nonsocial to some students.) How do students move from the dialogues of debates and discussions to written monologues? One way to do this is through collaborative reports, written by a team of students (Guthrie, McGough, Bennett, & Rice, 1996; Keys, 1994). Collaborative writing of this type has proved to be both motivational and effective in enhancing content knowledge.

Writing Should Require Analysis and Synthesis

Again and again, as we saw in the research studies analyzed earlier writing that required complex analysis led students to a deeper and more complex understanding (Langer & Applebee, 1987; Marshall, 1987). Writing assignments should require students to divide information into its component parts and to relate these parts back together again. The analysis of an issue or problem into problem–cause/problem–solution sets, the subdivision of concepts into hierarchical subcomponents, and the comparison and relation of concepts one to another, force a writer to come to terms with the basic content of a subject matter. Such writing often requires multiple reviews of the material to be learned and multiple attempts at writing the analytical paper; thus, these assignments can fit both theories of writing to learn. For example, a writing assignment might require a description of the structure and role of neutrons, electrons, and protons within an atom of hydrogen, and comparison of their similarities and differences. To complete such an assignment, a student might be wise to read the relevant parts of a biology chapter several times, once to gain access to information about neutrons, another time to add the proton information, and so on.

Analytical writing also requires students to deal with the knowledge structures that are common to a discipline, and that can have a real impact on reading, writing, and an understanding of the content (Durst, 1984). For example, social science writing tends to be patterned as descriptive summaries (i.e., sequential events) or into summaries of semiautonomous sections (with different parts of the presentation being summarized in turn), or such writing might provide a more interpretive summary, with commentary on the content in each section. It is also common for such writing to take the form of a compare-and-contrast essay that leads to some generalization or conclusion. Students who are trying to engage in an analysis of the content being studied should be expected to organize the information in a manner that is consistent with the structures used in that disciplinary area.

Another important issue in writing to learn is the idea of synthesis. In this case, *synthesis* refers to students' ability to pull together information from a variety of texts or other sources. When a student is asked to write a report using information from two or more texts (as well as videos, class presentations, experiments, and so on), a valuable learning possibility is posed. Studies suggest that good and poor readers–writers have some real difficulty with such assignments, but these difficulties tend to reveal weaknesses in students' conceptions of the content, so real learning is likely to result from attention to these issues.

Writing Should Be Evaluated

One basic reason many teachers don't like to assign writing is because of the demand for evaluation. Let's face it: It takes a lot of time to read a stack of student essays, if we are expected to evaluate the quality of the work. Most secondary teachers just don't feel that they have the time to do that much grading, so they find ways not to have kids write very much. Here is where I am supposed to suggest that most of these assignments don't need to be graded, and that when they are graded they only need to be examined in terms of one criterion or another, possibly no more than placing the paper on some holistic scale. And although I agree with both of those pieces of advice, I really believe that evaluation—even grading—is central to the idea of turning writing into an approach that will foster more effective content-area thinking on the part of students.

Here, I turn to the seemingly little-known work of James Howard (1983), who described a professional development project that he conducted with 32 high school teachers, in which they focused on writing to learn. Through these workshops, the teachers learned to do a number of worthwhile things, including how to make every writing assignment worthwhile (in terms of the content learning that it was to engender or expose), how to design assignments that were doable (in terms of the thinking and time required), but more than anything, how to grade the work. The guidelines for this evaluative work were determining grading criteria for marking their papers, validating their criteria by reading some of the papers, and grading rather than correcting papers. The approach really does involve grading—from A's down to F's.

I used this approach when I cotaught some middle school math classes. It was just amazing how much better learning came about as a result of this effort. We simplified the approach a bit for our use, but this meant having fewer grading categories (A, C, and F rather than the full range). The teachers would assign math problems for homework and class assignments, but they started including a writing item in each assignment. Typically, these assignments required writing an explanation of a particular formula or process, or a comparing arithmetic sentences or some other appropriate, meaty, content-specific writing. The teachers and I would then sit down and read these written responses together. Given the nature of mathematics, these were not especially long pieces of writing, but even if they had not been so brief, we would still have read them very quickly. Howard's admonition to grade rather than correct is a valuable one. Our interest was in whether the writing reflected a clear understanding of the content. If it did, without mistakes or ambiguity in the mathematical reasoning, it went into the A pile. If it did not, we had to decide what the mistake was. Usually, the papers divided into three sets (and we really sorted as much as graded): full understanding (A), generally correct but with some minor problems—comparable to setting up an equation properly but making a minor error when it was being carried out (C), and serious misunderstanding of the concept, formula, or process (F). Sometimes the C pile broke into two distinct sets, depending on the nature of the error.

Now the teachers have three—or four—sets of papers, with each pile reflecting different levels of understanding and proficiency. The teachers can see how their lesson miscarried, what proportion of students understood the problems, and who was lacking a particular grasp of the subject matter. Besides recording grades on the papers, what has to be done? Howard's next step is to share the criteria and evaluations with the students, and that makes great sense. The teachers would usually start off the next class by laying out the criteria and handing back the papers. By showing students sound answers and not-so-sound ones, there is a great opportunity to target reteaching of concepts. Papers improved over time, but so did the math reasoning of the students. None of these teachers ever gave up on this tool, because they felt it was the clearest insight that they ever had into their students' thinking. The grades give students a clear picture of where they stand, and the criteria give them a clear understanding of the distance between the new and the known.

WHAT STILL NEEDS TO BE KNOWN?

Sad to say, the research community is paying less attention to writing these days than was true a decade ago. Currently, there is not a great deal of exploration into how to teach students to write better, or to teach them to use writing in ways that lead to more extensive content learning. From the work that has been done, it is evident that we can teach students to write better (Hillocks, 1986), and that writing can benefit content learning

(Tierney & Shanahan, 1991), but we would benefit from much more detailed analyses of how to do these things more effectively—particularly in the context of disciplinary classrooms. Until that occurs, the guidelines included in this chapter will have to suffice.

REFERENCES

Bean, T. W., & Steenwyck, F. L. (1984). The effects of three forms of summarization on sixth graders' summary writing and comprehension. *Journal of Reading Behavior, 16,* 297–306.

Buerger, J. R. (1997). *A study of the effect of exploratory writing activities on student success in mathematical problem solving.* Unpublished doctoral dissertation, Columbia University, New York, NY.

Chomsky, N. (1957). *Syntactic structures.* The Hague: Mouton.

Copeland, K. A. (1987). *Writing as a means to learn from prose.* Unpublished doctoral dissertation, University of Texas, Austin.

Durst, R. K. (1984). The development of analytic writing. In A. N. Applebee (Ed.), *Contexts for learning to write: Studies of secondary school instruction* (pp. 79–102). Norwood, NJ: Ablex.

Greenwald, E. A., Persky, H. R. Campbell, J. R., & Mazzeo, J. (1999). *NAEP 1998 Writing: Report Card for the nation and the states.* Washington, DC: National Center for Educational Statistics.

Guthrie, J. T., McGough, K., Bennett, L., & Rice, M. E. (1996). Concept-oriented reading instruction: An integrated curriculum to develop motivations and strategies for reading. In L. Baker, P. Afflerbach, & D. Reinking (Eds.), *Developing engaged readers in school and home communities* (pp. 165–190). Mahwah, NJ: Erlbaum.

Hayes, D. A. (1987). The potential for study in combined reading and writing activity. *Journal of Reading Behavior, 19,* 333–352.

Hillocks, G., Jr. (1986). *Research on written composition.* Urbana, IL: National Conference on Research in English.

Howard, J. (1983). *Writing to learn.* Washington, DC: Council of Basic Education.

Hynd, C. R., McWhorter, J. Y., Phares, V. L., & Suttles, C. W. (1994). The role of instructional variables in conceptual change in high school physics courses. *Journal of Research in Science Teaching, 31,* 933–946.

Keys, C. W. (1994). The development of scientific reasoning skills in conjunction with collaborative writing assignments: An interpretive study of six ninth-grade students. *Journal of Research in Science Teaching, 31,* 1003–1022.

Langer, J. A., & Applebee, A. N. (1987). *How writing shapes thinking.* Urbana, IL: National Council of Teachers of English.

Marshall, J. D. (1987). The effects of writing on students' understanding of literary texts. *Research in the Teaching of English, 21,* 30–63.

Martin, M. A., Konopak, B. C., & Martin, S. H. (1986). Use of the guided writing procedure to facilitate comprehension of high school text materials. In J. Niles & R.

Lalik (Eds.), *Solving problems in literacy: Learners, teachers, and researchers* (pp. 66–72). Rochester, NY: National Reading Conference.

Mason, L. (2001). Introducing talk and writing for conceptual change: A classroom study. *Learning and Instruction, 11,* 305–329.

McGee, L. M., & Richgels, D. J. (1990). Learning from text using reading and writing. In T. Shanahan (Ed.), *Reading and writing together: New perspectives for the classroom* (pp. 145–169). Norwood, MA: Christopher-Gordon.

McGinley, W. (1989). *The role of reading and writing in the acquisition of knowledge: A study of college students' self-directed engagements in reading and writing to learn.* Unpublished doctoral dissertation, University of Illinois, Urbana–Champaign.

McGinley, W., & Tierney, R. J. (1989). Traversing the topical landscape: Reading and writing as ways of knowing. *Written Communication, 6,* 243–269.

Monopli, M. M. (2002). *Composing from science sources: Relationships to literacy skills, prior knowledge, and interest.* Unpublished doctoral dissertation, Universidad de Guadalajara, Mexico.

National Commission on Writing. (2003). *The neglected "R": The need for a writing revolution.* New York: College Entrance Examination Board.

Newell, G. E. (1986). Learning from writing: Examining our assumptions. *English Quarterly, 19,* 291–302.

Newell, G. E. (1989). The effects of writing in a reader-based and text-based mode on students' understanding of two short stories. *Journal of Reading Behavior, 21,* 37–57.

Newell, G. E. (1996). Reader-based and teacher-centered instructional tasks: Writing and learning about a short story in middle-track classrooms. *Journal of Literacy Research, 28,* 147–172.

Newell, G. E., Suszynski, K., & Weingart, R. (1989). The effects of writing in a reader-based and text-based mode on students' understanding of two short stories. *Journal of Reading Behavior, 21,* 37–58.

Newell, G. E., & Winograd, P. (1989). The effects of writing on learning from expository text. *Written Communication, 6,* 196–217.

Newell, G. E., & Winograd, P. (1995). Writing about and learning from history texts: The effects of task and academic ability. *Research in the Teaching of English, 29,* 133–163.

Penrose, A. M. (1992). To write or not to write: Effects of task and task interpretation on learning through writing. *Written Communication, 9,* 465–500.

Taylor, B. M., & Beach, R. W. (1984). The effects of text structure on middle-school students' comprehension and production of expository text. *Reading Research Quarterly, 19,* 134–146.

Tierney, R. J., & Shanahan, T. (1991). Research on the reading–writing relationship: Interactions, transactions, and outcomes. In R. Barr, M. L. Kamil, P. Mosenthal, & P. D. Pearson (Eds.), *Handbook of reading research* (Vol. 2, pp. 246–280). New York: Longman.

Tierney, R. J., Soter, A., O'Flahavan, J. F., & McGinley, W. (1989). The effects of reading and writing upon thinking critically. *Reading Research Quarterly, 24,* 134–173.

Wittgenstein, L. (1953). *Philosophical investigations.* New York: Macmillan.

Teaching Science through Literacy

CYNTHIA SHANAHAN

Recently, I asked a laboratory scientist how much time he spent in reading and writing activities associated with his job. He said that he read and wrote approximately 99% of the time he was at work. Scientists read to keep abreast of new developments. They write proposals to test hypotheses they create as a result of their reading and research, they gather and analyze data in written form, they confer in writing with other scientists, they write for publication, and so on. This particular scientist said that he became interested in science when he was younger, as a result of reading the biographies of great scientists. To be a scientist, sophisticated reading and writing about science is an integral part of the profession and may be key to one's motivation.

Reading and writing about science is also required of anyone who wishes to be an informed consumer or an engaged citizen. New findings, such as the discovery of a gene that determines how severely individuals feel pain, controversial issues, such as whether we should encourage cloning, and claims by drug companies about products all require sophisticated, critical reading. Engaged citizens write their Congressmen, engage in debate with others, and join lobbyist groups. To be a contributing member of society, critical reading and writing about science is an integral part of the process.

Yet, because reading and writing about science is often difficult, it is sometimes eschewed in schools (Holliday, in press; Holliday, Yore, & Alvermann, 1994). Class discussion, hands-on manipulatives, and laboratory work, as a part of "inquiry-based" science, are honored; textbooks or other reading materials are not. It is not just the notion that reading is difficult. Discovering science on one's own is also thought to be preferable to learning it from books, and books are seen as counterproductive to that discovery. However, an approach that does not include teaching students to read and write within the disciplines of science leaves students disadvantaged. Also, the notion that the hundreds of years of scientific discovery can be duplicated in classrooms is erroneous. Chinn (1998) discusses the difficulty in deriving scientific principles from the kinds of experimentation that are possible in classroom environments, where instrumentation is imprecise and error is high. Hynd, McNish, Lay, and Fowler (1995) document that students do not always come to scientific conclusions from their own experiments. Indeed, without the explanations that textbooks and other scientific readings contain, students would have trouble understanding scientific phenomena; they would surely be less likely to engage in or understand scientific experimentation and discovery without reading and writing. In addition, they would be less likely to be informed consumers and citizens. Most citizens read about new scientific discoveries and issues rather than "discover" them. Furthermore, science classes that do not include reading and writing instruction fail to meet criteria, such as the National Science Standards, in which reading and writing play a key role.

On the other side of the coin, some teachers appear to rely too heavily on science textbooks alone to teach science. Holliday et al. (1994) have found that, indeed, among high school science classes, textbook reading is the most prevalent activity. This prevalence is despite the fact that the students who read them often do not understand them, that instruction in how to read science textbooks is often absent. Craig and Yore (1995) point out that middle school students' strategies for reading science texts are about as good as younger students' readings of narratives. Textbook-dominant classes deprive students of opportunities to engage in hands-on experimentation and learn about the application of science outside of the classroom. In addition, textbook-dominant classes keep students from engaging in more authentic scientific reading and writing. I do not believe that science textbooks are useless or unnecessary. As I mention earlier, they have an important place in the curriculum. However, textbook reading should be balanced with laboratory experimentation and a variety of reading and writing activities that show students what it is like to engage in the processes of science, as well as to learn the body of knowledge that scientists have created.

INFLUENCES IN SCIENCE LEARNING

What does it mean to learn science? If students are to do it, they need to draw on various motivations and/or focus on several kinds of knowledge.

Motivations and Dispositions

Pintrich, Marx, and Boyle (1993) discuss the varying kinds of motivation associated with learning scientific information. Interest is a key motivation. Students who are interested in a topic in science will likely learn it better than do students who lack that interest. Schiefele (1991) found that students who were intrinsically interested used appropriate learning strategies to process text more deeply and reported having a higher quality learning experience.

There are other motivations as well. Pintrich et al. (1993) add that students who perceive the information as useful, as helping them meet their goals, and as related to their lives in some way are more likely to persist in learning scientific information. Hynd, Holschuh, and Nist (2000) reported on a study in which students who saw how science helped them understand everyday life used various deep-thinking strategies for learning new information, whereas students who did not believe that science was useful employed more surface-level strategies.

Paris, Lipson, and Wixon (1983) suggest that, in addition to the motivations already mentioned, learners' assessments of their efficacy in a particular setting may influence learning. Students who have a sense of self-efficacy exert more control over their own learning; thus, they persist more than those who do not feel capable of learning.

Luque (2003) discusses the need for students to be self-regulated. *Self-regulation* refers to students' metacognitive awareness of their own understanding (or lack of it). To be metacognitively aware, students must engage in ongoing monitoring and evaluation. Self-regulation also refers to students' purposeful use of activities to control their learning, such as regulating their attentional resources and learning strategies, or attending to their comprehension breakdowns once they are aware of them. Students need to employ strategic tools to aid their understanding, tools that they consciously use, and this requires a disposition to be self-regulated. Learners vary in the degree to which they regulate their learning even when their strategic knowledge is the same. For example, two students may both use concept cards to learn new vocabulary and understand how to monitor their understanding, but one will memorize without monitoring, whereas the other will engage in meaningful processing with ongoing monitoring. Both know how to self-regulate, but only one follows through.

It may be that epistemology also plays a role in whether students are self-regulated. Students' varying beliefs about knowledge and learning can influence how they learn. Students who believe that information that is difficult will never be learned may not persist in employing strategic tools to aid their understanding or regulate their attentional resources.

Epistemology may explain not only the quantity but also the quality of strategic effort that is employed. Students who believe that knowledge is what is told to them by an authority, and that it is certain and unchanging (the Truth) will be indisposed to viewing scientific knowledge as evolving, contextualized within a certain era and political context, or limited by instrumentation. Thus, they may approach scientific reading, writing, and experimentation as activities in which there are right and wrong answers; they would employ only surface-level strategies to learn "the facts." Schommer (1990) found that college students who believed that knowledge was certain, and that learning had to be easy, comprehended a science text less well than did students with more mature views of knowledge and learning.

Knowledge

As students move toward expertise in the discipline of science, their epistemologies may mature. Scientists have more sophisticated notions of scientific knowledge than do novices, because they know more about how their discipline operates. Thus, students need to learn about the discipline of science. Disciplinary knowledge in science is knowledge of science as a field. It includes understanding how knowledge is created (through scientific experimentation and discovery), how it is reported (in journals and newspapers), and how it is evaluated (through peer reviews, replication, prediction, and validation). It also includes how power structures interact with scientific activity to privilege some kinds of scientific understanding over others. For example, power relations explain why Galileo's ideas about the universe were not immediately accepted. Disciplinary knowledge is an understanding of the processes that define the daily life of a scientist. Knowing these processes allows students to think critically about scientific information and to understand its constantly changing status.

Other kinds of knowledge include topic knowledge and strategic knowledge. If students already know something about a topic, they are more likely to learn new information easily and have more sophisticated notions about how new and existing knowledge are related. Students who have strategic knowledge, then, are more likely to engage in successful self-regulatory behavior.

The Interaction of Knowledge and Dispositions

Our beliefs, dispositions, and motivations interact with knowledge to produce learning. Patricia Alexander and her colleagues (e.g., Alexander, 1997; Alexander, Jetton, & Kulikowich, 1995; Alexander & Judy, 1988) discuss the idea that strategic knowledge, topic knowledge, and interest interact to explain growth in scientific understanding; that is, if students lack prior knowledge of scientific information, they are likely to engage in inefficient, global strategies for learning that information and will lack intrinsic interest in the topic. If students' interests are piqued, if they gain some key understanding, or if they learn more efficient strategies, however, the change in one of these influences will likely result in changes in the other two. A student who becomes interested in the way the eye works, for example, will persist in learning about it and use strategies such as constructing diagrams that show how the different parts of the eye work together in an integrated process rather than merely memorizing the different parts. Or a student might learn to construct a diagram and, by doing so, gain a deeper understanding of how the eye works and find it more interesting than if he or she had merely engaged in memorization. Although Alexander and her colleagues have only studied the interactions of topic knowledge, interest, and strategic knowledge, other interactions, such as with disciplinary knowledge, self-regulative behavior, and other types of motivation are likely to occur.

Thus, students who are most likely to learn, think about, and engage in science are those who are interested and see science as related to their lives and useful to their ability to understand their world. These students understand how scientists go about their work. They are strategic in their approach to reading and writing about science, and they see interconnections in the information they learn. They understand both the processes and the products of scientific investigation. Literacy is at the core of those understandings.

Are there ways to infuse reading and writing into science lessons that make sense, in ways that would help students become scientists, consume scientific information independently, and/or critically think about that information? What do educators know about reading and writing in science that can be translated into appropriate instruction toward those aims? My purpose in this chapter is to discuss literacy (reading and writing) in science, in terms of both the research that has been done and the implications of that research for practice. I focus the rest of this chapter on various topics that science–reading researchers have identified in sections on *what we know* and *what we can do.*

SCIENCE TEXTS

What We Know

Reading and writing in science has been the focus of research for a number of years, and much of this research has been on the science textbooks themselves. Science textbooks have been found wanting in a number of key areas. For one, vocabulary loads are high, and little is done to develop fully readers' understanding of key terms (Konopak, 1988). Also, as Beck and Dole (1992) discuss, authors of science texts often fail to write coherent explanations: "Science texts, like their social studies counterparts, fail to expose the underlying conceptual frameworks which hold ideas together" (p. 6). Furthermore, science texts fail to make ties to students' prior knowledge, confront students' misconceptions, or provide real world, age–appropriate examples (Beck & Dole, 1992). Beck, McKeown, and Worthy (1995) refer to these kinds of texts as *inconsiderate*, in that they do not consider ties to students' experiences and knowledge. Students have to attempt to make inferences that they are incapable of making because of their lack of prior knowledge (Britton, 1996; Britton & Gulgoz, 1991). Guzzetti, Hynd, Skeels, and Williams (1995) asked high school physics students about their textbooks and got a number of critical responses. The illustrations were either superfluous to the text or the connection between the text and illustrations was unclear. The graphs and charts were often difficult to read. The writing seemed stultifying and archaic; it lacked "voice" (Beck et al., 1995). Problems at the end of chapters were not keyed to particular text that might help explain how to solve them. Yore and Schymanski (1991) noted these and other problems. For example, there were numerous errors in content or the scientific information was out of date. No wonder that even "good" science students had difficulty with the reading. One high school honors physics student described it this way: "It's like a house with no foundation." She explained that she did not have the resources to make the connections between her own "ground" of prior knowledge and the information the textbook was trying to explain (Guzzetti et al., 1995).

What We Can Do

In addition to asking high school students to critique their textbooks, Guzzetti et al. (1995) asked students' what they would do to improve science textbooks. These students' suggestions for publishers and authors included rectifying the many shortcomings just listed. One student, for example, suggested that each chapter be accompanied by a frequently asked questions (FAQ) section to address students' most common misconceptions and difficulties with the concepts. But making these changes takes time, and teachers are often not the authors of textbooks. So what can teachers do?

Engage in Careful Textbook Adoption

Teachers are often pressured to adopt textbooks without developing a good idea of their quality. Most teachers have been in situations in which the main criterion for a choice is whether the illustrations are beautiful. But the following characteristics, derived largely from my conversations with students about their texts, are more important than beauty:

- New terms that are essential to understanding the underlying concepts are fully explained and illustrated, and are positioned in relation to other terms associated with that concept.
- The scientific knowledge is up-to-date and accurate.
- The scope and sequence make sense and are closely aligned with national, state, and local standards.
- Age-appropriate, "lively" language is used.
- Students' prior knowledge and common intuitive understandings are addressed.
- Familiar examples are used to illustrate concepts.
- There are explicit ties between graphs, charts, and other illustrations and relevant text, and between problems students are asked to solve and relevant text.
- Marginal notations help students understand and think about the content.
- Reading and writing activities suggested in the student text and/or teacher's edition aid understanding, engage students in the processes that scientists use, and encourage critical thinking (synthesis, analysis, evaluation).
- The student text and teacher's edition provide direction in *how* to read and write in science classes, not just *what* to read and write.
- Students are taught how to solve problems.
- The textbooks are supplemented with texts and writing activities that represent the various genres of science.

In adopting a textbook, adoption committees should rate the quality of these features (using a rubric) rather than simply checking them off if they are present in any form.

Use Materials Other Than Textbooks

Commonly, educators confuse the textbook with the curriculum, allowing the textbook to determine the scope and sequence of content presentation and literate activity. If you ask those educators what they are teaching, they may answer, "Chapter 15." But the curriculum is determined by national, state, and local standards, through curriculum departments, committees, and individual teachers, and is not embodied in a particular book. For example, projectile motion may be a topic in the curriculum that is not adequately "covered" in the text; the district's knowledge standards for that topic would not be met if the textbook is the only source used. The science teachers in the school, however, may create a *curriculum* for the topic that includes film, trade books, articles, experiments, and laboratory reports in addition to those suggested by the textbook. They may embed those materials in a particular scope and sequence of lessons that may differ from the scope and sequence of the book. If the textbook were the curriculum, then appropriate learning would not take place. However, when the curriculum includes the textbook, but within a larger context of lessons, it is more likely that learning standards will be met. Therefore, science textbooks can be supplemented with other texts, such as nonfiction trade books, scientific magazines and articles, newspaper reports and editorials, fiction dealing with science topics, biographical accounts of scientists, examples of scientist's lab reports and proposals, websites, and so on—all materials that can have a place in the curriculum (Swann, 1993). The Guthrie, McGough, Bennett, and Rice (1996) integrated curriculum project, content-oriented reading instruction (CORI), provides evidence that integrating reading and writing instruction into science instruction using trade books is an effective way to engage elementary school students in learning about science.

The different kinds of written materials that can be used in science classes are referred to as *genres*. For example, one genre is the scientific research article which has a particular structure, uses specific language, and focuses on specific scientific information and processes that differentiate them from other kinds of science text. Research articles are organized into sections detailing a research question, its background, methods used in answering the question, findings, results, and conclusions. A science article may also be an issue-oriented article, an example of another genre. Issues-oriented texts may take the form of an argument, with a thesis statement, and supporting evidence and conclusions. Science textbooks, which represent still another genre, are usually structured around systems and processes, rely on specific definitions of sometimes common words, use a variety of illustrations and diagrams, and are often focused on problem solving that uses specific formulae. Reading a scientific research article, an issues-oriented article, and a textbook are different experiences and require different strategies. Using various genres ensures that the texts used in science classes are representative of the kinds of texts that continue to be a part of a scientist's or an informed citizen's life. Neither scientists nor citizens commonly read science textbooks; yet they often read articles, editorials, and other genres in the field of science.

CONCEPTUAL CHANGE

What We Know

Researchers have also investigated the role of text in helping students to undergo conceptual change; that is, believing one thing, then changing that belief to something different, is a common goal of science instruction. Many of us have intuitive beliefs that are not verified by scientific investigation. For example, many believe that the seasons are the result of the Earth being closer or farther from the Sun, yet that is not the case. The seasons are affected by the Earth's tilt, which causes the Sun to hit the Earth at various angles during its orbit. To learn scientific information about the seasons, students with contradictory beliefs would have to change them; that is, they would have to favor scientific understanding over intuitive understanding, and begin to use the scientific understanding to explain the phenomena they are encountering.

Change involves more than just assimilating the new information, because a shift, or an accommodation (Piaget, 1980), is necessary. In assimilation, ideas that are compatible to prior knowledge are added to it, expanding the depth of one's understanding; but when ideas are incompatible, individuals need to change their prior beliefs to accommodate the new one. This change has been hypothesized to take place in various ways. Vosniadou (2003) describes a type of conceptual change that occurs gradually, over time, without conscious effort; that is, individuals do not seem to be aware that their ideas are changing, but they are. For example, individuals may not believe in global warming, but may make slight, imperceptible shifts in their thinking each time new evidence is presented, until, at one point, they believe in global warming.

Others hypothesize that conceptual change occurs in a more abrupt fashion, involving a radical shift (Sinatra & Pintrich, 2003). This kind of shift is more likely to involve some form of conscious decision making, or metacognition, and researchers have referred to it as *intentional conceptual change*. This is the type of conceptual change that I have observed in my research about science learning.

Students' intuitive ideas are notably resistant to instruction. There are a number of ways that individuals keep believing what they believe. Chinn and Brewer (1993) say that individuals ignore, discount, explain away, change their ideas in superficial ways, compartmentalize, and otherwise fail to believe in information that contradicts their prior knowledge. In order for students to *change* their conceptions, they must recognize that their ideas are different from the scientific ideas, and the new information must be understandable, believable, and fruitful (Posner, Strike, Hewson, & Gertzog, 1982). Chinn and Brewer (1993) explain how information that is more likely to lead to change is repeated, exists in multiple forms, and seems credible.

Reading helps students learn information that is counterintuitive, especially if the text explicitly refutes intuitive understandings. Guzzetti, Snyder, Glass, and Gamas (1993), in a meta-analysis of experimental studies of conceptual change, found that refutational texts were effective in helping students overcome intuitive understandings in favor of scientific thinking. Most of these were laboratory studies not conducted in classroom settings. But since that meta-analysis, my colleagues and I (Hynd, McNish, Qian, Keith, & Lay, 1994) have shown that refutational texts positively affect student learning of counterintuitive concepts even when they are a part of ongoing, intensive classroom instruction, including demonstration, laboratory experimentation, lecture, and discussion, at least for students enrolled in regular and basic high school science classes.

What is refutational text? It is text that actively and explicitly refutes common intuitive concepts by acknowledging and then discounting them. An example of a refutational passage follows:

> The horizontal (forward) component of motion for a projectile is no more complicated than the horizontal motion of a bowling ball rolling freely along a level bowling alley. If the floor did not produce friction to slow the bowling ball, it would continue to move forward down the alley at a constant speed. *Despite the fact that many people think that a ball will slow or stop on its own, this will not happen.* In fact, scientists have created frictionless environments that prove that it doesn't. Moving objects will keep moving at a constant rate unless they are slowed or stopped, or their direction is changed because of an *outside* force such as friction.

In this passage, students are told about a common conception. Then are told that this conception does not reflect current scientific understanding; it is wrong. The text goes on to explain the scientific conception, contrasting science with intuition, and showing that the scientific conception provides the better explanation of the phenomenon. The text ties the scientific conception to real-life examples.

When we asked students to tell us about the effect of the text on them (compared to other genres of text covering the same scientific information), they explained that the text tied to their prior knowledge ("At least my idea was there!"), provided enough information to be understood ("All of my questions were answered"), and was useful in helping them explain an everyday phenomenon ("It's just like real life"). They overwhelmingly preferred it to nonrefutational text. Thus, we have qualitative evidence that refutation works in the ways hypothesized by various theorists in conceptual change (Chinn & Brewer, 1993, Pintrich et al., 1993).

Reading refutational texts may be even more important than other forms of instruction, such as discussion, when conceptual change is necessary. In one study (Hynd, McWhorter, Phares, & Suttles, 1994), we found evidence that discussion can make it *less* likely that students learn counterintuitive information and profit from subsequent reading. In this study, students who engaged in discussion of counterintuitive concepts or saw a demonstration that contradicted their knowledge and then discussed it, did *not* learn information as well as did those who read a refutational text. In addition, those who discussed the information prior to reading did not do as well as those who simply read. Transcripts of students' conversations revealed that they often talked each other out of scientific explanations in favor of intuitive ones, and that once this discussion took place, students' intuitive ideas appeared to have solidified, making them more immune to scientific ideas. The finding is in line with previous research showing that activation of prior knowledge before reading meant that students with alternate ideas would learn less (Alvermann & Hynd, 1989). These studies suggest that reading is important in overcoming nonscientific understandings, but that teachers must be vigilant in monitoring the discussion that takes place around that reading.

What We Can Do

Assess Students' Prior Knowledge

The finding that prior knowledge can debilitate the learning of counterintuitive information does not mean that students' prior knowledge should remain unactivated. Unless students make ties between new information and their previous ideas, true learning will not take place. Rather, new ideas will be compartmentalized and remain inaccessible or forgotten. The importance of background knowledge to subsequent reading and understanding was documented repeatedly in the comprehension research of the 1980s. An honor's physics teacher I once worked with believed that because his students were smart and motivated, they understood his scientific explanations, knew how to solve problems, and were deriving important scientific principles from experimentation, so he did not ask them what they were thinking. As I talked to them, however, I discovered that they, like other students, had significant difficulties understanding counterintuitive material and were frustrated with their inability to solve problems or explain their experiments. In fact, at one point, they confronted the teacher with the difficulties they were having, pleading with him to help them understand their textbooks and even to lecture more. This teacher learned an important lesson and changed his instruction to include more guided reading and discussion. He also learned to assess what his students knew.

One way to assess students' prior knowledge is through the use of anticipation guides, in which students must read statements and agree or disagree with them. For example, students would be asked whether they agreed with the following statements about projectile motion:

An object comes to a stop after its energy is spent.
If an object were shot horizontally from a cannon off a cliff, it would travel out for a while before it began to drop.
If a heavy and a light object were dropped from a tall building, the heavy object would land first (discounting air resistance).

These statements, all false, are examples of common misconceptions that students have about projectile motion as a result of their intuitive understandings of the way objects behave. Having students react to these statements gives teachers a chance to learn students' intuitive but scientifically naive ideas.

Assess Prior Knowledge, But . . .

In order for students to really learn information that is counterintuitive, they must activate their prior knowledge, then recognize the disparity between that knowledge and the new information. They must also find that the new information is better (e.g., it is better at explaining phenomena, more understandable, believable, and useful; Posner et al., 1982). In one study, simply telling students that their previous ideas might be wrong and that they should pay attention to the counterintuitive information in the text was enough to increase learning (Alvermann & Hynd, 1989). In real classrooms, teachers must counteract the solidification of intuitive conceptions by helping students see the disparities between intuitive and scientific information, and by providing explanations that are understandable and useful.

Use Refutational Text

Texts that explicitly confront students' conceptions can be powerful items in a teacher's toolkit. Refutational texts connect with students' prior knowledge, then help change it. Therefore, if refutational texts exist about intuitive conceptions, teachers should use them. Alternatively, they can construct their own text for those occasions when they find students have intuitive, nonscientific conceptions.

Present Information in Multiple Formats

Students learn counterintuitive information better when it is presented in more than one way. Thus, we provide students with multiple opportunities to encounter scientific principles, through reading in different formats (such as textbooks, trade books, the Internet, and articles), discussion, demonstration, and laboratory investigations.

COMPREHENSION STRATEGIES

What We Know

In their analysis of comprehension research, the National Reading Panel (NRP) report specified a number of effective comprehension strategies. These include (1) asking students questions and helping them to ask their own questions, teaching students to (2) construct idea maps or other graphic representations, (3) write summaries, (4) monitor their understanding, (5) answer questions, and (6) work with others in cooperative groups, and (7) engage in multiple strategies. Science educators have typically focused their investigations on the use of graphic organizers and questioning. They find that graphic organizers, especially those that students create as a result of reading the text, help students understand scientific ideas (Holliday & Benson, 1991). Furthermore, questions that focus students' attention on key points either in relation to the graphic organizers or to the text aid understanding of key ideas (Guzzetti, et al., 1993). Finally, research evidence suggests that teaching students to recognize text organization aids comprehension. Helping students to recognize different genres and their organizational elements in science is one way to help students understand what they read. These strategies, taught through direct instruction, can help students understand the scientific information they read.

What We Can Do

We can teach students to understand their science texts. By teaching, I mean that rather than merely assigning reading, teachers need to explain, model, provide guided practice, and engage students in independent practice. The strategies found effective by the National Reading Panel are general strategies, but they have specific applications in science; that is, teaching students to make a graphic organizer of science content is different than teaching students to make a graphic organizer of historical or literature content. Thus, science teachers can be better teachers of science reading strategies than are English teachers.

Textbook companies that provide science textbooks could improve understanding of their texts by providing instruction in science reading; that is, textbooks could include instruction in making graphic organizers, in recognizing the various scientific text genres and organizational styles, in asking good questions, or in engaging in cooperative activity. If science textbooks do not provide that instruction, though, teachers will have to do it.

WRITING

What We Know

Writing in science has not been the focus of extensive research. However, those studies that have been done generally show that students who are taught to write enjoy increased learning. Tucknott and Yore (1999) found, for example, that 4th graders improved their understanding of simple machines when they learned how to take notes, make summaries, and write sentence and paragraph explanations for drawings and labels.

Prain, Hand, and their colleagues have engaged in a series of studies of models of writing in science. The research using this model suggests that students benefit from instruction that involves them in writing for a variety of purposes to a variety of audiences, and in a variety of genres (Hand, 1999; Hand & Prain, 2001; Hand, Prain, & Wallace, 2002; Prain & Hand, 1999). The model specifies variation across the categories of (1) topic, (2) genre type, (3) purpose, (4) audience, and (5) method of text production. For example, if the topic were projectile motion, the writer could write a narrative, a set of instructions, a brochure, a poem, a diagram, an explanation, a report, a letter, a script, and so on. Students might write for the purpose of clarifying ideas, applying the ideas, or persuading readers. Their readers might be peers, teachers, younger students, visitors, or a government agency. A student might work with another student or in a group, using pencil and paper or a computer.

What We Can Do

Science teachers can do many things to help their students become more proficient writers in science. Probably one of the biggest drawbacks to traditional science instruction is that students are not taught to write. It may be true that writing is assigned, but assigning is not the same as teaching. To teach writing, teachers need to help students understand the characteristics of each of the genres of scientific writing they introduce. For example, there are specific formats scientists use for proposing studies and for writing up their results. Students use other formats of writing when they answer essay questions, take notes, explain scientific processes, and so on.

Yore, Hand, and Prain (1999) suggest that writing be focused on writing to learn. They recommend these instructional practices: reaction papers and collaborative explanatory essays. The reaction paper involves reading and writing. Students read an article and write a summary and reflection. They are taught summarizing skills (deleting redundancies, identifying relevant ideas, synthesizing those ideas into a unified text representative of the original author's intentions). They are also taught to make quality reflections that include evaluation and questioning of the ideas and methods, and connections between the text, other sources, and their own ideas. The collaborative essay involves students in expert teams developing written essays after inquiry into various topics in science. These essays are then shared with "home" groups that act as reviewers and ultimately are responsible for learning the information written in the essay.

Another strategy for writing is to provide students with skeletons for writing in different genres. For example, if students are to learn to write a research proposal, a skeleton of the parts of that proposal and sentences demonstrating the macrostructural elements are handed out to students. Students fill in the structure with their individual proposals. As students become more proficient in writing in that genre, the skeleton is faded and students become more independent.

The common element in these strategies is the idea of genre. To become scientists or contributing members of society, students must know how to write more than the five-paragraph theme, and science classes are the most likely place for teaching students the genres of science writing.

CONCLUSIONS

In summary, teachers who teach science are also in key positions to teach the kind of reading and writing that scientists do and the kind that citizens need to know if they are to be consumers of scientific information. Students do not learn how to read and write in science by reading only literature and writing only essays. They learn it by engaging in scientific activity which always involves reading and writing. Research evidence suggests that students can increase reading achievement and learn scientific information through the use of reading strategies. In addition, evidence suggests that text, especially refutational text, can help students change their conceptions to more current scientific thinking. Finally, writing strategies that focus on different scientific genres appear to increase understanding of scientific principles.

What do we still need to learn? The research on reading and writing in different scientific genres needs to be expanded. Specifically, we need to analyze fully the genres of reading and writing in science, so that instruction can focus on helping students more closely approximate authentic literate scientific activity. Once these genres are fully characterized, we need to engage in experimental research to determine which genres are most conducive to learning about science and what strategies in reading and writing succeed in those genres. Qualitative studies of students engaging in research proven activity can help us understand why certain instruction works.

Equally important is research that helps us determine how science learning should be organized. As I have argued in this chapter, reading and writing need to be a part of science learning. Reading and writing can be processes used when students engage in "hands-on" science, such as participating in experimentation, interpreting and writing up results, and so on. But text that explains what scientists know can also play a role. In other words, literate activity might be most effective when it is used both to learn about the products of science and to engage in the processes in which scientists engage. But the appropriate mix of activities has not yet been determined through research.

Finally, research about science textbooks needs to continue. We already know a good deal about what makes textbooks considerate. How well-written textbooks are used and what effects they have on science learning is an area that still needs to be studied.

REFERENCES

Alexander, P. A. (1997). Mapping the multidimensional nature of domain learning: The interplay of cognitive, motivation, and strategic forces. *Advances in Motivation and Achievement, 10*, 213–250.

Alexander, P. A., Jetton, T. L., & Kulikowich, J. M. (1995). Interrelationship of knowledge, interest, and recall: Assessing a model of domain learning. *Journal of Educational Psychology, 87*, 559–575.

Alexander, P. A., & Judy, J. E. (1988). The interaction of domain-specific and strategic knowledge in academic performance. *Review of Educational Research, 58*, 375–404.

Alvermann, D. E., & Hynd, C. R. (1989). Effects of prior knowledge activation modes and text structure on nonscience majors' comprehension of physics. *Journal of Educational Research, 83*, 97–102.

Beck, I. L., & Dole, J. A. (1992). Reading and thinking with history and science text. In C. Collins & J. N. Mangieri (Eds.), *Teaching thinking: An agenda for the twenty-first century* (pp. 3–21). Hillsdale, NJ: Erlbaum.

Beck, I. L., McKeown, M. G., & Worthy, J. (1995). Giving a text voice can improve students' understanding. *Reading Research Quarterly, 30*, 220–239.

Britton, B. K. (1996). Rewriting: The arts and sciences of improving expository instructional text. In C. M. Levy & S. Ransdell (Eds.), *The science of writing: Theories, methods, individual differences, and applications* (pp. 104–130). Mahwah, NJ: Erlbaum.

Britton, B. K., & Gulgoz, S. (1991). Interactive learning environments and the teaching of science and mathematics. In M. Gardner, J. G. Greeno, F. Reif, A. H. Schoenfeld, A. DiSessa, & E. Stage (Eds.), *Toward a scientific practice of science education* (pp. 111–140). Hillsdale, NJ: Erlbaum.

Chinn, C. (1998). A critique of social constructivist explanations of knowledge change. In B. Guzzetti & C. Hynd (Eds.), *Perspectives on conceptual change: Multiple ways to understand knowing and learning in a complex world* (pp. 77–116). Mahwah, NJ: Erlbaum.

Chinn, C. A., & Brewer, W. F. (1993). The role of anomalous data in knowledge acquisition: A theoretical framework and implications for science instruction. *Review of Educational Research, 63*(1), 1–49.

Craig, M. T., & Yore, L. D. (1995). Middle school students' metacognitive knowledge about science reading and science text: An interview study. *Reading Psychology, 16*(2), 169–213.

Guthrie, J. T., McGough, K., Bennett, L., & Rice, M. E. (1996). Concept-oriented reading instruction: An integrated curriculum to develop motivations and strategies for reading. In I. Baker, P. Afflerbach, & D. Reinking (Eds.), *Developing engaged readers in school and home community* (pp. 165–190). Mahwah, NJ: Erlbaum.

Guzzetti, B., Hynd, C., Skeels, S., & Williams, W. (1995). What students have to say about their science texts. *Journal of Reading, 38*, 656–665.

Guzzetti, B. J., Snyder, T. E., Glass, G. V., & Gamas, W. S. (1993). Meta-analysis of instructional interventions from reading education and science education to promote conceptual change in science. *Reading Research Quarterly, 28*, 116–161.

Hand, B. (1999). A writing in science framework designed to enhance science literacy. *International Journal of Science Education, 21*(10), 1021–1035.

Hand, B., & Prain, V. (2002). Teachers implementing writing-to-learn strategies in junior secondary science: A case study. *Science Education, 86*(6), 737–755.

Hand, B., Prain, V., & Wallace, C. (2002). Influences of writing tasks on students' answers to recall and higher-level test questions. *Research in Science Education, 32*(1), 19–34.

Holliday, W. G. (in press). Getting serious about reading instruction in science. In W. Saul (Ed.), *Crossing borders.* International Reading Association.

Holliday, W. G., & Benson, G. (1991). Enhancing learning using questions, adjunct to science charts. *Journal of Research in Science Teaching, 28*(6), 523–535.

Holliday, W. G., Yore, L., & Alvermann, D. E. (1994). The reading–science learning–writing connection: Breakthroughs, barriers, and promises. *Journal of Research in Science Teaching, 31,* 877–894.

Hynd, C., Holschuh, J., & Nist, S. (2000). Learning complex, scientific information: Motivation theory and its relation to student perceptions. *Reading and Writing Quarterly: Overcoming Learning Difficulties, 36*(1), 23–58.

Hynd, C., McNish, M. M., Lay, K., & Fowler, P. (1995). *High school physics: The role of text in learning counterintuitive information* (Reading Research Report, No. 27). Athens, GA: National Reading Research Center.

Hynd, C., McNish, M., Qian, G., Keith, M., & Lay, K. (1994). *Learning counterintuitive physics principles: The effect of text and educational environment* (Reading Research Report No. 16). Athens, GA: National Reading Research Center.

Hynd, C., McWhorter, Y., Phares, V., & Suttles, W. (1994). The role of instructional variables in conceptual change in high school physics topics. *Journal of Research in Science Teaching, 31,* 933–946.

Konopak, B.C. (1988). Effects of inconsiderate versus considerate text on secondary students' vocabulary learning. *Journal of Reading Behavior, 20,* 5–24.

Luque, M. L. (2003). The role of domain-specific knowledge in intentional conceptual change. In G. M. Sinatra & P. R. Pintrich (Eds.), *Intentional conceptual change* (pp. 133–170). Mahwah, NJ: Erlbaum.

Paris, S. G., Lipson, M. Y, & Wixon, K. K. (1983). Becoming a strategic reader. *Contemporary Educational Psychology, 8,* 293–316.

Piaget, J. (1980). *Experiments in contradiction* (D. Coltman, Trans.). Chicago: University of Chicago Press. (Original work published 1974)

Pintrich, P. W., Marx, R. W., & Boyle, R. A. (1993). Beyond cold conceptual change: The role of motivational beliefs and classroom contextual factors in the process of conceptual change. *Review of Educational Research, 63,* 167–199.

Posner, G. J., Strike, K. A., Hewson, P. W., & Gertzog, W. A. (1982). Accommodation of a scientific conception: Toward a theory of conceptual change. *Science Education, 66,* 211–227.

Prain, V., & Hand, B. (1999). Students' perceptions of writing for learning in secondary school science. *Science Education, 83*(2), 151–162.

Schiefele, U. (1991). Interest, learning, and motivation. *Educational Psychologist, 26,* 299–323.

Schommer, M. (1990). Effects of beliefs about the nature of knowledge on comprehension. *Journal of Educational Psychology, 82*, 498–504.

Sinatra, G., & Pintrich. P. (2003). The role of intentions in conceptual change learning. In *Intentional conceptual change* (pp. 1–18). Mahwah, NJ: Erlbaum.

Tucknott, J. M., & Yore, L. D. (1999, March). *The effects of writing activities on grade 4 children's understanding of simple machines, inventions, and inventors.* Paper presented at the annual meeting of the National Association for Research in Science Teaching, Boston, MA.

Vosniadou, S. (2003). Exploring the relationships between conceptual change and intentional learning. In G. Sinatra & P. Pintrich (Eds.), *Intentional conceptual change* (pp. 366–406). Mahwah, NJ: Erlbaum.

Yore, L. D., Hand, B. M., & Prain, V. (1999, January). *Writing to learn science: Breakthroughs, barriers, and promises.* Paper presented at the International Conference of the Association for Educating Teachers in Science, Austin, TX.

Yore, L. D., & Schymanski, J. A. (1991). Reading in science: Developing an operational conception to guide instruction. *Journal of Research in Science Teaching, 25*(3), 29–36.

Learning to Think Like a Historian
Disciplinary Knowledge through Critical Analysis of Multiple Documents

STEVEN A. STAHL
CYNTHIA SHANAHAN

It is a commonplace in the professional literature to say that history is not a "basketful of facts." Instead, the goal of history education should be that students develop what has been called *disciplinary knowledge* (e.g., Hynd & Stahl, 1998; Wineburg, 1991a), or knowledge of the processes of history. Individuals with disciplinary knowledge about history would know how new interpretations of history are created, how they are shared and evaluated, and what counts as quality. This was elegantly put by Mosborg (2002):

> School history is not fundamentally vocational. It is based on the premise that each of the academic disciplines offers unique criteria for examining phenomena, even as they share certain attributes of critical thinking and discourse. In keeping with the liberal arts tradition, history is one of several disciplines offered students so that they me [CH1]opposed to reason and deliberate with several lenses. What is learned by doing history, it is hoped, will transfer: If all goes well, students will be able to recruit and use historical knowledge throughout their political and cultural lives. (p. 324)

Wineburg (1991a) collected the thinking aloud of academically advanced high school students and professors of history as they examined depictions of a historical battle. No group was an expert in this battle, including the historians. The high school students read with the purpose of learning the facts. The historians processed the texts in ways that were different from those in high school, assumedly reflecting their disciplinary knowledge. The processes they used were conceptualized as comprising of three processes:

- *Corroboration*, or comparing and contrasting documents with one another;
- *Sourcing*, or looking first at the source of the document before reading the text itself to consider how the bias of the source might have affected the content of the document.
- *Contextualization*, or situating a text in a temporal and spatial context to consider how the time or place in which the document was written might have affected its content or the perspective taken.

In short, the historians tended to look for places where the documents overlapped (corroboration), to look at the source of the document for possible bias due to self-interest or political perspective (sourcing) and looked at the historical and social context of each document. The result was that historians tended to produce a more nuanced view of the events, even though they started out with knowledge equivalent to that of the high school students.

These differences were not simply due to differences in knowledge, because historians who did not know very much about the American Revolution still used the same reasoning processes in their think-alouds. Nor are the differences due to inability to detect bias. Previous research has demonstrated that students are capable of such detection. Both the college students in Perfetti, Britt, Rouet, Mason, and Georgi's (1993) study and the high school honor students in Stahl and Hynd's (1994) study could reliably detect bias in sources.

The differences between the groups seem to be related to their differing views of history. Unlike the professional historians (and educational scholars who study history education), the common view is to treat history as a narrative (a *story*, as it were). This is *not* to say that history really is seen as that "basketful of facts," but rather as a narrative of a people. We can see this emphasis on narrative not only in excellent history teachers (such as Coach Matthew Boggs, who has taught our children) but also in the discussions of history by marginalized groups, such as women or African Americans.

Possibly because of the way they have been taught, high school students tend to hold the common view; they view texts as narratives, as bearers of information, and believe that learning history is to learn the narrative as it is depicted in most history textbooks. Evidence for this observation is students' tendencies to rate textbooks as more trustworthy than source documents, a finding replicated by Perfetti et al. (1993), Rouet, Favart, Britt, and Perfetti (1997), and Stahl and Hynd (1994). Learning the narrative, however, does not ensure that students will be able to think critically about it. The students in Perfetti et al.'s study (1993) were able to grasp the basic "story" of the Panama Canal Treaty from documents describing the events leading up to the signing of the treaty in 1903. But, similar to the students in the 2002 National Assessment of Educational Progress (NAEP), when asked to analyze the events critically, they had difficulty providing evidence for their viewpoint.

Historians, on the other hand, tended to view texts as "speech acts" produced for particular purposes by particular persons, at particular times and places. To understand the text involves understanding both the person and the purpose, and to understand the nature of interpretation (that it is not "truth") involves comparing various perspectives, with an understanding of who produced the various texts and why. In the discipline of history, the "truth" is always an approximation, depending on who is doing the telling, the era in which it is being told, and the context of the event. Yet the high school students in these studies tended to see the task of history learning as "getting the story."

These two perspectives could be labeled *historiography* and *history*, reflecting the difference between history as a discipline of thought, and history as a narrative of a people's political and social changes over time. Teaching *history*, then, means teaching the narrative. The field of content-area reading has developed a great many techniques for teaching children strategies for learning the narrative of history (Vacca & Vacca, 2002), including use of graphic organizers, time lines (e.g., Armbruster, Anderson, & Meyer, 1991) and summarization (e.g., Rinehart, Stahl, & Erickson, 1986). Teaching *historiography*, on the other hand, means teaching the processes of history, focusing on the critical analysis of the various narratives that exist about any particular event or cluster of events. The field of content-area reading has not typically focused its efforts on strategies for historiography.

The purpose of this chapter, then, is to focus on multiple text strategies designed to develop disciplinary knowledge in history, or historiography. We plan to take an ecumenical view of history instruction, suggesting that both understanding of the narrative(s) of history and the discipline of history are needed to fulfill the goals of history education. Our intent is to concentrate on techniques for integrating the information in multiple texts to provide a complement to the well-developed content-area reading strategies discussed earlier. First, we discuss some of the difficulties high school students have learning disciplinary knowledge in history using multiple source documents. Second, we discuss some principles that we feel should govern instruction in using multiple-source documents to develop disciplinary knowledge in history. Finally, we speculate on some approaches that might be used to develop such knowledge. Some of these techniques discussed have been developed for working with a single textbook, such as *Questioning the Author* (Beck, McKeown, & Worthy, 1995; McKeown, Beck, & Worthy, 1993) or collaborative reasoning strategies (Chinn & Anderson, 1998; Chinn, Anderson, & Waggoner, 2001).

USING HISTORY TO UNDERSTAND CURRENT EVENTS

Certainly, the overriding purpose of developing historical understanding is for students to understand the present using the lens of the past, a purpose that fits in both the historied and historiographic approaches to history education. Surprisingly, we have found only one study that examined whether the study of history actually does this. Mosborg (2002) interviewed 5 students in a college-preparatory academy and 5 students from a Christian high school, both with high academic standards, about two current events topics—Starbucks's treatment of workers in Guatemala, and allowing prayer in public schools. She found, as might be expected, that the groups of students differed markedly in their response to these topics. Although their understandings were rooted in different "background narratives," both groups used historical understanding to support their beliefs. On the prayer issue, for example, the students in the college-preparatory school used a background narrative centered on the establishment clause of the Constitution and the separation of church and state; the students in the Christian school used a narrative centered on the persecution of religious beliefs by secular institutions and a letter by Thomas Jefferson to argue that the establishment clause did not suggest that religion should be eliminated from schools.

A major difference between this study and the others is Mosborg's (2002) use of prompts. She began her interview by stating that the purpose of the study was to "find out how your knowledge of American history helps you understand the daily news" (p. 358). She continued by saying, "After you read each set of articles, I'm going to ask you, What does this remind you of from American history or the past?" (p. 358). As students mentioned key terms, such as Constitution and Bill of Rights or tension between religion and government, she probed their meaning. Thus, Mosborg was far more direct than others in asking students to make explicit connections between the history content and the information in the articles. This explicitness may account for the richness of the connections between current events and the understanding of history reported by her subjects. It also could be that the direction, going from the present to the past rather than the other way around, may be more relevant to students.

The students in Mosborg's (2002) study, with only one exception, stayed within their own historical narratives. Critical analysis, such as that desired by the historiographers, would involve stepping outside of one's personal narrative and examining the documents as speech acts made by a particular person for a particular reason. Mosborg does not report that the students she interviewed did so. Instead, they used historical information to shore up their own perspective, not seeing the other side.

CRITICAL ANALYSIS

The critical facilities developed through schooling are necessary for people to participate in a democracy, because such intelligent participation involves critical evaluation of alternatives in relation to the people's prior experience, knowledge, and beliefs (Botstein, 1991). Seeing the other side of an argument is the *raison d'être* of critical analysis. Thus, although Mosborg's (2002) study suggests that academically able high schoolers can draw on historical information to apply to current events, they do not necessarily do so in a critical manner, instead using historical information to reinforce their currently held ideas. Nor do we want students to see *only* the other side. Changing one's opinion from one side to the other is not critical analysis any more than is passive acceptance of received wisdom. Hoffman (1992) describes his daughter's coming home to report that Christopher Columbus was an absolute villain, who made the natives give him impossible quantities of gold, and, if they could not, his men cut their arms off. This is graphic but no more true than the views of Columbus as the beneficent discoverer of the New World.

It may be a function of students' beliefs about knowledge that makes it difficult for them to consider various positions. Both Belenky, Clinchy, Goldberger, & Tarule (1986) and Perry (1970) present similar views of the development of intellectual activity in college-age students. In both accounts, students are seen as moving from positions in which knowledge that is presented to them is true. As students understand that there are different positions on the "truth" of that knowledge, they move toward a stance that all knowledge is relative, and that there is no absolute "truth." Hoffman's young daughter, who took an "Everything we know is wrong" position, exemplifies this stance. Students gradually move toward a stance based on personal belief. Those taking this stance can accept that there are many viewpoints on a subject, and can accept that they have one view and others hold different views, but they will not critically examine their views in light of others. Only a few participants in either the Belenky et al. (1986) or the Perry (1970) study moved to the more advanced stance toward knowledge, using information learned to critically examine their own beliefs. Students exemplifying this stance not only use their beliefs as an lens to examine learned information but also reflexively use new information to examine, and sometimes modify, their own beliefs. (Indeed, we see quite a few of our academic colleagues who will not do this.) Perry describes this stage as "commitment within relativism."

Why multiple documents? When historians write textbooks, the tradition is that they write them as a narrative of unfolding events. What is unseen are the processes they used to create that narrative. Events happen, but the relation among various events, or the narrative, is created in the observer's mind. Thus, historians engage in research to find different narratives and, through critical analysis, create their own. What is left out of the text are the other versions of the story. Historians, knowing this, often create "revisionist" and "postrevisionist" histories. A historian uncovers new or neglected narratives and uses these to persuade readers to change the accepted narrative. But students are not often asked to consider textbook information as a creation, and the textbooks themselves do not encourage such consideration; thus, they tend to believe in the truth of the narrative they are reading.

Students might confront that belief, however, if they are presented with a range of narratives, especially if those narratives conflict or represent widely different perspectives. As Wineburg's (1992) study suggests, students are not likely to confront their stances toward history texts without instruction. However, without the use of multiple texts, and the various perspectives and interpretations they bring to light, it is much more difficult to encourage that confrontation, even with instruction. Multiple, conflicting texts provide instructional opportunities to teachers, in that they lay bare the notion that history is interpretation rather than truth.

When examining multiple documents, we do not want students to accept each document uncritically, nor do we want students to reject documents based on their own beliefs. Instead, we want students to use critical analysis to understand *why* each document is written the way it is, based on the *source* of the document and the biases of that source, the *context* in which the document was written, and how the information in that document is *corroborated* (or not corroborated) by information in other documents, either those presented in the same set or documents (including textbooks) that have been previously read.

HIGH SCHOOL STUDENTS' USE
OF DISCIPLINARY KNOWLEDGE IN HISTORY

How much do academically able high school students use corroboration, sourcing and contextualization while reading multiple-source documents in history? Using a variety of methods and a variety of historical periods (the American Revolution, the Panama Canal conflict, Christopher Columbus's voyages, and the Vietnam conflict), the answer is generally that high school students do not respond critically to the documents they read, as Wineburg's study suggests. For example, Stahl, Hynd, Britton, McNish, and Bosquet (1996) and Hynd, Stahl, Britton, and McNish (1996) found that high school students are not effective at using multiple texts to learn historical information. These studies focused on the Gulf of Tonkin incident and the subsequent Senate resolution that became President Johnson's justification for escalating the Vietnam War. Stahl et al. (1996) found that students did gain in the consistency of their mental models after reading at least two documents, but they did not make any further gains after that. When compared to lay experts, they failed to achieve any growth after a first reading. Examining their notes, we found that students tended to take literal notes, regardless of the final task, which suggests that they used the initial readings to garner the facts about the incident or the resolution. If students were asked for a description, they tended to stay close to the text. If asked for an opinion, however, they tended to ignore the information in the texts they read, even though they may have taken copious notes.

Of the 44 students, only one made a notable number of comments that suggested use of corroboration, sourcing, and contextualization. This student was one of three judged to be knowledgable about the Vietnam War. The majority of his comments were merely noting the source rather than discussing how the perspective of the source may have affected the viewpoint. There was very little corroboration or contextualization observed in any of the students' notes or comments. These observations suggest that high school students may not be able to profit from multiple texts, especially those presenting conflicting opinions, without some additional instruction.

Text Effects

It is possible that the texts themselves may have reduced the amount of critical analysis. The texts dealt with a relatively unknown subject (for our high school participants who were born long after the Vietnam War ended) and were difficult. It is possible that a more familiar, but still controversial, topic might have induced more critical analysis. Stahl, Hynd, Montgomery, and McClain (1997) had high school honor students read conflicting texts about Christopher Columbus and his effect on the Americas, and perform similar analysis. One of the texts, an encyclopedia article, represented the "conventional" narrative about Columbus; another represented a revisionist viewpoint, castigating Columbus for his treatment of native peoples. Two others, a synthesis written by a prominent historian and articles from news magazines, represented moderate viewpoints. Stahl et al. found that students' reported rating of Columbus dropped significantly after one reading and stayed at the same level thereafter. Although none of the texts were textbooks per se, the news magazine stories had the greatest effect on students' attitudes toward Columbus, partially because they were perceived as the most balanced source. The revisionist text, which had a more strident tone than the others, was less effective in changing attitudes. This confirms the findings of Perfetti, Britt, and Georgi (1995) and Stahl et al. (1996) that high school students can accurately perceive bias. Finally, misconceptions about Columbus proved difficult to change, even after multiple readings. These statements were all common misconceptions about Columbus, such as "Columbus was the first to believe that the world was round" or "Columbus was regarded as a great man during his time." In spite of clear refutation in the texts, students tended to hold on to these misconceptions.

Group Processes

Hynd et al. (1996), using the Gulf of Tonkin texts, observed advanced-placement high school students working in groups discussing the different texts. They found that most of the processing during the group work was superficial, focusing either on the task itself, or on expressing opinions about each text, without integrating the texts. One group, perhaps the exception in this class of relatively serious students, took notes during reading, but discussion centered on group members' weekend plans more than on the documents they were reading and taking notes on. More typical is this group of three boys, two African American and one European American, who spent very little time (roughly 3%) off task. However, 40% of their time was spent deciding on procedures, with half of that procedural time spent discussing what the task was, 20% deciding on how they were going to complete the task (who would do what), and 27% on how to negotiate the computer (most of the computer talk was on the first day). The following excerpts exemplify their talk:

> MIKE: I think the Tonkin Gulf Resolution (*reading on his sheet about what major topic they should pick*). [task]
>
> JAKE: Who they voted for. [task]
>
> JOHN: Go to it. [computer]
>
> JAKE: Do you want to skim? Which one do you want to skim? [how to complete the task]
>
> MIKE: I don't care. Flip a coin. [how to complete the task]
>
> JAKE: There's five of them. We can't do that too well. [how to complete the task] I want to see the glossary. [computer]
>
> MIKE: When you are done previewing, click on the box you would like to read. [computer/task]

They spent a good deal of time talking about procedures, but they spent even more time talking about the content of the articles, either in asking for clarification (38%) or stating their opinions about them (13%). The following excerpts illustrate these comments:

> JOHN: Whoa, who, whoa, whoa, whoa. They're talking about the attack where nothing happened? [clarification] Okay! For real! [opinion] Oh, see, that's cheap right there. [opinion] Whoa, whoa. This is getting a lot more interesting. [opinion]
>
> MIKE: Yeah, it is. [opinion]
>
> JOHN: So they, when they were (*inaudible*), they decided that they had been attacked when they obviously hadn't been, that's what it said, right? [clarification] But let's tell them. And so, then, like an hour later, they started bombing, just cause someone messed up. [clarification]
>
> JAKE: They said something like 20 torpedoes. [clarification]

The rest of the talk during reading was about how much they knew or did not know (4%) and their opinions about the project itself (4%). The thing that most distinguished this group from others, however, was the decision to read out loud; thus, group members read together and eliminated wait time. Although reading aloud is generally thought to be less efficient than reading silently (Wilkinson & Anderson, 1995), this group covered as many or more texts than the other groups in this study. They read the first text silently but read the subsequent texts out loud. During one text, they took turns reading the cards. During another, the fastest reader (Jake) read the whole text, and during yet another, because it was a transcript of a congressional hearing, they took the parts of different Senators. Possibly because of their oral reading, they did not take notes. Each student had notes about the first text (the notes were almost identical) but none (except for one sentence) on subsequent texts.

This study represented a naive approach to using group processes both to observe critical analysis of the various texts (through examination of transcripts such as those discussed earlier) and to induce critical analysis. It was assumed that having students discuss the texts in groups would encourage them to make explicit comparisons between the different texts (corroboration) and to bring in information about the source and the context of the documents. The task was described generally and involved the development of either a description of the Gulf of Tonkin incident or an opinion about whether the Gulf of Tonkin incident should have led to war. From the amount of time spent on discussing the task, it is clear that this task was not clearly specified. The group work did not notably improve the amount of disciplinary processes observed. However, students did engage in some high-level discussions of the content of the text, allowing for some critical thought. As we discuss later, we believe that group discussion creates a context for critical analysis of the text, including corroboration, sourcing and contextualization, but the results of this study suggest that is not sufficient for this analysis to occur.

These students, as well as those in other, similar studies (Perfetti, Britt, & Rouet, 1995; Rouet et al., 1997), were able students—Advanced-Placement students, honor students, or college students in selective universities. If the tasks of integrating information by paying attention to the relations between the information in the texts, the biases from the various sources, and the context of each source are difficult for children who are academically accomplished and motivated, then average children would find this impossible.

PARADIGMS FOR TEACHING CHILDREN
TO ANALYZE HISTORICAL TEXTS

We have found only one instructional approach designed to teach children to compare multiple documents: Hoffman's (1992) I (or Inquiry) charts. This approach uses graphic organizers to teach children to compare and compile the information in multiple texts to learn about historical events. It was developed for upper-elementary-level students, but aspects of the approach might be useful for older children.

Prior to using the I chart, the teacher needs to plan a topic and a set of focal questions that can be answered in multiple texts. These are used to construct a chart used to guide the inquiry process. These questions should be the two, three, or four most important points in the text. For the Columbus unit, these questions are "Why did Columbus sail?"; "What did he find?"; "What important things did he do when he got there?"; and "How was Columbus regarded by others?" For older children, questions might include an evaluation of the effects of Columbus's voyages on the natives and whether he handled his conquests in a moral manner.

During reading, the teacher begins by probing the students about their prior knowledge and dispositions toward the topic, asking them how they would answer the focal questions prior to reading. These answers are put on the chart. During this phase, the teacher also solicits other interesting facts that students have in their background knowledge, as well as other questions that they might have about Columbus.

After the prior-knowledge phase, the teachers and students read the various sources that have been put together. Information from these sources regarding the focal questions is put in the chart. The recording process should be as accurate as possible, including quotations from the text. Thus, the chart can be used to make specific comparisons between texts on the crucial points. After all the texts are read and summarized in the chart, these summaries are themselves summarized across the different texts to determine what the different texts, as a whole, say about the focal questions.

I charts are a valiant approach to teaching difficult concepts to elementary and middle school children. We do not see them as viable without modification when the texts radically contradict each other, as in the case of historical documents, or when the texts are only obliquely focused on the focal questions. The focus on I charts is to get some sort of summary statement, a "truth," as it were, from different sources. In historical reasoning, it is important to understand these documents from different perspectives, and how these perspectives affected the way the documents were worded. This level of critical analysis may not be possible to achieve with younger children (but see Luke, 1992). However, an I chart can be used in a modified way as a springboard for a discussion focusing on the differences in focal issues. The credibility of the various documents given their unique sources and the contexts can be questioned if students see that there is disagreement. Instead of a summary, students could write a conclusion that represents their evaluation of the different perspectives.

Two other approaches, Questioning the Author (QtA; Beck, Mc-Keown, Hamilton, & Kucan, 1997; Beck, McKeown, Sandora, Kucan, & Worthy, 1996) and Collaborative Reasoning (Chinn et al., 2001; Chinn & Anderson, 1998) can be informative about the kinds of processes that might be taught in multiple-document lessons. Both of these approaches were developed, however, for use with single documents. Collaborative Reasoning was developed to use with literature but has clear applications for historical documents.

Questioning the Author (Beck et al., 1996, 1997; Sandora, Beck, & McKeown, 1999) is an instructional strategy designed to help students increase their effectiveness in encounters with text. It may be used with narrative or expository text and is based on a constructivist view of reading. The cognitive perspective is that readers need to use information interactively to construct meaning from text. QtA involves students in an active search for meaning during a first reading. Teachers and students grapple through segments of text using a reviser's eye to analyze the difficult portions. QtA has been used successfully with upper-elementary-level and middle school students (e.g., Beck et al., 1996)

The purpose of QtA is to have children understand that each text has a human, fallible author. The instructional procedure teaches children to "question" the unseen author in order to construct his or her meaning intended in that text. The teachers read the text before teaching in order to identify the major understandings, relate the text to curriculum needs, anticipate potential student difficulties, segment text, and develop queries.

QtA can be initiated by a teacher-modeling protocol used to demonstrate how a reader might think through the ideas in the text (Beck et al., 1996). This would involve modeling the processes of reflecting and evaluating text statements. For example, a statement in the text used by Beck et al. reads, "Russia has used rockets to put a new moon in the sky." The teacher might say, "Hmmmm. I don't know what the author means. How can you put another moon in the sky?", modeling the type of self-questioning desired.

Using QtA, teachers would use two types of queries to initiate and focus discussion. These queries help propel the discussions and facilitate students' construction of meaning during reading, unlike questions that tend to test recall after reading. Initiating queries such as "What is the author trying to say?" make the author's message public. Follow-up queries provide focus and integrate content, such as "That's what the author says, but what does it mean?" See Table 5.1, adapted from Beck et al. (1996).

A set of six "moves" is used by teachers to help orchestrate student ideas and make improvisational decisions during a dynamic discussion. There are three "moves" in response to student comments: *marking* for

TABLE 5.1. Teacher Queries to Meet Educational Goals

Goal	Queries
Initiate discussion.	What is the author trying to say?
	What is the author's message?
	What is the author talking about?
Help students focus on the author's message.	That's what the author says, but what does it mean?
Help students link information.	How does that connect with what we've already been told?
	How does that fit in with what we already know?
	What information has the author added here that connects with or fits in with _____?
Identify difficulties with the way the author has presented information or ideas.	Does that make sense?
	Is that said in a clear way?
	Did the author explain that clearly? What do we need to figure out or find out?
Encourage students to refer to the text either because they've misinterpreted a text statement or to help them recognize that they've made an inference.	Did the author tell us that?
	Did the author give us the answer to that?

emphasis, *turning back* to the students or text, and *revoicing* or rephrasing. More direct teacher "moves," used for helping students develop ideas, are *modeling, annotating,* or *recapping.*

Although QtA was developed for elementary school and has been used with single textbooks or narrative texts, it is not difficult to understand these procedures. The emphasis on the author as human rather than omniscient is needed to remember that texts are speech acts, developed by a person for particular needs. This is as true of textbooks as it is of political screeds. Research (Stahl et al., 1996) suggests that students are overly trusting of textbooks and less trusting of documents that have a personal perspective. Emphasizing the author forces students to examine the source and realize that a document is a product of its time and place, as well as its author.

Collaborative Reasoning (Chinn et al., 2001; Chinn & Anderson, 1998; Waggoner, Chinn, & Anderson, 1995) is another approach for encouraging critical thinking through discussion. Unlike QtA, but like

Document-Based Questions, Collaborative Reasoning discussions begin with a focal question, which is asked after children read silently. For a story used by Chinn and Anderson, "Making Room for Uncle Joe," which describes a family whose members decide to invite an uncle with Down syndrome to live with them permanently, the question was "Did the family make the right decision?"

After the central question is posed, students indicate their initial positions by raising their hands. Initial positions can include "not sure." Students begin the discussion by advancing reasons and supporting evidence for their position. They are encouraged to use textual evidence ("What in the text made you say that?"), as well as personal experience. Collaborative Reasoning discussions are student-led, with teachers intervening as little as possible. Students are expected to listen to and carefully evaluate each other's arguments, providing counterarguments when they disagree. As the discussion progresses, students are supposed to weigh the reasons for each position and, if need be, change their position. Teachers are to be active participants in the discussion, but the purpose of their participation is to spur students' growth in reasoning rather than to ensure that certain content is mastered. This is a different role than many teachers are used to and Chinn and Anderson (1998) and Chinn et al. (2001), have observed that it is difficult for some teachers to relinquish control. Beck et al. (1996) have made a similar observation in relation to QtA.

Similar to Alvermann's (1991) Discussion Web, Collaborative Reasoning emphasizes the discourse leading to critical thinking. Because it was developed for use with literature, it does not stress the kind of disciplinary thought needed specifically for history texts, but the structured discussions are equally useful in having students examine historical documents critically.

Alvermann's (1991) Discussion Web differs from Collaborative Reasoning in that a pair of students comes to a consensus only after recording both sides of the issue, using the text(s) the students are reading to provide that support. Once that pair has considered both sides of the evidence and has come to a conclusion, it joins another pair and works again for consensus, viewing both sides of the evidence. Then, a whole-group discussion ensues. Although the Discussion Web is used most often with one text, there is no reason why it cannot be used with multiple, conflicting texts.

DEVELOPING CRITICAL ANALYSIS

We feel that any effective approach to teaching students to analyze critically multiple documents in history has three components. The first involves group processes. In spite of the failure of group work to produce substantial amounts of critical analysis in the Hynd et al. (1996) study, we take a Vygotskyean view that "the higher functions of child thought first appear in the collective life of children in the form of argumentation and only then develop into reflection for the individual child" (cited in Chinn et al., 2001, p. 385). Au and Mason (1981) suggest that if there exists a "balance of rights" within the classroom between teacher and students, the students are more likely to adopt critical stances. In our observations of group functions, we did see more critical analysis of the texts in the process of discussion. Had there been less discussion about the final task product, which could have been controlled with more discussion about the task prior to beginning group work, we might have observed a higher percentage of critical analysis.

What we did not see was increased instances of Wineburg's (1991a, 1991b) three processes. The relatively small amount of sourcing, corroboration, and contextualization might have been increased by explicit teaching prior to instruction in the process of historiography, discussing the importance of each process, and providing guiding questions. Second, we suggest that students, even capable high school students, require some sort of *procedural facilitator* (Baker, Gersten, & Scanlon, 2002), which is an organizer that spells out explicitly strategies used to achieve certain academic goals. Procedural facilitators are generally used with children with learning problems and might include the use of formal story grammar to aid narrative comprehension (Beck & McKeown, 1981) or prompts to help students organize expository essays (Englert, Raphael, Anderson, Stevens, & Anthony, 1991). However, such facilitators can be useful in helping able students learn to internalize cognitively difficult processes.

The third component of multiple-document instruction is a written essay as a final product. Writing forces students to integrate the information in the various texts into a coherent product. We review each of these aspects in turn.

Group Processes

We realized in this work, unlike our naive earlier work, that effective group processes need to be carefully modeled and directed. Meloth and Deering (1999) suggest that instruction needs precede effective peer-group interactions. Such instruction should make clear that the purpose of the peer-group work is cognitive, including both critical and metacognitive components. This can be done using at least one whole-class session led by the teacher. The whole-class session includes focal questions and documents chosen to address that question. Such a session might begin with a think-aloud, such as that done in QtA (Beck et al., 1996), and might include a structured discussion of a series of short historical documents. The teacher might use the queries discussed earlier. As each document is read, the teacher models the use of the procedural facilitators we discuss later. The class discussion stresses the critical analysis of the various documents, including *sourcing, corroboration,* and *contextualization.* After the class discussion, the teacher and class jointly reflect on the process of the discussion itself, including a discussion of the queries used by the teacher and the various strategies he or she used to elicit critical analysis. The queries might be put on a chart in the room for later reference. A writing task used as a follow-up is usually a written response to the focal question.

There is evidence that discussion with a teacher can help students gain disciplinary knowledge. In an interview of college students studying multiple documents about the Tonkin Gulf, Hynd, Holschuh, and Hubbard (in press) asked students what historians did and how they did it. Most students' initial answers suggested that they viewed historians as documenters of facts. Fewer students' answers suggested that they considered historians to be arbiters looking carefully at different documents to find the "real" story. But as students considered *how* historians went about that documentation, their ideas shifted. By the end of the study, students who had believed that historians were mere documenters came to believe that they were arbiters, and those who originally believed they were arbiters came to believe that historians were, perhaps inadvertently, still biased. Without discussing the nature of historiography, Hynd et al. conclude that the students would not have changed their positions so readily, even given the multiple texts they were reading. Students also were asked to consider the credibility of the sources they were reading. Most students wanted to believe that an author was credible if he or she had participated in the event that was the focus of writing. For example, they wanted to believe that Dean Rusk, Secretary of State at the time of the Tonkin Gulf incident, was a credible source because he had been involved. Hynd et al. asked these students, "Does 'being there' make someone a reliable source of information?" In the process of answering that question, students struggled with the notion. One student's response is typical:

> "[I take into account] who they are and what role they had and who they know in Vietnam and if they had any involvement because one of them was involved, so you have to take that into consideration. I think experience gives you more of an edge about what's going on. You know it happened if you're there, but I don't know . . . I don't know . . . that gives you a firsthand thing. I don't know . . . people who have involvement, they're going to make themselves or the people who are affiliated with them look, you know, not look as bad, so they're a little sketchy in terms of

reading what they put down so, I don't know. Historians, they can have biases, too."

The point is, students need to grapple with these issues. A discussion that focuses on issues brings them to light.

If the teacher is sure that the students can function as critical analysis groups, then another assignment is given to groups of four to six students, whose task is to examine the documents critically, with the aim of preparing for individually written essays. The teacher monitors the discourse in each group, intervening with probes when necessary.

Procedural Facilitators

Because the processes involved in disciplinary knowledge are difficult, we include a set of procedural facilitators to encourage students to read each document with regard to its source and context, and actively compare information across documents. Such comparisons might include an analysis of how the political and social contexts of the documents led to differences in what is included or not included, and how others, with a different perspective, might have included different information or written the document differently.

The procedural facilitators might be a set of guiding questions. These questions can be posted and used by the groups to increase attention to these aspects of the documents. A set of questions might include the following:

Sourcing

1. Who produced this document?
2. What biases or predispositions did the author or authors have?
3. How might these biases have affected the content of the document?
4. What other voices might have been included in this document?

Context

1. When was this document produced?
2. Where was this document produced?
3. What was occurring in the time and place that this document was produced?
4. How might the context have affected this document?

Corroboration

1. What information in this document is similar to that of other documents (either in this set or other documents that you know about)?

2. What information contradicts information in other documents?
3. How might the source or the context explain some of the contradictions?
4. What is *not* said in this document that should be included? How does what is left out relate to the source and context?

Another approach might be to adapt the guiding questions of Luke, O'Brien, and Comber (2001). Their approach, which is for use in examining everyday materials, is intended to have students make texts the object of study, including the political and social implications of texts, and how power relationships are established and negotiated. They suggest that literacy programs include examination of texts to include (1) the institutional conditions in which the text was created and interpreted (i.e., the *context*); (2) talk about the ideologies underlying the text, including silences (who is not heard) and absences (who is not included in the text) (the *source*); (3) analysis of the way the text is written, including textual and linguistic techniques that relate to the conditions in which the text was created and the ideologies underlying the text. This includes a close examination of how the way the text was written conveys the underlying meanings intended, that is, a close analysis of the language used in the text. They suggest an examination of texts using the following questions:

1. What is the topic?
2. How is it being presented? What themes and discourses are being used?
3. Who is writing to whom? Whose voices and positions are being expressed?
4. Whose voices and opinions are not being expressed?
5. What is the text trying to do to you?
6. What other ways are there of writing about the topic?
7. What was not said about the topic? Why?

The teacher should encourage the students to use the procedural facilitators to both guide discussion and to compose the focal essay.

Written Products

We recommend a written final product for a number of reasons. The process of critical analysis of historical texts, using source materials to support the thesis, is how historians communicate their ideas. In addition, the activity of producing a persuasive essay, using source materials to back up reasoning, is consonant with language arts goals as well. Greene (1994) discusses how history students and history professionals differ in terms of their conceptualization of what comprises a history essay. Students tend to believe in the importance of having a thesis that covers everything, structured in terms of major and minor topics. Historians, on the other hand, tend to want to see such essays conceptualize the topic, using information from sources, to compare and evaluate different ideas. Historians see history writing as a "constructive, rhetorical act that establishes possibilities" (Greene, 1994, p. 92). In other words, the essay should recapitulate the critical analysis in the discussion.

The historiography approach is used as part of the Advanced-Placement History tests in the Document-Based Questions. The test provides a set of questions from two to six different documents that relate to a single question. The student is to write an essay synthesizing the sources to answer that question. The emphasis is on critical analysis and integration of the sources, not on merely parroting the information. For example, the first question on the 2002 Advanced-Placement U.S. History Examination (Educational Testing Service, 2003) reads, " 'Reform movements in the United States sought to expand democratic ideals.' Assess the validity of this statement with specific reference to the years 1825–1850" (p. 2). Students are then directed to use 10 short documents, ranging from the Fourth Annual Report, Society of the Reform of Juvenile Delinquents in the City of New York 1829, to an engraving from 1835, to a segment from the *McGuffey Reader* from 1836. The Document-Based Questions are intended to require students to synthesize information creatively from a number of sources, drawing on their knowledge of the period and the story of history, as well as their analytical abilities.

CONCLUSIONS

We see history as a source for cognitive growth, to help students develop the critical analysis of ideas in relation to other historical concepts and to current events. The lens of history should include not only seeing the present in terms of trends from the past but also understanding that history is produced and interpreted by humans. We want students not only to know the "facts" of history, as much as they can be ascertained, and also to understand that the interpretation of these facts depends on who is interpreting them, but also to reflect on the interpretations by the authors of historical documents and on their own interpretations.

REFERENCES

Alvermann, D. E. (1991). The Discussion Web: A graphic aid for learning across the curriculum. *Reading Teacher, 45,* 92–99.

Anderson, R. C., Chinn, C. A., & Waggoner, M. A. (2001). Patterns of discourse in two kinds of literature discussion. *Reading Research Quarterly, 36,* 378–411.

Armbruster, B. B., Anderson, T. H., & Meyer, J. L. (1991). Improving content-area reading using instructional graphics. *Reading Research Quarterly, 26,* 393–416.

Au, K. M., & Mason, J. M. (1981). Social organizational factors in learning to read: The balance of rights hypothesis. *Reading Research Quarterly, 17,* 115–152.

Beck, I., & McKeown, M. G. (1981). Developing questions that promote comprehension: The Story Map. *Language Arts, 58,* 913–918.

Beck, I., McKeown, M. G., Hamilton, R. L., & Kucan, L. (1997). *Questioning the Author: An approach for enhancing student engagement with text.* Newark, DE: International Reading Association.

Beck, I. L., McKeown, M. G., Sandora, C., Kucan, L., & Worthy, J. (1996). Questioning the Author: A yearlong classroom implementation to engage students with text. *Elementary School Journal, 96,* 385–414.

Beck, I. L., McKeown, M. G., & Worthy, J. (1995). Giving a text voice can improve students' understanding. *Reading Research Quarterly, 30,* 220–238.

Belenky, M. F., Clinchy, B. M., Goldberger N. R., & Tarule J. M. (1986). *Women's ways of knowing.* New York: Basic Books.

Botstein, L. (1991). Damagaed literacy: Illiteracies and American democracy. In S. R. Graubard (Ed.), *Literacy: An overview by 14 experts* (pp. 55–84). New York: Hill & Wang.

Chinn, C. A., & Anderson, R. C. (1998). The structure of discussions that promote reasoning. *Teachers College Record, 100*(2), 315–368.

Educational Testing Service. (2004). The United States History Exam. Available online at: *http://apcentral.collegeboard.com/members/article/.collegeboard.com*

Englert, C. S., Raphael, T. E., Anderson, L. M., Stevens, D. D., and Anthony, H. M. (1991). Making writing strategies and self-talk visible: Cognitive strategy instruction in writing. *American Educational Research Journal, 28,* 337–373.

Greene, S. (1994). The problems of learning to think like a historian: Writing history in the culture of the classroom. *Educational Psychologist, 29*(2), 89–96.

Hoffman, J. V. (1992). Critical reading/thinking across the curriculum: Using I-Charts to support learning. *Language Arts, 64*(2), 121–127.

Hynd, C., Holschuh, J., & Hubbard, B. (in press). Thinking like a historian: College students' reading of multiple historical documents. *Journal of Literacy Research.*

Hynd, C. R., & Stahl, S. A. (1998). What do we mean by knowledge and learning. In C. R. Hynd (Ed.), *Learning from text across conceptual domains* (pp. 15–44). Hillsdale, NJ: Erlbaum.

Hynd, C. R., Stahl, S. A., & McNish, M. (1996, April). *Group processes involved in studying multiple documents in history.* Paper presented at the annual meeting of the American Educational Research Association, New York, NY.

Litchfield, A. B., & Owens, G. (1984). *Making room for Uncle Joe.* Morton Grove, IL: Albert Whitman.

Luke, A. (1992, May). Reading and critical literacy: Redefining the "great debate." Paper presented at the annual New Zealand Conference on Reading, Wellington, New Zealand.

Luke, A., O'Brien, J., & Comber, B. (2001). Making community texts objects of study. In H. Fehring & P. Green (Eds.), *Critical literacy: A collection of articles from the Australian Literacy Educators' Association* (pp. 139–149). Newark, DE: International Reading Association.

McKeown, M. G., Beck, I. L., & Worthy, M. J. (1993). Grappling with text ideas: Questioning the author. *Reading Teacher, 4,* 560–566.

Meloth, M. S., & Deering, P. D. (1999). The role of the teacher in promoting cognitive processing during collaborative learning. In A. M. O'Donnell & A. King (Eds.), *Cognitive perspectives on peer learning: The Rutgers Invitational Symposium on Education Series* (pp. 235–255). New Jersey: Rutgers University Press.

Mosborg, S. (2002). Speaking of history: How do adolescents use their knowledge of history in reading the daily news? *Cognition and Instruction, 20,* 323–358.

Perfetti, C. A., Britt, M. A., & Georgi, M. C. (1995). *Text-based learning and reasoning: Studies in history.* Hillsdale, NJ: Erlbaum.

Perfetti, C. A., Britt, M. A., Rouet, J. F., Mason, R. A., & Georgi, M. C. (1993, April). *How students use text to learn and reason about historical uncertainty.* Paper presented at the annual meeting of the American Educational Research Association, Atlanta, GA.

Perry, W. G. (1970). *Forms of intellectual and ethical development in the college years.* New York: Holt, Rinehart & Winston.

Rinehart, S. D., Stahl, S. A., & Erickson, L. G. (1986). Some effects of summarization training on reading and studying. *Reading Research Quarterly, 21*(4), 422–438.

Rouet, J. F., Favart, M., Britt, M. A., & Perfetti, C. A. (1997). Studying and using multiple documents in history: Effects of discipline expertise. *Cognition and Instruction, 15,* 85–106.

Sandora, C., Beck, I. L., & McKeown, M. (1999). A comparison of two discussion strategies on students' comprehension and interpretation of complex literature. *Reading Psychology, 20,* 177–212.

Stahl, S. A., & Hynd, C. R. (1994, April). *Selecting historical documents: A study of student reasoning.* Paper presented at the annual meeting of the American Educational Research Association, New Orleans, LA.

Stahl, S. A., Hynd, C. R., Britton, B. K., McNish, M. M., & Bosquet, D. (1996). What happens when students read multiple source documents in history? *Reading Research Quarterly, 31,* 430–456.

Stahl, S. A., Hynd, C. R., Mongomery, T., & McClain, V. (1997). " *In fourteen hundred and ninety-two Columbus sailed the ocean blue": Effects of multiple document readings on student attitudes and prior concepts* (Report No. 82). Athens, GA: National Reading Research Center.

Vacca, R. T., & Vacca, J. L. (2002). *Content area reading: Literacy and learning across the curriculum* (7th ed.). Boston: Allyn & Bacon.

Waggoner, M. A., Chinn, C. A., & Anderson, R. C. (1995). Collaborative Reasoning about stories. *Language Arts, 72,* 582–589.

Wilkinson, I. A. G., & Anderson, R. C. (1995). Sociocognitive processes in guided silent reading: A microanalysis of small-group lessons. *Reading Research Quarterly, 30,* 710–740.

Wineburg, S. S. (1991a). On the reading of historical texts: Notes on the breach between school and academy. *American Educational Research Journal, 28,* 495–519.

Wineburg, S. S. (1991b). Historical problem solving: A study of the cognitive processes used in the evaluation of documentary and pictorial evidence. *Journal of Educational Psychology, 83,* 73–87.

Wineburg, S. S. (1992). Probing the depths of students' historical knowledge. *Perspectives of the American Historical Association, 30,* 20–24.

PART II

Teaching Adolescents with Literacy Difficulties

6

Adolescents Who Struggle with Word Identification
Research and Practice

MARY E. CURTIS

For many teachers, students' skill in identifying words is synonymous with their ability to translate words from print to speech—a process akin to "announcing" the words, if you will. But successful word identification during reading requires much more than simply being able to name the words on a page. It also entails accessing the meaning of those words in a way that facilitates comprehension of what is being read.

In understanding the research and practice related to adolescents' difficulties in word identification, three aspects of the problem are relevant: word analysis, word recognition, and semantic encoding. *Word analysis* refers to the processes involved in understanding and using the sounds that make up a word, as well as the letters that correspond to those sounds. *Word recognition* refers to facility in knowing that a group of letters represents a particular word. *Semantic encoding* refers to availability of and access to information about a word's meaning.

My goal in this chapter is to describe the nature of problems in word identification in adolescents as it relates to these first two of these factors: word analysis and word recognition. In the first section, I discuss research concerned with the development of word identification in typical adolescents and what we know about what has failed to develop (or has developed differently) in readers who struggle. Following that, I summarize findings from research designed to apply what we know in order to improve skill in word identification. Finally, I identify some questions that remain for future research to address.

WHAT WE KNOW ABOUT ADOLESCENTS' WORD IDENTIFICATION

Word Analysis

Skilled readers understand and are adept at using the sounds that make up a word, as well as the letters that correspond to those sounds. In English, we use several hundred letters and letter combinations to represent 40 or so speech sounds (Moats, 2000; Venezky, 1999). For the most part, these letter–sound relationships are mastered by the time students reach 5th grade. But for some teens, struggles with these kinds of print-based processing are the primary source of their reading problems.

Although research underscores the importance of letter recognition in reading development, most researchers and clinicians would agree that "the language skills that most reliably distinguish good and poor readers are specific to the phonological, or speech sound, processing system" (Moats, 2000, p. 8). These include functions such as segmenting and blending the speech sounds that combine to make words, as well as identifying words and syllables.

Even among less-skilled readers, though, word analysis seems to improve with age. When 14-year-olds with reading problems were compared to 10-year-olds experiencing reading difficulties, the older group was found to be significantly better than the younger cohort at phonological processing (Ackerman, Weir, Metzler, & Dykman, 1996). Despite any relative successes, however, word analysis skills in disabled adolescent readers often remain weak in an absolute sense. For example, when Ackerman and her colleagues compared accuracy in reading nonsense words between the previously mentioned 14-year-olds and a reading-age control group (i.e., younger students reading at the same level but without difficulty), the older readers made significantly more errors than did the younger ones.

In longitudinal studies of individuals with and without reading difficulties, growth in phonological processing slows down considerably for both groups by the time they reach adolescence (Flowers, Meyer, Lovato, Wood, & Felton, 2001; Francis, Stuebing, Shaywitz, Shaywitz, & Fletcher, 1996). The major difference between the skilled and less-skilled readers seems to be the level (not the age) at which their word analysis skills plateau, suggesting that phonological processing difficulties stem more from some sort of deficit than from a developmental lag. With regard to level, performance of high school–age disabled readers on phonological processing tasks is comparable to that of 5th grade nondisabled readers.

I have found in my clinical work that as many as one out of every 10 adolescents has serious difficulties in identifying words (Curtis & Longo, 1999). These difficulties usually stem from problems associated with the phonological aspects of word analysis, and are compounded by the tendency to abandon the process of trying to read a word and, instead, to guess at it based on context.

Students experience phonological processing difficulties for any number of reasons (Moats, 2000). Lack of awareness about phonemes may be the source of the problem. A phoneme is the smallest part of spoken language that makes a difference in the meaning of a word. Notice how changing the middle phoneme in *mop* from /o/ to /a/ affects the meaning of the following queries: "Did you remember to bring the *mop*?" and "Did you remember to bring the *map*?" Awareness of phonemes in words is a prerequisite for proficient reading in English and other alphabetic languages, because readers need to understand how the sequence of letters in a word maps onto the sequence of phonemes in it (a relationship referred to as the "alphabetic principle").

When learners experience typical reading development, their awareness of phonemes increases with their age and skill in reading. But for those who encounter difficulties with reading (like individuals with dyslexia), deficits in phoneme awareness present problems regardless of age or reading level (Bruck, 1992). To illustrate, imagine that I ask you to say *smack*. Then say it again, but don't say /m/ (Rosner, 1973). Among the teens with reading difficulties with whom I have worked, about 5% are unable to come up with *sack*. And, even though what they are being asked to do is auditory (no reading at all is involved), their level of success in completing these kinds of tasks will often be a better predictor of their reading comprehension ability than a test of listening comprehension would be (see also Weaver & Rosner, 1979). Again, this is because readers with difficulties in manipulating the phonemes in spoken words also have problems associating those phonemes with letters and letter combinations in printed words.

An even more common source of phonological processing problems among adolescents is difficulty in translating words from print to speech. This can occur either because of a lack of knowledge of letter–sound correspondences, or problems in applying that knowledge (Sanders, 2001). For example, students who read "not" for *note*, or who write LACK for *lake* are missing an understanding of silent-*e* word and syllable patterns. Other students may not know the sound that -*dge* makes at the end of words like *edge* or *badge*. Often, however, students know patterns but do not apply them consistently. They may demonstrate understanding when presented with words in isolation, but when faced with words in context, they find it easier to guess than to apply their knowledge (like the student who, immediately after reading the word *President*, read "Clinton" for *Kennedy*).

By far, the most common source of difficulty in word analysis faced by adolescent readers is their lack of facility in dealing with multisyllabic words. Sometimes it is the case that students are unfamiliar with the patterns found in longer words (e.g., they need to learn about suffixes such as *-tion/-sion*). As grade level increases, basic morpheme patterns (i.e., prefixes, suffixes, roots) of Latin and Greek origin are found increasingly in content-area textbooks. These tend to be patterns with which older students with reading difficulties are unfamiliar (Henry, 1999). Knowledge of common English suffixes also grows considerably between fourth grade and high school, and is related to reading ability (Nagy, Diakidoy, & Anderson, 1993). Difficulty with multisyllabic words can also occur because the words being analyzed are not part of the student's vocabulary. For instance, a student may say "mon-o-po´-ly" for *monopoly*, or "mon-o-tone´-us" for *monotonous*, not because of a problem with analyzing the words, but because of a lack of semantic access.

Quite often, students exhibit difficulty with multisyllabic words because they fail to analyze them fully, opting instead to make a guess based on their analysis of the first part of word. For instance, a student will read *permit* for *permanent*, or *favorite* for *favorable*. These students are engaging in what has been called "compensatory" reading (Spear-Swerling & Sternberg, 1996). They understand the alphabetic principle and can perform some word analysis, but because of weaknesses in their phonological skills, they tend to rely on other knowledge and skills (e.g., context) to assist them in identifying words. Over time, such readers can end up engaging more in composing what they read than in comprehending what has been written.

Conversely, students can be unsuccessful in word identification because they approach every word as if it can be "sounded out," leading to enormous frustration when they encounter words that are exceptions (e.g., *some, because, know*). These students are unable to use other abilities such as contextual skills (using the information from the setting in which a word occurs to aid in word identification) and sight-word knowledge (recognition of a word as a whole).

Research-based practices found to be effective in improving teens' word analysis skills are described, but first I turn to what is known about adolescents' word recognition processes.

Word Recognition

Becoming skilled at reading ultimately involves being able to recognize groups of letters as words, with an investment of minimal effort. This requires that readers develop automatic word identification, meaning that decoding (translating print into speech) occurs without needing to attend to it consciously. Jeanne Chall referred to this as "ungluing from print" (1983/1996), meaning that students become less and less tied to the need to sound out every word. Also required is facility in dealing with words that cannot be sounded out because of phonetic irregularities (e.g., *the* and *to*).

Differences among adolescents in word-identification skill appear to be strongly related to the extent of their experiences with print. For instance, among readers in the fifth through ninth grades, the degree of their exposure to written materials (as measured by their ability to recognize titles of books) seems to account for a significant amount of variance in word identification, independent of skill in phonological processing (McBride-Chang, Manis, Seidenberg, Custodio, & Doi, 1993).

Exposure to print most likely influences success in *orthographic processing*, that is, the ability to recognize letter patterns. As studies of spelling development reveal, children's knowledge of orthographic features progresses steadily. Ganske (1999, 2000) has summarized this development as follows: Between ages 4 and 9, students spell by sound, matching the names of the letters to the sounds they hear (e.g., writing MGRT for *majority*). Between ages 6 and 12, they learn to use letter–sound patterns (MUJORTEA). Between ages 8 and 12, their awareness about patterns in multisyllabic words grows (MEJORATY). Beginning about age 10, students learn that spelling patterns often remain constant for related words, even when those words are pronounced differently (*major, majority*). Reading affords the experiences with written words that result in increased familiarity with those features.

Experience with print also promotes automaticity in dealing with letter–sound relationships, a requirement for fluent reading. As noted earlier, *automatic processing* means that words can be identified without conscious effort, enabling readers to focus all of their available attention on the comprehension of what is being read (Perfetti, 1985). Fluency—as measured by oral reading rate—has been found to differ significantly between skilled and less-skilled readers through adolescence (Shaywitz et al., 1999), and difficulty with quickly accessing the names of letters and words that are known has been linked to reading disability (Wolf & Bowers, 1999).

A student who is constantly struggling with word analysis misses out on the opportunity to develop fluent word recognition. Dysfluent word recognition may lead the student to avoid reading, which in turn has negative consequences for the development of vocabulary knowledge. These interactions are all examples of what are now commonly known as "Matthew effects" (Stanovich, 1986), instances in which good readers continue to get more skilled, while poor readers continue to fall farther and farther behind.

Another illustration of how difficulty in one aspect of word identification can be related to the development of another comes from a longitudinal study of the reading development of low-income children as they advanced from grades 2–7 (Chall, Jacobs, & Baldwin, 1990). Through grade 3, the children's reading achievement progressed fairly typically. Beginning in grade 4, however, their knowledge of word meanings started to decelerate, followed next by their word recognition and spelling, and finally, by their ability to read text, both orally and silently. Differences in reading skill among the low-income children themselves also became apparent as they reached fourth grade. Some of the children experienced an earlier and more intense slump in reading development than did others, with differences in fluency being the first to emerge.

Chall and her colleagues (1990) argued that their results point to a need for more direct teaching of reading by using challenging materials, along with widespread reading for continued practice. As they observed, the earlier that children slip behind in their knowledge of the meanings of more academic and abstract words, the faster and farther they fall behind in other aspects of identifying words.

In the section that follows, research looking at the effectiveness of instruction in word identification is examined. Can adolescents' difficulties in word analysis and word recognition be overcome? If so, what are the significant features of successful remedial programs?

APPLYING WHAT WE KNOW

Word Analysis

Experts agree that significant improvements in adolescents' phonological processing skills can result from intensive systematic instruction and practice in procedures for analyzing words. A difference in opinions can be found relative to whether instructional emphasis is best placed on mastery of the phonetic patterns that characterize the relationships among sounds and letters, or on development of an implicit understanding of those phonic generalizations via examples and discussions.

A number of programs have been created to teach students to identify the various sound and letter patterns that make up words (Clark & Uhry, 1995; Greene, 1996; Kennedy & Backman, 1993). However, many clinicians believe that instructional focus is better placed on helping students to recognize and generalize letter–sound relationships than on mastery of specific patterns (Chall & Popp, 1996; Gaskins et al., 1988; Moats, 2000; Tuley, 1998). Research suggests that both approaches can be effective (Lovett & Steinbach, 1997), and that a combination of the two—beginning first with an emphasis on pattern mastery, then shifting to a focus on pattern generalization—may be most productive (Lovett, Lacarenza, & Borden, 2000).

In my own work, I have found that spelling—with a focus on syllable types—can be a powerful tool for teaching word-analysis skills to adolescents (Curtis & Longo, 1999). One reason is that many teens seem to be more comfortable in admitting concern about how well they spell than about how well they decode. As a result, instruction that seeks to improve their ability to go from sounds to letters holds more value for them than traditional phonics instruction. Progress in learning to spell can also be easier to demonstrate to students than progress in learning to read, making instruction in letter–sound relationships via spelling especially motivating.

Instruction on the most common types of syllables (consonant–vowel–consonant; consonant–vowel; vowel–consonant–*e*; *r*-controlled vowel; vowel–vowel; and consonant-*le*) puts the focus on the role of vowel sounds in word parts, building students' confidence in their ability to read and spell multisyllabic words. Using syllables also provides an opportunity to review the most important letter–sound correspondences (e.g., short vowels, long vowel variants, etc.). Syllables also enable use of words that are part of students' listening vocabularies but not their reading vocabularies. For instance, when working on the consonant–vowel–consonant pattern, words such as *tendon, hectic,* and *magnet* can be used as examples, providing material that is difficult enough to offer a challenge, but also consistent enough to enable students to make a generalization and recognize other words that fit the pattern.

Among adolescents with more advanced needs in word analysis, instruction that focuses on teaching them strategies for dealing with unknown words can be valuable as well. Among the strategies that have been shown to be effective is DISSECT, a series of steps that students are taught to take when they encounter an unknown word (Lenz & Hughes, 1990): "Discover the context": try to take a guess at what the word is, based on what would fit with the meaning of what is being read; "Isolate the prefix": look to see if the first syllable matches a list of prefixes that has been taught; "Separate the suffix": check the last syllable for a match with what has already been taught; "Say the stem": check to see if you recognize what remains of the word after the previous two steps; "Examine the stem": try to divide it into syllables, based on location of the vowels; "Check with someone"; and "Try the dictionary."

Word identification by analogy is another successful strategy (Gaskins et al., 1988). Students learn how to use familiar words that rhyme with unfamiliar word parts to aid in their word identification. For example, students are able to read the word *faffle* because they are already familiar with the word *baffle*. Self-talk is also an important component of Gaskins's program, in which students learn how to engage in thinking about the number of letters and sounds represented in words and word parts, and their relationships to other words.

Still another strategy students can be taught to improve their word identification is called "vowel variations" (Lovett et al., 2000). After learning that vowels frequently have multiple pronunciations in English, students are taught how to attempt different pronunciations until they come up with a word that they know. For example, imagine being unfamiliar with the word *thread*. You would learn to start with the vowel sound in *bead*, and when that did not result in a word you knew, you would know to try next the vowel sound in *bread*.

Beyond instruction and practice in analyzing words, providing students with opportunities to apply what they have learned is also an essential part of improving their reading ability. At least two features of application appear to be important. First, application needs to occur with words that require students to use the knowledge and skills they are acquiring. For example, multisyllabic words such as *cockroach* and *scapegoat* provide students with a chance to generalize understanding of the sound of *oa* in ways that practice with words such as *boat* and *coat* do not (Curtis & Chmelka, 1994). Second, application needs to occur in context, so that students can be encouraged to use their developing word-analysis skills to read unknown words on the page (rather than relying on the context to guess at them). In this regard, oral reading is increasingly being recognized for its effectiveness with older as well as younger readers (Allinder, Dunse, Brunken, & Obermiller-Krolikowski, 2001; National Institute of Child Health and Human Development, 2000), a point that I examine next in more detail.

Word Recognition

Like many skills, becoming proficient at word recognition involves practice. Practice improves students' abilities to identify words in an effortless manner and to read with appropriate intonation, stress, and phrasing—all hallmarks of fluent processing. And as reading becomes fluent, attention can be directed toward making meaning out of what is read.

Given the relationships among fluency, comprehension, and practice, it is not surprising that simply providing students with opportunities to read aloud can improve their comprehension (Allinder et al., 2001). For teens with a history of difficulties in word identification, however, structured approaches to building fluency in word recognition have produced promising results as well.

One approach involves providing students with speeded practice in reading elements such as letters, syllables, words, phrases, and texts (Mercer, Campbell, Miller, Mercer, & Lane, 2000). Another approach involves reading the same passage over and over, until a preestablished criterion rate is reached (Samuels, 2002). Regardless of the units being practiced, such interventions—referred to as *repeated reading techniques*—are very effective in improving fluency (as measured by rate) in older as well as younger students. However, gains in comprehension appear to be less striking (Thomas & Clapp, 1989), and may be confined to improved processing at the sentence level (Carver & Hoffman, 1981; O,Shea, Sindelar, & O'Shea, 1987).

Providing students with a model of fluent reading, along with a means for monitoring their growth, has been emphasized by some proponents of the use of repeated reading with adolescents (Harris, Marchand-Martella, & Martella, 2000; Hasbrouck, Ihnot, & Rogers, 1999). Based on their review of fluency research conducted with both younger and older students, Stahl and Kuhn (2002) also conclude that such "assisted" repeated reading produces better results than an unassisted approach.

The secondary school students and teachers with whom I have worked have been successful using a fluency technique adapted from an approach we used at the Harvard Reading Laboratory (Chall & Curtis, 1987; Curtis & Longo, 1999). Called *collaborative oral reading* (or *popcorn reading* by some), a group of four to six students reads aloud with a teacher from a high-interest adolescent novel for about 20 minutes each day. Every member of the group takes turns reading, passing the turn around every three to five lines to anyone in the group that the current reader chooses, and at any point in a text that he or she selects (midparagraph, mid-sentence, or even midword).

Collaborative oral reading works similarly to repeated reading in that, with a novel, many of the same words and language structures reoccur. With a teacher participating in the group, a model of fluent reading is provided, and students can be directed to recurring words and prosodic patterns. The technique works best when students are grouped with others who are reading at about the same level, however, so that anxiety about performance is alleviated and a sense of community is promoted. The novels must also be at a level where students can be accurate, so that instructional time is focused on reading smoothly, without hesitation, and with comprehension.

Computer activities and games can also be helpful in promoting fluent word recognition. Multiple opportunities need to be provided for practicing recognition of the same words, though, and feedback needs to be provided about reading rate. The best activities require students to process word meanings while they are practicing word recognition, promoting consolidation of word–reading skills with semantic encoding ability (Curtis & Longo, 1999; Wolf, Miller, & Donnelly, 2000). For example, software programs such as Ultimate Word Attack (1983; Davidson) provide the options of customizing students' word lists and adjusting the rate of speed at which they complete various activities requiring word reading, spelling, and meaning. Activities such as "Word Detective" designed by Wolf and her colleagues (2000), give students opportunities to ask and answer questions about words: "What does it start with?"; "What does it sound like?"; "What is it similar in meaning to?"

Conclusions

A number of suggestions for helping adolescents who struggle with word identification have emerged from the work of researchers and clinicians:

• *Systematic, explicit, and direct instruction produces the best results.* Identification of sounds and letter–sound relationships should be modeled, demonstrated, and applied in a logical and systematic manner (National Institute of Child Health and Human Development, 2000). Lessons should be fast-paced, multisensory, lively and brief, and include materials that encourage students to apply the knowledge and skills being learned (e.g., see Curtis & Chmelka, 1994; Curtis & McCart, 1992).

• *High-frequency sound–spelling relationships and words should be the focus of instruction.* When working with older readers, instruction should include the major sound–spelling relationships of consonants and vowels, syllable types, and basic reading–spelling vocabularies (e.g., see Graham, Harris, & Loynachan, 1993). Emphasis should be placed on assisting teens in identification of the most common syllables found within multisyllabic words (e.g., see Blevins's list [2001]).

• *Instruction should be reflective.* Learning to recognize patterns and making generalizations from and about them—not memorizing rules— should be the goal of instruction. When a rule is introduced, teachers should present it as a rule of thumb (i.e., a heuristic) rather than a recipe (i.e., an algorithm), and emphasis should be placed on flexibility in rule use.

- *Opportunities to practice identification of words in context should be frequent.* Word identification should never be viewed by students as an end in itself; it must always be seen a means to an end. To accomplish this, regular opportunities to engage in oral reading—in a setting where teens are comfortable with taking risks—should be provided.

- *Fluent reading should be modeled, with numerous opportunities for students to practice.* Reading with fluency—without hesitation, with expression and comprehension—comes first and foremost from practice. Teachers should read aloud with their students, directing their attention to the rhythms in written language. Teens need to be provided with opportunities and encouragement to read independently as well.

- *Connections among word analysis, word recognition, and semantic access should be emphasized.* To be successful, word identification must involve accessing the meaning of a word in such a way so as to facilitate understanding of what is being read. By providing opportunities to relate words and word parts to word structure (affixes, roots) and word origin (e.g., Anglo-Saxon, Latin, Greek), teachers enhance students' ability not only to recognize words but also to access word meanings (e.g., see Henry, 1990).

WHAT WE STILL NEED TO KNOW

Word Analysis

As noted earlier, we know from studies of word-attack skills in adolescent poor readers that development of these skills seems to level off around the fifth-grade reading level. What research has yet to examine, though, is the extent to which decoding skills plateau in adolescence because they receive less instructional emphasis as less-skilled readers get older. A number of instructional programs focus specifically on improving teens' word analysis through the use of intensive multisensory phonics instruction. What is needed next are data on the growth in word-analysis skills of older readers who have received these specialized programs, allowing us to establish whether (and how much) teens' ability to decode can be improved.

Comparisons are also needed to determine whether word-analysis programs differ in their effectiveness. Because decoding difficulties in adolescence can stem from any number of different sources, ranging from the inability to segment sounds in words to difficulties in generalizing what is known, does program effectiveness vary as a function of how well programs provide instruction in what students need to know?

For example, phonemic analysis is at the basis of the Lindamood–Bell (1975) learning process. Using colored blocks to stand for sounds, students learn to represent sounds within syllables before being taught the connections between those sounds and letters. In Corrective Reading (1980), vowels and vowel combinations are central. Lessons provide students with practice on long and short vowels, vowel digraphs (successive vowels representing a single sound, such as *oa* in *boat*), and dipthongs (adjacent vowels in the same syllable whose sounds blend together, such as *oi* in *oil*). The focus of the program Language (1995) is decoding and encoding patterns at the levels of sounds, words, sentences, and texts. Word identification instruction occurs within the context of a cumulative program addressing reading, writing, spelling, vocabulary, grammar, language use, and composition. In Wilson Reading (1988) instruction is based on recognition of syllable types. Students are taught finger-to-thumb tapping of phonemes, and left-to-right marking of vowels and syllables. In Project Read (1969), analyses of affixes and root words play a major role for instruction with older students. Students learn to look for known parts in words (e.g., *adjust* in *readjustment*) and how to create phrases that describe words (*readjustment* means the process of adjusting again). In Reading Is FAME (1992), the most common letter–sound correspondences are taught through spelling. Opportunities are provided each day to practice applying the phonic generalizations that are being learned, while reading aloud from young adult novels.

Are some programs better than others? Do the different emphases in these programs lead to different results? In what ways might programs be differentially effective for different students?

Word Recognition

The nature of the relationship between accuracy and fluency in word recognition in teens with reading difficulties is an area requiring further study. For instance, it is not at all unusual to find teens who read accurately at the fourth- and fifth-grade level at rates much slower than typically developing fourth and fifth graders. A large gap between the grade level at which materials can be read accurately versus fluently is also quite common among adolescent struggling readers (Curtis, 1997).

We know that reading rates in teens with reading difficulties can be improved via instruction that emphasizes practice (Kuhn & Stahl, 2003). What is not evident is who benefits most from this kind of intervention, or how much improvement in reading rate is necessary and sufficient to improve comprehension. As noted earlier, when instructional techniques such as repeated reading have been found to improve comprehension, gains seem to occur in efficiency in processing at the local (i.e., sentence) level.

But the value of other kinds of fluency instruction, such as prosodic modeling and techniques to improve ease of access to word meanings, merits further study.

The value of repeated reading of the same text compared to frequent practice in reading aloud also needs more investigation, as do the effects of fluency instruction that takes place orally versus silently.

In all aspects of word identification, more investigation is called for in the area of how technology can best be incorporated into improving adolescents' knowledge and skills. For example, programs such as Inspiration (2002) afford students ease in manipulating the kinds of visual representations that are at the core of approaches such as semantic mapping and semantic feature analysis. Does students' comprehension improve when they use such a tool? And what about digital text? Can providing students with the opportunity to click on a word and get immediate information about its pronunciation and meaning make a difference in vocabulary growth?

Finally, more research is needed on the relationships that exist among adolescents' word analysis, word recognition, and semantic access. As discussed earlier, we know that for teens who struggle with reading, deficits in semantic knowledge can result from difficulties in reading words, which in turn lead to less reading, and ultimately, to decreased academic expectations and demands. Similarly, though, as students grow older, familiarity with the semantic aspects of words becomes an increasingly integral part of their success in reading them. For example, as noted earlier, variant pronunciations of the letter string *monopoly* are reasonable according to the rules governing the relationship between print and speech. However, only one pronunciation is acceptable for the semantic unit that those letters represent. More information is needed about how adolescents' lack of vocabulary knowledge sets limits on their accuracy in word analysis and word recognition. Also needed is a careful examination of the possibility that as adolescents' difficulties in word recognition lessen, their ability to access meanings becomes more important for increased efficiency in word identification (Torgesen, Rashotte, & Alexander, 2001).

REFERENCES

Ackerman, P. T., Weir, N. L., Metzler, D. P., & Dykman, R. A. (1996). A study of adolescent poor readers. *Learning Disabilities: Research and Practice, 11,* 68–77.

Allinder, R. M., Dunse, L., Brunken, C. D., & Obermiller-Krolikowski, H. (2001). Improving fluency in at-risk readers and students with learning disabilities. *Remedial and Special Education, 22,* 48–54.

Blevins, W. (2001). *Teaching phonics and word study in the intermediate grades.* New York: Scholastic.

Bruck, M. (1992). Persistence of dyslexics' phonological awareness deficits. *Developmental Psychology, 28,* 874–886.

Carver, R. P., & Hoffman, J. V. (1981). The effect of practice through repeated reading on gain in reading ability using a computer-based instructional system. *Reading Research Quarterly, 16,* 374–390.

Chall, J. S. (1983, 1996). *Stages of reading development.* New York: Harcourt Brace. (Original work published 1983)

Chall, J. S., & Curtis, M. E. (1987). What clinical diagnosis tells us about children's reading. *Reading Teacher, 40,* 784–788.

Chall, J. S., Jacobs, V. A., & Baldwin, L. E. (1990). *The reading crisis: Why poor children fall behind.* Cambridge, MA: Harvard University Press.

Chall, J. S., & Popp, H. M. (1996). *Teaching and assessing phonics (a guide for teachers).* Cambridge, MA: Educators Publishing Service.

Clark, D. B., & Uhry, J. K. (1995). *Dyslexia: Theory and practice of remedial instruction.* Baltimore: York Press.

Corrective reading. (1980). Chicago: Science Research Associates.

Curtis, M. E. (1997). Teaching reading to children, adolescents, and adults: Similarities and differences. In L. R. Putnam (Ed.), *Readings on language and literacy* (pp. 75–88). Cambridge, MA: Brookline Books.

Curtis, M. E., & Chmelka, M. B. (1994). Modifying the Laubach Way to Reading Program for use with adolescents with LDs. *Learning Disabilities Research and Practice, 9,* 38–43.

Curtis, M. E., & Longo, A. M. (1999). *When adolescents can't read: Methods and materials that work.* Cambridge, MA: Brookline Books.

Curtis, M. E., & McCart, L. (1992). Fun ways to promote poor readers' word recognition. *Journal of Reading, 35,* 398–399.

Flowers, L., Meyer, M., Lovato, J., Wood, F., & Felton, R. (2001). Does third grade discrepancy status predict the course of reading development? *Annals of Dyslexia, 51,* 49–71.

Francis, D. J., Stuebing, K. K., Shaywitz, S. E., Shaywitz, B. A., & Fletcher, J. M. (1996). Developmental lag versus deficit models of reading disability: A longitudinal, individual growth curves analysis. *Journal of Educational Psychology, 88,* 3–17.

Ganske, K. (1999). The developmental spelling analysis: A measure of orthographic knowledge. *Educational Assessment, 6,* 41–70.

Ganske, K. (2000). *Word journeys: Assessment-guided phonics, spelling, and vocabulary instruction.* New York: Guilford Press.

Gaskins, I. W., Downer, M. A., Anderson, R. C., Cunningham, P. M., Gaskins, R. W., Schommer, M., et al. (1988). A metacognitive approach to phonics: Using what you know to decode what you don't know. *Remedial and Special Education, 9,* 36–41.

Graham, S., Harris, K. R., & Loynachan, C. (1993). The basic spelling vocabulary list. *Journal of Educational Research, 86,* 363–368.

Greene, J. F. (1996). LANGUAGE!: Effects of an individualized structured language curriculum for middle and high school students. *Annals of Dyslexia, 46*, 97–121.

Harris, R. E., Marchand-Martella, N., & Martella, R. C. (2000). Effects of a peer-delivered corrective reading program. *Journal of Behavioral Education, 10*, 21–36.

Hasbrouck, J. E., Ihnot, C., & Rogers, G. H. (1999). "Read Naturally": A strategy to increase oral reading fluency. *Reading Research and Instruction, 39*, 27–37.

Henry, M. K. (1990). *WORDS: Integrated decoding and spelling instruction based on word origin and word structure*. Austin, TX: PRO-ED.

Henry, M. K. (1999). A short history of the English language. In J. R. Birsch (Ed.), *Multisensory teaching of basic language skills* (pp. 119–133). Baltimore: Brookes.

Inspiration (Version 7.0). (2002). [Computer software]. Portland, OR: Inspiration Software.

Kennedy, K. M., & Backman, J. (1993). Effectiveness of the Lindamood Auditory Discrimination in Depth program with students with learning disabilities. *Learning Disabilities Research and Practice, 8*, 253–259.

Kuhn, M. R., & Stahl, S. A. (2003). Fluency: A review of developmental and remedial practices. *Journal of Educational Psychology, 95*, 3–21.

Language. (1995). Longmont, CO: Sopris West.

Lenz, B. K., & Hughes, C. A. (1990). A word identification strategy for adolescents with learning disabilities. *Journal of Learning Disabilities, 23*, 149–163.

Lindamood phoneme sequencing program for reading, spelling, and speech. (1975). San Luis Obispo, CA: Lindamood-Bell Learning Processes.

Lovett, M. W., Lacerenza, L., & Borden, S. L. (2000). Putting struggling readers on the PHAST track: A program to integrate phonological and strategy-based remedial reading instruction and maximize outcomes. *Journal of Learning Disabilities, 33*, 458–476.

Lovett, M. W., & Steinbach, K. A. (1997). The effectiveness of remedial programs for reading disabled children of different ages: Does the benefit decrease for older children? *Learning Disability Quarterly, 20*, 189–210.

McBride-Chang, C., Manis, F. R., Seidenberg, M. S., Custodio, R. G., & Doi, L. M. (1993). Print exposure as a predictor of word reading and reading comprehension in disabled and nondisabled readers. *Journal of Educational Psychology, 85*, 230–238.

Mercer, C. D., Campbell, K. U., Miller, M. D., Mercer, K. D., & Lane, H. B. (2000). Effects of a reading fluency intervention for middle schoolers with specific learning disabilities. *Learning Disabilities Research and Practice, 15*, 179–189.

Moats, L. C. (2000). *Speech to print: Language essentials for teachers*. Baltimore: Brookes.

Nagy, W. E., Diakidoy, I. N., & Anderson, R. C. (1993). The acquisition of morphology: Learning the contribution of suffixes to the meanings of derivatives. *Journal of Reading Behavior, 25*, 155–170.

National Institute of Child Health and Human Development. (2000). *Report of the National Reading Panel*. Washington, DC: Author.

O'Shea, L. J., Sindelar, P. T., & O'Shea, D. (1987). The effects of repeated reading and attentional cues on the reading fluency and comprehension of learning disabled readers. *Learning Disabilities Research, 2*, 103–109.

Perfetti, C. A. (1985). *Reading ability.* New York: Oxford University Press.

Project Read. (1969). Bloomington, MN: Language Circle Enterprise.

Reading Is FAME. (1992). Boys Town, NE: Girls and Boys Town.

Rosner, J. (1973). *Perceptual skills curriculum.* New York: Walker Educational Books.

Samuels, S. J. (2002). Reading fluency: Its development and assessment. In A. E. Farstrup & S. J. Samuels (Eds.), *What research has to say about reading instruction* (3rd ed., pp. 166–183). Newark, DE: International Reading Association.

Sanders, M. (2001). *Understanding dyslexia and the reading process: A guide for educators and parents.* Boston: Allyn & Bacon.

Shaywitz, S. E., Fletcher, J. M., Holahan, J. M., Shneider, A. E., Marchione, K. E., Stuebing, K. K., et al. (1999). Persistence of dyslexia: The Connecticut Longitudinal Study at Adolescence. *Pediatrics, 104,* 1351–1359.

Stahl, S. A., & Kuhn, M. R. (2002). Making it sound like language: Developing fluency. *Reading Teacher, 55,* 582–584.

Spear-Swerling, L., & Sternberg, R. J. (1996). *Off track: When poor readers become "learning disabled."* Boulder, CO: Westview Press.

Stanovich, K. E. (1986). Matthew effects in reading: Some consequences of individual differences in the acquisition of literacy. *Reading Research Quarterly, 21,* 360–407.

Thomas, A., & Clapp, T. (1989). A comparison of computer-assisted component reading skills training and repeated reading for adolescent poor readers. *Canadian Journal of Special Education, 5,* 135–144.

Torgesen, J. K., Rashotte, C. A., & Alexander, A. W. (2001). Principles of fluency instruction in reading: Relationships with established empirical outcomes. In M. Wolf (Ed.), *Dyslexia, fluency, and the brain* (pp. 333–355). Timonium, MD: York Press.

Tuley, A. C. (1998). *Never too late to read: Language skills for the adolescent with dyslexia (Based on the work of Alice Ansara).* Baltimore: York Press.

Ultimate Word Attack. (1998). [Computer software]. Torrance, CA: Davidson.

Venezky, R. L. (1999). *The American way of spelling.* New York: Guilford Press.

Weaver, P. A., & Rosner, J. (1979). Relationships between visual and auditory perceptual skills and comprehension in students with learning disabilities. *Journal of Learning Disabilities, 12,* 617–621.

Wilson reading system. (1988). Millbury, MA: Wilson Language Training.

Wolf, M., & Bowers, P. G. (1999). The double-deficit hypothesis for the developmental dyslexias. *Journal of Educational Psychology, 91,* 415–438.

Wolf, M., Miller, L., & Donnelly, K. (2000). Retrieval, Automaticity, Vocabulary, Orthography (RAVE-O): A comprehensive, fluency-based reading intervention program. *Journal of Learning Disabilities, 33,* 375–386.

Teaching Struggling Adolescent Readers to Comprehend What They Read

TERRY UNDERWOOD
P. DAVID PEARSON

Middle and high school teachers face a daunting challenge when they attempt to use reading as a primary means of stimulating higher level learning and thinking among their students about important topics within the various disciplines (Alvermann & Phelps, 1998; Davey, 1988). As we show in this chapter, the unfortunate fact is that the majority of adolescent readers in our schools routinely struggle when it comes to comprehending what they read as part of their academic assignments. Although part of the challenge stems from the poor quality of textbooks teachers usually have on hand (Commeyras & Alvermann, 1996; Paxton, 1999), another part arises when students experience cognitive roadblocks as they attempt to negotiate complex texts for academic purposes, whether those texts are well-written or not (Block & Pressley, 2002). In this chapter, we argue that a solution lies in asking teachers to use instructional interventions that help learners "fend for themselves" as they resolve difficulties encountered, regardless of the quality of the texts they must face, and we explain the designs of three classroom-based instructional interventions aimed at doing just that.

Data from the most recent National Assessment of Educational Progress (NAEP; 1998) suggest that far too many eighth- and 12th-grade students do not have the capacity to perform the higher order cognitive work required for deep learning of content through reading. According to the NAEP rubric, a "Basic" level at eighth grade means that readers can

- demonstrate a literal understanding of what they read,
- [are] able to make some interpretations,
- can identify specific aspects of the text that reflect overall meaning,
- can extend the ideas in the text by making simple inferences, [and]
- can recognize and relate interpretations and connections.

In contrast, eighth-grade students performing at the "Advanced" level can

- describe the more abstract themes and ideas of the overall text,
- analyze both meaning and form and support their analyses explicitly with examples from the text, [and]
- extend text information by relating it to their experiences and to world events.

Advanced performance is characterized by student responses that are "thorough, thoughtful, and extensive." Similar distinctions between "Basic" and "Advanced" reading performance apply to the reading achievement descriptors at the 12th-grade level in that Basic performance indexes an incapacity to be successful at higher order reading tasks.

How do older readers fare on these national assessments? Table 7.1 presents the NAEP-reported average reading scores for adolescents and young adults over the past decade (the "Basic" score band for eighth grade is 243–281, for 12th grade 265–302). In the current era in which higher order literacy performances are required for effective functioning in the workplace, community work, and politics, these data suggest that the pool of older readers whom we might characterize as "struggling" is quite large. To sharpen our focus on precisely who these learners are, consider the average scores in 1998 for older readers based on their eligibility for free or reduced-price lunch (Table 7.2). It is interesting to note the average scale score for low-income 12th graders is about the same as the average for

TABLE 7.1. Average NAEP Reading Scores over Time for All Readers

	8th grade	12th grade
1992	260	292
1994	260	287
1998	264	291

TABLE 7.2. Average NAEP Reading Scores (1998) for Readers Based
on Socioeconomic Status

	8th grade	12th grade
Eligible for free or reduced-price lunch	246	271
Not eligible for free or reduced-price lunch	270	292

higher income eighth graders. Even though the NAEP performance levels are far from perfect (see DeStefano, Pearson, & Afflerbach, 1997, or Linn, Glaser, & Bohrenstedt, 1997), the performance of students, particularly economically poor students at eighth and 12th grade, as it might be indexed by any standard, is inadequate compared to the expectations of subject matter curricula, texts, and teachers.

In this age of high standards for complex learning, during which no child is supposed to be left behind, and in light of the NAEP data, which show that the average adolescent is indeed being left behind, we argue in this chapter that these forgotten readers ought to receive at least as much intervention—and attention—as beginning readers have received in recent years. Richard Vacca, former president of the International Reading Association, has characterized the current state of affairs involving middle and high school learners as "the benign neglect of adolescent literacy" (Vacca, 1997, as cited in California Department of Education, 2000, p. 1). We only wonder if the characterization of the neglect as "benign" is appropriate; the costs of this neglect to our society in terms of economic productivity, civic participation, and personal efficacy are certainly not benign. The three instructional projects discussed in this chapter have identifiable approaches to adolescent literacy that have been tested in the real world of middle and high schools with culturally, linguistically, and economically diverse student populations, populations likely to include more than a fair share of adolescent readers at or below NAEP's "Basic" level of performance. Recognizing that not nearly enough research has been conducted to provide a universal solution to this problem, we offer these approaches partly as interventions that might be emulated in schools, and partly as design models that might guide colleagues in inventing, modifying, and validating even more ambitious and even more effective programs.

By way of preview, we simply assert that each of the models presented embody what must surely by now be commonsense assumptions of literacy instruction with no need for further documentation: When instruction is designed to engage students in more reading and in reading more widely than they might otherwise do, when instruction is planned so that students write about their reading, students build their capacity to comprehend. These assumptions are born out by the NAEP data, crude as the NAEP survey instruments are: Students in eighth grade who reported reading more than 11 pages per day scored roughly 25 points higher than students who reported reading fewer than 5 pages per day; 12th-grade students who reported reading more than 11 pages per day scored roughly 30 points higher than students who reported reading fewer than 5 pages per day. Moreover, students in both eighth and 12th grade who reported having assignments in school during which they wrote long answers to questions at least once per week scored between 30 and 40 points higher than students who reported hardly ever or never engaging in writing activities that involved reading. Granted, these are broad correlational findings, but they come with the support of research from natural experiments (e.g., Anderson, Wilson, & Fielding, 1988; Langer, 2001), as well as instructional experiments and analyses of best practice (Langer, 2001).

Our focus on instructional interventions delivered when learners are adolescents and young adults should not be taken as evidence that we believe that the challenges of teaching students to comprehend should be postponed until children actually reach these age levels. The past two decades of work among comprehension researchers have yielded considerable evidence that comprehension instruction should be carried out for all schoolchildren regardless of age or developmental level, even as early as the primary grades (Pearson & Duke, 2002). The current emphasis on decoding and fluency in the elementary school, necessary as these elements are as a foundation for comprehension, may actually exacerbate the problems of struggling adolescent readers. As they move through the grades, learners must process increasingly more information from increasingly more complex texts; at some point, the knowledge acquisition task posed by these texts reaches the point at which getting the words right and reading with greater facility and expression just does not cut it. An early emphasis on decoding and fluency must be truly balanced with a deliberate and systematic approach to comprehension from the earliest stages of formal schooling. We make the argument that just as an instructional imbalance with a tilt toward meaning may create students who cannot read the words accurately, an instructional imbalance with a tilt toward fluency may create students who can rattle off the words but cannot fathom the ideas, much less their significance.

CRITICAL RESEARCH

Reading educators have attended to the notion that comprehension depends on fluency and have taken seriously the role of word perception in the construction of meaning, leading to an intense instructional emphasis on print skills (Adams, 1990; Pressley, 1998). Indeed, the call from the 1990s for balanced instruction with decoding at center stage has had an influence on how teachers are prepared to serve as reading teachers in classrooms, if the reading methods textbooks published for use in preservice programs can be counted as indices of the content of teacher education programs. Recently, however, reading educators have begun to build a case grounded in empirical evidence for a balance that does justice to issues of comprehension, writing in response to reading, and critical examinations of text. Block and Pressley (2002) and others have argued persuasively that exemplary reading instructional programs provide students with rich opportunities to learn to comprehend printed text, while still providing a focus on the teaching of decoding skills, promoting growth in sight words, and providing opportunities and incentives for easy recreational reading.

It seems clear that although an intense instructional focus on fluency may pay short-term dividends, the cost–benefit analysis of such an emphasis for adolescent learners looks less attractive. We are not the first to point out that too many learners move from elementary into secondary school with serviceable levels of skill in decoding and fluency, yet are unable to comprehend what is read (Brown, 2002; Greenleaf, Jiménez, & Roller, 2002; Wilhelm, 1996). In California, where a heavy emphasis on instruction in fluency in the elementary grades has been the state's prescription for several years now, standardized test data reveal a sizable drop in reading comprehension scores across the state when students make the transition to secondary school. Table 7.3 summarizes the percentage of students scoring at or above the 50th national percentile rank on the Stanford 9 Test given each year to all of California's students and shows quite clearly the magnitude of this drop (California Department of Education, 2002). Fluency—along with its attendant correlates, accuracy and automaticity—may indeed be a necessary, but surely not sufficient, condition for comprehension.

So what does research say about how we intervene to teach struggling adolescents to comprehend what they read, once we have agreed that a

TABLE 7.3. Percentage of California Students Scoring at or above the 50th NPR by Grade Level between 1998 and 2002

	1998–1999	1999–2000	2000–2001	2001–2002
4th grade	41	45	47	49
8th grade	47	49	50	49
9th grade	34	35	35	34
11th grade	35	36	37	37

focus on comprehension is an instructional necessity? We might begin by scrutinizing what researchers mean by "struggling" and by "intervene." Researchers have pointed out repeatedly that "struggling" is definable only with reference to a particular context and a particular standard; there exist, out there somewhere, a situation and a criterion that will reduce all of us to the "struggling" label under certain circumstances (e.g., O'Brien, 2001). The competencies that emerge quite readily in some contexts (e.g., home or community settings) may not show up in the classroom (Rogers, 2002). Even so, teachers do indeed sometimes encounter high school students reading at a second-grade level, who struggle with decoding and fluency issues for which specific interventions related to technical skills may be needed. Let's be clear about our sense of the nature of the struggle in question: Far too many adolescents struggle when they must use literacy as a tool for academic learning. That said, it seems equally clear that interventions must help learners bridge from strengths to new capabilities, from home and popular discourse to academic discourse. There is no longer space for models of instruction driven by theories of deficits and remediation.

Lately, the term *intervention* itself has been explored in an effort to unpack assumptions sometimes surrounding it (Greenleaf et al., 2002). Jiménez wrote about a concern with the term stemming from "the idea that we . . . as educators . . . can enter a setting for a limited period and believe that as a consequence we bring about permanent and lasting change" (p. 485). Jiménez added, "We have to move away from the view of interventions as *deus ex machina*-type events and move toward more collaborative-type affairs involving researchers, teachers, students, and their families" (p. 487). We agree with Jiménez that the notion of intervention ought not be construed as a "quick fix" and argue that an intervention, in order to promote genuine learning potential among students, must possess two characteristics: a commitment to long-term, durable, permanent, measurable change, and an inclusive, collaborative framework of activity for involving all participants in the local setting in the work of raising the performance levels of struggling adolescents. Brief encounters with an isolated teacher in an isolated classroom, while everyone else goes on with business as usual, will not help students meet the textual challenges they face in schools.

The collaborative spirit must extend to teachers who engage in the design of the learning environment and to students who actually use the strategies taught to them in these learning environments. Interventions ought to be carefully crafted on the basis of strong theoretical knowledge of the basic processes of reading comprehension and learning from text *and* rich knowledge of local contexts, after which interventions should be refined on the basis of carefully designed local experiments and finally validated in something approximating randomized experiments. Our fear in the current milieu is that, in our rush to find panaceas to fix the problem that vexes us all, we will inadvertently ignore all but the last step in the scientific process. That would be a mistake, because we would end up trying to validate interventions that had neither the backbone of sound general theory nor the grounded validity of local knowledge.[1]

Fortunately, the good work of the past several decades has provided useful theoretical tools to organize instructional interventions with the promise of making a real difference in the academic lives of students. Here, we define *instruction* as *a staging of purposeful activity over an extended time frame. Furthermore, we expect that instruction will help students comprehend text and learn something about how one comprehends within particular academic discourse settings—settings that self-consciously integrate knowledge, cultural, and language resources brought into the classroom by the learners.* Just as researchers have said for many decades, instruction includes planned activity for purposeful learner engagement in cognitive and metacognitive work before, during, and after reading; our definition of *instruction* makes explicit the notion that the intellectual capital learners bring with them to learning activities must play a vital part in advancing their academic capital.

In the following paragraphs, we lay out a model of four levels of instructional interventions and tie each of these levels to research in reading comprehension. These levels are nested, in that the characteristics of a level 1 intervention are necessary but not sufficient for a level 2 intervention; similarly, the characteristics of a level 2 intervention are necessary but not sufficient for a level 3 intervention. As the level of the intervention rises, characteristics are added to the intervention, not taken away. In general, interventions at levels 1 and 2 are rooted in comprehension research done in accordance with an information-processing model of reading, which assumes that information is taken in and manipulated via cognitive processes such as attention and memory, so that readers construct mental representations of the propositional content of texts (e.g., Kintsch, 1998). By studying the kinds of cognitive processes good readers use as they construct these mental representations, researchers have identified a list of cognitive

---

[1] *Local knowledge* is a term that the eminent anthropologist Clifford Geertz (1983) popularized to describe the power of the belief systems of particular cultural groups in explaining their worldviews and everyday activity. We use it here as a rough approximation to Collins, Brown, and Duguid's notion of situated cognition (1989). Our emphasis is on the notion that cognitive strategies that are not culturally adapted are not likely to succeed, prosper, and achieve any sort of continued cultural transmission across generations.

strategies that are appropriate as a focus for instruction (see Dole, Duffy, Roehler, & Pearson, 1991).

We propose that instructional interventions aimed at helping older struggling readers comprehend texts in an academic discourse setting can have a greater effect on a larger number of learners when the elements of information–processing models (e.g., Afflerbach & Pressley, 1995) are integrated with social and cultural models (e.g., Smagorinsky, 2001). The result is a level 3 intervention. To explain what we mean by this integration, we have created a three–part conceptual framework for comprehension instruction that we believe captures lessons from research over the past few decades and points in the direction of future interventions that meet the Jiménez criteria of permanent change and local collaborative work.

Level 1 interventions focus primarily on the reader and the text, and aim to teach learners cognitive strategies for creating mental representations of the content of a text (what Kintsch has called a *text model*). As Anderson and Pearson (1984) and others have demonstrated, the role of prior knowledge in comprehension is a critical consideration in planning instruction to help readers activate, draw on, and build schemas before, during, and after reading—and learners need opportunities to examine how prior knowledge works during reading, a characteristic of level 1 intervention. As Rosenblatt (1978) explained, the activity of the reader as he or she moves through a reading event is shaped by the stance the reader takes toward the text along an aesthetic–efferent continuum (in which aesthetic stances privilege impressionistic reader response, and efferent stances tilt toward the workman–like extraction of meaning from "the text")—and teachers using a level 1 intervention provide opportunities for students to take up and examine their thought processes at various points on this continuum. As Meyer, Brandt, and Bluth (1980) and Taylor (1980) demonstrated, good readers look for structure in texts and differentiate between important and less important ideas; level 1 interventions include the teaching of strategies such as graphic organizers to help readers gain control of the macrostructure of texts. Level 1 interventions aim to help readers develop the cognitive and metacognitive strategies that good readers use to create mental models of texts.

Level 2 interventions include all of the characteristics of level 1 interventions but bring the author into the equation. Much of the research done over the past few decades to illuminate the cognitive processes of expert readers has used think–aloud methods (Afflerbach & Pressley, 1995; Kucan & Beck, 1997). Findings from these studies converge on the point that expert readers are active, that they question not just the text, but the text and its author(s), and that they engage, sometimes automatically and other times self-consciously, in all of the cognitive behaviors identified by researchers as central to effective comprehension (Dole et al., 1991). Level 2 interventions include learning activities related to constructing a mental representation of text, but they also teach learners to use their own knowledge and understanding as the basis for asking and answering questions that involve the learners "on their own," and that involve "the author and you" as per the instructional strategy Question–Answer Relationship (QAR; Raphael, 1982, 1984, 1986). Beck, McKeown, Hamilton, and Kucan's (1997) work with the strategy Questioning the Author is an example of a level 2 intervention. Using this strategy, teachers help learners understand that texts are framed or staged by an author to work in particular ways more or less effectively; authors are seen as fallible and intentional, and readers have the right to question them.

Level 3 interventions extend the explanatory power of information-processing theory to account for the emergence and deployment of cognitive behaviors within particular sociocultural contexts and activity settings (cf. Smagorinsky, 1998). Instructional interventions designed to stimulate the higher order cognitive behaviors of expert readers must take into account the relationship between the social context and these cognitive behaviors. Smagorinsky (2001) has developed a cultural model of reading that could form the basis for an exploration of level 3 activity, with an emphasis on the relationship between cognition and context in reading events. Smagorinsky's model is grounded in activity theory and "rel[ies] on the notions of tool and sign to describe what a text is and how a reader constructs meaning through joint activity with the text and other mediators . . . [and views] culture [as] the basis for meaning, serving to mediate the development of what Vygotsky (1978) called higher mental processes" (p. 134).

In a level 3 intervention, there is concern with academic discourse as one of many contexts of language use that readers must master, but there is also a concern for the reader's identity as an "agent of culture" rather than simply a "bearer of culture" (Ochs, 1996, p. 416), and with motivation for and access to legitimate participation in communities of literacy practice (Lave & Wenger, 1991) in just and fair ways. There is also a focus on structured opportunities for teachers to collaborate as they build a common professional knowledge base about instructional practices, examine student work for insights into the effects of practices, and articulate strategies for engaging learners as responsible agents in the academic culture of schooling. At the heart of level 3 intervention is the goal of helping learners regulate their own cognitive and social activity, in and out of the classroom, in ways that balance their own perspectives with the perspectives of the communities in which they engage in literacy acts.

Baker (2002) has provided a useful perspective on the relationship between metacognition and comprehension instruction: "Just as the engagement perspective and the learner-centered principles have made it clear that we need to go beyond cognitive factors to understand reading comprehension and learning, so too do we need to recognize that motivation and social interaction also influence metacognition" (p. 78). Baker discusses the importance of affective and motivational factors in metacognition, grounding her arguments in the Vygotskian notion of internalization: "There is a sequence of development from other-regulation to self-regulation. This notion provides the framework for virtually all instructional programs in which the goal is to enable students to take responsibility for their own learning" (p. 78). From this point of view, motivation and emotional states are central to accomplishing the cognitive goal, because it is unlikely that behavior will change in the absence of volition.

Motivational orientations are linked closely to social environment (e.g., Covington, 1992). If motivation and affect are central to cognition/comprehension and metacognition, if achievement motivation and overall affect are shaped at least partly during social interactions, then comprehension instruction itself must be social and cultural, both in theoretical grounding and in everyday implementation. From the perspective of cultural–historical psychology, teaching sequences designed as comprehension instruction qualify as "practices" or "activities" or "events" and ought to be examined in what Cole (1995) has called "the supra-individual envelope of development: activity and practice, situation and context." Cole employs Engestrom's basic structure of an activity system as a useful "framework for understanding the development of thought in culture" (p. 117). A number of recent reading and literacy theorists have echoed in one way or another Cole's insistence on the examination of individual behaviors, including reading behaviors, as inseparable from the materials, resources, affordances, and values of the social and historical surround (e.g., Gee, 1996; Rogers, 2002; Sarroub, 2002; Smagorinsky, 2001; Street, 1984, 1993). We agree with Baker in her argument that instruction in cognition and metacognition must involve concerns for motivation and affect, and we find the elaboration of this argument by anthropologically or socioculturally oriented literacy theorists (e.g., Gee, 1996) useful in our effort here to transform a *theory* of comprehension instruction for older readers, who all struggle at one point or another, into *practices* that add value to the their lives.

To expand our understanding of level 3 interventions, we see a need for researchers to address the role of context in reading far more explicitly than in the past, with an eye toward revising the role of the teacher from coach of the learning team to player (or perhaps a player/coach) in the learning game. Moreover, the roles and status of learners must be explored in an effort to provide social scaffolds that compel them to become more deeply involved in complex learning in classrooms. The three approaches we describe in the next section point in these directions. We also envision a level 4 set of interventions on the horizon, involving intermediality and the Internet (O'Brien, 2002) and film, together with other visual symbols systems. We return to a brief discussion of level 4, an admittedly speculative and sketchy construct in our minds, in our conclusion.

Over the past 25 years, important insights into reading comprehension and instruction have been generated in cognitive psychology, reading education, and English education. Programs and practices have been reported in the scholarly literature that should have had a major impact on student achievement, but the promise of this scholarship has not been realized in everyday classroom practice. The question is not, How do we teach learners to comprehend?—though many perplexing research issues remain in answering that question; the question is, How can we help teachers implement instructional interventions that integrate and capitalize on family, community, and school resources in a way that actually makes a permanent difference in the lives of students? We argue that attention to the levels of intervention framework can help.

AN ONGOING LEVEL 3 INTERVENTION: THE PATHWAY PROJECT

The Pathway Project, a collaborative intervention between the University of California, Irvine, a California Writing Project (UCIWP), Santa Ana Unified School District (SAUSD), and Santa Ana College (SAC), began during the 1996–1997 year after getting funded via the University of California Regents Diversity Initiative (see Olson, 2003, for a thorough report on the project). At this writing, the Pathway Project receives funds from the U.S. Department of Education Office of Bilingual Education and Minority Languages Affairs (OBEMLA). Designed specifically to provide a pathway of language arts classes to prepare English-language learners (ELLs) for effective participation in academic literacy settings at the high school and college levels, this intervention serves a student population made up almost entirely of minority groups: 88.9% Hispanic, 5.6% Asian/ Pacific Islander, 1.3% black—75% of whom live below the poverty level. Santa Ana College is significant in the partnership, because 53% of all SAUSD graduates matriculate to SAC, where they must apply whatever skills they have developed in academic literacy during their high school years. Indeed, the vision has been to develop learners' academic English proficiency using all of the cognitive strategies identified in the research; to keep these learners in high school; and to see them go to 2- or 4-year postsecondary institutions.

The Jiménez criteria of durability and local collaboration as non-negotiable characteristics of an intervention are well exemplified by the Pathway Project. Having sustained itself for 7 years with an accumulation of data providing an evidentiary basis of its effectiveness, the project has mobilized large groups of individuals involved in schooling in articulated, coordinated activity keyed to the goals and vision of the project. In answer to questions about reasons for the project's success, Olson (2003) points to the stability and commitment of teachers, motivated by their own professional growth and by the long-term development of the literacy of their students, who participate regularly in school site teams, grade-level teams, and vertical (6–12) cluster teams, including 6 full-released days at UCI per year.

The project has grown from 14 teachers and 490 students in 1996–1997 to 46 teachers in 54 classrooms in 9 middle schools and 4 high schools, and 1,890 students in 2002–2003. Even the project evaluation strategy was designed to get real, useful information back to students through the deployment of UCI undergraduate students as raters of the learners' pretest essays. Learners get their pretests back with feedback from a Pathway Project reader, then revise their pretest timed essay into a multiple-draft essay, using cognitive strategies taught in their class. Weeks later, they evaluate their pre- and posttest essays, and write a reflection on their growth as learners. Pathway Project teachers come to adopt a strong cognitivist orientation toward comprehension pedagogy, in that the menu of strategies often associated with comprehension instruction (e.g., Dole et al., 1991) are staples of instruction. Olson (2003) summarized this orientation as follows:

> One of the key principles of instructional scaffolding is internalization—the transferring of control from the teacher to the students as they gain competence and can apply the strategies independently. To do this, students need to move beyond declarative and procedural knowledge to develop conditional knowledge, to know when and why to apply various strategies and to "orchestrate" their use (Paris, Lipson and Wixon, 1983).

This emphasis on extending beyond declarative and procedural knowledge into conditional knowledge (the why and when of strategy use) is another aspect of the Pathway Project that moves it to a level 3 intervention. To learn conditional knowledge, students must be construed as participants in activity settings, and, of course, the activity settings in the Pathway Project necessarily entail those in which one form or another of academic discourse is critical for successful performance. Although the Pathway Project appears not to have a strong, or at least a transparent, focus on developing identity and agency, it brings together resources to help learners gradually assume more responsibility for completing academically valued work and for participating meaningfully in academic discourse communities.

Data supporting the effectiveness of the Pathway Project are impressive. The main instrument used to measure growth in reading and writing is a pre- and posttest, timed direct-writing assessment administered in October and again in April/May. The prompts direct students to write an interpretation of a literary work, a well-structured essay with evidence, supporting details, comments, and interpretive statements—precisely the sort of work the NAEP might classify as "proficient" or even "advanced." Since 2000, an average of 3,000 learners, 1,500 Pathway and 1,500 controls, have taken the pre- and posttest each year. Pre–posttest differences in gain scores between Pathway and control students have been statistically significant for 6 consecutive years. Other measures have favored the Pathway cohorts as well. Six variables are reported in Olson (2003) for 2000-2001: GPA, absences, SAT-9 Reading and Total Languages scores, and fluency. The Pathway group was statistically superior in every comparison except for days absent, suggesting that it is not mere presence that matters most, but what the students do while they are present in the school setting.

ANOTHER LEVEL 3 INTERVENTION: THE PORTFOLIO PROJECT

Designed and implemented during the peak of interest in alternative assessments of the 1990s, in particular, portfolios, we refer to the second instructional intervention we discuss as "the portfolio project" (see Murphy & Underwood, 2000; Underwood, 1996, 1998, 1999; Underwood, Murphy, & Pearson, 1995). This project resulted from the collaborative efforts of teachers in an English department serving an ethnically and linguistically diverse population that attended an urban middle school in northern California to create classroom cultures that invited learners to take up responsibility for their own learning.

For one thing, the idea was for students to develop literacy work habits like those seen in craftspeople or artists. Indeed, the intervention was grounded in the metaphor of the artist's portfolio, as Wolf (1987–1988) expressed it:

> First, in the arts, the ability to find interesting problems is . . . as important as being able to answer someone else's questions. . . . Second, learning in the arts often occurs in very large chunks spread out over a long period of time. . . . Third, it is

essential for young artists . . . to develop a keen sense of standards and critical judgment. Consequently, in the arts, [work] cannot be restricted to highly structured problems or just to finished products. (pp. 26–27)

The intervention was also rooted in what Bereiter and Scardamalia (1987) termed the *intentional model of learning* in contrast to the *knowledge-based model*:

> Within [the knowledged-base model] . . . the competence that a student will display depends on interest and intention, and these in turn influence the constructive activity that lead to future development. . . . [But] at any one moment student motives are taken as givens, [though] they are also thought of as evolving and capable of being stifled or nurtured by the teacher. The same notions apply to the [Intentional Learning model], except that in [this model] interests and intentions are not just mediators of competence, they are *part of a person's competence—something to be developed.* (p. 14, emphasis added).

The starting point for this intervention, then, was a theory of the learner as an agent with aesthetic inclinations responsible for developing not only academic knowledge and skills but also dispositions and habits that could sustain challenging and complex literacy work over time.

This theory of the learner was also informed by the work of researchers in the area of achievement motivation, who examined the centrality in academic accomplishment of the will and the drive to learn and to improve in life (e.g., Covington, 1992; Nicholls, Cobb, Wood, Yackel, & Patashnick, 1990). Beginning in the 1970s, achievement motivation theorists developed a goal-oriented model of motivation that aligned well with the student-as-artisan aspect of portfolio approaches. Dweck and Leggett (1988) and Midgley (1993), for example, explained that students who persist in the face of challenge, and who engage deeply in tasks, tend to exhibit a learning goal orientation, that is, they exert effort because they believe that effort will improve them intrinsically; students who do not persist, or who do not deeply engage in tasks, tend to exhibit a performance goal orientation; that is, they exert effort only to advance their status, to gain approval, or to avoid disapproval. The portfolio project, with its emphasis on student ownership, choice, task engagement, and reflective analysis, was intended to help students become oriented toward learning goals by helping them to develop interests and intentions, then to satisfy those interests and intentions through reading and writing.

In alignment with California's assessment system and curricular framework for language arts current in the mid-1990s, the English teachers took as their instructional objective the teaching of literary reading, as the construct was defined by Rosenblatt (1938/1983, 1978) and elaborated by Langer (1985, 1987, 1989). According to this perspective, readers transact with texts in one of two dominant stances: an aesthetic stance or an efferent stance. Readers assuming an aesthetic stance in Rosenblatt's sense transact with text in order to evoke an intensely personal inner response, a vicarious experience, the value of which lies in the experience of the event in itself. Readers assuming an efferent stance transact with text in order to carry away information; readers' responses to reading events in themselves are irrelevant so long as accurate or useful information is gained.

Rosenblatt argued that English teachers, most likely as a result of the long "apprenticeship of observation" (Lortie, 1975) they have served in school and university classrooms, have long taught readers to approach *all* texts, even poems, in the efferent stance, by privileging the reader's ability to answer questions or to show evidence to prove that he or she carried away information. The teachers at this middle school were acutely aware that Rosenblatt's model did *not* give readers permission to distort or miscomprehend textual information—neither was the state's reading assessment (long since abandoned) built on this assumption. But they also understood that the essence of Rosenblatt's aesthetic reading is constituted of a reader's response. Taking on the teaching of aesthetic reading as the primary instructional objective fit well with the learner-as-artist metaphor at the heart of the portfolio system, and it opened up space in the classroom for learners to focus their literacy work on their own interests, intentions, and purposes.

The elements of the instructional intervention were designed to engage students in goal-setting and self-monitoring activities, to provide direct instruction in cognitive strategies useful in understanding and responding to texts (e.g., predicting, visualizing, questioning, clarifying, connecting prior knowledge), to give students formal and informal qualitative and evaluative feedback on their work, and to hold them accountable for completing their work in a thoughtful and thorough manner. Students in the intervention classrooms were graded according to explicit criteria spelled out on a rubric. For example, to earn an A, students had to provide evidence in their portfolios of reading done habitually almost every day, often for long periods of an hour or two; of readings that not only entertain but also challenge and stretch capabilities; and of reading widely and experimenting with new authors and forms. Moreover, students had to provide evidence in their daily text logs (learning log–type entries) that they were transferring cognitive strategies taught directly in their classes to the reading of self-chosen books. At the end of every trimester, these students would submit both self-selected and required classwork in their portfolios to a committee of English teachers that examined this work by applying the criteria of the rubric, issued a letter grade for the students' report card, and wrote individual commentaries for each student describing the student's strengths and areas for improvement. (For more information see Murphy & Underwood, 2000; Underwood, 1999.)

A quasi-experimental design was employed to help determine the effectiveness of the intervention using matched pairs of pre–/posttest scores on a reading test representing 246 students from nonintervention classrooms at the three schools and 211 students from intervention classrooms. Patterned after the California Learning Assessment System (CLAS) reading test developed in California in the early 1990s (Claggett, 1996) and vaguely reminiscent of the NAEP performance levels, the test employed at the middle school asked students to write responses to open-ended questions, which were independently rated by two scorers using a 6-point scale wherein score points 1 and 2 represented confused and/or partial understanding; 3 and 4 represented control of the literal facts of the passage, with perhaps some thoughtfulness; and 5 and 6 represented sophisticated, agile, resistant reading, nonetheless evidencing firm grounding in the text. Table 7.4 presents mean scores and standard deviations for these students on this measure.

A mixed-model analysis of variance (ANOVA) was conducted, with reading achievement as the dependent variable measured across time, placement (portfolio vs. nonportfolio classroom placement) as a fixed explanatory variable, and the teacher as a nested, random, explanatory variable. There was a significant interaction between reading scores across time and placement ($F_{1, 451}$, MS error [1.31] = 7.57, $p < .05$). In other words, participation in the portfolio intervention classrooms had a statistically significant positive effect on reading achievement as measured by the site's direct reading assessment. According to the Jackson and Brashers (1994) recommendation for analysis of random, explanatory variables such as "teachers," it is probable that the average effect of the intervention on reading achievement, if it were implemented across a wide variety of teachers, would be positive for students' reading achievement. (For a full account of the statistical analysis, see Underwood, 1998.)

TABLE 7.4. Pre–/Posttest Reading Scores for Intervention versus Nonintervention Students

	Nonintervention students	Intervention students
Pretest	$M = 2.76$ $SD = .97$	$M = 2.97$ $SD = .83$
Posttest	$M = 2.52$ $SD = .79$	$M = 3.13$ $SD = 1.01$

TABLE 7.5. Means and Standard Deviations on Three Dimensions of Goal Orientation

	Approval goals	Learning goals	Advancement goals
Intervention students ($n = 265$)	$M = 21.19$ $SD = 6.7$	$M = 27.86$ $SD = 6.2$	$M = 32.65$ $SD = 6.2$
Nonintervention students ($n = 183$)	$M = 20.92$ $SD = 6.6$	$M = 25.91$ $SD = 9.9$	$M = 32.65$ $SD = 7.3$

Students in the intervention and the nonintervention classrooms were also surveyed near the end of the academic year with an adaptation of Hayamizu and Weiner's (1991) achievement motivation survey to gather data regarding three aspects of goal orientation: (1) the learning goal orientation, wherein effort is exerted to acquire knowledge, to improve skills, or to learn about the world; (2) a performance-approval orientation, wherein effort is exerted to be better than others, to gain the immediate social reward of favorable recognition, or to avoid the immediate social punishment of unfavorable recognition; and (3) a performance-advancement orientation, wherein effort is exerted to move forward in the institution in order to enhance one's life chances. Table 7.5 reports findings from this survey for each goal orientation (minimum possible score per dimension was 8, maximum was 40). Simple, one-way ANOVAs used as post hoc analyses, with each scale as a separate dependent variable and placement as a fixed explanatory variable, revealed that students in the portfolio classrooms registered significantly higher scores on the learning orientation scale than did students in the nonportfolio classrooms ($F_{1, 446}$, MS error [42.05] = 9.82, $p < .01$), but that there was no difference between the groups on either the approval or the advancement scales. Inspection of the respective mean scores for each group, as reported in Table 7.5, shows that each placement condition was very similar on the advancement and approval scales, but not on the learning scale, where almost two points separated the groups. These analyses suggest that the intervention did indeed have an effect on the motivational stance of students.

A THIRD LEVEL 3 INTERVENTION: THE READING APPRENTICESHIP

Like the portfolio project, the final intervention we discuss, which we refer to after the program designers as the *reading apprenticeship*, was created and implemented during the mid-1990s, also with the firsthand involvement of practicing classroom teachers (see Greenleaf, Schoenbach, Cziko, & Mueller, 2001; Schoenbach, Greenleaf, Cziko, & Hurwitz, 1999). As head of the English Department at Thurgood Marshall High School in San Francisco, an urban school that opened in 1994, serving one of San Francisco's poorest communities, Christine Cziko began working in 1995 with researchers from WestEd to develop an instructional approach that might solve the problem identified during the first 2 years of the school's operation: "[A] high number of our students were having difficulty getting through heavy reading requirements that our curriculum demanded" (Schoenbach et al., 1999, p. 46). Having tried alternative strategies such as designing and implementing interdisciplinary community-based projects with improvement in student engagement but little consequence for their reading abilities, Christine Cziko and Lori Hurwitz, two English teachers at Thurgood Marshall, decided to require a course called Academic Literacy for all freshmen: "We believed strongly that all freshman could benefit from becoming more conscious of the mental strategies involved in reading different types of texts [and] that diverse readers would learn from each other" (Schoenbach et al., 1999, p. 47).

The result of this decision to create and implement a course aimed at promoting growth in academic literacy among students, most of whom entered ninth grade reading at NAEP's basic or below level, is an approach to instructional intervention that has begun to have an impact across the nation (cf. Greenleaf et al., 2001). The heart of this particular intervention is an instructional framework that recognizes not only the central importance of cognitive strategies and metacognitive awareness in comprehension but also that comprehension in academic settings is shaped by personal and social elements that must be accommodated. During the first weeks of the course implemented at Thurgood Marshall, for example, the instructional focus was on neither text structures nor graphic organizers, but on helping students develop a sense of why anyone might want to read better in the first place: "It was clear to us that unless students could develop their own authentic reasons for reading, there was little chance that anything they learned in Academic Literacy would have a lasting impact" (Schoenbach et al., 1999, p. 59). In parallel with its approach to professional development for practicing teachers, the reading apprenticeship course was designed as an inquiry into reading carried out by these adolescents themselves as apprentices working with their teachers as master readers. As part of this inquiry, students were guided through investigations such as the following: "Investigate . . . the people who read in our society, what they read, why they read, and how reading affects their lives; investigate . . . the people who do not read in our society and how not reading affects their lives" (p. 25).

Just as the portfolio project combined direct teaching of cognitive strategies with plenty of opportunity for students to read self-chosen materials, the reading apprenticeship instructional plan involves reading of common texts using comprehension strategies and the use of Sustained Silent Reading in a closely monitored and collaborative setting. The reading apprenticeship intervention relies heavily on the "mental toolbelt" of Reciprocal Teaching, as this strategy was developed by Palinscar and Brown (1983). In this approach, students are first taught a variety of questioning strategies for several weeks and then to focus on summarizing, clarifying, asking questions, and predicting. Once students have some depth of experience with these strategies in situations in which they have read personally and socially relevant texts, they begin to practice reciprocal teaching by orchestrating all of the strategies at once in small groups. As part of this ongoing work, teachers teach strategies such as ReQuest and QAR, and those who participate in the Strategic Literacy Initiative's ongoing professional development activities devise and revise their own instructional strategies to share with colleagues. (For more information see Schoenbach et al., 1999, or Greenleaf et al., 2001).

During the 1996–1997 academic school year at Thurgood Marshall, students in the Academic Literacy course were tested before and after the course by alternate parallel forms of the Degrees of Reading Power (DRP) test. Because the students in the intervention could not be compared with a control group, WestEd researchers decided to use a norm-referenced test like the DRP to index the growth of these ninth-grade students against "default growth expectations" provided by the national population of ninth-grade students represented by the norming sample. The DRP has an additional attribute that makes it appealing for measuring reading growth: among the indices it provides is one on which both student achievement and text difficulty (using a fairly large sample of classics in children's and adolescent literature) have been scaled. Thus, the DRP can locate the most difficult kind of text a particular reader, with a particular test score, is likely to negotiate effectively. As a group, the ninth-grade students in the original Academic Literacy course gained 4 DRP units over the year, representing a statistically significant difference when compared with what is expected of ninth graders in the larger group ($t = 7.558$, $df = 215$, $p = .000$). When referenced by trade materials, this gain suggests that students improved from the ability to read children's magazines to the ability to read teen fiction and adult fiction magazines. Survey results indicated that students had changed in other ways as well. For example, when surveyed at the beginning of the course, students claimed to have read a mean of 5.58 novels in the previous year; on the end-of-course survey, students claimed to have read a mean of

10.99 books during the year. (For more information see Schoenbach et al., 1999, or Greenleaf et al., 2001).

COMMONALITIES IN DESIGN

Aspects of level 1 comprehension intervention can be found in each of the approaches to instruction we have discussed. The Pathways Project taught students in the SAUSD several strategies to use in constructing the gist of a passage, including ways to identify main ideas in a text and to note organizational patterns. At Charles Ruff Middle School, learners were taught strategies for depicting the content of their readings and writings in ways that promoted the skill of identifying text structures; they were taught simple strategies for story mapping, for example, and they learned to use narrative retelling strategies such as Herringbone. At Thurgood Marshall, learners apprenticed on such tasks as summarizing expository text, previewing, and making graphic organizers, and learned a great deal about structural and organizational shifts in texts. In both schools, teachers placed an emphasis on understanding the propositional content of texts.

Aspects of level 2 comprehension intervention, marked by attention to reader, text, and author, are also present in each of the approaches to instruction. Pathway Project teachers support students in learning to generate questions about topic, genre, author–audience, purpose, and related issues; students learn to analyze the author's craft. At Charles Ruff and Thurgood Marshall alike, teachers were keenly aware of the instructional need to help students find books they liked and that were within reach; readers were encouraged to come to know how and which authors craft the kinds of texts in which they could engage with some enthusiasm. This concern for a reader–text match intersected in both approaches with helping students access challenging texts in a cumulative and frequent fashion to stimulate intertextuality, build knowledge of content and genre, increase fluency, and understand the place of the author in reading events. In both approaches, teachers understood that students need to make a transition from familiar and inherently interesting texts to less familiar texts that actually show up much more often in academic discourse. Holding dialogues with the author—and with characters or figures within texts—also permeated instruction in both approaches. At Thurgood Marshall, Taffy Raphael's QAR was a staple, because it distinguishes so clearly among text- and reader-based activity. At Charles Ruff, students questioned the authors and the characters in their text logs, in class discussions, and in role-playing performances.

In each example program, we find several important aspects of Level 3 intervention. First, at the heart of each approach is a concern with the development of the reader's identity as an agent (thus, as a social and cultural being) and as an individual with a clear understanding of what literacy can and cannot do for him or her. This is exemplified in the programs' common insistence on student choice in books, including the right to abandon a book that is not working out. In each approach, local classroom and school libraries became centrally important to student success. To communicate with students about the reality of schooling in the modern world, each approach made full use of the notion of "institutional credit" and "grades" as the cultural capital of school. Indeed, the Pathway Project went to great lengths to help students see the link between their secondary school work and the local community college. The idea was this: Students needed to learn that they could achieve a high level of literacy for their own benefit—and that such achievement was valued in the institution.

Moreover, each approach recognized and took seriously the notion that academic literacy practices entail deep and critical processing of complex text across a range of genres. Learners in the Pathway Project were taught the pinnacle skill of writing an analytical/expository essay stemming from the serious study of serious works of literature. Adolescents participated in carefully scaffolded writing instruction to help them understand the difference between argument, commentary, and evidence. At Thurgood Marshall, the main goal of the class was to promote growth in students' capacity to engage and learn from nonfiction texts, to develop persistence and stamina, and the will to read complex texts. Like the Pathway Project, at Charles Ruff, the main goal was to create students who could participate effectively in the kind of reading and interpretation of literature that English teachers have long valued in schools. Reading was seen as a way to think and participate within one or more disciplines, a theme that was discussed explicitly with students. To build capacity to teach students academic ways with words involved changing how teachers went about their work in classrooms, to be sure, but it also involved collaboration across classrooms in an effort to create a culture of literacy for students that spanned classrooms. In both approaches, the aim was not simply to prepare teachers for the delivery of one or another instructional model, but to change the very nature of student–teacher interactions.

It is not irrelevant in these approaches that teachers *volunteer* to teach in a manner consistent with the routines and practices of the approach; teacher attitude and motivation are central to the intervention. Just as students worked at choosing books for themselves, the teachers worked at choosing how best to teach their students based on their growing understanding of theory and practice in an environment of inquiry and experiment. But let's be clear: This is not pedagogical or interpretive relativism, where anything goes for either teacher practice or student interpretation. Students and teachers exercised agency and choice but always within the context of providing evidence, argument, and warrant for the choices they made and the stances they took.

Assessment in level 3 interventions also tends to be broader based than that in lower levels. In each approach, students were given frequent opportunities to reflect on and assess their work in both informal writing and class discussions. Self-assessment and self-regulation were emphasized in a context of accountability and responsibility, where effort was prized and willingness to work through bouts of confusion was valued. But external assessment was also valued. The Pathway Project assessed students using a direct writing assessment strategy and standardized test data; at Charles Ruff, students took an externally scored reading exam and submitted their portfolios for external evaluation as a measure of pre- and postperformance; at Thurgood Marshall, students took a commercially prepared reading test to serve these purposes. In each approach, qualitative and quantitative data alike were collected on issues of student motivation, attitudes, and engagement.

CODA

We are encouraged by both the content and the results of these Level 3 interventions. Our encouragement stems from several key features of the interventions. First, each manages to balance the potential conflict that arises regarding the question of which of the four faces of reading comprehension (reader, text, author, or context) should be privileged in building a program for adolescents' text comprehension. Second, each faces up to the accountability of external assessment by recognizing that a good program should help student achievement in not only its own curriculum-embedded assessments but also in more general indicators of student progress, such as standardized tests and standards-based measures. Third, each does what all good programs should do: It turns over the reins of responsibility for text understanding just as soon as possible to those who deserve to control these processes and activities—the students. But each program is careful not to turn over this responsibility too soon, not before the students can handle it under supported learning conditions. In a sense, each embodies the principle of "gradual release of responsibility"(Duke & Pearson, 2002; Pearson & Gallagher, 1983) in its instructional delivery. Fourth, each provides practical tools that students can use on a daily basis to negotiate the slippery slopes of complex, conceptually dense, and sometimes inconsiderately written subject-matter texts. And it is this last point upon which all reading interventions for adolescents should be judged, for it remains the Achilles' heel in the lives of so many of our older readers and a thorn in the side of so many secondary school subject-matter teachers.

One final parting note: It was just beyond our conceptual reach (and way beyond our empirical evidence) to work out a level 4 in our conceptualization of comprehension instructional approaches. Whatever we do in level 4, it will involve a shift to an even broader view of context than is present in level 3 (which already includes reader, text, author, and social context). We see at least two big changes in level 4—what counts as text, and what counts as context. What counts as a text in level 3 remains largely a traditional written text, probably one that would most likely be encountered in schools. Many scholars and teachers have been at work trying to expand our notion of what counts as text, extending the construct to imaginal texts, electronic texts, hypermedia texts, and experiential texts—all of which would be in level 4. The biggest shift in thinking required in expanding the notion of text is the resulting expansion of the construct of intertextuality, which necessarily entails the juxtaposition of just about "everything" (very much in a Bakhtinian tradition). When the definition of comprehension instruction stretches to include guided activities not only in negotiating meaning with printed text in its local context but also in linking strings of meaning created in transaction with printed and other textual utterances, as well as in response to nonlinguistic elements, layers of instructional complexity emerge. Clearly, the requirements of long-term memory and socialization processes become central issues—learning as development, in short.

This expansion of the notion of text requires a parallel shift in our thinking about context, for it suggests that what is "read" as a text in one setting might well serve as context in another. Hence, what is text and what is context depends entirely on the purpose and focus of a particular reading situation. Another topic that has received much recent attention from scholars and teachers alike, family literacy, will also figure prominently in any interventions that qualify as level 4. As a dominant part of the context that is currently neither understood nor accommodated instructionally, family literacy and the related question of funds of knowledge, to borrow Moll's (1992) term (cultural and multicultural capital), will be privileged—and assessed—in level 4 instruction. That said, we are not quite sure where to go with level 4, because we cannot point readily to any clear programmatic instances of it. Even so, we mention it in the hope that we can interest others in working either in partnership or in parallel efforts to lay out and assess the efficacy of some exemplars.

REFERENCES

Adams, M. (1990). *Beginning to read.* Cambridge, MA: Harvard University Press.

Afflerbach, P., & Pressley, M. (1995). *Verbal protocols of reading: The nature of constructively responsive reading.* Hillsdale, NJ: Erlbaum.

Alvermann, D., & Phelps, S. (1998). *Content reading and literacy* (2nd ed). Needham Heights, MA: Allyn & Bacon.

Anderson, R. C., & Pearson, P.D. (1984). A schema-theoretic view of basic processes in reading. In P. D. Pearson (Ed.), *Handbook of reading research* (pp. 255–291). Elmsford, NY: Longman.

Anderson, R. C., Wilson, P., & Fielding, L. (1988). Growth in reading and how children spend their time outside of school. *Reading Research Quarterly, 30*(3), 285–303.

Baker, L. (2002). Metacognition in comprehension instruction. In C. C. Block & M. Pressley (Eds.), *Comprehension instruction: Research-based best practices* (pp. 77–95). New York: Guilford Press.

Beck, I., McKeown, M. G., Hamilton, R., & Kucan, L. (1997). *Questioning the author: An approach for enhancing student engagement with text.* Newark, DE: International Reading Association.

Bereiter, C., & Scardamalia, M. (1987). An attainable version of high literacy: Approaches to teaching higher-order skills in reading and writing. *Curriculum Inquiry, 17*(1), 9–29.

Block, C. C., & Pressley, M. (Eds.). (2002). *Comprehension instruction: Research-based best practices.* New York: Guilford Press.

Brown, R. (2002). Scaffolding two worlds: Self-directed comprehension instruction for middle schoolers. In C. C. Block & M. Pressley (Eds.), *Comprehension instruction: Research-based best practices* (pp. 337–350). New York: Guilford Press.

California Department of Education. (2000). *Strategic teaching and learning: Standards-based instruction to promote content literacy in grades four through twelve.* Sacramento: Author.

California Department of Education. (2002). DataQuest. Retrieved February, 2002, from *http://data1.cde.ca.gov/dataquest*

Claggett, F. (1996). *A measure of success: From assignment to assessment in English language arts.* Portsmouth, NH: Heinemann.

Cole, M. (1995). The supra-individual envelope of development: Activity and practice, situation and context. *New Directions for Child Development, 67,* 105–118.

Collins, A., Brown, J. S., & Duguid, P. (1989). Situated cognition and the culture of learning. *Educational Researcher, 18*(1), 32–42.

Commeyras, M., & Alvermann, D. (1996). Reading about women in world history textbooks from one feminist perspective. *Gender and Education, 8*(1), 31–48.

Covington, M. (1992). *Making the grade: A self-worth perspective on motivation and school reform.* New York: Cambridge University Press.

Davey, B. (1988). How do classroom teachers use their textbooks? *Journal of Reading, 31,* 340–345.

Destefano, L., Pearson, P. D., & Afflerbach, P. (1997). Content validation of the 1994 NAEP in reading: Assessing the relationship between the 1994 assessment and the reading framework. In R. Linn, R. Glaser, & G. Bohrnstedt (Eds.), *Assessment in transition: 1994 trial state assessment report on reading: Background studies* (pp. 1–50). Stanford, CA: National Academy of Education.

Dole, J., Duffy, G., Roehler, L., & Pearson, P. D. (1991). Moving from the old to the new: Research on reading comprehension instruction. *Review of Educational Research, 61*(2), 239–264.

Duke, N., & Pearson, P. D. (2002). Effective practices for developing reading comprehension. In A. Farstrup & J. Samuels (Eds.), *What research has to say about reading instruction* (3rd ed., pp. 205–242). Newark, DE: International Reading Association.

Dweck, C., & Leggett, E. (1988). A social-cognitive approach to motivation and personality. *Psychological Review, 95*(2), 256–273.

Gee, J. (1996). *Social linguistics and literacies: Ideologies in discourse.* London, UK: Falmer Press.

Geertz, C. (1983). *Local knowledge: Further essays in interpretive anthropology.* New York: Basic Books.

Greenleaf, C., Jiménez, R., & Roller, K. (2002). Conversations: Reclaiming secondary reading interventions: From limited to rich conceptions, from narrow to broad conversations. *Reading Research Quarterly, 37*(4), 484–496.

Greenleaf, C., Schoenbach, R., Cziko, C., & Mueller, F. (2001). Apprenticing adolescent readers to academic literacy. *Harvard Educational Review, 71*(1), 79–129.

Hayamizu, T., & Weiner, B. (1991). A test of Dweck's model of achievement goals as related to perceptions of ability. *Journal of Experimental Education, 59*(3), 226–234.

Jackson, S., & Brashers, D. (1994). *Random factors in ANOVA* (Sage University Paper series on Quantitative Applications in the Social Sciences, No. 07–098). Thousand Oaks, CA: Sage.

Kintsch, W. (1998). *Comprehension: A paradigm for cognition.* New York: Cambridge University Press.

Kucan, L., & Beck, I. (1997). Thinking aloud and reading comprehension research: Inquiry, instruction, and social interaction. *Review of Educational Research, 67*(3), 271–299.

Langer, J. (1985). Levels of questioning: An alternative view. *Reading Research Quarterly, 20*(5), 586–602.

Langer, J. (1987). Envisionment: A reader-based view of comprehension. *California Reader, 20*(3), 4–6.

Langer, J. (1989). *The process of understanding literature* (Center for the Learning and Teaching of Literature, Report Series 2.1). Albany, State University of New York.

Langer, J. A. (2001). Beating the odds: Teaching middle and high school students to read and write well. *American Educational Research Journal, 38*(4), 837–880.

Lave, J., & Wenger, E. (1991). *Situated learning: Legitimate peripheral participation.* New York: Cambridge University Press.

Linn, R., Glaser, B., & Bohrnstedt, G. (Eds.). (1997). *Assessment in transition: 1994 Trial State Assessment Report on Reading: Background studies.* Stanford, CA: National Academy of Education.

Lortie, D. (1975). *Schoolteacher: A sociological study.* Chicago: University of Chicago Press.

Meyer, B. J. F., Brandt, D., & Bluth, G. (1980). Use of top-level structure in text: Key for reading comprehension of ninth grade students. *Reading Research Quarterly, 16,* 72–103.

Midgley, C. (1993). Motivation and middle level schools. In M. Maehr & P. Pintrich (Eds.), *Advances in motivation and achievement: Motivation and adolescent development* (pp. 217–275). Greenwich, CT: JAI Press.

Moll, L., & Greenberg, J. (1992). Creating zones of possibilities: Combining social contexts for instruction. In L. Moll (Ed.), *Vygotksy and education.* New York: Cambridge University Press.

Murphy, S., & Underwood, T. L. (2000). *Portfolio practices: Lessons from schools, districts, and states.* Norwood, MA: Christopher-Gordon.

Nicholls, J., Cobb, P., Wood, T., Yackel, E., & Patashnick, M. (1990). Assessing students' theories of success in mathematics: Individual and classroom differences. *Journal for Research in Mathematics Education, 21*(2), 109–122.

O'Brien, D. G. (2001, June). "At-risk" adolescents: Redefining competence through the multiliteracies of intermediality, visual arts, and representation. *Reading Online, 4*(11). Available at *http://www.readingonline.org/newliteracies/lit_index.asp?*

Ochs, E. (1996). Linguistic resources for socializing humanity. In J. J. Gumperz & S. C. Levenson (Eds.), *Rethinking linguistic relativity* (pp. 407–437). New York: Cambridge University Press.

Olson, C. B. (2003). *Teaching strategic reading and analytical writing to English language learners in secondary school: Curricular approaches from the Pathway Project.* Report for the U.S. Department of Education, Office of English Language Acquisition.

Palinscar, A. S., & Brown, A. L. (1983). *Reciprocal teaching of comprehension-monitoring activities* (Technical Report No. 269). Cambridge, MA: Bolt, Beranek, & Newman.

Paxton, R. (1999). A deafening silence: History textbooks and the students who read them. *Review of Educational Research, 69*(3), 315–339.

Pearson, P. D., & Duke, N. (2002). Comprehension instruction in the primary grades. In C. C. Block & M. Pressley (Eds.), *Comprehension instruction: Research-based best practices* (pp. 247–258). New York: Guilford Press.

Pearson, P. D., & Gallagher, M. C. (1983). The instruction of reading comprehension. *Contemporary Educational Psychology, 8,* 317–344.

Pressley, M. (1998): *Reading instruction that works: The case for balanced teaching.* New York: Guilford Press.

Raphael, T. (1982). Question-answering strategies for children. *Reading Teacher, 36,* 186–191.

Raphael, T. (1984). Teaching learners about sources of information for answering comprehension questions. *Journal of Reading, 27,* 303–311.

Raphael, T. (1986). Teaching question–answer relationships. *Reading Teacher, 39,* 516–520.

Rogers, R. (2002). Between contexts: A critical discourse analysis of family literacy, discursive practices, and literate subjectivities. *Reading Research Quarterly, 37*(3), 248–277.

Rosenblatt, L. (1978). *The reader, the text, the poem: The transactional theory of the literary work.* Carbondale: Southern Illinois University Press.

Rosenblatt, L. (1983). *Literature as exploration* . New York: Modern Language Association of America. (Original work published 1938)

Sarroub, L. (2002). In-betweenness: Religion and conflicting visions of literacy. *Reading Research Quarterly, 37*(2), 130–149.

Schoenbach, R., Greenleaf, C., Cziko, C., & Hurwitz, L. (1999). *Reading for understanding: A guide to improving reading in middle and high school classrooms.* San Francisco: Jossey-Bass.

Smagorinsky, P. (2001). If meaning is constructed, what is it made from?: Toward a cultural theory of reading. *Review of Educational Research, 71*(1), 133–169.

Smagorinsky, P. (1998). Thinking and speech and protocol analysis. *Mind, Culture, and Activity, 5*(3), 157–177.

Street, B. (1984). *Literacy in theory and practice.* New York: Cambridge University Press.

Street, B. (Ed.). (1993). *Cross-cultural approaches to literacy.* New York: Cambridge University Press.

Taylor, B. (1980). Children's memory of expository text after reading. *Reading Research Quarterly, 15,* 399–411.

Underwood, T. (1996). Introduction and interpretive summaries. In *NCTE middle school portfolio tool kit.* Urbana, IL: National Council of Teachers of English.

Underwood, T. (1998). The consequences of portfolio assessment: A case study. *Educational Assessment, 5*(3), 147–194.

Underwood, T. (1999). *The portfolio project: Assessment, instruction, and the realities of school reform.* Urbana, IL: National Council of Teachers of English.

Underwood, T., Murphy, S., & Pearson, P. D. (1995). The Paradox of Portfolios. *Iowa English Bulletin, 43,* 73–86.

Wilhelm, J. (1996). *"You gotta BE the book": Teaching engaged and reflective reading with adolescents.* New York: Teachers College Press.

Wolf, D. (1987–1988). Opening up assessment. *Educational Leadership, 45*(4), 24–29.

Helping Adolescent Readers through Explicit Strategy Instruction

JEFFERY D. NOKES
JANICE A. DOLE

Last year, a prospective teacher completed his student teaching in the Social Studies department at Jeff's high school. He was eager to glean what he could from each of the teachers and spent time observing every classroom. One afternoon, he popped into Jeff's history class as Jeff was discussing with students ways that they could use their textbook structure to get the most out of their study time. At the end of class, the student teacher told Jeff what a great idea it was to teach students about the textbook, commenting that he wished someone had taught him how to use the textbook better when he was a high school student. Jeff responded that almost everyone wishes that he or she would have been taught while in high school how to use different study strategies, such as how to use textbooks to study.

This chapter is about *explicit strategy instruction*—instruction that explicitly teaches students how to use strategies such as how to use their textbooks to help them comprehend and learn better. The goal of the chapter is to provide the research foundation, as well as practical considerations, for teaching strategies to middle and high school students.

Why do students need explicit strategy instruction? After all, it is true that some students figure out certain strategies themselves, without help and assistance from teachers. Think how many of us figured out how to study without explicit instruction. As most of us spent our first and second year in college, we learned how to study—largely through trial and error. However, wouldn't most of us have preferred being taught, very explicitly and clearly, *how to study* in high school? Most of us would reply with an enthusiastic "Yes!" Early college life would have been easier. So it is with many high school students, most of whom would benefit from explicit strategy instruction.

But there is an even more important reason to teach strategies to students. Many students will not figure out strategies on their own. So if someone does not teach them, they will never learn them. How many students enter college and drop out, not because they party too much, but because no one taught them how to study and they did not learn how to do it on their own? How many high school students fail their biology tests, not because they cannot read their textbooks but because no one taught them how to sort out the relevant from the irrelevant information? Or because no one taught them how to look for what the teacher thought was important as opposed to what they themselves thought was important?

In this chapter, we look at explicit strategy instruction and how it can assist students, especially struggling readers, in comprehending and learning better. We discuss the research that forms the foundation of explicit strategy instruction. As we do this, we discuss the dimensions of teaching strategies explicitly, and how those dimensions assist readers in gaining the knowledge they need to use strategies as they read. Next, we consider the research studies on specific programs designed to teach strategies to students. We conclude with some final reflections on the use of strategy instruction for high school students.

FOUNDATIONS OF EXPLICIT STRATEGY INSTRUCTION

Three concepts are foundational to explicit strategy instruction: (1) comprehension strategies, (2) metacognition, and (3) explicit instruction. We discuss each of these concepts and how they apply to readers' ability to comprehend text.

Comprehension Strategies

Over the last quarter-century, there has been an explosive increase in reading comprehension research. During this time, and even today, the definition of *comprehension strategy* has undergone numerous revisions. Some researchers have described specific actions taken by a reader to make sense of text, such as the use of visual imagery (Gambrell & Bales, 1986) or the generation of questions (Davey & McBride, 1986). Other researchers have described strategies, not as isolated skills but as configurations of tactics used to accomplish a reading task (Wade, Woodrow, & Schraw, 1990). Today, most researchers agree with the latter definition, favoring multiple components of comprehension simultaneously as collections of tactics rather than specific behaviors (Duffy, 2002; Duffy et al., 1987; Pressley, 2002).

Strategies can be distinguished from skills in numerous ways. First, skills are often drilled to the point of automaticity, whereas strategies are used consciously and intentionally. Skills generally involve more specific behaviors than do strategies. For example, discovering the main idea of a passage would be considered a strategy, whereas deleting trivial material, which is useful in finding the main idea, would be considered a skill. Reading instruction at the middle and secondary levels traditionally have taught skills rather than strategies (Dole, 2000).

Much of the research on reading comprehension has attempted to identify what strategies proficient readers use. Studies have compared experts and novices to find out what specific behaviors experts exhibit that novices do not (Bransford, Vye, & Stein, 1984). Over the years, an extensive list of strategies has been developed. Paris, Wasik, and Turner (1991) showed that expert readers employ strategies before, during, and after reading. Pearson, Roehler, Dole, and Duffy (1991) listed seven strategies that distinguish proficient from struggling readers. Good readers activate and use relevant prior knowledge to make sense of text. They monitor their comprehension as they read and repair comprehension when it breaks down. Good readers determine what is important in a text passage and attempt to synthesize information across large portions of text. They continuously make inferences and ask questions as they read.

Pressley (2000, 2002) decomposed these strategies into some of their component skills. He contended that good readers set a purpose for reading and keep this purpose in mind as they read. They preview the text to see whether it is relevant to their purpose before they begin reading, and they read selectively, skipping passages that are irrelevant. Good readers use the context of novel words to interpret their meaning. They use mental imagery and create summaries as they proceed. They often read forward and backward in a text rather than linearly. Good readers make predictions and evaluate them as they proceed through a passage. They take steps to remember what they read. Good readers make numerous interpretations and evaluate the accuracy and worth of a text. They mentally review text after reading.

Trabasso and Bouchard (2002) described trained readers' use of graphic organizers, mnemonic devices, and text structure to improve comprehension and recall of items in a text. Numerous studies have produced verbal protocols as expert readers have thought aloud during the reading process and revealed their normally hidden cognitive processes. Pressley and Afflerbach (1995) have reviewed the verbal protocol research and written an extensive description of comprehension strategies that have been revealed by expert readers in these protocol studies. Lists of strategies are also provided in a literature reviews by Afflerbach (2002) and by Palincsar and Brown (1984).

Metacognition

> Being strategic is not a skill that can be taught by drill; it is a method of approach to reading and reading instruction. Much more than knowing a strategy, being strategic calls for coordinating individual strategies, altering, adjusting, modifying, testing, and shifting tactics as is fitting until a reading comprehension problem has been solved. (Trabasso & Bouchard, 2002, p. 186)

Metacognition is the consideration, monitoring and control of one's cognitive activities (Baker, 1994; Flavel, 1979; Paris, Cross, & Lipson, 1984). It includes an understanding of ourselves, our task and available strategies (Baker, 2002; Garner, 1992; Gourgey, 1998). Gourgey (1998) has provided helpful elaboration on each of these elements of metacognition. Knowing ourselves includes knowing how we learn, knowing when we do or do not understand, and knowing our strengths and weaknesses. Knowing our task involves an awareness of the nature of the task, its difficulty, and its demands in regard to time and cognitive resources. Knowing strategies involves an awareness of cognitive activities in which we can engage to increase the likelihood of our success.

Nicholson (1984) suggests that less proficient readers do not understand themselves and the difficulty of the task they face. Perhaps what distinguishes proficient from struggling readers, then, is their level of strategic knowledge. Proficient readers know when they know, and they know when they do not know. On the other hand, struggling readers do not know when they know, and they do not know when they do not know.

A proficient reader's metacognitive and cognitive elements interact during self-regulated reading through the *monitoring* and *control* of comprehension (Hacker, 1998). During monitoring, students' cognitive and metacognitive elements inform them regarding the success or failure of cognitive operations. When comprehension is proceeding smoothly, the cognitive element works relatively unchecked. Things "click" (Garner, 1992). When a problem arises, students' metacognitive level informs them of a problem. Things "clunk" (Garner, 1992). At this stage, the metacognitive level begins to inform the cognitive level and take control of the comprehension process. Self-regulated comprehension proceeds as strategies are employed to correct the problem that has been detected (Hacker, 1998). Strategy training provides less proficient readers with a repertoire of measures to fix-up comprehension problems.

But strategic knowledge does not *guarantee* the proper application and use of strategies. It is through metacognition that strategies are selected and put to use. Schraw (1998) contends that a teacher can improve students' metacognitive abilities by making them aware of the existence of metacognition; teaching them strategies and how to evaluate strategies; showing them how to regulate, adapt, and adjust strategies; and fostering a metacognitive environment by attributing student success to strategy use.

Thus, some of the cognitive behaviors described as strategies, such as monitoring comprehension and applying fix-up strategies, can be considered metacognitive in nature. Metacognition applies to the other cognitive strategies, in that through metacognition, an individual recognizes the need for a strategy, weighs potential strategies, determines which strategy to apply, adjusts strategies to meet the needs of specific situations, and evaluates the effectiveness and efficiency of strategy use.

Explicit Strategy Instruction

In the early stages of explicit strategy research, Roehler and Duffy (1984) compared and contrasted two teachers in regard to the explicitness of their strategy instruction. They noticed key differences between the two teachers and developed a teaching model based on the methods used by the teacher they perceived to be superior. This teacher explained mental processes to the students and explained why the processes helped. He was proactive, in that he spent the beginning of the lesson discussing strategies with the students, anticipating possible problems, and forewarning students about potential pitfalls before giving them an opportunity to practice. The other teacher was more reactive, providing little instruction at the outset of the lesson, and spending more time correcting problems as they occurred. The researchers thought the flow of the first teacher's lesson was much better, with explanations followed by guided practice and corrective feedback. Since that time, much explicit strategy instruction has been based on this model originally discerned by Roehler and Duffy.

Roehler and Duffy (1984), as well as numerous other researchers, have pointed out the need for students to be taught the *declarative, procedural,* and *conditional knowledge* associated with reading strategies (Afflerbach, 2002; Duffy, 2002; Ogle & Blachowicz, 2002; Paris et al., 1984; Pearson & Dole, 1987; Pearson et al., 1991). *Declarative knowledge* is knowing what the strategy is called. Having a common label for the strategy allows students and teachers to discuss the strategy openly, with a mutual understanding. *Procedural knowledge* is the awareness of how to apply the strategy. Readers with procedural knowledge know what must be done to use a strategy. *Conditional knowledge* is an awareness of when and where a strategy may be useful. Conditional knowledge leads to flexible strategy use, because readers with conditional knowledge are more likely to transfer strategies to unique settings (Baker, 2002).

Conditional knowledge also includes an affective component. Readers must have some awareness of the utility value of a strategy. Because strategy use is often demanding, students are not likely to engage in a strategy unless they are convinced that it will help them succeed (Baker, 1994; Garner, 1992; Gourgey, 1998). Thus, strategy use involves not only cognitive and metacognitive elements but also a motivational component.

Roehler and Duffy's (1984) original model of instruction has provided a framework for the explicit teaching of strategies. Vygotsky's research on social interaction, particularly his concept of the zone of proximal development, has also been influential (Baker, 1994). According to the concept of zone of proximal development, the optimal difficulty level of a task is beyond the learner's ability to complete the task, but not beyond his or her ability to complete the task with the help of a more capable individual. Optimal learning activities are located within this zone. Teachers and peers provide various types of support for learners as they engage in activities with which they need help. Typical comprehension strategy lessons organize this support in the form of (1) explicit training, including teacher modeling; (2) guided practice; and (3) independent practice. In the next section, we describe each of these stages in some detail, then give a general description of some of the characteristics of explicit strategy instruction.

Explicit Training and Teacher Modeling

Almost all researchers agree that in the earliest stages of a lesson, the teacher should provide support by giving explanations of a strategy in a sensible and meaningful manner (Afflerbach, 2002; Baker, 1994, 2002; Duffy, 2002; Ogle & Blachowicz, 2002; Paris et al., 1984; Pearson & Dole, 1987; Pressley et al., 1994). Roehler and Duffy's (1984) study revealed that the more effective strategy lessons begin with a great deal of teacher talk. It is during this stage of the lesson that teachers make sure students possess declarative, procedural, and conditional knowledge concerning strategies.

Teachers are very explicit in their instruction. Students know the name of the strategy. They are told how to use the strategy and given examples of when the strategy might be useful both within and outside the current setting. Teachers may discuss possible adjustments to the strategy to meet different task demands. The instrumental value of the strategy is also made clear. Teachers may go to great lengths to convince students that the use of the strategy is worth the effort. All of this is typically done at the beginning of the lesson.

Different studies have employed either a lecture or a discussion format during the training phase of the lesson. Literature reviews do not recommend one format over the other. Teachers using either lecture or discussion, or a combination of the two, have been equally successful in promoting students' use of strategies.

Researchers also recommend that teachers model the use of strategies as part of their explicit instruction (Baker, 1994; Collins & Smith, 1982; Duffy, Roehler, & Hermann, 1988; Pearson & Dole, 1987; Pressley, 2002; Pressley et al., 1994). In a review of the literature on explicit instruction, Duffy et al. (1988) give a thorough description of teacher modeling. They explain that teachers should reveal to the students the invisible mental processes used by expert readers. Teachers can accomplish this by pausing and thinking aloud as they read. Students observe as the teacher decides which strategy to use and employs the strategy. Although teachers may focus on an individual strategy at times, they can also demonstrate the flexible nature of strategy use by moving from one strategy to another as needed. This is a good way to review strategies that have been taught earlier and preview strategies that will be taught later. More importantly, it shows students metacognition in action as the teacher considers out loud which strategy may be employed to solve the current comprehension challenge.

Researchers have experimented with different aspects of thinking aloud. Silven and Vauras (1992) hypothesized that students might benefit from teacher modeling of incorrect ways of thinking or using strategies in order to make them aware of common comprehension problems. However, they found that including incorrect modeling and other minute differences in the nature of thinking aloud did not affect students' performance after a short (6-week) training period. Other researchers have found that modeling is most effective when combined with explicit instruction. Bereiter and Bird (1985) found that students did not benefit from teacher modeling, unless it was accompanied by explicit training.

However, it appears that thinking aloud is extremely important, because it reveals to struggling readers that even skilled readers are faced with comprehension challenges. Think-alouds demonstrate the flexible use of strategies, remind students about the specific steps involved in a strategy, and make otherwise invisible reading practices apparent to struggling readers who would otherwise lack strategic knowledge.

Guided Practice

In the next phase of explicit strategy instruction, guided practice, some researchers are emphatic about the need for students to have time to practice a strategy with assistance from the teacher and peers (Pearson & Dole, 1987; Pressley, 2002; Rosenshine & Meister, 1997; Silven & Vauras, 1992). Other researchers describe the gradual release of responsibility from the teacher to the student (Pearson & Gallagher, 1983). In other words, as the period of guided practice proceeds, the teacher takes a less active role and the student takes a more active role in both cognitive activity and metacognitive choices. Silven and Vauras (1992) found that extensive teacher guidance of student think-alouds during a period of guided practice resulted in greater transfer of strategy use.

The term *scaffolding* is often used to describe the temporary, adjustable, removable support that teachers provide for students. Rosenshine and Meister (1997) provide a comprehensive description of the scaffolding that a teacher might provide for struggling students. They argue that scaffolding bridges the gap between the student's current abilities and the intended learning goal. They suggest that teachers can accomplish this by reducing the complexity of an activity; breaking a challenging activity down into simplified steps; completing part of a task for students; forewarning students of common errors; providing simple reading materials; giving checklists, cue cards, or other procedural prompts; reverting to explicit instruction or modeling as needed; or allowing small groups of students to practice a strategy together.

Other researchers agree that allowing students to work in groups is critical during the guided practice phase of explicit strategy instruction. Social collaboration has been shown to be extremely motivating in regard to strategy use (Guthrie, Anderson, Alao, & Rhinehart, 1999; Swan, 2003). Pressley (2002) contends that small-group practice is a key to the internalization of a strategy. It seems that students working in groups are forced to defend their choice of strategy and to explain their cognitive processes. Such interaction provides a review of the declarative, conditional and procedural knowledge for both the explainer and the listener. Hacker (1998) contends that the interaction between an individual's metacognitive and cognitive functioning is a closed system. This creates the possibility of the reinforcement of errors in both content and strategic knowledge. The learner may think that he or she understands, when in reality, he or she does not. Allowing students to work in groups provides learners with a source of feedback outside of their closed system, increasing the likelihood that errors will be detected and corrected.

The possible types of activities that can be used during guided practice are limited only by the teacher's imagination. Brown (2002) recommends that teachers provide students with *inconsiderate* text (i.e., text that is incoherent or assumes that readers have more prior knowledge than they do) during periods of guided practice. By doing so, teachers give the students real-world practice, while providing them with scaffolding. As time proceeds, the teacher takes a less active role in students' practice. Eventually, the teacher may assume simply a corrective role, interceding only when students make a mistake (Collins & Smith, 1982).

(handwritten margin note: what about could build? Endur?)

Independent Practice

In the final phase of strategy instruction, independent practice, teachers provide students with the opportunity to practice a strategy without assistance. This may be done through homework reading assignments or individual in-class work. Researchers contend that independent practice is essential if students are to internalize strategies and apply them in new situations (Baker, 1994; Ogle & Blachowicz, 2002; Pressley, 2002). Students can see whether they really understand and can use the strategy. One of the key elements of independent practice is the opportunity to transfer strategies to new situations. Effective independent practice activities increase the chance that transfer will occur.

General Characteristics of Explicit Strategy Instruction

The numerous literature reviews on explicit strategy instruction agree on several fundamental characteristics of effective instruction:

- *Effective strategy instruction is flexible and opportunistic.* Teachers move back and forth from strategy to strategy according to students' needs and the opportunities that arise in class. Teachers constantly monitor student progress through formal and informal means. They may repeat any of the phases of instruction listed earlier as needs arise. Teachers regularly model metacognitive activity and strategy use. They repeat explanations of behaviors associated with strategies as needed. They provide multiple opportunities for students to practice. They are constantly trying to motivate students to use strategies by reminding them of the instrumental value of the strategies. Lessons are not scripted but emerge through the recognition of students' needs and the opportunities that arise as teachers and students engage with various texts. Although the same text may be read 2 years in a row, the direction that a lesson takes may be completely different.

• *Effective strategy instruction deals with not only multiple strategies but also relatively few strategies* (Anderson & Roit, 1993; Pressley, 2002; Sinatra, Brown, & Reynolds, 2002). In order for students to become metacognitive, they must have a repertoire of strategies from which to choose. They are not being metacognitive if every time they experience a comprehension challenge, they employ visual imagery to try to correct the problem. Although teachers may choose to focus on a single strategy during a lesson, they should model the metacognitive activity associated with selecting and employing the best strategy to compensate for the current comprehension challenge in every lesson. This can only be accomplished when students are aware of more than one strategy. Researchers warn, however, that teaching too many strategies may overwhelm students' cognitive resources (Anderson & Roit, 1993; Sinatra et al., 2002). If too many strategies are taught, students may have a large repertoire of strategies that they do not know when or how to use effectively.

• *Effective strategy instruction takes time.* Students should not be expected to grasp a strategy fully after a single lesson. Explicit training, modeling, and practice should be an ongoing process throughout the school year (Ogle & Blachowicz, 2002). In fact, some strategy training programs have focused on relatively few strategies over several years of training (El-Dinary, 2002; Pressley et al., 1994). Studies on the effects of strategy instruction, with very few exceptions, have generally taken weeks to show any results, and months to show long-term adoption of strategic reading.

• *Explicit strategy instruction has not occurred in America's schools in the past and is not happening in many schools today* (Baker, 2002; Dole, 2000; Durkin, 1979; Ogle & Blachowicz, 2002; Paris et al., 1984: Pearson & Dole, 1987; Pressley, 2002). Traditionally one of the most common methods of "instruction" has been the IRE model. The teacher *initiates* interaction with a student by asking a question, the student *responds*, and the teacher *evaluates* the student's response. There is no formal instruction according to this model, simply a chance for students to try out an answer and find out whether it was correct. For many years this model has dominated reading instruction. Durkin (1979) observed hundreds of hours of classroom instruction and was appalled by the lack of comprehension instruction. Recently, there have been some changes in comprehension instruction. Pressley (2002) observed that the publication and widespread use of the teacher training book *Mosaic of Thought* (Keene & Zimmermann, 1997) has increased teachers' awareness and excitement about strategy instruction. But the lack of a specific teaching model in *Mosaic of Thought* has left many teachers floundering, with the desire but not the know–how to teach strategies effectively.

RESEARCH ON STRATEGY INSTRUCTION

Research on strategy instruction has undergone two major phases (Pressley, 2000). The earliest studies of the 1970s and early 1980s often investigated whether students could be trained to use a single strategy in a relatively short amount of time. Some of these early studies included no real training but simply the suggestion of a certain strategy to students. In the mid-1980s, researchers began to consider the use of strategies from a more holistic perspective. Coherent packages of strategies were taught with the use of experimental methods of instruction. Metacognitive training sometimes accompanied the teaching of repertoires of strategies. In this section, we review a sample of the numerous studies that have (1) encouraged strategy use without training, (2) trained students in the use of a single strategy, and (3) taught students multiple strategies.

Strategy-Encouraging Studies

Numerous researchers have investigated the teaching of individual strategies. Baker (1984) used embedded inconsistencies in a text to study students' monitoring of their comprehension. Half of the students were warned specifically about the types of problems, while a control group was given the generic instruction to look for problems in the text. Baker discovered that specific warnings about the problems benefited better readers more than it helped poorer readers. Baker concluded that skilled readers are able to pick up a strategy quickly. She warns that this type of rapid, one-shot training could result in poorer readers falling further behind their more proficient peers. Other researchers however have found that both struggling and proficient readers have made moderate gains in their ability to comprehend texts after simply being told to generate mental images (Guttmann, Levin, & Pressley, 1977) or to produce self-explanations periodically while reading (Chi, DeLeeuw, Chiu, & LaVancher, 1994).

Individual Strategy-Training Studies

Numerous other researchers have studied the effects of more extensive training in an individual strategy on student comprehension. The National Reading Panel's (2000) meta-analysis of reading instruction reveals that explicit instruction in visual imagery, comprehension monitoring, and question generating, among other strategies, yielded positive results.

Visual Imagery

Several studies have been conducted to determine the value of teaching children to create visual imagery. Gambrell and Bales (1986) worked with 124 poor readers in fifth grade. Half of this group was given 30 minutes of training and practice in the creation of mental imagery. The other 62 children did not receive the training. The following day, both the trained and untrained students were given two texts with embedded problems. The young readers that had been trained in visual imagery detected the inconsistencies at a much higher rate than did those who had not been trained. The trained group reported using mental imagery as a strategy during the reading. Few students in the untrained group reported using visual imagery. Gambrell and Bales concluded that the strategy of visual imagery is not employed spontaneously by many students, can be taught relatively easily, and can be an effective tool for improving comprehension. Struggling students should be introduced to and trained in this basic strategy.

Comprehension Monitoring

Baker and Zimlin (1989) wondered whether training would improve fourth-grade students' monitoring of their comprehension. Above-average and average fourth-grade readers who participated in this study were assigned to one of three groups. Two groups received 20–30 minutes of training on the recognition of two different types of text problems. The third group received no training. Students were then given two texts, with different types of problems, to read. Baker and Zimlin found that students were most skillful in the recognition of the problems for which they had been trained. However, students who had been trained to look for either type of problem tended to recognize the types of problems in the text for which they had not been trained more often than did the control group. The researchers conclude that training students to recognize problems in a text helps them realize that texts are not infallible. This realization leads readers to become more critical of text and more aware of problems in the text, even when they have not been trained to look specifically for the types of problems they encounter. Although the students who had undergone training did better than those who had not been trained, a discouragingly low percentage of all students successfully recognized the embedded problems in the text, probably due in part to the short duration of the training.

Question Generation

Davey and McBride (1986) conducted a study on the effects of question-generation training on sixth-grade students. Five 40-minute training sessions were conducted over a 2-week period. Training focused on teaching students how to ask questions that connected information across sentences and highlighted the main ideas. Training consisted of explicit instruction, practice, and feedback. Trained students were compared with students who had practiced answering either literal questions or inferential questions instead of training. They found that the trained students outperformed both the students who had practiced literal questions and those who had practiced inferential questions on a posttest that required them to answer inferential questions. Trained students outperformed the students who had practiced answering inferential questions and did as well as those who had practiced answering literal questions on a literal question posttest. They seemed to be more metacognitive, as determined by their awareness of their comprehension. They knew what they knew and what they did not know in more cases than did the students who had not been trained to generate questions. They wrote higher quality questions that connected concepts globally and focused on main ideas rather than on trivial material. Training seemed to help poor and good readers alike. The researchers concluded that training in question generation is a worthwhile activity. Practice in answering questions does not promote strategic reading, deep processing, or metacognitive awareness as much as does creating questions.

Several patterns are apparent in the research on the teaching of individual strategies. First, strategy instruction is generally short term, lasting from a few minutes to a couple of weeks in length. Second, strategy instruction involves a limited use of the explicit teaching model described earlier. Teachers may explain or model the strategy and provide opportunities for guided or independent practice, but they generally have not incorporated all of the elements of explicit strategy instruction. Third, strategy instruction generally does not include metacognitive elements. Students may be taught the declarative and procedural knowledge, but are rarely taught the conditional knowledge required for them to be metacognitive about strategy selection. Beyond this, the instrumental value of the strategy is rarely discussed. We doubt the likelihood of students transferring strategic knowledge from one setting to another without metacognitive training. Fourth, surprisingly, the studies on the teaching of individual strategies have demonstrated improved student comprehension and recall. In most cases, students who are taught individual strategies have been shown to monitor their comprehension better, process texts more deeply, read more critically, and become more aware of their own comprehension, at least under experimental conditions. It would be interesting to see whether students in these experiments transferred strategies to unique settings or continued to use the strategies for a long period of time.

Integrated Strategy Instruction

Since the mid–1980s researchers have begun to investigate the teaching of packages of strategies to students. Trabasso and Bouchard (2002) contend that the teaching of multiple strategies at once is very powerful, claiming that "there is strong empirical, scientific evidence that the instruction of more than one strategy in a natural context leads to the acquisition and use of reading comprehension strategies and transfer" (p. 184). We now discuss some of the research and instructional models that led to these conclusions, including early multiple strategy research, reciprocal teaching, informed strategies for learning, collaborative strategy instruction, transactional strategy instruction, and several other instructional models.

Early Multiple-Strategy Research

As described earlier, Roehler and Duffy (1984) conducted a study contrasting the explicitness of two teachers. As a follow-up to that study, they attempted to train other teachers to follow the model of the more effective teacher. Three trained teachers and three untrained teachers were observed over an 8-week period. It was found that the trained teachers were not equally successful in applying the concepts learned in the training sessions. One of the trained teachers had such management difficulties that he was not able to apply much from the training. A second teacher applied some aspects of the training, while the third teacher was able to follow the teaching model with great precision. The researchers found that students in both the control teachers' classes and those of the teacher with management difficulties improved very little in reading comprehension. The students in the second trained teacher's class made moderate improvements. The students of the teacher who was able to follow the model improved dramatically. The researchers admit that the small sample size and numerous other confounding variables make the reliability of their study questionable. However, they contend that the patterns they discovered in this trail-blazing study should promote further investigation into teacher training and explicit strategy instruction. Indeed, it has.

Bereiter and Bird (1985) conducted a two-part study involving the teaching of multiple strategies. In their first study, they analyzed the verbal protocols of adult readers who thought aloud while reading several texts. From these protocols, it was determined that adults employed four teachable strategies while reading, namely, formulating problems, backtracking, restating ideas, and demanding relationships. In a second study, they investigated whether modeling was enough to teach the strategies or whether explicit instruction was also needed. Eighty seventh and eight graders were assigned to one of four experimental groups. A control group received no training. A second group was given independent exercises involving the four target strategies. The teacher modeled the four strategies for the third group. The fourth group was given explicit instruction on the strategies as well as the chance to observe the teacher model the strategy. Bereiter and Bird found that students in the first three groups benefited little from their training; however, students who received both explicit instruction and a model improved in the four strategies. Bereiter and Bird concluded that modeling is not enough to ensure students' use of strategies. They argued that explicit instruction helped students attend to the relevant cognitive activities demonstrated in the modeling. However, in order for modeling to be effective, students should be given a description of the declarative, procedural, and conditional aspects of a strategy.

Reciprocal Teaching

A second, extremely influential early study was conducted by Palincsar and Brown (1984). Their often-cited research is particularly influential, because it provides an empirically supported yet practical instructional model. They considered four strategies that lie at the heart of reading comprehension, namely, summarization, questioning, predicting, and clarifying. A reciprocal teaching lesson began with the teacher modeling these four strategies during a discussion of text with a small group of students. As the discussion continued, the teacher would increasingly draw students into the dialogue. Eventually, one of the students would be designated discussion leader and the discussion would continue. The teacher would maintain an active role in the discussion as needed, but would gradually withdraw as the student leader properly modeled each of the four target strategies. Later researchers successfully added an element of explicit instruction that was lacking in Palincsar and Brown's original model (Anderson & Roit, 1993).

The results of reciprocal teaching are extremely promising. The types of questions and summaries students produce improves, as does the depth of the dialogue in which the small groups engage. Students employ the strategies in their other classes. Evidence suggests that the strategies are internalized. And these improvements last for months after the small-group sessions had ended. The poor readers in the original study went from below-average to average on comprehension tests. The research by

Palincsar and Brown (1984) has attracted significant attention from both the education and research communities.

Informed Strategies for Learning

At about the same time that Palincsar and Brown (1984) were developing reciprocal teaching, Paris et al. (1984) created an instructional model called informed strategies for learning (ISL). Like other researchers, this team was concerned about the lack of comprehension instruction in America's schools. The stated goals of their program were to increase children's meta-cognition and use of strategies. An important aspect of ISL was convincing children that strategies were of instrumental value and would improve their comprehension. Strategy training was conducted for 30 minutes twice a week over 4 months in several third- and fifth-grade classes. Target strategies included setting a purpose for reading, skimming, monitoring comprehension, and summarizing. Training included all of the major elements of explicit strategy instruction. Empirical studies of ISL reported benefits similar to that of reciprocal teaching (Paris et al., 1984; Pearson & Dole, 1987). Cloze and error-detection tasks showed that students' comprehension improved.

Collaborative Strategy Instruction

Researchers and teachers worked together to design an instructional model that has been labeled collaborative strategy instruction (Anderson & Roit, 1993; Baker, 2002; Duffy et al., 1987). The model was developed during three 3-hour sessions attended by researchers and teachers. Researchers brought strategic knowledge to these discussions. Teachers brought practical concerns and an awareness of students' immediate needs. In the end, teachers were provided principles to follow during strategy instruction rather than specific scripts or rules.

Although this model was a result of collaboration between researchers and teachers, it gets its name from the collaboration that takes place between teachers and students as strategies are explored. Collaborative strategy instruction focused on teachers and students working together to solve comprehension problems. The solution to these problems often involved the use of multiple strategies. Students, rather than the teacher, were sometimes the source of the strategies. Often, students spontaneously used unsophisticated forms of strategies that were refined during discussions with their teachers. Other researchers have found that students do not enter the classroom as blank slates when it comes to strategic knowledge (Wade et al., 1990). Students were encouraged to share a variety of their personal strategies, so that others could enlarge their repertoire based on the success of their peers. The entire process of instruction reinforced metacognitive activity by demonstrating the intentional, efficient, and flexible use of strategies. It not only gave students the freedom to construct their own interpretation of the text but also the freedom to construct their own repertoire of strategies. Collaborative strategy instruction resulted in significant paradigm shifts by both teachers and students as comprehension concerns were more commonly expressed and openly discussed in search of socially constructed solutions based on research-supported strategies.

Transactional Strategy Instruction

An instructional model similar to collaborative strategy instruction, called transactional strategy instruction, was designed by a coalition of researchers (El-Dinary, 2002; Pressley et al., 1994). Transactional strategy instruction gets its name from the social construction of meaning that occurs as a transaction takes place among readers, a text, their peers, and the teacher. Like other successful multiple-strategy instruction, transactional instruction encourages teachers to use explicit training on when, where, why, and how to employ strategies. The teacher models the strategies for the students. Multiple strategies, but not too many strategies, are taught in coordination with each other. Teachers provide scaffolding that is gradually removed, over the course of years of practice in some cases (Pressley et al., 1994). Teachers must be opportunistic, seizing teaching moments when they arise. Authentic texts are used. Lessons follow the flow of class discussions, with skilled teachers constantly monitoring students, determining their needs, and leading the lesson to address those needs. Although some teachers struggle with the demands of Transactional Strategy Instruction (El-Dinary, 2002), some elementary schools have chosen to promote it at all grade levels, with a gradual reduction of scaffolding over the years. This multiple-year approach to training contrasts sharply with the 20-minute training sessions employed by early researchers of individual strategy instruction. Transactional Strategy Instruction has also yielded positive results in regard to students' comprehension.

Other Instructional Models

Strategy instruction is an important element in several other instructional packages. One of the earliest empirically studied programs was the Kamehameha Early Education Project (KEEP) designed for use with Hawaiian students. This culturally sensitive instructional model used an inundation–discovery approach to teaching strategies. Students received little explicit instruction but, as in reciprocal teaching, were immersed in strategy use. It was hoped that students would discover and begin to use the strategies independently (Pearson & Dole, 1987). A recently designed instructional model, Concept-Oriented Reading Instruction (CORI), blends explicit strategy instruction with social collaboration, hands-on experiences, student autonomy, and the reading of multiple, authentic texts. Reading instruction takes place within the context of either science or social studies. Studies have shown that CORI is an effective way to build deep conceptual knowledge, while promoting strategic reading (Guthrie et al., 1999; Swan, 2003). Individual teachers who are aware of research on strategy instruction, or based on their own intuition, have also taught metacognitive strategies to their students without any formal instructional model (Gourgey, 1998).

CONCLUSIONS

Researchers have collected much evidence that supports explicit strategy instruction. As teachers and researchers, we have observed firsthand the effects of strategy instruction on students. When we began our careers, we had the same attitude that many secondary teachers have: The elementary years are for students to *learn to read*, but at the secondary level, students should *read to learn*. We have found that there are numerous students who struggle to make sense of the challenging and sometimes inconsiderate texts adolescents face. Hearing secondary teachers lament year after year that "these kids just don't know how to read a textbook" has helped us to realize that secondary teachers have a responsibility to teach students to read the textbooks from which they want them to learn. This instruction does not have to do with teaching decoding or other basic skills, but involves the teaching of strategies and the promotion of deep thinking about text.

The teaching of strategies empowers readers, particularly those who struggle, by giving them the tools they need to construct meaning from text. Instead of blaming comprehension problems on students' own innate abilities, for which they see no solution, explicit strategy instruction teaches students to take control of their own learning and comprehension. They learn that they can solve their comprehension problem through the use the appropriate reading strategies. This realization is particularly motivating for students. Once they begin to attribute success to the proper use of strategies and effortful reading rather than to "being smart," poor readers are more willing to put forth the effort needed to succeed. And success breeds success. As teachers, there is no greater reward than seeing the "light go on" for struggling students who use a strategy and experience a successful reading experience for the first time since fourth grade.

REFERENCES

Afflerbach, P. (2002). Teaching reading self-assessment strategies. In C. C. Block & M. Pressley (Eds.), *Comprehension instruction: Research-based best practices* (pp. 96–111). New York: Guilford Press.

Anderson, V., & Roit, M. (1993). Planning and implementing collaborative strategy instruction for delayed readers in grades 6–10. *The Elementary School Journal, 94,* 121–137.

Baker, L. (1984). Spontaneous versus instructed use of multiple standards for evaluating their comprehension: Effects of age, reading proficiency and type of standard. *Journal of Experimental Child Psychology, 38,* 289–311.

Baker, L. (1994). Fostering metacognitive development. In H. Reese (Ed.), *Advances in child development and behavior* (Vol. 25, pp. 201–239). San Diego: Academic Press.

Baker, L. (2002). Metacognition in comprehension instruction. In C. C. Block & M. Pressley (Eds.), *Comprehension instruction: Research-based best practices* (pp. 77–95). New York: Guilford Press.

Baker, L., & Zimlin, L. (1989). Instructional effects on children's use of two levels of standards for evaluating their comprehension. *Journal of Educational Psychology, 81,* 340–346.

Bereiter, C., & Bird, M. (1985). Use of thinking aloud in identification and teaching of reading comprehension strategies. *Cognition and Instruction, 2,* 131–156.

Bransford, J. D., Vye, N. J., & Stein, B. S. (1984). A comparison of successful and less successful learners: Can we enhance comprehension and mastery skills? In J. Flood (Ed.), *Understanding reading comprehension* (pp. 216–231). Newark, DE: International Reading Association.

Brown, R. (2002). Straddling two worlds: Self-directed comprehension instruction for middle schoolers. In C. C. Block & M. Pressley (Eds.), *Comprehension instruction: Research-based best practices* (pp. 337–350). New York: Guilford Press.

Chi, M. T. H., DeLeeuw, N., Chiu, M., & LaVancher, C. (1994). Eliciting self-explanations improves understanding. *Cognitive Science, 18,* 439–477.

Collins, A., & Smith, E. E. (1982). Teaching the process of reading comprehension. In D. K. Detterman & R. J. Sternberg (Eds.), *How and how much can intelligence be increased?* (pp. 173–185). Norwood, NJ: Ablex.

Davey, B., & McBride, S. (1986). Effects of question-generation training on reading comprehension. *Journal of Educational Psychology, 78,* 256–262.

Dole, J. A. (2000). Explicit and implicit instruction in comprehension. In B. M. Taylor, M. F. Graves, & P. van den Broek (Eds.), *Reading for meaning: Fostering comprehension in the middle grades* (pp. 52–69). New York: Teachers College Press.

Duffy, G. (2002). The case for direct explanation of strategies. In C. C. Block & M. Pressley (Eds.), *Comprehension instruction: Research-based best practices* (pp. 28–41). New York: Guilford Press.

Duffy, G., Roehler, L. R., & Hermann, B. A. (1988). Modeling mental processes helps poorer readers become strategic readers. *Reading Teacher, 41,* 762–767.

Duffy, G. G., Roehler, L. R., Sivan, E., Rackliffe, G., Book, C., Meloth, M. S., et al. (1987). Effects of explaining the reasoning associated with using reading strategies. *Reading Research Quarterly, 22,* 347–368.

Durkin, D. (1979). What classroom observations reveal about reading comprehension instruction. *Reading Research Quarterly, 14,* 481–533.

El-Dinary, P. B. (2002). Challenges of implementing transactional strategies instruction for reading comprehension. In C. C. Block & M. Pressley (Eds.), *Comprehension instruction: Research-based best practices* (pp. 201–215). New York: Guilford Press.

Flavel, J. H. (1976). Metacognitive aspects of problem solving. In L. B. Resnick (Ed.), *The nature of intelligence* (pp. 231–235). Hillsdale, NJ: Erlbaum.

Gambrell, L. B., & Bales, R. J. (1986). Mental imagery and the comprehension monitoring performance of fourth and fifth-grade poor readers. *Reading Research Quarterly, 21,* 454–464.

Garner, R. (1992). Metacognition and self-monitoring strategies. In S. J. Samuels & A. E. Farstrup (Eds.), *What research has to say about reading instruction* (pp. 236–252). Newark, DE: International Reading Association.

Gourgey, A. F. (1998). Metacognition in basic skills instruction. *Instructional Science, 26,* 81–96.

Guthrie, J. T., Anderson, E., Alao, S., & Rhinehart, J. (1999). Influences of concept-oriented reading instruction on strategy use and conceptual learning from text. *The Elementary School Journal, 99,* 343–366.

Guttmann, J., Levin, J. R., & Pressley, M. (1977). Pictures, partial pictures and young children's oral prose learning. *Journal of Educational Psychology, 69,* 473–480.

Hacker, D. J. (1998). Self-regulated comprehension during normal reading. In D. J. Hacker, J. Dunlosky, & A. C. Grasser (Eds.), *Metacognition in educational theory and practice* (pp. 165–191). Mahwah, NJ: Erlbaum.

Keene, E. O., & Zimmermann, S. (1997). *Mosaic of thought: Teaching comprehension in a reader's workshop.* Portsmouth, NH: Heinemann.

National Reading Panel. (2000). *Report of the National Reading Panel.* Washington, DC: National Institute of Child Health and Human Development.

Nicholson, T. (1984). Experts and novices: A study of reading in the high school classroom. *Reading Research Quarterly, 19,* 436–451.

Ogle, D., & Blachowicz, C., L. Z. (2002). Beyond literature circles: Helping students comprehend informational texts. In C. C. Block & M. Pressley (Eds.), *Comprehension instruction: Research-based best practices* (pp. 259–274). New York: Guilford Press.

Palincsar, A. S., & Brown, A. L. (1984). Reciprocal teaching of comprehension-fostering and comprehension-monitoring activities. *Cognition and Instruction, 1,* 117–175.

Paris, S. G., Cross, D. R., & Lipson, M. Y. (1984). Informed strategies for learning: A program to improve children's reading awareness and comprehension. *Journal of Educational Research, 76,* 1239–1252.

Paris, S. G., Wasik, B. A., & Turner, J. C. (1991). The development of strategic readers.

In R. Barr, M. Kamil, P. Mosenthal, & P. D. Pearson (Eds.), *Handbook of reading research* (Vol. 2, pp. 609–640). Elmsford, NY: Longman.

Pearson, P. D., & Dole J. A. (1987). Explicit comprehension instruction: A review of research and a new conceptualization of instruction. *Elementary School Journal, 88,* 151–165.

Pearson, P. D., Roehler, L. R., Dole, J. A., & Duffy, G. G. (1991). Developing expertise in reading comprehension. In J. S. Samuels & A. E. Farstrup (Eds.), *What research has to say about reading instruction* (2nd ed., pp. 145–199). Newark, DE: International Reading Association.

Pressley, M. (2000). What should comprehension instruction be the instruction of? In M. Kamil, P. Mosenthal, P. D. Pearson, & R. Barr (Eds.), *Handbook of reading research* (Vol. 3, pp. 546–561). Mahwah, NJ: Erlbaum.

Pressley, M. (2002). Comprehension strategies instruction: A turn-of-the-century status report. In C. C. Block & M. Pressley (Eds.), *Comprehension instruction: Research-based best practices* (pp. 11–27). New York: Guilford Press.

Pressley, M., & Afflerbach, P. (1995). *Verbal protocols of reading: The nature of constructively responsive reading.* Hillsdale, NJ: Erlbaum.

Pressley, M., Almasi, J., Schuder, T., Bergman, J., Hite, S., El-Dinary, P. B., & Brown, R. (1994). Transactional instruction of comprehension strategies: The Montgomery County, Maryland SAIL program. *Reading and Writing Quarterly: Overcoming Learning Difficulties, 10,* 5–19.

Roehler, L. R., & Duffy, G. G. (1984). Direct explanation of comprehension processes. In G. G. Duffy, L. R. Roehler, & J. Mason (Eds.), *Comprehension instruction: Perspectives and suggestions* (pp. 265–280). Elmsford, NY: Longman.

Rosenshine, B., & Meister, C. (1997). Cognitive strategy instruction in reading. In S. A. Stahl & D. A. Hayes (Eds.), *Instructional models in reading* (pp. 85–108). Mahwah, NJ: Erlbaum.

Schraw, G. (1998). Promoting general metacognitive awareness. *Instructional Science, 26,* 113–125.

Silven, M., & Vauras, M. (1992). Improving reading through thinking aloud. *Learning and Instruction, 2,* 69–88.

Sinatra, G. M., Brown, K. J., & Reynolds, R. E. (2002). Implications of cognitive resource allocation for comprehension strategies instruction. In C. C. Block & M. Pressley (Eds.), *Comprehension instruction: Research-based best practices* (pp. 62–76). New York: Guilford Press.

Swan, E. A. (2003). *Concept-Oriented Reading Instruction: Engaging classrooms, lifelong learners.* New York: Guilford Press.

Trabasso, T., & Bouchard, E. (2002). Teaching readers how to comprehend texts strategically. In C. C. Block & M. Pressley (Eds.), *Comprehension instruction: Research-based best practices* (pp. 176–200). New York: Guilford Press.

Wade, S., Woodrow, T., & Schraw, G. (1990). An analysis of spontaneous study strategies. *Reading Research Quarterly, 25,* 147–166.

Strategies for Struggling Second-Language Readers

JANETTE K. KLINGNER
SHARON VAUGHN

Every teacher must be prepared to teach students who are English-language learners. Though this is seemingly a bold statement, consider the following:

- The majority of incoming kindergarten students in both Texas and California are English language learners.
- Though California and Texas have experienced significant increases in the number of students who are English language learners, these states are not the only ones. In 2000, the percentage of the school-age population speaking a different home language than English in California was 42.6%, and in Texas it was 32.4%; in Arizona, Florida, Nevada, New Jersey, New Mexico, New York, and Rhode Island, the percentage was over 20% and in several other states (12) the percentage surpassed 10% (U.S. Bureau of the Census, 2003).
- Latinos have passed African Americans as the largest minority group in the United States (U.S. Bureau of the Census, 2001).
- Hispanic students have higher dropout rates than do non-Hispanics (Education Statistics Quarterly, 2000).
- Although the Hispanic–white achievement gap narrowed in the 1970s and 1980s, it then widened in the late 1980s and 1990s, and is still large (Lee, 2002).

Although some preservice and inservice programs have made adjustments to ensure that practicing secondary teachers have the knowledge and skills to teach English language learners, the overwhelming number of teachers are ill-prepared to teach reading to English language learners. Thus, the majority of teachers have little or no knowledge or experience in effective practices for enhancing the literacy skills or text learning of adolescent English language learners.

OVERVIEW OF THIS CHAPTER

One of our first tasks was to identify and review all relevant research on adolescent students who are English language learners. To assist with our search, we defined *adolescents* as youngsters in grades 6 through 12, or (when grades were not specified) ages 12–17. Thus, we used the descriptors *secondary, middle school,* and *high school* to locate relevant articles. We defined *English language learners* as individuals described as English language learners, English as a second language learners (ESL) or bilingual. We used the key words *literacy* and *reading* in combination with these other descriptors. In addition, we searched for "second-language reading" in combination with our descriptors defining adolescence. We also conducted hand searches of major literacy and EES journals for articles published in the last 5 years that included English language learning adolescents and reading interventions.

Using this process and these criteria, we located numerous articles, as well as three syntheses, that addressed students who were English language learners and in which the research focused on reading (Fitzgerald, 1995a, 1995b; Gersten & Baker, 2000). All three sought to locate and review all articles across age groups, so we were able to use these syntheses as critical sources for locating relevant research.

We have divided this chapter into four sections: the contexts within which literacy instruction and learning take place; research on the cognitive processes of English language learners while engaged in reading; research on instructional practices; and a research agenda that defines what we still need to learn about adolescent second-language readers.

CONTEXTS FOR LITERACY INSTRUCTION

The cultural and social contexts within which literacy instruction takes place are of critical importance (Alvermann, in press; Au, 1995; Moore, 1996). Alvermann suggests that it is possible to close the achievement gap for culturally and linguistically diverse students by changing their learning contexts. Similarly, Reyes (1992) emphasizes the importance of tailoring literacy instruction to account for the cultural and linguistic diversity of all students. These adaptations cannot be an afterthought, but should instead begin with the assumption that every learner "brings a valid language and culture to the instructional context" (p. 427).

Contexts for literacy instruction should be culturally responsive, grounded in the belief that culturally and linguistically diverse students can excel in academic endeavors if (1) they are provided access to high-quality teachers, programs, curricula, and resources; (2) they are taught with the most effective practices; and (3) their culture, language, heritage, and experiences are valued and used to facilitate their learning and development (Nieto, 2002). An important aspect of culturally responsive teaching is tapping into and building on students' "cultural funds of knowledge" (Moll, 1990, 1992; Moll & González, 1994). As noted by Langer (1997), "Literacy learning is dependent upon the uses and forms of literacy that people in particular cultures and social traditions deem valuable. Thus, connection to the community is critical" (p. 607). Building on students' "funds of knowledge" does more than help them access schemas and make connections between new and prior knowledge: It is a way of fundamentally validating their ways of thinking, acting, and being.

Langer (1997) builds a case for using literature as a particularly inviting context for learning both a second language and literacy. She describes a project that focused on literacy acquisition among middle school students from the Dominican Republic, attending a school on Manhattan's lower East Side. Students participated in a book-writing project focused on "stories from home." The project engaged students, taught them ways both to discuss and to think, and fostered their literacy acquisition through literature.

Students have affirmed these views. Zanger (1994) involved Spanish-speaking high school students in a panel discussion of their experiences as Latinos. Students shared that they felt marginalized by their teachers and other students, and felt a need to be accepted and respected for who they were. They wanted to learn English and learn about American culture but did not want to have to give up their native language and culture.

Rosowsky (2000) explored the relationship between cultural knowledge and English reading among secondary-age bilingual pupils and found that different conceptual frameworks and schemas related to text reading may actually misguide culturally and linguistically diverse students. Students' expectations about story grammar and plot development may vary, causing dissonance and confusion. Also, cause–consequence chains and symbols (e.g., superstitions) may differ across cultures and cause a breakdown in understanding. There also may be differences in what is attended to closely, what is ignored, or what is superfluous. Teachers who strive to understand the backgrounds of their students are able to aid students' comprehension by making these differences explicit.

A challenge for many teachers and teacher-educators is to improve their understanding of how to alter contexts for learning, so that they are more culturally and linguistically responsive. Practicing teachers crave concrete examples that relate to the ages, cultural groups, and linguistic groups they teach. They are eager to learn how to develop contexts and respond to students situated within their daily practice—yet so little of this knowledge is available.

UNDERSTANDING BILINGUAL STUDENTS' COGNITIVE READING PROCESSES

Fitzgerald (1995a) conducted a critical review of research performed in the United States on the cognitive reading processes of English language learners. Nineteen of the 67 studies reviewed related to adolescents or students in grades 6–12. Overwhelmingly, results showed a transfer of native-language knowledge to ESL reading.

The Relationship between Second-Language Oral Proficiency and Second-Language Reading

In general, ESL oral proficiency and ESL reading are positively related, particularly at higher grade levels (Devine, 1987, Fitzgerald, 1995a; García-Vasquez, 1995; Tregar & Wong, 1984). Among middle and high school students, this relationship seems to be stronger than other relationships, such as those between native-language literacy and level of acculturation. Tregar and Wong's sample included 200 Cantonese and 200 Hispanic third-through eighth-grade students who had been in bilingual education programs. The best predictor of English reading at grades 3–5 was native-language reading ability, but in grades 6–8, the best predictor was oral English proficiency. In a study with 23 Mexican American students in grades 7–9, García-Vazquez (1995) investigated the relationship between students' level of acculturation to the school environment and to their own culture with reading achievement in English on the Iowa Test of Basic Skills. She found that students' English reading was not related to scores on either measure of acculturation but was related to level of English language proficiency.

There may be a threshold level of oral proficiency in the second language that must be achieved before reading in that language is strongly correlated. In a study by Lee and Schallert (1997), 809 Korean third-year middle school and first-year high school students exhibited a wide range in reading ability in both Korean and English, and a wide range in English proficiency. Measures included an English language proficiency test, an English reading comprehension test (the Metropolitan Achievement Test), and a Korean reading comprehension test. Students with low levels of English proficiency showed little relationship between their native- and second-language reading, whereas learners with higher levels of English oral proficiency showed a positive relationship between native- and second-language reading performance. In other words, learners needed some knowledge of their second language before they could successfully draw on their native-language reading abilities when reading in their second language.

Controversy exists about the level of second-language oral proficiency needed to support reading in that language. Wong-Fillmore and Valadez (1986) contend that second-language reading for English language learners should not be introduced until a fairly high level of second language proficiency has been achieved. However, others, such as Anderson and Roit (1996) and Gersten (1996), assert that instruction focused on second-language comprehension can be helpful to learners across a range of proficiency levels, even for English language learners with learning disabilities, as found by Klingner and Vaughn (1996). There seems to be a reciprocal relationship between oral proficiency and reading achievement, with instruction in second-language reading comprehension facilitating gains in second-language oral skills (see also, Elley, 1981). An important factor is whether or not the first language is valued and its development is nourished. Additional research is needed that untangles issues related to the relationships among level of first language oral proficiency, second-language oral proficiency, native language literacy, and English literacy. Furthermore, we need to understand oralcy better and its contribution to beginning reading for students whose first language and English oralcy skills are the same, and for students for whom oralcy skills are low.

Differences between More and Less Proficient Second-Language Readers

Most of what we know about differences between more and less proficient second-language readers in the upper grades can be gleaned from the work of Jiménez and colleagues. Jiménez, García, and Pearson (1995) compared the cognitive and metacognitive knowledge of a proficient bilingual reader with that of a marginally proficient bilingual reader and a monolingual reader. Differences were found in how the proficient bilingual reader navigated unknown vocabulary in both languages, how she viewed the purpose of reading, how she interacted with text, and how she took advantage of her bilingualism. The authors concluded that explicit knowledge of the relationship between Spanish and English facilitated the proficient bilingual student's reading comprehension.

Jiménez, García, and Pearson (1996) examined the strategic reading processes of 8 sixth- and seventh-grade bilingual Latina/o children who were considered successful English readers and compared their reading processes to those of 3 successful English readers and 3 less successful bilingual Latina/o readers. Their primary objective was to study how bilingualism and biliteracy affect metacognition (the ability of readers to monitor their understanding or "know what they know"). They found that the successful Latina/o readers (1) actively transferred information across languages; (2) translated from one language to another, but most often from Spanish to English; and (3) openly accessed cognates when they read, especially in their less dominant language (cognates are words that are similar in more than one language, such as *television* in English and *televisión* in Spanish). Also, the successful Latina/o readers frequently encountered unknown vocabulary words, whether reading in English or Spanish, but were able to draw upon multiple strategic processes to determine the meanings of these words. The less successful Latina/o readers used fewer strategies and were less effective resolving comprehension difficulties in either language. When they encountered unknown vocabulary items, they had difficulty constructing plausible interpretations of the text. The authors recommended that finding and nurturing the strengths of successful bilingual readers can go a long way toward "developing positive pedagogical and research traditions for school-aged children from linguistically diverse backgrounds" (p. 107). They suggest that teachers would benefit from an awareness of the benefits of transfer and an understanding of how native-language reading ability can facilitate English language literacy. Though some students seem to figure this out on their own, and can point out the benefits of cross-linguistic transfer, others need explicit instruction.

Though most of the following studies were not with adolescents, some tentative conclusions can be drawn from research about differences between more and less proficient older or younger second-language readers. More proficient second-language readers tend to (1) use more schematic knowledge (Ammon, 1987; third through fifth graders); (2) use more meaning-oriented strategies (Langer, Bartholome, Vasquez, & Lucas, 1990; fifth graders); (3) use a greater variety of metacognitive strategies, and use them more frequently (Anderson, 1991; 28 Hispanic university students); (4) take more action on plans to solve breakdowns in comprehension and check their solutions more often (Block, 1992; 14 Chinese- and Spanish-speaking university students); and (5) make better and/or more inferences (García, 1991; 53 Hispanic fifth and sixth graders).

Differences between Second-Language Readers and Native-English Readers

Jiménez et al. (1995) noted that for the bilingual readers in their study, unknown vocabulary presented an obstacle that it did not present to the monolingual reader, and that the cultural and linguistic familiarity of reading passages facilitated comprehension for the monolingual reader. Jiménez et al. (1996) added that the skilled English-only readers they studied seldom needed to monitor their comprehension overtly the way second-language readers needed to, because they rarely encountered unknown vocabulary and had well-developed background schemas that were relevant to the text they read. They found that their good second-language readers focused much more on word meaning than did their good monolingual readers, presumably because this was a great source of difficulty for them. The authors concluded that translation, cognate awareness, and information transfer (across languages) are strategies unique to bilingual reading. On the other hand, strategies that successful bilingual readers share with successful monolingual readers include making inferences or drawing conclusions; integrating prior knowledge, information, and experiences into ongoing meaning construction; and asking questions when comprehension breaks down (Jiménez, 1997).

In a study of ninth-grade second-language and native English readers, although the fluent second-language readers were able to identify cohesive signals (e.g., anaphora, or referents such as *them*, *it*, and *they*) as well as native English speakers, they were less able to apply this knowledge to their understanding of text (e.g., by making inferences) (Duran & Revlin, 1994). Another difference between first- and second-language readers seems to be that proficient readers use their syntactic, morphemic, and semantic knowledge to fixate unconsciously on high-information items in the text (Rayner & Pollatsek, 1989). Yet because the signals that indicate high-information items differ from language to language, second-language readers, not knowing which items are most important, may use inefficient fixation patterns when reading in their second language (Bernhardt, 1987).

Second-language readers even at the college level, did not use context as well as first-language readers (Carrell, 1983; Carrell & Wallace, 1983). Research reports indicate that younger second-language readers (third through fifth grade) use fewer metacognitive strategies than do native English speakers, and they select strategies with different relative frequencies

(Knight, Padrón, & Waxman, 1985; Padrón & Waxman, 1988). Yet more proficient second-language readers more frequently used a wider variety of metacognitive strategies. Field (1996) addressed challenges faced by fourth-grade bilingual children transitioning to literacy in English when answering reading comprehension questions requiring interpretation and synthesis of information related to fictitious characters' thoughts. She noted that understanding a character's perspective seemed to depend more on inference than on lexical content within the text.

Influence of Schemas

Most studies emphasizing schemas or prior knowledge utilization have been conducted with college-level participants. Results from these studies clearly indicate that participants better comprehend and/or remember passages that either are compatible with their native cultures or are considered more familiar (Carrell, 1981, 1987; Fitzgerald, 1995a; Johnson, 1981, 1982). In studies with fifth- through seventh-grade students (García, 1991; Jiménez, 1997; Langer et al., 1990) and 11th-grade students (Pritchard, 1990), similar results have been found. Familiarity with content promotes reading comprehension when reading in either a first or second language (Carrell, 1987; Fitzgerald, 1995a; Johnson, 1981). When texts are inconsistent with the reader's expectations, comprehension is negatively affected (Bransford & Johnson, 1972), and recall may be distorted (Reynolds et al., 1982; Steffensen, Joag-Dev, & Anderson, 1979). These effects are strongest with ambiguous material. It is important not to assume that students have (or should have) the same shared, common knowledge set, and to ensure that adequate time is spent previewing critical information and concepts from text and tapping related background knowledge.

Text Structure

Another schematic element is knowledge of text structure (the way the text is organized to guide readers in identifying key information and making connections between ideas). Research on the influence of text structure has been carried out almost exclusively with college-age students. These studies have found that different types of text structure affect comprehension and recall (Bean, Potter, & Clark, 1980; Carrell, 1984), and the type of information recalled (high- vs. low-level) (Carrell, 1984, 1992). In general, passages organized in a familiar structure are easier to comprehend and remember than passages structured in a less familiar way (Carrell, 1984; Fitzgerald, 1995a; Hinds, 1983). Text structures are culturally determined, and knowing them takes a great deal of implicit learning, though explicit instruction can help. In a study of 70 sixth-grade students studying English as a foreign language, Amer (1992) found that direct instruction in text structure facilitated students' comprehension and recall.

Metacognition and Use of Strategies

As already noted, metacognition is an important component of successful second-language reading (Jiménez et al., 1996). Pritchard (1990) investigated how 20 Spanish-background high school students used metacognitive skills to monitor their comprehension. He found that students used the same metacognitive strategies in English as in Spanish, but with less monitoring while reading in English. In a study with fifth graders, Langer et al. (1990) examined the meaning-making strategies of 12 Mexican American bilingual fifth graders. The focus of the study was on determining how students used strategies in both languages, and how this use facilitated their comprehension and recall. The authors concluded that "apart from the need for a basic knowledge of English, students' comprehension of both English and Spanish texts depended on their ability to use good strategies for making meaning" (p. 427). The better readers were distinguished more by their use of strategies than by their fluency in English, and students who did well in one language generally did well in the other (also see Au, 1995). Further research is needed to clarify these relationships further.

Importance of Vocabulary

Vocabulary knowledge is strongly related to effective text comprehension and appears to be a highly significant variable in second-language readers' success (Fitzgerald, 1995a; National Reading Panel, 2000). In a study with 10 second- through sixth-grade students with little prior English experience, Saville-Troike (1984) found that only oral English vocabulary production strongly correlated with English reading. In a study with 104 fifth and sixth graders, García (1991) found that vocabulary knowledge was even more important than prior knowledge of content in affecting performance on a reading comprehension test. English language learners with higher oral proficiency levels made more and/or better inferences. Qian (1999) explored the relationships between depth and breadth of vocabulary knowledge and comprehension in second-language reading, and found that scores on vocabulary size, depth of vocabulary knowledge, and reading comprehension were highly and positively correlated.

Zimmerman (1997) conducted a 10-week, classroom-based study with postsecondary students in a university-preparatory intensive English course to find out whether explicit instruction or incidental learning would lead to greater vocabulary gains. Students were divided into two groups. One group received 3 hours of interactive vocabulary instruction weekly plus an assignment to read self-selected materials, and the other group was assigned only self-selected materials to read. Interactive vocabulary instruction had a significant positive effect on vocabulary scores.

Cognates

García and Nagy (1993) conducted an investigation with 81 Hispanic fourth- through sixth-grade bilingual students, and Nagy, García, Durgunoglu, and Hancin (1993) included 74 Hispanic fourth- through sixth-grade bilingual students in two investigations of cognate knowledge. On the whole, second-language readers recognized cognate vocabulary fairly well, yet there was substantial variation in cognate recognition among participants, with students at higher ESL proficiency levels making better use of cognates. These findings are consistent with those of Jiménez et al. (1995, 1996). Rodriguez (2001) successfully taught 20 bilingual middle school students how to use cognates to facilitate their second-language reading.

RESEARCH ON INSTRUCTIONAL APPROACHES

Studies of School and Classroom Effectiveness

Studies of school and classroom effectiveness can add much to our understanding of the factors that promote successful learning for culturally and linguistically diverse students. Berman et al. (1995) studied eight schools, grades 4–8, nominated for providing "outstanding learning opportunities for [limited-English-proficient] LEP—and all students" (cited in August & Hakuta, 1997, p. 206). Classroom-level attributes included (1) effective language development strategies, and (2) curricula and instructional strategies that engaged students in meaningful, in-depth learning. Lucas (1996) studied six exemplary high schools. Attributes of these schools were that (1) the students' native language and culture were valued, (2) teachers had high expectations for student success, (3) parent involvement was high, and (4) school personnel were committed to "empowerment through education." Students benefited from a challenging academic curriculum (access to quality academics) while learning English (Collier & Thomas, 2001), and a theme-based curriculum (Lucas, Henze, & Donato, 1990).

Studies of Classroom Literacy Instruction

Typically teaching English language learners how to use comprehension strategies has received little attention even in upper grades, because teachers tend to focus on word recognition and pronunciation (Gersten, 1996). The focus of instruction for students not fully proficient in English is often on reading aloud, pronouncing words correctly, and answering literal interpretation questions (Fitzgerald, 1995b). Reyes (1991) used a case study approach in her investigation of the literacy instruction of 10 sixth-grade Hispanic bilingual students. The students received no explicit instruction in selecting, analyzing, and discussing books. Reyes therefore concluded that their English reading comprehension suffered.

Students' Perceptions

Thompson (2000) collected narratives from 10th graders whose first language was Spanish. She asked them to identify teaching practices that aided or hindered their acquisition of English. Students identified literature-based activities, oral practice, individual help from tutors and aides, peer interaction, and games as helping. They specified as ineffective or harmful having to read aloud in class and being interrupted or corrected when reading or speaking.

INTERVENTION RESEARCH ON ADOLESCENTS WHO ARE ENGLISH LANGUAGE LEARNERS

Although the research with adolescent English language learners and reading is sparse, there is an early knowledge base to draw from to inform instruction. In a research synthesis of reading instruction for ESL students, Fitzgerald (1995b) identified 24 studies that addressed instructional methods. Because she did not restrict this review to adolescents, studies that addressed all age groups were included. Only one of the 24 studies focused exclusively on adolescents between sixth and 12th grades (Neuman & Koskinen, 1992), and one additional study included sixth graders along with younger students in its sample (Saracho, 1982).

Neuman and Koskinen (1992) addressed instruction targeting specific student knowledge in vocabulary. Seventh- and eighth-grade English language learners more than 2 years below grade level participated in learning new English vocabulary in science one of four ways: watching captioned television, watching television, just reading text, or reading and listening to text. Students learned the most new words in English from watching captioned television. Saracho (1982) investigated the effectiveness of computer-assisted instruction with third- through sixth-grade Hispanic migrant students and found that students' English reading achievement improved when the computer-assisted instruction was used to supplement other forms of instruction.

In the Gersten and Baker synthesis (2000), only one study met criteria for addressing reading comprehension in adolescent English language learners (Klingner & Vaughn, 1996). Klingner and Vaughn investigated the effectiveness of an adapted version of reciprocal teaching (Palincsar & Brown, 1984) for improving the content-area reading comprehension of 26 middle schools students with learning disabilities (LD) who were also English language learners. Students participated in 15 days of teacher-facilitated strategy instruction while reading grade-level expository passages. They were then randomly divided into two groups of 13 students. One group was assigned to a cross-age tutoring condition, and the other to a cooperative learning condition. Students in the first group tutored younger English language learners with LD in the comprehension strategies, and students in the other group continued applying the strategies while working in small, peer-led groups. No significant differences were found between groups, but students in both groups showed substantial progress in reading comprehension over the entire course of the study, as measured by the Gates–MacGinitie Reading Comprehension Test, passage comprehension tests (Palincsar & Brown, 1984), and a strategy interview. A key finding was that a greater range of students benefited from strategy instruction than had been predicted: Students who began the study with comprehension levels substantially higher than their decoding levels, as well as students who were adequate decoders but initially lower in comprehension, benefited. Intelligence (as measured by the English Wechsler Intelligence Scale—Revised) did not seem to affect performance. However, initial decoding level and oral language proficiency did. Students with very low initial decoding skills, below a third-grade level on the Woodcock–Johnson Tests of Achievement, were least likely to show improvement. Students with an intermediate or lower level of oral language proficiency in English and, interestingly, in Spanish, were also less likely to benefit from the intervention. All of those students with English and Spanish proficiency scores of 3 or lower on the Language Assessment scales (on a scale of 1–5) showed less growth on outcome measures than did those students with higher oral proficiency, with one exception. One student was different than other students with low oral proficiency, in that she had close to grade-level scores in decoding—her score on the Gates–MacGinitie increased by 27 percentile points.

PROMISING PRACTICES FOR ENHANCING THE LITERACY SKILLS OF ADOLESCENT ENGLISH LANGUAGE LEARNERS

Improving the Quality of Teacher–Student Queries, Answers, and Dialogue

Even when there are large numbers of students who are English language learners in classrooms, traditional discourse reflects a recitation approach, with little conversation (Cazden, 1988; Moll, 1988; Oakes, 1986). This approach to question asking by the teacher and student recitation does little to extend the language, vocabulary, or concept development of any of the students and is particularly unproductive for English language learners. Improving the quality of conversations and questions in secondary classrooms has been extremely slow to change. In no small part, this may be a result of the learning experiences most teachers have had. They are likely to use the question–answer approach to instruction that was the foundation of much of their own instruction. Cazden (1995) emphasized the importance of examining the composition of classroom talk and its relation to specific curriculum goals, noting the usefulness of examining patterns of participation, and the forms and functions of students' language when determining teaching goals.

However, it is very difficult to improve the vocabulary learning, concept development, and language learning of students when the classroom discourse focuses consistently on the teacher's presentation, the teacher's questions, and little meaningful interactive discourse between teacher and students, or between students and students. These skills of knowing what to ask, when to ask, how to scaffold student responses, and how to organize student pairs and small groups for responding are not easy tasks, and this may be one of the reasons they occur so infrequently in middle and high schools.

Promoting Reading Comprehension with Adolescent English Language Learners

Various practices appear promising for improving the reading comprehension of adolescent English language learners. Anderson and Roit (1990, 1993, 1996) have worked extensively with English language learners in Canada and the United States, with the expressed goal of assisting teachers in providing strategy instruction in reading comprehension. For the purposes of this chapter, we have reviewed their recommended practices and selected those that seem most appropriate for adolescent learners.

Mapping Vocabulary Words

Anderson and Roit (1996) recommend that traditional approaches to vocabulary mapping be modified for English language learners. First, the vocabulary maps need to be kept "alive" and available to students, so that words can be revisited and additional relationships and descriptions can be added. Second, they suggest that a limited number of words be taught at one time, and that they be frequently revisited. Overwhelming students with too many words is unlikely to be profitable. They also suggest that vocabulary words can be taught in units with superordinate and subordinate key words.

Expanding Contexts

Providing contexts from which words or concepts are taught, as well as enabling students to use words and concepts framed within their own experiences, is useful. For example, when students are learning about *canyons*, teachers can frame the word around the context in which students will be learning about canyons within their reading. They can also integrate students' background and related experiences about canyons. These expanding contexts need to be considered within the multiple teachings of the text the students are reading and learning.

Predicting

Prediction can be better situated to assist English language learners when teachers first establish the context for a story, then help students relate the context to their prior experiences. Written cues and ideas can be written down to aid students while they are reading (Gersten & Jiménez, 1994). Students should later return to their predictions to assess how accurate they were.

Text Structures

Explicitly teaching text structures can increase English language learners' comprehension. In one procedure (Anderson & Henne, 1993; McLaren & Anderson, 1992), teachers teach students a new text structure, such as problem–solution, by prompting them to ask a series of questions about the text that corresponds to its structure. For example, "What is the problem? What is the cause of the problem? What will happen if the problem continues? How can the problem be solved?"

Culturally Relevant Material

Selecting materials that represent culturally familiar material that also is based on students' prior knowledge and experience is valuable. Brozo, Cantú Baleiro, and Salazar (1996) implemented a learning unit on Hispanic American culture in a class of eighth graders at a predominately Latino/a school. As participant observers, the authors gathered information about the class and students. Literacy engagement greatly increased. The authors recommended giving students a greater range of options for responding to text by including literature that is culturally relevant and appealing, establishing home–school connections, and using the community as a cultural resource.

Teaching Reading Comprehension Embedded within Content Instruction

Graves (1998) observed more than 20 middle school classrooms in which some form of English language development was provided for students who were English language learners. She concluded that teachers who taught reading comprehension explicitly benefited these students. She observed teachers who combined minilessons in reading by proactively and specifically teaching reading strategies that students needed to succeed in their content-area classes—such as finding the main idea or comparing two items. Graves further notes that these reading comprehension strategies can be taught through extended conversations in which thinking and learning from text is promoted. Goldenberg (1992–1993) and Echevarria (1995) refer to these as instructional conversations.

Cognitive Academic Language Learning Approach (CALLA)

CALLA was developed as an instructional program for English language learners preparing to participate in mainstream academic content instruction (Chamot & O'Malley, 1996; O'Malley & Chamot, 1990). Unfortunately, information about the effectiveness of CALLA is limited. However, the authors state that initial findings are promising. Though the program does not focus specifically on literacy, reading comprehension is clearly an important aspect of the program. The CALLA model targets the development of academic language skills through direct instruction in learning strategies. CALLA lessons include both teacher-directed and learner-centered activities. Each lesson is divided into five phases:

1. *Preparation*: The teacher finds out what students already know about the concepts in the subject to be presented, what gaps in prior knowledge need to be addressed, and what strategies students already know. The teacher explains the lesson's objectives.

2. *Presentation*: The teacher presents and explains new information in English, supported by contextual clues such as demonstrations and visuals. Learning strategies are taught.

3. *Practice*: Students engage in hands-on practice. The teacher acts as a facilitator during this phase, helping students to assimilate new information and apply learning strategies.

4. *Evaluation*: The teacher and students check the level of students' performance and understanding.

5. *Expansion activities*: Students are given a variety of opportunities to think about and apply the new concepts and skills they have learned. They continue to develop academic language and exercise higher order thinking skills.

Learning strategies taught in the CALLA model include metacognitive strategies, cognitive strategies, and social and affective strategies:

Metacognitive strategies

- Advance organization (previewing the text)
- Advance preparation (rehearsing the language needed for an oral or written task)
- Selective attention (focusing on key information)
- Self-monitoring (checking one's own comprehension while listening or reading)
- Self-evaluation (judging how well one has accomplished a task)
- Self-management (seeking or arranging conditions that facilitate one's learning)

Cognitive strategies

- Grouping (classifying words and concepts)
- Note taking (writing down key words and concepts)
- Summarizing (making a mental or written summary of key information)
- Imagery (using visual images to understand and remember information)
- Auditory representation (rehearsing a sound, phrase, or fact to assist with recall)

- Elaboration (relating new information to prior knowledge)
- Transfer (applying what is already known)
- Inferencing (using text information and prior knowledge to guess meanings)

Social and affective strategies

- Clarification (eliciting an explanation or verification from a teacher or peer)
- Cooperation (collaborating with peers to solve problems).

Graphic Organizers

In a synthesis of the effects of graphic organizers on the reading comprehension of students with LD (most of whom had identified reading problems), Kim, Vaughn, Wanzek, and Wei (in press) synthesized available research on graphic organizers for students with LD. Of the 21 studies identified, only three were conducted with English language learners (Bos & Anders, 1992, studies 1, 3, 5), and these studies were with elementary-age students. Although overall findings across studies of the use of graphic organizers on reading comprehension of secondary students were high (e.g., Kim et al., in press), as with many interventions, we were unable to identify studies that specifically addressed secondary students who are English language learners. For example, in study 1 conducted by Bos and Anders (1992), 42 elementary-age bilingual students with LD were randomly assigned to one of four groups: semantic mapping, semantic feature analysis, semantic/syntactic feature analysis, or definition instruction. Students participated in group instruction for three practice sessions (50 minutes each) and three treatment session (50 minutes each) over a 2-week period. Effect sizes for the treatment groups compared with the definition instruction group were high (effect size = .81). This suggests that elementary-age students who are bilingual benefit from graphic organizers to learn key concepts and vocabulary. However, implications for secondary school bilingual students are speculative, because empirical documentation with this group is not available.

Collaborative Strategic Reading (CSR)

CSR, an instructional approach for English language learners that combines cooperative learning (e.g., Johnson & Johnson, 1989) and reading comprehension strategy instruction (Klingner & Vaughn, 1996; Palincsar &

Brown, 1984), was designed to promote content learning, language acquisition, and reading comprehension in diverse classrooms (Klingner, Vaughn, & Schumm, 1998). Students of mixed reading and achievement levels work in small, cooperative groups to assist one another in applying four reading strategies to facilitate their comprehension of content area text: (1) *preview* (prior to reading a passage, students recall what they already know about the topic and predict what the passage might be about); (2) *click and clunk* (students monitor comprehension during reading by identifying difficult words and concepts in the passage and using fix-up strategies when the text does not make sense); (3) *get the gist* (during reading, students restate the most important idea in a paragraph or section); and (4) *wrap-up* (after reading, students summarize what has been learned and generate questions "that a teacher might ask on a test"). Initially, the classroom teacher presents the strategies to the whole class using modeling, role playing, and teacher think-alouds. Students learn why, when, and how to apply the strategies (Klingner, Vaughn, Dimino, Schumm, & Bryant, 2001).

As students develop proficiency with the strategies, they are divided into small groups of four, five, or six students. Each student in a group performs a different role. Roles are explicitly taught by the classroom teacher. Initially, students use cue cards with prompts that specify how to carry out the different roles. As students become confident in how to fulfill their roles, they are encouraged to set aside the cue cards to enable a more natural discussion to take place. Students record their ideas in CSR Learning Logs and complete various follow-up activities (e.g., semantic maps and games to reinforce vocabulary).

We (Klingner & Vaughn, 2000) investigated the frequency and means by which bilingual fifth-grade students helped each other and their LEP peers while working in small, heterogeneous CSR groups and found that, overall, students spent nearly all of their time engaged in academic-related strategic discussion and almost no time (less than 1%) engaged in procedural negotiation. Students assisted one another in understanding word meanings, getting the main idea, asking and answering questions, and relating what they were learning to previous knowledge. Students' scores on English vocabulary tests improved significantly from pre- to posttesting.

Bryant and colleagues (2000) studied the integration of CSR into middle school instructional teams and the role of peer-mediated strategies in improving academic outcomes. Average-achieving, low-achieving, and students with LD (many of whom were also English language learners) improved in accuracy of oral reading and fluency, word identification, and comprehension. However, a subgroup of very poor readers made little or no gains in reading achievement.

Peers Working with Peers: Classwide Peer Tutoring

Arreaga-Mayer (1998; Arreaga-Mayer & Greenwood, 1986) and her colleagues at the Juniper Garden's Children's Project at the University of Kan-
sas have developed, implemented, and evaluated the effectiveness of
Classwide Peer Tutoring (CWPT) in reading and spelling with culturally
and linguistically diverse students. They have designed spelling and reading
materials that can be used by pairs of students from the same class or different classes to tutor and practice reading and spelling. All of their CWPT
approaches include rewards to encourage cooperation between pairs,
rewards for the class to encourage group functioning, individual accountability to ensure that all students profit from the tutoring, and specific and
well-organized task structures to ensure that students acquire critical
knowledge in reading and spelling. Teachers serve in the role of selecting
appropriate materials and monitoring student progress. Students co-teach
each other and provide support and feedback. Overall, the CWPT
approach has been effective for improving the performance of participating
students, and the practice holds great promise for English language learners.

WHAT DO WE STILL NEED TO KNOW
ABOUT LITERACY INSTRUCTION
FOR STRUGGLING SECOND-LANGUAGE LEARNERS?

The easiest and most apparent answer to this question is, "Everything."
Despite the growth in culturally and linguistically diverse populations, and
the obvious need to understand instructional practices for these groups
better, the amount of research on English language learners is exceedingly
sparse. Although research with elementary school students is very limited
and often of poor quality, it is bountiful in comparison to research with
adolescents. We crave a broader foundation of empirical studies to inform
decision making.

However, to ensure that the research is useful and reliable, the overall
quality of research needs to be enhanced. Fitzgerald (1995b) notes that
"the exercise of research methodologies in much of the ESL reading instruction research might be characterized as appallingly lax, or at the very
least, less than rigorous" (p. 145). The lack of quality research is a function
of how difficult this research is to do given the complexities of doing
school-based research in general, but particularly with culturally and linguistically diverse populations. Some of the most important questions are
the hardest to address. Furthermore, obtaining adequately large sample sizes

and providing random assignment to groups are often demands that can be met in very few circumstances.

As a field, we face a serious problem in that we continue to make decisions for all students based on data from only some students. Students who are English language learners and not fully proficient in English are often left out of research samples, or their unique needs are not addressed. We offer a few examples of how we believe the knowledge base for English language learners might be expanded through research.

It may be possible to create common protocols for recording descriptive variables, so that a common database might be available across studies. This would allow for ready comparison and combination of samples. These descriptive variables might include such factors as specific family background; amount of first-language text available in the home and community; language spoken in the home, community, and by extended family; language proficiency; and number of years educated in the United States and other countries.

We suggest that, when conducting studies, researchers include students who represent culturally and linguistically diverse groups and disaggregate the data for these students, so that findings might be better understood. Often student English language learners are included in large samples, but without disaggregated data, and without the previously requested descriptive data, these findings are not meaningful for groups of English language learners.

Developing and using adequate measures of language dominance and proficiency are critical components of improving knowledge about English language learners. This valuable information will provide researchers with the opportunity to describe outcomes for these students and inform others about their language proficiency. Thus, findings can be generalized to classroom contexts and future studies.

We have identified several research questions that we believe would contribute greatly to addressing the literacy skills of adolescent English language learners. By no means do we believe that this is an adequate research agenda: It is merely a beginning, and in only one small area related to English language learners.

- Perhaps one of the most challenging issues for adolescent English language learning readers is their background knowledge and understanding within both narrative and expository text. Research to investigate classroom practices that can enhance outcomes in these areas is much needed.
- Feasible effective practices for teachers to implement that enhance

vocabulary knowledge and use across content areas would benefit students and teachers.

- Issues regarding the extent to which the knowledge base in reading comprehension for monolingual students is appropriate to generalize to student English language learners need to be addressed.
- In the growing number of adolescents who are new to our country, models that effectively integrate this population into schooling are required.
- We need to understand better the relationship between oral language development and literacy with adolescent English language learning students. Though often considered only a challenge at the elementary school level, there are many students whose literacy instruction is influenced significantly by their low oral language development. There is limited knowledge on how to address these issues for adolescent English language learners.
- It is simply not possible to make adequate progress in the education of English language learning students without research on how to conduct effective teacher preparation. Though the "call" to improve teacher preparation is ongoing, research on practices that might actually affect teacher education are missing.

In summary, in this chapter, we have discussed the contexts within which literacy instruction and learning take place, the cognitive processes of English language learners while engaged in reading, various promising instructional practices, and a research agenda. We have pointed out the importance of valuing and using students' culture, language, heritage, and experiences to facilitate their learning and development. We have shared research results indicating that bilingual students are able to transfer native-language knowledge to ESL reading, that ESL oral proficiency and reading are positively related, and that there are key differences between more and less proficient second-language readers, as well as between second-language readers and native English readers. We have discussed the influence of schemas (background knowledge), metacognition, and vocabulary, and have noted that, in effective schools, teachers had high expectations for student success, parent involvement was high, and students benefited from a challenging academic curriculum while learning English. We have described several instructional approaches that show promise with adolescent English language learners. Finally, we have noted that despite the growth in culturally and linguistically diverse populations across the United States, research on adolescent English language learners is still quite sparse. Much remains to be learned.

REFERENCES

Alvermann, D. (in press). Exemplary literacy instruction in grades 7–12: What counts and who's counting? In J. Flood & P. Anders (Eds.), *The literacy development of students in urban schools: Research and policy*. Newark, DE: International Reading Association.

Amer, A. A. (1992). The effect of story grammar instruction on EFL students' comprehension of narrative text. *Reading in a Foreign Language, 8*(2), 711–720.

Ammon, M. S. (1987). Patterns of performance among bilingual children who score low in reading. In S. R. Goldman & H. T. Trueba (Eds.), *Becoming literate in English as a second language* (pp. 71–105). Norwood, NJ: Ablex.

Anderson, N. J. (1991). Individual differences in strategy use in second-language reading and testing. *Modern Language Journal, 75*, 460–472.

Anderson, V., & Henne, R. (1993). (1993, December). *Collaborative, integrated reading and writing strategy instruction*. Paper presented at the annual meeting of the National Reading Conference, Charleston, SC.

Anderson, V., & Roit, M. (1990, December). *Developing active reading behaviors with disabled adolescent learners*. Paper presented at the National Reading Conference, Miami, FL.

Anderson, V., & Roit, M. (1993). Planning and implementing collaborative strategy instruction for delayed readers in grades 6–10. *Elementary School Journal, 94*(2), 121–137.

Anderson, V., & Roit, M. (1996). Linking reading comprehension instruction to language development for language minority students. *Elementary School Journal, 96*(3), 295–309.

Arreaga-Mayer, C. (1998). Language-sensitive peer-mediated instruction for culturally and linguistically diverse learners in the intermediate elementary grades. In R. M. Gersten & R. T. Jiménez (Eds.), *Promoting learning for culturally and linguistically diverse students* (pp. 73–90). Belmont, CA: Wadsworth.

Arreaga-Mayer, C., & Greenwood, C. R. (1986). Environmental variables affecting the school achievement of culturally and linguistically different learners: An instructional perspective. *Journal of the National Association of Bilingual Education, 10*(2), 113–135.

Au, K. (1995). Multicultural perspectives on literacy research. *Journal of Reading Behavior, 27*, 85–100.

August, D., & Hakuta, K. (Eds.). (1997). *Improving schooling for language minority children: A research agenda*. Washington, DC: National Academy Press.

Bean, T. W., Potter, T. C., & Clark, C. (1980). Selected semantic features of ESL materials and their effect on bilingual students' comprehension. In M. Kamil & A. Moe (Eds.) *Perspectives on reading research and instruction: Twenty-ninth yearbook of the National Reading Conference* (pp. 1–5). Washington, DC: National Reading Conference.

Berman, P., McLaughlin, B., McLeod, B., Minicocci, C., Nelson, B., & Woodworth, K. (1995). *School reform and student diversity: Volume II. Case studies of exemplary practices for LEP students*. Berkeley, CA: National Center for Research on Cultural Diversity and Second Language and BW Associates.

Bernhardt, E. B. (1987). Cognitive processes in L2: An examination of reading behaviors. In J. P. Lantolf & A. Labarca (Eds.), *Research in second language learning: Focus on the classroom* (pp. 35–50). Norwood, NJ: Ablex.

Block, E. (1992). See how they read: Comprehension monitoring of L1 and L2 Readers. *TESOL Quarterly, 26*(2), 319–343.

Bos, C. S., & Anders, P. L. (1992). Using interactive teaching and learning strategies to promote text comprehension and content learning for students with learning disabilities. *International Journal of Disability, Development and Education, 39*, 225–238.

Bransford, J. D., & Johnson, M. K. (1972). Contextual prerequisites for understanding: Some investigations of comprehension and recall. *Journal of Verbal Learning and Verbal Behavior, 4*(2), 717–726.

Brozo, W. G., Cantú Baleiro, P., & Salazar, M. M. (1996). A walk through Gracie's garden: Literacy and cultural explorations in a Mexican American junior high school. *Journal of Adolescent and Adult Literacy, 40*, 164–170.

Bryant, D. P., Vaughn, S., Linan-Thompson, S., Ugel, N., & Hamff, A. (2000). Reading outcomes for students with and without learning disabilities in general education middle school content area classes. *Learning Disability Quarterly, 23*(3), 24–38.

Carrell, P. L. (1981). Culture-specific schemata in L2 comprehension. In R. Orem & J. Haskell (Eds.), *Selected papers from the Ninth Illinois TESOL/BE Annual Convention, First Midwest TESOL Conference* (pp. 123–132). Chicago: Illinois Teachers of English to Speakers of Other Languages/Bilingual Education.

Carrell, P. L. (1983). Three components of background knowledge in reading comprehension. *Language Learning, 33*(2), 183–207.

Carrell, P. L. (1984). Evidence of a formal schema in second language comprehension. *Language Learning, 34*(2), 87–112.

Carrell, P. L. (1987). Content and formal schemata in ESL reading. *TESOL Quarterly, 21*(3), 461–481.

Carrell, P. L. (1992). Awareness of text structure: Effects on recall. *Language Learning, 42*(1), 1–20.

Carrell, P. L., & Wallace, B. (1983). Background knowledge: Context and familiarity in reading comprehension. In M. Clarke & J. Handscome (Eds.), *On TESOL '82* (pp. 295–308). Washington, DC: Teachers of English to Speakers of Other Languages.

Cazden, C. B. (1988). *Classroom discourse: The language of teaching and learning.* Portsmouth, NH: Heinemann.

Cazden, C. B. (1995). New ideas for research on classroom discourse. *TESOL Quarterly, 29*, 384–387.

Chamot, A. U., & O'Malley, J. M. (1996). The cognitive academic language learning approach (CALLA): A model for linguistically diverse classrooms. *Elementary School Journal, 96*(3), 259–273.

Collier, V., & Thomas, W. (2001). *A national study of school effectiveness for language minority students' long-term academic achievement final report: Project 1.1.* Santa Cruz, CA: Center for Research on Education, Diversity, and Excellence.

Devine, J. (1987). General language competence and adult second-language reading. In J. Devine, P. Carrel, & D. Eskey (Eds.), *Research in reading in English as a second lan-*

guage (pp. 73–86). Washington DC: Teachers of English to Speakers of Other Languages.

Duran, R., & Revlin, R. (1994). Showcasing center projects: Diagnostic and dynamic assessment of comprehension and reasoning skills. *Focus on Diversity, 4,* 608.

Echevarria, J. (1995). Interactive reading instruction: A comparison of proximal and distal effects of instructional conversations. *Exceptional Children, 61*(6), 536–552.

Education Statistics Quarterly. (2000). High school dropouts, by race/ethnicity and recency of migration. *Education Statistics Quarterly, 2*(3), 25–27.

Elley, W. B. (1981). A comparison of content-interest and structuralist reading programs in nine primary schools. *New Zealand Journal of Educational Studies, 15*(1), 39–53.

Field, M. (1996). Pragmatic issues related to reading comprehension questions: A case study from a Latino bilingual classroom. *Issues in Applied Linguistics, 7*(2), 209–224.

Fitzgerald, J. (1995a). English-as-a-second-language learners' cognitive reading processes: A review of research in the United States. *Review of Educational Research, 65,* 145–190.

Fitzgerald, J. (1995b). English-as-a-second-language reading instruction in the United States: A research review. *Journal of Reading Behavior, 27,* 115–152.

García, G. E. (1991). Factors influencing the English reading test performance of Spanish speaking Hispanic children. *Reading Research Quarterly, 26*(4), 371–392.

García, G. E., & Nagy, W. (1993). Latino students' concept of cognates. In D. J. Leu & C. K. Kinzer (Eds.), *Examining central issues in literacy research, theory, and practice: Forty-second yearbook of the National Reading Conference* (pp. 367–373). Chicago: National Reading Conference.

García-Vazquez, E. (1995). Acculturation and academics: Effects of acculturation on reading achievement among Mexican-American students. *Bilingual Research Journal, 19,* 305–315.

Gersten, R. (1996). The language-minority student in transition: Contemporary instructional research. *Elementary School Journal, 96*(3), 217–219.

Gersten, R., & Baker, S. (2000a). What we know about effective instructional practices for English-language learners. *Exceptional Children, 66*(4), 454–470.

Gersten, R., & Jiménez, R. (1994). A delicate balance: Enhancing literacy instruction for students of English as a second language. *Reading Teacher, 47,* 438–449.

Goldenberg, C. (1992/1993). Instructional conversations: Promoting comprehension through discussion. *Reading Teacher, 46,* 316–326.

Graves, A. (1998). Instructional strategies and techniques for middle school students who are learning English. In R. M. Gersten & R. T. Jiménez (Eds.), *Promoting learning for culturally and linguistically diverse students* (pp. 167–186). Belmont, CA: Wadsworth.

Hinds, J. (1983). Contrastive rhetoric: Japanese and English. *Text, 3*(2), 183–195.

Jiménez, R. T. (1997). The strategic reading abilities and potential of five low-literacy Latina/o readers in middle school. *Reading Research Quarterly, 32,* 224–243.

Jiménez, R. T., García, G. E., & Pearson, P. D. (1995). Three children, two languages, and strategic reading: Case studies in bilingual/monolingual reading. *American Educational Research Journal, 32,* 67–97.

Jiménez, R. T., García, G. E., & Pearson, P. D. (1996). The reading strategies of bilingual Latino students who are successful English readers: Opportunities and obstacles. *Reading Research Quarterly, 31,* 90–112.

Johnson, D. W., & Johnson, R. T. (1989). Cooperative learning: What special educators need to know. *The Pointer, 33,* 5–10.

Johnson, P. (1981). Effects on reading comprehension of language complexity and cultural background of a text. *TESOL Quarterly, 15*(2), 169–181.

Johnson, P. (1982). Effects on reading comprehension of building background knowledge. *TESOL Quarterly, 16*(4), 503–516.

Kim, A., Vaughn S., Wanzek, J., & Wei, S. (in press). A synthesis of research on graphic organizers and their effect on reading comprehension for students with learning disabilities. *Journal of Learning Disabilities.*

Klingner, J. K., & Vaughn, S. (1996). Reciprocal teaching of reading comprehension strategies for students with learning disabilities who use English as a second language. *Elementary School Journal, 96,* 275–293.

Klingner, J. K., & Vaughn, S. (2000). The helping behaviors of fifth-graders while using Collaborative Strategic Reading (CSR) during ESL content classes. *TESOL Quarterly, 34,* 69–98.

Klingner, J. K., Vaughn, S., Dimino, J., Schumm, J. S., & Bryant, D. (2001). *From clunk to click: Collaborative Strategic Reading.* Longmont, CO: Sopris West.

Klingner, J. K., Vaughn, S., & Schumm, J. S. (1998). Collaborative Strategic Reading during social studies in heterogeneous fourth-grade classrooms. *Elementary School Journal, 99,* 3–21.

Knight, S. L., Padrón, Y. N., & Waxman, H. C. (1985). Cognitive strategies used by ESL students. *TESOL Quarterly, 19,* 789–792.

Langer, J. A. (1997). Literacy acquisition through literature. *Journal of Adolescent and Adult Literacy, 40,* 606–614.

Langer, J. A., Bartholome, L., Vasquez, O., & Lucas, T. (1990). Meaning construction in school literacy tasks: A study of bilingual students. *American Educational Research Journal, 27,* 427–471.

Lee, J. (2002). Racial and ethnic achievement gap trends: Reversing the progress toward equity. *Educational Researcher, 31,* 3–12.

Lee, J., & Schallert, D. L. (1997). The relative contribution of L2 language proficiency and L1 reading ability to L2 reading performance: A test of the threshold hypothesis in an EFL context. *TESOL Quarterly, 31,* 713–739.

Lucas, T. (1996). *Promoting secondary school transitions for immigrant adolescents* [Report No. EDO-FL-97-04]. (ERIC Document Reproduction Service No. ED402786)

Lucas, T., Henze, R., & Donato, R. (1990). Promoting the success of Latino language-minority students: An exploratory study of six high schools. *Harvard Educational Review, 60*(3), 315–339.

McLaren, J., & Anderson, V. (1992, December). *Instruction in two text structures: Effects on understanding and written production of expository text by elementary school students.* Paper presented at the National Reading Conference, San Antonio, TX.

Moll, L. (1988). Some key issues in teaching Latino students. *Language Arts, 65*(5), 465–472.

Moll, L. (1992). Bilingual classroom studies and community analysis: Some recent trends. *Educational Researcher, 21*(2), 20–24.

Moll, L., & González, N. (1994). Lessons from research with language-minority children. *Journal of Reading Behavior, 26*(4), 439–456.

Moll, L., & Ruiz, R. (2002). The schooling of Latino students. In M. Suarez-Orozco & M. Paez (Eds.), *Latinos: Remaking America* (pp. 362–374). Berkeley: University of California Press.

Moll, L. C. (Ed.). (1990). *Vygotsky and education: Instructional implications and applications of sociocultural psychology.* New York: Cambridge University Press.

Moore, D. W. (1996). Contexts for literacy in secondary schools. In D. J. Leu, C. K. Kinzer, & K. A. Hinchman (Eds.), *Literacies for the 21st century: Research and practice, Forty-fifth yearbook of the National Reading Conference* (pp. 15–46). Chicago: National Reading Conference.

Nagy, W. E., García, G. E., Durgunoglu, A., & Hancin, B. (1993). Spanish–English bilingual children's use and recognition of cognates in English reading. *Journal of Reading Behavior, 25*(3), 241–259.

National Reading Panel. (2000). *Report of the National Reading Panel.* Washington, DC: National Institute of Child Health and Human Development.

Neuman, S. B., & Koskinen, P. (1992). Captioned television as comprehensible input: Effects of incidental word learning from context for language minority students. *Reading Research Quarterly, 27,* 95–106.

Nieto, S. (2002). *Language, culture, and teaching: Critical perspectives for a new century.* Mahwah, NJ: Erlbaum.

Oakes, J. (1986). Keeping track: Part 2. Curriculum inequality and school reform. *Phi Delta Kappan, 68*(2), 148–154.

O'Malley, J. M., & Chamot, A. U. (1990). *Learning strategies in second language acquisition.* Cambridge, UK: Cambridge University Press.

Padrón, Y., & Waxman, H. C. (1988). The effect of ESL students' perceptions of their cognitive strategies on reading achievement. *TESOL Quarterly, 22,* 146–150.

Palincsar, A. S., & Brown, A. L. (1984). Reciprocal teaching of comprehension-fostering and comprehension-monitoring activities. *Cognition and Instruction, 1*(2), 117–175.

Pritchard, R. (1990). The effects of cultural schemata on reading processing strategies. *Reading Research Quarterly, 25*(4), 273–295.

Qian, D. D. (1999). Assessing the roles of depth and breadth of vocabulary knowledge in reading comprehension. *Canadian Modern Language Review, 56,* 282–307.

Rayner, K., & Pollatsek, A. (1989). *The psychology of reading.* Englewood Cliffs, NJ: Prentice-Hall.

Reyes, M. de la Luz. (1991). A process approach to literacy using dialogue journals and literature logs with second language learners. *Research in the Teaching of English, 25*(3), 291–313.

Reyes, M. de la Luz. (1992). Challenging venerable assumptions: Literacy instruction for linguistically diverse students. *Harvard Educational Review, 62,* 427–446.

Reynolds, R. E., Taylor, M. A., Steffensen, M. S., Shirley, L. L., & Anderson, R. C.

(1982). Cultural schemata and reading comprehension. *Reading Research Quarterly,* *17,* 353–366.

Rodriguez, T. A. (2001). From the known to the unknown: Using cognates to teach English to Spanish-speaking literates. *Reading Teacher, 54*(8), 744–746.

Rosowsky, A. (2000). Reading and culture: The experience of some of our bilingual pupils. *English in Education, 4*(2), 45–53.

Saracho, O. N. (1982). The effects of a computer-assisted instruction program on basic skills achievement and attitudes toward instruction of Spanish-speaking migrant children. *American Educational Research Journal, 19*(2), 201–219.

Saville-Troike, M. (1984). What really matters in second language learning for academic achievement? *TESOL Quarterly, 18*(2), 199–219.

Steffensen, M .S., Joag-Dev, C., & Anderson, R. (1979). A cross-cultural perspective on reading comprehension. *Reading Research Quarterly, 15*(1), 10–29.

Thompson, G. L. (2000). The real deal on bilingual education: Former language-minority students discuss effective and ineffective instructional practices. *Educational Horizons, 78*(2), 80–92.

Tregar, B., & Wong, B. F. (1984). The relationship between native and second-language reading comprehension and second language oral ability. In C. Rivera (Ed.), *Placement procedures in bilingual education: Education and policy issues* (pp.152–164). Clevedon, UK: Multilingual Matters.

U.S. Bureau of the Census. (2001, April 2). *U S. Census Bureau, Population Division.* Retrieved March 26, 2003, from *http://www.census.gov/population/www/cen2000/phc-t1.html*

U.S. Bureau of the Census. (2003, February, 25). *U.S. Census Bureau, Population Division.* Retrieved March 26, 2003, from *http://www.census.gov/population/www/cen2000/phc-t20.html*

Wong-Fillmore, L., & Valadez, C. (1986). Teaching bilingual learners. In M. Wittrock (Ed). *Handbook of research on teaching* (pp. 648–685). New York: Macmillan.

Zanger, V. V. (1994). "Not joined in": The social context of English literacy development for Hispanic youth. In B. M. Ferdman, R. Weber, & A. G. Ramirez (Eds.), *Literacy across languages and cultures* (pp. 171–198). Albany: State University of New York Press.

Zimmerman, C. B. (1997). Do reading and interactive vocabulary instruction make a difference? *TESOL Quarterly, 31,* 121–140.

10

Literacy Intervention Programs at the Middle and High School Levels

DONNA E. ALVERMANN
LESLIE S. RUSH

We subscribe to the view that intervention programs aimed at improving adolescent literacy achievement must address the complex issues around youth's engagement with texts, both traditional print texts and those of the new media and information communication technologies that surround us on all sides. This view calls for rethinking the teaching of youth whose motivations to read (or not to read) hinge on a wide range of factors, including the cognitive, social, and cultural, for starters. It involves rethinking intervention programs, perhaps along the lines of what Cole and Griffin (1986) earlier, and Luke and Elkins (2000) more recently, have alluded to as re/mediating adolescent literacies. It also involves rethinking our definition of text, broadening it to include both visuals and print, as suggested by the New London Group's (2000) framework of multiliteracies.

Drawing on some interesting derivatives for *medium, media,* and *mediate,* Luke and Elkins (2000) point out that these are concepts for communicating, framing, and scaffolding ideas and relationships among people and their material worlds. In much the same way, the concept of re/mediation involves rethinking or reframing the way we think about intervening in students' reading lives. It calls for moving beyond fruitless searches for some method (or magic bullet, if you will) that promises to fix kids' so-called deficits in reading. Re/mediation, in the sense that Luke and Elkins (2000) used the term, involves fashioning instructional conditions that enable us as educators "to come to grips with the contextual variables in adolescent lives, all of the complex causes and consequences of any given action and intervention, and the multiple relations between media technologies that adolescents juggle every day" (p. 397). In a metaphoric sense, then, re/mediation involves fixing the conditions in which students learn rather than fixing the students per se.

Teaching with an eye to re/mediation requires letting go of (or at the very least rethinking) some old adages. For example, the popular motto "Every teacher, a teacher of reading" sounds like a good idea, but a brief look at the literature on content area literacy instruction for the last five decades clearly shows that it is a motto seldom taken up by more than a few staunch supporters in a few isolated instances (O'Brien, Stewart, & Moje, 1995). Perhaps more detrimental, however, is the often-repeated saying that "Students learn to read before they read to learn." Not only is this wrongheaded, it is also potentially damaging from an instructional point of view. Separating the act of reading from one of its functions—reading to learn *something*—makes no sense. Though it can be argued that, developmentally, beginning readers are different from skilled readers, the difference between these two age groups lies more with the content or subject-matter materials they are expected to read than with any overall purpose for reading.

Another continual favorite—"reading across the curriculum"— sounds simple and straightforward. However, if taken literally, this saying can be somewhat misleading. For example, "reading across the curriculum" would suggest that individuals who can apply a set of reading skills in one disciplinary area will be equally successful when applying that same set of skills in another disciplinary area. Yet, as any proficient reader knows, the structures of disciplines (e.g., history, science, mathematics, literature) differ greatly, and so do the text structures that support them in the content area textbooks a student reads. Ways of talking about science, engaging in science experiments, and being recognized as a scientist are vastly different from the ways of talking about history, writing a history book, and being recognized as a historian. These discourses and their corresponding differences make it imperative that a reader approach any given text by asking critical questions about whose message is being conveyed, by what means, and for what purposes. Not only will the answers to such questions vary from one content area to another, but so also will the skills a reader brings to the task.

Finally, rethinking the dominance of print in teaching and learning from (and with) texts may take some doing on everyone's part. The close association between print and "text" has been the norm for so long that it is almost second nature to equate the two. Yet sweeping changes in interactive communication technologies require that we prepare students to interpret and respond to multimedia and hypermedia texts, with their richly integrated uses of print, visual, and auditory elements (Bean, Bean, & Bean, 1999; Elkins & Luke, 1999; Rush, 2003). The necessity of preparing students to comprehend and respond to these kinds of texts challenges educators to move beyond narrowly conceived notions of literacy.

In the process of moving beyond outmoded conceptions, we might also begin to rethink the kinds of interventions necessary for re/mediating the conditions in which struggling readers learn. The importance of doing so seems self-evident and is backed by efforts on many fronts. For example, consider the Carnegie Foundation's innovative initiative, Schools for a New Society (*http://www.carnegie.org/sub/news/sns.html*). This initiative, which was launched in October 2001, is in response to the fact that, in the United States, close to 50% of the incoming ninth graders in this country's comprehensive, public high schools cannot comprehend the texts that their teachers assign. Students who have not had opportunities to engage critically with the textual practices and discourses common to the subject matter they are expected to read not surprisingly end up failing their courses and eventually dropping out of school.

This chapter is divided four ways. In the first part, we focus on middle and high school literacy intervention programs that are currently in use at the district, state, or national level and that are supported by research—though not necessarily independently conducted research, a factor to which we return later in the chapter. In the second part, we offer a critique of these programs in terms of how they fit within the re/mediation perspective introduced earlier. Specifically, do the programs involve interventions for fixing the conditions in which students learn, or do they simply attempt to fix the students? Our belief in the need to re/mediate the conditions for student learning in subject matter classrooms is perhaps best mirrored in Greenleaf, Jiménez, and Roller's (2002) redefinition of the term *intervention*. In their words, it is "integrated, strategic, meaningful, and, if necessary, intensive curriculum and instruction to powerfully enrich and expand adolescents' reading lives" (p. 495). In the third part, we offer a set of educator guidelines for applying what can be learned from the critique in part two to classroom practice. Finally, in part four, we conclude with a discussion of several issues that make broad implementations of adolescent literacy programs problematic and the research that might address these issues.

INTERVENTION PROGRAMS

In an effort to cast a fairly wide net in our search for literacy intervention programs designed for teaching and learning at the middle and high school levels, we posted questions on the National Council of Teachers of English (NCTE) listserv and on the International Reading Association's (IRA) Adolescent Literacy Commission listserv that asked for program nominations. We also attended sessions at the annual meetings of the NCTE, the IRA, the American Reading Forum (ARF), and the National Reading Conference (NRC) that addressed issues concerning intervention programs for youth who find school literacy a challenge. In addition, we did a hand search of *Reading Research Quarterly, Journal of Literacy Research*, and *Reading Research and Instruction* for articles related to this topic. The seven programs described here were the results of that effort.

Accelerated Reader

Accelerated Reader (AR) is a program for computer-assisted, student self-assessment of reading comprehension. Originally published by Advantage Learning Systems, now called the School Renaissance Institute, it is described as both a reading motivation program and a learning information system, through which teachers can manage the reading practice of their students. Students begin the program by taking a Standardized Test for Assessment of Reading (STAR), which is a computerized cloze test, with no accompanying test of oral reading comprehension or teacher observation of reading behaviors. Once a reading or grade level has been established for a student, he or she selects a trade book to read from a list of over 13,000 titles. Each book is assigned a certain point value, based on the number of words in the book and its readability. After reading the chosen book, the student takes a computerized, multiple-choice comprehension test on the content of the book. The computer scores the test, awards the student points based on test results, and keeps a complete record of results. The software originated in the United States and is supported by extensive staff development known as Reading Renaissance. AR is currently used in over 40,000 schools in the United States, and its use is spreading to other countries.

Although the Renaissance Learning website (*www.renlearn.com*) listed 87 research abstracts on AR at the time of this writing, we found very little in the way of peer-reviewed, published research reports. Many of the reports listed on the website are district reports written by district personnel, including curriculum supervisors and teachers. These district reports present a positive picture of AR's success in percentages of improvement on standardized reading test scores, increased library circulation, and improved attitude toward reading. In addition to district reports are several reports conducted as dissertations or other graduate school projects (Kambarian, 2001; Mathis, 1996). Kambarian (2001) analyzed scores on the California Test of Basic Skills (CTBS) Terra Nova test for second- through sixth-grade students in two groups, one of which had been exposed to AR, and the other, which had not, over a 3-year period. The study found that the youngest cohort of students—second through fourth grade—that had been exposed to AR showed the greatest improvement. Mathis analyzed the Stanford Achievement Test scores of 30 sixth-grade students both before and after their use of the AR program. Results indicated no significant increase in reading comprehension scores. These conflicting findings indicate that further research is necessary.

Findings in published articles on AR (Pavonetti, Brimmer, & Cipielewski, 2002; Topping & Paul, 1999; Vollands, Topping, & Evans, 1999), when taken together, are mixed. Pavonetti et al. (2002) used a Title Recognition Test to examine whether seventh graders who had used AR in elementary school tended to read more books than those seventh graders who had not. Their results do not support AR's claim that the use of their product leads to the development of lifelong readers. Vollands et al. (1999) contains two action research projects; in both of these projects, groups of students using AR are compared to groups using other reading programs. The authors claim that the use of AR yielded gains in reading achievement for at-risk readers.

READ 180

READ 180, which is a Scholastic computerized program based on the work of Ted Hasselbring and the Cognition and Technology Group at Vanderbilt University, Janet Allen and the Orange County Literacy Project in Florida, and the development staff at Scholastic, targets students in grades 4–12 who are reading below grade level. It allows students to work on improving vocabulary, reading, and writing skills through computer-based programs with supplemental books and audiotapes. According to the Scholastic website (*http://teacher.scholastic.com/read180/research/timeline.htm*), Hasselbring's research in 1985 led to the development of a software program that used individual student performance data to differentiate reading instruction. Originally called the Peabody Learning Lab, this software was combined with Janet Allen's literacy workshop model for use in the Orange County (FL) Literacy Project. This project, piloted in three middle school classrooms in 1994–1995, was extended to 13 classes in 1996, and districtwide in 1997. Scholastic became involved with the project in 1997, and published it under the name of READ 180 in 1999–2001. The program is currently available for use at the elementary school level (Stage A), middle school level (Stage B), and high school level (Stage C). The program has four main components: interactive CD-ROM software for students and management software for teachers; audiobooks; leveled paperbacks for independent reading; and various teacher resources. Each segment of the software begins with a video and a passage that summarizes the video. As students move through the software, they are given both opportunities to complete activities that repeat words from the passages and immediate feedback on errors, as well as strategies for remediation. Repeated readings and review of words are used to enhance fluency. Support for English language learners is provided in the software through both clickable translations of passage text and Spanish summaries of the videos and reading passages. READ 180 is currently being used in a number of schools in the United States and in Department of Defense schools.

Research on the piloting of the Orange County Literacy Project's use of the software found that students in the Literacy Project made significantly larger gains than the nationally normed group on the Degrees of Reading Power test (Scholastic, 2002). Given that the READ 180 version for grades 9 and above was released in August 2002, no research is yet available on the effectiveness of the program with high school students.

Reading Is FAME

Reading Is FAME is designed as an intervention program for adolescents who lack the decoding ability and/or word knowledge needed to comprehend reading materials at grade level. The initial piloting of this program took place at Father Flanagan's Boys and Girls Town in Nebraska, where the average participant is 15 years old and is in residence from 18 to 22 months. Adolescents are sent to Boys and Girls Town because of "chronic neglect and abuse, illegal and antisocial behaviors, and academic failure" (Curtis & Longo, 2001, p. 1). The Reading is FAME program was designed by Mary Beth Curtis and Anne Marie Longo based on Chall's (1983) stages of reading development. The program comprises four courses, each 16 weeks in length. The first course, Foundations of Reading, which is aimed at students in grades 7–12 who are reading below a fourth-grade level, teaches relationships among most common letter combinations. The second course, Adventures in Reading, for students in grades 7–12 reading between fourth- and sixth-grade levels, is designed to promote fluency in word recognition and knowledge of word meaning. The third course, Mastery of Meaning, is designed to build vocabulary knowledge of students in grades 9–12 who read between sixth- and eighth-grade levels, and the fourth course, Explorations, for students in grades 9–12 reading above an eighth-grade level, involves improving integration of text information through reading and writing. Reading Is FAME programs are in place in Nebraska, Iowa, Wyoming, Utah, South Carolina, New York, Texas, Georgia, and Washington, D.C. (Curtis & Longo, 1999). Research on Reading Is FAME at its initial site found that students gained about a year in reading achievement, as measured by the Woodcock–Johnson Psycho-Educational Battery, for every semester's worth of instruction. Similar gains were found in a public high school implementation of the program (Curtis & Longo, 1999).

Supported Literacy Approach

The Supported Literacy Approach (SLA), a project within the larger, multidisciplinary and programmatic REACH Institute (2001), was designed by Catherine Morocco, Alisa Hindin, and associates at the Education Development Center in Newton, MA. Supportive literacy instruction is focused on advancing diverse groups of middle school students' (especially those with disabilities) understanding of literature. The SLA draws from research conducted within a sociocultural perspective on the learning process, which basically adheres to the notion that students learn to read by participating in group activities that are mediated by students' and teachers' uses of language, such as whole-class, small-group, and peer-led discussions. Research on the SLA (Hindin, Morocco, & Aguilar, 2001; Morocco & Hindin, 2002) has shown that integrating peer-led discussions with reading and writing about young adult literature enables students with disabilities to perform similarly to their peers in regular education.

Strategic Literacy Initiative

The Strategic Literacy Initiative is a professional development and research program of WestEd that focuses on improving adolescents' literacy by building teachers' expertise in teaching reading in their subject matter areas. The program's codirectors, Ruth Schoenbach and Cynthia Greenleaf, have developed with their WestEd colleagues what they call a reading apprenticeship model that takes into account adolescents' interests and provides instruction in guided reading, reciprocal teaching, vocabulary, metacognition, and other useful teaching and learning strategies taught in regular content area classes. The model, which is viewed as an alternative to pull-out remediation programs for underprepared high school students, was evaluated during the 1996–1997 academic year in the San Francisco

Bay area. The results of that evaluation showed that struggling ninth-grade readers enrolled in a regular education classroom in a culturally diverse high school achieved 2 years' growth in a 7-month period, as measured by a standardized test of reading comprehension (Greenleaf, Schoenbach, Cziko, & Mueller, 2001). Since then, professional staff developers at the National Institute in Reading Apprenticeship have launched similar reading apprenticeship programs in urban school districts outside the Bay area. According to Greenleaf and Schoenbach (2004), new cohorts of students in regular content-area classrooms show gains similar to those achieved by students in the 1996–1997 study, with those who are furthest behind at the beginning of the school year making the greatest gains.

Project CRISS

CReating Independence through Student-owned Strategies (CRISS) was originally developed by Carol Santa and her colleagues in Kalispell, Montana. Its purpose was to support secondary teachers of science, social studies, English, mathematics, and reading as they worked together to develop practical approaches for helping students learn from (and with) their content area texts. Santa and her colleagues met in teams to read the research and professional literature on applying key principles from cognitive psychology to classroom reading instruction (Santa, Havens, & Maycumber, 1996). They also designed teacher researcher studies that permitted them to examine the effectiveness of Project CRISS in actual classroom practice.

In 1985, the U.S. Department of Education and the Joint Dissemination Review Panel recognized Project CRISS as an exemplary high school program—one that uses research-based reading and writing strategies to help students improve their learning in content area classes—and named it as part of the National Diffusion Network. This validation of the project led to further development over the next 15 or so years by Carol Santa and Lynn Havens. For example, in 1993, national validation of the project was expanded by the U. S. Department of Education and the Program Effectiveness Panel to include grades 4–12 (Killion, 1999; Project CRISS, 1996). Project CRISS-based practices, which had been largely literacy-oriented, were extended to include professional development models of teaching, reading engagement, and school change, all built on evidence-based research across several disciplinary areas. There is also a professional development component for parents, including a workbook available in English, Spanish, and, soon, in Vietnamese.

During the 2001–2002 school year, Project CRISS evaluators conducted an extensive study of the effectiveness of the program in the Granite County School District of Salt Lake City, Utah. The study's design included experimental and control classrooms at each of three grade levels: grade 4, grade 7, and grade 10 biology classes. Pre- and posttest measures were administered to both experimental and control groups at the beginning and end of the school year. The intervention consisted of the experimental group teachers receiving professional development in how to integrate Project CRISS principles and strategies into their teaching. Students in the experimental condition were taught by the specially trained teachers for one school year. At the end of the year, students in each of the experimental classrooms showed statistically significantly larger gains than the control group on tests of comprehension and recall of information in age-appropriate social studies or science selections, 4–8 pages in length. Similar results were found in earlier evaluations of Project CRISS in Colorado, Florida, Montana, and Virginia (Killion, 2002a, 2002b; Personal communication, Lynn Havens, April 22, 2003).

Talent Development High School Literacy Program

The Talent Development High School (TDHS) Literacy Program is designed to accelerate the literacy growth of underprepared high school students. It was developed by the high school reform team at the Center for Education of Students Placed at Risk (CRESPAR) and the Center for Social Organization of Schools at Johns Hopkins University. This yearlong program, which currently serves only underprepared students at the ninth-grade level (Personal communication, James McPartland, March 24, 2003), consists of four components. The first component involves students in block-scheduled instruction for 90 minutes a day in math and English for a whole year. The second consists of two semester-long blocks. In the first semester, students enroll in three courses designed to help them overcome their lack of preparation: (1) a course on Strategic Reading; (2) one on Transition to Advanced Mathematics; and (3) the Freshman Seminar. The Strategic Reading course uses four approaches to improve students' fluency and comprehension: read-and-think-aloud demonstrations by the teachers; minilessons on specific comprehension and writing strategies (e.g., skimming and identifying elements of various genres); cooperative learning teams to practice new vocabulary and develop fluency; and self-selected reading and writing activities (high interest fiction and nonfiction). The second semester course uses the district's English I syllabus. In the third component, teachers receive intensive and sustained professional development that includes 25–30 hours of course-specific sessions and weekly in-classroom coaching provided by teachers on special assignment and instructional facilitators from Johns Hopkins University. The fourth component, the Ninth-Grade Success Academy, is located in a separate part of the main school building. In this component, students receive instruction from teachers who have a common planning period in which to coordinate efforts related to student outreach and recovery (Balfanz, 2002).

Although several evaluation studies have been conducted on the TDHS instructional interventions in reading and literacy between 1999–2001, only data from those pertaining to the TDHS Literacy Program are included here. In 1999–2000, the literacy intervention was used in 20 regular education classes by eight teachers in three Baltimore nonselective neighborhood high schools. The curriculum coaches rated one teacher as a high implementer, five as medium implementers, and two as medium-low implementers. In the three control schools, students received 90 minutes a day of mathematics and English instruction for one school year. Students in both the experimental and control schools had attendance rates of 87% to 89%, which suggests that they were present frequently enough to have been impacted by the interventions. Overall, students in the experimental schools significantly outperformed students in the control schools on standardized measures of reading. During the 2000–2001 school year, similar results were found in two supplemental studies of the TDHS Literacy Program when it was implemented in 11 high-poverty, nonselective high schools in Newark, Philadelphia, Baltimore, and New York City (Balfanz, 2002).

A CRITIQUE FROM THE STANDPOINT OF RE/MEDIATION

Attempting to fix, or intervene, in the material conditions in which middle and high school students learn, as opposed to trying to change something about the learners themselves, is a distinguishing characteristic of Luke and Elkins's (2000) notion of re/mediation. It is a far cry from earlier uses of the term *remediation*, minus the slash mark, which typically meant sorting students by reading ability level, then removing the lowest performing students from their regularly assigned classes in order to work with them in one-on-one or small-group settings. Sometimes referred to as the medical model of remediation, the assumption was that something was inherently wrong in a young reader's development, and that it was up to the reading specialist to "diagnose" the problem and to fix it with the appropriate instructional materials available. In some of the intervention programs we overviewed earlier, this older model is still in operation.

For example, although Accelerated Reader (AR) is advertised as a motivating program for reluctant readers, its use seems to be based on the assumption that students with reading difficulties lack practice in reading, and that providing practice with books at their reading level will improve their fluency and comprehension. Although this assumption has appeal, a problem that arises with it in this case is the blanket application of the program to students, teachers, and learning contexts regardless of their unique qualities. Here, the problem is perceived as residing within the student, and the solution is to turn that student over to a computer program for assistance. This perception can be seen throughout the program, because testing through STAR is relied on as an assessment of students' silent reading comprehension without reference to any other factors. This testing is then used to assign students' reading level, and students are directed toward and tested on appropriate-leveled books.

Even if AR is seen purely as a tool for reading motivation, problems arise. It is our belief, because of what we know about the problems of extrinsic motivation for reading (Baker & Wigfield, 1999; Cameron & Pierce, 1994; Gambrell & Marinak, 1997; Sweet, 1997; Wigfield & Guthrie, 1997), and from the research of Pavonnetti et al. (2002), that even though AR may motivate some students to read temporarily, it has little effect on reading comprehension abilities, and little long-term effect on reading motivation.

To a lesser degree, we place READ 180 in the same category as AR. Like AR, READ 180 is a computerized program designed to assist students who struggle with reading. We find the program to be much more sophisticated than that used by AR, in that it provides feedback to students, makes use of video and audiotape components, and provides support for English language learners. However, we find that READ 180 is based on the same assumptions about students who struggle with reading: that the problem lies within the student, and that a program such as this can fix the problem. Another concern with both of these programs is the ease with which it is possible for teachers to turn students who struggle with reading over to computerized programs, instead of working to understand how classrooms and instructional methods could be changed to meet the complex and multiple conditions of adolescents' needs.

Reading Is FAME is based on the assumption that reading problems for adolescents largely stem either from an inadequate vocabulary base or from problems with phonological processing. Naturally, Reading is FAME attempts to resolve this issue with intensive instruction in decoding and word meaning throughout the program. Although we applaud this work in its focus on a worthwhile goal, improving adolescents' ability to recognize and use words, we find its focus a bit limited and limiting. Reading Is FAME lacks the contextual support and flexibility that we would hope for in a reading program that could expand to meet the complex needs of adolescents, as is required in a program that fits into the re/mediation framework.

The Supported Literacy Approach (SLA) is a good example of a program couched within a re/mediation framework. Its success among middle school students with disabilities in language processing is attributed to teachers' abilities to scaffold whole-class, small-group, and peer-led discussions of young adult literature in ways that teach valuable comprehension skills as students talk about highly motivating material. Although this is a step forward in changing the learning conditions to meet individual needs, the SLA is limited at the present time to a focus on literary texts. Whether this approach would work equally well with content area texts is unknown.

The Strategic Literacy Initiative(SLI) and Project CRISS take the re/mediation model to a new level of sophistication. Instead of simply changing conditions of learning for a particular type of student reading a particular type of text, these two programs concentrate on professional development courses for secondary content area teachers that support them in helping students learn from (and with) the various subject matter texts they assign. By working directly with teachers of science, social studies, English, mathematics, and reading, the professional development staffs of the SLI and Project CRISS are able to introduce teachers to strategies and skills that extend beyond literacy-oriented instruction in various disciplinary areas. For example, teachers in the SLI learn to use the apprenticeship model as a means of helping students who struggle with reading to become more capable learners in their subject matter classes. Students can see for themselves how the use of teacher-guided comprehension and vocabulary strategies can move them along the continuum from apprentice to expert learner. In Project CRISS, teachers are encouraged to engage in action research projects of their own choosing to improve learning conditions within their own classrooms. Although the changes initially may be local, that is, classroom-focused, the possibility exists for influencing broader, districtwide changes as well. What is missing in these two programs, as well as in the ones discussed earlier, is an outside source to evaluate how effective they are. To date, the evaluations that have been conducted are internal to the various programs under investigation.

The absence of an external evaluation program is also a concern for the TDHS Literacy Program. Although this program has been the object of fairly large-scale assessments using well-known standardized reading tests in high-poverty urban schools, it has been staff at CRESPAR who have conducted them. This is not to say that an independent outside evaluator would find different results, of course, in any of the program evaluations just discussed. What sets the TDHS Literacy Program apart from the other programs we have described is its comprehensive, schoolwide teaching and learning components. For example, teachers and students in this program are involved in yearlong professional development and special courses coordinated in a manner that changes the conditions not only for learning but also for the curriculum. Rather than trying to fit within a school's particular prescribed curriculum, those involved in the TDHS Literacy Program are the beneficiaries of re/mediation at its best.

What we could not determine from the available literature on any of the programs we examined is the degree to which the various interventions took into account the need for direct instruction in critical and evaluative reading. As noted earlier, disciplinary structures differ, and so do the skills necessary for reading them critically and evaluatively. Certainly, some of the interventions discussed here incorporated strategies (e.g., guided reading, peer-led discussions, skimming, and identifying elements of various genres) that would seem to encourage students to discuss critically the material at hand and to use elements of the writer's craft to point out textual inconsistencies. In this regard, the SLA, the SLI, Project CRISS, and the TDHS Literacy Program appear to do a credible job.

However, not one of the programs under review seems overtly concerned with the various nonprint literacies that adolescents use today—visual and digital literacies that can extend print-based learning and provide struggling readers with alternative pathways to comprehending disciplinary content. We believe this is a serious oversight, especially given that these same literacies account for a significant amount of adolescents' learning outside school (Alvermann, 2002; Hull & Schultz, 2001; Moje, 2000).

EDUCATOR GUIDELINES

In a re/mediation approach to intervening instructionally, the emphasis is not so much on ensuring that every teacher is a teacher of reading as it is on taking into account the complexities of teaching and learning in content area classes. When teacher-educators and other professional development experts work with classroom teachers in ways that demonstrate the futility of thinking of any literacy program as simply a means for superimposing a set of basic reading skills that can be applied without regard to a specific discipline's discourse and textual practices, they accomplish what we propose is the first step to trading in the old remediation model for the newer concept of re/mediation. We realize that this is not a one-step process, and we also acknowledge that re/mediation itself is not the magic bullet that will "fix" every problem adolescents encounter in learning to read from (and with) their content area texts. Still, we believe that a fundamental change in teachers' and teacher educators' expectations for what needs changing—students or the conditions in which they learn—will lead to the development and implementation of better and more effective literacy intervention programs. With this in mind, and working from what is now available in the literature discussed earlier in this chapter, we propose the following guidelines for educators interested in choosing a program to use with students who struggle to read their content area texts.

1. Choose programs that show promise for intervening in the instructional conditions in which students are expected to learn. Criteria that might be used in making such choices should address issues of feasibility (e.g., is a program's practical implementation likely given the current level of administrative support?) and context (e.g., what changes in teacher and student practices would need to be considered, or what supplementary services, in terms of professional development and technological support, would need to be in place?).

2. Examine the assumptions underlying these programs. For example, is one of the assumptions that students with reading difficulties lack practice in reading and, therefore, simply providing more practice with materials judged to be at their appropriate reading level will increase their fluency and comprehension? Is there sufficient research evidence to back such an assumption? If one subscribes to the findings of the National Reading Panel (2000), the idea that more practice leads to better reading achievement is not supported, though, arguably, this idea is still open to investigation using a broader research paradigm than the one that guided members of the panel.

3. Determine the degree to which teachers are expected to lend a guiding hand in helping students become more motivated and proficient learners. Literacy intervention programs that merely turn instruction over to a computer are not likely to assess accurately (and, thus, respond appropriately) to the complexities involved in working with youth whose motivations to learn may vary greatly according to time, place, and context. Thus, any program that promises a blanket solution to students' literacy learning without considerable teacher involvement should be approached with caution.

4. Analyze what assumptions seem to be operating in a literacy intervention program that treats subject matter as transparent and not open to critical and evaluative questioning by teachers or students. Treating disciplinary knowledge as if it were easily seen through and unchangeable across time and different contexts is equivalent to acting in the interests of what Freire (1972) and others have described as the banking approach to education—that is, filling students' heads with information in an unproblematic way, such that the delivery apparatus takes precedence over what might be learned through questioning and debating the very material being presented.

In addition to the previous programmatic guidelines, teachers who are working individually to improve student reading in their own classrooms may want to consider implementing aspects of the reviewed programs that seem promising. One aspect of AR and READ 180 that seems promising is access to large amounts of high quality reading materials for students who struggle with reading. Teachers who provide students with plenty to read give those students options that they might otherwise not have. Mirroring the work of the SLI, teachers may choose to integrate peer-led discussions with reading and writing about young adult literature in their classrooms. Similarly, teachers might follow the lead of READ 180 and provide feedback on errors and strategies for improving reading comprehension, or that of Reading Is FAME and give students plenty of intensive instruction in vocabulary from texts they are required to read. It is our hope that teachers will also reflect on their instructional practices in light of the re/mediation framework, considering perhaps how this framework may assist in changing classroom learning environments in ways that meet the literacy needs of individual students.

SOME CONCLUDING THOUGHTS ON WHAT WE STILL NEED TO KNOW

Of course, as we look at all of these programs and the research done on them, we find that several questions are still left unanswered. Several of the programs we reviewed are for-profit ventures owned by companies that make fairly extensive claims for their programs. Others are the work of educational interest groups and individual researchers. Although each has undergone evaluation of varying magnitude and duration, in each instance, that evaluation has been internal rather than external. Independent sources of evaluation would add immeasurably to the pool of data that is currently available. Publishing this information in easily accessible formats and through well established national networks (e.g., North Central Regional Educational Lab, WestEd) would make it widely available and subject to frequent updates.

We would also like to see research carried out that looks at the complex settings adolescents in schools experience, and how these programs interact with those settings. We see this type of research as providing more depth than that which measures individual student or group performances on particular tasks. This type of research could answer questions such as the following: What happens when experienced teachers implement these programs? How do the programs change? What happens to student learning? How do students with learning disabilities fare in the programs? What about students who are English language learners? We believe that research conducted by evaluators external to a particular company or group promoting a particular program, as well as research that looks at the complex settings and interactions of both students and teachers, would provide a more compelling picture of the worth of these programs than is presently available.

Finally, we are left wondering whether the bias toward print-based literacy exhibited in each of the seven programs reviewed here is a telltale sign of an aging teaching and program development force—one not accustomed to, or perhaps not fully comfortable with, the multiple literacies (e.g., visual, digital, and spatial) that millennial youth have at their disposal and use daily outside school. Are intervention programs that focus exclusively on print-based literacy too shortsighted? Might they be limiting the options available for developing a wide range of literacies in youth who struggle to read print? What might researchers working from a re/mediation perspective learn about conditions that support interventions having a broader view of reading than the current one?

REFERENCES

Alvermann, D. E. (Ed.). (2002). *Adolescents and literacies in a digital world*. New York: Peter Lang.

Baker, L., & Wigfield, A. (1999). Dimensions of children's motivation for reading and their relations to reading activity and reading achievement. *Reading Research Quarterly, 34*, 452–477.

Balfanz, R. (2002). *Catching up: Impact of the Talent Development High School's ninth grade instructional interventions in reading and mathematics*. Unpublished manuscript, Baltimore, MD: Johns Hopkins University, Center for Social Organization of Schools.

Bean, T., Bean, S., & Bean, K. (1999). Intergenerational conversations and two adolescents' multiple literacies: Implications for redefining content area literacy. *Journal of Adolescent & Adult Literacy, 42*, 438–449.

Cameron, J., & Pierce, W. D. (1994). Reinforcement, reward, and intrinsic motivation: A meta-analysis. *Review of Educational Research, 64*, 363–423.

Chall, J. S. (1983). *Stages of reading development*. New York: Harcourt Brace.

Cole, M., & Griffin, P. (1986). A sociohistorical approach to remediation. In S. deCastell, A. Luke, & K. Egan (Eds.), *Literacy, society, and schooling* (pp. 110–131). Cambridge, UK: Cambridge University Press.

Curtis, M. B., & Longo, A. M. (1999). *When adolescents can't read: Methods and materials that work*. Cambridge, MA: Brookline Books.

Curtis, M. B., & Longo, A. M. (2001). Teaching vocabulary to adolescents to improve comprehension. In *Reading online*. Available at *http://www.readingonline.org/articles/art_index.asp?href=/articles/curtis/index.html*

Elkins, J., & Luke, A. (1999). Redefining adolescent literacies. *Journal of Adolescent & Adult Literacy, 43,* 212–215.

Freire, P. (1972). *Pedagogy of the oppressed.* Harmondsworth, UK: Penguin.

Gambrell, L. B., & Marinak, B. A. (1997). Incentives and intrinsic motivation to read. In J. T. Guthrie & A. Wigfield (Eds.), *Reading engagement: Motivating readers through integrated instruction* (pp. 205–217). Newark, DE: International Reading Association.

Greenleaf, C., Jiménez, R., & Roller, C. M. (2002). Reclaiming secondary reading interventions: From limited to rich conceptions, from narrow to broad conversations. *Reading Research Quarterly, 37,* 484–496.

Greenleaf, C., & Schoenbach, R. (2004). Building capacity for the responsive teaching of reading in the academic disciplines: Strategic inquiry designs for middle and high school teachers' professional development. In D. Strickland & M. L. Kamil (Eds.), *Improving reading achievement through professional development* (pp. 97–127). Norwood, MA: Christopher-Gordon.

Greenleaf, C. L., Schoenbach, R, Cziko, C., & Mueller, F. L. (2001). Apprenticing adolescent readers to academic literacy. *Harvard Educational Review, 71,* 79–129.

Hindin, A., Morocco, C. C., & Aguilar, C. M. (2001). "This book *lives* in our school": Teaching middle school students to understand literature. *Remedial and Special Education, 22,* 204–213.

Hull, G., & Schultz, K. (2001). Literacy and learning out of school: A review of theory and research. *Review of Educational Research, 71,* 575–611.

Kambarian, V. (2001). *The role of reading instruction and the effect of a reading management system on at-risk students.* Unpublished doctoral dissertation, St. Louis University, MO.

Killion, J. (1999). *What works in the middle: Results-based staff development* (Project CRISS, pp. 166–169). Oxford, OH: National Staff Development Council. Retrieved April 23, 2003, from *http://www.nsdc.org/midbook/criss.pdf*

Killion, J. (2002a). *What works in the high school: Results-based staff development* (Project CRISS, pp. 118–121). Oxford, OH: National Staff Development Council and the National Education Association. Retrieved April 23, 2003, from *http://www.nsdc.org/resultsbased/hswhatworks.pdf*

Killion, J. (2002b). *What works in the elementary school: Results-based staff development* (Project CRISS, pp. 182–185). Oxford, OH: National Staff Development Council and the National Education Association. Retrieved April 23, 2003 from *http://www.nsdc.org/resultsbased/hswhatworks.pdf*

Luke, A. (2001). Foreword. In E. B. Moje & D. G. O'Brien (Eds.), *Constructions of literacy: Studies of teaching and learning in and out of schools* (pp. ix–xiii). Mahwah, NJ: Erlbaum.

Luke, A., & Elkins, J. (2000). Re/mediating adolescent literacies. *Journal of Adolescent & Adult Literacy, 43,* 396–398.

Mathis, D. (1996). *The effect of the Accelerated Reader program on reading comprehension* (Unpublished report) (ERIC Document Reproduction Service No. ED398555; summary available online at *www.edrs.com*)

Moje, E. B. (2000). "To be part of the story": The literacy practices of gangsta adolescents. *Teachers College Record, 102,* 651–690.

Morocco, C. C., & Hindin, A. (2002). The role of conversation in a thematic understanding of literature. *Learning Disabilities Research & Practice, 17,* 144–159.

National Reading Panel. (2000). *Report of the National Reading Panel.* Washington, DC: National Institute of Child Health and Human Development.

New London Group. (2000). A pedagogy of multiliteracies: Designing social futures. In B. Cope & M. Kalantzis (Eds.), *Multiliteracies: Literacy learning and the design of social futures* (pp. 9–37). New York: Routledge.

O'Brien, D. G., Stewart, R., & Moje, E. B. (1995). Why content area literacy is difficult to infuse into the secondary curriculum: Strategies, goals, and classroom realities. *Reading Research Quarterly, 30,* 442–463.

Pavonetti, L., Brimmer, K., & Cipielewski, J. (2002). Accelerated Reader: What are the lasting effects on the reading habits of middle school students exposed to Accelerated Reader in elementary grades? *Journal of Adolescent & Adult Literacy, 46*(4), 300–311.

Project CRISS. (1996). *Educational programs that work: The catalogue of the National Diffusion Network* (21st ed.). Longmont, CO: Sopris West.

REACH Institute. (2001). [Special themed issue]. *Learning Disabilities Quarterly, 24*(1).

Rush, L. (2003, April). Taking a broad view of literacy: Lessons from the Appalachian Trail thru-hiking community. *Reading Online, 6*(7). Available online at *http://www.readingonline.org/newliteracies/lit_index.asp?href=rush/*

Santa, C., Havens, L., & Maycumber, E. (1996). *CReating Independence through Student-owned Strategies.* Dubuque, IA: Kendall/Hunt.

Scholastic. (2002). *Scholastic's READ 180: A heritage of research.* Retrieved January 11, 2003, from *http://teacher.scholastic.com/read180/research/pdf/heritage_of_research.pdf*

Sweet, A. P. (1997). Teacher perceptions of student motivation and their relation to literacy learning. In J. T. Guthrie & A. Wigfield (Eds.), *Reading engagement: Motivating readers through integrated instruction* (pp. 86–101). Newark, DE: International Reading Association.

Topping, K., & Paul, T. (1999). Computer-assisted assessment of practice at reading: A large scale survey using Accelerated Reader data. *Reading & Writing Quarterly, 15*(3), 213–232.

Vollands, S., Topping, K., & Evans, R. (1999). Computerized self-assessment of reading comprehension with the Accelerated Reader: Action research. *Reading & Writing Quarterly, 15*(3), 197–212.

Wigfield, A., & Guthrie, T. (1997). Relations of children's motivation for reading to the amount and breadth of their reading. *Journal of Educational Psychology, 89,* 420–432.

11

Differentiating Instruction
A Synthesis of Key Research and Guidelines

CAROL ANN TOMLINSON

Contemporary middle and high schools are marked by the irony that as their populations become exponentially more academically diverse (Fletcher, Bos, & Johnson, 1999; Wlodkowski & Ginsberg, 1995), pressures increase to ensure that all of those students perform similarly, on the same time lines, and under virtually identical conditions. Despite all we know about human variability in learning—particularly during adolescence (National Middle School Association, 1995)—we seem to pursue a path that suggests we jettison decades of accumulated knowledge about learner variance in favor of pedagogy that ignores rather than plans proactively for student differences (Archambault et al., 1993; McIntosh, Vaughn, Schumm, Haager, & Lee, 1993; Schumm & Vaughn, 1991, 1992, 1995; Tomlinson, 1995; Westberg, Archambault, Dobyns, & Salvin, 1993).

The reasons for our one-size-fits-all approach to teaching and learning are many. We teach so many students that the idea of attending to them as individuals seems hopeless. We lack images of classrooms in which student variance is effectively addressed. We view ourselves as content specialists who teach best when we tell what we know. We have only one textbook, despite the variability of student readiness to read it. Classroom furniture invites inflexibility. And we feel compelled—often politically as much as educationally—to "cover" vast amounts of information in protracted amounts of time in order to "prepare" students for high stakes tests of one kind or another (Callahan, Tomlinson, Moon, Brighton, & Hertberg, 2003; Schumm & Vaughn, 1995).

Yet seated before us among "grade-level" learners are students who are learning English, those with learning disabilities and other cognitive challenges, students who are advanced in their learning, those from a range of cultures and economic groups, and many who fit in more than one of these categories. Evidence seems clear that one-size-fits-all classrooms persistently fail many of these learners (Delpit, 1995; Fuchs, Fuchs, & Fernstrom, 1993; Gamoran, Nystrand, Berends, & LePore, 1995).

Thus, we find many professional groups calling for instruction that attends to learner variance rather than ignoring it. For example, in *Turning Points 2000*, a publication that assesses the current state of middle schools and offers counsel for future development, Jackson and Davis (2000) say, "Classes should include students of diverse needs, achievement levels, and learning styles, and instruction should be differentiated to take advantage of the diversity, not ignore it" (p. 23).

Reflecting on his landmark study of high schools, Theodore Sizer (1985) advises, "That students differ may be inconvenient, but it is inescapable. Adapting to that diversity is the inevitable price of productivity, high standards, and fairness to students" (p. 194). Furthermore, citing the National Board for Professional Teaching Standards, Ring and Reetz (2002) advise: "Teachers recognize individual differences in their students and adjust their practice accordingly. Failure to do so results in inappropriate instruction and evaluation for those who lack prerequisite skills, as well as for those who clearly are beyond the grade level standards and need expanded opportunities to develop" (p. 12).

Educators who seek to address literacy needs of adolescents effectively live in the midst of this dilemma. Students differ as learners. Teachers who address those differences in instructional planning and teaching are more likely to be effective with the populations they teach. Yet few of us find ways to attend systematically and robustly to student differences. Understanding the principles and practices of differentiated instruction is important in making decisions about the kinds of classrooms we develop.

BACKGROUND ON DIFFERENTIATION

The concept of "differentiated instruction" is neither recent nor novel. It is, rather, a way of thinking about teaching and learning that keeps at the forefront of teachers' attention the belief that we teach not only content but also individuals (Tomlinson, 2003). If we are to teach content effectively, we must teach individuals effectively; that is, we must respond to the varying learning needs of the adolescents we teach.

The principles and practices of differentiated instruction are based on theory and research suggesting that students learn more effectively and efficiently when teachers address their readiness levels, interests, and learning profiles. *Readiness* has to do with a student's current performance relative to specific knowledge, understanding, and skill. Evidence suggests that individuals learn when tasks are a bit beyond their reach, and when adults or peers support students in spanning the gap between the known and familiar and that which is currently somewhat beyond reach (Bransford, Brown, & Cocking, 1999; Cskiszentmihalyi, Rathunde, & Whalen, 1993; Howard, 1994; Jensen, 1998; Rohrkemper, 1990; Sousa, 2001; Vygotsky, 1978, 1986; Wolfe, 2001).

Interest refers to a student's desire to learn about a particular topic or to work with a particular set of skills, and is strongly linked to motivation to learn. When tasks, problems, and questions are interesting to them, students are more likely to remain engaged with the task, find the work rewarding, function more creatively, work more independently, be more productive, feel more competent, and sustain a higher level of intrinsic motivation (Amabile, 1983; Bruner, 1961; Collins & Amabile, 1999; Herbert, 1993; Renninger, 1990; Sharan & Sharan, 1992; Vallerand, Gagne, Senecal, & Pelletier, 1994; Zimmerman & Martinez-Pons, 1990). Smith and Wilhelm (2002) make a potent case for connecting literacy with learner interest (as well as gender and culture) in *Reading Don't Fix No Chevys: Literacy in the Lives of Young Men.*

Learning profile refers to preferred modes of learning and is shaped by an individual's learning style, intelligence preferences, gender, culture, or a combination of these factors (Tomlinson, 1999). Research evidence favors instruction that attends to students learning styles (Sullivan, 1997), intelligence strengths (Sternberg, 1996, 1997; Sternberg, Torff, & Grigorenko, 1998), and culture (Dunn & Griggs, 1995; Garcia, 1995; Ladson-Billings, 1994; Sternberg & Grigorenko, 1997). Finally, although research suggests that gender shapes learning (Baker Miller, 1986; Belenky, Clinchy, Goldberger, & Tarule, 1986; Gilligan, 1982; Gurian, 2001; Lasley & Matczynski, 1997; Tannen, 1990), there is not a substantial body of research pointing to achievement gains based on adjusting instruction for gender preferences.

Key also to the success of differentiation is teacher understanding of the importance of student affect in learning and the role of a positive *learning environment,* in which the value of each learner is recognized by teacher and students alike (Tomlinson, 2003). Such environments actively respond to the need of each student for affirmation, contribution, challenge, purpose, and power (Tomlinson, 2003).

Each of these elements (readiness, interest, learning profile, learning environment) is critical to making effective adaptations in secondary literacy instruction, if that instruction is to attend to the varied needs of large numbers of adolescent learners with wide-ranging needs for support in developing literacy competencies. It is likely that teachers who systematically attend to all of the elements will be most effective in addressing academic diversity in their classrooms. Rooted in research and theory of psychology and education, differentiated instruction asks teacher to do the following:

- Actively work with students to develop learning environments that are positive for each learner.
- Routinely engage in reflection on learners as individuals as well as on learners as a group.
- Systematically assess learner knowledge, understanding, and skill via preassessment, formative assessment, and summative assessment in light of desired learning goals.
- Purposefully modify instruction in response to learner need and to extend learner proficiency from its current point base, as indicated by assessment and reflection.
- Consistently adapt content (what students learn, or how students get access to what they need to learn), process (activities, or how students learn), and/or products (how students show what they know, understand, and can do) based on learner readiness, interest, and learning profile (Tomlinson, 1999, 2001).

Differentiated teaching would be flexible teaching. The teacher would use time, materials, student groupings, instructional approaches, and other classroom components as flexibly as possible to ensure optimum learning for various students (Tomlinson, 1999, 2001). Rather than a "keep them on the same page" mind-set, the teacher would work from a "let's find the right page for this student" perspective.

RESEARCH ON THE CURRENT STATE OF DIFFERENTIATION

Critical to understanding the scope of the task of helping teachers develop appropriately responsive classrooms is a body of research examining the degree to which differentiation is evident in contemporary classrooms. To enable readers to have a sense of the nature of several key studies yielding information on that broad question, this section first provides a synopsis of nine studies whose methods and findings are both complementary and distinctive. Following the description of key questions, methods, and findings, central themes derived from the nine studies are presented and briefly discussed.

Survey of Classroom Teachers, Varied Levels

Schumm and Vaughn (1991) conducted a survey of teachers at elementary ($n = 25$), middle ($n = 23$) and high school ($n = 45$) levels to determine the desirability and feasibility of making adaptations for students with learning disabilities (LD) in their classrooms. The teachers were drawn from two elementary schools, two middle schools, and two high schools in a metropolitan school district in the southeastern United States. Schools were selected because student ethnic distribution was representative of many urban areas and of the county in which the study was conducted. The research sample mirrored the district as a whole. All middle and high school teachers surveyed were English teachers. Researchers developed the Adaptation Evaluation Instrument, a Likert-type scale that asked teachers to rate the desirability and feasibility of 30 possible classroom adaptations for students with LD. The Wilcoxon Matched–Pairs Signed Ranks Test was used to compare the difference between desirability and feasibility ratings for each of the 30 items. A Kruskal–Wallis one-way analysis of variance (ANOVA) was used to compare differences among elementary, middle, and high school respondents.

There were few differences in findings between elementary, middle, and high school teachers. Adaptations teachers listed as most desirable related to socioemotional adjustment of students (e.g., providing reinforcement and encouragement for the student, establishing personal relationships with the student). Adaptations teachers listed as least desirable would require of the teacher systematic evaluation of goals and adjustment of instructional materials (e.g., adapting regular materials, using alternate materials, and providing individualized instruction).

Survey of Elementary Teachers

Archambault et al. (1993) surveyed approximately 7,300 third- and fourth-grade teachers nationwide using standard stratified random sampling procedures. The Classroom Practices Questionnaire addressed four research questions:

1. Do classroom teachers modify curriculum and instruction to meet the needs of gifted and talented students?
2. Do classroom teachers in different parts of the country and in communities of different size provide different services for gifted students?
3. What instructional practices are used with gifted and talented students in classrooms across the country?
4. Are there differences in the types of regular classroom services provided for gifted students in districts with and without formal gifted programs?

A total of 39 items was in the classroom practices portion of the survey, and teachers rated the frequency of their use with each practice for both general and identified gifted students. Analyses of responses were performed using mainframe and microcomputer versions of the Statistical Package for the Social Sciences (SPSS-X) and the Statistical Analysis System (SAS), and included descriptive analyses performed at the item and scale levels, and multivariate analyses of variance (MANOVAs) with repeated measures performed at the scale level.

Teachers made only minor modifications in the regular curriculum to address the needs of gifted students. This was the case across geographic regions, types of schools, and student population types—and in schools both with and without special programs for gifted learners.

Observations of Students in General Education Classrooms

McIntosh et al. (1993), observed 20 elementary teachers, 20 middle school teachers, and 20 high school teachers to examine the extent to which the teachers accommodated mainstreamed students with LD and treated those students differently from classmates. All teachers in the study were selected because their principals felt they were effective in meeting the needs of mainstreamed students with LD. Early data from participating teachers corroborated that the teachers also felt they addressed the needs of these learners. Researchers examined teacher instructional practices such as grouping of students, monitoring student work and progress, adapting materials, and so on. They also examined teacher–student interactions, including fairness and impartiality, negative comments, asking students questions, asking students to volunteer, and so on. Teachers were observed with the Classroom Climate Survey, with 180 observations of approximately 50 minutes each comprising the data set. Observers recorded information on both students with LD and their general education classmates. A Wilcox on Signed

Ranks two-tailed test was used to test differences between paired ratings for each item.

Teachers made some instructional modifications of mainstreamed students with LD at the elementary level, but few at the middle and high school levels. Target students were treated like general education classmates at all levels. Although this is positive in regard to teacher acceptance of students, it is negative in regard to differentiating instruction to meet the academic needs of mainstreamed students with learning disabilities, particularly at the middle and high school levels.

Case Study of a Middle School

Tomlinson (1995) used case study methodology to examine the experiences of teachers in a middle school in the Midwest over a period of 18 months as teachers began working under a school board mandate to differentiate instruction. Data sources included interviews with teachers, students, and parents (totaling 28 hours), classroom observations (totaling 30 hours), and attendance at and participation in teacher team meetings (11 hours), faculty meetings (4-½ hours), and staff development sessions (34 hours), as well as documents. Transcribed tape recordings, field notes, and researcher memos were hand-coded and ultimately analyzed for recurring coding categories leading to themes.

Most modifications for students were reactive (improvisational adaptations) rather than proactive (preplanned). When modifications were made, they were more likely in response to struggling rather than to advanced learners. In general, teachers lacked a rationale for differentiation, as well as a clear definition of what would constitute appropriate differentiation. They also struggled with issues related to implementation of more flexible classroom management and more student-centered instruction. Early subscribers were inquirers about students, who saw disequilibrium in their practice as a positive catalyst for change.

Survey of Middle-Grade Teachers

Moon, Tomlinson, and Callahan (1995) conducted a national survey of middle school principals and teachers to determine attitudes, practices, and curricular structures related to instruction in academically diverse middle-level classrooms. The study employed a representative stratified random sample of 1988 middle schools, and used both open and closed survey questions to gather data. Middle school principals and teachers of the core subjects in their schools responded to the survey. Descriptive statistics were calculated using the mainframe version of SPSS to determine the prevalent belief structures, practices, and policies regarding instructional practices as they relate to meeting the needs of academically diverse middle schoolers. Qualitative analysis of open ended questions included content analysis and used each discrete suggestion of respondents as a unit of analysis, resulting in patterns reflecting the most common responses.

Among findings from the survey portion of the study are that teachers generally feel that middle schoolers are concrete thinkers, easily discouraged, work best with routine, and are extrinsically motivated. Teachers generally cited external reasons for not differentiating instruction (e.g., lack of planning time, short class periods) or seeing no need to differentiate. Principals generally cited factors internal to teachers as reasons they might not differentiate instruction (e.g., lack of knowledge about how to differentiate, fear of loss of control). Of 18 instructional strategies that might be used to respond to student differences (e.g., preassessment, peer tutoring, tiered lessons, interest groups, mentorships), teachers generally reported only scant use of any of the strategies. Structural approaches to addressing learner variance (e.g., use of parent volunteers to assist students) were also seldom used—with the exception of offering before- and after-school help. Fewer than 5% of open-ended responses indicated robust or proactive teacher routines for addressing academic diversity.

Survey of Secondary Teachers

Hootstein (1998) conducted a survey of high school teachers to determine (1) the importance to the teachers of addressing students' academic differences; (2) which instructional methods teachers most often use to address students' academic differences; (3) which instructional methods teachers feel are most effective for this purpose, and why they thought so; and (4) which factors inhibit and facilitate teachers' ability to differentiate instruction. A stratified random sample of teachers was drawn from 28 high schools in seven school districts of the Metropolitan Educational Research Consortium, which sponsored the study. The Differentiation Practices Survey, developed by representatives from the 7 participating districts, was sent to 386 high school teachers. A response rate of 74% (284 teachers) was achieved. The survey included both Likert-type rating scales and an open-ended question. Descriptive statistics and multiple comparisons were calculated with the use of SPSS on the rating scales. Open-ended responses were coded inductively to derive categories that subsumed all responses.

Almost all respondents (90%) indicated that they felt addressing academic differences was important. Modifications most frequently used to differentiate for varied learner needs included modeling, varied materials, adjusting questions, and lecture with questions and answers. Least used modifications included those that require proactive planning by teachers, such as tiered assignments, independent projects, and curriculum compacting. The majority of modifications were directed at students with learning difficulties rather than extension of the learning of advanced students.

Case Studies of Bilingual Education Teachers

Fletcher et al. (1999) studied two elementary teachers deemed effective at meeting the academic needs of diverse learners. The study was conducted in a metropolitan school district of about 14,000 in the southwestern United States. Using case study methodology, they observed two teachers and interviewed them over a 4-month period during, and related to, their language art instruction. Inquiry was focused on understanding how the teachers address the needs of students with LD in their bilingual classrooms. An adaptation of the Classroom Climate Scale (McIntosh et al., 1993) was used in observation. Interviews were conducted with a semi-structured interview protocol that encouraged teachers to elaborate on their instructional thought and planning. Mean ratings were obtained from the observation scale. Coding for themes was used with field notes and interview transcripts. A constant comparison method was used to determine consistencies between the two teachers.

Although both teachers were novices, one was more confident and innovative in her approach to the target students. The two cases provide an interesting contrast in how two teachers in similar settings vary in their thought and practice regarding students with dual special learning needs in their classrooms. Researchers concluded that both teachers most frequently used whole-class, undifferentiated instruction. Typical adjustments included variations in seating, use of pairs and cooperative groups, and adjustments in expectations and amount of time given to complete work.

Extended Case Studies of Multiple Middle Schools

Callahan et al. (2003) studied teachers in nine middle schools located in three states in the South and mid-Atlantic regions of the country over a 3-year period. The larger study consisted of several investigations in which both quantitative and qualitative methods were used. The study involved two treatment groups of three schools each, and three control schools. Teachers in treatment group 1 worked for 3 years in large-group, small-group, and individual coaching sessions to extend their competencies in teaching academically diverse middle-level learners by directly studying and implementing a model of differentiated instruction. Teachers in treatment group 2 worked for 3 years, with an emphasis on assessment as a means for understanding student needs and differences. The supposition with treatment group 2 was that if teachers became more aware of student needs and strengths as a result of a focus on varied forms of assessment, they might determine a need to teach in a more differentiated fashion. Control teachers received no staff development or support related to differentiated or responsive instruction during the span of the study. Investigators wanted to determine the relative impacts of the two treatments on teachers' skill and will related to differentiation. In addition, researchers examined impacts on student achievement of the two approaches.

A grounded theory case study method that used persistent observations and interviews, and data analysis leading to grounded theory revealed that teachers in the differentiation treatment were more likely to teach in a responsive or differentiated manner than those in the assessment treatment. Teachers in both groups, however, found it very difficult to change their teaching patterns. Key impediments to differentiation were teachers' lack of reflection on students, their lack of clarity about the basic structure and nature of the subjects they taught, discomfort with flexible classroom management, and a paucity of instructional strategies to support differentiation. Principal support for the initiative was an encouragement for change. High-stakes standards tests were a major discouragement for change toward more responsive classrooms. Quantitative analysis of student achievement data found small but statistically significant differences in favor of the differentiation group.

Key Themes from Multiple Studies

The nine studies distilled here are both qualitative and quantitative in nature. They examine small and large sample sizes in a variety of geographic and economic contexts. Their questions target general student populations, mainstreamed students with LD, second-language learners with LD, and students identified as gifted. Teachers who participated in the studies not only teach in a range of grades (although emphasis here is placed on studies including or limited to secondary teachers) and subjects but also cover the spectrum of experiential levels in the profession of teaching. They also span over a decade of investigation. It is worthy of note, then, that from such variety comes such a clear set of themes. Following are five key themes that, in each case, derive from more than one of these studies. In addition to noting which of the nine studies contributes to a given theme, citations from other relevant studies beyond the nine are also included to support further investigation by interested educators. In some instances, related themes from studies beyond the nine discussed here are also noted.

1. Many teachers—including those at the secondary level—are aware of both the presence of academically diverse learners in their classrooms and the desirability of addressing that diversity in instruction (Hootstein, 1998; Moon et al., 1995; Schumm & Vaughn, 1991). Teachers generally seem accepting of their academically diverse students (Fletcher et al., 1999; McIntosh et al., 1993). An exception to this generality may be students with emotional and behavior problems (Schumm & Vaughn, 1992).

2. Most teachers do not make significant modifications in instruction for their academically diverse learners (Archambault et al., 1993; Baker & Zigmond, 1990; Callahan et al., 2003; Delpit, 1995; Fletcher et al., 1999; Fuchs, Fuchs, & Bishop, 1992; Hootstein, 1998; McIntosh et al., 1993; Morocco, Riley, Gordon, & Howard, 1996; Schumm & Vaughn, 1991, 1992, 1995; Tomlinson, 1995; Westberg et al., 1993). When teachers do make modifications, they are likely to be reactive or improvisational rather than proactive or preplanned (Callahan et al., 2003; Hootstein, 1998; McIntosh et al., 1993; Schumm & Vaughn, 1991, 1992; Tomlinson, 1995), and most often relate to socioemotional needs rather than academic ones (Schumm & Vaughn, 1991). Adaptations for students with learning problems often focus on lowering expectations for those students (Deno, 1994; Fletcher et al., 1999; Fuchs & Fuchs, 1998; Tomlinson, Callahan, Tomchin, et al., 1997). Although adjustments are not the norm for any category of student, they are more likely to be made for struggling students than for learners who are advanced (Callahan et al., 2003; Hootstein, 1998; Moon et al., 1995; Tomlinson, 1995; Tomlinson, Callahan, Tomchin, et al., 1997). Students with multiple learning exceptionalities (including cultural differences, language differences, advanced ability, learning difficulties, and so on) may find classrooms particularly unresponsive to their learning needs (Fletcher et al., 1999; Minner, 1990; Reis, Neu, & McGuire, 1997).

3. Teachers often do not reflect systematically on learners as individuals or on variance among those learners (Callahan et al., 2003; Moon et al., 1995; Tomlinson, 1995; Tomlinson, Callahan, Tomchin, et al., 1997), and often do not make important connections between formative assessment, student needs, and instructional modifications (Callahan et al., 2003; Fuchs & Fuchs, 1998; McIntosh et al., 1993), perhaps seeing those connections as ineffective (Hootstein, 1998) or not feasible (Callahan et al., 2003; Schumm & Vaughn, 1991).

4. Factors internal to teachers that may impede their willingness or ability to modify curriculum and instruction for academically diverse learners include (a) lack of clarity about essential knowledge, understanding, and skills in the content areas which serves as a basis for substantive differentiation (Callahan et al., 2003; Moon et al., 1995; Tomlinson, 1995;

Tomlinson, Callahan, & Lelli, 1997); (b) limited knowledge about and/or implementation of a repertoire of instructional strategies for creating student-centered classrooms that are more likely to support differentiation (Archambault et al., 1993; Hootstein, 1998; Moon et al., 1995; Schumm & Vaughn, 1991; Tomlinson, 1995; Tomlinson, Callahan, Tomchin, et al., 1997; Tomlinson, Callahan, & Lelli, 1997); (c) lack of comfort with managing a flexible classroom (Callahan et al., 2003; Moon et al., 1995; Tomlinson, 1995; Tomlinson, Callahan, & Lelli, 1997; Vaughn & Schumm, 1994); and (d) deep-seated beliefs about teaching and learning, including teaching as telling, learning as absorbing, assessment as giving back information, content as factual, students as dependent, and time as fixed (Callahan et al., 2003; Moon et al., 1995; Tomlinson, 1995).

5. External factors reported by teachers as having a negative impact on their willingness and/or ability to differentiate instruction for academically diverse populations include (a) pressure for content coverage and heavy emphasis on standardized test scores (Callahan et al., 2003; Schumm & Vaughn, 1995; Tomlinson, Callahan, & Lelli, 1997); large class size (Callahan et al., 2003; Vaughn & Schumm, 1994); lack of effective administrative support (Callahan et al., 2003; Fletcher et al., 1999; Hootstein, 1998; Tomlinson, 1995; Vaughn & Schumm, 1994); inadequate resources (Hootstein, 1998); lack of preservice and inservice preparation to support differentiation (Archambault et al., 1993; Fletcher et al., 1999; Hootstein, 1998; Scruggs & Mastropieri, 1996; Tomlinson, Callahan, Tomchin, et al., 1997); lack of images and models of how differentiated classrooms would look (Tomlinson, 1995); lack of time for planning (Fletcher et al., 1999; Hootstein, 1998; Scruggs & Mastropieri, 1996) limited collaboration (Archambault et al., 1993; Fletcher et al., 1999; Hootstein, 1998); and issues related to grading (Callahan et al., 2003). Conversely, when positive attitudes, a clear vision for change, effective staff development options, teacher choice about the focus of change, material resources, and support from administrators and colleagues are realities, teachers may be more likely to enact change (Johnsen, Haensly, Ryser, & Ford, 2002).

ADDITIONAL RESEARCH-BASED IMPLICATIONS FOR DIFFERENTIATION

At least three additional research findings are important to educators who want to develop classrooms responsive to academically diverse students. All three point directly to instructional adaptations likely to benefit student achievement.

1. A meta-analysis of literature on the effects of within-class grouping on student achievement (Lou et al., 1996) finds that flexible grouping of students in classrooms is beneficial to student achievement. Student achievement is greater when students have the chance to work in small groups (generally 3 or 4 students) compared with students not working in small groups. Small-group arrangements give teachers time to work more closely with varying learner needs than does whole-class or large-group instruction. In addition, using small groups allows the teacher greater opportunity to adjust learning goals and/or materials than does whole-class instruction. Small groups are also likely to support student sense making, motivation, and development of social and communication skills (Lou et al., 1996).

2. Student achievement gains are likely to be greatest when the teacher varies instructional materials for the needs of small groups of learners rather than using the same materials for all students regardless of their needs (Kulik & Kulik, 1991; Lou et al., 1996).

3. Flexible pacing is important in addressing learner variance (Ben Ari & Shafir, 1988; Dahloff, 1971; Oakes, 1985). When the instructional pace is too rapid or two slow for a particular student, learning is impeded. Thus, teachers should consider varying time allotments for student work based on varied student needs rather than assuming that time must be fixed and invariable.

DIFFERENTIATION TO PROMOTE ADOLESCENT LITERACY

Theory, research, and practice related to differentiated or responsive instruction suggest the importance of at least three key elements for effective instructional practice related to adolescent literacy: reflection on learners as individuals, attention to quality curriculum, and flexibility in instruction. Teachers who attend to adolescent variance in literacy competencies and needs likely subscribe to and work toward the following beliefs and practices:

1. The teacher believes adolescents vary broadly in their proficiency, with a range of skills in reading and writing, and understands that literacy is a gatekeeper to academic success for all adolescents. Every adolescent needs active support for continuing growth in literacy. What particular skills and support students need in a given class to grow in competence and confidence with the components of literacy will vary, but the teacher accepts the premise that each student should grow from his or her starting point, and that it is a role of the teacher to facilitate that growth.

2. The teacher is a determined "student of students," working to learn how gender, culture, varied learning exceptionalities, and varied experiences have shaped and continue to shape his or her students as learners. The teacher uses virtually everything students do and create as a source of data about students, becoming a "hunter and gatherer" of insights about individuals and the group as a whole.

3. The teacher knows the specific scope of reading and writing skills and understandings important for proficiency as a literate adolescent and adult. That knowledge provides the compass for assessment, instruction, coaching, and feedback for students. Students may use varying materials, time allocations, and/or support systems. They may apply the skills or understandings to areas of particular relevance to them as individuals. They may work in a variety of modes. It is the teacher's clarity about essential skills and understandings that enables students to have options for their work, while the teacher retains accountability for focus on essential outcomes.

4. The teacher uses his or her knowledge of those skills and understandings to preassess learners at multiple points during the school year; to plan instruction for the whole class, for small groups, and for individuals; to develop activities and products; and to both develop and interpret ongoing or formative assessment for the purpose of informing subsequent instruction.

5. The teacher continually works to develop curriculum that is inviting to adolescents as a group and individually, helps students make meaning of what they learn, is focused on products that are relevant to adolescents, and clearly identifies essential knowledge, understanding, and skill (including skills of literacy) for both teacher and students. A key goal of this focus is promoting adolescents' motivation to learn and apply skills of literacy.

6. The teacher works to achieve maximum flexibility in instruction within the parameters of curricular non-negotiables. The teacher learns to use time flexibly rather than expecting all students to achieve mastery of critical goals at the same pace. The teacher consistently designs whole-class, small-group, and individual teaching/learning opportunities. The teacher provides a variety of materials for student use in order to address readiness, interest, and learning preference. The teacher consistently and purposefully groups students in varied configurations to address readiness, interest, and learning preference needs. The teacher uses a growing range of instructional strategies to maximize learning for the full range of students in a class.

7. The teacher is aware that a sense of community in which individuals and the group are fully respected is necessary for maximum growth in

literacy. The teacher leads the group in understanding that each learner is in the process of growing, that where a student is in his or her growth at the moment is not nearly as important as that the student *is* growing, that teacher and students share responsibility to ensure that every member of the class have what they need to grow as much as they can, and that everyone in the class shares responsibility to make the class work.

8. The teacher and class adopt a *growth orientation*. Everyone understands that there is a continuum of knowledge, understanding, and skill along which each learner is growing. The teacher, with ongoing student input, will assess to determine learner needs, and will work to ensure that students have the support necessary to grow along that continuum. In turn, each student has the responsibility to work hard to achieve maximum growth. When growth is achieved, it is acknowledged. Grades reflect two factors: individual growth and current status relative to benchmarks, goals, or outcomes.

That such aspirations are demanding is undeniable. That they are important in classrooms increasingly marked by student variance is also undeniable. Teaching is a profession in which members work toward expertise on a day-by-day basis. The solution to more responsive teaching of adolescents is day-by-day attention to development of the attitudes, skills, and beliefs that support such teaching.

Many avenues to differentiated teaching are low in teacher preparation and disruption of current classroom routines. Among these are preassessing to understand students' varied readiness levels, interests, and/or preferred ways of learning; using oral strategies such as think-alouds and close reads to support student cognition and metacognition; using graphic organizers to help students understand the framework and flow of ideas in a topic or unit of study; giving students choices of working conditions or ways of expressing what they are learning; supporting the option of reading partners, using small-group instruction to revisit or extend ideas for students with particular needs; using Exit Cards to assess student understanding and skill quickly, offering minilessons to students while the class is engaged in desk work; asking students to make suggestions for modifications to class routines and work that would benefit them; and encouraging students to apply key understandings and skills to areas of interest to them. Initially, teachers can use approaches that require more intensive teacher preparation (e.g., tiered assignments, RAFTs [role, audience, format, topic] assignments, learning contracts, independent investigations, rubrics) at a pace that is feasible for the teacher—building to more frequent use of such approaches as the teacher's repertoire and comfort level grow. For information on a range of options for responsive teaching, see Billmeyer and Barton, 1998; Burke, 2000, 2001, 2002, and Tomlinson, 1999, 2003.

Susan Ohanian (1999) is no doubt correct when she reminds teachers of two important and confounding truths of teaching. First, she notes, no matter how much we do as teachers, we will always feel that it is not enough. At the same time, however, she reminds us, that just because we cannot do everything is no excuse to do nothing. Small, daily actions in a desirable direction—over time—transform teachers and classrooms.

CONTINUING TO LEARN ABOUT AND IMPLEMENT DIFFERENTIATION FOR ADOLESCENT LITERACY

There are certainly questions to be answered relative to differentiated or responsive teaching and adolescent literacy. For example, we would benefit from qualitative and quantitative studies of classrooms in which teachers of adolescents do actively support growth in literacy for each learner. Such studies would confirm or disconfirm our current understanding of the need to modify content, process, and product based on learner readiness, interest, and learning profile, specifically in the area of literacy. These studies should provide evidence of short- and long-term achievement benefits for a range of learners of instruction that responds to the literacy needs of learners, as well as impacts of such instruction on student motivation to learn, and student and teacher efficacy. Of equal importance, such studies would be helpful in providing images of the beliefs and routines that support such classrooms.

Conversely, it would be beneficial to research impacts of single-text, single-model, and scripted-text approaches to teaching reading to the full range of academically diverse adolescents. A reasonable hypothesis based on current understandings about differentiation is that well-informed approaches to literacy development that are more flexible would more robustly address the full range of adolescent needs for continual growth in literacy than would more limited or rigidly prescribed approaches.

Nonetheless, our greatest challenge in promoting adolescent literacy in middle and high school classrooms that are becoming more diverse year by year is perhaps in understanding how we might assist in a change process that would enable more teachers to apply what they already know to be sound classroom practice. Key among questions that could guide research in the area of teacher change for responsive literacy instruction are the following:

- How do we engage secondary educators in systematic consideration of belief systems about learners and learning, and the impacts of those beliefs on whom we teach, where we teach, what we teach, and how we teach?
- How do we help secondary teachers become more knowledgeable and reflective about the adolescents they teach—including impacts of gender, culture, past schooling experiences, current proficiency levels, predilections for modes of learning, and interest in the learning process?
- How do we help teachers of adolescents develop sufficient clarity about the precise skills of literacy that such knowledge becomes a gateway to effective instructional assessment and planning?
- How do we work with issues of quality curricula in a time of high-stakes testing—just as at other times—to ensure that adolescents find learning a source of meaning, possibility, and power in this critical developmental stage?
- How do we help teachers of adolescents develop proficiency and comfort with more flexible teaching routines in settings that have a long history of inflexibility?
- How do we find the will to engage in prolonged staff development toward modeling differentiation for teacher needs, just as we expect those teachers to differentiate for students needs?

Although complex to implement with consistency and quality in the secondary classroom, the concept of differentiation is nothing more than an outgrowth of our knowledge about human development and learning. We do not develop as learners on a unitary timetable. We are not motivated to learn by identical factors. Our neurological wiring, culture, gender, and past experiences cause us to go about learning in different ways. To the degree that learning opportunities match the learner's need, they are more likely to be catalysts for effective and efficient learning. A mismatch is a predictor of discomfort, discouragement, and diminished learning. There is much to do with what we already know about the need to translate these understandings into defensible classroom practice that is responsive to each learner whose academic welfare is entrusted to us.

REFERENCES

Amabile, T. (1983). *The social psychology of creativity.* New York: Springer-Verlag.

Archambault, F., Westberg, K., Brown, S., Hallmark, B., Emmons, C., & Zhang, W. (1993). *Regular classroom practices with gifted students: Results of a national survey of classroom teachers* (Research Monograph No. 93102). Storrs, CT: University of Connecticut, National Research Center on the Gifted and Talented.

Baker, J., & Zigmond, N. (1990). Are regular education classes equipped to accommodate student with learning disabilities? *Exceptional Children, 56,* 515–526.

Baker Miller, J. (1986). *Toward a new psychology of women* (2nd ed.). Boston: Beacon.

Belenky, M., Clinchy, B., Goldberger, N., & Tarule, J. (1986). *Women's ways of knowing: The development of self, voice, and mind.* New York: Basic Books.

Ben Ari, R., & Shafir, D. (1988). *Social integration in elementary school.* Ramat-Gan, Israel: Institute for the Advancement of Social Integration in the Schools, Bar Ilan University.

Billmeyer, R., & Barton, M. (1998). *Teaching reading in the content areas: If not me, then who?* Aurora, CO: Mid-Continent Regional Educational Laboratory.

Bransford, J., Brown, A., & Cocking, R. (Eds.). (1999). *How people learn: Brain, mind, experience, and school.* Washington, DC: National Academy Press.

Bruner, J. (1961). The act of discovery. *Harvard Educational Review, 31,* 21–32.

Burke, J. (2000). *Reading reminders: Tools, tips, and techniques.* Portsmouth, NH: Heinemann.

Burke, J. (2001). *Illuminating texts: How to teach students to read the world.* Portsmouth, NH: Heinemann.

Burke, J. (2002). *Tools for thought: Graphic organizers for your classroom.* Portsmouth, NH: Heinemann.

Callahan, C., Tomlinson, C., Moon, T., Brighton, C., & Hertberg, H. (2003). Feasibility of high end learning in the middle grades. Charlottesville: University of Virginia, National Research Center on the Gifted and Talented.

Collins, M., & Amabile, T. (1999). Motivation and creativity. In R. J. Sternberg (Ed.). *Handbook of creativity* (pp. 297–312). New York: Cambridge University Press.

Csikszentmihalyi, M., Rathunde, K., & Whalen, S. (1993). *Talented teenagers: The roots of success and failure.* New York: Cambridge University Press.

Dahloff, M. (1971). *Ability grouping, content validity, and curriculum process analysis.* New York: Teachers College Press.

Delpit, L. (1995). *Other people's children: Cultural conflict in the classroom.* New York: New Press.

Deno, S. (1994). *Effects of support conditions on teachers' instructional adaptation and student learning.* Paper presented at the 2nd annual Pacific Coast Research Conference, LaJolla, CA.

Dunn, R., & Griggs, S. (1995). *Multiculturalism and learning style: Teaching and counseling adolescents.* Westport, CT: Praeger.

Fletcher, T., Bos, C., & Johnson, L. (1999). Accommodating English language learners with language and learning disabilities in bilingual education classrooms. *Learning Disabilities Research and Practice, 14,* 80–91.

Fuchs, D., Fuchs, L., & Fernstrom, P. (1993). A conservative approach to special education reform: Mainstreaming through transenvironmental programming and curriculum-based measurement. *American Educational Research Journal, 30,* 149–177.

Fuchs, L., & Fuchs, D. (1998). General educators' instructional adaptation for students with learning disabilities. *Learning Disability Quarterly, 21,* 23–33.

Fuchs, L., Fuchs, D., & Bishop, N. (1992). Instructional adaptation for students at risk for academic failure. *Journal of Educational Research, 86,* 70–84.

Gamoran, A., Nystrand, M., Berends, M., & LePore, P. (1995). An organizational analysis of the effects of ability grouping. *American Educational Research Journal, 32,* 687–715.

Garcia, G. (1995). Equity challenges in authentically assessing students from diverse backgrounds. *Educational Forum, 59*(1), 64–73.

Gilligan, C. (1982). *In a different voice: Psychological theory and women's development.* Cambridge, MA: Harvard University Press.

Gurian, M. (2001). *Boys and girls learn differently: A guide for teachers and parents.* San Francisco: Jossey-Bass.

Herbert, T. (1993). Reflections at graduations: The long-term impact of elementary school experiences in creative productivity. *Roeper Review, 16*(1), 22–28.

Hootstein, E. (1998). *Differentiation of instructional methodologies in subject-based curricula at the secondary level.* Richmond, VA: Metropolitan Educational Research Consortium. (ERIC Document Reproduction Service No. ED427130).

Howard, P. (1994). *An owner's manual for the brain.* Austin, TX: Leornian Press. Jackson, A., & Davis, G. (2000). *Turning points 2000.* New York: Teachers College Press.

Jensen, E. (1998). *Teaching with the brain in mind.* Alexandria, VA: Association for Supervision and Curriculum Development.

Johnsen, S., Haensly, P., Ryser, G., & Ford, R. (2002). Changing general education classroom practices to adapt for gifted students. *Gifted Child Quarterly, 46*(1), 45–63.

Kulik, J., & Kulik, C. (1991). *Research on ability grouping: Historical and contemporary perspectives.* Storrs, CT: University of Connecticut, National Research Center on the Gifted and Talented. (ERIC Document Reproduction Service No. ED350777)

Ladson-Billings, G. (1994). *The dreamkeepers: Successful teachers of African American children.* San Francisco: Jossey-Bass.

Lasley, T., & Matczynski, T. (1997). *Strategies for teaching in a diverse society: Instructional models.* Belmont, CA: Wadsworth.

Lou, Y., Abrami, P., Spence, J., Poulsen, C., Chambers, B., & d'Apollonia, S. (1996). Within-class grouping: A meta-analysis. *Review of Educational Research, 66,* 423–458.

McIntosh, R., Vaughn, S., Schumm, J., Haager, D., & Lee, O. (1993). Observations of students with learning disabilities in general education classrooms. *Exceptional Children, 60,* 249–261.

Minner, S. (1990). Teacher evaluations of case descriptions of LD gifted children. *Gifted Child Quarterly, 34*(1), 37–39.

Moon, T., Tomlinson, C., & Callahan, C. (1995). *Academic diversity in the middle school: Results of a national survey of middle school administrators and teachers* (Research Monograph No. 95124). Charlottesville, VA: National Research Center on the Gifted and Talented.

Morocco, C., Riley, M., Gordon, S., & Howard, C. (1996). The elusive individual in teachers' planning. In G. Brannigan (Ed.), *The enlightened educator* (pp. 154–176). New York: McGraw-Hill.

National Middle School Association. (1995). *Developmentally responsive middle level* schools: A position paper of the National Middle School Association. Columbus, OH: Author.

Oakes, J. (1985). Keeping track: How schools structure inequality. New Haven, CT: Yale University Press.

Ohanian, S. (1999). One size fits few: The folly of educational standards. Portsmouth, NH: Heinemann.

Reis, S., Neu, T., & McGuire, J. (1997). Case studies of high-ability students with learning disabilities who have achieved. Exceptional Children, 63(4), 1–12.

Renninger, K. (1990). Children's play interests, representations, and activity. In R. Fivush & J. Hudson (Eds.), Knowing and remembering in young children (Emory Cognition Series, Vol. 3, pp. 127–165). Cambridge, UK: Cambridge University Press.

Ring, M., & Reetz, L. (2002). Grading students with learning disabilities in inclusive middle schools. Middle School Journal, 34(2), 3–11.

Rohrkemper, M. (1990). Self-regulated learning and academic achievement: A Vygotskian view. In D. Shunck & B. Zimmerman (Eds.), Self-regulated learning and academic achievement: Theory, research, and practice (pp. 143–167). New York: Springer-Verlag.

Schumm, J., & Vaughn, S. (1991). Making adaptations for mainstreamed students: General classroom teachers' perspectives. Remedial and Special Education, 12(4), 18–27.

Schumm, J., & Vaughn, S. (1992). Planning for mainstreamed special education students: Perceptions of general classroom teachers. Exceptionality, 3, 81–98.

Schumm, J., & Vaughn, S. (1995). Getting ready for inclusion: Is the stage set? Learning Disabilities Research and Practice, 10(3), 169–179.

Scruggs, T., & Mastropieri, M. (1996). Teacher perceptions of mainstreaming/inclusion, 1958–1995: A research synthesis. Exceptional Children, 63, 59–74.

Sharan, Y., & Sharan, S. (1992). Expanding cooperative learning through group investigation. New York: Teachers College Press.

Sizer, T. (1985). Horace's compromise: The dilemma of the American high school. Boston: Houghton Mifflin.

Smith, M., & Wilhelm, J. (2002). Reading don't fix no Chevys: Literacy in the lives of young men. Portsmouth, NH: Heinemann.

Sousa, D. (2001). How the brain learns (2nd ed.). Thousand Oaks, CA: Corwin.

Sternberg, R. (1996). Successful intelligence: How practical and creative intelligence determine success in life. New York: Plume.

Sternberg, R. (1997). What does it mean to be smart? Educational Leadership, 55(7), 20–24.

Sternberg, R., & Grigorenko, E. (1997). Are cognitive styles still in style? American Psychologist, 52, 700–712.

Sternberg, R., Torff, B., & Grigorenko, E. (1998). Teaching triarchically improves student achievement. Journal of Educational Psychology, 90, 374–384.

Sullivan, M. (1997). A meta-analysis of experimental research studies on the Dunn and Dunn learning styles model and its relationship to academic achievement and performance. National Forum of Applied Educational Research Journal, 10(1), 3–10.

Tannen, D. (1990). *You just don't understand: Women and men in conversation.* New York: Ballentane.

Tomlinson, C. (1995). Deciding to differentiate instruction in middle school: One school's journey. *Gifted Child Quarterly, 39,* 77–87.

Tomlinson, C. (1999). *The differentiated classroom: Responding to the needs of all learners.* Alexandria, VA: Association for Supervision and Curriculum Development.

Tomlinson, C. (2001). *How to differentiate instruction in mixed ability classrooms* (2nd ed.). Alexandria, VA: Association for Supervision and Curriculum Development.

Tomlinson, C. (2003). *Fulfilling the promise of the differentiated classroom: Strategies and tools for responsive teaching.* Alexandria, VA: Association for Supervision and Curriculum Development.

Tomlinson, C., Callahan, C., & Lelli, K. (1997). Challenging expectations: Case studies of high-potential, culturally diverse young children. *Gifted Child Quarterly, 41*(2), 5–17.

Tomlinson, C., Callahan, C., Tomchin, E., Eiss, N., Imbeau, M., & Landrum, M. (1997). Becoming architects of communities of learning: Addressing academic diversity in contemporary classrooms. *Exceptional Children, 63,* 269–282.

Vallerand, R., Gagne, F., Senecal, G., & Pelletier, L. (1994). A comparison of the school intrinsic motivation and perceived competence of gifted and regular students. *Gifted Child Quarterly, 36,* 68–72.

Vaughn, S., & Schumm, J. (1994). Middle school teachers' planning for students with learning disabilities. *Remedial and Special Education, 15*(8), 152–161.

Vygotsky, L. (1978). *Mind in society.* Cambridge, MA: Harvard University Press.

Vygotsky, L. (1986). *Thought and language* (A. Kozulin, Trans. & Ed.). Cambridge, MA: MIT Press.

Westberg, K., Archambault, F., Dobyns, S., & Salvin, T. (1993). *An observational study of instructional and curricular practices used with gifted and talented students in regular classrooms* (Research Monograph No. 93104). Storrs, CT: University of Connecticut, National Research Center on the Gifted and Talented.

Wlodkowski, R., & Ginsberg, M. (1995). *Diversity and motivation: Culturally responsive teaching.* San Francisco: Jossey-Bass.

Wolfe, P. (2001). *Brain matters: Translating research into classroom practice.* Alexandria, VA: Association for Supervision and Curriculum Development.

Zimmerman, B., & Martinez-Pons, M. (1990). Student differences in self-regulated learning: Relating grade, sex, and giftedness to self-efficacy and strategy use. *Journal of Educational Psychology, 82,* 51–59.

PART III

Critical Issues in Adolescent Literacy

12

Motivated Reader, Engaged Writer
The Role of Motivation in the Literate Acts of Adolescents

JOYLYNN HAILEY REED
DIANE LEMONNIER SCHALLERT
ALICIA D. BETH
ALTHEA L. WOODRUFF

> Zoe13185: Hey
>
> Jdawg04: SUP? [What's up?]
>
> Zoe13185: NM. U? I was ROFL bout u today. [Not much. What about you? I was rolling on the floor laughing about you today.]
>
> Jdawg04: OIC, thought it was funny? [Oh, I see, you thought it was funny?]
>
> Zoe13185: Yeah. GTG TTYL. [Got to go. Talk to you later.]
>
> Jdawg04: K, C ya [Okay, See you.]

This Instant Message (IM) conversation, quite typical in form and content, illustrates an activity played out among adolescents more often than adults probably imagine. And with the confluence of Internet access and cell phones, we can expect that IMing will become even more prevalent in students' lives. Although the teachers and parents of these adolescents may attend to IMing only to ensure that they are not neglecting their schoolwork and more traditional communication channels, we believe there is something important to be learned about motivation and literacy from looking at what students do when they IM their friends. When adolescents are engaged in IMing and other forms of online communication, we see highly motivated young people who are fully involved in literacy activities. Yet teachers, administrators, and parents often worry about the fact that adolescents are not reading as much as they should and wonder why kids who can read choose not to. In response to what is seen as an issue of *aliteracy*, they try to get children and students interested in books, to give them writing topics that they hope will be engaging, and they work hard to figure out how to encourage children to spend more time with literacy activities. In terms of adolescent literacy, it may help to address explicitly what it is exactly that is worrisome. Is it that adolescents are not reading books as much as previous generations? Is it that they are not able to write cogent arguments? In terms of promoting an appreciation of the motivation needed to develop ever more sophisticated literacy practices, we believe that looking at what adolescents are doing can inform what we want them to do.

Thus, it may be that these adolescents are actually reading and writing extensively, but the literacy activities that captivate them are not the ones that their teachers and parents traditionally value. Recently, an article in the *Austin American-Statesman* (Ly, 2003) described how the FBI had hired three eighth-graders to help train agents, so that undercover FBI users of IM communication could "pass" as adolescents, and locate and prosecute individuals who are making the Internet a dangerous place for young people. Like this example in which adults have come to value the literacy activities of the current generation of youth, perhaps we, as educators and educational researchers, can learn much from taking adolescents' self-chosen literacy acts more seriously. With a touchstone for the psychological processes in which adolescents engage, we can learn about what it means to be fully involved in reading and writing, and perhaps be more effective in designing traditional, school-based literacy activities that adolescents will find engaging.

Although we believe strongly that students have a great deal to learn about how to use and evaluate online information, this chapter is not about media literacy. Despite the fact that we refer to salient aspects of the current adolescent culture, this chapter is not about cultural literacy. Instead, we want to examine the role of motivation in adolescents' interaction with literacy activities, and learn from their positive approach to media and popular culture to understand their response to more traditional literacy. We begin by reviewing models and empirical findings that relate to motivation and adolescent literacy, organizing this rich literature into three areas: motivation, the adolescent experience, and adolescent literacy. Next, we address how this literature can inform practice and how it might be used to help improve adolescents' views of literacy activities, particularly those they encounter in school. In our final section, we discuss research that is needed to explore further adolescent literacy and related motivational processes.

MOTIVATION, ADOLESCENCE, AND LITERACY

With our concerns about how and why adolescents approach or avoid traditional literacy activities, we are following in the footsteps of such thoughtful researchers as Donna Alvermann (e.g., 2001a; 2001b; Alvermann & Heron, 2001) and Lesley Rex (2001), who have described the work of young adults using print to negotiate their multiple identities. Like these researchers, we see what young people do with enthusiasm and a sense of self-chosen pleasure as a resource to help us understand why they are often so much less motivated by forms of literacy activities that adults in school and society choose for them to do. For our purposes, we examine the psychological and educational literature in three areas, beginning broadly before sharpening our focus. First, we discuss motivation, focusing on those characteristics we believe are central to understanding adolescent literacy. Second, we describe adolescent development, focusing on identity and the reasons students sometimes are not engaged in school. Finally, we review the research that brings together issues of motivation, literacy, and adolescent readers–writers.

Motivation

When we use the term *motivation* to explain any kind of human behavior, we are referring to the goals that humans are striving to reach, the choices they make among several actions, and their persistence exhibited when they encounter difficulties in pursuing their goals. Because motivation has been of such great interest to psychologists in the last 20 years, it would be overwhelming to review all that might be relevant to an understanding of adolescents' motivation for literacy. We have chosen to review the work based on three concepts that we believe have special relevance. First, in explaining how individuals respond to the circumstances of their lives, Deci (1980) and colleagues (Deci, Vallerand, Pelletier, & Ryan, 1991; Ryan & Deci, 2000, 2002) noted how critical it is for people to feel a sense of control and competence. This work has spawned a flurry of research on what is called the *self-determination* perspective. A second concept, *self-regulation*, or how individuals make plans and use strategies to reach their sometimes competing goals (Zimmerman, 1990; Zimmerman & Schunk,

2001) includes two kinds of thoughts: knowing ourselves to direct our own thinking, and motivating ourselves to accomplish our goals. The third construct we review, *involvement*, is defined by a combination of cognitive, emotional, and motivational aspects (Reed & Schallert, 1993). Involvement is more than attention to and interest in tasks; it refers to a process during which one is wholly absorbed by what he or she is doing. Certainly most young people experience deep involvement during an active bout of IMing.

Self-Determination

When using motivation in discussions of educational problems, teachers and parents are likely to think of the dichotomy that pits intrinsic against extrinsic motivation. In such a view, extrinsic motivation is the "bad" sort of motivation, a necessary but less than ideal impetus, whereas intrinsic motivation is seen as a worthy, even virtuous, reason for engaging in a task. This contrast between extrinsic and intrinsic motivation is often reflected in the early work on motivation. One of the more interesting developments in the field of motivation has been the focus on an explanation of extrinsic and intrinsic motivation using the concept of self-determination most notably associated with Deci and Ryan and their colleagues (Deci, 1980; Deci et al., 1991; Ryan & Deci, 2000). In this view, extrinsic and intrinsic motivation represent ends of a continuum, with different degrees of individual autonomy as the underlying dimension. Autonomy, one of three basic needs, along with competence and affiliation, refers to the need to have control over one's life. Researchers have found that the perception of being in control over one's own life, of being an agent rather than a passive recipient in situations, is related to several socially valued outcomes, such as higher academic achievement (Miserandino, 1996), higher self-esteem and self-worth (Ryan & Grolnick, 1986), and more positive affect (Ryan & Connell, 1989).

It seems sensible to predict that when students are engaged in tasks that are fully self-chosen, and for reasons that are highly important to them, they are intrinsically motivated to engage in those tasks. However, the particular strength of the self-determination perspective is that we can acknowledge that a student might not find the task intrinsically motivating or captivating, yet be perfectly willing on his or her own to complete it. After all, students perceive that many school tasks are more chore than delight. Students may choose a task because they identify it as personally important, or because they endorse it and see it as congruent with their own goals, values, and beliefs. This means that there are different forms of extrinsic motivation, some of which occur because students have control over their own engagement in tasks.

A very important thought about motivation is that control is highly susceptible to what is in the student's surroundings, both physical and psychological. In a review of the research on applications of the self-determination perspective to educational settings, Reeve (2002) documented the many ways in which teachers can be more or less supportive of students' need for control and help them accomplish more, while increasing their feelings that they can succeed. In addition, having control in a task increases one's enjoyment. Anytime students are given some degree of choice, their feelings of self-determination increase, and they move closer to the intrinsic end of the motivation continuum. Teachers and parents can do much by giving students just a little more autonomy. In addition, when that little bit of choice and control support is combined with the other two basic needs identified by Deci and colleagues (1991), the need to feel a sense of competence and the need to connect with others, students' eagerness and pleasure for the activities and tasks that make up a school day are likely to increase. An analysis reveals that the IMing task has all three basic needs nicely intertwined: affiliation needs, which are clearly a part of what motivates young people to want to contact and connect with many friends at once; competence needs, which are fulfilled as they manage from four to 10 conversations at once, successfully keeping track of what is appropriate to say with each friend; and control needs, which are amply gratified because the task is nearly always self-chosen and incorporates many aspects of choice ("To whom should I respond next?"; "How long should I wait before my next response?"; "What creative ways can I think of to communicate succinctly what I want to say?"; etc.). School tasks that are challenging enough to appeal to competence, that allow for authentic choice, and that encourage peers to work together are the kinds of tasks recommended from a self-determination perspective.

Self-Regulation

When writing this chapter, we surrounded ourselves with wonderful books, journals, and each other. We had a great time reading about motivation and an even better time talking with each other. Inevitably, our conversation would turn to personal topics, because we are long-term friends. After we spent some time digressing from our work, one or the other of us would mention that we had spent 30 minutes away from our task of writing and that perhaps we should get back to work. Sometimes the conversation on personal topics would be too fascinating to stop immediately, but we would state explicitly that it had a time limit: "We'll start back to work at 2:00." Other times, when we faced an impasse in our reasoning and the words simply would not come, one of us would ask the others, "Okay, now summarize what we were talking about in this section." These, among our other strategies for making sure we made progress in our writing, are examples of self-regulation. Thus, self-regulation occurs when a person consciously steers performance toward achieving a goal and engages strategies to get back on track, if the goal seems unlikely given the current trajectory of activities.

This simple definition implies a rich explanation of how people monitor themselves. First, no one has just one goal. Instead, we are always pursuing many goals at the same time. In fact, if we tried to write a list of all of our goals, or *current concerns*, as Klinger (1977) called them, then the task would be virtually impossible, because we are all pursuing an almost infinite number of interweaving and overlapping goals simultaneously, many of them not easily accessible to conscious awareness. However, it is possible to identify at least some of the more immediate goals or tasks that allow us to keep track of what we need to do in the finite limits of time and energy. Second, as Winne and Perry (2000) explained, the components of self-regulation include having some knowledge of the subtasks that comprise a task. For example, an adolescent assigned to write an essay on *The Catcher in the Rye* (Salinger, 1951) would need to know that reading the novel and jotting down notes while reading are important things to do as part of writing this essay. Third, a person must have knowledge of the strategies necessary for accomplishing a given task (Winne & Perry, 2000). While writing the essay, the student would need to know how to figure out the boundaries of what the teacher expected in terms of content for the essay, how to construct a thesis statement and make coherent sentences that develop the thesis, and how to integrate what she has learned reading the novel, what has been talked about in class, and what she wants to include in the essay. Finally, individuals develop strategies to help monitor performance on these tasks to get back on track when they perceive they are not accomplishing the tasks as effectively or efficiently as they want to do them. These are what have been called *self-regulation strategies* (Zimmerman & Schunk, 2001).

In an interesting approach to helping students learn these strategies and become better at using them, Randi and Corno (2000) taught high school students in a literature class to ferret out self-regulation strategies from stories about heroes and their quests, such as the Greek myth about Odysseus. Students were allowed to choose a story about a hero on a quest and were then asked to discuss and outline the archetypal patterns in such stories (e.g., accepting the call to start the hero on a journey, meeting with challenge, etc.). The common metaphor relating a hero's quest and the student's learning journey was presented to help the students transfer their understanding about questing to learning strategies. In small-group meetings and whole-class discussions, the students were able to identify and categorize heroes' activities and relate them to self-regulation strategies involved in their own learning.

Knowing how and when to use such strategies is an important aspect of self-regulation. Suppose our student writing the essay on *The Catcher in the Rye* had a strategy of asking the teacher for help after school. She would need to know when it would be most helpful for her to request the meeting with her teacher, as well as how to phrase her request to the teacher. The student would also need to assess how much time and effort she would need to spend writing her essay to achieve her goal for the assignment (to get an A, to finish the task, to write something she is proud of). In fact, her knowledge of herself as both a writer and a reader would be crucial to her estimate of time allocation for the task. A very slow reader and writer who is motivated to finish the assignment might choose to start it very early and even give up some well-liked social activity to fulfill the goal. Conversely, a reader who is able to speed through the novel, or a writer who is fluent and finds it easy to put words to thoughts, might be able to set aside less time to complete the assignment. In addition, the student would need to step back from reading and writing periodically. A self-regulated student would disengage, assess whether he or she is progressing toward the goal, and decide what to do if a change in approach were needed. In contrast, and often simply because they lack confidence in their ability to monitor themselves, some students do not monitor their performance and even seem unaware that self-regulation is an option for them. Such students relinquish control over their goals and performance to others.

Schunk and Zimmerman (1997) proposed that self-regulation is the culmination of four phases: observation, imitation, self-control, and self-regulation. Zimmerman and Kitsantas (1997) tested this model with high school girls learning a complex physical skill, dart throwing. They measured the girls' actual abilities in hitting targets, reactions to their success levels, intrinsic interest, beliefs in their own capability for dart throwing, and the reasons they gave for performing well or not. The researchers were interested in two types of goals. First, they considered process goals, which are goals that learners must adopt in order to learn *how* to do a task well. Second, they looked at outcome goals, or goals learners make that relate to the end state of an activity. In this task, the process goals that some girls set were those that would help them become better at throwing darts. The outcome goals that other girls set were those that tracked their scores while they threw the darts. In some respects, these kinds of goals are similar to Dweck and Leggett's (1988) distinction between learning versus mastery orientations. Zimmerman and Kitsantas (1997) reported that girls who were encouraged first to set process goals until they developed some level of automaticity and then to set outcome goals were more successful on several measures than girls who simply set one kind of either process or outcome goal. This research suggests that process goals encourage a learner to observe the steps involved in a task and to gain control over those steps. Once this is achieved, the learner is well on the way to being able to use self-regulation strategies in working toward outcome goals.

Although self-regulation is usually helpful, it is possible to be overly self-regulating, to the point of making it difficult actually to accomplish a task. Accomplishing a task can become impossible when interruptions become too frequent and too much focus is placed on what needs to be done to improve performance. This problem is particularly relevant to writing tasks, as Peter Elbow (1981) discussed when he described how writers often "flex" both their "creative muscles" and their "critical muscles" at the same time. His point was that creativity in generating ideas does not blossom in an atmosphere of strong criticism of those ideas. Writer's block arises, in part, because a writer is too self-regulating, when he or she should be focusing on getting any and all words down on the paper. When Zimmerman and Kitsantas (2002) tested the effects of modeling and feedback on college students' skill in revising writing, they found that watching writers slowly struggle to improve their writing helped students learn more about how to revise sentences than watching a model who was already extremely adept at the task. Without the benefit of watching the struggles of the process-focused model, students seemed to work too hard too early at self-regulation, before they had had time to develop effective writing skills.

Finally, the amount of confidence in one's ability to use self-regulation strategies influences whether these strategies are even invoked in a task. Chen and Zimmerman (2003) reported that seventh-grade math students with higher self-confidence were better able to evaluate their performance and adjust their efforts on math tasks than classmates with lower self-confidence. As adolescents experience the pull from several attractive activities and see themselves fail repeatedly at regulating themselves in order to accomplish academic goals, they can develop a feeling of helplessness about their own self-control. In a study of ninth graders engaged in reading and writing tasks, Miller, Heafner, Massey, and Strahan (2003) found that these students were unable to study at home, because they did not have the self-regulation skills to allow them to get rid of competing distracters. At school, the students were able to show sophisticated comprehension and writing strategies. The teacher's presence acted as a motivational protector. When at home,

> most students preferred to study on the couch, while simultaneously listening to music, talking to friends on a phone, and watching occasionally the television in the background. Teacher exhortations to limit distractions were successful with some students, but the effects did not appear to last very long. . . . An inability or unwillingness to limit distractions appeared to be the primary reason why students could not transfer what was practiced in a classroom to home. (pp. 18–19)

Given these complex pulls on adolescents' task commitments, it is perhaps not surprising that Pajares and Valiante (2002) found that students' beliefs that they can control their own learning decrease steadily from elementary to high school years.

In summary, self-regulation occurs when individuals have a repertoire of strategies to help themselves solve problems that arise when they attempt a task. What has perhaps been less often considered in the existing literature is what happens when multiple, sometimes incompatible, goals are in place. For adolescents, the problem of competing multiple goals may be a very frequent experience. For example, the students in the study by Miller et al. (2003) were sincere in wanting to do well on their reading and writing assignments. However, at home, other goals competed, such as needing to rest, wanting to enjoy social connections with friends, and enjoying the entertainment of radio and television programs. At issue is not whether we can persuade students to have the same goals as adults, but whether we can help these students learn how to regulate themselves when dealing with the multiple, sometime antagonistic goals they have, both in and out of school.

Involvement

It is always a delight to see students enjoying themselves, to be so caught up in an academic task that they are hard to distract. Unfortunately, this kind of excitement is not common in classrooms. Although we have proposed that self-determination and self-regulation are important aspects of what helps to create enthusiasm for literacy tasks, we believe that one of the most integral aspects for motivation is the experience of involvement. When students are lost to the world, fully attentive to what they are writing or reading, they go through the kind of pleasurable, invigorating experience that can motivate them to reengage in the future in other, similar tasks. In this section, we discuss the nature of involvement (what it means to be engrossed rather than merely engaged in a task), and why it is important when considering adolescent motivation.

In previous work (Reed, Hagen, Wicker, & Schallert, 1996; Reed & Schallert, 1993; Reed, Schallert, & Deithloff, 2002), we described how involvement is both a process and a state of mind that includes cognitive, motivational, and affective processes. It is closely related to the concept of engagement (Guthrie et al., 1996); in fact, we maintain that involvement is a particular kind of engagement. Whereas engagement refers to any motivated, strategic, activity-related process, involvement refers to those processes in which the person becomes totally absorbed by a task, so much so that nontask-related emotions, motivations, or metacognitive thoughts are excluded. Individuals regularly report being involved in a movie, book, or conversation and finding that several hours have flown by without any monitoring of time or awareness of what was happening in the background. The experience of involvement, or *flow*, as Csikszentmihalyi (1990) would call it, waxes and wanes over time, and shows sensitivity to antecedents (such as interest), concomitants (such as a lack of awareness of time), and consequences (such as an affinity for the involving task). Finally, like flow, involvement tends to occur when a person undertakes a task that is at just the appropriate level of difficulty, appropriately challenging without being too difficult, something that requires concentration but is comprehended.

What connects involvement to motivation is that being involved generally leads to positive affect after an activity is finished, and these positive emotions about the activity then lead to wanting to engage in it again. Thus, having experienced deep involvement while reading a book by a particular author, we look for books by the same author. For example, Nell (1988) reported that students engaged in what he called *ludic reading* (and what we could call involvement) reported an avid joy in reading books, gobbling up whatever fit their affinities for reading material. Csikszentmihalyi (1990) reported that being in flow was a driving force behind the pursuit of many activities. Csikszentmihalyi and Nakamura (1989) further noted, after following adolescents throughout their school day, that students were rarely "in flow" while engaged in official school tasks. To the contrary, students often were bored in school. They were not much more engaged while watching television but were most likely to report all the concomitants of a flow experience when interacting with friends.

As positive an experience as involvement is, it is not one that is easily engineered from the outside. Reed, Schallert, and Goetz (1993) found that it is unlikely that a task can be designed in itself to guarantee involvement.

When tasks do not allow enough of the lead-in time necessary for the process of "falling into involvement," and when too many distractions from other factors occur early on, involvement does not happen. Students may finish the task, and they may be engaged in it, but they will not be involved. In fact, even making something interesting is not a guarantee of involvement. Whereas interest can certainly trigger involvement by signaling that a task includes attractive content, a book on an interesting topic, for example, might be too easy or too difficult for the student and, therefore, not be at all involving.

We conclude our discussion of the interesting work that has been reported in the three separate areas of self-determination, self-regulation, and involvement by pointing to the strong interconnections we see among these three concepts when we use them to address issues of motivation in adolescent literacy. Guthrie and Wigfield (1997) proposed that motivational concepts (i.e., involvement and self-regulation strategies) are as important to literacy development as learner-centered instruction and social interaction. In their view, motivations for reading differ in different classroom contexts. In our current thinking, Guthrie and Wigfield have encouraged us to make connections across the different literature sources we reviewed earlier.

First, although self-regulation may seem antithetical to the state of deep involvement, it can become quite relevant in describing what one can do before a task in order to "fall into involvement." By using self-regulation strategies, a reader or writer can make him- or herself begin a task and then "get into" it (Reed et al., 1996; Reed et al., 2002). For example, a student might need to know that it is sometimes important to read the first chapter of a book rather quickly, when the early parts are confusing, with the expectation that the book will get better later.

Second, self-determination comes into play when one sets goals and chooses involving tasks that have proved pleasurable in the past. Enjoyment of involving literacy tasks is generally an assessment made *after* the task is completed, or after the involving episode. The memory of that pleasure becomes motivating as it is carried forward to the next time a similar task is approached. It might even be what motivates a student to attempt and complete a task (Ryan & Deci, 2000).

Third, an adolescent who knows how to use strategies relevant to a particular literacy task is likely to become involved in it. Coupled with a growing confidence in his or her abilities, the result of this involvement is joy and pleasure.

By focusing our discussion on self-determination, self-regulation, and involvement, we have left out many crucial motivational variables, such as self-efficacy and goal setting (e.g., Schunk, 1996; Shell, Murphy, & Bruning,

1989), goal orientations (e.g., Pintrich, 2000), risk taking (e.g., Clifford, 1991), and motivational resources in the classroom environment (e.g., Ruddell & Unrau, 1997). These and other aspects of motivation all play important roles in adolescents' motivation. We believe that motivation is so complex and multifaceted that much remains to be done before we gain a more detailed and complete understanding of what entices adolescents to approach, engage in, and even enjoy literacy tasks.

The Adolescent Experience

Adolescence is considered one of the most interesting, important, and meaningful developmental periods that we experience as human beings. Adults remember this time in their lives, sometimes with longing, but more often with relief that it is over, as they recall the incredible growth that their bodies and minds underwent. From Piaget (in Goldhaber, 2000) to Ogbu (Fordham & Ogbu, 1986), researchers have struggled to understand what it means to be an adolescent negotiating the social contexts that have been created both by the individual and by society as a whole. Of particular relevance to this chapter is the affective development that takes place during this time in life and how such growth relates to adolescents' attitudes toward literacy. Because of the relationships that can be drawn between theories of affect development and motivation, we have chosen to focus on one aspect of the literature on adolescence: the motivational consequences one can expect when an adolescent does or does not identify closely with school tasks that involve literacy. In what follows, we first discuss theories of identity/self-concept. We then bring in the interesting work on disidentification and disengagement, concepts used to describe what happens when individuals relinquish their personal connections to a domain and lower their motivation for its pursuits. Finally, we turn to the empirical findings that have linked the concept of identity with motivational processes, and then to the research that has connected identity to literacy in particular.

Identity/Self-Concept Theories

Before beginning a discussion of theories of identity and self-concept, a brief explanation of terms is in order. In the literature on the self, a distinction is made between the *me* (i.e., the self-concept) and the *I* (i.e., the identity) of the self. Although making such distinctions may be important in certain academic discussions, the distinction does not seem as important as bringing together both aspects in our quest to understand how identity may be related to adolescents' motivation. In what follows, we use the term *identity/self-concept* to describe the processes involved as a young person connects with a role or an activity and envisions him- or herself as a legitimate agent and participant in that activity.

Much of the research on identity/self-concept processes originated with Erikson's (1956) theories of social–emotional development, in which identity and the processes of identity formation lie at the center. Erikson focused on how critical these processes are during adolescence and placed emphasis on the importance of social context in identity formation, on adolescents' finding their "niche" in society: "In finding it [a niche] the young adult gains an assured sense of inner continuity and social sameness which will bridge what he *was* as a child and what he is *about to become*, and will reconcile his *conception of himself* and his *community's recognition* of him" (p. 111). Erikson's theory placed identification at the heart of social–emotional growth, an idea upon which contemporary researchers have expanded. For example, some theorists define identity/self-concept not as one entity in and of itself but rather as multidimensional and multicontextual. In this vein, Susan Harter (1985, 1988) described how self-perception changes in different domains, including scholastic, social, and physical domains, and how adolescents develop their self-perceptions within these different realms. With her colleagues (Harter, Bresnick, Bouchey, & Whitesell, 1997), Harter described how social and cognitive processes contribute to a "proliferation of role-related selves during adolescence" (p. 835) and the "emergence of different selves in different relational contexts" (p. 837). These different views of the self in different contexts make it very likely that intraindividual conflicts will occur. For example, an adolescent may act very differently with a group of friends than with his parents at home. As the adolescent develops, these multiple selves become greater in number and present conflicts that, in early adolescence, the child may not yet be equipped to handle cognitively. With age, however, the adolescent gains the cognitive ability to "normalize the construction of multiple selves, that allow one to selectively occupy those contexts in which self-evaluations are more favorable, and that provide for a phenomenological sense of unity through the construction of a meaningful narrative on one's life story" (p. 851). Harter and her associates focused not only on the different selves adolescents create in their relationships with other people (Harter & Monsour, 1992; Harter et al., 1997) but also on how competence and motivation within the academic domain can be affected by contextual factors (Harter, Whitesell, & Kowalski, 1992). Thus, the transitions from elementary school to middle school and from middle school to high school represent challenges, even threats, to adolescents' sense of who they are as students and what they find motivating about school tasks. By drawing on these two lines of research, one focusing on conflicting selves in adolescence and the other on changing competence and motivation in specific domains, we can better understand the developing motivational processes adolescents experience while trying to achieve and learn in different academic domains.

The Process of Disidentification

A different approach to understanding the development of multiple identities/self-concepts within different domains is to consider the proverbial other side of the coin, what Steele (1997) called *disidentification*. Whereas *identification* refers to persons connecting and defining their multiple selves within different domains, both academic and nonacademic, *disidentification* indicates the process by which individuals separate and disconnect from such domains. Similarly, Major, Spencer, Schmader, Wolfe, and Crocker (1998) stated that disidentification occurs when individuals "define or redefine their self-concepts in such a way that those domains are no longer a basis of their self-evaluation" (p. 35).

Connected to disidentification is another, similar process termed *disengagement* (Crocker, 1999; Major et al., 1998). When individuals receive feedback that they perceive as somehow damaging to the self within a specific context, they separate themselves or disconnect from this feedback to protect or preserve their self-image. Just like identity/self-concept and identification, both disengagement and disidentification are redefining processes that allow individuals to create and recreate who they are within particular contexts.

Although some researchers have examined disengagement and disidentification in relation to group differences within specific domains (e.g., African Americans vs. European Americans; Major et al., 1998; overweight and normal weight women; Crocker, 1999), all persons experience these processes across a variety of domains and contexts. For example, Osborne (1997) demonstrated that all students, no matter their gender or ethnic background, disidentified from academics to some extent as they progressed through high school. In addition, the different domains and contexts in which a person participates should not be viewed as having isolated effects on the self. In other words, identity/self-concept processes do not occur strictly within each context separately; instead, these ongoing processes work in coordination to create a "working" identity at a specific time and in a specific place. To illustrate, Aronson, Blanton, and Cooper (1995) discussed how a threat to one area of the self-concept can lead to "affirming some valued aspect of the self-concept not necessarily related to the threat" (p. 986), causing a person to change his or her self-concept. Specifically, students in their study modified their self-concepts by dis-identifying with the aspect of the self-concept that had been threatened, then identifying with some other aspect that was not related to this threat, thereby demonstrating that disidentification with one domain could lead to identification with other domains.

Fluctuations of identity/self-concept, identification, disidentification, and disengagement become important as children enter adolescence. During this time, young persons experience an exploding number of different contexts within which they must relate who they are. This proliferation of contexts increases the number of transitions that an individual must make across contexts, thereby also enhancing the nature and complexity of the person's identity/self-concept. Due to the ever-changing nature of these aspects of the self, particularly during this time in life, it is no surprise that adolescents experience fluctuations in all aspects of their lives, including their motivation and interest in domains such as reading and writing.

Research on Identity as It Relates to Motivation

When parents and family witness the variability and inconsistency that adolescents begin to display in their interactions with the world, they often explain these changes as the result of moods or hormones. By contrast, identity researchers explain these fluctuations as resulting from the different contexts an adolescent must negotiate and the different identities that must be coordinated. Negotiating these different contexts and identities is not easy work, and it begins to take its toll and show its effect in a similar ebb and flow (or maybe just ebb) of motivation for many areas of life, particularly those such as schoolwork, which are perceived as imposed by adults.

And this is where we can make a link to an earlier topic, self-determination theory (Deci et al., 1991; Ryan & Deci, 2002). In developing self-determination theory, Deci, Ryan, and their colleagues described how individuals experienced more internalized motivation as they perceive themselves to have more control over what happens in a specific context. Because of autonomy and control, self-determination becomes connected to identity/self-concept. The individual's sense of control (i.e., identity), anytime it is supported, leads to more internally focused motivation, which, as discussed earlier, is often preferred over more external forms of motivation. Thus, an adolescent who becomes an expert at something that is self-chosen, for example, one who takes an after-school job assisting a veterinarian, may find that she is developing an identity and sense of self as a responsible worker who is good with animals. It is even possible that this identification with the after-school job may undermine, by way of the contrast between two contexts that are very different in autonomy support, the adolescent's sense of connection to school.

Similarly, Woodruff and Schallert (2003) explicitly linked the two processes of motivation and identity/self-concept. In a study of how college student/athletes managed to coordinate both academics and athletics, Rosenberg's (1979) definition of self-concept as a "motivational system" (p. 25) is useful in showing how identity work and motivational processes are enmeshed with each other. In essence, student/athletes defined themselves differently in these two contexts, taking on the roles, values, and goals necessary to succeed by their own definitions. Motivational processes played a central role as students decided "Who will I be" in the different contexts they negotiated.

Identity Related to Literacy

Some literacy researchers have called on the concept of identity/self-concept to clarify issues of adolescent literacy, focusing on the importance of culture and cultural messages. Although various authors conceive of culture differently, there is general agreement that culture is an important component in the literacy process. For example, in his theoretical article on literacy, Ferdman (1990) discussed the importance of the relationship of cultural identity to literacy. He began with the basic premise that belonging to a group leads to forming an identity with that group. Ferdman argued that being a member of a group (e.g., an ethnic minority) affects what literacy means to an individual, and that being literate can have a different meaning for each individual depending on that "person's view of social reality" that "is mediated by collective representations of that reality" (p. 186). He explained the concept of institutional control of what it means to be literate: An individual within institutions (e.g., school) must make a choice. One must either identify and internalize the institution's perspective of what it means to be literate or experience continual conflict within the institution when defining oneself as a reader and/or writer. Alvermann also focused on issues of control and meaning making in her research (Alvermann, 2001b; Alvermann & Heron, 2001), emphasizing the effect of adolescent culture itself on the relationship between identity and literacy, rather than membership in other cultures, such as those created through ethnic or gender differences. She studied adolescents who have struggled within educational institutions and been labeled to some degree or other as nonliterate. Alvermann argued that such labels derive from a cultural perspective that does not recognize the different forms of literate behavior that these individuals demonstrate.

Although different cultures are represented in any educational setting, as Alvermann (2001b) pointed out, all readers–writers and their literacy identities are "part and parcel of the wider culture" (p. 683). Through relationships within and between cultures, an adolescent experiences the processes of identity/self-concept and the fluctuations within these processes. Rex (2001) described these processes and variabilities as *positions,* or *orientations,* that both students and teachers experience as they participate in literacy processes. She proposed that "orientation is at the center of individual students' reading and reading improvement" (p. 310), and that power and status relationships also influence such positioning of students and teachers within a literacy environment. Indeed, power and status seemed central to Dutro's (2002–2003) description of the ways that different masculinities played out in how young adolescents did or did not identify with reading.

The relationship between identity/self-concept and literacy processes highlights how cultures and individuals are continually in the process of making meaning, remaking themselves, constructing and reconstructing, and becoming and being. In this flux of defining and redefining themselves, literacy plays an integral role. Synthesizing these different areas of literature and incorporating identity/self-concept, motivation, and literacy processes allows for a broader perspective of what *adolescent motivation in literacy* means. First, several ongoing processes are acknowledged, such as those of adolescence, identification, disidentification, motivation, and culture that overlap and connect with one another in meaningful ways. In the connections and relationships that one can then draw among these processes, a larger theme emerges: individual control. Individuals need to feel in control of who they are, what they experience, and how they experience specific contexts. A lack of such control can lead to disidentification, decreased motivation, and behavior that could be labeled as nonliterate by those who have the power and status to do such labeling.

The paradox here lies in the fact that at a time when individuals could be gaining a greater sense of control and autonomy through the development of more complex, multiple identities/self-concepts across domains, they are given less and less control over many aspects of their lives, including what it means to be literate and to experience literacy. Thus, it is not surprising that activities such as IMing are so captivating to so many adolescents. Unlike face-to-face or phone conversations, these kinds of activities allow participants to adopt various identities and play out those self-concepts with people who may not know them in person. An adolescent who would like to try on different personas as often as changing T-shirts could find this kind of environment highly attractive. Clearly, some of the new media allow for a type of literacy engagement that affords adolescents a great deal of autonomy and opportunities to stretch themselves in ways never tried before.

Studies of Adolescent Literacy and Motivation

A number of researchers (e.g., Oldfather & McLaughlin, 1993) have noted that children's intrinsic motivation to read decreases as they move from elementary to middle school. This finding, along with current ideas of the multiple and expanded literacies, and the constantly evolving technologies associated with reading and writing, suggest that new and thoughtful reconsiderations of adolescent literacy are needed. Moore, Bean, Birdyshaw, and Rycik (1999) called for renewed research on adolescent literacy and highlighted the need for a focus on literacy issues beyond the early grades:

> Adolescents entering the adult world in the 21st century will read and write more than at any other time in human history. They will need advanced levels of literacy to perform their jobs, run their households, act as citizens, and conduct their personal lives. They will need literacy to cope with the flood of information they will find everywhere they turn. They will need literacy to feed their imaginations so they can create the world of the future. (p. 99)

In this section, we discuss what research on adolescent literacy and motivation tells us about literacy acts that adults have traditionally valued, and about those that have been introduced under the umbrella of *new literacies* (e.g., IMing).

Adolescents' Motivation for Traditional Literacy Activities

Findings on motivation for traditional literacy activities in adolescence have centered on a number of concepts. One is control, or what we referred to earlier as *self-determination*. Literacy studies that focus on control use a variety of terms (e.g., agency, choice, ownership, preference) but all share the idea that students who perceive that they have greater control over their reading or writing are more motivated.

For example, Ivey and Broaddus (2001) investigated students' perceptions about what motivates them to read, and found that personal choice was closely related to positive reading experiences. Most students preferred free reading periods, in which they selected their own reading materials and read silently in their classrooms, even to activities such as reading class novels or participating in discussion groups over books. On the one hand, when asked, "What makes you want to read in this class?", students mentioned that they were motivated by good reading materials, typically judged by their titles, and by having some control over the selection of these materials. Students' worst experiences, on the other hand, involved lack of control over their reading. With assigned readings, they frequently mentioned being bored and experiencing difficulties with comprehension.

Increased motivation for reading materials with interesting titles, however, does not mean that adolescents are interested exclusively in genres of action or adventure. Although Worthy, Moorman, and Turner (1999) found that students most preferred scary books and stories, comics and cartoons, and magazines about popular culture and sports, Moss and Hendershot (2002) suggested that adolescents also are motivated by reading nonfiction materials on topics about which they are passionate. They argued that nonfiction is an untapped resource for promoting motivation in language arts classrooms in middle schools. They suggested that simply expanding students' choices for self-selected reading materials beyond what is typically available in classroom libraries (i.e., drama, fiction, and poetry) would improve motivation for reading. Ivey and Broaddus (2001) shared this concern that classroom libraries typically do not fulfill the needs of students. They found that only 28% of the nearly 1,800 sixth graders in their study reported that they could find books they liked to read in their own classrooms. Similarly, only 25% thought that their teachers or librarians were good sources for recommending reading materials. Worthy and colleagues (1999) found that students' access to preferred reading materials was severely limited, and even low-income students ranked their classroom libraries as their last source for good reading materials.

Adolescents' motivation to read personally meaningful texts continues to be important as they grow older. Moss and Hendershot's (2002) findings with young adolescents echo those of Wade, Buxton, and Kelly (1999), who reported that the characteristics of a text played a critical role in undergraduate students' motivations for reading. Specifically, undergraduates were more interested in texts that presented (1) important or valuable information, (2) unexpected or surprising information, (3) information that students could connect with their prior knowledge, (4) a great deal of imagery or descriptive language, and (5) connections among topics.

Research suggests that control is also important in writing. Abbott (2000), for instance, investigated the flow (or involvement) experiences of two young adolescent boys as they engaged in self-sponsored writing. Both boys experienced heightened states of concentration and motivation when they exercised control and choice in their writing and were allowed to express their own interests. Abbott's findings are supported by other research (e.g., Bruning & Horn, 2000; Fairbanks & Broughton, 2003; Singer & Hubbard, 2002-2003) that highlights broadly the importance of authentic writing tasks for promoting motivation.

This research on the importance of control over traditional literacy activities clearly suggests a number of implications for language arts teachers and classrooms, and is centered on somehow allowing students to take control whenever possible of what they are asked to undertake as literacy activities. Building choices into language arts activities, however, may not be as simple as one might expect. Orange and Horowitz (1999) found that the literacy tasks students preferred did not match what their language arts teachers *perceived* they preferred. So even if teachers want to offer choices among a variety of literacy activities designed to promote motivation, they may not recognize which of these choices actually would be motivating for their adolescent students.

Finally, we acknowledge that motivation for literacy activities, whether encountered in the language arts classroom, the composition class, or in the content areas, is more complicated and multidimensional than just the issue of students' control over their literacy activities. Gee (2001) suggested that literacy should be understood broadly as involving a number of cognitive and language processes, and framed within the contexts of society, culture, and social interaction. Accordingly, research suggests that in order to understand students' complex motivations for reading and writing in classrooms, one also must consider a variety of contextual factors, including students' backgrounds and motivational histories (Baker & Wigfield, 1999; Gee, 2000; Smagorinsky & O'Donnell-Allen, 1998) and social relationships among members of the class, both students and teachers (Heron, 2003; Ivey & Broaddus, 2001; Smagorinsky & O'Donnell-Allen, 1998).

Thus, individual learners' motivations for reading and writing are intricate and influenced by any number of factors interacting in the sociocultural context. Ivey (1999) argued that previous research has failed to address the complexity of individual and contextual factors that influence reading motivations and behaviors. She illustrated this complexity with case studies of 3 sixth graders who, even though she selected them based on the vast differences in their performances on school reading tasks (one was categorized as struggling, another was moderately successful, and the last was highly successful), she found that she was unable to classify them accurately or exclusively as skilled or unskilled, motivated or unmotivated. Cole (2002-2003) reported similar complexities with younger readers. Even readers as young as age 7 were motivated to read by a complex set of factors, including their beliefs about reading and about themselves as readers, their reasons and purposes for reading, and their affective reactions to reading.

Adolescents' Motivation for Other Literacy Activities

Recent research on students' motivation for literacy activities has included a look at popular media and computer technologies, and has suggested that adolescents' views of literacy often are broader and more inclusive than those of their parents and teachers. Reinking (1997) referred to adults' narrow perspectives on literacy as *literacy ethnocentrism*, "our deep and abiding prejudice for books" (p. 634). In the same way, Lewis and Fabos (2000) described the contrast between adults' narrow understandings of literacy and adolescents' broader abilities to handle multiple media simultaneously:

> Like it or not, we have entered the world of the Internet—as teachers, researchers, and, for some, as parents. We have witnessed multinational mergers of information and entertainment technologies. We have been flooded with images from popular narratives and media—the indelible iconography of a blue dress or a Teletubby. We have seen the faces of ethnic cleansing and heard the euphemistic discourse of smart and precise bombs. The juxtaposition of these disparate images and technologies sends us reeling, but it does not have the same effect on the teenagers we know well, who have come into literacy and life in the midst of new technologies. Competing images don't confuse them as they do us. (p. 462)

Bean, Bean, and Bean (1999) traced the multiple literacies of two adolescent girls over the course of 2 weeks. They found that, along with classroom textbooks, the girls' multiple literacies included phones, cell phones, and pagers; computers, Internet, and e-mail; video games; and a variety of music and art forms. Similarly, Fisherkeller (2000) described the multiple literacies students use daily as they encounter television, novels and magazines, and photographs and posters. As Moje and Young (2000) explained, "Being literate no longer means just learning to read and write traditional print texts; people need to be sociotechnically literate" (p. 402).

These kinds of technologies, however, cannot be justified in education simply because they are possible and available. As Reinking (1997) suggested, "It is legitimate, and important, to ask the question 'Why bother?' with using computers in classrooms. I don't think that it's valid to reply, like the mountain climber, 'Because it's there' " (p. 636). Computer-based technologies, in particular, can support student-centered, socioconstructivist learning environments in ways never before possible (Reinking, 1997; Salomon & Almog, 1998), but these technology-rich, *new literacy* environments (Kist, 2000, 2002) must be designed thoughtfully to enhance students' motivations to become independent researchers and writers.

Research on computer-based literacies commonly draws the distinction between technologies used primarily for communication purposes and those used for information purposes (e.g., Hoadley & Enyedy, 1999). Communication technologies support interactions and collaborations among individuals (e.g., chat rooms, e-mail, IMing), whereas information technologies help people locate, organize, and process information (e.g., databases).

Adolescents' use of communication technologies in school includes literacy activities such as e-mail (Doherty & Mayer, 2003), Internet chat rooms (Albright, Purohit, & Walsh, 2002), and both synchronous and asynchronous computer-mediated discussions (e.g., Love, 2002). Synchronous computer-mediated discussions are especially interesting to literacy researchers, because they blur the line between reading and writing (McGrath, 1998). These real-time interactions, strangely similar to and yet unlike traditional classroom discussions, unfold in a written medium. In addition, a number of teachers and researchers (e.g., Albright et al., 2002; Bean, Valerio, Senior, & White, 1999; Love, 2002) have reported that students' motivation and engagement with content are enhanced during electronic discussions.

Adolescents also use technologies in school that support information-related purposes. New literacy activities, sometimes described as extensions of traditional literacy, include hypermedia composition (Garthwait, 2001) and publication (Karchmer, 2001), both of which have been found to promote engagement. Students' critical assessment of the credibility of Internet information also has become an important goal for literacy instruction (Rekrut, 1999).

Communication technologies are particularly motivating for activities outside of school. Lewis and Fabos (2000), for example, studied two adolescent girls' use of IMing and found that they viewed it as a particularly satisfying literacy activity, one in which they were uniquely able to draw on the knowledge and intimacies they shared with peers. The girls were highly sophisticated, easily able to carry on multiple conversations simultaneously. One girl who had been restricted by her parents in the number of friends she could keep on her America Online (AOL) "buddy list," typically IMed four to eight people at a time. The other juggled 20 or more conversations simultaneously. Both adapted the breadth, depth, language, subject matter, and tone of their messages according to the people with whom they were communicating. In addition, they routinely completed homework assignments, ate, listened to music, watched television, or talked on the phone at the same time. Clearly, the level of engagement that these technologies can engender for literacy activities is tremendous.

In conclusion, we argue that these kinds of complex multiple literacies are valuable and should be incorporated into a broader definition of literacy. Literacy is increasingly important in the 21st century, not less so. Appreciating adolescents' electronic literacies, in particular, and drawing on their sophisticated abilities to navigate these technologies successfully, may help us to understand how to support their motivation for more traditional literacy activities.

WHEN THIS KNOWLEDGE IS APPLIED TO THE CLASSROOM, WHAT DOES IT LOOK LIKE?

Considering the complexities in adolescents' lives, the social and academic contexts that must be traversed, the physical growth, emotional and intellectual maturation, and change in sense of identity that is going on, and the increased demands and responsibilities that becoming a young adult requires, it is easy to become paralyzed in awe at the enormity of the task that these young people and their teachers and parents face. Yet there is much excitement and joy involved as well, and there is no escaping the responsibilities that all parties face in teaching and learning the keys to greater autonomy and a worthwhile life, with literacy as a major doorway to such a future. Thus, with some trepidation, we want to consider some ways in which the literature we have reviewed might inform our understanding of adolescents' motivation for literacy activities.

Such recommendations for motivating adolescents to engage in and learn from classroom literacy tasks can easily become "tricks" and "tools" instead of embodying systemic changes in ways teachers and students understand literacy goals. It is seductive to think, as Alvermann (2001a) noted, that teachers could entice students into becoming motivated for traditional literacy tasks simply by allowing them to read or write "cool" and "fun" assignments. For example, Alvermann and Heron (2001) discussed how asking students to overlay an academic analysis on their freely chosen literacy activities might not be received with any enthusiasm and instead leave the students bemused about why a teacher would ask them to do such things. This worry came from Alvermann and Heron's interactions with Robert, a student who described himself as not interested in reading, yet spent hours on the Internet perfecting his expertise, knowledge, and appreciation of a Japanese cartoon figure, an anime called "Dragon Ball Z." When they asked him to compare the structure of the stories and the characters involved to Greek myths and more traditional literature, Robert did not seem in any way to respond to the task, find it engaging, or understand its purpose. Alvermann and Heron quickly dropped this approach, commenting on how genuine play may be a better avenue for literacy development more broadly defined than any academic exercise contrived to make school tasks more interesting by hijacking students' out-of-school interests.

Robert's response exemplifies the ways the social, cultural, and motivational systems intersect even in a seemingly innocuous assignment a teacher might use to get a student interested in classroom literacy tasks. We believe that it underscores the notion that a classroom environment in which the adolescent's identity and learning needs, the teacher's learning goals, the school's curriculum, and society's needs for literate people must somehow all be brought together to inform an understanding of not only the specifics of literacy tasks (e.g., writing coherent paragraphs or being able to describe an author's point of view) but also the types of literacies that are likely to populate the students' future. Guided by the expectation that classrooms can look different than they do currently, we have four points to present.

First, when it comes to addressing specifically the motivational processes of adolescents in literacy-focused classrooms, the single most powerful suggestion we can make is to encourage teachers to develop learning environments that are autonomy-supportive. Different from merely trying to get students to read and write what the teacher thinks might interest adolescents, an autonomy-supportive environment means giving students authentic choices wherever possible, and supporting adolescents' burgeoning sense of self-control. It is important that teachers keep in mind the adolescents' identification processes and how quickly students will disidentify when they are asked to do school tasks they do not believe are interesting, useful, or necessary. Reeve (2002) identified several teacher behaviors that create the sort of environment that supports students' sense of autonomy: Teachers who listen more, who allow for independent work, who give fewer criticisms and more praise of quality performance, who show empathy and the ability to take the students' perspective, and who have learned to recognize when their students' interest is at its peak or is waning are doing what they can to help students feel self-determined.

A discussion of the motivational concerns of teachers and students in the classroom naturally leads to our second point: It is important to engage students in helping society redefine what is meant by literacy. Currently, teachers develop and choose literacy tasks for their classrooms, assuming a notion of literacy that nearly always excludes a large portion of the literacy activities in which adolescents are engaged. The distance between teachers' definitions of literacy and students' actual practices needs to be bridged in order to increase the likelihood of deep engagement and genuine excitement in school-based literacy events. Certainly, teachers have goals for their students in terms of what adolescents need to know, to be able to do, and to experience as a result of their instruction. However, it is likely that teachers have overlooked the extension of literacy to new literacies, literacies that may prove as essential in students' futures as the traditional tasks that currently make up the curriculum. Close observation, clear appreciation for the strengths and abilities their students have developed, and openness to new ways of thinking about literacy will help teachers fulfill their goals of addressing the motivational barriers they see in their class-rooms. We recommend that teachers engage their students in an explicit discussion of what is meant by literacy in the 21st century. In this context of negotiating goals for and definitions of literacy, teachers and students will develop not only shared understandings but also mutual respect for each other's tasks as teachers and learners of literacy.

In addition to encouraging students and teachers explicitly to define literacy through discussion in individual classrooms, it would be worth-while to consider these same issues with other faculty in order to examine the underlying curricular goals for promoting literacy and making them explicit throughout a school. With all its portents of turmoil and require-ment for adjustment, change does always bring with it the gift of allowing reflection on what was and choice of a new vision for what will be. Teachers and curriculum coordinators would benefit from a fresh consid-eration of what students need to learn for the 21st century. For example, the concept of media literacy is a response to the need for the Internet generation, young and old, to develop critical thinking and analytical skills. In addition, discussions might center on how literacy learning translates into relevant, effective communication skills. Learning to read and write is so much broader than it ever has been, and an open discussion of how to decide what to replace and what to include in the curriculum is long over-due. If these learning goals were shared among teachers and students, we believe that many insights would reveal ways these goals could be met and implemented that transcend the more typical classroom tasks and assign-ments.

Finally, taking advantage of adolescents' propensity to search for who they are and their tendency to introspect, we can teach them motivational strategies, such as self-regulation and volitional control, that depend on an awareness of one's intellectual and motivational processes. We can make clear how these strategies can be specifically applied to literacy tasks, as well to other areas central to their identity development. One source of insight for how best to teach such strategic approaches to school tasks is to engage adolescents in self-observation of how they apply self-regulation and voli-tional strategies when they engage in out-of-school literacy tasks. For example, how do they carry on 20 IM conversations simultaneously? How do they engage with the Internet, while also completing homework assign-ments? What are the mechanisms of their abilities to multitask? We suspect that students would enjoy answering these kinds of questions. For their part, teachers could gain interesting insights into how adolescents think by not only asking the questions but also giving their students a vocabulary for answering.

QUESTIONS FOR THE FUTURE

In conclusion, we have three ideas for future research that seem intriguing given these perspectives on adolescents and motivation for literacy tasks. First, it would be interesting to examine how and why students differ in their tendency to become involved in literacy tasks. From earlier research on involvement, Schallert and Reed (1997) concluded that there are likely to be individual differences in people's propensity to get involved. In our discussion here, we have suggested that these individual differences may have something to do with adolescents' goals, their identification with school, or their sense of self-determination and control. We would like to answer the question of whether there is a trait-like propensity for deep involvement, and if so, of what can be done, in terms of structure and design of literacy tasks, to help students who find it difficult to get involved in any school-related tasks.

As a second question, we would like to test with adolescents our model of the involvement process, with its waxing and waning, and its potential tie to self-regulation strategies (e.g., Reed et al., 1996, 2002). In previous research, we found that undergraduate students reported more or less involvement at any given point as they undertook academic tasks. We are interested in determining whether, when adolescents "fall out" of involvement, they use self-regulation strategies to get back into flow. In addition, we propose that at least three aspects of self-regulation would apply to this waxing and waning of involvement: knowing that one is no longer involved, identifying that one needs self-regulation strategies to get reinvolved, and knowing *which* self-regulation strategies to invoke. Having tested this model and determined the kinds of self-regulation knowledge and strategies students have, we would suggest that the next question would involve determining how teachers can best proceed to encourage situated strategy instruction.

Finally, we are fascinated by the question of what exactly the literacies are that will be required in the future and how students' motivational processes will come into play when dealing with these literacies. When we think about the IMing that adolescents love, we wonder, what equally attractive academic goals would entice students in school learning? In a world where students might read fewer book-length texts than any previous generation, we would find it interesting to learn what teachers, students, parents, and administrators believe will comprise the literacy acts they can and should include in the classroom of the future. In this future world, we believe that students' relationships with texts, authors, and the authority of the printed word will be much different even than at present. Research at the curriculum level and policy analysis about adapting to the underlying goals for literacy instruction in the future could address these issues, as well as make explicit the hallmarks of an adolescent who is considered by teachers to be literate.

REFERENCES

Abbott, J. A. (2000). "Blinking out" and "having the touch": Two fifth-grade boys talk about flow experiences in writing. *Written Communication, 17,* 53–92.

Albright, J., Purohit, K., & Walsh, C. (2002). Louise Rosenblatt seeks *QtAznBoi@aol.com* for LTR: Using chat rooms in interdisciplinary middle school classrooms. *Journal of Adolescent and Adult Literacy, 45,* 692–705.

Alvermann, D. (2001a). Some "wonderings" about literacy and teacher education. *Journal of Reading Education, 27,* 9–13.

Alvermann, D. (2001b). Reading adolescents' reading identities: Looking back to see ahead. *Journal of Adolescent and Adult Literacy, 44,* 676–690.

Alvermann, D., & Heron, A. (2001). Literacy identity work: Playing to learn with popular media. *Journal of Adolescent and Adult Literacy, 45,* 118–122.

Aronson, J., Blanton, H., & Cooper, J. (1995). From dissonance to disidentification: Selectivity in the self-affirmation process. *Journal of Personality and Social Psychology, 68,* 986–996.

Baker, L., & Wigfield, A. (1999). Dimensions of children's motivation for reading and their relations to reading activity and reading achievement. *Reading Research Quarterly, 34,* 452–477.

Bean, T. W., Bean, S. K., & Bean, K. F. (1999). Intergenerational conversations and two adolescents' multiple literacies: Implications for redefining content area literacy. *Journal of Adolescent and Adult Literacy, 42,* 438–448.

Bean, T., Valerio, P. C., Senior, H., & White, F. (1999). Secondary English students' engagement in reading and writing about a multicultural novel. *Journal of Educational Research, 93,* 32–44.

Bruning, R., & Horn, C. (2000). Developing motivation to write. *Educational Psychologist, 35,* 25–37.

Chen, P., & Zimmerman, B. (2003, April). *Accuracy of middle school math students' self-efficacy beliefs and its effects on academic self-regulation.* Paper presented at the meeting of the American Educational Research Association, Chicago, IL.

Clifford, M. M. (1991). Risk taking: Theoretical, empirical, and educational considerations. *Educational Psychologist, 26,* 263–297.

Cole, J. E. (2002-2003). What motivates students to read?: Four literacy personalities. *Reading Teacher, 56,* 326–336.

Crocker, J. (1999). Social stigma and self-esteem: Situational construction of self-worth. *Journal of Experimental Social Psychology, 85,* 89–107.

Csikszentmihalyi, M. (1990). *Flow: The psychology of optimal experience.* New York: HarperCollins.

Csikszentmihalyi, M., & Nakamura, J. (1989). The dynamics of intrinsic motivation: A study of adolescents. In C. Ames & R. E. Ames (Eds.), *Research on motivation in education: Vol. 3. Goals and cognitions* (pp. 45–71). San Diego: Academic Press.

Deci, E. L. (1980). *The psychology of self-determination.* Lexington, MA: Heath.

Deci, E. L., Vallerand, R. J., Pelletier, L. G., & Ryan, R. M. (1991). Motivation and education: The self-determination perspective. *Educational Psychologist, 26,* 325–346.

Doherty, C., & Mayer, D. (2003). E-mail as "contact zone" for teacher–student relationships. *Journal of Adolescent and Adult Literacy, 46,* 592–600.

Dutro, E. (2002–2003). "Us boys like to read football and boy stuff": Reading masculinities, performing boyhood. *Journal of Literacy Research, 34,* 465–500.

Dweck, C., & Leggett, E. (1988). A social-cognitive approach to motivation and personality. *Psychological Review, 95,* 256–273.

Elbow, P. (1981). *Writing with power.* New York: Oxford University Press.

Erikson, E. H. (1956). The problem of ego identity. *Journal of the American Psychoanalytic Association, 4,* 56–121.

Fairbanks, C. M., & Broughton, M. A. (2003). Literacy lessons: The convergence of expectations, practices, and classroom culture. *Journal of Literacy Research, 34,* 391–428.

Ferdman, B. M. (1990). Literacy and cultural identity. *Harvard Educational Review, 60,* 181–204.

Fisherkeller, J. (2000). "The writers are getting kind of desperate": Young adolescents, television, and literacy. *Journal of Adolescent and Adult Literacy, 43,* 596–606.

Fordham, S., & Ogbu, J. U. (1986). Black students' school success: Coping with the "burden of 'acting white.'" *Urban Review, 18,* 176–206.

Garthwait, A. (2001). Hypermedia composing: Questions arising from writing in three dimensions. *Language Arts, 78,* 237–244.

Gee, J. P. (2000). Teenagers in new times: A new literacy studies perspective. *Journal of Adolescent and Adult Literacy, 43,* 412–420.

Gee, J. P. (2001). Reading as situated language: A sociocognitive perspective. *Journal of Adolescent and Adult Literacy, 44,* 714–725.

Goldhaber, D. E. (2000). *Theories of human development: Integrative perspectives.* Mountain View, CA: Mayfield.

Guthrie, J. T., Van Meter, P., McCann, A. D., Wigfield, A., Bennett, L., Poundstone, C. C., et al. (1996). Growth of literacy engagement: Changes in motivations and strategies during concept-oriented reading instruction. *Reading Research Quarterly, 31,* 306–332.

Guthrie, J. T., & Wigfield, A. (1997). Reading engagement: A rationale for theory and teaching. In J. T. Guthrie & A. Wigfield (Eds.), *Reading engagement: Motivating readers through integrated instruction* (pp. 1–12). Newark, DL: International Reading Association.

Harter, S. (1985). *Manual for the Self-Perception Profile for Children.* Denver, CO: University of Denver Press.

Harter, S. (1988). *Manual for the Self-Perception Profile for Adolescents.* Denver, CO: University of Denver Press.

Harter, S., Bresnick, S., Bouchey, A. A., & Whitesell, N. R. (1997). The development of multiple role-related selves during adolescence. *Development and Psychopathology, 9,* 835–853.

Harter, S., & Monsour, A. (1992). Developmental analysis of conflict caused by opposing attributes in the adolescent self-portrait. *Developmental Psychology, 28,* 251–260.

Harter S., Whitesell, N. R., & Kowalski, P. (1992). Individual-differences in the effects of educational transitions on young adolescents' perceptions of competence and motivational orientation. *American Educational Research Journal, 29,* 777–807.

Heron, A. H. (2003). A study of agency: Multiple constructions of choice and decision making in an inquiry-based summer school program for struggling readers. *Journal of Adolescent and Adult Literacy, 46,* 568–579.

Hoadley, C. M., & Enyedy, N. (1999). Between information and communication: Middle spaces in computer media for learning. In C. Hoadley & J. Roschelle (Eds.), *Proceedings of the Computer Support for Collaborative Learning (CSCL) 1999 conference* (pp. 242–251). Mahwah, NJ: Erlbaum.

Ivey, G. (1999). A multicase study in the middle school: Complexities among young adolescent readers. *Reading Research Quarterly, 34,* 172–192.

Ivey, G., & Broaddus, K. (2001). "Just plain reading": A survey of what makes students want to read in middle school classrooms. *Reading Research Quarterly, 36,* 350–377.

Karchmer, R. A. (2001). The journey ahead: Thirteen teachers report how the Internet influences literacy and literacy instruction in their K–12 classrooms. *Reading Research Quarterly, 36,* 442–466.

Kist, W. (2000). Beginning to create the new literacy classroom: What does the new literacy look like? *Journal of Adolescent and Adult Literacy, 43,* 710–718.

Kist, W. (2002). Finding "new literacy" in action: An interdisciplinary high school Western Civilization class. *Journal of Adolescent and Adult Literacy, 45,* 368–377.

Klinger, E. (1977). *Meaning and void.* Minneapolis: University of Minnesota Press.

Lewis, C., & Fabos, B. (2000). But will it work in the heartland?: A response and illustration. *Journal of Adolescent and Adult Literacy, 43,* 462–469.

Love, K. (2002). Mapping online discussion in senior English. *Journal of Adolescent and Adult Literacy, 45,* 382–396.

Ly, P. (2003, June 6). Maryland eighth-graders tutor FBI agents in ways of teen-agers. *Austin American-Statesman,* pp. A25, A27.

Major, B., Spencer, S., Schmader, T., Wolfe, C., & Crocker, J. (1998). Coping with negative stereotypes about intellectual performance: The role of psychological disengagement. *Personality and Social Psychology Bulletin, 24,* 34–50.

McGrath, C. (1998). A new voice on Interchange: Is it talking or writing? Implications for the teaching of literature. *Journal of Educational Technology Systems, 26,* 291–297.

Miller, S. D., Heafner, T., Massey, D., & Strahan, D. (2003, April). *Students' reactions to teachers' attempts to create the necessary conditions to promote the acquisition self-regulation skills.* Paper presented at the meeting of American Educational Research Association, Chicago, IL.

Miserandino, M. (1996). Children who do well in school: Individual differences in perceived competence and autonomy in above average children. *Journal of Educational Psychology, 88,* 203–214.

Moje, E. B., & Young, J. P. (2000). Reinventing adolescent literacy for new times: Perennial and millennial issues. *Journal of Adolescent and Adult Literacy, 43,* 400–410.

Moore, D. W., Bean, T. W., Birdyshaw, D., & Rycik, J. A. (1999). Adolescent literacy: A position statement. *Journal of Adolescent and Adult Literacy, 43,* 97–112.

Moss, B., & Hendershot, J. (2002). Exploring sixth graders' selection of nonfiction trade books. *Reading Teacher, 56,* 6–17.

Nell, V. (1988). The psychology of reading for pleasure: Needs and gratifications. *Reading Research Quarterly, 23,* 6–50.

Oldfather, P., & McLaughlin, H. J. (1993). Gaining and losing voice: A longitudinal study of students' continuing impulse to learn across elementary and middle school contexts. *Research in Middle Level Education, 3,* 1–25.

Orange, C., & Horowitz, R. (1999). An academic standoff: Literacy task preferences of African American and Mexican American male adolescents versus teacher-expected preferences. *Journal of Adolescent and Adult Literacy, 43,* 28–39.

Osborne, J. W. (1997). Race and academic disidentification. *Journal of Educational Psychology, 89,* 728–735.

Pajares, F., & Valiante, G. (2002). Students' self-efficacy in their self-regulated learning strategies: A developmental perspective. *Psychologia, 54,* 211–221.

Pintrich, P. R. (2000). Multiple goals, multiple pathways: The role of goal orientation in learning and achievement. *Journal of Educational Psychology, 92,* 544–555.

Randi, J., & Corno, L. (2000). Teacher innovations in self-regulated learning. In M. Boekaerts, P. Pintrich, & M. Zeidner (Eds.), *Handbook of self-regulation* (pp. 651–685). New York: Academic Press.

Reed, J. H., Hagen, A. S., Wicker, F. W., & Schallert, D. L. (1996). Involvement as a temporal dynamic: Affective factors in studying for exams. *Journal of Educational Psychology, 88,* 101–109.

Reed, J. H., & Schallert, D. L. (1993). Discourse involvement: An exploration of a cognitive/motivational construct in academic discourse tasks. *Journal of Educational Psychology, 85,* 253–266.

Reed, J. H., Schallert, D. L., & Deithloff, L. F. (2002). Investigating the interface between self-regulation and involvement processes. *Educational Psychologist, 37,* 53–57.

Reed, J. H., Schallert, D. L., & Goetz, E. (1993, April). *Interest happens but involvement takes effort: Distinguishing between two constructs in academic discourse tasks.* Paper presented at the meeting of the American Educational Research Association, Atlanta, GA.

Reeve, J. (2002). Self-determination theory applied to educational settings. In E. L. Deci & R. M. Ryan (Eds.), *Handbook of self-determination research* (pp. 183–203). Rochester, NY: University of Rochester Press.

Reinking, D. (1997). Me and my hypertext:) A multiple digression analysis of technology and literacy [*sic*]. *Reading Teacher, 50,* 626–643.

Rekrut, M. D. (1999). Using the Internet in classroom instruction: A primer for teachers. *Journal of Adolescent and Adult Literacy, 42,* 546–557.

Rex, L. A. (2001). The remaking of a high school reader. *Reading Research Quarterly, 36,* 288–313.

Rosenberg, M. (1979). *Conceiving the self.* New York: Basic Books.

Ruddell, R., & Unrau, N. (1997). The role of responsive teaching in focusing reader intention and developing reader motivation. In J. Guthrie & A. Wigfield (Eds.), *Reading engagement: Motivating readers through integrated instruction* (pp. 102–125). Newark, DL: International Reading Association.

Ryan, R. M., & Connell, J. P. (1989). Perceived locus of causality and internalization: Examining reasons for acting in two domains. *Journal of Personality and Social Psychology, 57,* 749–761.

Ryan, R. M., & Deci, E. L. (2000). Intrinsic and extrinsic motivations: Classic definitions and new directions. *Contemporary Educational Psychology, 25,* 54–67.

Ryan, R. M., & Deci, E. L. (2002). Overview of self-determination theory: An organismic dialectical perspective. In E. L. Deci & R. M. Ryan (Eds.), *Handbook of self-determination research* (pp. 3–33). Rochester, NY: University of Rochester Press.

Ryan, R. M., & Grolnick, W. S. (1986). Origins and pawns in the classroom: Self-report and projective assessments of individual differences in children's perceptions. *Journal of Personality and Social Psychology, 50,* 550–558.

Salinger, J. D. (1951). *The catcher in the rye.* Boston: Little, Brown.

Salomon, G., & Almog, T. (1998). Educational psychology and technology: A matter of reciprocal relations. *Teachers College Record, 100,* 222–241.

Schallert, D. L., & Reed, J. H. (1997). The pull of the text and the process of involvement in one's reading. In J. T. Guthrie & A. Wigfield (Eds.), *Reading engagement: Motivating readers through integrated instruction* (pp. 68–85). Newark, DE: International Reading Association.

Schunk, D. H. (1996). Goal and self-evaluative influences during children's cognitive skill learning. *American Educational Research Journal, 33,* 359–382.

Schunk, D. H., & Zimmerman, B. J. (1997). Social origins of self-regulatory competence. *Educational Psychologist, 32,* 195–208.

Shell, D., Murphy, C., & Bruning, R. (1989). Self-efficacy and outcome expectancy mechanisms in reading and writing achievement. *Journal of Educational Psychology, 81,* 91–100.

Singer, J., & Hubbard, R. S. (2002-2003). Teaching from the heart: Guiding adolescent writers to literate lives. *Journal of Adolescent and Adult Literacy, 46,* 326–336.

Smagorinsky, P., & O'Donnell-Allen, C. (1998). The depth and dynamics of context: Tracing the sources and channels of engagement and disengagement in students' response to literature. *Journal of Literacy Research, 30,* 515–559.

Steele, C. M. (1997). A threat in the air: How stereotypes shape intellectual identity and performance. *American Psychologist, 52,* 613–629.

Wade, S. E., Buxton, W. M., & Kelly, M. (1999). Using think-alouds to examine reader–text interest. *Reading Research Quarterly, 34,* 194–216.

Winne, P. H., & Perry, N. E. (2000). Measuring self-regulated learning. In P. Pintrich, M. Boekaerts, & M. Zeidner (Eds.), *Handbook of self-regulation* (pp. 531–566). Orlando, FL: Academic Press.

Woodruff, A. L., & Schallert, D. L. (2003). Identification and disidentification: What can be learned about motivation from student-athletes' perspectives? Manuscript in preparation.

Worthy, J., Moorman, M., & Turner, M. (1999). What Johnny likes to read is hard to find in school. *Reading Research Quarterly, 34,* 12–27.

Zimmerman, B. J. (1990). Self-regulated learning and academic achievement: An overview. *Educational Psychologist, 25,* 3–17.

Zimmerman, B. J., & Kitsantas, A. (1997). Developmental phases in self-regulation: Shifting from process to outcome goals. *Journal of Educational Psychology, 89,* 29–36.

Zimmerman, B. J., & Kitsantas, A. (2002). Acquiring writing revision and self-regulatory skill through observation and emulation. *Journal of Educational Psychology, 94,* 660–668.

Zimmerman, B. J., & Schunk, D. H. (2001). *Self-regulated learning and academic achievement: Theoretical perspectives.* Mahwah, NJ: Erlbaum.

Motivating Adolescent Readers through Concept-Oriented Reading Instruction

EMILY ANDERSON SWAN

Research has shown that students' intrinsic motivation to read begins to declines from grade 4 on (Gottfried, 1985; Guthrie & Davis, 2003). Intrinsic reasons for reading include reading to learn, to satisfy curiosity, or to pursue personal interests. Perhaps part of the decline relates to the middle and secondary school climate that becomes increasingly extrinsic in nature. For example, emphasis at the upper grade levels tends to be oriented toward grades, standardized test scores, competition, teacher control, and discipline (Eccles, Wigfield, Midgley, Reuman, MacIver, & Feldlaufer, 1993). Thus, the decrease in motivation may in fact be due to a changing classroom context that increasingly emphasizes performance as opposed to learning (Guthrie & Davis, 2003). These changes are problematic for all readers, but especially for struggling readers. As a result, many students lose their motivation to read.

Motivation to read and learn in middle and high school is not inborn but may instead be the result of the changing context in higher grades (Wigfield, Eccles, MacIver, Reuman, & Midgley, 1991). For example, students can be motivated and competent in some school circumstances, whether they struggle with reading or are competent readers (Ivey, 1999a).

Case studies of middle school students indicate that motivation may be a result of the context itself. In one case, a struggling reader performed extremely well when he was given a text that was both personally interesting and at an appropriate reading level. He used cognitive strategies, was persistent, and remained invested in the reading. Yet in another case study, when a student classified as a high-achieving reader was given extremely difficult or personally irrelevant reading material, she demonstrated weak use of cognitive strategies and lower motivation, similar to that of disengaged learners (Guthrie & Davis, 2003; Ivey, 1999a). Ivey (1999a) concluded that engagement in reading was a function of the person–context relationship. The students' engagement was determined by their purposes, the texts they read, and their links to personal circumstances.

Thus, classroom contexts are critical for students in determining their level of motivation to read and engage in learning. *But how do teachers create the kinds of contexts that engage and motivate adolescent readers?* This is the question this chapter seeks to address.

In this chapter, I describe an instructional framework that can be used to assist teachers in designing a classroom context and instruction that motivates students to read, think, and learn. The instructional framework, called concept-oriented reading instruction, or CORI, was developed by Guthrie and his colleagues (Guthrie & Davis, 2003; Guthrie et al., 1998), and I was part of the initial development and evaluation of the original CORI model.

This chapter describes the four phases of the CORI instructional framework that guide teachers in planning their curriculum and instruction. Next, I illustrate how CORI instruction may look in secondary school classrooms by using examples from teachers who have used this framework in different content areas. Finally, I will discuss the research on CORI and its effectiveness for creating engagement in reading, including ideas for future research.

CONCEPT-ORIENTED READING INSTRUCTION

CORI is an instructional framework designed to help teachers at any grade level motivate their students to think and learn. When this framework is implemented, teachers can provide students with the strategic learning tools and classroom support to gain deep, conceptual knowledge about content—whether in earth science, U. S. history, biology, or English. One goal of CORI—deep conceptual knowledge of content—is critical for all content-area teachers; they want their students to learn the content of their domain. Another goal of CORI—independent, competent learners—is consistent with goals desired by all content-area teachers. Teachers want students to know how to be in charge of themselves, take responsibility for and have some control over their choices, and to increase their ability to become knowledgeable in all content areas. Teachers can use the CORI framework to teach their students how to read to learn.

Reading to learn involves thinking about text, reflecting on and evaluating what is read, understanding and making personal connections to what is read, as well as finding the resources needed to answer questions and, ultimately, to share knowledge with others. When reading instruction is focused on learning content knowledge, both motivation and comprehension are increased (Grolnick & Ryan, 1987). The result of motivated, strategic learning is knowledge (Guthrie & Anderson, 1998). When students learn that they can "get smarter" by reading, and by using strategies for searching for information and comprehending text deeply, they continue to be motivated to learn (Stipek & Seal, 2001). This upward spiral is fueled by the need to share their knowledge with others. Motivated, strategic, knowledgeable, and socially interactive students are engaged learners (Guthrie & Anderson, 1998). For some students, this opportunity to learn may be the first time they succeed in school.

Guiding Principles of Concept-Oriented Reading Instruction

CORI revolves around several research-based principles that create a context for engagement in reading (Guthrie & Davis, 2003; Guthrie et al., 1998; Swan, 2003). These principles work together to help students become self-directed, self-motivated, and competent learners (Guthrie, Anderson, Alao, & Rinehart, 1999). The guiding principles include (1) goals for learning, (2) autonomy support, (3) social collaboration, (4) strategy instruction, (5) interesting texts, and (6) real-world interaction.

Goals for Learning

The goals of learning principle refers to core learning goals that are codeveloped by the teacher and students in conjunction with state core curriculum standards. When teachers' goals for students are about learning the concepts and understanding more than just getting the right answer, students are more likely to believe that they can do the hard work of gaining knowledge. Students who are learning-goal-oriented are likely to be engaged, use cognitive strategies, and link their new knowledge to old (Meece, Blumenfeld, & Hoyle, 1988). In contrast, students whose goals are to outperform others or to demonstrate their competence through competition are less engaged in learning (Meece et al., 1988).

Teachers can create learning goals by using long-term *conceptual themes* to organize instruction. Conceptual themes are broad concepts that students can learn about in a variety of ways. For example, one conceptual theme that teachers have used is civil rights. Civil rights apply to every person, regardless of culture or gender. Other conceptual themes can include genetics, biological adaptation, immigration, the Civil War, and so forth.

Researchers discuss the value and importance of students taking ownership in the learning process (Deci & Ryan, 1987). Thus, students participate in establishing goals for learning. Ownership is important in the process of empowering students toward quality performance and increased self-control and self-determination. If reading comprehension and learning are valued for their own sake, they become learning goals. If they are valued for points, grades, or competition, they become performance goals whose purpose is just to get the job done, for a grade, or to win. Little learning takes place.

Autonomy Support

Reading classrooms at the secondary school level typically tend to minimize student choice (Guthrie & Davis, 2003). However, giving students opportunities to "self-rule" and "self-determine" can make learning more personally meaningful and intrinsically motivating (Deci & Ryan, 1985; Deci, Vallerand, Pelletier, & Ryan, 1991; Ryan & Powelson, 1991). Teachers can ask students to assume responsibility and have some control over their learning by helping them to select topics, tasks, texts, and media for learning about the conceptual theme. The opportunity to make choices may help students' volition, or voluntary sustained effort, when learning may otherwise seem uninteresting or irrelevant to their lives. Allowing students choices does not mean that they have complete freedom to do whatever they want. Rather, it is allowing students to make decisions within the boundaries that teachers set. Students who set their own goals for studying, reading, finding resources, and answering their individual questions are more invested in school and have a greater sense of control over their learning (Ames, 1992; Ames & Ames, 1984; Deci et al., 1991; Stipek & Seal, 2001).

Social Collaboration

Social activity and friendships seem to dominate adolescents' thinking and time. Students also seem to have a strong need to belong and to be part of a social network (Deci et al., 1991). Channeling this social energy toward learning about concepts such as the circulatory system, human rights, and the root causes of war can benefit both teachers and students. Engaged students discuss topics found in texts and share their ideas and reactions (Almasi, 1996). These students can also make decisions, solve problems, explain their understanding (Chi, DeLeeuw, Chiu, & LaVancher, 1994; Wong, 1985), and increase their knowledge when they collaborate with others (Guthrie, Schaefer, Von Secker, & Alban, 2000). Students who are involved in discussions also learn how to develop communicative competence, interact socially, and take responsibility for their own learning (Almasi, 1996).

In concept-oriented classrooms, students can work together to share ideas and learn from text. In addition, reading itself can be a very social process. Students who are engaged in what they are reading and learning want to talk about it (Guthrie, Schafer, Wang, & Afflerbach, 1995). Collaborative classrooms provide an opportunity for students to work together toward common goals (Wentzel, 1993, 1996).

Strategy Instruction

All students have a need for competence (Deci et al., 1991). Competence breeds motivation, because it allows students to self-direct their learning and provides them with the ability to succeed in school on their own (Deci et al., 1991; Stipek & Seal, 2001). Often at the middle school or high school level, teachers assume that students already know "how to learn," or at least believe that they should know how to learn. In many state curricula, though, strategies such as searching for information are not taught until the fifth grade (Armbruster & Armstrong, 1993). Many classroom teachers argue that their middle-level students do not have any idea how to begin to research a topic or write a meaningful report, much less comprehend text at a deep level.

The purpose of strategy instruction is to help students become competent readers, writers, and thinkers. In short, strategy instruction helps students learn how to learn. Strategies included in CORI include (1) asking appropriate and answerable questions; (2) locating, integrating, and synthesizing information; (3) understanding texts of all genres; and (4) organizing and remembering ideas.

Teachers can facilitate students' learning of these strategies through explicit instruction and by using a gradual release of responsibility model of instructional delivery (Pearson & Gallagher, 1983). First, careful explicit instruction, which includes demonstrating and modeling the strategy, clearly explaining the name of the strategy, *why* it is important to pay attention to it, *when* to use it, and *how* it will help students better understand the text or assignment. Next, teachers can provide authentic opportunities and activities for students to practice these strategies with teacher support and assistance. Instruction is coherent when students can see how the direct application of these strategies connects to their increased competence and learning about a concept (e.g., the Civil Rights Movement). Allowing students to practice these strategies as they work with partners or peers to complete assignments and discuss topics provides needed practice toward independence.

Over time, as students become independent users of the strategies, teachers release their support of students. This competence for learning increases students' conceptual knowledge, which in turn motivates them (Guthrie & Anderson, 1998). Students become excited when they gain more control over their learning by having the tools to unlock meaning in texts. Strategies are the tools by which students gain competence, as well as autonomy and control. Competence is a powerful motivator for students (Deci et al., 1991; Stipek & Seal, 2001).

Interesting Texts

Sometimes it is difficult for adolescents to believe that reading is not boring. Yet upon careful and honest analysis, most teachers would conclude that many of the texts used in classrooms are, in fact, boring. One seemingly obvious way to increase engagement and competence in reading is the next principle in concept-oriented reading classrooms: Teach using interesting texts. *Interesting texts* are defined here as texts that are easy to read, have vivid details, and contain relevant information (Schraw, Bruning, & Svoboda, 1995). The principle of interesting texts is important in a concept-oriented classroom, because the goal is to create lifelong learners. Teachers know that the texts students read, including the variety in topic and genre, the level of text difficulty, and the accessibility of books and other resources, are important factors to consider when planning conceptual units for instruction. However, it is also critical that students have interesting books that are colorful, information-filled, and perhaps controversial or provocative. Furthermore, they need lots of them (Guthrie & Davis, 2003; Swan, 2003).

Interesting texts can include newspaper and magazine articles, children's picture books, trade books, textbooks, reference books, electronic databases, and all varieties of literature, such as novels, poetry, and folk tales. Adolescents have background knowledge that is rich and diverse. They are creative and curious about themselves and the world around them, and they can think abstractly about various situations and ideas. These characteristics alone are a great springboard for discussions and debates about issues in texts. Guthrie, Schafer, et al. (2000) found that when students have a plethora of texts within the classroom and access to community resources outside of the classroom, such as libraries and the Internet, students become motivated and reading achievement improves (Guthrie & Davis, 2003).

Real-World Interaction

In addition to reading interesting texts, students need concrete, real-world connections to what they are learning. They need to connect the concept themes about what they are studying to their lives in ways that make personal sense to them.

The purpose of real-world interactions is to create and sustain interest in a concept. This is commonplace to many content areas, such as science. For example, many science (and other) teachers believe that "hands-on" experiences capture students' interests and attention (Hootstein, 1995). Scientific observation is widely viewed as motivating for students (Ross, 1988). Many science teachers also use demonstrations and hands-on activities to teach concepts. Simulations, experiments, field trips to parks, museums or concerts, and creating models are great ways to link science to real life.

In other content areas, however, real-world interactions are more abstract. Teaching students about the Great Depression of 1929, colonization, derivatives, elements of light value in artwork, Shakespeare's sonnets, and the three branches of government may not be as concrete and straightforward as the circulatory system, the life cycle of an animal, or the structure of a human cell. Yet on a continuum from abstract to concrete examples or experiences, the more concrete teachers can make a concept, the more powerful the connection becomes for students.

Four Phases of Concept-Oriented Reading Instruction

Based on one or more of the guiding principles, what is the instructional framework itself? What do CORI classrooms look like? The CORI instructional framework has four phases, or purposes, for instruction. These phases, which help teachers focus their instruction and intentionally build the assessment, curriculum, and instructional triangle that constantly informs teaching, are (1) Observe and Personalize, (2) Search and Retrieve, (3) Comprehend and Integrate, and (4) Communicate to Others. Using the four phases, teachers can develop, implement, and evaluate CORI conceptual themes and units of instruction in any content area. The phases are described next. Figure 13.1 illustrates how the framework for a unit is planned.

	Goals for learning	Autonomy support	Social collabor- ation	Strategy instruction	Interesting texts	Real-world interaction
Observe and personalize						
Search and retrieve						
Comprehend and integrate						
Communicate to others						

FIGURE 13.1. The concept-oriented reading instructional framework.

Observe and Personalize

The purpose of this phase is to create interest in the topic to be learned, whether the topic is the American Revolution, the circulatory system, or civil rights issues in society. Teachers may choose the principles of real-world interaction and social collaboration to create interest. Creating interest in these topics can occur in a variety of ways that range on a continuum from concrete to abstract.

A concrete example of teaching the life cycle of a frog is to have a live tadpole in the classroom, so students, over time, can see the tadpole grow and change into a frog. Another concrete example is for students to watch a video of this metamorphosis. More abstract ways to teach the life cycle of a frog might include photographs, diagrams, or simply describing this change. *The more concrete the activity is for students, the easier it is for them to see the value in learning about it, and the more interest it generates.* In content areas such as life science or chemistry, it is easier to generate interest and curiosity by providing concrete examples than in other content areas, such as history or English. Nevertheless, teachers should always think about the most concrete examples possible.

The following section illustrates several different examples of how various content-area teachers implement Observe and Personalize in their classrooms.

ENGLISH

Colli is a middle school English teacher who integrates English with history. Colli had been teaching reading strategies for years, yet her students did not seem to be engaged in her instruction. Things changed when Colli began teaching them English and history centered on a conceptual theme, such as civil rights.

Colli generates interest in the conceptual theme by helping her students make personal connections to civil rights in a variety of ways. Some ideas include (1) conducting a role play in class, in which specific students are discriminated against; (2) reading and discussing a gripping story about a real person; and (3) reading and discussing current events in newspapers and magazines to help students "observe and personalize" the more abstract concept. Colli's room is also full of picture books about various groups of people, including biographies of famous men and women who have experienced discrimination. She reads several picture books to the class to generate interest in people who struggled with discrimination or persecution and how they overcame their struggles. Colli uses Japanese Americans to model for her students and provide examples of people within this group who struggled in internment camps during World War II in the United States. Because there is an old internment camp not far from where these students live, the discussion generates interest and engages students.

HISTORY

Jeff is a high school history teacher with a passion for history. Jeff's guiding principle has been to engage his students in history through real-world or simulation experiences. This principle of real-world interaction helps Jeff connect important historical events to students' lives. When Jeff teaches the concept of revolution, he shows a 10-minute clip from an episode of *The Simpsons*, in which Bart takes over a summer camp. The kids at the camp are being abused in numerous ways. When they complain about being fed gruel, the camp cook reveals that it is really imitation gruel. The arts-and-crafts class has become a wallet-producing sweatshop, and nature hikes have become "grim death marches." Finally, when Bart has had enough, he and his followers chase the camp staff away and take over the camp. Needless to say, the students in Jeff's class are drawn into the concept of "revolution" by this video (Nokes, 2003). Jeff and his students then develop a general pattern of revolution in the class discussion that follows the video clip. This activity builds wonderful background knowledge and stimulates many questions as students continue to learn more about the concept of revolution.

Jeff has found that thought-provoking video clips can allow students to see, hear, and feel historical events in ways that produce questions. For example, Jeff shows a video clip on Henry VIII from the movie *Anne of the Thousand Days,* and students have numerous questions about the English royal lineage. After showing a clip from *The Messenger*, students think of numerous questions about Islam, Muhammad, Saudi Arabia, and styles of warfare. As with any other activity, it is essential that the teacher have a purpose for each video clip and provide students with guidance in the important, interesting, and relevant things to observe (Nokes, 2003). These are several of the ways that abstract concepts can become real to students.

One last example of Observe and Personalize from Jeff's classroom is when he teaches his students about the Holocaust each year. To help students relate to this important event in history, Jeff creates tickets for students, much like the tickets one receives when entering the Holocaust Museum in Washington, DC. These tickets contain information about a real Holocaust survivor or victim. Jeff's students are able to identify with these real people, and with some of the horror they endured.

SCIENCE

Science teachers, such as Thom, may also use Observe and Personalize to teach students the scientific method. Students may conduct experiments, gather data, and observe things over time. Thom teaches the concept of cell division by having students create a human cell out of clay. Students make the cell wall, the mitochondria, the capillaries, and so on, and paint the various parts. This model then serves as the starting point for questions and further searches for information and integration of knowledge about the human cell. Dissecting frogs to learn about the parts of the body, demonstrations, simulations, or experiments are common and important ways to build background knowledge and create interest in science topics.

Creating interest in a topic can be achieved with anything from a guest speaker to a carefully chosen piece of literature or music to create a situation in which students make a personal connection to the topic. Once students connect and relate to the topic, their curiosity is piqued and they begin to have questions. *This is the beginning of engagement in learning.*

Search and Retrieve

In the second phase of the CORI instructional framework, Search and Retrieve, the purpose is to help students learn more information about the topic and answer their questions. The guiding principles that this phase may employ include (1) goals for learning, (2) autonomy support, (3) strategy instruction, and (4) interesting texts. This phase includes teaching students how to access information and find relevant resources, such as print or media to gather information, so they can read and learn about the topic at hand. Students learn how to search for information in a variety of texts, including documents, graphs, charts, and the Internet. Students also learn how to determine which information is most relevant and important, how to take notes, and how to organize data or information gathered.

This phase can also be applied to any content area. Students may learn about the history of Greek theater, the life of Beethoven, or the dangers of certain chemical reactions. Teaching students how to be strategic and resourceful when searching for answers to any question they have provides an important life skill.

Here are more examples from middle and secondary CORI teachers' classrooms.

ENGLISH

In Colli's class, students learn about the Civil Rights Movement by choosing to study a person from one of four different minority groups in Colli's class who influenced the movement—Mexican Americans, Native Americans, African Americans, and women. Students select one group and read several picture books to learn about common issues these groups faced and overcame. All students are required to choose one person from any group and research his or her life.

Colli teaches her students how to take notes, and how to determine relevant information and what is important in texts they read. She also teaches them how to use the Internet to search for information. While Colli teaches her students how to write and use all the parts of speech, she is also teaching them to write about someone who has made a difference in the Civil Rights Movement. Teaching students about the process of learning is key in content-area classes. This is the way students transfer strategies to different content.

HISTORY

In Jeff's U.S. history class, he has his students research music and bands from the 1980s. He has his students choose different types of music, such as rap, rhythm and blues, country western, funk, hard rock, and reggae. Jeff teaches his students how to use the Internet and periodicals such as *Rolling Stone* magazine to find out about major events within a music era. For example, the hard-rock group researched one band, Nirvana, and found out about Curt Cobain and his tragic life story. The students were amazed that Cobain kept a journal, and that it had been published. Jeff's students were fascinated to find out about a rock star's personal struggles and the way he handled them. Jeff used music to help the students connect to U.S. history, as well as to teach them to search for information, take notes, determine what is important and relevant, and organize information from multiple sources.

SCIENCE

Thom teaches his students the strategies that they need to make sense of the texts they read in his biology class. In the Search and Retrieve phase, Thom focuses his instruction on helping students be more strategic, resourceful readers. He teaches lessons in text structure and how to repair or fix confusion while reading. Students learn to go back and reread, and to look at the title and the illustrations to help them make sense of biology concepts about which they are reading. He teaches them how to read charts, diagrams, graphs, tables, and other valuable elements of text structure. He teaches them how to ask questions that will lead to deeper levels of knowledge. Thom teaches them about the Internet and how to access information that is relevant to their topic and purpose for searching.

Comprehend and Integrate

The third phase of the CORI instructional framework, Comprehend and Integrate, is phase is the heart of Concept-Oriented Reading Instruction: comprehension and knowledge. The guiding principles that may be employed in this phase include (1) strategy instruction, (2) goals for learning, (3) autonomy support, and (4) interesting texts. This phase includes teaching students how to use comprehension strategies to make connections to what they read, how to read critically, how to think deeply, how to integrate and organize information from a variety of sources, how to write about what they know, and how to make sense of the problems they may encounter.

Comprehending and integrating also means thinking about and comparing new information to students' preexisting knowledge. Teachers can help students in any content area learn new information if their instruction begins with what their students already know. This is true in art, music, chemistry, English, or advanced-placement biology. The key is to find out what students know or can already do, find out what they need to know to be able to progress to a deeper level of knowledge, then help them reach that deeper level.

Here are examples of Comprehending and Integrating from CORI upper-level classrooms.

ENGLISH

Colli's emphasis in the Comprehend and Integrate phase is to teach her students how to makes sense of what they read relative to a conceptual theme. For her American Revolution conceptual theme, Colli reads with her students the historical fictional novel *Johnny Tremain*. Her purpose for choosing this book is threefold. One purpose is to teach her students about making inferences as a comprehension strategy. Another is to teach the students about narrative text structure, specifically, historical fiction. The third purpose is to help students understand more about the specific purposes of the American Revolution. This book teaches the students about a boy their age who has many challenges, and how he overcomes them. Through Johnny's struggles, he meets and works for men involved in the American Revolution. Eventually, this book provides Colli's students with circumstances they can relate to, and it helps them identify with and appreciate the purpose of the American Revolution.

Colli focuses her comprehension instruction on specific strategies such as inference, author-determined importance, reader-determined importance, task-determined importance, summarizing, and synthesis. She focuses on one or two strategies per quarter (see Figure 13.2). For her English curriculum, she teaches students about the writing process and writing

1st Quarter **Immigration**	2nd Quarter **13 Colonies**	3rd Quarter **American Revolution**	4th Quarter **Civil Rights**
Reading goals • Activate background knowledge • Questioning/predicting • Determining importance Reader-determined Teacher-determined	**Reading goals** • Same as 1st quarter	**Reading goals** • Inference • Visualization • Determining importance Author-determined Text structure Compare–contrast Problem–solution	**Reading goals** • Determining importance Author-determined • Synthesis
Writing • Essays • Writing process	**Writing** • Same as 1st quarter	**Writing** • Historical fiction • Writing process	**Writing** • Same as 3rd quarter
Six Traits • Ideas and content • Organizing information	**Six Traits** • Same as 1st quarter	**Six Traits** • Word choice • Voice • Sentence fluency and convention	**Six Traits** • Same as 3rd quarter

FIGURE 13.2. Colli's reading and writing goals for the year.

evaluation. Her students write about a piece of historical fiction, using the information they have gathered and synthesized from small working groups.

HISTORY

Jeff, like Colli, teaches his students the comprehension strategies that good readers use, as well as strategies for synthesizing multiple texts, writing a research paper, and using all of the learning strategies that go along with critical analysis of texts. Jeff uses interesting texts to teach his students about comprehending and integrating, and he piques their interest in historical topics.

For example, when Jeff teaches his students about making inferences when they read, he constantly searches the newspaper and current periodicals for relevant articles of interest. Part of Jeff's 11th-grade U.S. history class, is a unit on the 1940s and World War II. One of Jeff's lessons is a discussion of life on the home front during World War II. Jeff discusses the internment of Japanese Americans. The text Jeff uses for this lesson is an obituary of a Japanese American man, which he found in a local newspaper.

As students read the obituary of an elderly man, Jeff helped them read this short piece of text slowly, so they could experience deep-level processing of the text passage. As the class read the obituary together, the students began to observe several important facts as they read. One student first noticed the man's name and inferred from his picture that the man was Japanese. Another student noticed the dates of his birth and death; this man died at age 94 from natural causes, at the Willow Wood Care Center. Another student noticed that "Kay" was in the middle of this man's name. The inference this student made was perhaps that this was his nickname, or perhaps an "Americanized" version of his Japanese name.

As the class continued to read, the text indicated that "shortly after marriage he and Stesu (his wife) were relocated to Cityville and held at the Topaz Internment Camp during World War II." Students observed that this sentence was written in a passive voice. The students had background knowledge of internment camps, so they made several inferences at this point about this man's life. As they continued to read, Jeff guided them as they linked the text clues with their background knowledge to make inferences about the man's life.

Jeff's purpose and goal to help his students understand an aspect of history were combined with his strategy instruction and careful selection of relevant and poignant text. The lesson not only taught students about the value of a slow, close read, but also about the usefulness of making inferences to develop deeper understanding of text. These students developed an appreciation and respect for this man and his epic life. The strategy instruction was a means to the greater goal: conceptual knowledge about important events in the history of the United States.

SCIENCE

While the students in Thom's class searched for information about diseases or genetic defects, a group of students became particularly interested in cleft palates. Because of this interest, Thom showed his students a video of reconstructive surgery for cleft palates. Students learned all about the layers of skin and muscles in the mouth and how the surgical procedure is done. One group of students became so interested in this topic and the way surgery can help children with this genetic problem, that they started a fund-raising effort in the community and raised money for Operation Smile. Teachers know that their students understand a concept deeply when they are able to communicate this knowledge to others.

Communicate to Others

In the fourth phase, Communicate to Others, the purpose is to teach students how to communicate and share their knowledge to others in a variety of ways. This is especially valuable for struggling middle school readers (Ivey, 1999b). The guiding principles that may be employed in this phase are (1) autonomy support and (2) social collaboration. These principles can include writing persuasively, writing descriptively, explaining, demonstrating, performing, presenting, or simply collaborating with others to share and exchange knowledge. Students learn many ways to communicate their knowledge to audiences both small and large. Students who think and pay attention to what they are learning use language to process their new knowledge. Students need to talk and discuss what they are thinking to make it more tangible; writing is another way to process information. They learn how to communicate to others academically, respectfully, and creatively.

ENGLISH

Colli's students work in pairs, individually, or in small groups, depending on the assignment, to demonstrate their knowledge. Through these projects, Colli evaluates and grades her students. She provides a grading rubric with each assignment. The students know upfront what constitutes an A, B, and C grade. Students can then "choose" which grade they want to achieve. The important factor here is that quality is not compromised. All students have to consistently produce work of high quality. For example, writing an essay is worth 100 points. Students earn the 100 points when they have completed a high-quality essay. They are allowed to rewrite their essays until they are done well. So when students hand in essays without a thesis statement or without a conclusion, Colli simply hands them back to be rewritten, rather than giving students partial credit. This teaches students that the most important part of the class is learning. The minimum requirement is to learn to write a high-quality essay. If students write two essays or more, their grades are raised. The difference between a B and an A is therefore a difference of quantity, and not of quality. Figure 13.3 illustrates an example of Colli's rubric for her Civil Rights unit. Colli's students present their group projects to the class. This way, all students learn about the civil rights study of other groups, in addition to their own. Colli's students also write about a piece of historical fiction, participate in daily assignments, and do other activities in which they write and communicate their knowledge.

HISTORY

Like Colli, Jeff has his students present only projects done in groups. For example, the music of the 1980s research project leads to an engaging presentation for all members of the class. Each type of music group plays three or four examples of music from its category. Students are required to have a visual aid, including a time line, as well as a written report. Group presentations allow students to choose their group membership based on interest. The presentation guidelines are rigorous, providing a challenge for the students. Jeff's students claim that this project is one of their favorites, and they all learn the material well. They also write individual research reports and, like Colli's students, are responsible for several types of assignments that demonstrate their knowledge.

SCIENCE

Thom has his students communicate to others in a "metacognitive" way on a continuous basis, which means that he is constantly talking with his students about how they know that they understand something. His goal is for his students ultimately to learn that by paying attention to what they think and read, and how they connect these two strategies to what they already know, their understanding expands. Thom has his students commu-

These things are required for an A	These things are required for a B	These things are required for a C
• Read one chapter book dealing with a civil rights issue (100 points).	• Read one chapter book dealing with a civil rights issue (100 points).	• Read one chapter book dealing with a civil rights issue (100 points).
• Complete your historical fiction project (100 points).	• Complete your historical fiction project (100 points).	• Complete your historical fiction project (100 points).
• Complete an individual project dealing with a civil rights issue (100 points).	• Complete an individual project dealing with a civil rights issue (100 points).	• Complete an individual project dealing with a civil rights issue (100 points).
• Complete an individual project dealing with a civil rights issue (100 points).	• Complete an individual project dealing with a civil rights issue (100 points).	• Read 15 picture books dealing with civil rights issues (150 points).
• Read 15 picture books dealing with civil rights issues (150 points).	• Read 13 picture books dealing with civil rights issues (130 points).	• Complete 70% of daily assignments (70 points).
• Complete 100% of daily assignments (100 points).	• Complete 80% of daily assignments (80 points).	• Complete a learning portfolio (100 points).
• Complete a learning portfolio (100 points).	• Complete a learning portfolio (100 points).	• Due Date: May 30
• Due Date: May 30	• Due Date: May 30	

Description of Requirements

All requirements must have my signature in order to receive credit. Remember that you may have to go back and revise before you get credit. You will have half of every class period to complete requirements.

1. *Chapter book.* The chapter books must relate to the topic of civil rights movements and/or violations anywhere in the world. When you complete your book, write a synthesis of your thinking.

2. *Historical fiction project.* You've already received the requirements for this project.

3. *Individual projects.* The topic for your projects must deal with a civil rights issue somewhere in the world. The following are the requirements for the projects:

   • You must have at least four sources for your research.
   • You must include a bibliography.
   • You must include your K-W-L (Know–Want to know–Learned) notes for your research.
   • You must show evidence of taking your projects through the writing process.
   • Your projects must represent a synthesis of what you have learned about your topic.
   • Your projects may take the form of an essay, a piece of historical fiction, or a poem. In corporate your knowledge of text structure into the writing.
   • Your final product must have correct spelling, punctuation, and grammar.
   • You must share your projects with the class.

4. *Picture books.* In order for a picture book to count, it must be about civil rights issues. You may read about civil rights issues, however, outside of the topics chosen for your group work and individual projects. For example, if you are in the Native American group, you may choose to read about civil rights issues relating to African Americans, if you want to.

5. *Daily assignments.* You will be working in groups a great deal this quarter. You will choose to be in the Native Americans African American, women's, or Mexican American group. Most daily assignments will focus around what you'll be learning within your groups.

6. *Portfolios.* Your portfolios will involve work from all four of your team classes. You'll receive more details on this later.

FIGURE 13.3. Colli's grading rubric for her Civil Rights unit.

nicate their knowledge about everything, from the meaning of a paragraph on renal function to their knowledge about all of the systems in the human body. He continually builds on what students know.

Thom does not allow his students to get away with saying that they do not know anything. He continues to push his students to take responsibility for their role in learning. Students communicate their knowledge through regular written responses and classroom discussions. Thom also gives more formal assessments, in which his students write and present their understanding in traditional ways.

These four phases provide teachers with four specific purposes that guide their instruction. When instruction is planned around teachers' learning goals for each phase, the guiding principles of engagement are naturally integrated.

Research on Concept-Oriented Reading Instruction

There is now a substantial body of research on Concept-Oriented Reading Instruction. Early research on CORI classrooms showed significant effects on students' conceptual knowledge and motivation to read compared to traditional methods of reading instruction (Guthrie et al., 1998). Students who received Concept-Oriented Reading Instruction were better able to answer questions about the main ideas in expository text and the characters or plot in narrative text than students who received traditional instruction (Guthrie et al., 1998).

A study by Guthrie, Anderson, Alao, and Rinehart (1999) compared middle school CORI students' and traditional students' reading comprehension in a life science topic they had studied and also the ability to transfer these skills to a new, less familiar knowledge domain: earth science. CORI students scored higher than traditional students on both the familiar and new domains, although all students scored higher on the familiar knowledge domain than on the unfamiliar one. In narrative text comprehension, CORI students scored higher than traditional students on both the familiar and the new domain.

In another study, Guthrie and his colleagues (1998) found that CORI students outperformed traditional students in their ability to search for, integrate, and comprehend information from multiple sources to answer specific questions. CORI students were more proficient than traditional students in locating texts relevant to the topic, had better reasoning for selection of the texts, and took better quality notes on the topic of study over time. CORI students' motivation to read was increased compared to that of traditional students. This motivation increased students' strategy use in searching for and comprehending both informational and narrative texts (Guthrie, Wigfield, & Von Secker, 2000; Guthrie et al., 1998).

CONCLUSION

Concept-Oriented Reading Instruction can work in any content area, because the instructional framework is not about one particular content, but about teaching students how to learn. Students learn by experiencing, identifying, and relating their own lives and interests to the content. This is true whether learning is about civil rights, understanding the circulatory system and how it relates to other systems in the body, knowing the parts of speech, writing a persuasive letter, or thinking deeply and responding to text. These are concepts and skills that adults use all the time. As teachers, our job is not only to teach the content but also to help students learn the concepts and become smarter. Knowledge is a the center.

CORI classrooms need to be implemented with purposeful goals. CORI is not a program or a package of lessons and activities to be used off the shelf. I have found that all effective CORI teachers have one thing in common: They are all learners themselves. I find that there are fine classroom teachers in every school, but the difference I am noticing is that beyond all the frameworks these teachers have in place, beyond their years of experience, beyond the support of their principals, effective CORI teachers love to learn. Most of them have tried everything. They continue to remain open to new ideas and are avid readers. Many have advanced degrees and hours of professional development. These teachers understand the power of the *language* they use in their classrooms. They empower their students in the ways they discuss, explain, demonstrate, and honor their students. These teachers have figured out how to talk in such a way that their students understand, individually, what they need to learn.

Many teachers have taught me how CORI looks in secondary classrooms. These classrooms are all different, but the teachers all know that their job is to help their students learn how to think and learn. The success their students exhibit, not only in test scores but also in becoming responsible, literate, capable learners is the ultimate payoff for these teachers.

REFERENCES

Almasi, J. F. (1996). The nature of fourth graders' sociocognitive conflicts in peer-led and teacher-led discussion of literature. *Reading Research Quarterly, 30,* 314–351.
Ames, C. (1992). Achievement goals and the classroom motivational climate. In D. H.

Schunk & J. L. Meece (Eds.), *Student perceptions in the classroom* (pp. 327–348). Hillsdale, NJ: Erlbaum.

Ames, C., & Ames, R. (1984). Goal structures and motivation. *Elementary School Journal, 85*, 39–52.

Armbruster, B. B., & Armbruster, J. O. (1993). Locating information in text: A focus on children in the elementary grades. *Contemporary Educational Psychology, 18*, 139–161.

Chi, M. T. H., DeLeeuw, N., Chiu, M., & LaVancher, C. (1994). Eliciting self-explanations improves understanding. *Cognitive Science, 18*, 439–477.

Deci, E. L., & Ryan, R. (1985). *Intrinsic motivation and self-determination in human behavior.* New York: Plenum Press.

Deci, E. L., & Ryan, R. (1987). The support of autonomy and the control of behavior. *Journal of Personality and Social Psychology, 53*, 1024–1037.

Deci, E. L., Vallerand, R. J., Pelletier, L. G., & Ryan, R. M. (1991). Motivation and education: The self-determination perspective. *Educational Psychologist, 26*, 325–346.

Eccles, V. S., Wigfield, A., Midgley, C., Reuman, D., MacIver, D., & Feldlaufer, H. (1993). Negative effects of traditional middle schools on students' motivation. *The Elementary School Journal, 93*(5), 553–574.

Gottfried, A. (1985). Academic intrinsic motivation in elementary and junior high school students. *Journal of Educational Psychology, 77*, 631–645.

Grolnick, W. S., & Ryan, R. M. (1987). Autonomy in children's learning: An experimental and individual differences investigation. *Journal of Personality and Social Psychology, 52*(5), 890–989.

Guthrie, J. T., & Anderson, E. (1998). Engagement in reading: Processes of motivated, strategic, knowledgeable social readers. In J. T. Guthrie & D. E. Alvermann (Eds.), *Engaged reading: Processes, practices, and policy implications* (pp. 17–45). New York: Teachers College Press.

Guthrie, J. T., Anderson, E., Alao, S., & Rinehart, J. M. (1999). Influences of concept-oriented reading instruction on strategy use and conceptual learning from text. *Elementary School Journal, 99*(4), 343–366.

Guthrie, J. T., & Davis, M. H. (2003). Motivating struggling readers in middle school through and engagement model of classroom practice. *Reading and Writing Quarterly, 19*, 59–85.

Guthrie, J. T., Schafer, W., Von Secker, C., & Alban, T. (2000). Contributions of integrated reading instruction and text resources to achievement and engagement in a statewide school improvement program. *Journal of Educational Research, 93*, 211–226.

Guthrie, J. T., Schafer, W. D., Wang, Y. Y., & Afflerbach, P. (1995). Relationships of instruction of reading: An exploration of social, cognitive, and instructional connections. *Reading Research Quarterly, 30*, 8–25.

Guthrie, J. T., Van Meter, P., Hancock, G. R., McCann, A. D., Anderson, E., & Alao, S. (1998). Does concept-oriented reading instruction increase strategy-use and conceptual learning from text? *Journal of Educational Psychology, 90*, 261–278.

Guthrie, J. T., Wigfield, A., & Von Secker, C. (2000). Effects of integrated instruction on motivation and strategy use in reading. *Journal of Educational Psychology, 92*(2), 331–341.

Hootstein, E. W. (1995). Motivational strategies of middle school social studies teachers. *Social Education, 59*, 23–26.

Ivey, G. (1999a). A multicase study in the middle school: Complexities among young adolescent readers. *Reading Research Quarterly, 34*, 172–192.

Ivey, G. (1999b). Reflections on teaching struggling middle school readers. *Journal of Adolescent and Adult Literacy, 42*, 428–436.

Meece, J., Blumenfeld, P., & Hoyle, R. (1988). Students' goal orientations and cognitive engagement in classroom activities. *Journal of Educational Psychology, 80*, 514–523.

Nokes, J. D. (2003). Concept-oriented reading instruction in high school history classes: Phase one. Observe and personalize. Unpublished manuscript.

Pearson, P. D., & Gallagher, M. C. (1983). The instruction of reading comprehension. *Contemporary Educational Psychology, 8*, 317–344.

Ross, J. A. (1988). Controlling variables: A meta-analysis of training studies. *Review of Educational Research, 58*, 405–437.

Ryan, R., & Powelson, C. (1991). Autonomy and relatedness as fundamental to motivation and education. *Journal of Experimental Education, 60*(1), 49–66.

Schraw, G., Bruning, R., & Svoboda, C. (1995). Source of situational interest. *Journal of Reading Behavior, 27*, 1–17.

Stipek, D., & Seal, K. (2001). *Motivated minds: Raising children to love learning.* New York: Holt.

Swan, E. A. (2003). *Concept-oriented reading instruction: Engaging classrooms, lifelong @reftext = learners.* New York: Guilford Press.

Wentzel, K. R. (1993). Motivation and achievement in early adolescence: The role of multiple classroom goals. *Journal of Early Adolescence, 13*(1), 4–20.

Wentzel, K. R. (1995). Social and academic motivation in middle school: Concurrent and long-term relations to academic effort. *Journal of Early Adolescence, 16*, 390–406.

Wigfield, A., Eccles, J. S., MacIver, D., Reuman, D. A., & Midgley, C. (1991). Transitions during early adolescence: Changes in children's domain-specific self-perceptions and general self-esteem across the transition to junior high school. *Developmental Psychology, 27*, 552–565.

Wong, B. (1985). Self-questioning instructional research: A review. *Review of Educational Research, 55*, 227–268.

14

Addressing the Literacy Needs of Adolescent English Language Learners

GEORGIA EARNEST GARCÍA
HERIBERTO GODINA

> If the teacher feels there is no hope in an immigrant child, then the child will think, "Well, if the teacher who's helping me thinks that I can't go anywhere, then I might as well give up myself."
>
> —QUOTE FROM AN IMMIGRANT STUDENT (in Igoa, 1995, p. 100)

The English literacy performance of adolescent English language learners (second-language learners of English) is a topic that researchers and educators generally have overlooked. Yet, as the opening quotation indicates, school life for English language learners in grades 5–12 can be difficult, both instructionally and emotionally. Dropout statistics for this group of students also are high, highlighting the importance of developing effective programs to address their needs. In 1995, English language learners with limited English proficiency accounted for 44% of the students who did not complete high school (U.S. Bureau of the Census, 1997). Although English language learners come from a range of ethnic, national, and language backgrounds, over two-thirds of this population are Latino, with the majority from Mexico (Kindler, 2002). Some of the other language groups include speakers of Vietnamese, Hmong, Cantonese, Korean, Arabic, Mandarin, Polish, Russian, and Hindi (Kindler, 2002).

Adolescent English language learners vary considerably in their educational backgrounds (DevTech Systems, 1996; Waggoner, 1999). Some may have participated in U.S. schools at the elementary school level, but their English needs may not have been appropriately addressed. These students may be orally proficient in English, but may not have been given the length of time and type of instruction necessary to develop their academic English proficiency (reading and writing skills, along with content knowledge) to further their learning in English (Collier & Thomas, 1989; Cummins, 1981). Others may have participated in school in their home countries and immigrated to this country with their families. This student population frequently enters U.S. schools with a high level of literate and cognitive development in their native (home) languages. They also may have acquired some instruction in English as a foreign language. Once they acquire oral proficiency in English, they often can transfer what they have learned in their native language to their English learning. Still others may have been refugees. These students frequently have had serious interruptions in their schooling. They may not be very literate in their native language and may enter U.S. schools with very little or no English and limited academic knowledge.

Many English language learners at the middle and secondary school levels are of low socioeconomic status (DevTech Systems, 1996). They often have to work while in school or move with their families, so that their parents can find work. As a result, the education of some English language learners is characterized by high student mobility and student disappearance for lengthy periods of time (DevTech Systems, 1996). Because parents and students frequently have immigrated to the United States from countries with a centralized system of education, they may not understand that it is not unusual for each state or district in the United States to have its own graduation requirements. They often do not understand that course credits acquired in one district for graduation do not always transfer to another district.

Valdés (1996) reported that educational dissonance sometimes occurs between school personnel and English language learners' families due to different cultural expectations. She found that low-income parents from Mexico had minimal involvement in the U.S. school setting but were inclined to attend ceremonial functions, such as graduation ceremonies. The parents' working-class status limited the amount of time that they had available to visit schools and interact with teachers. School personnel assumed that parents did not care about their children's education. However, school personnel did not understand that parents tended to defer control and authority over educational issues to their children's teachers.

Two sets of researchers found that Mexican American high school students were more inclined to drop out of school due to school practices rather than parental influences (Falbo, 1996; Lucas, Henze, & Donato, 1990). Falbo sampled 100 Mexican American 15-year-olds who were labeled "at risk" and found that their parents were positively oriented toward their children's completion of high school. He reported that grade retention, exit-level standardized testing, and tracking negatively influenced the students' attitudes toward school, lowering their self-esteem and expectations. Students in the lower tracks were most likely to drop out of school because of repeated failure on exit tests.

Unfortunately, few school districts have developed coherent programs of instruction at the middle and high school levels to address the various needs of English language learners (Faltís, 1999). Although some instruction in the native language would allow English language learners to continue to develop their content knowledge as they acquire English, less than 25% of middle or high schools provide instruction in the native language (Kindler, 2002). Instead, most adolescent English language learners receive instruction in English as a second language (ESL) or all-English classrooms. Many school districts place English language learners together in the same ESL classroom, irrespective of their previous educational experiences and literacy levels in their native languages. Students typically receive 1 or 2 years of pull-out ESL instruction that is not coordinated with instruction in content-area classes. Although they may receive specialized instruction in the ESL classroom, their instruction in the content classrooms generally has not been changed (Harklau, 1999). Often, their ESL instruction focuses on oral English proficiency, not academic English proficiency. Sometimes tutors who speak the same native languages as the students are assigned to help students in the all-English-content classrooms. However, tutors rarely receive training in ESL techniques, may not be knowledgeable about the content-area classrooms, and rarely are provided with opportunities to coordinate their efforts with those of the classroom teachers.

The lack of coordinated planning is complicated by the fact that adolescent English language learners face high academic and cognitive demands, especially at the high school level. For example, they have to acquire English at the same time that they are supposed to use it to develop and further their academic knowledge in a range of domains (e.g., history, science, mathematics, literature). They not only have to further their cognitive development, but they also have to learn the discourses, or ways of thinking and talking, that characterize each of the academic domains. Collier and Thomas (1989; Thomas & Collier, 1996) report that English language learners at the secondary level who already are highly literate and knowledgeable in their native languages generally need 4–6 years of instruction in the United States before they can perform at grade level (50th percentile) in English. They note that it takes a much longer period of time for English language learners who do not already have high levels of literate and cognitive development in their native languages.

Unfortunately, the number of researchers who have investigated the literacy development or instruction of adolescent English language learners is relatively small. To provide guidance to teachers and administrators, we have organized this chapter so that we first review key research findings that either add to our knowledge about the literacy performance and instruction of English language learners in grades 5–12 or that raise important issues. Next, we present a brief review of the effective schools' literature for English language learners and propose guidelines for the effective literacy instruction of English language learners. We conclude the chapter by summarizing key issues that still need to be investigated relative to the literacy performance and instruction of English language learners.

RESEARCH ON THE LITERACY PERFORMANCE AND INSTRUCTION OF ENGLISH LANGUAGE LEARNERS

A few researchers have investigated the reading–writing performance and instruction of adolescent English language learners. In this section of the chapter, we first review findings from several key studies related to adolescent bilingual or English language learners' reading and writing performance. Then, we focus on instructional literacy programs that specifically have been developed for English language learners in grades 5–12. Due to the dearth of research on this age group, we also have reviewed findings from multiage studies with younger students, as long as fifth graders are included in the studies.

Literacy Performance of English Language Learners

Findings from a qualitative, think-aloud study conducted by Jiménez, García, and Pearson (1995, 1996) shed some light on the effective reading strategies of Spanish-speaking English language learners. Jiménez et al. compared the reading strategies (cognitive and metacognitive) of bilingual, Latino sixth and seventh graders who were successful and marginally successful English readers with those of monolingual, native-English-speaking sixth and seventh graders who were successful English readers. They found that both groups of Latino students faced more unknown vocabulary and unfamiliar topics in their English reading compared to the monolingual, native-English speakers. However, the Latino students who were successful

English readers had a repertoire of high-level reading strategies (e.g., invoking prior knowledge, making inferences, using context, asking questions, summarizing) that they used strategically to monitor and repair their reading comprehension. In contrast, the Latino students who were less successful English readers tended to use a limited range of low-level strategies (e.g., decoding, restating, identifying unknown vocabulary). Although they could identify comprehension problems, they infrequently repaired them.

The Latino successful English readers also had a unitary view of reading across Spanish and English that focused on comprehension (Jiménez et al.. 1995, 1996). They not only utilized knowledge and strategies acquired while reading in one language to approach reading in the other language but also employed several types of strategies unique to bilinguals. For example, to figure out the meaning of a vocabulary item, they sometimes tried out an English word in a Spanish text (code mixing), or while discussing the meaning of a text, they sometimes switched between Spanish and English while referring to the text (code switching). Occasionally, they translated the text into the other language or made use of a cognate (ancestrally related words in Spanish and English that look similar and have similar meanings, such as *climate* and *clima*) to figure out an unfamiliar word in the other language. In contrast, the less successful English readers thought that they had to keep reading in their two languages separate or they would become confused. They rarely used any of the strategies unique to bilinguals.

Other researchers also have reported that Spanish-speaking English language learners in fifth and sixth grade sometimes make use of cognates in their English reading to enhance their English reading comprehension. For example, Nagy, García, Durgunoğlu, and Hancin (1993) reported that fourth-, fifth-, and sixth-grade Spanish-speaking English language learners' knowledge of specific Spanish cognates and their recognition of cognate relationships significantly predicted their comprehension of unknown English cognates while reading in English, after their knowledge of English vocabulary had been controlled. The fifth and sixth graders' recognition of cognates was significantly greater than that of the fourth graders, suggesting that recognition of cognates might be developmental. Because none of the students made full use of the Spanish cognates that appeared in the English readings (García & Nagy, 1993), Nagy and his colleagues (1993) thought that the students, especially those in fifth and sixth grade, could benefit from instruction on how to use cognates in their English reading.

Not too many researchers have analyzed or described the writing performance of English language learners at the middle or high school level. In a study of Latino high school students from limited school backgrounds, García (1999) pointed out the importance of finding out what students can do in the native language, and of building on that expertise. In a survey of home reading and writing practices, she and her colleagues reported that the students wrote more in Spanish than they read. Although the students were verbally articulate in Spanish, their oral reading lacked fluency, and they did not always comprehend what they read. However, when the female students were given the opportunity to write in journals, they demonstrated the ability to write and comprehend *pensamientos*, or love poems, in Spanish. García thought that the *pensamientos* presented more complex and appropriate text for the students to read than the simple texts that were provided in the Spanish or ESL classrooms.

Valdés (1999) analyzed the writing performance of three middle school Latino students who started school in the United States with no English. She was concerned that the structural emphasis of some of the ESL classrooms, with a focus on students' correct use of grammar in speaking and writing English, seriously limited their English writing development. Students in the structurally oriented ESL classrooms tended to write according to what they could say orally, and, in some cases, seemed to transfer their knowledge of writing from Spanish to English. Because the students were not strong writers in Spanish, cross-linguistic transfer, in this situation, was not particularly helpful. The teachers tended to use "guided composition strategies" or "controlled composition" techniques (p. 147), in which students completed sentences by selecting the appropriate phrases. Valdés attributed students' lack of voice in their English writing to their lack of experience with process writing approaches. Given the limited writing development of the English language learners, and the ESL classrooms' focus on linguistic structure, Valdés questioned whether the students would be able to develop the writing skills needed to attend college if they continued to be placed in these types of ESL classrooms. She raises the issue of an "ESL ghetto," in which English language learners ironically become marginalized by the very ESL programs that are supposed to help them to communicate in English.

Other researchers have pointed out that teachers need to be aware of the challenges that adolescent English language learners often face when they are asked to participate in all-English instruction in content domains, such as history, literature, and science, or to comprehend academic English text. García (1991) conducted a study that compared the English reading test performance of Spanish-speaking, Latino fifth and sixth graders and their native-English-speaking Anglo classmates. She reported that the Latino students, regardless of English reading level, were less familiar with the range of topics on the standardized test passages and knew much less of the vocabulary in the passages and test items compared to their Anglo classmates. Latino low- and average-performing readers also tended to interpret the passages literally compared to the low- and average-performing Anglo readers. Because the students had not received instruction adapted to their needs as second-language learners of English, García speculated that they had not fully benefited from current and past instruction in all-English classrooms to the same degree as their native-English-speaking peers.

Adamson (1991) reported that English language learners from a variety of language backgrounds and proficiency levels needed additional help before they were able to participate effectively in the type of instruction that characterized all-English academic classrooms at middle, high school, and college levels. For example, the students particularly had difficulties in classrooms that were teacher fronted and emphasized teacher lecturing, note taking, textbook reading, and multiple-choice tests. Students benefited when they were interested in the topics being studied, and when individual tutors provided them with *realia* (photos, objects, illustrations) and hands-on experiences to increase their background knowledge about key topics covered in the classes.

In a series of case studies, Adamson (1991) revealed the types of strategies that English language learners used to accomplish academic tasks. Those students who could "tolerate less than a complete understanding of the text and just concentrate on the main points" tended to do better than other students, who overrelied on dictionaries to look up unknown English vocabulary (p. 84). Adamson concluded that much of the material that students were assigned in the all-English academic classrooms was beyond their comprehension, and, as a result, students often hid their lack of comprehension by memorizing and copying material. He noted that English language learners benefited when they received ESL instruction related to the academic domains that took into account the problems he reported.

Literacy Instruction of English Language Learners

Several experts in second-language literacy have advocated process literacy approaches for English language learners (Peregoy & Boyle, 2001; Pérez & Torres-Guzmán, 2002). Some basic characteristics of process literacy approaches include the use of trade books; writing from multiple drafts; integrating reading and writing activities; peer interactions; a student-centered curriculum, or students' choice for reading and writing, along with inquiry-based projects; and open-ended activities in which students are encouraged to explore the various meanings of texts (Atwell, 1987; Graves, 1994; Hiebert & Fisher, 1990). Valdés (1999), in particular, thought that the middle-school English language learners she observed would have benefited more from the writing process approaches that their English-speaking classmates received in the all-English classrooms than they did from the structural linguistic approach used by some of their ESL teachers. She noted the success of one teacher who combined writing process approaches with structured writing opportunities to scaffold English language learners' writing in English. In this instance, the teacher assigned the students an essay about themselves, entitled "A Decade of Differences." She provided a general frame for the essay and encouraged students to write in their journals about topics that they could include in the different parts of the essay. She also showed them how to take notes about themselves and to cluster their ideas for paragraph development. With this type of help, students participated in the different stages of the writing process, including writing conferences and peer-response groups.

Other researchers have warned that strict adherence to process writing approaches often fails to provide students from diverse linguistic backgrounds with specific information about the code of Standard English, which they need, if they are to participate successfully in the "culture of power" (Delpit, 1988; Reyes, 1991, 1992). In an analysis of the literacy development of 10 fifth-grade Latino students enrolled in a bilingual education classroom, Reyes (1991) noted that the students did not benefit as much as they should have from a process literacy approach, because the instruction was not adapted for second-language learners of English. For example, the students did not know how to select appropriate English texts for their independent reading; rarely understood the complex events that took place in their English texts; and did not improve their use of Standard English writing conventions, even though they participated in daily writing conferences, peer conferences, and minilessons. Although the students were allowed to write in dialogue journals in Spanish or English, they were required to use English in their literature responses, limiting their ability to respond to or communicate what they were reading in English.

Several educational researchers have specifically developed instructional programs for English language learners based on what is known about their literacy and academic performance in U.S. schools. For example, once English language learners are exited from a bilingual education or ESL program, they rarely receive additional services, even though their academic English proficiency still may not be developed enough to perform at grade level in English. Saunders and Goldenberg (1999) have tried to offset this problem by developing a transitional literacy program for Spanish-speaking English language learners in grades 4–5, who previously were enrolled in transitional bilingual education (a program that initially presents students with instruction in Spanish as they acquire ESL proficiency). Their literacy program is based on the experience–text relationship (ETR) approach (Mason & Au, 1986), in which the teacher uses themes to help students make connections between assigned texts and personal experiences. Saunders and Goldenberg's literacy program is characterized by two key elements: (1) the use of literature logs, in which students write, in response to prompts, about a text being read; and (2) instructional conversations, in which small groups of students discuss and reflect on a text by critically analyzing the text and relating it to their own personal experiences. Other components of their literacy program include explicit strategy instruction, teacher read-alouds, writing projects, independent reading, weekly dictation, explicit instruction on writing conventions, and pleasure reading.

Saunders and Goldenberg (1999) were especially interested in evaluating the impact of the literature logs and instructional conversations on students' English reading comprehension. They used factual, interpretive questions and thematic essay writing to compare the pre- and poststory comprehension of four groups of students who, over a period of 10–15 days, were randomly assigned to participate in one of four groups: literature logs, instructional conversations, combined literature logs and instructional conversations, or a control group. The students in the instructional conversation group and combined literature log and instructional conversation group significantly outperformed the other two groups on the factual and interpretive questions, with the students in the combined group doing slightly better than the instructional conversation group. No group had a significant advantage on the essay writing, because students' performance on this measure tended to vary according to their English proficiency. The fluent English speakers in all three experimental groups outperformed the control group, whereas the limited-English-proficient students in the combined literature log and instructional conversation group outperformed the limited-English-proficient students in the other three groups.

Igoa (1995) describes the type of instruction that she provided in a pull-out Sheltered English Classroom for fifth- and sixth-grade English language learners from a range of countries (among others, Afghanistan, American Samoa, China, Mexico, the Phillipines, Romania, and Vietnam). Through ethnographic portrayals of the children's experiences in her classroom, she demonstrates how she combined the use of the native language; the integration of English reading, writing, speaking, and listening; and explicit individualized instruction on English vocabulary, phonics, mechanics, and grammar with authentic literacy tasks. One of the most effective activities was individual children's development of filmstrips in English, complete with illustrations, narrative, and sound effects, which they shared with other students in the class. Igoa points out the anxieties that many immigrant students experience as they try to appear knowledgeable in all-English settings when they do not fully understand what is occurring. She also reveals the psychological importance of valuing students' native languages and home cultures, and of helping them to make home–school connections.

Based on his earlier findings on bilingual reading (Jiménez et al., 1995, 1996), Jiménez (1997) conducted a formative experiment with 5 low-literacy seventh-grade Latino students that previously had been designated English language learners. After observing the students' reading instruction and performance in English, he designed eight cognitive strategy lessons, which he taught to the students over a period of 2 weeks. His strategy lessons emphasized improving students' reading fluency by having them repeat oral readings of culturally familiar text, as well as teaching students how to figure out unknown vocabulary, ask questions, make inferences, search for cognates, and use knowledge acquired in one language to approach the other. He also wanted students to talk about and reflect on what they were reading. He reported that the students were more engaged with the instruction, talked more about the text, and improved their inferences when culturally relevant text was used, and when the students were encouraged to use Spanish and English to discuss English text.

Klingner and Vaughn (2000) investigated the effect of Collaborative Strategic Reading on the science reading vocabulary of 37 fifth graders (35 of whom were Spanish–English bilingual but of varying English proficiency). Collaborative Strategic Reading emphasizes a variety of comprehension strategies: how to preview text; identify difficult concepts and words in a passage and figure out repair strategies; restate the most important idea in a section or paragraph; and summarize what was learned, as well as generate teacher-like test questions. It involves cooperative learning, teacher modeling, role playing, think-alouds, and peer assistance. After a month of Collaborative Strategic Reading instruction, Klingner and Vaughn compared the students' ability, prior to the study and after the study, to write definitions for words in two science book chapters. Although all of the students made significant gains on the pre–posttest measures, the students with greater English proficiency did the best. Their findings suggest that students with low levels of English proficiency may need more explicit vocabulary support than what the intervention provided.

Based on a longitudinal analysis of immigrant students' performance in U.S. schools, Thomas and Collier (1996) reported that secondary students who entered U.S. schools with grade-level performance in their native language had the best opportunity for success when they received content-based ESL instruction, which involves teaching subject matter, such as science and social studies, by utilizing ESL techniques that shelter (support) students' comprehension of the material (see Peregoy & Boyle,

2001). In content-based ESL instruction, students acquire English in the context of furthering their knowledge or acquiring knowledge about a specific domain. Teachers integrate reading, writing, speaking, and listening at the same time that they use gestures, physical action, visuals, dramatizations, and *realia* to make instruction comprehensible. Some teachers also modulate their speech for beginning ESL students by slowing down the pace, enunciating clearly, and reducing the use of paraphrasing until they are sure that students understand what is being said.

Chamot and O'Malley (1996) have developed a content-based ESL program of instruction for intermediate ESL learners that they call the Cognitive Academic Language Learning Approach (CALLA). They argue that when students are taught content material through the use of sheltered English, they acquire not only the domain knowledge but also the necessary vocabulary, syntax, and discourse relevant to the domain. Their method specifically teaches students how to use three types of strategies to interact with content-area material in mathematics, social studies, science, or literature. Students explicitly are taught metacognitive strategies, such as how to plan and monitor their comprehension of a content domain, cognitive strategies, which include strategies to process text and material (e.g., taking notes, summarizing, making inferences), and social strategies, such as asking questions for clarification or about how to cooperate with each other. Although ESL programs sometimes are based on Chamot and O'Malley's rationale for content-based ESL instruction, the use and evaluation of their specific program has not been extensively investigated.

PRINCIPLES FOR EFFECTIVE LITERACY INSTRUCTION OF ADOLESCENT ENGLISH LANGUAGE LEARNERS

In this section, we first present new information on effective schools for English language learners, then draw on these findings and those from our previous discussion to delineate guidelines that we think can be used to provide high-quality literacy instruction for English language learners. We draw on the effective schools' literature, because our earlier discussion revealed the importance of providing English language learners with a coherent and coordinated program of instruction.

Effective Schools for English Language Learners

Lucas et al. (1990) identified the consistent features of high schools deemed successful at teaching English language learners. These were high schools that state and federal agencies had identified as sharing high standards for academic excellence in the effective education of English language learners. Criteria for success included high-standardized test scores, low dropout rates, and subsequent college attendance. Unfortunately, not very many high schools met the exceptional criteria, although Lucas et al. did develop profiles for six high schools that were considered successful.

Lucas et al. (1990) reported that everyone at the successful schools, both students and school personnel, recognized and embraced high academic goals and expectations. Staff development was linked to instructional strategies specifically designed to benefit English language learners. School counselors placed special attention on the unique needs of English language learners. Parents were encouraged to participate in their children's education through contact with bilingual staff and by enrolling in ESL night classes held at the schools. The school curricula included a variety of programs that integrated English language learners' social and cultural knowledge, as well as capitalized on their native-language abilities. Instruction stressed high academic standards in both the students' native language and English. English language learners also were able to take Advanced Placement examinations for college credit in their native language as readily as fellow students who took the examinations in English.

In a study of the academic performance of immigrant students who entered U.S. schools at the secondary level, Thomas and Collier (1996) shared similar findings. They found that English language learners already literate in their native language benefited when instruction emphasized higher order thinking skills, students' prior knowledge, cooperative groups, respect for students' native languages and cultures, inquiry- and discovery-based learning, and multiple assessments.

Although continued instruction in the native language may seem counterintuitive, it is important to remember that what makes a difference in the academic learning of English language learners in U.S. classrooms is their academic proficiency in English, not their oral proficiency in English. Cummins (1981) reported that it may take English language learners only 2–3 years of English instruction to develop their ability to communicate orally with others, or what Cummins calls *basic interpersonal skills*. However, it often takes them 4–7 years to develop the type of *cognitive academic proficiency* necessary fully to comprehend and learn new material through English. In his interdependence hypothesis, Cummins also points out that bilinguals who have developed a cognitive base in one language should be able to transfer knowledge and strategies acquired in that language to a second language. When adolescent English language learners are provided with continued content-area instruction in their native language, as they acquire English, they are provided with the opportunity to continue their learning at the same time that they are in the process of developing their oral and academic proficiencies in English. They do not have to put their knowledge development on hold, until they have acquired enough academic English to be able to learn through English.

Guidelines for the Effective Literacy Instruction of English Language Learners

• Given the diversity of experiences that characterize adolescent English language learners, it is important for educational personnel to find out who these students are in terms of their language and sociocultural backgrounds, educational experiences, literacy levels in the native language, and levels of oral and academic English proficiency. Differences among the students should be taken into account in the development of a coherent instructional program for them.

• A coherent program of instruction needs to include continued instruction in the native language when at all possible; high-quality ESL instruction; and targeted placement in all-English classrooms, based on the assessment of English language learners' academic English proficiency, not their oral English proficiency.

• The type of instruction provided to English language learners in the native-language, ESL, and all-English classrooms needs to be coordinated, so that coverage of the school's curriculum standards occurs. Ideally, students should be introduced to new and difficult cognitive areas in the native-language and ESL classrooms before being expected to work in such areas in the all-English classrooms.

• Teachers who work with English language learners in ESL and all-English classrooms need to know how to shelter students' comprehension of English instruction through the integration of reading, writing, speaking, and listening, and the use of visuals, gestures, drama, physical activity, and *realia* (Peregoy & Boyle, 2001). They need to understand that English language learners will do better in classrooms that emphasize inquiry-based learning and small-group instruction or cooperative learning than they will in lecture-oriented, teacher-fronted classrooms (Adamson, 1991). They also need to open up their instruction, so that they become aware of how English language learners are interpreting and responding to instruction, and know when they need clarification, help with English vocabulary, or explicit instruction (García, 1991). Several researchers have pointed out that a bridging of home and school also needs to occur, so that English language learners are comfortable using their native language, prior knowledge, and previous experiences to approach topics presented in English (García, 1999; Igoa, 1995; Jiménez, 1997; Saunders & Goldenberg, 1999).

• The primary focus of ESL instruction should be on content-area instruction tied to the same content standards that guide the instruction of native-English speakers at the school. This type of instruction should integrate reading, writing, listening, and speaking in a particular academic domain (ESL language arts, ESL algebra, ESL biology, etc.). It should provide English language learners with the necessary vocabulary and discourse structures needed to further their learning in the specific domain. Sheltered techniques and native language support (such as, native-language reference materials, bilingual dictionaries, opportunities for students from the same native-language backgrounds to confer in their native languages) also should be provided. A strategic approach, such as that proposed by Chamot and O'Malley (1996), may be useful in helping students to acquire the metacognitive, cognitive, and social strategies needed to interact in specific academic domains.

• English language arts as a content area needs to be offered as an ESL course. Enough time needs to be allotted for this course, so that teachers can provide English language learners with opportunities to hear, read, discuss, and write about age-appropriate literature, as well as improve their English speaking, listening, reading and writing skills through their interactions with texts and writing activities. To motivate students and help them develop strong inferencing strategies, students should be provided with opportunities to read culturally familiar/relevant texts, as well as texts that are part of the all-English curriculum. Saunders and Goldenberg (1999), in particular, pointed out the importance of helping English language learners identify relationships between their personal experiences and texts that they read.

• Within the ESL language arts classroom, we recommend strategy instruction, in which the teacher models and gives students' guided practice in using cognitive strategies to monitor and repair their comprehension in English. Jiménez and his colleagues (Jiménez et al., 1995, 1996) pointed out that specific strategies—questioning, summarizing, making accurate inferences, using context to figure out unknown vocabulary—are characteristic of Spanish-speaking students who are successful English readers. We also recommend that teachers encourage English language learners to use knowledge and high-level strategies (e.g., invoking prior knowledge, noticing novelty) acquired while reading in their native languages to reading in English, as well as bilingual strategies (code mixing, code switching, cognates, etc.) (see Jiménez, et al., 1995, 1996; Nagy et al., 1993).

• Process writing approaches, in which students are given the opportunity to communicate their thoughts authentically through writing, seem important (see Valdés, 1999). However, Reyes (1991, 1992) also points out that this type of instruction should be combined with explicit instruction on topics/conventions unfamiliar to many English language learners (e.g., how to edit English writing, how to write specific genres). Valdés (1999) notes that some structured writing opportunities also may be helpful for beginning English writers.

• Finally, we think that process literacy approaches, combined with strategy instruction and explicit instruction, especially on topics/skills not automatically known to English language learners (e.g., how to select books in English for independent reading or English writing conventions), may be particularly helpful to English language learners. We note that a number of researchers (Igoa, 1995; Jiménez, 1997; Saunders & Goldenberg, 1999) have developed programs that emphasize this type of combined instruction.

KEY TOPICS THAT NEED TO BE ADDRESSED

Clearly, we need to know much more about the literacy performance and instruction of English language learners in grades 5–12. Longitudinal studies that track the literacy development, performance, engagement, and instruction of adolescent English language learners are imperative. In addition, we need experimental studies that develop and test instructional literacy programs for English language learners based on what we know about second-language acquisition, second-language literacy, and bilingualism; adolescent English language learners; and the demands of literacy instruction at the middle and high school levels. Given the high dropout rate of English language learners (U.S. Bureau of the Census, 1997), this is a research agenda that, as a nation, we cannot afford to delay and that we should give the highest priority.

REFERENCES

Adamson, H. D. (1991). *Academic competence: Theory and classroom competence: Preparing ESL students for content courses.* New York: Longman.

Atwell, N. (1987). *In the middle: Writing, reading, and learning with adolescents.* Portsmouth, NH: Heinemann.

Chamot, A. U., & O'Malley, M. (1996). The cognitive academic language learning approach: A model for linguistically diverse classrooms. *Elementary School Journal, 96*(3), 259–274.

Collier, V. P., & Thomas, W. P. (1989). How quickly can immigrants become proficient in school English? *Journal of Educational Issues of Language Minority Students, 16,* 187–212.

Cummins, J. (1981). The role of primary language development in promoting educational success for language minority students. In California Sate Department of Education (Ed.), *Schooling and language minority students: A theoretical framework* (pp. 3–49). Los Angeles: Evaluation, Dissemination and Assessment Center, California State University.

Delpit, L. (1988). The silenced dialogue: Power and pedagogy in educating other people's children. *Harvard Educational Review, 58,* 280–298.

DevTech Systems. (1996). *Executive summary, a descriptive study of the ESEA Title VII Educational Services provided for secondary school limited English proficient students.* Retrieved January 13, 2004 from *http://www.ncela.gwu.edu/miscpubs/devtech/secondary/*

Falbo, T. (1996). *Latino youth and high school graduation.* Toronto, CA: American Psychological Association (ERIC Document Reproduction Service No. ED401353).

Faltís, C. J. (1999). Introduction: Creating a new history. In C. J. Faltís & Paula Wolfe (Eds.), *So much to say: Adolescents, bilingualism, and ESL in the secondary school* (pp. 1–9). New York: Teachers College Press.

García, G. E. (1991). Factors influencing the English reading test performance of Spanish-speaking Hispanic students. *Reading Research Quarterly, 26,* 371–392.

García, G. E., & Nagy, W. (1993). Latino students' concept of cognates. In D. J. Leu & C. K. Kinzer (Eds.), *Examining central issues in literacy research, theory, and practice: Forty-second yearbook of the National Reading Conference* (pp. 171–177). Chicago: National Reading Conference.

García, O. (1999). Educating Latino high school students with little formal schooling. In C. J. Faltís & Paula Wolfe (Eds.), *So much to say: Adolescents, bilingualism, and ESL in the secondary school* (pp. 42–82). New York: Teachers College Press.

Graves, D. (1994). *A fresh look at writing.* Portsmouth, NH: Heinemann.

Harklau, L. (1999). The ESL learning environment in secondary school. In C. J. Faltís & P. Wolfe (Eds.), *So much to say: Adolescents, bilingualism, and ESL in the secondary school* (pp. 42–60). New York: Teachers College Press.

Hiebert, E. H., & Fisher, C. W. (1990). Whole language: Three themes for the future. *Educational Leadership, 47*(6), 62–63.

Igoa, C. (1995). *The inner world of the immigrant child.* Mahwah, NJ: Erlbaum.

Jiménez, R. T. (1997). The strategic reading abilities and potential of five low-literacy Latino readers in middle school. *Reading Research Quarterly, 32,* 224–243.

Jiménez, R. T., García, G. E., & Pearson, P. D. (1995). Three children, two languages, and strategic reading: Case studies in bilingual/monolingual reading. *American Educational Research Journal, 32,* 31–61.

Jiménez, R. T., García, G. E., & Pearson, P. D. (1996). The reading strategies of bilingual Latina/o Latino students who are successful English readers: Opportunities and obstacles. *Reading Research Quarterly, 31*(1), 2–25.

Kindler, A. L. (2002). *Survey of the states' limited English proficient students and available educational programs and services, 2000–2001 summary report.* Washington, DC: National Clearinghouse for English Language Acquisition and Language Instruction Educational Programs.

Klingner, J. K., & Vaughn, S. (2000). The helping behaviors of fifth graders while using collaborative strategic reading during ESL content classes. *TESOL Quarterly, 34*(1), 69–98.

Lucas, T., Henze, R., & Donato, R. (1990). Promoting the success of Latino language minority students: An exploratory study of six high schools. *Harvard Educational Review, 60*(3), 315–339.

Mason, J. M., & Au, K. H. (1986). *Reading instruction for today.* Glenview, IL: Scott Foresman.

Nagy, W. E., García, G. E., Durgunoğlu, A., & Hancin, B. (1993). Spanish–English bilingual children's use and recognition of cognates in English reading. *Journal of Reading Behavior, 25*(3), 241–259.

Peregoy, S. E., & Boyle, O. F. (2001). *Reading, writing, and learning in ESL: A resource book for K–12 teachers.* New York: Longman.

Pérez, B., & Torres-Guzmán, M. E. (2002). *Learning in two worlds: An integrated Spanish/English biliteracy approach* (3rd ed.). Boston: Allyn & Bacon.

Reyes, M. (1991). A process approach to literacy using dialogue journals and literature logs with second language learners. *Research in the Teaching of English, 25,* 291–313.

Reyes, M. (1992). Challenging venerable assumptions: Literacy instruction for linguistically different students. *Harvard Educational Review, 62,* 427–446.

Saunders, W. M., & Goldenberg, C. (1999). Effects of instructional conversations and literature logs on limited- and fluent-English proficient students' story comprehension and thematic understanding. *Elementary School Journal, 99*(4), 277–301.

Thomas, W. P., & Collier, V. (1996). Language-minority student achievement and program effectiveness. *NABE News, 19*(6), 33–35.

U.S. Bureau of the Census. (1997, October). *Current population surveys, 1992 and 1995.* Washington, DC: U.S. Printing Office.

Valdés, G. (1996). *Con respeto, bridging the distances between culturally diverse families and schools: An ethnographic portrait.* New York: Teachers College Press.

Valdés, G. (1999). Incipient bilingualism and the development of English language writing abilities in the secondary school. In C. J. Faltis & P. M. Wolfe (Eds.), *So much to say: Adolescents, bilingualism and ESL in the secondary school* (pp. 138–175). New York: Teachers College Press.

Waggoner, D. (1999). Who are secondary newcomer and linguistically different youth? In C. J. Faltis & P. M. Wolfe (Eds.), *So much to say: Adolescents, bilingualism, and ESL in the secondary school* (pp. 13–42). New York: Teachers College Press.

Culturally Responsive Practices for Youth Literacy Learning

ELIZABETH BIRR MOJE
KATHLEEN HINCHMAN

A great deal has been written about the importance of engaging in culturally responsive pedagogy in recent years (Banks & Banks, 2001; Ladson-Billings, 1994, 1999; Lee, 1995). Our purpose in this chapter is to examine what it means to talk about culturally responsive pedagogy and its many variants (e.g., culturally relevant pedagogy, multicultural pedagogy), particularly when enacted in secondary (middle, junior, and senior high) school content areas.

The first question to ponder is why a chapter on culturally responsive pedagogy is included in a book on best practice for youth literacy learning. How does it relate to the other best practices discussed in this text? What would it look like to engage in one of the other best practices but not be culturally responsive? Is culturally responsive literacy pedagogy different in the content areas of the secondary school, where young people are expected to study increasingly sophisticated concepts and discursive practices of the different disciplines?

We take the stance that all practice needs to be culturally responsive in order to be best practice. Young people, whether African American, European American, Latino/a, Asian American, or American Indians are, like all people, cultural beings. As cultural beings, young people deserve to experience pedagogy and curricula that respond to and extend their cultural experiences. Indeed, many recommended mainstream teaching practices *are* designed to be culturally responsive but are enacted in ways that are responsive only to a segment of students; that is, such practices are often, for a variety of reasons, situated in mainstream "ways with words" (Heath, 1983) and knowledges, making them inaccessible to those who do not share such cultural practices.

Our research with youth suggests to us that best practice needs to be responsive to more than culture, at least as culture is often defined, in terms of ethnic, racial, or—less often—social class backgrounds. Instead, best practice, as we see it, is responsive to the many funds of knowledge and Discourse (Gee, 1996) that shape and inform literate practice of youth learners. *Discourse*, as Gee defines it, emphasizes not only language itself but also the *ways* of knowing, doing, being, reading, writing, and talking that people in different communities enact, often without even realizing that their Discourses are unique to their group, whether a cultural, ethnic, gender, or professional group. A number of scholars have demonstrated that these Discourses—ways of knowing and "ways with words" (Heath, 1983)—are present in school and also influence how people teach and learn in school (Gee, 1996; Heath, 1983; Lemke, 1990; Luke, 1993). Based on such research, we argue that best practice attends to the knowledges and Discourses of the youths' homes; ethnic, racial, or geographic communities; and youth culture, popular culture, school culture, classroom culture, or discipline-specific culture.

In fact, rather than naming a particular sort of responsiveness (i.e., "cultural"), we prefer to talk simply about *responsive teaching*. By responsive teaching, we mean that which *merges* the needs and interests of youth as persons with the needs and interests of youth as learners of new concepts, practices, and skills. Such teaching also recognizes that needs and interests are always mediated by membership in many different groups of people and by activities engaged in many different times, spaces, and relationships. However, even as we offer this expanded notion of what it means to be responsive in teaching, we recognize that the cultural knowledges and practices of some students—most often, students of color, English language learners and recent arrivals to the United States, or students from low-income homes and communities—are often unrecognized or dismissed in attempts to build best practices, especially at the secondary level.

With these issues in mind, we offer a review of different perspectives on culturally responsive pedagogy and examples of culturally responsive pedagogy drawn from classrooms in which we have worked. To organize our review of the most important studies of culturally responsive pedagogy, we categorize studies into three different current perspectives on what it means to engage in culturally responsive pedagogy:

1. Culturally responsive pedagogy should use students' experiences as a *bridge* to conventional content and literacy learning.
2. Culturally responsive pedagogy should teach youth how to *navigate* cultural and discursive communities.
3. Culturally responsive pedagogy should also draw from students' experiences to *challenge and reshape* the academic-content knowledge and literacy practices of the curriculum. *often seen as argumentative?*

CRITICAL RESEARCH ON CULTURALLY RESPONSIVE PEDAGOGY: A REVIEW

Cultural Responsiveness as a Tool for Building Bridges

From this perspective, it is important to respond to the cultural backgrounds of all students to build bridges from knowledge and Discourses often marginalized in school settings to the learning of conventional academic knowledges and Discourses. Much of this work draws from cognitive and sociocognitive perspectives that seek to activate learners' prior knowledges and connect their existing knowledge to the target concepts. However, scholars who write from culturally responsive bridging perspectives would argue that the prior knowledge of nonmainstream learners often is either not understood or not acknowledged as valid and valuable (Moll, Veléz-Ibañéz, & Greenberg, 1989).

Much of the work in this area focuses on making available to teachers the rich funds of knowledge and cultural practices that youth from nonmainstream backgrounds might bring to school (e.g., Heath, 1983; Moll, 1994; Moll et al., 1989). Once teachers learn about the different forms of prior knowledge or the different discursive practices their students might bring to their classrooms, they can then build bridges between the mainstream academic knowledge and discourse, and the knowledge and discourse that students bring to classrooms (e.g., Gutiérrez, Baquedano-López, Alvarez, & Chiu, 1999; Heath, 1983; Hudicourt-Barnes, 2003; Lee, 1993; Lee & Fradd, 1999; Moll & Gonzalez, 1994; Warren, Ballenger, Ogonowski, Rosebery, & Hudicourt-Barnes, 2001). In this perspective, these bridges from nonmainstream to mainstream thus provide opportunities to learn mainstream forms of knowledge and discourse, while also making a space for voices and experiences that have not always been heard in classrooms (Gutiérrez et al., 1999).

In each of the preceding studies, researchers found, to varying degrees, that students showed gains in academic content learning as a result of the particular practice the teacher enacted. For example, Lee (1993) studied the use of *signifying* as a way to teach literary devices often used to interpret canonical literature. *Signifying*, as defined by Lee, is an African American discourse pattern practiced in many African American homes. To signify means to "speak with innuendo and double meanings, to play rhetorically upon the meaning and sounds of words, and to be quick and often witty in one's responses" (Lee, 1993, p. 11). Signifying, Lee argues, serves as a tool for defining oneself as an African American; it is a tool for achieving status and recognition, and a way of taking an insider role in many African American communities. Lee engaged youth in signifying practices that exploited the use of irony and metaphor, among other literary elements, to teach Shakespearean works. Lee's mixed-method design demonstrated the process of enacting the practice, how young people in her classrooms understood the practices, and the posttreatment learning gains that young people demonstrated, which were significant and broad. The work of the Cheche Konan group (Warren, Rosebery, & Conant, 1994; Warren et al., 2001) demonstrates similar gains in both student engagement and conventional academic concept learning, as does Moll and colleagues' (1989; 1994) work with teachers and students in the Southwest. In fact, each of the studies in this bridging perspective demonstrated gains in student engagement and participation. Few of the studies, however, measured student learning gains on content knowledge in explicit ways.

Cultural Responsiveness as Tool for Navigating Discourse Communities

This perspective argues that culturally responsive pedagogies should teach youth with varieties of cultural backgrounds how to navigate academic communities, such as school content areas, academic disciplines, or professions. This navigation is meant to equip students with access to knowledge and language conventions of different communities, so that youth can successfully navigate across those communities. This navigation needs to address the cultural values and norms of particular communities, such as knowing when it is appropriate for children and youth to ask questions or engage adults in debate (Heath, 1983; Philips, 1972). Navigation, however, in this perspective, needs also to address the different ways of talking, reading, and writing (the Discourses) within a community, such as understanding what types of oral and written texts are valued in a community (Delpit, 1988; Deyhle, 1991) or how different skills might be used to make meaning across communities (Lee, 1993; Moje, Collazo, Carrillo, & Marx, 2001; New London Group, 1996).

At the secondary level, this suggests a need to focus in particular on crossing the discursive boundaries posed by the different disciplines, or school content areas, as students progress into deeper and deeper, or more and more specialized texts of those areas (Hicks, 1995-1996; Hinchman & Young, 2001; Hinchman & Zalewski, 2001; Lemke, 1990; Luke, 2001; Moje, Ciechanowski, et al., 2004; New London Group, 1996). Research in this area explores youths' understandings and insights regarding their discipline-specific studies, considering the matches and mismatches in several aspects of classroom discourses. Researchers with this perspective claim that students must learn to navigate subject-specific discourse, as well as the more tacit meanings of classroom discourse. For instance, Lampert and Blunk (1998) investigated the relationships between talk and mathematics, including the ways teachers mediate students' understandings via classroom talk. Noting students' claims to understand material discussed in class, Hinchman and Zalewski (2001) explained that students' claim that "she puts it in such hard words" on tests reflected students' sense that, whereas they understood content in class lectures and discussions, something was different, and more difficult, about reading social studies material on tests. They theorized that this complaint may have reflected that the negotiation of meaning that takes place during classroom discussion makes meaning seem more accessible to students. Such negotiation cannot take place during text reading, especially that which occurs during a test. Students' reported difficulty may also have hinted of less familiarity with, and perhaps greater complexity of, the written discourse of the social studies test.

Some educators who work from this position also seek to make evident the power hierarchies inherent in school learning and in the different professions and disciplines outside of secondary schools (Luke, 2001; Moje, Young, Readence, & Moore, 2000; New London Group, 1996). For example, Lemke (1990) discovered that classroom discourse constructed a mystique that made science content accessible only to some students. Hinchman and Young (2001) discovered students who were silenced because they had understandings of discussion participation that disagreed with those of teachers and other class members. We have found that no studies have measured student gains as a result of treatments constructed with this perspective in mind, in part because the goal of such work is not to measure what students have learned according to mainstream perspectives, but to uncover the ways that power operates within discourse communities to silence or control certain language practices and to introduce possibilities for alternative ways of thinking, talking, reading, and writing the content and processes of various disciplines.

Culturally Responsiveness as a Tool for Social (and Epistemological) Change

Culturally responsive pedagogy should also use students' experiences to challenge and reshape the academic-content knowledge and literacy practices of the curriculum (Moje et al., 2001; Lankshear, 1997; Mahiri, 2003; Morrell, 2002). This perspective on culturally responsive pedagogy argues that it is not enough to bring cultural experiences into classrooms as a way of helping students to connect more effectively to new ideas or as a way of engaging and motivating students, despite the fact that these are important aspects of culturally responsive pedagogy. Instead, this perspective wants to make a permanent space in the classrooms and schools for knowledges and Discourses that have been traditionally marginalized. Educators working from this perspective want to integrate everyday knowledge and ways of knowing of all students with the knowledges and ways of knowing that have been valued in academic settings. The goal here is both to claim a space for marginalized voices and to construct new knowledge to the benefit of all parties involved in the educational process.

Very few studies of culturally responsive pedagogy (CRP) that challenges and reshapes the curriculum have been conducted, in part because so few classrooms represent this form of CRP. In fact, most studies that have been done have been conducted outside of classroom spaces (e.g., Barton, 2001; Duncan-Andrade, 2003; Edwards & Eisenhart, 2002). Some classroom-based studies in this area are paving the way, however. Morrell (2002), for example, reports on work with urban students in Los Angeles, who engaged in social action projects that required their learning conventional writing skills, historical analysis skills, and critical sociology. Similarly, Kirkland and Tate (2003) describe and analyze their work with young African American students in an English literature classroom as they used, analyzed, and critiqued hip hop and rap music, both as a way to learn critical analysis skills and to become critically literate.

What all three of these perspectives share is that they see culturally responsive pedagogy as a tool for enhancing the learning of all students. The type of tool depends on one's perspective on what schooling should accomplish. It is possible, of course, to engage in one version of culturally responsive pedagogy and reject or overlook the other versions. Like many of our colleagues, however, we do not see any of these perspectives as mutually exclusive. Instead, we take the stance that best practice in culturally responsive pedagogy brings together all of these perspectives. Indeed, many of the same scholars are represented in each of the three perspectives we present in the following review. We assert that this cross-representation is not a matter of indecisiveness on the part of the scholars, but is rather a function of the belief that a carefully constructed culturally responsive pedagogy could promote each of these ends (i.e., bridging, navigating, challenging, and reshaping content knowledge). In other words, there is value in learning mainstream forms of knowledge at the same time that one may work toward transforming that knowledge and generating new understandings of the world, informed by multiple perspectives and communicated via many different discursive practices.

With these perspectives in mind, we now turn to a description of some of the culturally responsive practices we have observed in classrooms in which we study and/or teach.

WHAT DOES CULTURALLY RESPONSIVE PEDAGOGY LOOK LIKE IN CLASSROOMS?

In what follows, each of us offers exemplars drawn from urban content-area classrooms. We chose these classrooms because we believe that they exemplify many of the different perspectives on responsive pedagogy that we have laid out. None of the classrooms represented completely captures all aspects of CRP, but we believe that few, if any, teachers (including ourselves) ever have perfected completely and uniformly responsive pedagogy. These teachers, however, represent many of what we later describe as the *principled practices* of cultural responsiveness.

Exemplars from an Urban Mathematics Class: Kathy's Case

Kathy's case is drawn from her work on a newly established mathematics and literacy research collaborative in a medium-size urban school district in the northeast United States. With roughly 22,000 students, recent data suggest that this school district is 46.2% African American, 44.5% European American, 6.7% Hispanic/Latino, and 2.5% Native American. Students with limited English proficiency make up 5.6% of the school district's population, and 68.4% of the students qualify for free or reduced lunch. The purpose of our collaboration is to understand what mathematics teachers need to know to support students' development of mathematical communication required by the 2000 reform of the National Council of Teachers of Mathematics (NCTM) *Principles and Standards for School Mathematics*. In particular, the new communication standard represents a dramatic shift in classroom focus for secondary school teachers by requiring that instructional programs "enable all students to organize and consolidate their mathematical thinking though communication; communicate their mathematical thinking coherently and clearly to peers, teachers, and others; analyze and evaluate the mathematical thinking and strategies of others; and use the language of mathematics to express mathematical ideas precisely" (National Council of Teachers and Mathematics, 2000). We are working with teachers through classroom observation and study-group collaboration to explore literacy demands and to develop literacy scaffolding tools, cases for teacher education tools, and a library of exemplary student work.

Dawn Williams, a European American seventh-grade teacher in a middle school in our collaborative, is an experienced teacher who has taught in the school for many years. In sharp contrast to the district average, in this middle school, 82% of students are African American or Latino, 89% of the students are eligible for free or reduced lunch, and 20% of the student body has been identified as having special educational needs; the school has been designated as among the lowest performing in the state. Kathy began observing in Dawn's classroom to gain a sense of the workings of the new mathematics curriculum. The class was taught by Dawn with the help of a special education teacher because, of the 23 students in her class, 5 students were identified as having special education needs. Dawn knows the students well; she attends sporting events and runs an after-school math club that does community service projects. Her language is sprinkled with smiles and affectionate terms, such as "honey" and "sweetie," to both boys and girls; she seems to enjoy her work and to like her students. Students respond in kind, asking her about upcoming school and community events, and volunteering often in class.

The curriculum adopted by Dawn's school district was organized so that students used mathematics in real-world simulations. The school district adopted materials developed by Michigan State University's Connected Mathematics Project (CMP) to facilitate this (Frey, Fitzgerald, Friel, Lappan, & Phillips, 2002). For example, in Dawn's seventh-grade class, a major organizing theme for a portion of the school year was the study of variables and patterns. Students conducted and charted the results of investigations outlined by the program or developed by the teacher, or they read about and charted others' exploits.

Dawn followed the principle of helping her students to use mathematics for problem solving in real-life situations in the activities she designed for the students as well. For instance, percentages were included in her district's seventh-grade curriculum but were not addressed explicitly in the CMP materials she was using. To address the use of percentages in real life, Dawn orchestrated an activity for students to complete in pairs, in which they imagined they were going to a restaurant with a certain amount of money to spend and needed to budget their orders, taxes, and tips accordingly.

Dawn began the lesson by saying,

"I am going to give a menu and an order check that would be used by a waiter or waitress to each pair. Figure out what you can afford to order, including the total for all the food you want to order, the tax, and the tip. If you look at the menu with me, you can see that, in this restaurant, lots of the food comes with extra side orders. Make sure you know what each entry says overall."

The menu given to each dyad read, "Larry's Lunch Place." It included entries for several "lunch specials," including roast turkey with dressing, gravy, and cranberry sauce; veggie *quesadillas* made of whole-wheat tortillas, tomatoes, peppers, and three kinds of cheeses; and chicken tenders with baked potato, coleslaw, and barbecue sauce. Other specials included meatloaf, spaghetti, and grilled chicken. The menu also included a section on burgers, seafood, desserts, and beverages. The order check received by each group included a two-column chart, with one column for items ordered and another for price.

Dawn said, "At Larry's Place, one of the specials is a platter. Who knows what a platter is?" No one volunteered an answer, so Dawn explained, "A platter is a plate with a main food and several side dishes."

Dawn asked again, "What is a combo? Do you see that on the menu? What does it come with?"

Charisse raised her hand and offered, "Fish and chips."

Dawn asked, "What are 'chips' with 'fish and chips'? Not potato chips, right?"

Boomer said, "French fries."

Dawn repeated, "Good. French fries."

To this end-of-the-day class, she explained, "The chocolate cake is $1.50. With ice cream, it's not $1.50 plus $1.95, but just $1.95, which isn't clear on this menu. Also, what is a root beer float?"

Monique raised her hand and replied, "Root beer soda and ice cream in a glass."

Dawn said, "Okay, good."

Putting an overhead transparency onto the projector in the front middle of the room, Dawn pointed out the handwriting on an order form and said, "Here are the kinds of things my family ordered," explaining what she, her daughter, and her son decided to order, with all the side dishes, desserts, and beverages as a model for the class. She showed the students how to estimate the cost quickly to see whether she would have enough money and asked what would happen if they ordered food they could not afford—to which students' response was laughter to indicate their understanding that this would be an inappropriate thing to do. Then she actually totaled up the items her family had ordered, and showed where and how she determined the tax—a process that was a review for students.

Dawn later explained that because of her experiences with her own children's preferences for fast-food, restaurants and knowing about the high poverty rate typical of students in her schools, she had been a little worried that her students would not have experienced restaurants with menus, tax, and tip. But completing this lesson with other sections of the same class, meeting earlier in the day, belied her fears and suggested the importance of not generalizing too much about the cultural relevance of a restaurant simulation, and instead respecting the different funds of knowledge that individuals' might bring to such discussions (e.g., Heath, 1983; Moje et al., 2000; Moll et al., 1989, 1994). Indeed, many of her students talked about having relatives who worked in restaurants, and the question of what percentage to tip was generated much discussion within groups.

The class Kathy observed met at the end of the day, and Dawn reported that she had learned from earlier classes that students had some difficulty interpreting the menu offerings of figuring out how to complete the order form. They tended to read only the heading for the menu item, without reading the side dishes that accompanied the main entrée. Dawn reported that her students also simply did not know what some of the food was. Not knowing whether this was due to inexperience anchored in culture or age, she'd learned that she could eliminate the need for answering a significant number of questions by providing students with a brief explanation of some menu entries and by modeling completion of the order form so that students could see how it was done.

Students worked diligently as Dawn and a special education teacher circulated to answer questions and to check students' mathematics, quietly totaling and estimating tax and totals as students talked with one another. When they found errors, they gently guided students back to their problem solving, pointing to segments that needed recalculation. Most students totaled orders appropriately. They struggled a bit with determining tax and tip, percentage problems that Dawn predicted would cause them the greatest challenge, and that were the focus of the experience.

When all the pairs had completed their work, Dawn went to her overhead projector in the front of the room and led another review. "I'm nosy. How many people picked the meatloaf as their choice for lunch?" No one raised a hand. "How about the burger?" Several students raised their hand, a tally Dawn noted on her transparency next to the item name. Several other students had ordered the *quesadillas*, and still others, the chicken tenders. "What kind of graph could I make that best shows the numbers of orders per item?"

LaBron raised his hand and offered, "Bar graph," and Dawn responded, "Good," and drew the beginnings of a small bar graph on her transparency to show how it might work.

Dawn noted, "I estimated totals to check your work, and found out that Boomer left an item out of his total. How did you complete your estimates?"

Madelaine explained, "I rounded to the closest 5s and 10s and added to see the total."

Dawn again replied, "Good. And what is tax on food in our state?"

José said, "Seven percent."

Dawn followed with, "So for every dollar, I pay 7 cents, right? And how do I figure it out? How do I write 7% in a decimal?"

Monique replied, "Point zero seven."

Dawn wrote this on her transparency and said, "How do you determine tax?"

Jose said, "Put subtotal in the calculator and multiple by .07."

Dawn said, "Good. But then look at your answer. If it is more than two decimals, you round up, right? So what does $1.2999 become?"

Charisse volunteered, "$1.30."

Kathy also observed a CMP group problem-solving activity. Students had worked in groups of three on the preceding day to record the number of jumping jacks that one person could complete in 2 minutes. For each group, one student had done the actual jumping jacks, while another counted the number of jumping jacks completed, and a third person recorded the number at 10-second intervals. Dawn showed the students how to record and construct written interpretations of the experiment. After a full class period of group investigation, she began the next day's instruction by putting a copy of a chart recording the responses from one group's investigation onto an overhead transparency for all to see as visual support for an interactive, whole-class explanation of how to put the variables onto a coordinating graph, with students recording definitions of coordinating graph, independent variable, and dependent variable in their notebooks as they worked.

While it might be argued that the jumping jacks experiment represented knowledge that was more a school-based than real-life orientation, the action was easily imitated by all students to some extent or another. The activity also had the potential to result in competitive teasing, but the supportive environment of Dawn's classroom did not allow this to happen. The activity was one that students found fun, especially as they noted the different rates at which students completed their jumping jacks and why, recognizing and celebrating different students' capabilities as they worked. Moreover, it was an experiment that allowed the students to see a relationship between rate and time as they recorded the progression of numbers of jumping jacks on a graph. They could talk with each other about why this had happened, talking their way into understanding the workings of tables and graphs as they worked (Davis, Jones, & Pearn, 1994; Lampert & Blunk, 1998).

Dawn's affectionate relationships with her students produced a classroom within which everyone was engaged and willing to share answers in front of peers (Dillon, 1989; Moje, 1996). As a seventh-grade teacher who knew that her students had likely not engaged in extensive reading, writing, and note taking, Dawn also helped them begin to understand how to do this, using a set of experiences that she knew they would find engaging (Draper, 2002). Dawn began her mathematical explanations with students' explanations for why the numbers progressed as they did, scaffolding their efforts to translate these into written text that would be acceptable for communicating such interpretations to others, and encouraging them to share their efforts with one another so that they could develop a sense of appropriate variations (Luke, 2001; Moje et al., 2000; New London Group, 1996). The special education teacher also helped to support students' literacy development, by noting areas with which students seemed to be struggling and helping students to understand practice their skills in these areas.

Following suggestions in the CMP curriculum, Dawn invited students to participate in experiences that would move them through a problem set to problem solving, graphic representation, and, eventually, algebraic representation, a tenuous trajectory for many students to follow (MacGregor & Stacey, 1995). Such efforts represented a classroom in transition, moving from a techniques-based curriculum to an inquiry-based one, scaffolding students' reading and writing efforts on the way toward inviting them to generate ideas more independently (Siegel, Borasi, & Fonzi, 1998). Thus, Dawn's classroom represents one in which the teacher was responsive to students' needs and interests by drawing from real-world experiences to which she felt all students could relate. She was not, however, explicitly focused on students' cultural backgrounds. The teacher in the next cases we present draws from both ethnic and youth cultures to build a responsive science pedagogy.

Exemplars from Urban Science Classrooms: Elizabeth's Cases

Elizabeth's cases are drawn from work done by a curriculum development, enactment, and research team comprised of Detroit public school teachers and administrators, and University of Michigan curriculum developers and researchers (Marx, Blumenfeld, Krajcik, & Soloway, 1997). The Detroit Public Schools are populated primarily by African American students (91.1%), followed by Latino/a students (4%), European American students (3.7%), Asian and Pacific Island students (0.9%), and American Indian students (0.2%). The average percentage of students eligible for the free or reduced lunch program throughout the district is 70%, although the percentage ranges from 35 to 90% at the schools in our project. The teachers who participate in our project represent a mix of ethnic, racial, and social-class groups, but the teachers in the subset represented in this chapter are African American and Latino/a in ethnic background. We work closely with these teachers, meeting for bimonthly professional and curriculum development work, and we videotape in classrooms and collect student and teacher work as artifacts of student learning. Student learning is also measured via pre- and postunit tests on science content and process knowledge, as well as on several performance tasks administered throughout the unit. We also interview a subset of students on their content knowledge, attitudes about and toward science, and strategies for sense making in the curriculum.

Our work is focused on science and scientific literacy learning in the middle and high school grades. In particular, we develop and enact "project-based" science units. The idea behind project-based science (or any project-based curricula) is that student learning is framed and motivated by real-world questions that are of interest to real people in real places. For example, our curricula revolve around questions such as "What affects the quality of air in my community?" (air quality—chemistry); "Can good friends make you sick?" (communicable diseases—biology); "What is the water like in my river?" (water quality—chemistry and ecology). Thus, the curricula themselves are an attempt to build *curricula* that are responsive to youths' everyday worlds because they are situated in the youths' communities, relationships, and physical spaces. Although the questions are designed to draw from the actual world of experience youth might have, whether or not the questions are of immediate interest to the youth in any given space and time is always an issue. In fact, it is an issue that begs a culturally responsive pedagogy, as the teachers in the group routinely demonstrate.

For example, Ms. Hall, a seventh-grade science teacher recently adapted the communicable diseases curriculum (which revolves around the question, "How can good friends make you sick?") because she believed that adding a particular reading at the start of the unit would better connect with the life worlds of the young people she teaches than would the article that had been included in the curriculum reader. Ms. Hall also believed that the article she had chosen would motivate the students to engage more thoughtfully in the activities—including the remaining read-ing and writing activities—of the curriculum.

Specifically, rather than beginning with an article on Nkosi, a 12-year-old African boy who was, at the time, living with AIDS, Ms. Hall decided to begin by having the students in her class read a teen magazine article on body piercing and tattooing. Although Ms. Hall valued the Nkosi article (and did have students read it during their next activity), she assessed her students' interests and experiences as more connected to the piercing and tattooing article. She knew that most of them knew people with piercings and tattoos, and that many of them desired piercings and tattoos. She also worried that her students would not be able to connect cognitively or affectively to Nkosi's experience because he lived in Africa, rather than the United States, and because the context for living with AIDS/HIV in Africa is so different from that of the United States. She did not assume that the students' African heritage would build a natural connection; instead, she looked for something that related to their particular everyday lived experience. Furthermore, Ms. Hall assessed the piercing and tattooing article, and found that it introduced many of the concepts that would be studied in the curriculum (including bacteria and the spread of infectious agents). She determined that the combination of connecting to students' interests, experiences, and desires, together with the important content introduced, made a good rationale for beginning with the piercing and tat-tooing article.

To introduce the article, Ms. Hall asked the students to write a response to the question of whether teens should be required to have parental consent before obtaining a body piercing or tattoo. According to Ms. Hall, the students immediately set to work writing a response and appeared to be engaged in putting their opinions in print. Then, without discussing the issue in detail, Ms. Hall asked the students to read the article. Following the reading, Ms. Hall led a whole-class discussion on the article. Students were highly engaged in this discussion, voicing their opinions and using both personal experience and information from the article to argue their points. Ms. Hall played the role of prober and facilitator during the discussion, offering neither her opinion nor any correction of students' views. She simply asked students to use information from the article to support their thinking. Ms. Hall then concluded the activity with another journal writing exercise; students wrote intently and appeared to be inter-ested in getting their opinions down.

In the activity, then, students' experiences were integrated with the social and scientific concepts they had read about in the article. Several of the students raised points about bacteria that were central aspects of the unit (and that they would study in later weeks). Their focus on bacteria in this article established a ground for their later investigations of the growth of bacteria in different parts of the school. And the next day, Ms. Hall returned to the curriculum as laid out by our team, asking students to read and discuss the article about Nkosi. She reported in our team meeting that she felt that her students had a better sense of the curriculum and the question, "Can good friends make you sick?" after reading the piercing and tattooing article, despite its seemingly loose connection to the driving question. Thus, Ms. Hall made a judgment about how to draw on, build, and maintain students' interest and knowledge throughout the curriculum unit. Although curriculum developers had included the Nkosi article in the hope of interesting students in someone of their own age living with a communicable disease, Ms. Hall recognized that the experiences of a boy living on another continent, no matter the age, would seem far removed to her students. She also knew that her students were familiar with the term *bacteria*, although they probably could not distinguish bacteria from *viruses*, at least in scientific terms. The article would build on a basic level of content knowledge, challenge some naive conceptions about both bacteria and piercing and tattooing, and would set a stage for further development of the concept of bacteria. Thus, Ms. Hall's practice responded to students as cultural and social beings of a certain age, with certain experiences and pressures, and certain levels of content knowledge.

In another exchange in Ms. Hall's classroom, Ms. Hall demonstrated her attention to the unique discourse of science by making connections from everyday experiences of the youth to the terminology they needed to learn in order to "talk (and read and write) science" (see Lemke, 1990). In the following discussion of the terms *reactants* and *products*, which the students had been asked to write about in their bell work (journal writing that they do at the beginning of each class period to help them focus on the day's activity), Mrs. Hall drew on the students' experiences in a peer discourse community to help them navigate the discourse of science. She also used humor to engage them in the conversation and performed her interpretation of a typical peer exchange in that community as a way to make the words more concrete and dramatic. The exchange begins with Ms. Hall focusing the students' attention on the words that they need to learn:

MS. HALL: Think about the word *react*. In order for something to react, it has to interact with somethin' else. For example, if I look at LaShayna, and LaShayna was lookin' at me like—(*tilts her head to the side, rolls her eyes, and flips her hand up in a dismissive gesture, flips her head and rolls her eyes once more, this time twirling her hand, with one finger pointed to the ceiling, the class laughs and looks at*

LaShayna)—and then, I'm lookin' at LaShayna, now I could do one of two things. Tell me if I do this, am I reactin'?

Ms. Hall walks across the room, past LaShayna, without looking in LaShayna's direction. A few students say "No," but others say, "Yes, yes."

Ms. HALL: Yes, I'm reacting by what?

STUDENT: Just walking away.

Ms. HALL: Just walking away. Okay, so, what will be the product of me just walking away?

STUDENT: No beatin' [inaudible].

Ms. HALL: No, what would be the end results of that?

STUDENT: No fighting.

STUDENT: No violence.

STUDENT: No fighting.

Ms. HALL: No fighting, no violence, things like that. But what if I did this, she's (*gestures and rolls her eyes*) and I'm like—(*again acts out a response, but this time she twists her body and gestures "back" at the LaShayna; she continues her dance-like, gesture-filled response*). Now is there a reaction, is there something goin' on between me an' LaShayna?

STUDENTS: Yes.

Ms. HALL: Okay, so we're reactin' to one another. And so what happens, we just keep doin', keep doin it, keep doin' it.

STUDENT: That would look kinda stupid. (*Everyone laughs, including Ms. Hall.*)

Ms. HALL: Okay, or, or I just start goin' (*raises her voice and puts a different, somewhat surly note in it*), "What you lookin' at? Don't be lookin' at me. I'm lookin' at you." And we keep goin' back and forth, we keep goin' back and forth. (*Students are laughing and looking around the room at each other.*) Is there a reaction goin' on in that situation?

STUDENTS: Yessss.

Ms. HALL: What's the end product of that?

STUDENTS: A bad situation.

STUDENTS: Maybe a fight.

STUDENTS: A argument.

STUDENTS: Conflict.

MS. HALL: Maybe an argument. Conflict . . . Reactants are saying what? Two things react together and then you can get an end product from that. For example, I'm a farmer. Jerry here is my sheep. (*laughter from the students*) He's baa, baa, baaing all the way around. And then I go up to him, and I, uh, shear his wool. It's called shearing when you take the wool off of a sheep.

STUDENT: [some sort of question that is inaudible]

MS. HALL: (*Laughs.*) No, no. Listen to the scenario, though. Okay, I take his wool. His wool doesn't just come to you when you have on a sweater, which is your product, it doesn't come directly from the sheep to you. What happens in-between, just give me one, I have wool, plus what.

STUDENTS: Well, you have to do the carpenting and all that stuff.

MS. HALL: The carpenting? Okay, don't get mixed up with, okay, I understood. I got the wool. What has to happen between the wool and the sweater?

STUDENT: It has to be cleaned?

MS. HALL: It has to be cleaned. What else?

STUDENTS: Put together.

MS. HALL: Put together. We look at that as the things that react, and then my end product is the what?

STUDENTS: A sweater. A coat.

MS. HALL: A sweater or a coat. Think about this, now based upon what I just told you. When I say "baking soda plus vinegar and I get carbon dioxide and water," what are my reactants in that situation?

STUDENTS: The uh, it'll start to bubble?

MS. HALL: No, I didn't say, "What happens?" I said, "What are my reactants?" Brian?

STUDENTS: Carbon dioxide?

MS. HALL: Uh, my reactants, the things that are reacting together?

BRIAN: Baking soda and vinegar?

MS. HALL: Baking soda and vinegar. (*Turns back to the boy who said "bubbling"*) You were on the right track because we saw that when they react together they do what?

STUDENT: Bubble

STUDENT: That's what we used in the volcano.

MS. HALL: And so, that's what we used, you're right, in the volcano. They *yield* carbon dioxide and water. Those are my products.

Ms. Hall's practice in this excerpt demonstrates four important aspects of CRP for young people in secondary school content areas. First, Ms. Hall saw her students as whole beings and engaged in practice that was responsive to them as cultural beings (e.g., using African American English in her performance), as youth (e.g., situating the scenario in the experiences of two young women), and as socially situated beings (e.g., performing a scenario that she had seen young people in the school engaged in on several occasions). Second, Ms. Hall's choices were not based on any of these qualities alone; that is, she did not choose a confrontational exchange on the basis of their race, age, social class, or geographic setting (an urban area). Nor did she assume that all the students would resonate with the scenario, as illustrated by her offering a second, and very different, scenario of a farmer shearing sheep.

Third, Ms. Hall was committed to developing students' understandings of content concepts and engaged in culturally responsive practice to support those understandings. She did not enact culturally responsive practice merely to draw the students' attention, although student engagement is a critical aspect of learning (e.g., Guthrie et al., 1996; Paris, Lipson, & Wixson, 1983). Engagement for the purposes of entertaining or managing the classroom, however, is not a feature of CRP. As in Ms. Hall's performance, the connections made must be between students' experiences and the content concepts. This example illustrates a form of bridging pedagogy and also begins to develop a navigating pedagogy, as youth begin to see different discourse practices around the same general concepts. Ms. Hall's use of the words *reactant, reaction,* and *products* across everyday and scientific discourse communities begins to make evident for students the differences in discourse communities. Her emphasis on the word *yield* demonstrates her cueing to students that *yield* is a word they would use in a scientific discussion of reactants and products, rather than in an everyday discussion. In this exemplar, Ms. Hall does not engage in any explicitly transformative responsive pedagogy, because she does not ask the students to merge their everyday knowledge and discourse with that of scientific knowledge and discourse. Yet her practice is transformative in the sense that she makes a space for the everyday experiences of youth in her classroom, even as she draws from those experiences to build bridges to the content area concepts.

PRINCIPLES OF CULTURALLY RESPONSIVE
YOUTH LITERACY PEDAGOGY

Whether a particular practice is a best form of culturally responsive youth literacy pedagogy is, we believe, an open question. As illustrated in the literature review and the exemplars presented in the previous section, the construct of cultural responsiveness connotes practice that is so intimately tied to relationships, activities, spaces, and times, that few generalizations can be made about the specifics of best practice. We can, however, offer general *principles* for engaging in CRP. Examining cases of culturally responsive practice allows us to see how different teachers and different students together construct classroom content-area spaces and activities to support the learning of content and literacy skills, as well as the construction of new perspectives on content and literacy. Other teachers can learn from such cases and can modify the practices they read about for their own classrooms. However, some principles of practice can be drawn from our cases to provide a framework for engaging in culturally responsive practice with youth.

Drawing from these cases, and borrowing from David Moore's (Moje et al., 2000) notion of principled practices that are connected to particular contexts (or are "ecologically valid") for adolescent literacy (see also Hoffman & Duffy, 2001), we want to propose a set of principled practices for best culturally responsive practice when working with adolescent literacy learners across the content areas of the secondary school (high school and middle school). What follows are the principles we have derived:

1. *Culturally responsive pedagogy should begin with the formation of relationships between teachers and students.* Teachers who cheer for youth playing basketball, who know their students' families and neighborhoods, and who have a sense for the kinds of things particular students care about, have several advantages. A number of education researchers (Noddings, 1984; Sizer, 1992) have suggested the importance of forming relationships with students, particularly in secondary content-area literacy classrooms (Dillon, 1989; Moje, 1996). Teachers who build relationships can more easily construct explanations and orchestrate experiences suited to students' existing understandings. They also can more easily read students' responses to their initiations and negotiate accordingly. Finally, when students know that someone cares about them, they more easily empathize with and even become excited about the interests of that person; as a result, students are more likely to believe or buy into a teacher's assertion that it is important to know some particular content-related generalization or a particular pro-

cess (see Moje, 1996). The difficulty for many of us as teachers, however, is that we do not understand—and sometimes even devalue—cultural experiences that are different from our own, making responsive teaching difficult.

Dawn Williams, the seventh-grade mathematics teacher represented in the previous section has supportive relationships with her students. She builds these relationships by attending extracurricular sporting events and shows, meeting parents at these and other community events, and is offering an after-school club herself. She invites students to work in groups so that she can observe their interactions and approaches to shared efforts. She knows her students well enough to know when someone does not feel well, to recognize when someone is especially agitated, or to see the excitement in the eyes of someone who has just solved a difficult problem. Likewise, Ms. Hall knows her students well enough to draw from the different ethnic and youth cultural practices that will resonate with them. They draw from those practices to make connections across everyday and academic discourse communities.

2. *Culturally responsive pedagogy should recognize and be respectful of the many different cultural experiences that any one person can embody.* In other words, it is important that CRP not essentialize members of a cultural group by assuming that an individual possesses certain characteristics or engages in particular practices simply by virtue of being an identifiable member of a group. Ms. Hall, the science teacher we represented, illustrates this principle in two ways. First, she did not assume that her students would connect with Nkosi, the young African boy described in the curriculum reader article, simply because they were all of African heritage. Second, she did not assume that they would resonate with his experience because they were the same age as Nkosi when the article was written. Instead, she chose an article that she knew would be of interest to them because she knew something about their particular youth cultural experiences. She also did not assume that all of her students would connect with the confrontation scenario that she performed to illustrate reactants and products, and so offered a different scenario about sheep shearing, wool gathering, and sweater production as an alternative explanation, one that may have been far removed from many of her urban students' experiences, but that connected to experiences some of them have when visiting relatives in rural settings. She thus challenged and expanded their thinking at the same time that she connected to many of their everyday experiences.

This principle is also supported a variety of cultural theories and research studies that position culture and identity as dynamic, fluid, and hybrid (Bhabha, 1994; Luke & Luke, 1999; Rosaldo, 1999). According to these theories, it is problematic to position a member of a cultural group in a particular way based on her cultural background, in part because cultures are always changing. Even in the most seemingly stable of cultures, it is dangerous to assume an essential set of practices for any given member of a cultural group, because individuals within a culture engage in a variety of experiences that shape their meaning making within those cultures. What is more, in a world in which access to information and transportation seems to grow exponentially, we cannot assume that people are members of only one cultural group. Access to the Internet, to popular cultures via television, movies, and music, and to actual experiences in spaces other than our own, make us all hybrid beings to some extent.

In addition to these theoretical perspectives, a number of classroom-based studies have complicated notions of what it means to be culturally responsive (Fecho, 1998; Obidah, 1998; Sarris, 1993), particularly in diverse classrooms, or in classrooms where teacher and students are of different ethnic and cultural backgrounds. Fecho, a European American teacher, for example, wrote of his own stumbles at what he thought would be a culturally responsive practice with African American students in a large, urban school district. Despite Fecho's extensive experience of working with African American students and of living in that district over 20 years, students nevertheless rejected his attempt to engage them in a particular piece of African American poetry, claiming that he mocked them in his efforts. Sarris (1983) presented a similar study of a white teacher working with American Indian students, who pointedly rejected her attempt to engage them in reading Indian folk tales, explaining that these were not their stories (the stories were stories told in their tribe, but Sarris reveals the complications of white teachers attempting to take up a group's cultural tales as part of the classroom experience).

3. *Culturally responsive pedagogy works with youth to develop applications and to construct understandings that are relevant to them.* Ms. Hall, the science teacher, followed this principle by organizing instruction around questions of interest to her students. Ms. Williams, the mathematics teacher, showed students the helpful connections between what they could observe around them and mathematical representations. Students responded to both initiations with energy, interest, and enthusiasm. They learned content typical for their grade level, and did so in ways that fostered their understanding of application.

A variety of educators have recommended such approaches. For example, the Wiggington (1977) Foxfire approach suggested negotiation of topics for inquiry around students' community realities. Wiggins and McTighe (1998) recommended inviting students to engage in inquiry around essential questions. Such approaches do not obviate the need for teachers' subject-specific expertise; teachers can add their expertise to the mix of perspectives discovered during the exploration and reporting processes. However, such problem-based pursuit of essential questions can put teachers in the position of sometimes not knowing answers to questions that will come up when students move forward to answer their own questions. Teachers can also find that their expertise gets challenged and even changed as a result of an insightful student comment, which is one of the benefits of engaging in pedagogy that responds to and incorporates students' cultural, ethnic, and community experiences.

4. *CRP depends on knowledge of discipline-related concepts.* This principle is important for two reasons. Too often, CRP is interpreted as drilling students who lack the cultural and linguistic capital (Bourdieu & Passeron, 1990) on facts to help them *compete* with those who hold such capital. This sort of practice is often justified by referring to Delpit's (1988) argument that nonmainstream (or nondominant) learners need access to the "culture of power," and do not need to be taught fluency or creativity. A careful reading of Delpit, however, illustrates that such an interpretation is an inaccurate reading of her argument; Delpit argues for teaching youth—of all cultural backgrounds—the skills necessary to engage with different sets of practices, and to traverse and negotiate different cultural spaces, especially those of the dominant power group. She does not advocate drilling students in such skills, however. Rather, she argues for teaching them skills of discourse communities other than their own by linking to deep concepts within those discourse communities, and by comparing and connecting those practices to communities in which the students are fluent and skilled.

This principled practice is important for a second reason. In contrast to the drilling method that sometimes is justified on cultural grounds, another interpretation of CRP is often to search for any and all cultural experiences to bring into the classroom, whether or not they connect to the content under study in deep ways. Such an approach is of limited value, however; although students may become temporarily engaged in an activity that may resonate with their cultural or social experiences, they often make few, if any, connections between the culturally situated experiences and the target concepts. For deep content learning to occur, the experiences drawn upon need to be relevant to the target concepts.

Each of these teachers illustrates this important principled practice. Ms. Hall, for example, links specific words and phrases (e.g., *reactant* and *product*) to youths' experiences and to their linguistic knowledge of words such as *react, reaction, end result, end product,* and *product,* all the way emphasizing the subtle differences in language (e.g., *reactant, yields*). Ms. Williams discusses the unique qualities of explanation writing in mathematics by emphasizing particular inferences associated with mathematical representation. She distinguishes between the kind of explaining that students might do to one another and that which they would do to represent and draw conclusions about causes for change over time.

5. *CRP invites youth to participate in multiple and varied discipline-specific, cross-discourse experiences that include reading, writing, speaking, listening and performing in the service of increasingly sophisticated knowledge construction.* As has been argued by a number of scholars, it is important to provide students with the opportunity to construct and represent understandings across different forms and genres of representation, including different types of print texts, as well as images, performances, electronic texts, and oral language (Eisner, 1994; Epstein, 1994; Gardner, 1983; Lemke, 1990). It is also important to engage students in communicating their understanding within and across different discourse communities (Hicks, 1995–1996; Lemke, 1990; Luke, 2001). CRP makes clear that no single form of representation—even print—can convey an author's meaning transparently or completely (Eisner, 1994). CRP makes clear to students that knowledge is best produced when people explore the world and experiment with many different ways that different cultural groups (ethnic, disciplinary, age, gender) use to represent their understandings.

The teachers and curricula that we have represented here provide examplars of this principled practice. Ms. Hall and her science colleagues in Detroit provide opportunities for students to engage with a number of different forms and discourses. They engage students in actual investigations, such as the investigation on bacteria growth. They take walks throughout the community, during which the students take photographs to provide evidence of air pollution. Students simultaneously record their observations on paper and report on what they observed in class. They conduct a series of experiments to determine whether air is matter and to examine the amount of particulate matter in the air around their school or emitted by different models of cars.

The classes also take trips to the river to collect data, or when field trips are prohibitive because of time and funding, students watch videos of the teachers at the river taking water samples and testing the water that they have brought back to the room in buckets for the students to test. They also "interact" with the river via a CD-ROM activity developed to provide a simulated river walk. In the communicable disease unit, students not only conduct their own investigation of bacteria, but they also engage in simulated epidemiology studies and develop contact maps to trace the spread of a simulated disease throughout their classroom.

Throughout each of these units, the students read not only from the curriculum readers developed to accompany these specific curricula but also from Internet articles they search for with modeling from the teacher using a strategy developed from a combination of several different content-area literacy strategies. They also write in journals (as illustrated in exemplars from Ms. Hall's class), at times writing in words, and at times representing their understanding in drawings, charts, tables, and graphs. The students work in both small and whole-class groupings, talking through ideas and critiquing each other's representations through a strategy the teachers label "museum walks," wherein each group displays its work and the students walk through the room, observing and commenting on each other's work.

In every case, the students practice communicating their ideas in multiple forms of representation, often with the task of having to translate across the forms as they move from raw data to drawing, to table, to graph, and finally, to verbal explanation. And in each case, the teachers encourage students to use their own words, their prior knowledge, their everyday experiences and their experiences, with science in the world and in the classroom to make sense of and to represent their understandings. At times, the teachers ask students to generate cartoons, posters, or rap lyrics to convey their understanding of the science, providing students an opportunity to convey ideas in forms familiar or engaging to them. The teachers also, however, make a concerted effort to help students understand the conventions of scientific Discourse, emphasizing that the way one might convey an idea to a friend or to one's mother is not necessarily how one would convey the same information to another scientist.

CRP also makes evident that the different forms and discursive practices valued in the discipline are human constructions, established over time as useful ways of communicating information and ideas, but are not necessary outgrowths of knowledge production in a given area. CRP thus makes clear to students that useful knowledge can be generated and communicated in forms not always valued in the different disciplines. Indeed, a CRP looks for other ways of knowing and representing the world, and engages students in those ways as a means of both validating multiple ways of knowing and of deepening the learning of traditional content concepts.

6. *CRP invites youth to develop and express new understandings of the world, understandings that merge mainstream content concepts with everyday knowledge in alternative, creative forms.* This is perhaps the most difficult principled culturally responsive practice for secondary school content teachers to enact. This principle requires a great deal of time to explore multiple perspectives on information, and requires that teachers have the background knowledge in their content area to be able to allow flexible interpretations, without promoting the construction of understandings that are, quite simply, inaccurate. Examples of this principled practice are illustrated by each of the teachers we have presented, who encourage their students to question the data or claims presented in the curriculum and in their community.

REMAINING QUESTIONS ABOUT CULTURALLY RESPONSIVE PEDAGOGY FOR YOUTH LITERACY LEARNERS

What does it look like when CRP encourages students to merge everyday knowledge with academic knowledge to construct new understandings of the world? Most forms of CRP that have been enacted and studied in classrooms have been bridging or negotiating pedagogies. As we have argued previously, these forms are not exclusive of a challenging and reshaping form of CRP, because new knowledge cannot be generated if current knowledges are not understood, and if young people cannot navigate across or negotiate the many different discourse communities they experience in any given secondary school day.

That said, however, we believe that there is a great deal of work to be done in literacy research, in teacher education, and in the content areas to support teachers in enacting CRPs that encourage young people to question existing academic knowledge and to apply academic knowledge to issues and problems in their own communities. We need to design experiments that investigate both the processes (teaching and learning) and products (i.e., learning gains) of such forms of CRP. Such work needs to consider not only how teachers interact with students but also how teachers facilitate students interacting with one another. We also need to understand better how to map curricula and topics in ways that invite experimentation with and transformation of knowledges and Discourses held by subject-area experts and by youth.

Indeed, we need research that investigates, in general, what is learned when young people experience CRP. As described in this review, some studies of bridging pedagogies have demonstrated learning gains (Lee, 1993; Warren et al., 2001), but most studies focus more on analyzing and interpreting the processes that teachers and students engage in as they enact CRP. Although these process-oriented studies are critically important in understanding how to enact CRP and why students and teachers make the meanings that they do from CRP, the field also needs analyses of what students learn in terms of conventional academic concepts, identities, and self-concepts, and in terms of new understandings and representations of the physical and social world. Such learning measures are especially important if we hope to affect education policies in secondary, content-area literacy.

Thus, research that will move the field forward includes both the ethnographies and discourse studies that will allow us to understand the processes of CRP in more detailed ways (e.g., Edwards & Eisenhart, 2002), as well as studies that will allow us to examine learner outcomes in varied ways, including alternative outcomes that arise from the transformed insights that are likely to result from CRP (e.g., Lee, 1993; Morrell, 2002). Ethnographies that examine how youth use language and texts in their homes and communities outside of school (e.g., Moje, Peek-Brown, et al., in press) can provide important information to teachers about what different groups of young people may bring to classroom learning. In addition, school-based ethnographies that examine how different content-area classrooms establish cultural norms and discursive practices can reveal the assumptions that both teachers and students make about the work of teaching and learning. Because these assumptions are often invisible to those who live and work inside particular contexts, the long-term and intensive data collection of a participant observer—the classroom or community ethnographer—can be critical in revealing these assumptions and offering information about how such assumptions get turned into classroom and community norms. Discursive studies can be embedded in ethnographies, with the researchers focusing on detailed, microanalyses of the "ways with words" of people in particular communities, classrooms, or content areas.

Thus, such work can include studies of youth out of school, of classrooms actually engaging in CRP, of community-based organizations and how they engage youth in social action projects, and studies that collect pre- and postinformation on the development of learning over time that results from particular CRP enactments; design experiments; and interventions. In short, mixed-method designs that illuminate processes, practices, and products are necessary for the field to move forward and offer practice that is responsive to all cultures for all students.

ACKNOWLEDGMENT

This chapter is based upon work supported by the National Science Foundation, under Grant No. REC 0106959 Amd 001. Any opinions, findings, and conclusions or recommendations expressed in this material are those of the authors and do not necessarily reflect the views of the National Science Foundation.

REFERENCES

Banks, J. A., & Banks, C. M. (2001). *Handbook of research on multicultural education.* San Francisco: Jossey-Bass.

Barton, A. C. (2001). Science education in urban settings: Seeking new ways of praxis through critical ethnography. *Journal of Research in Science Teaching, 38,* 899–917.

Bhabha, H. K. (1994). *The location of culture.* London: Routledge.

Bourdieu, P., & Passeron, J.-C. (1990). *Reproduction in education, society and culture.* London: Sage. (Original work published in 1977)

Davis, G. E., Jones, A., & Pearn, C. (1994). Voices in the dark: Making sense of talk in mathematics classes. In G. Bell, B. Wright, N. Leeson, & J. Geake (Eds.), *Challenges in mathematics education: Constraints on construction* (Vol. 1, pp. 187–195). Proceedings of the 17th Annual Conference of the Mathematics Education Research Group of Australia. Lismore, New South Wales: Mathematics Education Research Group of Australia.

Delpit, L. D. (1988). The silenced dialogue: Pedagogy and power in educating other people's children. *Harvard Educational Review, 58*, 280–298.

Deyhle, D. (1991). Empowerment and cultural conflict: Navajo parents and the schooling of their children. *International Journal of Qualitative Studies in Education, 4*, 277–297.

Dillon, D. R. (1989). Showing them that I want them to learn and that I care about who they are: A microethnography of social organization of a secondary low-track English-reading classroom. *American Educational Research Journal, 26*, 227–259.

Draper, R. J. (2002). School mathematics reform, constructivism, and literacy: A case for literacy instruction in the reform-oriented mathematics classroom. *Journal of Adolescent and Adult Literacy, 45*, 520–529.

Duncan-Andrade, J. (2003, April). *Critical pedagogy in a woman's varsity basketball program.* Paper presented at the annual meeting of the American Educational Research Association, Chicago, IL.

Edwards, L., & Eisenhart, M. (2002, November). *Middle school Latinas studying science: Using valued identities to enhance engagement.* Paper presented at the annual meeting of the American Anthropological Association, New Orleans, LA.

Eisner, E. W. (1994). *Cognition and curriculum reconsidered* (2nd ed.). New York: Teachers College Press.

Epstein, T. L. (1994). Sometimes a shining moment: High school students' representations of history through the arts. *Social Education, 58*(3), 136–141.

Fecho, B. (1998). Crossing boundaries of race in a critical literacy classroom. In D. E. Alvermann, K. A. Hinchman, D. W. Moore, S. Phelps, & D. Waff (Eds.), *Reconceptualizing the literacies in adolescents' lives* (pp. 75–102). Mahwah, NJ: Erlbaum.

Frey, J. T., Fitzgerald, W. M., Friel, S. N., Lappan, G., & Phillips, E. D. (2002). *Connected Mathematics Project.* New York: Prentice-Hall.

Gardner, H. (1983). *Frames of mind.* New York: Basic Books.

Gee, J. P. (1996). *Social linguistics and literacies: Ideology in discourses* (2nd ed.). London: Falmer Press.

Guthrie, J. T., Meter, P. Z., McCann, A., Wigfield, A., Bennett, L., Poundstone, C., et al. (1996). Growth in literacy engagement: Changes in motivations and strategies during concept-oriented reading instruction. *Reading Research Quarterly, 31*, 305–325.

Gutiérrez, K. D., Baquedano-López, P., Alvarez, H., & Chiu, M. M. (1999). Building a culture of collaboration through hybrid language practices. *Theory Into Practice, 38*(2), 87–93.

Heath, S. B. (1983). *Ways with words: Language, life, and work in communities and classrooms.* Cambridge, UK: Cambridge University Press.

Hicks, D. (1995-1996). Discourse, learning, and teaching. In M. W. Apple (Ed.), *Review of research in education* (Vol. 21, pp. 49–95). Washington, DC: American Educational Research Association.

Hinchman, K. A., & Young, J. P. (2001). Speaking but not being heard: Two adolescents negotiate classroom talk about text. *Journal of Literacy Research, 33*, 243–268.

Hinchman, K. A., & Zalewski, P. (2001). Interpreting language in global studies: Literacy and learning for two students in one tenth-grade class. In E. Moje & D. O'Brien (Eds.), *Constructions of literacy: Studies of teaching and learning in and out of secondary schools* (pp. 171–192). Mahwah, NJ: Erlbaum.

Hoffman, J. V., & Duffy, G. G. (2001). Beginning reading instruction: Moving beyond the debate over methods into the study of principled teaching practices. In J. Brophy (Ed.), *Advances in Research in Teaching: Subject-specific instructional methods and activities* (pp. 25–49). New York: Elsevier Science.

Hudicourt-Barnes, J. (2003). The use of argumentation in Haitian Creole science classrooms. *Harvard Educational Review, 73*, 73–93.

Kirkland, D., & Tate, S. (2003, April). *Critical pedagogy and critical literacy instruction in secondary classrooms.* Paper presented at the annual meeting of the American Educational Research Association, Chicago, IL.

Ladson-Billings, G. (1994). *The dreamkeepers: Successful teachers of African American children.* San Francisco: Jossey-Bass.

Ladson-Billings, G. J. (1999). Preparing teachers for diverse student populations: A critical race theory perspective. In A. Iran-Nejad & P. D. Pearson (Eds.), *Review of research in education* (Vol. 24, pp. 211–247). Washington, DC: American Educational Research Association.

Lampert, M., & Blunk, M. L. (1998). *Talking mathematics in school: Studies of teaching and learning.* Cambridge, UK: Cambridge University Press.

Lankshear, C. (1997). *Changing literacies.* Buckingham, UK: Open University Press.

Lee, C. D. (1993). *Signifying as a scaffold for literary interpretation: The pedagogical implications of an African American discourse genre* (NCTE Research Report No. 26). Urbana, IL: National Council of Teachers of English.

Lee, C. D. (1995). A culturally based cognitive apprenticeship: Teaching African American high school students skills in literary interpretation. *Reading Research Quarterly, 30*(4), 608–630.

Lee, O., & Fradd, S. H. (1999). Teachers' roles in promoting science inquiry with students from diverse language backgrounds. *Educational Researcher, 28*, 14–20.

Lemke, J. L. (1990). *Talking science: Language, learning, and values.* Norwood, NJ: Ablex.

Luke, A. (1993). Stories of social regulation: The micropolitics of classroom narrative. In B. Green (Ed.), *The insistence of the letter: Literacy studies and curriculum theorizing* (pp. 137–153). London: Falmer Press.

Luke, A. (2001). Foreword. In E. B. Moje & D. G. O'Brien (Eds.), *Constructions of literacy: Studies of teaching and learning in and out of secondary schools* (pp. ix–xii). Mahwah, NJ: Erlbaum.

Luke, C., & Luke, A. (1999). Theorizing interracial families and hybrid identity: An Australian perspective. *Educational Theory, 49*(2), 223–250.

MacGregor, M., & Stacey, K. (1995). The effect of different approaches to algebra on students' perceptions of functional relationships. *Mathematics Education Research Journal, 7*, 69–85.

Mahiri, J. (Ed.). (2003). *What they don't learn in school: Literacy in the lives of urban youth.* New York: Peter Lang.

Marx, R. W., Blumenfeld, P. C., Krajcik, J. S., & Soloway, E. (1997). Enacting project-based science. *Elementary School Journal, 97*, 34–358.

Moje, E. B. (1996). "I teach students, not subjects": Teacher–student relationships as contexts for secondary literacy. *Reading Research Quarterly, 31*, 172–195.

Moje, E. B., Ciechanowski, K. M., Kramer, K. E., Ellis, L. M., Carrillo, R., & Collazo, T. (2004). Working toward third space in content area literacy: An examination of everyday funds of knowledge and discourse. *Reading Research Quarterly, 39*(1), 38–71.

Moje, E. B., Collazo, T., Carrillo, R., & Marx, R. W. (2001). "Maestro, what is 'quality'?": Language, literacy, and discourse in project-based science. *Journal of Research in Science Teaching, 38*(4), 469–496.

Moje, E. B., Peek-Brown, D., Sutherland, L. M., Marx, R. W., Blumenfeld, P., & Krajcik, J. (in press). Explaining explanations: Developing scientific literacy in middle-school project-based science reforms. In D. Strickland & D. E. Alvermann (Eds.), *Bridging the gap: Improving literacy learning for preadolescent and adolescent learners in grades 4–12.* New York: Teachers College Press.

Moje, E. B., Young, J. P., Readence, J. E., & Moore, D. W. (2000). Reinventing adolescent literacy for new times: A commentary on perennial and millenial issues in adolescent literacy. *Journal of Adolescent and Adult Literacy, 43*, 400–411.

Moll, L. C. (1994). Literacy research in community and classrooms: A sociocultural approach. In M. R. Ruddell, R. B. Ruddell, & H. Singer (Eds.), *Theoretical models and processes of reading* (4th ed., pp. 179–207). Newark, DE: International Reading Association.

Moll, L. C., & Gonzalez, N. (1994). Critical issues: Lessons from research with language-minority children. *Journal of Reading Behavior, 26*, 439–456.

Moll, L. C., Veléz-Ibañéz, C., & Greenberg, J. (1989). *Year one progress report: Community knowledge and classroom practice: Combining resources for literacy instruction* (IARP Subcontract L-10, Development Associates). Tucson: University of Arizona Press.

Morrell, E. (2002). Toward a critical pedagogy of popular culture: Literacy development among urban youth. *Journal of Adolescent and Adult Literacy, 46*, 72–77.

National Council of Teachers of Mathematics. (2000). *Principles and standards for school mathematics.* Reston, VA: Author. Retrieved on June 4, 2003 from *www.nctm.org/ standards/standards.htm*

New London Group. (1996). A pedagogy of multiliteracies: Designing social futures. *Harvard Educational Review, 66*, 60–92.

Noddings, N. (1984). *Caring: A feminine approach to ethics and moral education.* Berkeley: University of California Press.

Obidah, J. (1998). Black mystory: Literacy currency in everyday schooling. In D. E. Alvermann, K. A. Hinchman, D. W. Moore, S. Phelps, & D. Waff (Eds.), *Reconceptualizing the literacies in adolescents' lives* (pp. 51–71). Mahwah, NJ: Erlbaum.

Paris, S. G., Lipson, M. Y., & Wixson, K. K. (1983). Becoming a strategic reader. *Contemporary Educational Psychology, 8,* 293–316.

Phillips, S. U. (1972). Participant structure and communicative competence: Warm Sorings children in community and classroom. In C. Cazden, D. Hymes, & W. J. John (Eds.), *Functions of language in the classroom* (pp. 370–394). New York: Teachers College Press.

Rosaldo, R. (1989). *Culture and truth: The remaking of social analysis.* Boston: Beacon Press.

Sarris, G. (1993). Keeping Slug Woman alive: The challenge of reading in a reservation classroom. In J. Boyarin (Ed.), *The ethnography of reading* (pp. 257–271). Berkeley: University of California Press.

Siegel, M., Borasi, R., & Fonzi, J. (1998). Supporting students' mathematical inquiries through reading. *Journal for Research in Mathematics Education, 29,* 378–413.

Sizer, T. R. (1992). *Horace's school: Redesigning the American high school.* Boston: Houghton Mifflin.

Warren, B., Ballenger, C., Ogonowski, M., Rosebery, A., & Hudicourt-Barnes, J. (2001). Rethinking diversity in learning science: The logic of everyday languages. *Journal of Research in Science Teaching, 38,* 1–24.

Warren, B., Rosebery, A., & Conant, F. (1994). Discourse and social practice: Learning science in a language minority classroom. In D. Spener (Ed.), *Adult biliteracy in the United States* (pp. 191–210). Washington, DC: Center for Applied Linguistics.

Wiggington, E. (1977). The Foxfire approach: It can work for you. *Media and Methods, 14*(3), 48–51.

Wiggins, G., & McTighe, J. (1998). *Understanding by design.* Alexandria, VA: Association for Supervision and Curriculum Development.

Adolescents, Computer Technology, and Literacy

HELEN S. KIM
MICHAEL L. KAMIL

As technological innovations transform traditional boundaries of communication, entertainment, and learning, technology infuses the lives of adolescents in more ways than ever imaginable. From authoring web pages to participating in Internet chat rooms, adolescents are engaging in activities that entail new skills and forms of participation. The consequences of this changing technological landscape include an expanded definition of literacy and a wider range of skills and competencies necessary to be successful when engaged in literacy activities. In this chapter, we review critical research in three areas of technology and literacy for adolescents in grades 5–12: (1) computerized literacy instruction, reading and writing; (2) the effects of social uses of technology on literacy development; and (3) factors that inform adolescents' attitudes toward computers.

Computerized literacy instruction has afforded both new opportunities to offer students reading guidance that extends beyond the printed text and specialized writing assistance. Although the widespread use of technology among adolescents has introduced exciting prospects that support learning and social interaction, it has also raised questions and concerns about how to use computers to facilitate literacy skills within this age group. This chapter explores the effects of computerized instruction and social uses of technology on literacy development, and some of the important factors that inform the attitudes and preferences of adolescents toward computers. In the context of these research findings, practical guidelines for the successful implementation of technology in the classroom are discussed, as well as their implications for effective instructional practices. We conclude by highlighting specific areas in need of continued investigation, with recommendations for future research that will deepen our understanding of how to facilitate adolescent literacy through technology.

CRITICAL RESEARCH AREAS RELATIVE TO COMPUTERS AND ADOLESCENCE

Computerized Literacy Instruction for Adolescents

As an alternative or adjunct to traditional reading instruction, computer-assisted instruction can offer students the opportunity to access customized support, to learn at a comfortable pace, and to process text actively. Prior research with adolescents suggests that computer-assisted reading instruction can facilitate reading comprehension. Reinking (1988) found that fifth- and sixth-grade students reading expository texts benefited from reading computer-mediated texts that included options for accessing additional information about the text, such as vocabulary definitions, simplified text, and background information. Students reading the computer-mediated texts scored higher on measures of reading comprehension than students who read the text off-line or on the computer without options, even after adjusting for the differences in reading time among the experimental conditions.

In a study with low-achieving fifth-grade students receiving traditional versus computer-assisted instruction, Weller, Carpenter, and Holmes (1998) found significant increases in standardized reading comprehension scores with the computer-assisted group. Weller et al. credited the augmented learning outcomes to students' daily interaction with computer-assisted instruction. Similarly, Boyd (2000) found that a self-paced computer based reading instruction helped to increase seventh- and eighth-grade students' independent reading levels. The computerized reading instruction included guided reading, cloze activities, and providing students with context clues. Students who interacted with the program over a period of 6 months increased their reading levels from a range of 1 to 5 levels.

However, not all studies of computerized reading instruction have found consistent benefits over traditional methods of instruction. In a study with fifth-grade students reading expository science texts, Kinzer, Sherwood, and Loofbourrow (1989) found that the non-computer group scored significantly higher than the computer group on posttest measures.

In the study, students in the computer group viewed computerized simulations, while the noncomputer group read a similar expository text. Kinzer et al. speculate that there could have been novelty effects with the computer group, difficulties with reading from the computer, as well as the potential for the computer animations to distract from efficient processing of the material. One important instructional variable to note is that the computer group learned in a whole-class environment, while the noncomputer group read the texts individually. As a result, the implementation of the computer-assisted instruction in this study was significantly different from some of the previous studies reviewed that assessed the benefits of providing individualized reading instruction.

These studies not only suggest that computerized literacy instruction can have the potential to augment reading comprehension but also underscore the importance of considering many other factors that can affect its successful implementation. Further research is necessary to assess the impact of offering individual versus group computer instruction for various types of learning tasks, as well as to identify the instructional practices that can facilitate its application to literacy development. Although previous studies have assessed the collective benefits of offering students several options for reading assistance, such as vocabulary assistance and guided reading activities, additional research is needed to investigate the types of assistance that are particularly effective for supporting reading. The computer-assisted instruction utilized in these studies was primarily conventional in nature. Future studies that investigate the application of some of the more advanced technologies may further enhance the kinds of learning interactions and instruction that can be supported, making it possible to move away from traditional forms of instruction to use the full potential of reading instruction delivered by computers. For example, the use of pedagogical agents, or electronic tools that accompany web pages or software programs, can offer assistance to readers of electronic and multimedia text. As progress is made in the area of speech synthesis technology, the capacity to convert text accurately to natural-sounding electronic speech may help to support students in areas such as decoding and spelling.

Even without reaching this full potential, there are benefits to using computers to teach reading. In the next section, we consider some specific strategies that may help to facilitate the successful implementation of computerized reading instruction for adolescents.

Computerized Instruction of Strategies for Adolescents

Prior research on developmental differences in the ability to comprehend the presentation of combined visual and verbal information reveals that even adolescents may need assistance to process various types of multimedia effectively. In a study of students in grades 5, 7, and 9 reading science texts with visual adjuncts, Moore and Scevak (1997) found that the ninth graders displayed a greater ability to link text and visual aid information explicitly than did the fifth- and seventh-grade students. The authors concluded that the explicit linking of text and diagrams, and the ability to think about ways a diagram can enhance text comprehension, are rare among fifth- and seventh-grade students. Even for the ninth graders, only about half in the study were found to engage in such thinking. Small, Lovett, and Scher (1993) discovered that even many adults do not attend to information in visuals, unless explicitly instructed to do so. They cited research findings that children often need directions to pay attention to visuals. In a study of high school students, Moore (1993) discovered that subjects were largely ineffective in processing the adjunct visuals, such as maps and graphs, that accompany text and took a passive role in interacting with the visual aids. In a study with fifth- and sixth-grade students and college students, Kirby (1993) emphasized that all students may need to be taught strategies and methods for complex and deep processing of visuals. Examples of important skills students are likely to require for processing visuals include learning how to extract salient information from graphs, maps and diagrams; how to use visuals to support their comprehension of text; and how to reference visual adjuncts when reading textual information.

These findings suggest that the ability to form referential connections between visual elements and text may reveal developmental trends, and that even adolescents and adults have difficulties in effectively processing visuals within text. Proficiency is not necessarily acquired as children progress through school, probably because they are offered little in the way of instruction. Many adolescents need explicit instruction and guided practice in applying strategies for processing nontextual information in meaningful contexts.

The ability to synthesize visual and textual information is a process that is influenced by many variables. One cluster of variables is related to conventional strategic reading skills that develop with age and practice. Another cluster is related to specific skills in which students must be instructed, such as readers' use of prompts to encourage processing of various sources of information actively. Merely presenting the texts and visual aids together is not sufficient for most readers, including adolescents, to process efficiently. Young children are not the only learners who will require additional assistance with these tasks: Older readers are also likely to benefit from specific instruction to process texts and visuals actively.

Another area of importance is reading and processing multimedia documents. Multimedia documents, such as hypertext, often have several user-controlled options for additional information, such as links to additional textual information, graphics, pictures, or audio. With these types of non-linear documents, adolescents may need specialized guidance and strategic instruction to read proficiently. In a study with seventh graders, Davidson-Shivers, Rasmussen, and Bratton-Jeffery (1997) found that the more successful readers of hypertext documents engaged in a variety of learning strategies, including comprehension monitoring and actively linking new information with their prior knowledge of the topic. Students who do not have a repertoire of strategies for reading and navigating multimedia documents are likely to benefit from specific instruction in tasks such as selecting relevant hyperlinks and considering the time and sequence of accessing additional information.

Structured Computer Learning Environments for Adolescents

One hallmark of computer technology is the ability to offer consistent and structured reading support and guidance for text processing. For example, computers can provide students who are reading electronic texts with immediate and continuous access to vocabulary definitions, photos, videos, and links to additional information. Computer technology can foster a structured learning experience by limiting user-controlled options. These restrictions might include providing students with selective access to relevant hyperlinks, or guiding students through text information in a prearranged order to facilitate comprehension. The next section reviews research on the provision of guidance in computerized reading instruction.

In an experiment with fifth-grade students, Gillingham, Garner, Guthrie, and Sawyer (1989) used varied levels of computer-assisted instruction to assist with text comprehension. They found that the fifth-grade students performed best in the condition in which they were given a high level of guidance. More specifically, students performed best when they were given computerized reading prompts, along with a specific suggestion for the type of assistance to use. In this structured learning condition, students were asked to reread the text, and were then prescribed a fixed sequence of assistance, including definitions of words, background information, and hints for how to locate and comprehend important text information. In contrast, the other two learning conditions were characterized by less structure. Students in the second condition were asked to reread the text and were given access to assistance, but, importantly, no prescription for the assistance was given. Students in the third condition were simply asked to reread the text, with no assistance made available. Gillingham et al. concluded that providing the opportunity for assistance was no guarantee that students would utilize the appropriate assistance on their own.

Similarly, Reinking and Rickman (1990) found that sixth graders reading text passages on the computer screen performed best in a mandatory vocabulary assistance condition. In this mandatory treatment condition, students received the vocabulary definitions of difficult target words while reading informational text. Another treatment condition studied the effects of providing optional vocabulary assistance, and two other conditions explored the effects of having students read printed text with a dictionary or a glossary of the target words. Students who received mandatory assistance with the definitions of target vocabulary words in the experimental passage scored higher on measures of vocabulary and text comprehension than did students in the condition in which vocabulary assistance was optional.

These findings suggest that specific reading guidance may be necessary for adolescents to utilize a multimedia environment for learning successfully. Simply providing access to various options for reading support is not sufficient when readers do not know how to select and apply the relevant assistance accurately at the appropriate times. Adolescents are likely to benefit from the provision of specific reading prompts while reading on the computer, such as assistance with the definitions of difficult vocabulary words, becoming familiar with the structural elements of the text, and directives to attend to salient information in the text and multimedia elements. In addition, these studies suggest that adolescents may benefit from computerized reading instruction that includes an element of predetermined assistance, in which the assistance is highly structured and restrictions are placed on the amount of learner control students are given. These findings with adolescent readers are consistent with findings with younger children, which have revealed that children tend to do better in more structured computer-learning environments (e.g., Shin, Schallert, & Savenye, 1994). Whereas further research is needed that investigates the effects of learner variables, such as prior knowledge and reading ability, a tentative finding from the research studies is that highly structured learning environments and fixed levels of assistance help students learn more effectively from computer-assisted reading instruction.

Computerized Writing Instruction for Adolescents

The application of computer technology to writing tasks, such as the use of word processors, has been linked to increased motivation and task engagement (e.g., Daiute, 1983; Kamil, Intrator, & Kim, 2000). For example, McMillan and Honey (1993) found that the provision of laptop computers to eighth-grade students for completing assignments and writing journal entries was highly motivating. The authors associated the students' enhanced motivation with a number of writing improvements over the course of a year. However, the nature of the relationship between the provision of computer technology and improvements in the quality of writing is complex, and underscores the importance of considering several other instructional and learner variables that can mediate learning outcomes. As computers are increasingly being used to provide students with instruction and assistance with writing skills, the results have generally been mixed with respect to the increased effectiveness of computerized instruction compared to more traditional methods. In this section, we review studies that have compared the effects of computerized writing instruction with traditional instruction on the quality of adolescents' writing.

Palumbo and Prater (1992) found that ninth graders in a remedial English class who received a computer-based writing instruction program significantly increased their scores on pre–posttest measures of essay quality. The computer-based writing instruction, a software program named Writer's Helper, consisted of prewriting strategies and activities to assist students with writing persuasive essays. No significant differences were found in the essay quality between students in the computer-based writing-instruction group and the traditional instruction group, where students learned prewriting strategies from a teacher. Students in both the computer instruction group and the traditional instruction group demonstrated significant gains on pre–posttest measures.

Bonk and Reynolds (1992) investigated the efficacy of computer-based instruction that gave students prompts for higher level writing skills, metacognitive monitoring and the modeling of expert strategies. In the study, sixth-, seventh-, and eighth-grade students were divided into two groups of low and high writing ability. At the end of 6 weeks, Bonk and Reynolds found no significant differences on holistic scores of writing performance between the students who received the computer-based instruction and students in the control group. Significant main effects were found for the older participants in the study, with seventh and eighth graders generally performing better than sixth graders. Overall, students with higher writing ability also performed better. In the context of the minimal effects found for the computer-writing prompts, Bonk and Reynolds recommended that future research examine the efficacy of using more specific prompts that are customized to individual needs, abilities, and task demands.

In a study with older adolescents, Rosenbluth and Reed (1992) assessed the effects of computerized writing instruction and word processing on the writing and computer attitudes of 11th-grade students. The study included both remedial and accelerated 11th-grade students, who were divided into a computer instruction group and a control group that received no computer instruction. Over the course of 16 weeks, the experimental and control groups received writing-process-based instruction that included elements of prewriting, drafting, and revising. Improvements in the quality of the essays were found for the remedial writers regardless of whether they had used computers for writing. However, the authors found that accelerated writers demonstrated quicker improvements when working with a computer. Rosenbluth and Reed suggest that remedial writers may have needed a longer interaction with the computer to demonstrate similar gains compared to the accelerated writers, because of their lack of preexisting writing skills and strategies.

One general implication of this set of studies is that the successful application of technology to writing instruction is mediated by several learner, instructional, and task variables. Variables such as the proficiency of the students' writing skills (i.e., remedial vs. accelerated students), the quality of instructional support, and the students' grade level were found to influence the learning outcomes. Consistent with research findings in the area of computerized reading instruction, an emerging finding in the area of computerized writing instruction suggests that structured guidance, strategic instruction, and multiple interactions with the technology are likely to influence how successfully adolescents utilize multimedia environments for learning.

Social Development of Literacy Skills for Adolescents

Computers give adolescents opportunities to develop literacy skills through collaborative work and social interactions with each other. Computer-based communication, such as e-mail or chat rooms, places expectations on participants to respond in written formats to convey meaning accurately and effectively. Without the benefit of intonation, gestures, and facial expressions to help communicate a speaker's intent in spoken language, written communication relies solely on the use of words and symbols, such as punctuation, smiley faces, and familiar computer jargon, to convey emotion and intent. The following research studies underscore some of the social components involved with computer-based communication, and describe some of the new literacy skills that can develop from adolescents' participation in these activities.

Reporting on studies of seventh-grade students working on computers, Beach and Lundell (1998) observed that students engaged in computer-mediated communication (CMC), such as e-mail, posting messages, and online chats, learned literacy skills through the social exchanges. Computer technology can also provide a context for collaborative work, such as group writing projects in which students work together to share and revise drafts. Beach and Lundell found that the computerized format could encourage participation from students who tend to shy away from face-to-face discussions and facilitate the free expression of alternate views. The authors noted how these social contexts collectively require adolescents to participate in ways that call on them to infer social meanings, respond in ways that are socially appropriate, and accurately communicate their ideas to an audience.

Because students must communicate through reading and writing in computer- mediated environments, strong emphasis is placed on proficient literacy skills for participation. In a study with fifth graders, Moore and Karabenick (1992) assessed the effects of computer communications on reading and writing performance. Through the evaluation of written transcripts of the communication, the authors found that the quality of the students' written communication increased on measures such as clarity, and the inclusion of more examples and support for their ideas. The authors hypothesized that providing students with an audience and a clear purpose for their writing helped to motivate students to write longer passages and communicate their ideas effectively. An additional finding from this research was that the students' attitudes toward computer use became more positive through increased interactions with the computer. However, the study did not find changes in students' attitudes toward reading and writing because of their computer interactions. The authors suggested that these findings might have been different if students had had longer interactions with the computer, as well as a more explicit link between computer activities and the reading and writing curriculum.

In a study with 6 teenage girls ages 14–16, Merchant (2001) investigated the types of online activities in which students were involved, and found that the adolescents developed skills, from basic familiarity with mouse/keyboard use to complex skills, such as online navigation, and the sharing of pictures and exchange of website links. Through their participation, adolescents increased their proficiency with the conventions of *written conversation,* the term Merchant uses to describe the written communication of exchanges that are typically spoken. These conventions include common abbreviations and symbols used to convey emotions and shorthand, as students quickly learn the popular computer jargon and develop new ones. In addition, students have the opportunity to integrate various forms of media on the computer seamlessly, such as incorporating media files and links to websites into their written text. Merchant concludes that adolescents' participation in these online activities develop communication and literacy skills that may not always be recognized in more formal educational settings.

Variables That Influence Adolescents' Attitudes toward Computers

A compelling objective in the area of adolescent literacy and technology is to encourage all students to feel comfortable using computers, so that they will want to participate actively in computer-mediated activities. Although many adolescents feel proficient with the new technologies, many factors can cause adolescents to feel anxious or negative about using computers. In this section, we examine the role of some of these factors in forming adolescents' attitudes toward computers.

Students quite often report that they do not want to read what they are asked to read in school (Worthy, Moorman, & Turner, 1999). For many of these students, the lack of motivation may be interpreted as an inability to read. Alvermann et al. (2000) have shown that adolescents do read very difficult material in after-school contexts. The students that Alvermann et al. studied were particularly adept at reading complex computer and multimedia information. This suggests that computers do have a positive effect on adolescents' attitudes toward reading.

A few studies have found that gender can significantly influence adolescents' attitudes toward computers. In a study with ninth graders in Belgrade, Kadijevich (2000) found that the boys demonstrated a more positive attitude toward computers than did girls, although no differences were found in computer anxiety after controlling for computer experience. Interestingly, the gender differences in computer attitudes were significant even after taking into account the different amount of computer experience for girls and boys. In contrast, although Chen (1986) found that adolescent males reported more positive attitudes toward computers than did females, these differences were not significant once the amount of computer experience was controlled for between genders. These disparate findings on the role of computer experience on influencing attitudes toward computers underscore the importance of considering other possible variables that may be involved, such as age, socialization effects, and socioeconomic status.

In a 3-year longitudinal study of fourth- through 10th-grade students' perceptions of computers, Krendl and Broihier (1992) found that boys consistently had more positive attitudes toward technology. Girls described computers as more difficult and regarded computers as less instructionally effective than did the boys. Age was also found to be a significant variable, and older students in the study tended to be more skeptical than the younger students of the teaching ability of computers. Consistent with these findings, in a meta-analysis of gender differences in computer attitudes, Whitley (1997) found that males reported higher computer self-efficacy, as well as a larger incidence of sex-role stereotyping of computers than females, especially among the high school students in the study. Whitley suggests that socialization factors may contribute to the larger effect sizes found for high school students' than for the younger students' gender-related differences in attitudes toward computers; that is, by the time elementary school students reached high school, the effects of years of gender stereotyping of computer attitudes may have become stronger.

Another variable hypothesized to relate to adolescents' interests in computers is socioeconomic status. In an earlier study with seventh-grade students from urban and suburban schools, Pulos and Fisher (1987) found evidence for a relationship between social-class differences and computer interest. Although the authors found that most adolescents in the study demonstrated an indifferent or neutral attitude toward computers, they found evidence for an increased interest in computers among students from the lower socioeconomic school, who had less exposure to computers than students in the higher socioeconomic school, perhaps suggesting that a novelty effect could be driving the augmented interest. Another interesting aspect of this study was that many adolescents in the study, particularly those who themselves were not interested in intellectual activities, described students who liked computers to be the smart kids.

In another early study of students in grades 5–12, Campbell (1988) found that the most significant predictor of computer anxiety was students' perceptions of the effects of their computer ability on their interpersonal relationships. Campbell noted that this finding was consistent with the importance of peer status and interpersonal relationships among adolescent students. Campbell also found that adolescents who were not afraid of using computer hardware were likely to have low computer anxiety. Students who had access to a computer at home and at school were also likely to have lower computer anxiety. These findings suggest that computer experience, or increased exposure to computers, can have positive effects on reducing computer anxiety. In addition, this study found no gender or grade differences with respect to levels of computer anxiety. However, it is important to note that the Pulos and Fisher (1987) and Campbell (1988) studies are old enough to preclude the ability to make generalizations from these data.

Schools may have an ameliorating effect on the attitudinal differences among students from various socioeconomic levels. More school-age children in the nation use computers at school than at home (Newburger, 2001). Because the majority of the instructional computers in schools are connected to the Internet, a wide variety of applications is likely to be found with those computers. Access may even extend beyond regular school hours. A total of 78% of secondary schools made computers available to students outside of regular school hours (U.S. Department of Education, 2002).

The availability of and access to school computers during and after school may have the effect of compensating for effects that may be attributable to socioeconomic levels, and perhaps to gender effects as well. Ultimately, it might be possible that these differences will simply disappear.

APPLYING WHAT IS KNOWN

In this section, we summarize the research findings in each of the areas of adolescent literacy and technology we have reviewed: computerized reading instruction, social aspects of adolescent literacy development and computers, and encouraging positive attitudes toward computers. These findings suggest practical implications for integrating technology into the classroom.

Computerized Reading Instruction in Classrooms

Research suggests that consistent interaction with computerized reading instruction in areas such as vocabulary assistance and guided reading instruction can help adolescents with reading and text comprehension (e.g., Boyd, 2000; Reinking, 1988). The studies also underscore the importance of specialized instruction for helping students develop strategies for learning in multimedia environments. In particular, adolescents can benefit from learning strategies for processing visual information, and learning how to integrate visual and textual information (e.g., Kirby, 1993; Moore and Scevack, 1997).

For proficient multimedia reading, adolescents also need specific strategies for navigating through linked text, and metacognitive strategies for thinking about the careful selection and timing of hyperlinks for obtaining additional information. Research suggests that adolescents may not have developed a sophisticated repertoire of strategies for learning with computers, and that structured multimedia learning environments can be beneficial for facilitating literacy development. Accordingly, special provisions, such as computer prompts for students to attend to important details in the text and to provide strategic reading assistance, may be necessary to help students successfully utilize multimedia environments for learning. Software that includes elements that compel adolescents to read and process the text, such as providing fixed rather than optional assistance, seems to have a stronger potential to be helpful (e.g., Reinking & Rickman, 1990). Specifically, students who are given access to reading assistance on a voluntary basis may opt not to use the help even when it is needed, and some students may encounter difficulties choosing the appropriate type of assistance. One alternative approach would be to offer computerized reading instruction that is highly structured, such as vocabulary assistance that routinely follows up difficult target words with definitions, or the strategic arrangement of specific reading hints and suggestions to help guide students through texts.

Computers and Writing Instruction

Although the effectiveness of computerized compared to traditional writing instruction is unclear, prior studies have found that computers can be one effective way to provide adolescents with writing assistance (e.g., Palumbo & Prater, 1992). In addition to the potential motivational benefits of applying computers to writing, computerized instruction can assist adolescents by providing detailed writing prompts, structured guidance with prewriting and drafts, as well as strategies and activities for writing essays. The review of the research also found that learner, task, and instructional variables are important to consider when implementing writing instruction and determining which students are most likely to benefit. One research finding (Rosenbluth & Reed, 1992) suggested that students with lower writing ability might need longer interactions with computerized writing instruction to achieve notable benefits. The provision of multiple and consistent opportunities to write with computers is likely to help students with a range of writing abilities gain valuable experience and proficiency with the conventions of composing on the computer.

Social Aspects of Adolescent Literacy and Technology

As the review of research on the social aspects of adolescent literacy and technology attests, giving adolescents the opportunity to engage in activities such as e-mail, chat rooms, and collaborative work on the computer can help them develop important literacy skills (e.g., Moore & Karabenick, 1992). In addition to increased proficiency with basic computer skills, such as word processing, many literacy skills are developed when adolescents use the computer to engage in written communication. For example, adolescents communicating on the computer learn how to respond in ways that are appropriate to the social situation, accurately communicate their ideas through writing, and infer meanings from written messages they receive from their peers (e.g., Merchant, 2001). Because of the time-sensitivity of online communication, adolescents are often required to formulate their responses quickly. An additional consideration that is unique to computer-mediated contexts is the capacity for adolescents to merge and integrate various media, such as attaching web links, photos, or music files to their written text.

In regard to guidelines for classroom practice, providing adolescents with opportunities to use the computer in social ways, such as to exchange e-mail, participate in online chat rooms, collaborate, and share their work with their peers, may help to develop an array of important literacy skills. Classroom projects that allow adolescents to use computers for shared literacy activities, such as collaborative writing projects, online journals, and chat room discussions, can provide good opportunities for students to share their work and receive feedback from their peers. CMC can place large demands on adolescents to develop a range of social, literacy, and technical skills in order to participate.

Instructional support may be necessary to help all students successfully participate in computer-literacy activities. For example, adolescents may need specific instruction in technical skills, such as authoring web pages and sharing media files, or an introduction to some of the conventions of CMC (e.g., common computer jargon). Teachers can encourage adolescents to use the computer to communicate in creative ways, such as choosing different font sizes and colors to emphasize key points, or representing their thoughts and ideas with various media. General etiquette for communicating on the computer is likely to be another important skill to discuss with adolescents. Adolescents can help to encourage the free exchange of ideas in the classroom by writing their responses in ways that are respectful and courteous of their peers, particularly when discussing controversial topics in which there are strong differences of opinion.

Encouraging Adolescents' Positive Attitudes toward Computers

Research findings in the area of adolescents' attitudes toward computers underscore the importance of considering various factors that can inform adolescents' attitudes toward computers. We reviewed previous studies in which gender was linked to differences in adolescents' attitudes toward computers (e.g., Kadijevich, 2000; Krendl & Broihier, 1992), with boys typically demonstrating more positive attitudes toward computers and higher levels of computer confidence than girls. Socialization factors appear to be an important factor in explaining the gender differences in attitudes toward computers. Consequently, a greater sensitivity to computer-access issues, software choices that appeal to both genders, and structured group activities in the classroom may encourage all students to feel more included in computer-literacy activities.

Although our review of research found conflicting evidence regarding the role of computer experience in influencing adolescents' attitudes toward computers, one study (Campbell, 1988) found that having access to computers either in school or at home was related to lower levels of computer anxiety. One practical implication of this finding is that providing adolescents with multiple exposures to computers may help them to feel more comfortable in computer-related activities. For adolescents who do not have access to computers at home, providing free access to computers through schools, libraries, community programs, and after-school programs may be an important variable for helping them to develop confidence with new technologies.

WHAT WE STILL NEED TO KNOW ABOUT ADOLESCENTS AND COMPUTERS

This chapter has identified some of the specific variables related to improving adolescent literacy through technology and the role of computerized instruction, social factors, and computer attitudes in literacy development. Continued research is necessary to investigate these findings systematically and to explore further how learner, task, and socialization factors affect adolescent literacy development through technology. One general finding from the research is that the successful application of technology to facilitate adolescent literacy entails a careful consideration of the interaction among many variables. Despite continued progress in the research on adolescent literacy and technology, there is much we still need to know to move forward.

With respect to computerized literacy instruction, questions remain regarding the optimal use of individual versus group instruction for adolescents. Additional research in this area may help to underscore important task and learner variables that impact how effectively adolescents can benefit from individual and group resources to learn different literacy skills. Many of the instructional research studies reviewed in this chapter have investigated students' interactions with software that offered a comprehensive array of instructional assistance, such as vocabulary definitions, reading strategies, and guided reading. Subsequent studies that systematically compare the learning outcomes associated with specific design manipulations are important next steps in determining which variables are particularly important for supporting instructional goals. One area that appears to be particularly important to explore is the effect of mandatory versus optional computerized reading assistance for different learners and learning tasks.

Future research is necessary to assess the potential for strategic instruction to help students read and process multimedia documents more proficiently.

A particularly interesting variable identified for further exploration was the role of gender, a factor that was tenuously linked to differences in adolescents' attitudes toward computers. Additional research on the role of computer experience in influencing adolescent's attitudes toward computers and their levels of computer anxiety may help to identify ways to provide adolescents with structured experiences and opportunities that encourage active participation in computer-literacy activities. It is clear that we cannot just place students in front of a computer without prior instruction and expect exceptional results. Adolescents need structured guidance, consistent support, and targeted assistance to learn how to utilize a multimedia environment for learning successfully.

The studies reviewed here offer a glimpse into the kinds of instructional support that are possible with the available technology. Developments in the near future will surely push the envelope, with innovations that can support an even wider range of social interactions and individualized instruction for adolescents. Some of these innovations include the integration of speech recognition and speech synthesis technologies to allow students to interact with the computer through a combination of text and speech. In addition, advances in artificial intelligence may offer new opportunities for the real-time assessment of student responses, and the capacity to provide immediate corrective feedback. One important consequence of exploring the relationship between adolescent literacy and technology is a deepened understanding of the process and pathways for the acquisition and instruction of a wide range of literacy skills. Future research designs that follow children, adolescents, and adults over repeated interactions with technology are important for bringing to bear new insights on how literacy skills are learned and transferred to new contexts.

REFERENCES

Alvermann, D. E., Hagood, M. C., Heron, A. H., Hughes, P., Williams, K. B., & Jun, Y. (2000). *After-school media clubs for reluctant adolescent readers* (Final report, Spencer Foundation Grant No. 199900278). Chicago: Spencer Foundation.

Beach, R., & Lundell, D. (1998). Early adolescents' use of computer-mediated communication in writing and reading. In D. Reinking, M. C. McKenna, L. Labbo, & R. Kieffer (Eds.), *Handbook of literacy and technology: Transformations in a post-typographic world* (Vol. 379, pp. 93–112). Mahwah, NJ: Erlbaum.

Bonk, C. J., & Reynolds, T. H. (1992). Early adolescent composing within a generative–evaluative computerized prompting framework: Computer use in the improvement of writing [Special issue]. *Computers in Human Behavior, 8,* 39–62.

Boyd, R. (2000, Winter). Computer based reading instruction: The effectiveness of computer based reading instruction in positively influencing student scores in science. *CSTA Journal*, pp. 17–23.

Campbell, N. J. (1988). Correlates of computer anxiety of adolescent students. *Journal of Adolescent Research, 3*, 107–117.

Chen, M. (1986). Gender and computers: The beneficial effects of experience on attitudes. *Journal of Educational Computing Research, 2*(3), 265–282.

Daiute, C. (1983). *Writing and computers*. Reading, MA: Addison-Wesley.

Davidson-Shivers, G. V., Rasmussen, K. L., & Bratton-Jeffery, M. F. (1997). Investigating learning strategies generation in a hypermedia environment using qualitative methods. *Journal of Computing in Childhood Education, 8*, 247–261.

Gillingham, M. G., Garner, R., Guthrie, J. T., & Sawyer, R. (1989). Children's control of computer-based reading assistance in answering synthesis questions. *Computers in Human Behavior, 5*, 61–75.

Kadijevich, D. (2000). Gender differences in computer attitude among ninth-grade students. *Journal of Educational Computing Research, 22*, 145–154.

Kamil, M. L., Intrator, S., & Kim, H. S. (2000). Effects of other technologies on literacy and literacy learning. In M. Kamil, P. Mosenthal, P. D. Pearson, & R. Barr, (Eds.), *Handbook of reading research* (Vol. 3, pp. 773–788). Mahwah, NJ: Erlbaum.

Kinzer, C. K., Sherwood, R. D., & Loofbourrow, M. C. (1989). Simulation software vs. expository text: A comparison of retention across two instructional tools. *Reading Research and Instruction, 28*, 41–49.

Kirby, J. R. (1993). Collaborative and competitive effects of verbal and spatial processes. *Learning and Instruction, 3*, 201–214.

Krendl, K. A., & Broihier, M. (1992). Student responses to computers: A longitudinal study. *Journal of Educational Computing Research, 8*, 215–227.

McMillan, K., & Honey, M. (1993). *Year one of Project Pulse: Pupils using laptops in science and English: A final report* (Technical Report No. 26). New York: Center for Technology in Education.

Merchant, G. (2001). Teenagers in cyberspace: An investigation of language use and language change in Internet chatrooms [Special issue: Literacy, home and community]. *Journal of Research in Reading, 24*, 293–306.

Moore, M. A., & Karabenick, S. A. (1992). The effects of computer communications on the reading and writing performance of fifth-grade students [Special issue: Computer use in the improvement of writing]. *Computers in Human Behavior, 8*, 27–38.

Moore, P. J. (1993). Metacognitive processing of diagrams, maps and graphs. *Learning and Instruction, 3*, 215–226.

Moore, P. J., & Scevak, J. J. (1997). Learning from texts and visual aids: A developmental perspective. *Journal of Research in Reading, 20*, 205–223.

Newburger, E. (2001). *Home computers and Internet use in the United States: August 2000* (U.S. Bureau of the Census current population reports). Washington, DC: U.S. Bureau of the Census.

Palumbo, D. B., & Prater, D. L. (1992). A comparison of computer-based prewriting strategies for basic ninth-grade writers [Special issue: Computer use in the improvement of writing]. *Computers in Human Behavior, 8*, 63–70.

Pulos, S., & Fisher, S. (1987). Adolescents' interests in computers: The role of attitude and socioeconomic status. *Computers in Human Behavior, 3,* 29–36.

Reinking, D. (1988). Computer-mediated text and comprehension differences: The role of reading time, reader preference, and estimation of learning. *Reading Research Quarterly, 23,* 484–498.

Reinking, D., & Rickman, S. S. (1990). The effects of computer-mediated texts on the vocabulary learning and comprehension of intermediate-grade readers. *Journal of Reading Behavior, 22,* 395–411.

Rosenbluth, G. S., & Reed, W. M. (1992). The effects of writing-process-based instruction and word processing on remedial and accelerated 11th graders [Special issue: Computer use in the improvement of writing]. *Computers in Human Behavior, 8,* 71–95.

Shin, C., Schallert, D., & Savenye, W. (1994) Effects of learner control, advisement, and prior knowledge on young students' learning in a hypertext environment. *Educational Technology Research and Development, 42,* 33–46.

Small, M., Lovett, S., & Scher, M. (1993). Pictures facilitate children's recall of unillustrated expository prose. *Journal of Educational Psychology, 85,* 520–528.

U.S. Department of Education, National Center for Education Statistics. (2002). *Internet access in U.S. public schools and classrooms: 1994–2001* (NCES Report No. 2002-018, by A. Kleiner & E. Farris. Project Officer: B. Greene). Washington, DC: Author.

Weller, L. D., Carpenter, S., & Holmes, C. T. (1998). Achievement gains of low-achieving students using computer-assisted vs regular instruction. *Psychological Reports, 83*(4), 1440–1441.

Whitley, B. E., Jr. (1997). Gender differences in computer-related attitudes and behavior: A meta-analysis. *Computers in Human Behavior, 13,* 1–22.

Worthy, J., Moorman, M., & Turner, M. (1999). What Johnny likes to read is hard to find in school. *Reading Research Quarterly, 34,* 12–27.

Assessing Adolescent Reading

PETER AFFLERBACH

My goal in this chapter is to describe how assessments can be conceptualized, developed, and used to promote adolescent students' growth and achievement in reading. I examine current knowledge of adolescent reading and reading assessment, and consider three questions that are central to successful assessment: Why do we assess? What do we assess? How do we assess adolescents' reading? I develop a definition of adolescent reading, with a focus on the reading that adolescents do in school, namely, the reading and learning of information in the different content areas. I characterize the skills, strategies, motivations, and mind-sets that contribute to adolescent reading development. I then discuss a model of effective assessment (Pellegrino, Chudowsky, & Glaser, 2001) and how we may determine the suitability of adolescent reading assessment (Liepzig & Afflerbach, 2000). I present an overview of the different types of assessment, including performance assessments, portfolio assessments, and teacher observation and questioning that can help us better understand adolescent reading development. I also describe the nature and influence of high-stakes tests. To complete the chapter, I consider important issues in need of further research and exploration.

THREE IMPORTANT QUESTIONS FOR THE ASSESSMENT OF ADOLESCENT READING

A first important question to ask of any assessment is, "Why do we assess?" Reading assessment must be conducted with the goal of helping students become better readers. Although there are different paths to the goal, this purpose guides our efforts to develop or choose those assessments best suited to promoting adolescents' achievement in reading. It also allows us to question assessment practices that do not have a clear and positive influence. A second important question is, "What do we assess when we assess reading?" Our answer to this question is determined, in part, by the breadth or constraint with which we conceptualize adolescent reading. I believe that it is in students' best interest that we conceptualize adolescent reading richly and in accordance with current knowledge, as described in the chapters in this volume. Yet I note that we have much to learn about adolescent literacy, and that some of what we do know is rarely acknowledged or used productively in classrooms (Alvermann, 2001; Moje et al., 2004). Perhaps a compromise vision is one in which enacted curriculum and instruction will foster students' reading strategies, content-domain knowledge, motivation to read, and their understanding of the importance and power of reading, while providing the means to ably assess them. The question, "What do we assess?", requires us to examine our assessments in light of our knowledge, values, and beliefs related to adolescents' literacy and their development. It serves the good purpose of having us examine the relationship between the things we teach and the things we assess. The third question, "How do we assess adolescent reading?", helps us to focus on the materials and procedures of reading assessment and the contexts in which reading assessments take place. This question is addressed later in this chapter, as we consider different types of assessment that are available to help us chart accomplishment and growth in adolescent reading.

DEFINING READING

The assessment of adolescent reading must be linked clearly to a detailed definition of what reading "is." Our attention to the details of the construct of adolescent reading is important, for it allows us to consider assessments that are sensitive to both the obvious and more nuanced aspects of growth that adolescent readers experience in productive school environments. Where might we begin? A strategic and goal-oriented conceptualization of adolescent reading serves as a foundation for the Program for International

Student Assessment (PISA), which is used to assess adolescents' (age 15 years) reading achievement in 32 countries. PISA defines reading literacy as "understanding, using and reflecting on written texts, in order to achieve one's goals, to develop one's knowledge and potential, and to participate in society" (Organization for Economic Cooperation and Development, 2000, p. 18). Note that the PISA definition begins with the assumption of understanding: Adolescent readers must possess the requisite skills, strategies, and other knowledge that are necessary to construct meaning from text. This fairly anticipates the nature of most assessments of adolescent reading, in which acquiring and remembering content-domain knowledge is the focus while reading ability is unexamined. We must contrast this assumption of student understanding of text content with the fact that there a considerable number of adolescent readers struggle to construct meaning from even relatively simple texts.

Nevertheless, the PISA definition provides a valuable starting point from which we can develop a more detailed definition of reading and suggest the areas in which reading assessment is needed. A strong point of this definition is that it reminds us that we rarely read for reading's sake. We read to understand and then use that which we comprehend. We are fortunate to have research and theory related to adolescent reading, although we are far from a full understanding of it (Snow, 2002). Adolescent readers must be able to read fluently and demonstrate command of decoding skills, and we assume that for many adolescent readers these skills are well developed. They must have increasingly rich general and content-domain-specific vocabularies. They must have the strategies to determine the meaning of unfamiliar vocabulary words.

Adolescent readers must use sophisticated reading comprehension strategies as they work with increasingly complex texts and tasks. Pressley and Afflerbach (1995) describe dynamic and accomplished readers who use strategies to identify and remember important aspects of text, monitor the process of constructing meaning, and evaluate different aspects of reading. From the descriptions of accomplished reading given in think-aloud protocols, Pressley and Afflerbach provide a foundation for us to consider the reading skills and strategies that adolescents must have to read well in school. Readers will use strategies that lead to appropriate inferences and predictions, and that allow for summarization and synthesis of information. Readers will move beyond both the literal and inferential comprehension of text to appraise critically the accuracy and worthiness of an author's message or a text's claims. Successful readers continuously monitor their progress toward near and far goals. Closely related to the construction of meaning is the application and use of the knowledge constructed from reading.

In school, adolescent reading is predominantly situated in the content domains. Alexander's model of domain learning (2003) details the interaction of the strategic, cognitive, and motivational factors that are involved in content-domain learning and that shape students' learning and growth. Alexander's model allows us to situate reading skills and strategies (Pressley & Afflerbach, 1995; Snow, 2002) that students must use to read well in school. Equally important, the model suggests the manner in which content-domain knowledge grows and the ability to read and learn in content domains develops. The demand to read and learn content-area materials increases in size and complexity across adolescent readers' years in school. Adolescent readers must develop and use an extensive array of reading skills and strategies on demand, and they must learn and remember vast amounts of content-domain information. Students are expected to apply their reading skills and strategies to construct meaning from content-area texts. We expect that students will demonstrate that they understand what is read in the content areas of history, science, literature, and the arts through performances that include describing, comparing, synthesizing, and evaluating.

If we return to the definition of reading that guides the PISA (Organization for Economic Cooperation and Development, 2000), we can augment it with the following: Adolescent reading is best considered an ongoing, developmental process. Reading strategies get better as readers become more experienced, although many adolescents in the United States do not develop to proficient or advanced levels of reading (Donahue, Finnegan, Lutkus, Allen, & Campbell, 2001). We learn and use new reading skills and strategies in relation to the different content domains and reading contexts that are encountered. Adolescent reading in the content domains (most often represented by specific school subjects, such as biology and American history), when working well, is marked by the development of both reading ability and content-domain knowledge. With these qualifications, we can propose the following definition of adolescent reading:

> *Adolescent reading involves the use of skills, strategies, and prior knowledge to construct meaning from text. Adolescent readers continue to develop the ability to construct meaning from text, and use and reflect on the information gained from written texts, so that they may achieve goals, develop knowledge and potential, and participate in society.*

Adolescents need to read to learn, and as they do so, they are becoming better readers. The dynamics and complexities of reading become apparent in this definition and reflect what should be a duality of the assessment of adolescents' reading ability and content-domain learning. An informed and accurate definition of adolescent reading provides considerable power, because it allows us to propose new assessments that honor the construct of adolescent reading (best representing what we hope our students achieve) and to evaluate existing assessments that may (or may not) describe the richness of adolescent reading and its development.

Might we expect that reading assessment has a dual focus on content-domain learning and reading ability? This is not the case. The majority of adolescent reading in school is centered on different content domains, and reading assessment is skewed toward the determination of how much content-area learning a student has experienced through reading. There is often precious little assessment done in relation to students' ongoing reading development. In fact, most adolescent readers must exhibit considerable difficulties with reading even to be considered for the types of assessment that focus on the development of reading strategies and skills. Thus, much adolescent reading assessment reflects but a portion of the construct of reading: reading and understanding content domain texts, then giving back this information and using it, with the assumption that readers' skills and strategies are working well enough to result in the prerequisite construction of meaning. The clear need that arises from this observation is a balance in reading assessment between reading development and content-area learning.

A second balance is also called for: Too many adolescent reading assessment efforts focus on summative (and not formative) reading assessments. The majority of assessment that adolescents encounter in school, including surprise quizzes, end-of-chapter tests, unit tests, and district- and statewide year-end tests are summative in nature. These assessments provide important information about the accomplishments of students in relation to common school tasks and time frames. They document learning but they do not inform teaching. They tell us how well students learn the material in content domains. These assessments are decidedly "after the fact" and give summary statements of achievement rather than detailed developmental accounts of achievement. Often missing in an adolescent reader's school experience is a core of assessments that can provide valuable diagnostic information related to content-area learning and reading development. Such assessments help shape, or form, instruction and learning.

SUCCESSFUL ASSESSMENT OF READING

We are fortunate that as our knowledge of adolescents' reading development evolves, there is a concurrent evolution in the understanding of how best to assess student learning. A recent book, *Knowing What Students*

Know: The Science and Design of Educational Assessment (Pellegrino et al., 2001), describes the integral components of cognition, observation, and interpretation that are necessary for successful assessment, and suggests how we might develop and use reading assessment materials and procedures. We touch on these components whenever we assess, although we may not have considered them in such formal terms.

Cognition

The *cognition* component of reading assessment focuses on what students do when they read and the content that we expect them to learn through reading. To the degree that we can specify what adolescents need to do as successful readers, we can use this information to specify the things we would like to assess. For example, if we ask students to compile information from a chapter and to describe the central issues, we might develop an assessment that intends to describe students' ability to synthesize important information in text. We can also specify the content-domain learning that is expected of students. Thus, we may characterize one learning goal in 10th-grade biology as understanding the concept of cell division that is described in the biology textbook. When we enlarge the grain size of the word *understanding,* we see that it involves adolescent readers' engaging relevant prior knowledge, applying necessary and available reading strategies, and constructing meaning from text through their interaction. Both reading skill, strategy and content-domain learning, and knowledge should receive assessment attention. Our characterization here is critical for two reasons: It must accurately reflect what a reader does and anticipate the nature of the assessment we might use to determine how well the biology text is understood. A result of considering the cognition aspect of reading assessment should be a list of the important processes and products that we may choose to assess in content-area reading.

Observation

Within the model of assessment, a second important focus is *observation,* or how we might go about assessing those things we deem critical to reading success and content-area learning. The *observation* component of reading assessment must represent our best knowledge and effort related to three particular domains: reading, the particular content area in which students read, and assessment. Applied to adolescent reading, we should identify assessments that create situations that reflect classroom reading practice, and that demand appropriate performances of students.

Imagine a series of multiple-choice assessment items similar to the following:

The word that we use for *division of cells* is
  A. regeneration
  B. mitosis
  C. mitochondria
  D. symbiosis

An adolescent reader's correct choice of *mitosis* may demonstrate fact learning, memorization of a definition of mitosis, and the student's ability to recall information. It may indicate a thorough understanding of this critical biological process, or it may demonstrate a good guess. Our observation must be scrutinized, for it will be asked to bear the weight of the inferences we make about student learning. Compare this item with a constructed response item that asks 10th graders to write in relation to the following prompt:

Apply your knowledge of mitosis and describe differences in mitosis with normal and cancerous cells.

Such a comparison might involve the application of knowledge of cell division to related biological knowledge and the ability to compare and contrast knowledge of normal and cancerous cells. It will also involve the student's ability as a writer. In all cases, it will assume a level of understanding of the content-domain material.

Our choices related to the observation of reading must be guided by our estimation of what best allows students to demonstrate their abilities and achievements. Both the multiple-choice item and the written comparison focus on knowledge of mitosis, but they require of students different thinking (or cognition) to determine or construct the correct response. The constructed response item may demand more complex thinking and allow students to demonstrate what may be qualitatively different understanding. An important question here is whether or not a particular type of assessment is suitable for the task of describing the depth and breadth of what students learn in a particular curriculum. The observation component reminds us that an effective assessment will be informed by our understanding of how adolescents read in relation to particular tasks, texts, and settings. This will then be reflected in the reading assessment materials and procedures that are available to help us observe and record such learning and knowledge.

Interpretation

Interpretation is the third component of the good assessment. Assessment always involves interpretation, which involves a series of inferences that we make from assessment information. Our understanding of the nature of adolescent reading must be combined with our understanding of appropriate assessment materials and procedures. To return to the consideration of the multiple-choice item and the written comparison, we can make inferences that are more or less justified from the evidence that the assessment observation provides us. Related but different strategies and knowledge are needed for the adolescent reader to respond successfully to each type of item. One demands the knowledge of a definition, and the other demands the ability to apply conceptual knowledge.

Would we want to infer that an adolescent reader has the ability to perform the task of comparing mitosis in normal and cancerous cells from that reader's ability to answer the multiple-choice item? In all cases, an important goal is to develop adolescent reading assessments that allow us to make high-faith inferences about adolescent reading achievement and ability. I note that the preceding example of assessment of knowledge of the concept of mitosis focuses on content-domain knowledge and assumes competence in reading. We may make inferences about student reading based on the work that students do in an assessment, but, in this case, our inferences about reading ability would be decidedly indirect, because we infer that reading went well (or did not go well) based on content-domain-driven responses. To augment this particular assessment, we might develop an assessment that better allows us to understand student strategy use while reading.

Pellegrino et al. (2001) focus on the cognitive aspects of reading. However, we can and should conceptualize reading assessment in relation to the aspects of adolescent reading that are other than cognitive (cf. Alexander, 2003). If we were to develop a list of important outcomes of reading instruction, we would include motivation to read, high self-esteem as a reader, and a perception of self-efficacy as a reader, along with students' increased understanding of, and appreciation for, content-area learning. We must develop assessments of such instructional outcomes with the same rigor and attention to detail that is present in current assessments of reading achievement. These efforts should be guided by consensus understanding of the range of positive outcomes of high-quality teaching and engaging curriculum. For example, an assessment of students' motivation for reading must demonstrate a clear relation to the construct of motivation and specify what aspects of motivation are to be assessed. Our understanding of the complexity of reading should inform the development of the observation instrument and procedures, and guide the interpretation of results.

DETERMINING THE SUITABILITY OF READING ASSESSMENTS

When combined, clear definitions and characterizations of adolescent reading and assessment can help us to conceptualize and develop assessments of adolescent reading that provide valuable information. Yet this is not all that is needed to create useful assessments. Assessment is socially situated and politically influenced. The reading assessment agenda is quite crowded, with assessments chosen or mandated by different groups. Often, the most powerful assessments are those imposed from outside the school community, and these may take resources from other, valuable assessments. Thus, it is important to make decisions for or against using particular assessments based on a wide range of criteria.

The CURRV framework for determining the suitability of reading assessments (Leipzig & Afflerbach, 2000) allows us to situate assessment in such social and political contexts. It allows for examination of the Consequences of the assessment, the Usefulness of the assessment, the Roles and responsibilities related to the assessment, and the Reliability and Validity of the assessment. The first three criteria of the CURRV framework were included because of the traditional and privileged use of the psychometric standards of reliability and validity as the arbiters of good assessment. Although reliability and validity are critical aspects of any worthwhile assessment, reading assessments may be chosen based only on these two criteria. The CURRV framework reminds us that the assessment of adolescent literacy must be considered in relation to the consequences of the assessment, the usefulness of the assessment, and the particular roles and responsibilities related to an assessment.

The application of the CURRV framework allows us to identify characteristics and anticipate issues that are related to particular assessments of adolescent reading. A sample of the types of issues and questions addressed with the CURRV framework are presented in Table 17.1. For example, assessments of adolescent literacy may have positive or negative consequences. Low test scores may gain funding for a school district, or they may result in the loss of funding for a school district. Teacher feedback during class can have the consequence of guiding students to better accomplishment or of alienating particular students. Reading assessments that are mandated by states or the federal government may not prove useful to teachers, parents, and students, whereas the careful observation and recording of student performance does. Multiple-choice tests are accompanied by roles and responsibilities that teachers and students know only too well. If a performance assessment is initiated, will students and teachers understand the active roles and responsibilities that are necessary to make the use of the performance assessment worthwhile?

TABLE 17.1. Using the CURRV Framework: Sample Questions That Help Determine the Suitability of Assessments of Adolescent Reading

Consequences

What are possible consequences related to the use of the assessment?
Are there positive consequences?
Are there negative consequences?

Usefulness

How useful is the assessment?
What purpose(s) will the assessment serve?
What audience(s) will the assessment serve?

Roles and responsibilities

What are there particular roles and responsibilities that the assessment creates
    For teachers?
    For students?
    For administrators?
    For parents?
    For other stakeholders?

Reliability

How reliable is the assessment?
Is the assessment consistent in how it measures and describes reading?
Is the assessment subject to bias? Does the assessment treat each student fairly?

Validity

How valid is the assessment?
Does the assessment sample from what we consider to be important aspects of
    adolescent reading?
Do the assessment tasks and materials fairly reflect the type of tasks and materials
    that adolescent students normally encounter in the classroom?

TYPES OF ASSESSMENTS FOR ADOLESCENT READING

We have considered a working definition of *adolescent reading*, a model for developing effective assessment, and a means for determining the suitability of different assessments for the adolescents who read in our classrooms. In this section, I examine several potentially useful types of reading assessment. The success of instructional programs and the continued development of adolescent students' reading achievement demand that we select and use reading assessments that represent the best union of our purposes for assessing and our current knowledge of how best to assess. In this section, I consider different types of assessment, including performance assessments, portfolio assessments, teacher observation and questioning, and high-stakes tests. Each is described in terms of the particular characteristics, uses, and notable strengths and weaknesses of the assessment.

Performance Assessments

Performance assessments are particularly well suited to helping us understand adolescent students' ability to use what is learned from text in content-area classrooms. Performance assessment prompts are often crafted so that they result in complex tasks for students. A performance assessment might ask a student to compare and contrast information learned from two texts written on the same topic from different perspectives. For example, Van Sledright (2001) had students take an investigative approach to reading and learning history. Students read two accounts of the Boston Massacre that appeared in newspapers in Boston and London. Students were required to read the two newspaper articles and account for the different descriptions and conclusions contained in each article. In doing so, students were able to perform and demonstrate sophisticated strategies involved in reading and thinking as historians. They were involved in learning facts, as well as learning how "facts" in history could differ and be in opposition. Van Sledright worked with fifth-grade students, and I believe this bodes well for the idea of increasingly sophisticated teaching and learning in different content areas, and describing them with performance assessments.

Performance assessment in other content domains might involve students in manipulating and applying knowledge gained from reading to write creatively or persuasively. The performance assessment might involve the development of dramatic and artistic performances. Performance assessments place students in assessment situations in which we seek to evaluate what has been learned from reading tasks that emulate and anticipate important content-domain and life performances. In this sense, they are authentic assessments.

Performance assessments are accompanied typically with rubrics, scoring guides and examples of performances (Baxter & Glaser, 1998). Rubrics contain the details that help teachers and students understand how the assessment defines different levels of performance at the task. The greater the detail of description in the rubric, the more guidance the student reader receives related to what must be included in the performance and how it will be graded. A sample rubric used in an American history class is provided in Table 17.2. Students are asked to determine whether a text is a primary or secondary source through their identification and use of partic-

TABLE 17.2. Representative Performance Assessment Rubrics: Determining Primary and Secondary Source Texts and Author's Purpose in American History Texts

---

General goal of curriculum

Determining the nature and trustworthiness of American History texts

Specific student performance

Uses cues to distinguish between primary and secondary source texts.

4   Uses three or more cues to determine primary or secondary source status of text.
3   Uses two cues to determine primary or secondary source status of text.
2   Uses one cue to determine primary or secondary source status of text.
1   Does not use cues to determine primary or secondary source status of text.

Specific student performance

Identifies the author's purpose in history texts.

3   Identifies author purpose and gives evidence to support determination of purpose.
2   Identifies author purpose but does not give evidence to support determination of purpose.
1   Does not identify author's purpose and does not give evidence to support determination of purpose.

---

ular text cues. Students are also asked to determine author purpose and to provide evidence to support their determination.

When concrete examples of performances are presented and discussed, a further opportunity for students and teachers to understand the details of performance is provided. In this sense, performance assessments can give students a blueprint of how they might execute a superior performance. The detail of the rubric also serves to guide teachers in the scoring of students' performances and in focusing instruction prior to assessment. As well, to the extent that teachers and students discuss the performance assessment, the scoring rubric, and the means to creating a superior performance, the assessment becomes public.

Black and Williams (1998) suggest that many students experience assessment as a black box: Students' work goes in, something mysterious happens to it, and it emerges with a grade. This provides little or no guidance to students who are interested in learning more about assessment. Discussions around performance assessments and their accompanying rubrics, along with the display of the rubrics and exemplar papers and performances, provide good levels of transparency to the task of doing the assessment. The opportunity for adolescent readers to work with performance assessments and their accompanying rubrics, scoring guides, and sample performances can contribute to a growing familiarity with the nature of assessment and the development of self-assessment ability. We expect that adolescent readers are capable of independent reading, but this is not possible without readers' strategies that allow for assessing the self. The discussion of rubrics and exemplar performances provides a forum for students to question assessment and develop a detailed understanding of how reading and reading assessment work. Less able readers may have their efforts short-circuited by performance assessments that assume a baseline understanding of text that has not been achieved.

Performance assessments allow us to make different inferences about adolescent students' reading development. They allow for the examination of how students use what they have understood. However, many performance assessments assume students' ability to comprehend text. Adolescent readers must understand what they read as a starting point in many performance assessments. We infer that students have understood text when they apply the knowledge contained in the text. This aspect of performance assessments means that there may be restricted opportunities to focus on students' reading ability and achievement in a formative manner.

There are several caveats related to the use of performance assessments with adolescent readers. First, performance assessments and their assumption of reading ability may provide relatively little useful information about the nature of students' reading skills and strategies. Second, when we assess reading through related student performance, we must be wary of confounds that are introduced. A written account of what an adolescent understands from text introduces students' writing ability into the assessment. A public performance related to what a student has read and understood can be subject to a particular student's characteristics that include creativity, anxiety, confidence, and self-esteem. The interjection of these factors can influence a performance assessment in a manner that results in our misinterpretation of reading achievement. Finally, successful performance assessments enlist the student and teacher as active participants in evaluation. Classrooms with relatively traditional or passive approaches to assessment, such as those that depend on quizzes, and chapter and end-of-unit tests, will need to have clear roles and responsibilities spelled out for students and teachers for performance assessments to work well. Finally, performance assessments are often difficult to score reliably. They demand considerable teacher expertise and time in pursuit of consistent scoring.

Portfolio Assessments

Portfolios provide different opportunities for students to conduct assessment, and they promote important habits of mind in those who successfully develop and use them. As much as the physical aspects of the portfolio differ from other assessments, such as high-stakes tests, so to do portfolios demand thinking and reflection that are unique to good assessment. In addition, portfolios provide a context in which students can learn and practice self-assessment, understand their ongoing and cumulative accomplishments related to reading, and be motivated to further reading (Tierney, Carter, & Desai, 1991).

Portfolios can take many forms. They may be realized in various formats that allow for the collection, access, and utilization of students' work: boxes, accordion folders, computer files, file folders, and the like. Many portfolio assessments derive from the model provided by creative artists and their large carry-around portfolios, which are capable of holding a considerable amount of student work. They are also flexible, in that the contents of the portfolio can be manipulated in relation to the purpose and audience for the assessment. Such large collection ability allows adolescent readers to gather the different types of work and evidence that reflect their development and accomplishment. More recently, computers offer promising possibilities for collection, storage, and access to the individual student's record of reading. For example, students can store, comment on, and work with artifacts of reading kept in electronic portfolios (Wiedmer, 1998). The learning logs, reading journals, performances, tests, quizzes, and related materials can be produced on a computer, or scanned and kept in an easily accessed series of files.

Through the use of portfolios, adolescent readers can gain a sense of their personal progress. Portfolios provide the means for students to work on assessment over time, including units, grading periods, and entire school years. Portfolio assessment can be flexible to accommodate students and their work. For example, consider a ninth-grade curriculum that encourages students to conduct their own investigations of scientific phenomena. A student determines that the groundwater pollution problem in his community is a worthy focus for his investigation. A portfolio assessment approach in the science classroom accommodates the student's copious field notes and observations, and readily provides these resources to a semester-long project. Another section of the portfolio holds the key vocabulary words that accompany the science curriculum and those that the student, through related reading, has determined to be central to the observed phenomena. Still another section contains a list of the resources consulted by the student in the school media center and on the Internet. In this section of the portfolio, the student can develop understandings of words such as *percolate* and *leach*, then refine these understandings throughout the semester. Yet another part of the portfolio can hold the student's learning log, in which explanations of observed phenomena are interpreted in relation to the weekly science laboratory and assigned readings. The semester project itself, in which the student proposes solutions to the problem of groundwater pollution, is kept in the portfolio also. The proximity of the project to the student's notes of scientific observation, key vocabulary, and the learning log represents a gathering of the important learning resources that the student must use to do well in the course. Although focused on the content domain of science, the portfolio provides a rich account of student development as reader and writer. The portfolio also serves the purpose of helping the student present work in progress and completed work to the teacher and to parents (Tierney & Clark, 1998).

Equally important, the capability of the portfolio to hold and help organize students' work must be complemented by students' active use of the portfolio as a forum for presentations of their work, and for reflection and assessment. Portfolio assessment encourages a culture of reflection and discussion around acts of assessment. This helps adolescent students become more knowledgeable about assessment and can encourage them to conduct regular self-assessment (Afflerbach, 2001). Students can attach entry slips to individual items in portfolios that contain students' written commentary and review. The portfolio offers opportunities for students to display and discuss their work with teachers, parents, and fellow students. Over time, such use of portfolios demonstrates to students that assessment done well takes time, and that taking the time is well rewarded.

The culture of portfolio assessment can provide students with ideas and motivations related to their reading and learning (Tierney & Clark, 1998). But the portfolio must be used actively, and the tendency to use portfolios as a storage facility rather than a forum must be avoided. For teachers and students considering the implementation of portfolio assessment of reading and content-area learning, portfolio assessment is demanding in unique ways. It requires that students become the center of assessment efforts. It requires that teachers be knowledgeable, so that they can model uses of the portfolio and suggest to students who are learning portfolios the means to undertake and learn their portfolio routines. Portfolio assessment done well is demanding of time, and students and teachers must have this time to make portfolios fruitful.

Teacher Observation and Questioning

Throughout their time in school, students should have opportunities to increase their prowess as readers. Adolescent readers face increasingly complex texts and reading tasks in the different content areas, and teachers are best positioned to observe and question students as a means of assessing and understanding their growth. As mentioned earlier in this chapter, not all teachers are able to focus on both the continuing development of students' reading ability and their learning of content-domain knowledge (Stiggins, 2002). Teacher observation and questioning are central to both goals of assessment. And when done well, there is no more powerful formative assessment than that which is conducted on a daily basis by the classroom teacher. Yet for most adolescent readers and their teachers, reading assessment serves the exclusive purpose of checking content-area learning. Classroom contexts that support teacher questions and observation for reading assessment must be developed to pursue the dual goals of understanding how students are learning content, and how their reading achievement is related to this learning.

Perhaps the most common form of reading assessment is teacher questioning. It is habit to have students read, then answer questions at the end of a paragraph or chapter. For the purposes of adolescent assessment, we do well to consider an expanded conceptualization of teacher questioning. We can construct three broad categories of questions: those that address student learning of content, those that address the development and use of reading skills and strategies, and those that serve as a model of the types of questions that adolescent readers may eventually ask themselves.

Our questions related to the content of student learning must allow students the opportunity to respond in a manner that describes the nature of their learning. From these responses, we may infer how students are progressing in relation to instructional goals and standards. We also may infer the quality of our instruction. Questions related to reading must be directed at the processes students use to construct meaning. This means that we should consider developing and using question sets like the following: What were climatic characteristics of the Devonian period? How did you determine your answer? In addition, the silent reading that marks most adolescent classrooms needs to be uncovered. When students think aloud as they read, they can provide accounts of the reading strategies that they use (Afflerbach, 2001; Kucan & Beck, 1997). Reading and thinking aloud may be unusual practice in adolescent classrooms, but it can serve the important purpose of providing details of students' reading strengths and weaknesses, and their relationship to content-area learning. Finally, the questions we ask of students can provide models of the types of questions that students might ask themselves. In this sense, our questioning provides examples of what independent readers ask themselves about the process and content of reading as they work strategically with content-area texts.

There are considerable challenges to the development of teacher expertise in observing and questioning in the service of assessment (Stiggins, 2002). Few teacher education programs have courses dedicated to reading assessment. When preservice and practicing teachers encounter material related to reading assessment in their course work, it is more often focused on test construction and the interpretation of test scores (Schafer & Lissitz, 1987). Yet we know that teacher observation and questioning can yield extremely useful information (Johnston, 1997). Reading Recovery succeeds, in part, because teachers are trained to conduct reading inventories that allow them to gather reliable assessment information about student reading. Admittedly, the main focus in such programs is on diagnostic reading instruction. The point is that when teachers are supported appropriately, they can conduct high-quality classroom assessments of reading that revolve around observation and questioning.

Two challenges arise from this observation, should we commit to assessment of adolescent reading in classrooms. First, teachers must receive professional development in reading assessment. Second, the typical school day for adolescents must be structured to allow for the high-quality, teacher-based assessment to occur. An ancillary demand is that content-area curriculum be structured so that there is time available for teachers to observe student reading in depth. This suggests a necessary trade-off in content coverage: Instead of pursuing content coverage goals that are extremely broad (and, in contrast, rarely deep), the curriculum must build in regular opportunities for teachers to observe their students as readers of content-area texts.

High Stakes Tests

All adolescent readers and their teachers are familiar with high-stakes tests. Federal law now mandates that children moving toward adolescence will be tested in grades 3–8 in reading. Many states are implementing exit tests that must be passed for students to receive credit for the different content-area courses and to graduate. This rampant testing practice has not contributed to new forms of high-stakes tests. In fact, the majority of today's high-stakes tests are quite similar to those that adults in the United States took while in school. Familiarity breeds complacency, and the widespread use of tests is based more on tradition and habit than on their ability to sample richly the important aspects of reading development.

For our purposes, it is important to note a central paradox in high-stakes testing. There are massive expenditures of time and money on training to take, administer, and score the tests. Yet they provide very little useful information that can positively impact the reading of adolescent readers in content domains. High-stakes tests receive the preponderance of school funding and media attention, all out of proportion to the benefits they provide (Afflerbach, 2002; Frederiksen, 1984). Despite considerable progress in our understanding of adolescent reading and good assessment, high-stakes tests are often developed in relation to views of reading and assessment that are dated. The results of high-stakes tests are not very useful to teachers and students.

High-stakes tests generally share several characteristics. They are most often norm-referenced and machine-scored, and they often include a majority of multiple-choice items, thereby limiting by design the detailed description of adolescent reading that they can provide (Afflerbach, 2002). These tests are standardized to attempt to provide the same experience and opportunity for all test takers, and this practice contributes to relatively high reliability. For adolescents, the high stakes associated with these tests include student retention in a grade or content area, school sanction, and graduation. In addition, the productive use of the vast majority of high-stakes test results is inhibited by the time lag between administration of the test and acting upon test results. Minimal turnaround and reporting back of test scores is at least several weeks, while more typical intervals for reporting are from 2 to 6 months.

Given the paradox of high-stakes testing, what are teachers of adolescent readers to do? Calkins, Montgomery, and Santman (2001) provide considerate guidelines for teachers who are accountable to both their students and themselves as professionals. Teachers must consider the possible high-stakes consequences that tests have for their students: Tests will figure in decisions of future class placements, educational opportunities, and life outside of school. Therefore, preparing students for testing may be considered a solemn duty. Helping students prepare for testing, while staying true to one's teaching philosophy, means that teachers who are helping their students will also focus on maintaining the integrity of the material that is taught, offering rich accounts of curriculum rather than test preparation items.

WHAT WE NEED TO KNOW NEXT

Our knowledge related to adolescent reading and how best to assess it affords us the opportunity to identify issues and questions that will benefit from research investigations. Thus, an important question is, "How can our most recent understanding of adolescent reading be combined with our most recent understanding of effective assessment?" It turns out that our knowledge about adolescent reading and reading assessment has little to do with how we assess adolescent reading. It is relatively rare to find a complex, well-done assessment that honors the intricacies of learning that are expected in many adolescents' schoolwork within content domains. Multiple-choice and short, constructed response items predominate in most school settings, while school, district, and state reading standards suggest that more effective and innovative assessments are needed. Work that brings together state-of-the-art knowledge is needed. We must reject, at all costs, the argument that the most appropriate assessments of adolescents' reading are too expensive.

A second priority must be assessment that describes adolescent students' reading ability and content-area learning. Current practice in assessment of adolescent reading focuses on assessing readers' learning and understanding of content-domain knowledge and fairly ignores students' strategic reading abilities when they interact with texts. It is as if reading assessment were constructed to reflect the naive conception that students transition from learning to read to reading to learn at some point in elementary school. In reality, readers in school, be they adolescents or elementary schoolers, will grow as strategic readers when reading and content area curricula challenge them to do so. In addition, content-area teachers have little time to conduct assessments that serve the diagnostic reading purpose, because they must spend all their time teaching and assessing content-area reading.

Lack of teacher professional development in reading assessment also works against the assessment of adolescents' strategic reading abilities. Training and support for teachers to become effective diagnosticians are lacking (Stiggins, 2002). Work that describes the types of assessment that can inform us about both content area learning and reading development is much needed. We must determine how professional development helps teachers become reading assessment experts. Despite accounts of the generally dismal assessment abilities of teachers (Stiggins & Conklin, 1992), there are success stories that describe what teachers can do with reading assessment when they are supported with professional development opportunities (Au, 1993; Hoffman, Baumann, & Afflerbach, 2000). We need to understand the characteristics of effective professional development that place more responsibility and expertise in the hands of teachers. This expertise represents a hybrid assessment effort: to know adolescents as both readers and as content-domain learners. Then, we must study the relationship between teachers' well-done assessment and adolescents' reading achievement.

Also important is the full understanding of the influence of reading assessment on reading achievement. High-stakes tests are mandated as measures of adolescent reading, but little attention is given to the disruptive influence of testing on teaching and learning in school (Smith, 1991). We should know better: We cannot claim that we support high standards for adolescent literacy if our tests have the effect of teaching to the test and shrinking an already limited curriculum. Studies that examine the influences of high-stakes tests on what is taught and learned in classrooms peopled by adolescents are needed. As well, we need to examine the beneficial effects of assessment on adolescent reading. Are there assessments that provide immediately useful information for teachers, students, and parents, that are also trusted and used in yearlong appraisals of schools and districts? Do particular assessments have the ability to contribute to adolescent readers' self-esteem, motivation, and knowledge of self as readers?

Across the country, reading assessment is selected, developed, and mandated in relation to different audiences and purposes. Choices of particular assessments emanate from outside and within the classroom as a result of local, district, state, and now national mandates and initiatives. Most reading assessment programs lack an organizing principle: Too often, there are major gaps and redundancies of assessment, while critical aspects of adolescents' reading development go unexamined. For example, could we justify a program that provides three different measures of adolescent students' literal comprehension of content-area textbook information, while fully ignoring changes in adolescents' motivation to read, their reading habits, and their ability to read critically advertisements and other persuasive text? Conducting inventories of reading assessment programs (in effect, assessing the assessment program) should provide information related to strengths and weaknesses of assessment when compared to the models of adolescent reading sketched earlier in this chapter.

Much of the discussion in this chapter revolves around the fact that adolescents are responsible for reading and learning immense amounts of content for school. Likewise, teachers are responsible for teaching these immense amounts of material, and coverage of most curricula involves a trade-off that sacrifices depth of treatment for coverage of broad topics. The opportunity cost involved in current approaches to content-domain curricula experienced by adolescents must be carefully examined. In the process of covering American history or biology in 180 days, options for conducting both formative and summative assessment of high quality may be limited. A teacher who is struggling to keep up with covering material from Native Americans to the role of the United States in the Middle East may have little time to conduct the ongoing assessment of students' developing knowledge of the content of U.S. history or current reading ability.

Finally, our understanding of reading is evolving continuously, and this evolution must be reflected in our assessments. Why is it that we have no district- and statewide assessments of student motivation to read, when there is general agreement as to the centrality of motivation for reading success (Guthrie & Wigfield, 1997)? We do have descriptions of the connection (or disconnection) between reading and literacy in school and out (Alvermann, 2001) that broaden the concept of adolescent reading. Might adolescents' literacy practices outside of school provide secure ground from which they do well in school? Without assessments to describe the detailed nature of student reading, in terms of both strength and need, opportunities to reach and teach students effectively are lost. There are sometimes stark contrasts between the literacies that adolescents use in and out of school and in content-area classrooms, and a general lack of effort to bring these related literacies together to good effect in school (Moje et al., 2004; Moll, 1992). This suggests that reading assessments might describe when adolescent students' reading knowledge and experience in and out of school are complementary, and when they may be problematic. Reading assessments to help us better understand the different resources some students bring (and other students lack) that contribute to adolescent reading development are needed.

REFERENCES

Afflerbach, P. (2000). Verbal reports and protocol analysis. In P. Pearson, M. Kamil, R. Barr, & P. Mosenthal (Eds.), *Handbook of reading research* (3rd ed., pp. 163–179). Hillsdale, NJ: Erlbaum.

Afflerbach, P. (2001). Teaching reading self-assessment strategies. In C. C. Block & M. Pressley (Eds.), *Comprehension instruction: Research-based best practices* (pp. 96–111). New York: Guilford Press.

Afflerbach, P. (2002). The road to folly and redemption: Perspectives on the legitimacy of high-stakes testing. *Reading Research Quarterly, 37*, 348–360.

Alexander, P. (2003, August). *Expertise and academic development: A new perspective on a classic theme.* Invited address at the European Association for Research on Learning and Instruction, Padua, Italy.

Alvermann, D. E. (2001). Reading adolescents' reading identities: Looking back to see ahead. *Journal of Adolescent and Adult Literacy, 44*(8), 676–690.

Au, K. (1993). Portfolio assessment: Experiences at the Kamehameha elementary education program. In S. Valencia, E. Hiebert, & P. Afflerbach (Eds.), *Authentic reading assessment: Practices and possibilities* (pp. 103–126). Newark, DE: International Reading Association.

Baxter, G., & Glaser, R. (1998). Investigating the cognitive complexity of science assessments. *Educational Measurement: Issues and Practice, 17*(3), 37–45.

Black, P., & William, D. (1998). Inside the black box. *Phi Delta Kappan, 80*, 139–148.

Calkins, L., Montgomery, K., & Santman, D., with Falk, B. (1998). *A teacher's guide to standardized reading tests: Knowledge is power.* Portsmouth, NH: Heinemann.

Donahue, P., Finnegan, R., Lutkus, A., Allen, N., & Campbell, J. (2001). *The nation's report card: Fourth-grade reading 2000.* Washington, DC: U.S. Department of Education.

Frederiksen, N. (1984). The real test bias: Influences of testing on teaching and learning. *American Psychologist, 39*, 193–202.

Guthrie, J., & Wigfield, A. (1997). *Reading engagement: Motivating readers through integrated instruction.* Newark, DE: International Reading Association.

Hoffman, J., Baumann, J., & Afflerbach, P. (2000). *Balancing principles for teaching elementary reading.* Hillsdale, NJ: Erlbaum.

Johnston, P. (1997). *Knowing literacy: Constructive literacy assessment.* York, ME: Stenhouse.

Kucan, L., & Beck, I. (1997). Thinking aloud and reading comprehension research: Inquiry, instruction, and social interaction. *Review of Educational Research, 67*, 271–299.

Liepzig, D., & Afflerbach, P. (2000). Determining the suitability of assessments: Using the CURRV framework. In L. Baker, M. Dreher, & J. Guthrie (Eds.), *Engaging young readers* (pp. 159–187). New York: Guilford Press.

Moje, E. B., McIntosh Ciechanowski, K., Kramer, K., Ellis, L., Carrillo, R., et al. (2004). Working toward third space in content area literacy: An examination of everyday funds of knowledge and discourse. *Reading Research Quarterly, 39*(1), 38–71.

Moll, L. C. (1992). Literacy research in community and classrooms: A sociocultural approach. In R. Beach, J. L. Green, M. L. Kamil, & T. Shanahan (Eds.), *Multidisciplinary perspectives in literacy research* (pp. 211–244). Urbana, IL: National Conference on Research in English and National Council of Teachers of English.

Organization for Economic Cooperation and Development. (2000). *Measuring student knowledge and skills: The PISA 2000 assessment of reading, mathematical and scientific literacy.* Paris: Author.

Pellegrino, J., Chudowsky, N., & Glaser, R. (2001). *Knowing what students know: The science and design of educational assessment.* Washington, DC: National Academy Press.

Pressley, M., & Afflerbach, P. (1995). *Verbal reports of reading: The nature of constructively responsive reading.* Hillsdale, NJ: Erlbaum.

Schafer, W., & Lissitz, R. (1987). Measurement training for school personnel: Recommendations and reality. *Journal of Teacher Education, 38*, 57–63.

Smith, M. (1991). Put to the test: The effects of external testing on teachers. *Educational Researcher, 20*, 8–11.

Snow, C. (2002). *Reading for understanding: Toward a research and development program in reading comprehension.* Santa Monica, CA: RAND Corporation.

Stiggins, R. (2002). Assessment crisis: The absence of assessment for learning. *Phi Delta Kappan, 83*, 758–765.

Stiggins, R., & Conklin, N. (1992). *In teachers' hands: Investigating the practices of classroom assessment.* Albany: State University of New York Press.

Tierney, R., Carter, M., & Desai, L. (1991). *Portfolio assessment in the reading–writing classroom.* Norwood, MA: Christopher-Gordon.

Tierney, R., & Clark, C. (with Fenner, L., Herter, R., Simpson, C., & Wiser, B.). (1998). Portfolios: Assumptions, tensions, and possibilities. *Reading Research Quarterly, 33,* 474–486.

Van Sledright, B. (2001). *In search of America's past: Learning to read history in elementary school.* New York: Teachers College Press.

Wiedmer, T. (1998). Digital portfolios: Capturing and demonstrating skills and levels of performance. *Phi Delta Kappan, 80,* 586–589.

18

Teacher Education
and Adolescent Literacy

THOMAS W. BEAN
HELEN J. HARPER

This chapter brings together two fields of study that have not had much intellectual contact: teacher education and adolescent literacy. Although it is true that teacher education courses in English/language arts methods, and more generally in "content-area literacy," may reflect some of the research emanating from adolescent literacy, by and large, the impact of this research on teacher education programs has been limited (Readence, Bean, & Baldwin, 2004). At best, teacher-educators may be sprinkling new material or strategies into their courses. This may reflect an earlier incantation of adolescent literacy as "secondary reading," which, according to Vacca (1998) "represented, more or less, a bag of tricks—text learning and remedial reading techniques—that were often out of synch with adolescent needs and the realities of subject-matter instruction" (p. xvi). This chapter considers more substantial content arising from recent research that we believe may speak more profoundly to reform in teacher preparation and professional development programs. We begin with a brief review of the research on adolescent literacy.

RESEARCH ON ADOLESCENT LITERACY

The "Adolescent" of Adolescent Literacy

Research in adolescent literacy over the last 15 years has provided highly contextualized descriptions of the lives of teenagers and their experiences with school literacy practices both in and outside of classrooms (Bean, Bean, & Bean, 1999; Cherland, 1994; Finders, 1997; Harper, 2000; Moje, 2000). These descriptions reveal that adolescent identity is complex, shifting, and varied and that, for many contemporary teens, literacy practices are equally complex, multifaceted, and multimodal. Yet this complexity is often unrecognized even by those who spend much of their time working or living with teenagers.

For example, it has been our experience that when teachers and/or preservice teachers are asked to free-associate words that come to mind when thinking of "teenagers," they often draw on the dominant, stereotypical, and masculinist discourse of the restless, defiant, alienated teen: the "bundle of raging hormones," "the sower of wild oats," "the tester of growing powers" (Finders, 1998; Hudson, 1984; Lesko, 2001). Such renditions categorize adolescents as a homogenized group with little individual variation. Oddly enough, these depictions are invoked not only in discussing teenagers in general but also in speaking about an individual teen, or about one's own personal experience of adolescence.

There is also a lengthy history, certainly within education, of speaking about adolescents as if they are working their way toward an adult destination, caught in the future rather than living in the present. This view renders adolescents as unfinished projects, occupying some temporal zone between child and adult (Lesko, 2001). Nancy Lesko in her 2001 text, *Act Your Age!: A Cultural Construction of Adolescence*, argued that educators need to break this mold of linear time and its developmental stage theory of adolescence. She suggested:

> Youth are simultaneously young and old, learning and learned, working and in school. This idea of time (that is, of past, present, and future) as holding seemingly opposing identities *simultaneously* is, I believe, a necessary dimension of a retheorizing of adolescence. (p. 197)

In this statement, Lesko begins to capture the complexity of adolescence evident in the research literature.

Other studies indicate the complexity of teenagers' literate lives. Investigations of teens in and out of the classroom literacy setting suggest that teens are often engaged in a variety of literacy activities, often quite sophisticated, that could be better represented in classroom contexts (cf. Alvermann, Hinchman, Moore, Phelps, & Waff, 1998; Bean, Bean, & Bean, 1999; Brozo, Walter, & Placker, 2002; Finders, 1998; Flores–Gonzalez, 2002; Worthy, 1998). For example, in a recent case study, Broughton and Fairbanks (2002) observed and interviewed Jessica, a sixth-grade Latina student in Texas, where high-stakes testing and daily preparation for these assessments are routinized classroom practices. Although Jessica was adept at "doing school," she viewed school literacy practices as boring. Fortunately, she did have rich experiences with texts outside of school. At home Jessica kept an elaborate personal journal and read series books and young adult novels voraciously. She acquired an interest in journaling not in school, but from a cartoon character on a television program. These and other literacy practices were not represented in Jessica's school experience. She saw few connections between classroom literacy and the literacy that was useful and important to her outside school. This disparity between in-school and out-of-school literacy is borne out in many other studies (cf. Hagood, 2002; Hinchman, Payne-Bourcy, Thomas, & Olcott, 2002; Lewis, 2001; Worthy, 1998).

Some of this research points specifically to the mismatch between print-based literacy that adolescents experience in school and the fast-paced information flow that many teens now enjoy outside of school vis-à-vis electronic real-time messaging, surfing the Internet, talking on a cell phone, using portable e-books, and the countless other evolving texts and modalities. Research and pedagogy in adolescent literacy is beginning to examine these newer text forms, including DVDs, CD-ROMs, the Internet, music, television, e-mail, chat rooms, instant messaging, film, video, video games, and teenzines (Alvermann, Moon, & Hagood, 1999). Given the pervasiveness of these texts in the out-of-school lives of at least some adolescents, it seems crucial to include such texts and modalities in classrooms wherever and whenever possible, and to reconfigure our notions of literacy and pedagogical practice in the process.

Recent studies indicate not only the discrepancy among in- and out-of-school literacy practices, texts, and modalities, but also how adolescents actively cope with varying and conflicting social contexts, identities, and literacy demands. For example, Hagood (2002) recently chronicled the problems encountered by Timony, a white, middle-class, high school student. Timony, like Jessica, was an avid reader of novels and engaged with myriad other texts, but these out-of-school literacies were largely ignored and untapped by his teachers. Instead, Timony was seen as a school troublemaker, partly based on his grunge rock T-shirts and unkempt appearance. Whereas this very identity—the rebel—made Timony vibrant and interesting to his friends, it made it difficult to acknowledge and negotiate an alternative or more complex interpretation of who he was, let alone his "hidden literacies," with school officials and school and state policies. Despite considerable if misguided efforts, Timony could not reposition himself, his life, and literacy in school contexts. Timony's efforts and his competencies were largely ignored, as was the school's own work in constructing the discourse of "good students and bad" and of "literates and illiterates."

Timony's experience is much like that of adolescent males in other studies (Brozo et al., 2002; Hinchman et al., 2002; Worthy, 1998) and, indeed, like other teenagers across a wide spectrum of gender, race, class, and ethnicity (Finders, 1997; Flores-Gonzalez, 2002; Harper, 2000; McDonald, 1999; Moje, 2000). Based on these studies and others, we agree with Hinchman et al. (2002) that essentialized identities of adolescents and their literacies are "not reflective," if they ever were, "of the identity fluidity that must be developed to survive in the postmodern world" (p. 242) or of the struggle to negotiate an identity, however fluid, in any world.

To summarize, the emerging field of adolescent literacy places teens at the center of inquiry and asks about their literacy practices, broadly defined. It assumes a connection between literacy practice in and outside of schools and identity formation. To date, research in this field reveals a large and disturbing gap between the lives and literacies of adolescents and the literacy practices and identities offered in school contexts. Reified categories naming "teens," "literacy," and "good pedagogy" do not capture the complexity or fluidity evident in teens' lived experience. This is hardly a surprise for, we hope, many educators, but as they and others may well remind us, reconfiguring pedagogy in light of a more complex and dynamic notion of teens and their literacy is not easily accomplished. It flies in the face of present-day conditions of schooling that allow for and, indeed, encourage simple explanations, quick solutions, and measurable outcomes. We know that the time and energy for the development of new lessons with new materials, let alone for professional reflection and reading, is limited (Hiebert, Gallimore, & Stigler, 2002). Certainly teaching literacy with and for complexity, fluidity, and plurality requires considerable forethought. Nonetheless, we believe more powerful literacy lessons are possible and indeed necessary, if we take into account the research emerging in the field of adolescent literacy. Exposure to this research and to embodied forms of pedagogical practice that embrace fluidity, complexity, and plurality in literacy lessons, together with sufficient time for critical inquiry and reflection, is needed in inservice and preservice programs, if change is to occur.

Research in Preservice and Inservice Teacher Education and Literacy

Systematic research in teacher preparation has been remarkably sparse, locally funded, and far too limited in scope (Wilson, Floden, & Ferrini-Mundy, 2002). In a review of research on teacher preparation, Wilson et al. found only 57 studies that were sufficiently rigorous to warrant attention. In their review of these studies, Wilson et al. found that preservice teachers' initial beliefs and knowledge acted as powerful predictors of what they might learn in education courses. With regard to the impact of practicum, they found wide variation in the nature and quality of clinical experiences. Cooperating teachers ranged from those intent on inculcating student teachers into the status quo of schooling and teaching, to those fostering innovation and independence. Most notably, student teachers who were able to engage critically in action research and inquiry seemed to gain more from this experience than those in more traditional apprenticeship field experiences (Wilson et al., 2002).

Much of the recent work aimed at studying teacher education explores themes of preservice and inservice teachers as reflective practitioners in communities of practice (Bean & Stevens, 2002; Bean & Zulich, 1989; Dewey, 1933; Munby, Russell, & Martin, 2001; Risko, Roskos, & Vukelich, 1999, 1992; Roskos, Vukelich, & Risko, 2001; Schon, 1983; Zulich, Bean, & Herrick, 1992). Such communities of practice would seem to offer the possibility of creating more dynamic, introspective, and informed pedagogical practice for all teachers, including those in literacy education. Unfortunately, there remains a strong and persistent image of the American schoolteacher as a rugged individual who works heroically to educate through sheer force of will, charisma, or some form of natural ability or insight, rather than through collective intellectual and practical effort (Britzman, 2003; Phillips, 2002; Weber & Mitchell, 1995).

This image of the rugged individual renders preservice and inservice programs largely superfluous, because at its extreme, this image, and the discourse that supports it, implies that student teachers are best left to sink or swim in their practicum as a test of their character and natural gifts, and thus their suitability for the profession; and that experienced teachers are also best left alone to do their magic with students, without attending to colleagues or to current research and theory. In such a view, the need for theory and for collegial support would be seen as unnecessary and/or a sign of professional inadequacy.

Fortunately, in the last 15 years, in the face of increasing turnover rates in which nearly 50% of new teachers leave the profession, there has been acknowledgment that experienced teachers need ongoing professional development, and that novice teachers are entitled to more mentoring and support than they have been receiving (National Commission Report, 2003). Some efforts are being made. However, an ongoing 5-year study of 50 new teachers, conducted by Harvard University, indicates how meager such support often is (Johnson & Kardos, 2002). Evident in this study, induction for a new teacher largely centered on district policy, union goals, and experienced mentors who were too busy to meet and address the new teachers' classroom concerns, let alone their own. The teachers in the Harvard Study felt marginalized and isolated. As in their student teaching experience, they were expected to be rugged individuals professing certainty and embodying authority, but struggling with this discourse, many began to question their career choice. In some ways, these novice teachers mirror the adolescents mentioned earlier in this chapter, in their inability to position themselves easily within these images/discourses about the teacher.

The view of teachers as reflective practitioners in communities of practice is antithetical not only to the image of the rugged individual but also to the more passive image of the teachers as technocrats of the state, following the dictates of a mandated curriculum enforced by high-stakes testing and increased teacher testing. Highly accountable, but with low levels of autonomy, these "technocrats" or "good employee" teachers are turned into semiprofessionals at best; their education and professional development are in effect state training (Schwartz, 1996). As characterized by Munby et al. (2001), within this view, "the delivery of teacher education is cast as course-work intensive, with inadequate time for reflection and with an emphasis on the teacher as technician and consumer of propositional knowledge rather than as reflective practitioner" (2001, p. 893). Because they are to follow the dictates of others, the technocrat teachers, like the rugged individualist teachers, have limited need for research or for critical reflection on that research or on school practices and policies, let alone state and national education directives. It is not surprising that the status quo is so easily reinscribed or that, for purposes of this chapter, the ability of teachers and schools officials to reflect and respond to the dynamic, complex, and contextual nature of adolescents' lives and literacies may be so limited.

As a counterforce to the status quo in teacher education, many educators and scholars have recommended that preservice and inservice teaching, including the work of mentoring, should be cast as a form of inquiry (Cochran-Smith, 2000; Elliot, 1990). However, the exact nature and content of this inquiry is highly disputed. Hiebert et al. (2002) have suggested that inquiry and discussion be directed at a series of case-based classroom lessons developed by the profession. Similar content is suggested by Hamilton and McWilliam (2001), who argue that there is a need for the "patient documentation of daily practice in teaching" (p. 35) in efforts to provide a foundation for discussion and inquiry. While grounding inquiry in local contexts and conditions, many have argued that the analysis of teaching and learning needs to address the wider social and economic power relationships that produce classroom and school practices (Freire, 1970, 1994; Freire, Fraser, Macedo, McKinnon, & Stokes, 1997; Giroux, 1988a, 1988b). From a related perspective, others have that suggested that teacher education needs to collect and examine the ways in which identities and ways of life are named and authorized in schools; to insist on choice, diversity, and the possibility of resistance (Phillips, 2002). Still others have suggested that inquiry focus on the psychoanalytic as well as social aspects of learning and teaching, and the knowledge and identities therein produced (Britzman, 1991, 2003; Britzman & Dippo, 2000). Britzman and Dippo suggest that the "grand themes of our present education" concerning affiliation, commitment, trauma, destruction, and community (p. 33) in their social-psychological dimensions should be the focus of teacher education in relation to the question, "How do people learn?" In an extensive review of research centered on how experienced teachers regard their professional identities, Van den Berg (2002) noted the profound role of emotions in thinking about teaching and in the construction of "the teacher's personal subjective educational theory" (p. 589). It is argued that these personal theories and their effects need to be the focus of inservice and preservice education through autobiographical study.

A focus on critical inquiry and reflection, whatever its form, suggests a more active position for both novice and experienced teachers, and, not incidentally, teacher-educators. Such a focus may provide impetus for examining current research and classroom- and/or school-based investigation (or action research). Collective reflection and inquiry concerning the lives and literacies of adolescents, for example, may encourage more profound reform in school literacy practices and school and district policies. Ongoing inquiry might allow for more relevant and responsive teaching. At the very least, multiple opportunities for thoughtful critical reflection, along with debriefing and discussion of teaching and learning events, are badly needed. However, reflection and inquiry in and of themselves may not enough.

Although early work on reflection in action by Schon (1983) caused a flurry of interest in teacher reflection, the work that followed continues to show the limitations and complexities of doing "reflection." For example, only minimal effects could be detected when reflection was treated as solitary writing about teaching literacy without group discussion of practice (Roskos et al., 2001). In addition, much of the research on preservice teacher reflection has been limited by an absence of careful scaffolding of classroom problems. Effective scaffolding of reflective writing and discussion of teaching events involves paying attention to both cognitive and affective elements (Lepper & Hodeell, 1984). Lepper and Hodeell suggest that the carefully scaffolded reflection of preservice teachers should include (1) appropriate selection of the activity or problem; (2) monitoring and debriefing teaching efforts; (3) the mentor's use of leading questions, direct instruction, demonstrations, think-alouds, analogies, and metaphors to deepen thought; (4) experimentation and further application; and (5) sensitive feedback.

Munby et al. (2001) promote a framework that provides a more student-centered approach than that of Lepper and Hodeell: "Student teaching can be a setting where prospective teachers identify what they already know (in action) and what they need to learn (in action) in a program of teacher education" (p. 893). But the technocratic rationality implied by these frameworks has been challenged. Whether student teachers or, for that matter, their teacher-educators, know what they know, can identify what they need to know and can then apply it unproblematically, denies the ambiguities, uncertainties, and emotive factors that influence learning and teaching, as well as the social positioning of teacher, learner, and knowledge that confounds easy transference or application (Britzman, 2003).

The knowledge that reflection and inquiry makes available, let alone its pedagogical implications, can be troubling to teachers because it can "bother their own understanding of education" (Britzman, Dippo, Searle, & Pitt, 1998, p. 19). It is not surprising that teachers may not choose to reflect deeply or critically, or may choose to depict easily solved problems, issues, or descriptions. This was evident in a recent study of teachers' responses to content-area reading strategies, inservice teachers' integrated personal beliefs, and pedagogical practice in reflective journals. For example, one high school English teacher noted in her reflections:

> I usually prepare students by accessing prior knowledge and setting the scene. I also guide students during reading stopping periodically to check for comprehension. Modeling reading strategies for students is also helpful. (in Bean & Stevens, 2002, p. 214)

Although this teacher and the others enrolled in a graduate content-area reading class were adept at describing and reflecting on the various dimensions of their own classrooms and related practices, their comments were largely confined to that local, immediate context. A focus on instrumental analysis of teaching fails to address larger issues of social justice and at the same time fails to engage the more basic perceptions about education and the boundaries and categories employed in thinking about school and curriculum (Fendler, 2003; Roy, 2003). In light of the research on adolescent literacies, such boundaries and categories should include, for example, "adolescents" (as good, bad, normal, deviant), "literacy and illiteracy," and what should count as "school texts."

There are other problems with reflective practice. In a recent critique of teacher reflection research, Lynn Fendler (2003), drawing on and extending the work of Zeichner (1996), suggests the privileging of university research over teacher research; and as we discussed earlier, the emphasis on teaching techniques and classroom management, the disregard of the social contexts and issues of social justice, and a focus on individual rather than collective reflection, undermine reflective practice. Of particular concern to the preparation of teachers who can provide dynamic and complex literacy education, reflective practice may serve to reinforce existing beliefs and practices rather than challenge assumptions. Fendler (2003) comments, "Some reflective practices may simply be exercises in reconfirming, justifying or rationalizing preconceived ideas" (p. 16). Moreover, Fendler suggests that the device of autobiographical narrative, often used in reflective work, may well function to create teachers who confess and confirm their identities (and we would add literacies) and those of their students in terms of categories that mirror existing popular assumptions and stereotypes. Inquiry and reflection that do more than perpetuate the status quo require considerable effort. Participants (students–teachers, teachers, teacher-educators) need to consider and critique basic assumptions and "commonsense" notions that underlie inquiry, reflection, and practice generally. They need to examine the limits of the concepts and categories, as well as the social and institutional history and contexts. In general, in acts of inquiry and reflection, we must look not for confirmation but for difference, that is, the unexpected, the surprise, the unpopular or "awful" thought that opens and extends our thinking and ultimately our practice (Britzman, 1991; Britzman & Dippo, 2000).

This difficult work is not often evident in teacher education. Teacher education has been called "a profession historically charged with fostering assimilation" (Florio-Ruane, 2001, p. 29), but we believe that this older model is ripe for change. Embracing a more introspective, critical, and complex view of teaching along the lines we are suggesting entails risk and a willingness to undertake a "process of critical engagement with self, others, texts, and ideas" (p. 139).

In our efforts to create these more critical engagements in teacher education, we do not want to lose sight of the practical context and structural reforms with regard to literacy education that are also needed (e.g., Ancess, 2003).

As noted by Alvermann et al. (2002), the context of the classroom and school is critical to successful school reform in adolescent literacy. In classroom and school contexts in which meaning making is taken seriously, teachers strive to provide adequate background knowledge and active, hands-on learning to prepare students for text reading and comprehension (Alexander & Jetton, 2000).

In an extensive knowledge development report on successful teaching with adolescents, Alvermann et al. (2002), with the support of a Carnegie Corporation grant, explored the nature of inservice teachers' principled practices and the school structures that were likely to support these efforts. At the center of these reform efforts, there is often a well-respected principal and school literacy leader. Under a school leadership teams' guidance, professional development is needed to translate a shared vision into daily lessons. Successful professional development models include (1) teacher study groups; (2) time and pay for teachers to study and plan; (3) site visits; (4) peer coaching and mentoring support; (5) action research in content-area literacy; and (6) the additional support of a reading specialist to work with struggling readers (Alvermann et al., 2002). Of course, there is no single blueprint for reform. The Carnegie knowledge development document (p. 93) concluded that there are no "quick fixes or prescriptions." Rather, we need to take the best knowledge derived from studies like that of Alvermann et al. and think carefully about local contexts and the implementation of change in both preservice and inservice teacher education.

Partnerships and consortia in which university professors and school district literacy leaders, including administrators, department chairs, core team leaders, reading teachers/coordinators, media specialists, community members, teachers, students, and other change agents collaborate offer a powerful vehicle for change (Alvermann et al., 2002). In particular, these consortia can seek and apply for external funding to focus on adolescent literacy needs.

IMPROVING LITERACY TEACHER EDUCATION
AND PROFESSIONAL DEVELOPMENT

We want to offer a number of alternatives to traditional teacher education that have their roots in, among other things, activity theory (Beach, 2000; Engestrom, Miettinen, & Punamaki, 1999), case study analysis (Hiebert et al., 2002), and reflective inquiry using practical argument (Bean & Stevens, 2002; Tidwell, 1995). Although each of these alternatives has limitations, they would seem to offer possibilities for more effective engagement in theory and practice to allow for more complex, responsive, and profound teaching and learning. In the section that follows, we provide a brief over-view of each of these topics, along with recommended readings. Most importantly, we believe that these alternatives should manifest themselves in our own preservice and inservice teacher education courses, practica, and programs. Much like the now well-known National Writing Project that immerses teachers in the act of writing to first explore their own approaches to this task, before envisioning how they want to engage students in writing and revision, we see a similar need for teacher-educators to risk incorporating these alternatives in their own practice, their own daily lessons, not simply as content but as embodied methodology. Of course, these possible alternatives need to be "reinvented" or "retooled" for the specific context in which they are deployed. These are suggestions only.

Activity Theory

Activity theory (Engestrom et al., 1999), a relatively new way of thinking about classroom lessons, conceives of a classroom as an activity system with a focus on problem-based learning. Activity theory has its roots in Marxist concepts of labor, with an emphasis on collective production using tools to accomplish object-driven goals. In its more recent forms, activity theory has been used to scaffold problem-based learning around activity systems (e.g., a classroom lesson), mediating artifacts, and psychological (conceptual) tools used to accomplish learning goals (Beach, 2000; Bean, 2002b; Grossman et al., 2000). Mediating artifacts include signs and tools we use each day, including television remote control units, a computer mouse, digital alarm clocks, or more mundane devices, such as a shovel or a pencil. These artifacts are used to solve problems. Ideally, concept learning in most content areas should include groups of students collaborating to solve problems through shared discourse centered around particular artifacts (Kozulin, 1998). Activity theory assumes that frameworks for thinking are learned through problem-solving actions with others in specific social contexts (Grossman et al., 2000). In this activity theory based model of learning, the teacher becomes a facilitator or field guide after carefully designing lessons. For example, if high school students in economics participate in a simulation in which they role-play creating a monthly budget, this problem represents the goal of the activity system. Calculators represent mediating artifacts that will assist students in figuring out a monthly budget, and formulas for adding and subtracting income and expenses offer psychological tools that visually depict mathematical solutions.

The discussions and collaborative social interaction that occur in a classroom activity system devoted to inquiry and problem solving drive student learning. For example, in a biology laboratory class, ninth graders might be engaged in dissecting a squid. Using a diagram (i.e., a conceptual tool) and various artifacts, including the preserved squid and a scalpel, their goal is to dissect and analyze the various anatomical features of the squid. In doing so, students are also asked to consider how the various tools and artifacts limit what can be known about the squid.

Activity systems should provide learners with "phenomena, situations, and tasks going beyond their actual possibilities to such a degree that a problem situation can arise" (Lompsher, 1999, p. 268). In this approach, learners need to consider what they do not know and form some collective learning goals. Therefore, lessons based on activity theory have two crucial elements: (1) Students' prior knowledge is incomplete; and (2) within a sociocultural framework, they are collectively and cooperatively engaged in an activity in order to achieve a goal, solve a problem, or examine an issue (Beach, 2000; Engestrom et al., 1999; Wertsch, 1998).

We propose that activity theory offers a vehicle for revamping both preservice and inservice teacher education through teacher reflection on daily lessons, with greater attention to contextual and social elements than in the past. Indeed, Bean (2002b) has developed a lesson planning and reflection framework that teachers can use to examine activity systems carefully in classrooms, including related artifacts, student response modes, social context, and target concepts to be learned. It is important to note that the development of this lesson framework was a conscious effort to move lesson design beyond its behavioral roots in most preservice teacher education programs. Blueprints for lesson design in most secondary methods texts focus on writing performance–based goals and objectives, with the learning activities flowing from those expected outcomes. Unlike activity theory, with its center on artifacts and cultural dimensions, traditional lesson planning tends to ignore learner characteristics, treating students largely as homogenized targets of instruction.

ARCC: Activity, Response, Context, and Concepts

ARCC is an acronym denoting four crucial elements of a lesson based on using artifacts and related discourse to explore an issue or inquire into a topic (Bean, 2002b). Detailed guidelines and a sample high school health lesson on sleep deprivation are listed in the recommended reading section of this chapter (Bean, 2002b). We suggest that combining ARCC with case study analysis and practical argument, described shortly, are dimensions of practice that need to be modeled in our own teacher education adolescent literacy and content-area reading classes. For example, ARCC and the other approaches we outline here can be used to examine existing lessons critically, with an eye toward improving the degree to which students feel they have an active role in any topic inquiry that is introduced. In essence, activity theory centers the project of learning concepts or questioning ideas on the learner, with the teacher in the role of a facilitator. ARCC consists of four lesson elements.

Activity

Lessons based on activity theory involve carefully selecting both the activity and mediating artifacts that lend themselves to inquiry. At this stage, a consideration of students' prior knowledge is important. For example, in a lesson on drought in the West, it is important to determine students previous direct or indirect experience of such conditions and their effects.

Response

Because student collaboration is a goal, cooperative responses such as making a display, writing a song, or designing a Web quest or advertisement are all possibilities. A lesson on drought lends itself to a variety of responses, including video shots of the effects of the drought on various people and places (farmers, boaters, forests, lakes, zoos, etc.).

Context

There is substantial evidence that how students are grouped in cooperative inquiry matters a great deal. As in all sociocultural situations, there is no neutral ground. Gender and cultural differences influence the flow of interaction in any group, and there is always the danger of some students being marginalized or excluded (Lewis, 2001). Thus, carefully considering how best to group students is crucial.

Concepts

A lesson that is developed to move students beyond listing concepts to a greater understanding of how these ideas weigh into the human condition is far more productive than the typical memorize-and-recall form of learning still prevalent in many content-area classrooms. For example, in addition to understanding the conditions that create drought and its effects, students can gain an appreciation of how natural phenomena impact human lives. They might take on roles that exemplify these differences such that the impact of a drought on farmers, zoo curators, boaters, fishing enthusiasts, environmentalists, and others becomes apparent. Examining the topic from various angles and positions should reveal those who are marginalized and those who are privileged. Looking behind texts at hidden agendas and biases is crucial (Luke, O'Brien, & Comber, 2001).

Wherever possible, teachers might consider using young adult literature within ARCC to support students' concept learning. A number of young adult novels treat topics relevant to various content areas (Bean, 2002a). For example, in a unit on drought, the award winning novel *Dust* (Slade, 2001) explores the impact of the Dust Bowl on Canadian farmers and their families through a fantasy plot involving a rainmaker who comes to town, promising a magical cloud seeding system, while spiriting away the town's children. This novel, and others, illuminate concepts in a literary way that is simply not possible in nonfiction texts.

In order to introduce preservice and inservice teachers to ARCC and lend a critical element to lesson design and analysis, we believe there is tremendous value in employing case studies and practical argument as critical frameworks for discussion.

Case Study Analysis and Reflection Using Practical Argument.

Practical argument offer a means to engage preservice and inservice teachers in critical reflection based on a two-level examination of daily lessons (Tidwell, 1995). In essence, a teacher reviews a particular teaching moment within a video, audio, or field-note transcription of a lesson using two very different perspectives. The first perspective involves critiquing the lesson, using the voice of the Teacher immersed in the context of the lesson, whereas the second perspective involves engaging the voice of the Other. The Other functions as a critical friend, observing, critiquing, and reflecting on the lesson from the outside (Tidwell, 1995). Alternatively, the Other may be an imaginary critic, who lends an alternative perspective to a case study critique, or a real mentor, such as a student teaching supervisor. For example, in a ninth-grade social studies class on the Industrial Revolution, a student teacher attempted to engage student interest by using a working scale model of a steam engine. Unfortunately, once the steam engine was introduced and running, its power as an item of interest quickly wore off as students listened to the student teacher lecture from his text-based notes. Some students fell asleep, others feigned attention, and a few faithfully "did school" by copying the teacher's lecture points off the PowerPoint presentation.

When the student teacher met with the cooperating teacher to go over the field notes on this lesson using practical argument, the voice of the Other quickly discerned that the attention-getting power of the steam engine could have been better placed as a culminating activity. In addition, this lesson took place in a community where factory workers had recently lost their jobs, yet no connection was made between this local event and the text discussion of the Industrial Revolution.

Practical argument can be used to reflect on preexisting case studies of daily teaching events, video cases, or the increasing number of Internet cases being developed by professional organizations. For example, the College Reading Association has a bank of literacy case studies at *http://literacy.okstate.edu.*

Tidwell (1995) noted:

> Practical argument as an instructional approach does provide preservice and novice teachers the opportunity to examine their own beliefs in the context of their own teaching. Through the use of their Other voice in practical arguments, these teachers move from concrete representation to a more thought-provoking and problem-solving way of thinking, thus enabling them to talk about the interaction of their beliefs and practice. (p. 373)

By using practical argument as a means to analyze positive and negative features of daily lessons in an activity system framework, ongoing reform of teaching and teacher education is centered on deepening classroom inquiry and reflection. At the close of this chapter, we offer recommended readings that provide additional information on activity theory, case study analysis, and practical argument.

WHAT STILL NEEDS TO BE KNOWN

Each of these alternative ways of conceptualizing and carrying out teacher preparation needs multiple lines of systematic research to gain an understanding of their contribution to moving teacher education in adolescent literacy ahead. The need for newer models of teacher education based on contemporary research on adolescents, and the value of critical reflective practice centered on daily lessons, should revitalize our practice. By critically exploring activity theory, case study analyses, practical argument, and the like, it may be possible to move the field of teacher education beyond simplistic models that merely indoctrinate teachers in the status quo. More systematic investigation of these alternatives and others is desperately needed. Such research and investigation, we hope, may lead to more critically informed, responsive teaching and learning for lives and literacies of adolescents, their teachers and their teacher-educators.

REFERENCES

Alexander, P. A., & Jetton, T. L. (2000). Learning from text: A multidimensional and developmental perspective. In M. L. Kamil, P. B. Mosenthal, P. D. Pearson, & R. Barr (Eds.), *Handbook of reading research* (Vol. 3, pp. 285–310). Mahwah, NJ: Erlbaum.

Alvermann, D., Boyd, F., Brozo, W., Hinchman, K., Moore, D., & Stutevant, E. (2002). *Principled practices for a literate America: A framework for literacy and learning in the upper grades.* New York: Carnegie Corporation.

Alvermann, D., Hinchman, K., Moore, D., Phelps, S., & Waff, D. (1998*). Reconceptualizing the literacies in adolescents' lives.* Mahwah, NJ: Erlbaum.

Alvermann, D., Moon, J., & Hagood, M. (1999*). Popular culture in the classroom: Teaching and researching critical media literacy.* Newark, DE: International Reading Association.

Ancess, J. (2003). *Beating the odds: High schools as communities of commitment.* New York: Teachers College Press.

Beach, R. (2000). Critical issues: Reading and responding to literature at the level of activity. *Journal of Literacy Research, 32*, 237–251.

Bean, T. W. (2002a). Making reading relevant for adolescents. *Educational Leadership, 60*, 16–19.

Bean, T. W. (2002b). Text comprehension: The role of activity theory in navigating students' prior knowledge in content teaching. In C. M. Roller (Ed.), *Comprehensive reading instruction across grade levels* (pp. 133–147). Newark, DE: International Reading Association.

Bean, T. W., Bean S. K., & Bean, K. F. (1999). Intergenerational conversation and two adolescents multiple literacies: Implications for redefining content and literacy. *Journal of Adolescent and Adult Literacy, 47*, 438–448.

Bean, T. W., & Stevens, L. P. (2002). Scaffolding reflection for preservice and inservice teachers. *Reflective Practice, 3*, 205–217.

Bean, T. W., & Zulich, J. (1989, Winter). Using dialogue journals to foster reflective practice with preservice, content area teachers. *Teacher Education Quarterly*, pp. 33–40.

Britzman, D. (1991). Decentering discourses in teacher education: Or, the unleashing of unpopular things. *Journal of Education, 173*(3), 60–80.

Britzman, D. (2003). *Practice makes practice: A critical study of learning to teach* (2nd ed.). Albany: State University of New York Press.

Britzman, D., & Dippo, D. (2000). On the future of awful thoughts in teacher education. *Teaching Education, 11*(1), 31–37.

Britzman, D., Dippo, D., Searle, D., & Pitt, A. (1998). Toward an academic framework for thinking about teacher education. *Teaching Education, 9*(11), 15–26.

Broughton, M. A., & Fairbanks, C. M. (2002). Stances and dances: The negotiation of subjectivities in a reading/language arts classroom. *Language Arts, 79*, 288–296.

Brozo, W. G., & Walter, P., & Placker, T. (2002). "I know the difference between a real man and a TV man": A critical exploration of violence and masculinity through literature in a junior high school in the hood. *Journal of Adolescent and Adult Literacy, 45,* 530–538.

Cherland, M. R. (1994). *Private practices: Girls reading fiction constructing identity.* London: Taylor & Francis.

Cochran-Smith, M. (2000). The future of teacher education: Framing the questions that matter. *Teaching Education Journal, 11*(1), 13–23.

Dewey, J. (1933). How we think. Lexington, MA: Heath. (Original work published in 1901)

Elliot, J. (1990). Teachers as researchers: Implications for supervision and teacher education. *Teaching and Teacher Education, 6*(1), 1–26.

Engestrom, Y., Miettinen, R., & Punamaki, R. (1999). *Perspectives on activity theory.* New York: Cambridge University Press.

Fendler, L. (2003). Teacher reflection in a hall of mirrors: Historical influences and political reverberations. *Educational Researcher, 32*(3), 16–32.

Finders, M. (1997). *Just girls: Hidden literacies and lives in junior high.* New York: Teachers College Press.

Finders, M. (1998). Raging hormones: Stories of adolescence and implications for teacher preparation. *Journal of Adolescent and Adult Literacy, 42,* 252–263.

Flores-Gonzalez, N. (2002). *School kids/street kids: Identity development in Latino students.* New York: Teachers College Press.

Florio-Ruane, S. (2001). *Teacher education and the cultural imagination.* Mahwah, NJ: Erlbaum.

Freire, P. (1970). *Pedagogy of the oppressed.* New York: Continuum Press.

Freire, P. (1994). *Pedagogy of hope: Reliving pedagogy of the oppressed.* New York: Continuum Press.

Freire, P., Fraser, J., Macedo, D., McKinnon, T., & Stokes, W. (1997). *Mentoring the mentor: A critical dialogue with Paulo Freire.* New York: Peter Lang.

Giroux, H. (1988a). *Schooling and the struggle for public life: Critical pedagogy in the modern age.* Minneapolis: University of Minnesota Press.

Giroux, H. (1988b). *Teachers as intellectuals.* Minneapolis: University of Minnesota Press.

Grossman, P. L., Valencia, S. W., Evans, K., Thompson, C., Martin, S., & Place, N. (2000). Transitions into teaching: Learning to teach writing in teacher education and beyond. *Journal of Literacy Research, 32,* 631–662.

Hagood, M. C. (2002). Critical literacy for whom? *Reading Research and Instruction, 41,* 247–266.

Hamilton, D., & McWilliam, E. (2001). Ex-centric voices that frame research on teaching. In V. Richardson (Ed.), *Handbook of research on teaching* (4th ed., pp. 17–43). Washington, DC: American Educational Research Association.

Harper, H. J. (2000). *Wild words dangerous desires.* New York: Peter Lang.

Hiebert, J., Gallimore, R., & Stigler, J. W. (2002). A knowledge base for the teaching profession: What would it look like and how can we get one? *Educational Researcher, 31,* 3–15.

Hinchman, K. A., Payne-Bourcy, Thomas, H., & Olcott, K. C. (2002). Representing adolescents' literacies: Case studies of three white males. *Reading Research and Instruction, 41*, 229–246.

Hudson, B. (1984). Femininity and adolescence. In A. McRobbie & M. Nava (Eds.), *Gender and generation* (pp. 31–53). Baskingstoke, UK: Macmillan.

Johnson, S. M., & Kardos, S. M. (2002). Keeping new teachers in mind. *Educational Leadership, 3,* 27–31.

Kozulin, A. (1998). *Psychological tools: A sociocultural approach to education.* Cambridge, MA: Harvard University Press.

Lepper, M. R., & Hodeell, M. (1984). Intrinsic motivation in the classroom. In R. Ames & C. Ames (Eds.), *Research on motivation in education: Vol. 3. Goals and cognitions* (pp. 73–105). San Diego: Academic Press.

Lesko, N. (2001). *Act your age!: A cultural construction of adolescence.* New York: Routledge/Falmer Press.

Lewis, C. (2001). *Literacy practices as social acts: Power, status, and cultural norms in the classroom.* Mahwah, NJ: Erlbaum.

Lompsher, J. (1999). Activity formation as an alternative strategy of instruction. In Y. Engestrom, R. Miettinen, & R. Punamaki (Eds.), *Perspectives on activity theory* (pp. 264–281). New York: Cambridge University Press.

Luke, A., O'Brien, J., & Comber, B. (2001). Making community texts objects of study. In H. Fehring & P. Green (Eds.), *Critical literacy: A collection of articles from the Australian literacy educators' association* (pp. 112–123). Newark, DE: International Reading Association.

McDonald, K. (1999). *Struggles for subjectivity: Identity, action and youth experience.* New York: Cambridge University Press.

Moje, E. (2000). "To be part of the story": The literacy practices of gangstra adolescents. *Teachers College Record, 102,* 651–690.

Munby, H., Russell, T., & Martin, A. K. (2001). Teachers knowledge and how it develops. In V. Richardson (Ed.), *Handbook of research on teaching* (4th ed., pp. 877–904). Washington, DC: American Educational Research Association.

National Commission Report. (2003). *Report on teaching and America's Future.* Washington, DC: Author.

Phillips, D. K. (2002). Female preservice teachers' talk: Illustrations of subjectivity, visions of "nomadic" space. *Teacher and Teaching: Theory and Practice, 8,* 9–27.

Readence, J. E., Bean, T. W., & Baldwin, R. S. (2004). *Content area literacy: An integrated approach* (8th ed.). Dubuque, IA: Kendall/Hunt.

Risko, V., Roskos, K., & Vukelich, C. (1999). Making connections: Preservice teachers' reflection processes and strategies. In T. Shanhan & F. Rodriguez-Brown (Eds.), *Perspectives on literacy research and practice: 48th yearbook of the National Reading Conference.* Chicago: National Reading Conference.

Roskos, K., Vukelich, C., & Risko, V. (2001). Reflection and learning to teach reading: A critical review of literacy and general teacher education studies. *Journal of Literacy Research, 33,* 595–635.

Roy, K. (2003). *Teachers in nomadic spaces: Deleuze and curriculum.* New York: Peter Lang.

Schon, D. (1983). *The reflective practitioner: How professionals think in action.* San Francisco: Jossey-Bass.

Schwartz, H. (1996). The changing nature of teacher education. In J. Sikula (Ed.), *Research on teacher education* (pp. 3–13). New York: Macmillan.

Slade, A. (2001). *Dust.* Toronto: HarperCollins.

Tidwell, D. (1995). Practical argument as instruction: Developing an inner voice. In K. Hinchman, D. J. Leu, & C. K. Kinzer (Eds.), *Perspectives on literacy research and practice: 44th yearbook of the National Reading Conference* (pp. 368–373). Chicago: National Reading Conference.

Vacca, R. (1998). Foreword. In D. Alvermann, K. Hinchman, D. Moore, S. Phelps, & D. Waff (Eds.), *Reconceptualizing the literacies in adolescents' lives* (pp. xvx–vi). Mahwah, NJ: Erlbaum.

van den Berg, R. (2002). Teachers' meanings regarding educational practice. *Review of Educational Research, 72,* 577–625.

Weber, S., & Mitchell C. (1995*). That's funny, you don't look like a teacher: Interrogating images and identity in popular culture.* London: Falmer Press.

Wertsch, J. V. (1998). *Mind as action.* New York: Oxford University Press.

Wilson, S. M., Floden, R. E., & Ferrini-Mundy, J. (2002). Teacher preparation research: An insider's view from the outside. *Journal of Teacher Education, 53,* 190–204.

Worthy, J. (1998). "On every page someone gets killed!": Book conversations you don't hear in school. *Journal of Adolescent and Adult Literacy, 41,* 508–517.

Zeichner, K. (1996). Teachers as reflective practitioners and the democratization of school reform. In K. Zeichner, S. Melnick, & M. L. Gomez (Eds.), *Currents of reform in preservice teacher education* (pp. 199–214). New York: Teachers College Press.

Zulich, J., Bean, T. W., & Herrick, J. (1992). Charting stages of preservice teacher development and reflection in a multicultural community through dialogue journal analysis. *Teaching and Teacher Education, 8,* 345–360.

RECOMMENDED READINGS

Activity Theory

Beach, R. (2000). Critical issues: Reading and responding to literature at the level of activity. *Journal of Literacy Research, 32,* 237–251.

Bean, T. W. (2002). Text comprehension: The role of activity theory in navigating students' prior knowledge in content teaching. In C. M. Roller (Ed.), *Comprehensive reading instruction across grade levels* (pp. 133–147). Newark, DE: International Reading Association.

Engestrom, Y., Miettinen, R., & Punamaki, R. (1999). *Perspectives on activity theory.* New York: Cambridge University Press.

Kozulin, A. (1998). *Psychological tools: A sociocultural approach to education.* Cambridge, MA: Harvard University Press.

Lewis, C. (2001). *Literacy practices as social acts: Power, status, and cultural norms in the classroom.* Mahwah, NJ: Erlbaum.

Lompshear, J. (1999). Activity formation as an alternative strategy of instruction. In Y. Engestrom, R. Miettinen, & R. Punamaki (Eds.), *Perspectives on activity theory* (pp. 264–281). New York: Cambridge University Press.

Case Study Analysis and Reflection Using Practical Argument

Fenstermacher, G. D. (1994). The place of practical arguments in the education of teachers. In V. Richardson (Ed.), *A theory of teacher change and the practice of staff development: A case in reading instruction* (pp. 23–42). New York: Teachers College Press.

Hiebert, J., Gallimore, R., & Stigler, J. W. (2002). A knowledge base for the teaching profession: What would it look like and how can we get one? *Educational Researcher, 31,* 3–15.

Tidwell, D. L. (1995). Practical argument as instruction: Developing an inner voice. In K. A. Hinchman, D. J. Leu, & C. K. Kinzer (Eds.), *Perspectives on literacy research and practice: 44th yearbook of the National Reading Conference* (pp. 368–373). Chicago: National Reading Conference.

PART IV

Reflections on Theory and Current Practice

The Need for Research
on Secondary Literacy Education

MICHAEL PRESSLEY

For most of the past decade, I have had little to nothing to do with middle schools and high schools, focusing instead on literacy instruction in the primary grades. My colleagues and I have found out a great deal about how excellent, primary-level, elementary educators develop literacy skills in their students (see Pressley, Allington, Wharton-McDonald, Block, & Morrow, 2001), including how to develop comprehension skills in young readers (Pressley, 2002; Pressley, El-Dinary, et al., 1992). Of course, as I present my findings about elementary education, from time to time, there have been questions addressed to me about literacy education during adolescence (i.e., middle school and high school). There is one point I can make about reading in adolescence with certainty, a point made prominently in the research literature.

COMPREHENSION STRATEGIES INSTRUCTION IMPROVES
SECONDARY STUDENTS' READING

Middle school and high school readers who have comprehension difficulties benefit when they are taught to use a repertoire of comprehension strategies (e.g., to use prediction, question asking, seeking clarification, and summarization; Anderson, 1992; Collins, 1991). The effective teaching of comprehension strategies (Pressley, El-Dinary, et al., 1992) begins with a teacher modeling and explaining comprehension strategies, for example, while reading stories aloud to students. This is followed by students' practicing the strategies, often with some teacher scaffolding while a group of students read a story together, with each student explaining his or her strategies activity to the group. For example, if the teacher decides to begin teaching prediction, he or she models predicting while reading aloud, perhaps also noting aloud reactions to events in the story that are either consistent or inconsistent with the predictions. As students become familiar and comfortable with making predictions, the teacher can model and explain additional strategies (e.g., constructing mental images representing ideas in the text). Then, the children are encouraged to make predictions and construct images as they read through text. Students may be given several weeks to focus on articulating these two strategies during reading. Once they are comfortable doing so, the teacher can model and explain a third strategy, perhaps summarizing (i.e., stopping during reading and attempting to recall the most important points in the text). Students then work on articulating predicting, imagining, and summarizing. And so it goes until students have built up a repertoire of perhaps a half-dozen or so strategies that they coordinate as they read text.

This approach to strategy instruction has been called "transactional comprehension strategies instruction" for several reasons (Pressley, El-Dinary, et al., 1992): (1) There is the transaction between the reader and text, with the reader responding to text (e.g., Rosenblatt, 1978); (2) there are transactions between students over text, with the students responding to the strategy attempts of each other (e.g., after one student reports an image, another relates that his or her image is different in some important way). During such transactions with text and other readers, students are anything but passive, thinking hard about what is being read, as well as the various reactions to the text that are being aired in the discussion. Doing this every day for a semester or a year, or longer, results in internalization and ownership of the strategic processes taught (Pressley, El-Dinary, et al., 1992); that is, participants eventually are making predictions themselves, as well as constructing images and asking questions, seeking clarification when confused, and summing up (Pressley, El-Dinary, et al., 1992).

Such teaching produces large, positive effects on comprehension and memory of text (Anderson, 1992; Collins, 1991). So even though I have not studied middle school or high school since the 1970s, I have always had something to say when asked, because others had done telling work at secondary level, producing outcomes that connect with some of my work at the elementary level.

NEW RESEARCH DIRECTIONS FOR ME

I have now decided to study teaching and learning in middle and high schools myself, in part, motivated by policymaker concerns and expectations about adolescent literacy. During the past academic year, I spent considerable time in two middle schools and one high school.

Concerns

As this chapter was being written, the 2002 National Assessment of Educational Progress (NAEP; *http://nces.ed.gov/nationsreportcard/reading/*) was released, with much more bad news than good news. Eighth graders improved slightly on the test relative to previous administrations, whereas 12th graders declined. Although almost three-fourths of eighth and 12th graders performed at or above the Basic level, only about one-third of students performed above the Proficient level; that is, although a clear majority of students had mastery of the basic skills for reading grade-4 and -8 material, respectively, only one-third of students were able to handle challenging material, use sophisticated analytical skills, or apply their reading skills broadly. There is plenty of room for improvement in reading at the middle and high school levels, as reflected in the NAEP results. Moreover, the country is demanding that there be improvement.

Policymakers' Demanding Literacy Expectations

As this chapter is being written, I am working on a committee charged to revise the Michigan kindergarten- to eighth-grade-level expectations with respect to literacy achievement. As my colleagues and I have done this work, we have become aware that groups vetting state standards (e.g., Achieve, Inc.; see *http://www.achieve.org*) have very broad and high expectations about literacy achievement in secondary schools.

Consider just the expectations with respect to reading. By grade 8, students should be capable of the following:

1. Words frequently encountered in texts should be recognized automatically (i.e., as sight words).
2. Others words should be easily sounded out (i.e., by middle school, students should have strong phonics skills).
3. Grade-8 students should be able often to determine the meaning of unfamiliar words from text context clues and know the meaning of words frequently encountered in text.

4. Students should be reading a range of texts, writings from different cultures, time periods, genres, and authors.

5. Students should be doing a great deal of reading during free time at school and at home. They should be enthused about reading.

6. Reading of grade-level texts should be fluent, including appropriate expression.

7. Students should be able to analyze a text with respect to the author's values, beliefs, and cultural-historical contexts.

8. Grade-8 students should be aware of how authors attempt to influence the reader through bias, stereotyping, omission, and emphasis.

9. Grade-8 students should be using automatically the essential comprehension strategies that are employed by skilled readers (see Pressley & Afflerbach, 1995). These include predicting, constructing mental images representing ideas in text, questioning, rereading or listening again if uncertain, and summarizing. Students should be able to relate their personal prior knowledge to themes, issues, and perspectives in text.

10. Grade-8 students should be monitoring their comprehension (i.e., be aware of whether they are understanding text), with such awareness guiding use of comprehension strategies (e.g., changing strategies if comprehension is not occurring).

11. Students should be able to follow the plot of a narrative (i.e., short stories, novels, plays), noting rising action, turning points, and falling action.

12. They should also be aware of how an author uses figurative language, irony, and symbolism in narratives.

13. They should be able to spot the main ideas versus supporting ideas in an informational text and recognize overarching conclusions that follow from such text.

14. Students should be aware of the various expository text structures (e.g., cause and effect, descriptions) and how authors use prologues, epilogues, previews, and reviews to make their points. They should be able to use knowledge of expository text structure to locate information in texts and construct meaning from text.

15. They should be able to construct generalizations over several texts relating to a particular theme (i.e., determine messages that are consistent with all of the texts read about a particular topic) and be able to do this for texts in various presentation modes, including written texts, pictures, multimedia productions, and drama.

16. Grade-8 students should be able to use the Internet to find information. They should be able to select among Web-based resources, explain the bases for their selection of Internet sources, and effectively use the sources on the Web to construct meaning.
17. Grade-8 students should be able to judge the aesthetic qualities and literary merits of texts they read, interpreting texts they read critically, judging the reasonableness of conclusions drawn, assessing the universality of messages in text, and determining whether arguments in text are persuasive.
18. Eighth graders should be able to engage in interpretive discussion with others about the content of a text.
19. They should be obtaining significant knowledge from what they read—knowledge they use to relate to social studies, science, and other content.
20. Grade-8 students should be able to apply the themes and univeral truths found in text to their own lives, for example, changing courses of action based on information gained from reading.

In summary, the expectations about what grade-8 students can do as they read are substantial expectations that are likely to be reflected in many more state standards documents that drive state testing in the near future. Literacy is more than reading, however, with the expectations for composing every bit as high and extensive. The same is true for both speaking and listening. A reasonable expectation is that there needs to be a great deal of teaching in middle school and high school aimed at all of these elements of literacy. I have my doubts that such intense teaching is occurring in contemporary American schools.

MY RECENT IMMERSION IN MIDDLE AND HIGH SCHOOL ENVIRONMENTS

During school year 2002–2003, I spent a great deal of time in three middle school and one high school environment. These were all good schools, producing between respectable and outstanding achievement in their students relative to other middle school and high school settings.

Students in these schools were asked to read a great deal not only as part of class assignments but also at home. They also wrote quite a bit, although, consistent with Applebee's (1984) insight, the most common writing was short answers to test questions or questions following a reading. More positively, longer writing did seem to be within a plan, draft, revise model (Flower & Hayes, 1980), with considerable demands with respect to both coherence and mechanics. Also, I witnessed quite a bit of vocabulary development in the schools I studied, and there were high demands for correct spelling.

Perhaps the greatest disappointment for me, although it was not a surprise, was little teaching of comprehension strategies. Yes, there were occasional teachers who encouraged prediction and/or making images and/or summarizing, but there was nothing like the intense and prolonged instruction of a small repertoire of comprehension strategies, that is, nothing like the transactional strategies instruction approach documented as effective in the literature (e.g., Anderson, 1992). As has been true since researchers started looking at this issue (Durkin, 1978-1979), there was a lot of testing of comprehension (i.e., asking students questions about what they read) but little teaching how to comprehend.

Just as salient in all of the settings I studied last year were students with substantial difficulties in reading, writing, and oral communications:

• Although most students in middle school and high school can sound out words, many do so slowly, with reading that is anything but appropriately expressive; that is, they are not fluent readers.

• Although there was much teaching of vocabulary, there were often obvious gaps in students' understanding of vocabulary commonly encountered in contemporary American discourse.

• The responses of many students to questions about what they read flagged the fact that many of them were failing to comprehend, with limited connecting of ideas newly encountered in a text to prior knowledge. Many responses to comprehension questions reflected literal knowledge of what they read and little else.

• I never saw any evidence of a single student attacking a text on a first reading using the complex repertoire of strategies that are used by skilled readers (Pressley & Afflerbach, 1995). In fact, students evidenced strategy use only when prompted by the teacher (e.g., the teacher asking, "What questions occurred to you as your read?" with students then coming up with questions that appeared to be made up in response to the teacher's probe). I left these schools with no sense that students were engaging in self-regulated use of comprehension strategies.

• I saw little evidence of students actively interpreting text, unless the teacher prompted them to be interpretive (i.e., again, through questioning).

• The quality of writing varied enormously among students, with many students having difficulties writing long compositions, and others having difficulties with mechanics and spelling.

• Students had relatively few opportunities to communicate orally about academic matters except in response to teacher questions. In particular, I observed little demand for students to plan and deliver substantial and coherent oral presentations. Often, even responding to teacher questions posed difficulties, with students not seeming to be able to express what they meant to say.

Although it is obvious to me that we should be teaching more language arts at the middle and high school level, as a well-read language arts researcher, I recognize there is a problem. We do not know how to teach middle school and high school students with respect to the most important language arts elements. That is, we know the elements that should be taught but not much else. As I reflected on the research literature and my observations in middle and high schools, I came to the following specific realizations:

• We know little about how to help those students who do not develop fluent reading by the middle school years except perhaps to have them read more, or even better, to have them receive feedback on their reading from a teacher (Kuhn & Stahl, 2003). Yes, there are some other suggestions in the language arts practitioner literature about how to stimulate fluency development, for example, to employ Reader's Theater, which requires students to read words quickly and with expression, or to have students do poetry slams, which also require automatic reading of words with expression. Even so, these methods are much better developed to be deployed in elementary schools, and even there, they are not evaluated as completely as they need to be in order to be certain of their efficacy (Blevins, 2001; Rasinski, 2003; Rasinski & Padak, 2001). We especially need to study how to develop fluency in students who are slow to become fluent. I saw enough examples of students reading slowly and showing no evidence of comprehension—most likely because all of their capacity was consumed by sounding out the words (LaBerge & Samuels, 1974)—to be confident that dysfluent middle school and high school readers are common.

• Although there are intervention programs to teach comprehension strategies to struggling adolescent readers (e.g., Deshler, Ellis, & Lenz, 1996), I did not see these approaches being employed. In fact, I have encountered more than a fair share of high school teachers who comment that high school students are supposed to be able to read already, that high school is about teaching substantive content; that is, they seem to believe that students should have learned how to read with high comprehension in the elementary years, that it is not their responsibility to teach students how to read and write.

• Perhaps worst of all, I saw little evidence of students reading really challenging texts. In fact, just yesterday I met with two local middle school principals to discuss reading in their schools. They confided to me that they knew their students were not reading the social studies and science texts, because they were poorly written and very difficult for the students to understand. Last year, I observed many ways that teachers compensate so that their students do not have to read such challenging texts: In particular, they give lots of worksheets and study questions that provide detailed information about what will be tapped on exams (i.e., often, these study sheets contain the exact questions that students will encounter on texts). Rather than reading the text to complete study sheets, students simply go searching for information in the text that is pertinent to the questions posed. Yes, text search is an important skill to learn, but it is a very different competency than reading to comprehend text (Guthrie, 1988). It is also a very difficult task for many students, especially if they lack much knowledge of the content being searched (Symons & Pressley, 1993), which was certainly the case for many of the middle and high school students we observed as they labored to find answers to questions.

• Despite the fact that science and social studies course work demanded the most reading of informational texts, when there was teaching to increase use of comprehension strategies, it usually occurred in language arts, typically, as students read narratives.

There is much reading of narratives (i.e., novels, short stories) in middle school and high school. On the positive side, often these do connect with important content knowledge. For example, in a study of a 100% African American school in Chicago (Pressley, Raphael, Gallagher, & diBella, in press), students read many novels about African Americans experiences in America that complemented the detailed focus on the African American experience in social studies. On the negative side, such reading and reading instruction was not preparing students to deal with informational texts, like the ones assigned in their content classes.

• Many middle and high school students do not know how to compose well. For some, it is a lack of higher order skills—not knowing how to plan, draft, and revise a paper. For others, however, it is a lack of lower order skills—not knowing grammar or mechanics well, so that most sentences written by such students have problems with them. In addition, many middle and high school students cannot spell. Again, there are compensatory programs to teach writing skills (Deshler et al., 1996)—programs that I did not observe being used during my visits to middle and high schools last year.

In short, a year of immersion in middle and high schools developed in me a concrete understanding that there is a need for more literacy instruction in middle and high schools, with little teaching aimed directly at increasing fluency at the word level, use of comprehension strategies above the word level, or writing (which demands that students comprehend multiple texts as they construct conclusions across texts). That said, most of the students I observed were not in academic trouble in the sense that they were in danger of failing in school, because they were generally meeting the most salient demand being made on them: They learn content knowledge well enough to pass tests administered to them. In fact, content-area instruction was the one very bright spot that I detected in the middle and high schools I visited—a bright spot with important implications for literacy.

DEVELOPMENT OF CONTENT KNOWLEDGE

For over a century, secondary schooling has focused on teaching of content (Cuban, 1993), with a prototypical high school student going through 6 ± 1 classes a day, each dedicated to some important content. In addition, a major shift has occurred for children in grades 5–8. As middle school students, fifth-, sixth-, seventh-, and eighth-grade students now experience a school day that more resembles what goes on in the high school than what went on in elementary schools in the middle part of the 20th century.

My colleagues and I did witness a great deal of content instruction in the middle and high schools that we visited this past year. Moreover, most of it was of content that definitely seemed important for young Americans to be learning. As I mentioned earlier in this chapter, teachers were well aware that students could not and would not learn the content from texts, with the result that teachers did a great deal of planning and organizing to ensure that the content was covered in class. Thus, not only did they provide study questions but also these questions were covered in class, so that all students would have a good set of guides to prepare for exams.

Implications of Content Learning for Comprehension

This development of content knowledge has vast implications for comprehension. Without a doubt, the most important contribution of the Center for the Study of Reading at the University of Illinois was that their work increased understanding that possessing background knowledge that can be related to new readings is a critical determinant in text comprehension (Anderson & Pearson, 1984). For example, students' cultural backgrounds very much determine how they interpret text, with Lipson's (1983) demonstration that the understandings of the same text by Jewish and Catholic students was filtered through their cultural knowledge, with Jewish students injecting Jewish ideas as they recalled a story about a Catholic event, and Catholic students injecting Catholic ideas as they recalled a text about a Jewish event. As a second example, consider that cultural knowledge developed through schooling can impact future learning, such as occurred in Brown, Smiley, Day, Townsend, and Lawton's (1977) demonstration that learning about American Native life through reading impacted subsequent comprehension of text about American Native life.

The content that is most likely to be taught is what is specified in a school's curriculum guides, with these often informed by the state. Some schools go so far as to buy textbooks that have been especially prepared for their state.

Encouraging Students to Use Their Prior Knowledge While Reading Text

Beyond acquiring worthwhile world knowledge, it is important that students use that knowledge to understand new texts and ideas that are encountered. Unfortunately, both children and adults possess prior knowledge that they could use to increase understanding and learning of new content, but they fail to use it (Pressley, Wood, et al., 1992); that is, young readers need to be taught to connect what they already know to ideas in texts being read (e.g., Keene & Zimmermann, 1997). The tactic that Pressley, Wood, et al. (1992) found to be very powerful in stimulating students to connect their prior knowledge during new learning was to teach students to reflect on why the facts being detailed in a text made sense. When students ask themselves why the new facts make sense and, in fact, try to figure out why the facts make sense, memory of the text improves dramatically. The research was sufficiently analytical to make clear that *why*-questioning orients students to relevant prior knowledge that explains the significance of the facts covered in text—knowledge that they typically would not activate when reading factual text (Martin & Pressley, 1991). In general, neither children nor adults seem to do much thinking about the significance of facts in text unless they are taught to do so (Pressley, Wood, et al., 1992).

Dangers in Encouraging Students to Relate Their Prior Knowledge to Ideas in Text

One danger in urging students to use their prior knowledge is that sometimes students possess errant prior knowledge, which is better left unactivated, for its activation can actually reduce comprehension and memory of related text (Alvermann, Smith, & Readence, 1985). Then, there are some adolescent readers who activate prior knowledge that is relevant to tangential information in the text rather than to the major ideas that should be the focus of the reading. Moreover, the ideas they relate are often idiosyncratic to the point that it is hard to know how they are connected to the text (Williams, 1993). Not surprisingly, this approach does not improve understanding of text. More positively, these students can be taught strategies to focus on the important ideas in text, to dig for the central ideas, with such instruction benefiting their comprehension (see Williams, 1998 and 2002, for reviews).

When I have talked about Williams's (1993) finding that there are weak readers who make strange prior knowledge associations to the texts they are reading and, hence, undermine their comprehension, I am always amazed at the number of teachers nodding their heads in agreement. When I ask these teachers how many have students who make such idiosyncratic associations, many hands go up. I have little doubt at this point, based not only on Alvermann et al.'s (1985) research and Williams's (1993) work, but also on my interactions with middle and high school educators, that there is a need to extinguish some types of knowledge connecting, at least by some students. Teaching such inhibition can then set the stage for teaching the students information that matters in text (e.g., the story grammar elements in a narrative), and how that information should be noted carefully and related to their existing prior knowledge as part of trying to understand a text (Williams, 1998, 2002).

Summary

The emphasis on content knowledge in middle and high school has great potential for improving the comprehension of students. That said, having content knowledge is one thing, and relating it appropriately to text in order to increase understanding is quite another. At one extreme are kids who relate to texts with ideas that are tangential to the main points in the reading and, thus, undermine their comprehension. They need to be taught to inhibit tangential responding as they are also taught to focus on and relate to the central ideas in text. The reaction of many students to texts they are reading, however, is passive, with students possessing prior knowledge that they could use to understand a text but not applying it. Such students need to be taught to relate their prior knowledge to the text—to be taught to make predictions about upcoming content based on prior knowledge, to connect what they already know to ideas encountered in text, and to ask themselves why the ideas in text make sense (i.e., to understand the significance of the claims made in text).

I close this section, noting that the emphasis on content in secondary schools is unquestioned by many secondary teachers, with a frequent assertion by high school teachers that their job is development of content knowledge in their students, not to teach students how to read, write, and communicate. The problem with this stance is that reading, writing, and communicating are essential skills, with the long-term negative consequences of illiteracy being much greater than the consequences of not learning the content covered in secondary schooling. An irony is that if content teachers would teacher their students to read and write more effectively, it is likely that content learning would increase. That returns this discussion to comprehension strategies instruction.

BUT COMPREHENSION STRATEGIES ARE COVERED IN THE LANGUAGE ARTS CURRICULUM!

Examination of teacher editions of secondary language arts anthologies confirms that there is some coverage of comprehension strategies. For example, in one seventh-grade volume, activating prior knowledge was covered on page 55, predicting on page 173, visualizing on pages 22, 344, and 527, questioning and clarifying on page 458, and summarizing on page 498. The problem, of course, is that effective comprehension strategies instruction involves coordinated use of the strategic processes habitually (see, e.g., Anderson, 1992); that is, there should be activation of prior knowledge and connecting to prior knowledge every time a students reads, with prior knowledge use driving predictions and affecting students' images in reaction to text. In the same story, an active reader asks questions and attempts to clarify when confused, ultimately making certain that he or she can summarize what has been read! As I reviewed this particular anthology, as well as its competitors in the marketplace, I just did not get the sense that the individuals preparing the lessons in these texts understood the transactional strategies instructional approach. Rather, they seem to know that use of the individual strategies does improve memory and comprehension, consistent with a great deal of evidence (see National Reading Panel, 2000; Pressley, Johnson, Symons, McGoldrick, & Kurita, 1989), but they do not seem to realize that good readers do not execute just one strategy at a time, but rather several strategies in a coordinated fashion (Pressley & Afflerbach, 1995).

As our understanding increases about what occurs in secondary language arts classrooms that work, there is additional motivation to teach strategies. Applebee, Langer, Nystrand, and Gamoran (2003) have documented that the most effective secondary language arts classes are ones where students engage in thoughtful dialogues about the texts they are reading. When such dialogues are examined, students do much predicting about text based on prior knowledge, make connections to other texts and their knowledge of the world, report envisionments of the stories being read, ask questions and look for answers, and interpretively summarize; that is, they use the processes that students are taught to use as part of transactional comprehension strategies instruction. Recall that as such strategies are being taught, students practice the strategies in small groups, dialoguing about their predictions, connections, images, questions, and summaries; that is, comprehension strategies instruction encourages exactly the same dialogical processes that are at the heart of dialogues in effective secondary classrooms (Applebee et al., 2003). Presumably, by participating in such dialogic practice of strategies, students will internalize the strategies (Vygotsky, 1978), coming to own them and eventually, habitually read the way excellent readers read (Pressley & Afflerbach, 1995). Comprehension strategies instruction, an approach that definitely makes sense in the contemporary secondary language arts classroom, promotes both dialogical skills and individual, self-regulated thinking during reading.

THE MIDDLE SCHOOL AND HIGH SCHOOL LITERACY INSTRUCTIONAL RESEARCH WE NEED

Just about everyone—more than 90% of parents, teachers, and the general public—believes it is more important for American students to emerge from secondary school with strong literacy skills than to acquire high content knowledge (e.g., knowledge of American history; Public Agenda Foundation, 1995). How can that occur? Well, here is my best thinking as I contemplate directing my professional life toward this problem.

Increase Public Awareness of High School Literacy Deficiencies and Possibilities

Something that absolutely must occur, and soon, is that the literacy shortcomings of American secondary students must be made clearer and more salient to the American public. More than NAEP scores on the Web are required. Parents must know what should be expected of secondary students and whether students are meeting those expectations. As I have worked on the Michigan expectations, I have heard again and again that no one understands much the existing expectations, the ones that would be replaced by the standards I am working on. Even teachers and principals who had read the previous standards documents often reported not knowing what the standards really meant.

I became determined that not only would the standards cover the breadth of literacy competencies that students need to acquire, and do so with sufficient depth, but they would also be written so that school administrators, teachers, parents, and even the students could understand the expectations. As the new expectations translate into assessments of competency, it is essential in my view that there be detailed reporting about both the literacy competencies that are developed well in secondary students and those that are not, with this information driving reform of literacy instruction in secondary schools. If more people understand the variety of literacy competencies that can and should be accomplished in secondary schools, as well know in detail the literacy education accomplishments and failures in contemporary secondary schools, there can be much better informed decision making than is occurring now.

Determine How to Get Secondary Schools to Teach Differently . . . to Teach Students How to Read and Write

Getting secondary schools to teach differently is not going to be easy. The commitment to content learning is deeply entrenched (Cuban, 1993). Secondary schools at the dawn of the 21st century look a lot like the junior and senior high school that I experienced when I was a student in the 1960s. There are a lot of content basals now, as there were then. Most relevant here, there still is very little teaching of high school students about how to read and compose. As I commented earlier, curricular materials support for teaching the reading process is not very compelling. Recall that the high school literature anthologies have scattered lessons on individual comprehension strategies rather than encouraging students to use the strategies as a repertoire consistently (i.e., with every single reading!). More positively, I am very impressed with some of the published composition basals I have seen. My problem is that they do not seem to be used much in school. Composition instruction could be much more complete than it is.

How can secondary schools be persuaded to change? With respect to reading, I think the most powerful lever might be the teachers themselves. According to the Public Agenda Foundation (1995), 98% of teachers recognize the importance of developing literacy skills in students. One possibility with respect to reading is that teachers are not very good readers themselves; hence, they are in no position to teach their students how to read better. In particular, they do not use comprehension strategies on their own, with the result that their own reading is not nearly as cognitively active as it needs to be for high comprehension and intelligent interpretation of text (Keene & Zimmermann, 1997). That hypothesis needs to be evaluated, and, if true, efforts made to improve the comprehension of teachers; that is, Keene and Zimmermann's hypothesis should be evaluated: If teachers learn to use comprehension strategies, then they will recognize the value of the strategies, be more receptive to teaching them, and understand better what is required to encourage students to use comprehension strategies. It is time to test this complex hypothesis.

With respect to writing, I suspect that the strongest lever in the next few years is the coming change in the Scholastic Aptitude Test (SAT), with 800 points added for a writing sample. That will certainly make clear to everyone that secondary students must learn how to write better. So, there is the motivation. What is also going to be required is education of teachers about how to teach writing, including how to teach writing in the content areas. We do not even have hypotheses about how to accomplish that. That is a problem that the best minds in writing instruction need to tackle and soon. One possibility is that a hypothesis analogous to that of Keene and Zimmermann (1997) might work: Educate the teachers in process writing to plan, draft, and revise, learning the most effective tactics for each of the three major stages of composition. As the teachers become better writers, they should begin to understand both the potential of similar instruction to improve their students' literacy and what is required to develop writing competence in students.

In short, determining how to increase teaching of comprehension and writing strategies in American secondary schools should be a high priority. There is enough evidence of the effectiveness of such teaching to be confident that increasing such teaching will make a difference. That such work should occur as soon as possible should not be interpreted to mean that teaching comprehension and composition strategies is all that is needed.

Expand Research on Development of Literacy in Secondary Schools

I urge everyone reading this chapter to study the research that was conducted at the National Research Center on English Learning and Achievement (CELA), with their work available at the CELA website: *http://cela.albany.edu/*. That center generated a great deal of data on which the literacy research and English teacher community should reflect as part of contemplating a larger, fuller research agenda.

What do we need to know? Basically, almost everything, given this history of understudy of literacy development in secondary schools: So just how well developed is the sight-word knowledge of secondary students? What proportion of secondary readers cannot use phonics skills to sound out unfamiliar words? What proportion of students are fluent (i.e., What proportion can read familiar words automatically? What proportion can read with appropriate expression?)? What do secondary students read? What proportion are reading the wide variety of texts that should be read by secondary students on their way to being culturally literate? How many secondary students are skilled at figuring out the meanings of words in text? How common is students' use of comprehension strategies to monitor their understanding of text and adjust reading in response to monitoring? In short, much needs to be known about what secondary students can do and what they cannot do, much more than is being tapped by the NAEP.

Beyond this is the need for instructional research that can improve the situation. Once more is known about the extent of the problems in reading and writing, this information can be used to target the greatest needs. That said, I suspect that many literacy needs require addressing, from increasing fluency at the word level, to increasing use of comprehension strategies, to increasing writing skills at all levels (i.e., from word processing to the higher order aspects of planning, drafting, and revising).

There is plenty here for researchers to do in anticipating reform of secondary education to increase the amount and quality of the literacy instruction that occurs there. As researchers do their work on instruction and student learning, they must also do research on how to motivate teachers to teach literacy processes. It is definitely time for some of the best research minds in literacy to spend some time in secondary schools. I hope to see many of my colleagues there as I continue my work at that level.

REFERENCES

Anderson, R. C., & Pearson, P. D. (1984). A schema-theoretic view of basic processes in reading. In P. D. Pearson (Ed.), *Handbook of reading research* (pp. 255–291). New York: Longman.

Alvermann, D. E., Smith, L. C., & Readence, J. E. (1985). Prior knowledge activation and the comprehension of compatible and incompatible texts. *Reading Research Quarterly, 20*, 420–436.

Anderson, V. (1992). A teacher development project in transactional strategy instruction for teachers of severely reading-disabled adolescents. *Teaching and Teacher Education, 8*, 391–403.

Applebee, A. N. (1984). *Contexts for learning to write.* Norwood NJ: Ablex.

Applebee, A. N., Langer, J. A., Nystrand, M., & Gamoran, A. (2003). Discussion-based approaches to developing understanding: Instruction and achievement in middle and high school English. *American Educational Research Journal, 40*, 685–730.

Blevins, W. (2001). *Building fluency: Lessons and strategies for reading success.* New York: Scholastic.

Brown, A. L., Smiley, S. S., Day, J. D., Townsend, M. A. R., & Lawton, S. C. (1977). Intrusion of a thematic idea in children's comprehension and retention of stories. *Child Development, 48*, 1454–1466.

Collins, C. (1991). Reading instruction that increases thinking abilities. *Journal of Reading, 34*, 510–516.

Cuban, L. (1993). *How teachers taught: Constancy and change in American classrooms 1890–1990* (2nd ed.). New York: Teachers College Press.

Deshler, D. D., Ellis, E. S., & Lenz, B. K. (1996). *Teaching adolescents with learning disabilities: Strategies and methods.* Denver, CO: Love.

Durkin, D. (1978–1979). What classroom observations reveal about reading comprehension instruction. *Reading Research Quarterly, 15*, 481–533.

Flower, L., & Hayes, J. (1980). The dynamics of composing: Making plans and juggling constraints. In L. Gregg & E. Steinberg (Eds.), *Cognitive processes in writing* (pp. 31–50). Hillsdale, NJ: Erlbaum.

Guthrie, J. T. (1988). Locating information in documents: Examination of a cognitive model. *Reading Research Quarterly, 23*, 178–199.

Keene, E. O., & Zimmermann, S. (1997). *Mosaic of thought: Teaching comprehension in a reader's workshop.* Portsmouth, NH: Heinemann.

Kuhn, M. R., & Stahl, S. A. (2003). Fluency: A review of developmental and remedial practices. *Journal of Educational Psychology, 95*, 3–21.

LaBerge, D., & Samuels, S. J. (1974). Toward a theory of automatic information processing in reading. *Cognitive Psychology, 6*, 293–323.

Lipson, M. Y. (1983). The influence of religious affiliation on children's memory for text information. *Reading Research Quarterly,*k *18*, 448–457.

Martin, V. L., & Pressley, M. (1991). Elaborative interrogation effects depend on the nature of the question. *Journal of Educational Psychology, 83*, 113–119.

National Reading Panel. (2000). *Report of the National Reading Panel.* Washington, DC: National Institute of Child Health and Development.

Pressley, M. (2002). *Reading instruction that works: The case for balanced teaching* (2nd ed.). New York: Guilford Press.

Pressley, M., & Afflerbach, P. (1995). *Verbal protocols of reading: The nature of constructively responsive reading.* Hillsdale, NJ: Erlbaum.

Pressley, M., Allington, R., Wharton-McDonald, R., Block, C. C., & Morrow, L. M. (2001). *Learning to read: Lessons from exemplary first-grade classrooms.* New York: Guilford Press.

Pressley, M., El-Dinary, P. B., Gaskins, I., Schuder, T., Bergman, J. L., Almasi, J., et al. (1992). Beyond direct explanation: Transactional instruction of reading comprehension strategies. *Elementary School Journal, 92*, 511–554.

Pressley, M., Johnson, C. J., Symons, S., McGoldrick, J. A., & Kurita, J. A. (1989). Strategies that improve memory and comprehension of what is read. *Elementary School Journal, 90*, 3–32.

Pressley, M., Raphael, L., Gallagher, D., & DiBella, J. (in press). Providence–St. Mel School: How a school that works for African-American students works. *Journal of Educational Psychology.*

Pressley, M., Wood, E., Woloshyn, V. E., Martin, V., King, A., & Menke, D. (1992). Encouraging mindful use of prior knowledge: Attempting to construct explanatory answers facilitates learning. *Educational Psychologist, 27,* 91–110.

Public Agenda Foundation. (1995). *Assignment incomplete: The unfinished business of education reform.* New York: Author.

Rasinski, T. V. (2003). *The fluent reader: Oral reading strategies for building word recognition, fluency, and comprehension.* New York: Scholastic.

Rasinski, T. V., & Padak, N. D. (2001). *From phonics to fluency: Effective teaching of decoding and reading fluency in the elementary school.* New York: Addison-Wesley/Longman.

Rosenblatt, L. M. (1978). *The reader, the text, the poem: The transactional theory of the literary work.* Carbondale: Southern Illinois University Press.

Symons, S., & Pressley, M. (1993). Prior knowledge affects text search success and extraction of information. *Reading Research Quarterly, 28,* 250–261.

Vygotsky, L. S. (1978). *Mind in society: The development of higher psychological practices.* Cambridge, MA: Harvard University Press.

Williams, J. P. (1993). Comprehension of children with and without learning disabilities: Identification of narrative themes and idiosyncratic text representations. *Journal of Educational Psychology, 85,* 631–641.

Williams, J. P. (1998). Improving the comprehension of disabled readers. *Annals of Dyslexia, 48,* 213–238.

Williams, J. P. (2002). Using the theme scheme to improve story comprehension. In C. C. Block & M. Pressley, *Comprehension instruction: Research-based best practices* (pp. 126–139). New York: Guilford Press.

Theories and Constructs That Have Made a Significant Difference in Adolescent Literacy
—But Have the Potential to Produce Still More Positive Benefits

MICHAEL F. GRAVES

Something like four decades ago, the cognitive revolution ushered in a host of theoretical insights, research findings, and instructional innovations. By and large, the effects of the cognitive revolution have been hugely positive. We know much more about reading and much more about teaching than we did 40 years ago. Yet, in a number of cases, our increased knowledge has not had as powerful an effect as it can have on students' learning. In this chapter, I discuss theories and constructs that have had substantial influence on the literacy education of adolescents but that, in my judgment, have the potential to produce still more positive benefits for adolescent learners.

In organizing the topics, I have grouped them under four headings: "Theories Worthy of the Name," "How to Teach," "What to Teach," and "Motivation and Engagement: The *Sine Qua Non* of Learning." In each section, I first define the theory or constructs being considered, then appraise the practical effects or influence the theory or construct has had thus far and suggest some additional effects or influence that it could, and in my judgment *should*, have.

THEORIES WORTHY OF THE NAME

Here, I discuss five theories, taking them up in the order in which they first became prominent influences in the field. The five theories are schema theory, the interactive model of reading, constructivism, reader response theory, and sociocultural theory.

Schema Theory

Schema theory is both one of the earliest and most influential constructs to emerge from the cognitive revolution. As described by schema theory, knowledge is packaged in organized structures termed schemata. According to Rumelhart (1980), schemata constitute our knowledge about "objects, situations, events, sequences of events, actions, and sequences of actions" (p. 34). We have schemata for objects, such as a house, for situations, such as being in a class, for events, such as going to a football game, and for sequences of events, such as getting up, eating, showering, and going to work. We interpret our experiences—whether those experiences are direct encounters with the world or vicarious experiences gained through reading—by comparing and in most cases matching those experiences to an existing schema. In other words, we make sense of what we read and of our experiences more generally by a tacit process that in essence tells us, "Aha. This is an instance of such and such."

One very important consequence of readers having these rich, internalized networks of schemata is that, once a particular schema is evoked, a huge store of knowledge becomes immediately available. Schemata assist the reader in initially making sense of what he or she reads, relating information newly acquired to prior knowledge, determining the relative importance of information in a text, making inferences, and remembering (Anderson & Pearson, 1984).

The field has certainly recognized the importance of some aspects of schema theory, most notably, the importance of students having the requisite background knowledge to read a particular text, and of teachers building or activating students' background knowledge as they begin a particular text. Less positively, the field appears not to have recognized the importance of students' internalizing a common body of knowledge that enables them to understand and be understood by each other, and that allows teachers to approach instruction with some understanding of what knowledge most of their student do and do not have. In our concern over what body of knowledge we ought to teach, we seem to have forgotten the importance of teaching some common body of knowledge.

The Interactive Model of Reading

While schema theory emphasizes the importance of the reader's knowledge in understanding a text, the interactive model of reading serves as a very important reminder that both the reader and the text play vitally important roles in reading. As described by the Rumelhart's (1977) interactive model, the reader arrives at his or her understanding of a text by simultaneously synthesizing information from a variety of sources, including word-level knowledge, syntactic knowledge, and various sorts of schemata that he or she has internalized. Good readers need to rely appropriately on the texts they are reading and their background knowledge to arrive at meaning, and teachers need to provide them with the sorts of texts and tasks that promote their doing so.

Over the past 30 years, some in the field—most notably, those with very strong reader response orientations—appear to have largely rejected the concept of reading as an interactive process. They have put the vast majority of emphasis on the reader and have given the text short shrift. Fortunately, the radical approach to reader response appears to be losing proponents, and several authorities who strongly endorse reader response (e.g., Appleman, 2000; Pirie, 1997) have recently discussed the excesses of the approach in minimizing the place of the text. Even more fortunately, the RAND Reading Study Group (2002), which has already had a strong influence and seems likely to have even more influence in the future, defined comprehension as "the process of simultaneously extracting and constructing meaning through interaction and involvement with written language" (p. 11), and went on to say that they deliberately used "the words extracting and constructing to emphasize both the importance and the insufficiency of the text as a determinant of reading comprehension" (p. 11). The fact that comprehension involves both "extracting and constructing meaning" needs to be universally understood, and the activities in which we engage students and our expectations of what they will learn need to reflect this fact.

Constructivism

Constructivism has many roots and many branches (Phillips, 2000), being in fact a philosophical (von Glaserfeld, 1984), political (Searle, 1993), and social (Gergen, 1985) construct, as well as a psychological one. Here, I use the term in its psychological sense. Used in this sense, *constructivism* makes it clear that comprehending a text is very much an active, constructive process. Consider this metaphor: The author of a text, like an architect who draws a blueprint, has created a representation of his or her ideas. The reader, like a builder, must take this representation and construct something. Much like the builder much construct a house, the reader must construct meaning. Constructivists often use the phrase "making meaning" to emphasize the reader's active role in comprehending texts. Students cannot just passively absorb meaning from texts. A truly passive reading would leave the reader simply having turned the pages. Instead, readers must actively engage with the text, consider what they are reading, and link the information they are gleaning from the text with ideas, topics, and events they already know. Moreover, the more difficult a text becomes for students—the more new and challenging information it presents—the more actively engaged readers must be.

In addition to describing the active nature of reading, constructivism emphasizes that the meaning a reader constructs from a text is subjective, the result of that particular reader's processing of the text. Just as no two builders construct exactly the same house from a blueprint, so no two readers construct exactly the same meaning from a text. A particular reader's processing is influenced by the sum total of his or her experience and unique intellectual makeup. Because of this, each reader constructs a somewhat different interpretation of the text, the text as he or she conceptualizes it (von Glaserfeld, 1984).

The claim that reading is an active process has been universally accepted, and it deserves this acceptance, because no text with information that the reader does not already know gives up its meaning without substantial effort from the reader. The second claim, that the meaning one constructs from a text is subjective, has also been very widely accepted, perhaps too widely so. As Stanovich (1994) has noted, texts differ dramatically in how much they constrain meaning. Many texts are meant to be, and can be, interpreted quite similarly by most readers. If people and nations are to understand each other, be able to work out their differences, and thereby live in peace, that is a very good thing. As I said in considering the interactive model and again say in considering reader response theory, both the text and the reader deserve appropriate consideration.

Reader Response Theory

I have already mentioned reader response theory in commenting on the interactive model of reading, but the theory deserves consideration in its own right. Reader response theory (Rosenblatt, 1938/1995, 1978) has much in common with constructivism. However, reader response theory differs from constructivism in that it has different roots than constructivism and focuses specifically on reading. As its name suggests, the theory puts a great deal of emphasis on the reader. It stresses that the meaning one gains from text is the result of a transaction between the reader and the text, and that different readers will have a range of responses to literary works. Many literary texts simply do not have a single correct interpretation; readers should be allowed and encouraged to construct a variety of interpretations of such texts.

However, one critical fact to keep in mind when considering reader response theory is that it applies primarily to certain types of texts and certain purposes for reading—to literary texts and to what Rosenblatt calls *aesthetic reading.* In aesthetic reading, the primary concern is with what happens to the reader as he or she is reading. The primary purpose when reading aesthetically is to experience the text—to "pay attention to associations, feelings, attitudes, and ideas" (Rosenblatt, 1978, p. 25) that the text arouses. For the most part, literature is written to provide an aesthetic experience. Most adults read literature for enjoyment; they do not read literature to learn it. Adolescent readers need to be given opportunities to do the same.

But there is another purpose of reading, which Rosenblatt calls *efferent* or *informational reading.* When doing informational reading, the reader's attention is appropriately focused on what he or she will take from the reading—what information will be learned. Much of the reading that adolescents do—much of the reading in such subjects as health, science, math, and geography—is for the sake of learning new information, answering questions, discovering how to complete a procedure, or gleaning knowledge that can be used in solving a particular problem. Informational texts, unlike many literary texts, often constrain meaning substantially, do not invite a variety of interpretations, and should yield quite similar interpretations for various readers. I believe that the field has often been guilty of ignoring the nature and importance of informational reading, and that adolescents are too often asked to emote in situations in which they should be asked to learn and understand. Students need to read a lot of informational texts, and they need to be guided and assisted in learning from and deeply understanding such texts.

Sociocultural Theory

Sociocultural theory is another construct that has much in common with constructivism. Like constructivism, it views learning as an active and constructive task, and what is learned as subjective. As described by its originator, Vygotsky (1978), or by Vygotskian scholars such as Wertsch (1998), sociocultural theory is complex. Here, I consider only three simple tenets of the theory. First, students' social and cultural backgrounds have a huge and undeniable effect on their learning. Unless we as teachers take students' social backgrounds and modes of learning and thinking into account, little learning is likely to occur. Second, much learning is social and takes place as groups of learners work together. Dialogue—give-and-take, face-to-face discussion in which students really strive to make themselves understood and to understand others—is a mainstay of learning. Third, the classroom, the school, and the various communities of students in a classroom are all social contexts with very strong influences on what is, or is not, learned in the classroom. Each of these contexts much be carefully considered in planning and carrying out instruction.

Sociocultural theory holds some extremely important lessons for teaching and learning. Still, some interpretations of the theory and implications that are drawn from it seem unfortunate. For example, in the process of recognizing and accommodating to students' social backgrounds and modes of learning and thinking, we also need to recognize that to exist as a society, all of us need to appreciate each other and share some things in common. Additionally, while it is certainly the case that much learning is social, it is also the case that much learning is individual. Classrooms need to be places that recognize and respect individuals, various social groups, and the society in which we all live.

HOW TO TEACH

Here, I discuss five topics: the tetrahedral model of learning, transfer, scaffolding, the gradual release of responsibility model, and direct explanation. Once again, the topics suggest opportunities in which some rethinking and fine-tuning could result in benefits for adolescent learners.

The Tetrahedral Model of Learning

The tetrahedral model of learning was originally developed by Jenkins (1977) in an effort to explain the diversity of results from psychological research on learning and memory. Jenkins noted that experiments that appeared to be dealing with the same phenomena often produced a variety of results. For example, consider some experiments on chess experts. As one might expect, experiments have shown that, compared to novices, chess experts have hugely superior memories for the arrangement of chess pieces on a board. However, experiments have also shown that this superiority does not always hold. If chess pieces are arranged randomly on the board, then both experts and novices have similar difficulty recalling their placement. The explanation is that it is the orderly arrangement of pieces in a way that makes sense in the game of chess that gives the chess expert the advantage. Jenkins employed the tetrahedral model to alert researchers that the outcome of an experiment will be influenced by at least four different factors—characteristics of the learner, the nature of the materials, the learning activities, and the criterial tasks.

Although Jenkins's (1976) model was constructed for psychologists doing research, it applies just a well to educators considering instruction. Some educators concerned with adolescent literacy have taken note of the model. The heuristic for reading comprehension developed by the RAND Reading Study Group (2002) considers three of Jenkins's factors, and the Scaffolded Reading Experience lesson framework that I am currently working on (Fitzgerald & Graves, 2004; Graves & Graves, 2003; Graves & Liang, 2002) considers all four factors. In many cases, however, the field appears to consider differences in the learner and the learning activities but to ignore differences in the materials and criterial tasks. Providing instruction that is shaped by all four factors will substantially increase the likelihood that *all* students will profit from our instruction.

Transfer

Transfer is the use of knowledge or skills learned in one context in another context. Knowledge and skills that transfer become tools that students can use throughout their lives. In a very real sense, transfer is the central purpose of schooling. Schools are future-oriented. Students attend school today so that tomorrow they can use what they learn. We want students to apply what they learn in the early grades to their learning in later grades; even more importantly, we want them to apply what they learn in school to the world outside of school.

Unfortunately, decades of research have repeatedly shown that students very frequently fail to use out of school what they learn in school (Perkins & Salomon, 1988). The student who adds and subtracts quite competently during math class fails when she tries to calculate how much allowance she has left. The student who writes a competent letter of complaint as a class exercise never thinks of writing the distributor when his magazine fails to arrive 2 months in a row. As British philosopher Alfred North Whitehead (1929) aptly put it over 50 years ago, the knowledge that students gain in school has all too frequently been *inert*—fragile, tip-of-the-iceberg knowledge that might enable them to choose a correct answer on a multiple-choice test but is not lasting, and does not serve much purpose in the real world.

To be sure, the field is well aware of the importance of transfer. If asked about its importance, any authority in adolescent literacy would answer that it is vitally important. Yet often we do not do as much as we can to facilitate it. For example, I know of no research in which a comprehension strategy taught to adolescents at one grade level has been systematically reviewed and retaught at subsequent grade levels. We must continually recognize the difficulty of transfer and do everything possible to maximize it.

Scaffolding

Since its introduction 25 years ago, the concept of instructional scaffolding has been investigated, elaborated, related to other instructional concepts, and strongly endorsed by virtually every major reading authority. Although different authors define *scaffolding* slightly differently, three closely related features are essential attributes of effective scaffolding. First, there is the scaffold itself, the temporary and supportive structure that helps a student or group of students accomplish a task they could not accomplish—or could not accomplish as well—without the scaffold. Second, the scaffold must place the learner in what Vygotsky (1978) has termed the *zone of proximal development*. As explained by Vygotsky, at any particular point in time, children have a circumscribed zone of development, a range within which they can learn. At one end of this range are learning tasks that children can complete independently; at the other end are learning tasks that they cannot complete, even with assistance. Between these two extremes is the zone most productive for learning, the range of tasks at which children can achieve *if* they are assisted by some more knowledgeable or more competent other. Third, over time, the teacher must gradually dismantle the scaffold and transfer the responsibility for completing tasks to students.

As I just noted, virtually every major reading authority endorses the concept of scaffolding. However, in talking to middle and secondary school teachers, I have found that many of them are simply not familiar with the concept. Moreover, consistent with Clark's (2002) findings with primary-grade teachers, my talks with middle and secondary school teachers and my observations of middle and secondary school classrooms have revealed that teachers have myriad definitions of the concept, that some of them are simply wrong, and that very little scaffolding takes place in many classrooms. Teachers need to understand fully the nature of scaffolding, and develop and use effective ways of scaffolding students' efforts.

The Gradual Release of Responsibility Model

The gradual release of responsibility model (Campione, 1981; Pearson & Gallagher, 1983) depicts a progression in which students gradually move from situations in which the teacher takes the majority of the responsibility for their successfully completing a reading task (in other words, does most of the work for them), to situations in which students assume increasing responsibility for the task, and finally to situations in which students take total or nearly total responsibility for the task. The model is very closely related to the concept of scaffolding; as I just noted, effective scaffolding includes gradually releasing responsibility to students.

Like scaffolding, the gradual release model is widely endorsed by reading authorities but is by no means frequently used by or even familiar to all teachers. Equally important, the "gradual" feature of the model seems very frequently to be truncated, particularly in the middle and secondary grades. The thinking is that adolescents are nearing maturity and ought therefore to become increasingly independent, and that is certainly the case as far as it goes. However, adolescents are asked to do increasingly complex tasks with increasingly challenging texts. As students progress through school, they should be expected to assume increased responsibility for their learning. Over time, the goal is to dismantle gradually the scaffolds we have built, so that students become increasingly independent readers. Yet students do not repeatedly read the same sorts of text or face the same tasks over time. Instead, over time, students deal with increasingly challenging texts and with increasingly complex tasks. At any particular point in time, students are likely to be—and should be—dealing with some texts and tasks that are more challenging and some that are less challenging. The scaffolding that teachers provide, and the extent to which they release responsibility to students, should always be dependent on the particular texts and tasks with which students are working (Collins, Brown, & Holum, 1991). Teachers should be just as prepared to scaffold advanced students' efforts at complex tasks as they are to scaffold less advanced students' efforts at simpler tasks.

Direct Explanation

Direct explanation is an approach to teaching that employs both scaffolding and gradual release of responsibility. Developed by Duffy, Roehler, and their colleagues (1986) nearly two decades ago, it continues to be highly recommended (Duffy, 2002; Duke & Pearson, 2002). Although direct explanation has most often been used to teach comprehension strategies, it can also be used to teach other sorts of procedural knowledge—word recognition strategies, strategies such as using word parts or context to learn word meanings, and many other strategies competent readers use. The procedure is straightforward and has repeatedly been proven very effective. As described by Duke and Pearson (2002), it comprises the following steps:

- An explicit description of the strategy and when, how, and why it should be used.
- The teacher's cognitive modeling of the strategy, and perhaps student modeling of it.
- Teacher and students using the strategy collaboratively.
- Guided practice in which students gradually assume increased responsibility for using the strategy.
- Independent use of the strategy by students.

Unlike scaffolding and the gradual release of responsibility model, direct explanation is not universally endorsed in the field. A sizable number of authorities in adolescent literacy appear to see it as too brittle and too direct, preferring some sort of inquiry (Beach & Myers, 2001) or transactional (Pressley, 2002) approach. I believe that this is very unfortunate, because I think it is often more efficient to use direct explanation. I believe inquiry can fairly frequently lead students in the wrong direction. And I am concerned that transactional instruction—because it is imbedded in the ongoing work of the class and not singled out as a separate part of the curriculum—is often left undone. Direct explanation is only one of many valid instructional approaches, but it is one that is frequently applicable and should be frequently used.

WHAT TO TEACH

Here, I consider five curricular areas well worthy of serious study by adolescents: vocabulary, text structure and functions, teaching comprehension strategies versus learning from text, higher order thinking, and teaching for understanding.

Vocabulary

Although interest in vocabulary has repeatedly waxed and waned with the research community and in elementary schools, vocabulary instruction has always been an interest of middle and secondary school teachers, probably because they recognize its importance and are familiar with procedures for teaching vocabulary. For the most part, however, the vocabulary instruction that adolescents receive has been less comprehensive and less systematic than it could be, more often than not consisting solely of teaching the meanings of a small number of difficult words that come up in the selections students are reading. Elsewhere (Graves, 2000; Ryder & Graves, 2003) I have described a comprehensive vocabulary program that includes teaching individual words, teaching word-learning strategies, and fostering word consciousness. Although this is certainly not the only framework for vocabulary instruction (see, e.g., Johnson, 2002), middle and secondary students deserve more than occasional instruction on individual words. Students who lack strategies for dealing with word parts and context would certainly profit from instruction in these word-learning strategies, and all students are likely to profit from attempts to increase their interest in and excitement about words. Adolescents need and deserve a comprehensive and well-planned program of vocabulary instruction.

Text Structure and Functions

Most middle and secondary schools lack a comprehensive approach to preparing students to deal with the variety of text structures they will encounter outside of school, or increasing their understanding of the various functions of text. There is, to be sure, a significant amount of instruction about text in English classes, but virtually all of that instruction is with literature and with narratives. Most English teachers do little to prepare students to deal with exposition or to help them understand the various purposes for which writers write and readers read—to inform, to persuade, to entertain, and the like. Unfortunately, the same can be said for most teachers in other content areas. There is simply very little in the middle and secondary school curriculum that addresses such matters. Much of the important reading that adults do involves expository texts (RAND Reading Study Group, 2002). Understanding foreign and domestic affairs, keeping informed on health issues, managing finances, voting intelligently, and even choosing entertainment and making vacation plans all require reading informational material. Adolescents deserve instruction that prepares them to deal with such material. Such efforts should include instruction in text structure, such as that recently investigated by Meyer and Poon (2001), and it should include instruction on the functions and purposes of different sorts of texts.

Teaching Comprehension Strategies versus Learning from Text

Some years ago, Tierney and Cunningham (1984) distinguished between two sorts of comprehension instruction: instruction in "learning from text," which is designed to assist students in reading, comprehending, and learning from a particular text, and "teaching comprehension strategies," which is designed to increase students' ability to understand and learn from the variety of texts that they will read over time. After a lengthy period of neglect, teaching comprehension strategies has once again become a topic of considerable interest to university researchers (National Reading Panel, 2000; Pressley, 2000; RAND Reading Study Group, 2002). Unfortunately, however, at the present time, comprehension strategies instruction is all too infrequent at the elementary level (Pressley, 2002) and, in my own experience, occurs even less frequently at the middle and secondary school level. Ideally, comprehension strategies instruction would begin in the primary grades, be continued in the elementary grades, and leave middle school and secondary teachers with the task of reviewing and refining already learned skills. However, if adolescents have not learned comprehension strategies during their elementary years, then they need to be taught them in middle or secondary school. Unfortunately, as is the case with text structure and functions, it is not clear where in the curriculum these strategies can be expected to be taught. This is particularly the case at the high school level.

The situation with learning from text is almost the opposite of that with teaching comprehension strategies. University researchers have recently shown very little interest in learning from text: The topic is not addressed in the Report of the National Reading Panel (2000); Pressley fails to even mention it in his "What Should Reading Comprehension Instruction Be the Instruction Of?" (2000); and the RAND Reading Study Group (2002) sees it as distinctly secondary to teaching comprehension strategies. On the other hand, many middle and secondary school teachers provide students with at least some assistance in learning from text. Unfortunately, that instruction is neither as widespread nor a strong as it might be. English teachers are by and large the most likely to provide instruction in learning from text, and because most of the texts they deal with are narratives, most of that instruction is with narratives. Moreover, when students do receive instruction in learning from text, it is often not robust—a few words briefly introduced, a bit about the author, and other somewhat weak supports.

With at least some texts and for some purposes, students need more assistance. Instructional frameworks such as the Scaffolded Reading Experience (SRE; Fitzgerald & Graves, 2004; Graves & Graves, 2003) provide guidelines for robust and powerful instruction in learning from text. Briefly, the SRE framework describes how teachers can (1) plan instruction in learning from text by considering the students they are teaching, the text they are reading, and the purposes for which they are reading; then (2) implement that plan with a series of prereading, during-reading, and postreading activities appropriate for that particular combination of students, text, and purposes. The SRE framework builds directly on Jenkins's (1976) tetrahedral model, it is consistent with all of the theories and constructs considered in this chapter, and it has substantial research support (Cooke, 2002; Fournier & Graves, 2002; Graves & Liang, 2002). Study scaffolding such as that provided by SREs has a definite place in middle and high school classrooms.

Higher Order Thinking

As Resnick (1987) notes, although there is universal agreement about the importance of higher order thinking, the concept is not easy to define. Still, she does an excellent job of listing its key features:

- Higher order thinking is nonalgorithmic. That is, the path of action is not fully specified in advance.
- Higher order thinking tends to be complex. The total path is not "visible" (mentally speaking) from any single vantage point.
- Higher order thinking often yields multiple solutions, each with costs and benefits, rather than unique solutions.
- Higher order thinking involves nuanced judgments and interpretation.
- Higher order thinking involves the application of multiple criteria, which sometimes conflict with one another.
- Higher order thinking often involves uncertainty. Not everything that bears on the task at hand is known.
- Higher order thinking involves self-regulation of the thinking process. We do not recognize higher order thinking in an individual when someone else calls the plays at every step.
- Higher order thinking involves imposing meaning, finding structure in apparent disorder.
- Higher order thinking is effortful. There is considerable mental work involved in the kinds of elaborations and judgments required. (p. 3)

Certainly, teachers at all levels want to develop such traits in their students, and many middle school and secondary teachers make it a point to ask higher order and open-ended questions. Yet there are at least two roads to higher order thinking, one of which is to repeatedly ask students to engage in such thinking—something that currently happens a lot, and the other of which is to deliberately teach higher-order thinking—something that happens much less frequently. Much more of the latter is needed. At the very least, teachers ought to be familiar with and directly attempt to promote specific sorts of higher order thinking, such as those listed in the recent revision of Bloom's Taxonomy (Anderson & Krathwohl, 2001), a brief version of which is listed here:

- Remembering: Retrieving relevant knowledge from long-term memory.
- Understanding: Constructing meaning from instructional messages, including oral, written, and graphic communications.
- Applying: Carrying out or using a procedure in a given situation.
- Analyzing: Breaking material into its constituent parts and determining how the parts relate to one another and to an overall structure or purpose.
- Evaluating: Making judgments based on criteria and standards.
- Creating: Putting elements together to form a coherent or functional whole, reorganizing elements into a new pattern or structure.

Teaching for Understanding

As noted by Perkins (1992), probably the most prominent proponent of teaching for understanding, understanding enables a person "to perform in a variety of thought-demanding ways . . . [to] explain, muster evidence, find examples, generalize, apply concepts, analogize, represent in a new way, and so on" (p. 13). To teach for understanding, teachers must go beyond simply presenting students with information and ensure that students understand topics deeply, retain important information, and actively use the knowledge they gain in the classroom in other classrooms and, more importantly, in the world outside of school. Students who have learned to read for deep understanding consciously to seek thoroughly understand and to use the knowledge they gain through reading. As the RAND Reading Study Group (2002) and many other national authorities make clear, the expectations of schooling, and the level of knowledge and skills that our society requires have risen dramatically in recent years and will continue to rise, perhaps even more dramatically, in the future. Yet, as these same authorities indicate, and as empirical data such as that produced by the National Assessment of Education Progress (NAEP; Campbell, Hombo, & Mazzeo, 2000) make clear, few American students are performing at the advanced levels that full participation in our society demands. Teaching for understanding can change this.

Unfortunately, while virtually all teachers want their students to develop the sort of understanding they need, doing so is not easy. Teaching for understanding is challenging work: It takes time, demands focus, and requires teachers and students to negotiate and grapple with the meaning of the texts they read (Prawat, 1989). It also requires teachers to analyze students' responses repeatedly in an effort to determine what they are thinking, to decide whether there is a problem of understanding, and if there is a problem, to diagnose it and come up with a solution. Several authorities (Newmann, 1996; Perkins, 1992; Wiggins & McTighe, 1998; Wiske, 1998) have described specific approaches to teaching for understanding. All of these programs provide insights that middle and secondary schools and teachers should consider and implement in some fashion, and schools and teachers need to work together, so that the curriculum give teachers the time and the opportunity to teach for understanding

MOTIVATION AND ENGAGEMENT: THE *SINE QUA NON* OF LEARNING

Sine qua non—that without which—specifically, that without which the theories and constructs I have discussed thus far do not matter very much. In fact, without students being motivated and involved in their learning, the concepts I have discussed thus far matter very little. Unless learners are seriously interested in learning, unless they want to learn and put some effort into doing so, there is almost no likelihood that significant learning will take place. This is hardly a new insight, yet until fairly recently, many educators have paid very little attention to motivation. In laying out their plan for improving student learning, the National Research Council (1999) divided the knowledge base into what it saw as two equally important domains—knowledge about cognition and learning on the one hand, and knowledge about increasing student motivation and engagement on the other. The National Research Council then went on to say that the task with cognition and learning is to put the vast knowledge base we already have to work in the classroom, while the task with motivation and engagement is to *develop* the knowledge base. In other words, it believes that we know all too little about motivation and engagement.

It is not that we know nothing about motivation and engagement (see, e.g., Bogner, Raphael, & Pressley, 2002; Dolezal, Welch, & Pressley, 2003; Graves, Juel, & Graves, 2004; Guthrie & Wigfield, 2000; Pressley, 2002). We know that students must develop positive attitudes about themselves as learners, about their ability to succeed in school, and about the instructional goals that they, their teachers, and their schools set. We know that success is crucial, that if students are going to learn effectively they need to succeed at the vast majority of learning tasks they undertake. We know that students can attribute their successes and failures to factors that are beyond their control, such as ability or luck, or to factors under their control, such as effort and perseverance; and that we want to do everything possible to help students attribute their success or failure to factors that are under their control. We know that students who repeatedly fail are apt to fall into a passive failure syndrome (Johnston & Winograd, 1985), a syndrome in which they repeatedly attribute their failure to forces beyond their control and, as a consequence, stop trying.

We also know that many teachers are outstanding motivators, but that many others are not. In two extremely informative studies of primary-grade classrooms studies that have significant implications for middle and secondary school classrooms, Bogner et al. (2002) and Dolezal et al. (2003) found that the best teachers literally "saturate" their classrooms with motivation. In all, these two studies list and give examples of more than 40 motivating behaviors of the best teachers. These reports are certainly worth reading and studying in detail. Here, however, are some of the recommendations that I find the most compelling:

- Demonstrate deep concern for students.
- Do everything possible to ensure students' success.
- Scaffold students' learning.
- Present appropriate challenges.
- Support risk taking and help students realize that failures will sometimes occur.
- Encourage students to attribute their successes to their efforts, and realize that additional effort can help avoid failures.
- Encourage cooperative learning and discourage competition.
- Favor depth of coverage over breadth of coverage.
- Communicate to students that many academic tasks require and deserve intense attention and effort.

Finally, both to parallel the qualifying remarks I have made on each of the previous topics in this chapter and because I believe it is essential to understand something that my emphasis on motivation does not mean, I conclude this final section with one more qualifying statement. The emphasis on motivation and engagement generally, and particularly the emphasis on success, must not be taken to mean that students should be spoon fed, told they are doing well when in fact they are not, or be faced with only easy tasks. As Csikszentmihalyi (1990) has shown in his more than 40 years of research, challenges are also important, and some of the very best learning comes when students are seriously challenged by a meaningful task and use the resources they have to achieve at that task. Many of today's adolescents are not doing well at the sorts of tasks they need to master in order to succeed in the 21st century (Campbell et al., 2000; Clinton, 2002; Lemke et al., 2002; Sum, Kirsch, & Taggart, 2002), and pretending to them or to ourselves that they are doing well is not going to change that situation. Rather, the plea here is to understand fully the powerful theories and constructs that have been developed in the field, and to make full use of this knowledge in designing instruction that is stimulating, challenging, and effective.

REFERENCES

Anderson, L. W., & Krathwohl, D. R. (2001). *A taxonomy for learning, teaching, and assessing: A revision of Bloom's Taxonomy of Educational Objectives.* White Plains, NY: Longman.

Anderson, R. C., & Pearson, P. D. (1984). A schema-theoretic view of basic processes in reading. In P. D. Pearson, P. Mosenthal, M. Kamil, & R. Barr (Eds.), *Handbook of reading research* (pp. 255–291). White Plains, NY: Longman.

Appleman, D. (2000). *Critical encounters in high school English. Teaching literary theory to adolescents.* New York and Urbana, IL: Teachers College Press and National Council of Teachers of English.

Beach, R., & Myers, J. (2001). *Inquiry-based English instruction.* New York: Teachers College Press.

Bogner, K., Raphael, L., & Pressley, M. (2002). How grade 1 teachers motivate literate activity by their students. *Scientific Studies of Reading, 6,* 135–165.

Campbell, J. R., Hombo, C. M., & Mazzeo, J. (2000). *NAEP 1999 trends in academic progress: Three decades of student performance.* Washington, DC: U.S. Department of Education.

Campione, J. (1981). *Learning, academic achievement, and instruction.* Paper presented at the 2nd annual Conference on Reading Research of the Center for the Study of Reading, New Orleans, LA.

Clark, K. C (2000). *Instructional scaffolding in reading: A case study of four primary grade teachers.* Unpublished doctoral dissertation, University of Minnesota, Minneapolis.

Clinton, P. (2002, September/October). Literacy in America: The crisis you don't know about. *Book,* pp. L4–L9.

Collins, A., Brown, J. S., & Holum, A. (1991). Cognitive apprenticeship: Making thinking visible. *American Educator, 15*(4), 6–11, 38–46.

Cooke, C. L. (2002, December). *The effects of scaffolding multicultural short stories on students' comprehension and attitudes.* Paper presented at the 51st annual meeting of the National Reading Conference, Miami, FL.

Csikszentmihalyi, M. (1990). *Flow: The psychology of optimal experience.* New York: Harper & Row.

Dolezal, S. E., Welch, L. M., & Pressley, M. (2003). How nine third-grade teachers motivate student academic engagement. *Elementary School Journal, 103,* 239–267.

Duffy, G. G. (2002). The case for direct explanation of strategies. In C. C. Block & M. Pressley (Eds.), *Comprehension instruction: Research-based best practices* (pp. 28–41). New York: Guilford Press.

Duffy, G. G., Roehler, L. R., Meloth, M. Vavrus, L., Book, C., Putnam, J., et al. (1986). The relationship between explicit verbal explanation during reading skill instruction and student awareness and achievement: A story of reading teacher effects. *Reading Research Quarterly, 21*, 237–252.

Duke, N. K., & Pearson, P. D. (2002). Effective practices for developing reading comprehension. In A. E. Farstrup & S. J. Samuels (Eds.), *What research has to say about reading instruction* (3rd ed., pp. 205–242). Newark, DE: International Reading Association.

Fitzgerald, J., & Graves, M. F. (2004). *Scaffolding reading experiences for English-language learners.* Norwood, MA: Christopher-Gordon.

Fournier, D. N. E., & Graves, M. F. (2002). Scaffolding adolescents' comprehension of short stories. *Journal of Adolescent and Adult Literacy, 40*, 30–39.

Gergen, K. J. (1985). The social constructionist movement in modern psychology. *American Psychologist, 40*, 266–275.

Graves, M. F. (2000). A vocabulary program to complement and bolster a middle-grade comprehension program. In B. M. Taylor, M. F. Graves, & P. van den Broek (Eds.), *Reading for meaning: Fostering comprehension in the middle grades* (pp. 116–135). New York: Teachers College Press.

Graves, M. F., & Graves, B. B. (2003). *Scaffolding reading experiences: Designs for student success* (2nd ed.). Norwood, MA: Christopher-Gordon.

Graves, M. F., Juel, C., & Graves, B. B. (2004). *Teaching reading in the 21st century* (3rd ed.). Boston: Allyn & Bacon.

Graves, M. F., & Liang, L. A. (2002). On-line resources for fostering understanding and higher-level thinking in senior high school students. In D. L. Schallert, C. M. Fairbanks, J. Worthy, B. Maloch, & J. V. Hoffman (Eds.), *51st National Reading Conference yearbook* (pp. 204–215). Oak Creek, WI: National Reading Conference.

Guthrie, J. T., & Wigfield, A. (2000). Engagement and motivation in reading. In M. Kamil, P. Mosenthal, P. D. Pearson, & R. Barr (Eds.), *Handbook of reading research (Vol. 3, pp. 402–422).* Mahwah, NJ: Erlbaum.

Jenkins, J. J. (1977). Four points to remember. In L. S. Cermak & F. I. M. Craik (Eds.), *Levels of processing in human memory* (pp. 429–446). Hillsdale, NJ: Erlbaum.

Johnston, D. D. (2002). *Vocabulary in the elementary and middle school.* Boston: Allyn & Bacon.

Johnston, P. H., & Winograd, P. N. (1985). Passive failure in reading. *Journal of Reading Behavior, 17*, 279–301.

Lemke, M., Calsyn, C., Lippman, L., Jocelyn, L., Kastberg, D., Liu, Y., et al. (2002). *Outcomes of learning: Results from the 2000 Program for International Student Assessment.* Washington, DC: U.S. Department of Education.

Meyer, B. J. F., & Poon, L. W. (2001). Effects of structure strategy training and signaling on recall of text. *Journal of Educational Psychology, 93*, 141–159.

National Reading Panel. (2000). *Teaching children to read: An evidence-based assessment of the scientific research literature on reading and its implications for reading instruction.* Bethesda, MD: National Institutes of Health.

National Research Council. (1999). *Improving student learning.* Washington, DC: National Academy Press.

Newmann, F. W. (1996). *Authentic achievement: Restructuring schools for intellectual quality.* San Francisco: Jossey-Bass.

Pearson, P. D., & Gallagher, M. (1983). The instruction of reading comprehension. *Contemporary Educational Psychology, 8,* 317–344.

Perkins, D. L. (1992). *Smart schools: From training memories to educating minds.* New York: Free Press.

Perkins, D. N., & Salomon, G. (1988). Teaching for transfer. *Educational Leadership, 46* (1), 22–32.

Phillips, D. E. (Ed.). (2000). *Constructivism in education.* Chicago: National Society for the Study of Education.

Pirie, B. (1997). *Reshaping high school English.* Urbana, IL: National Council of Teachers of English.

Prawat, R. S. (1989). Teaching for understanding: Three key attributes. *Teaching and Teacher Education, 5,* 315–328.

Pressley, M. (2000). What should reading comprehension instruction to be the instruction of? In M. Kamil, P. Mosenthal, P. D. Pearson, & R. Barr (Eds.), *Handbook of reading research: Volume III* (pp. 545–561). Mahwah, NJ: Erlbaum.

Pressley, M. (2002). *Reading instruction that works: The case for balanced teaching* (2nd ed.). New York: Guilford Press.

RAND Reading Study Group. (2002). *Reading for understanding: Toward an R&D program in reading comprehension.* Santa Monica, CA: RAND Education.

Resnick, L. (1987). *Education and learning to think.* Washington, DC: National Academy Press.

Rosenblatt, L. (1975). *Literature as exploration.* New York: Appleton–Century. (Original work published in 1938)

Rosenblatt, L. (1978). *The reader, the text, the poem: The transactional theory of the literary work.* Carbondale: Southern Illinois Press.

Rumelhart, D. E. (1977). Toward an interactive model of reading. In S. Dornic (Ed.), *Attention and performance* (Vol. 6, pp. 573–603). Hillsdale, NJ: Erlbaum.

Rumelhart, D. E. (1980). Schemata: The building blocks of cognition. In R. J. Spiro, B. C. Bruce, & W. F. Brewer (Eds.), *Theoretical issues in reading comprehension* (pp. 33–58). Hillsdale, NJ: Erlbaum.

Ryder, R. J., & Graves, M. F. (2003). *Reading and learning in content areas* (3rd ed.). New York: Wiley.

Searle, J. R. (1993). Rationality and realism, what is at stake? *Daedalus, 122*(4), 55–83.

Stanovich, K. E. (1994). Constructivism in reading education. *Journal of Special Education, 28,* 259–274.

Sum, A., Kirsch, I., & Taggart, R. (2002). *The twin challenges of mediocrity and inequality: Literacy in the U. S. from an international perspective.* Princeton, NJ: Educational Testing Service.

Tierney, R. J., & Cunningham, J. W. (1984). Research on teaching reading comprehension. In P. D. Pearson (Ed.), *Handbook of reading research* (pp. 609–654). White Plains, NY: Longman.

von Glaserfeld, E. (1984). An introduction to radical constructivism. In P. Watzlawick (Ed.), *The invented reality* (pp. 17–40). New York: Norton.

Vygotsky, L. S. (1978). *Mind in society: The development of higher psychological processes.* Cambridge, MA: Harvard University Press.

Wertsch, J. V. (1998). *Mind as action.* New York: Oxford University Press.

Whitehead, A. N. (1929). *The aims of education and other essays.* New York: Macmillan.

Wiggins, G., & McTighe, J. (1998). *Understanding by design.* Alexandria, VA: Association for Supervision and Curriculum Development.

Wiske, M. S. (1998). *Teaching for understanding: Linking theory with practice.* San Francisco: Jossey-Bass.

Index